International Law
Dictionary

International Law Dictionary

Ernest Lindbergh

BLACKSTONE
PRESS LIMITED

First published in Great Britain 1992 by Blackstone Press Limited,
9-15 Aldine Street, London W12 8AW. Telephone 081-740 1173

© Ernest Lindbergh, 1992

ISBN: 1 85431 119 0

British Library Cataloguing in Publication Data
A CIP catalogue record for this book is available from the British Library.

Typeset by Kerrypress Limited, Luton, Beds
Printed by Ashford Colour Press, Gosport, Hampshire

Contents

Acknowledgements

I wish to express my great appreciation and gratitude to Mrs Inge Shields and Mr Philippe Auclair who contributed to the German and French versions of this dictionary.

Preface

With the intensified communion of nations and the lifting of trade barriers in Europe there is increasing intercommunication at the legal level. An inevitable consequence of this is that not only European lawyers and administrators, but also their colleagues and counterparties at the global level, need to be able to understand each other's languages. This has created an urgent need for an international law dictionary.

This book contains English, French and German legal terms. It is divided into three sections in order to ease the search for the appropriate entry whether you set out from an English, French or German word. It covers not only the technical legal terms, but also general law-related terms from other fields, such as banking and finance and taxation. I have paid particular attention to terms and phrases which reflect the same or similar legal concepts in different countries, whilst excluding those which are falling into disuse.

The concept of this dictionary is simple — to provide, by the shortest possible route, the precise legal term sought.

E. Lindbergh
June 1992

Abbreviations, abréviations, Abkürzungen

English

cf.	*confer* (compare)
EC	European Community
EEC	European Economic Community
s.o.	someone
UK	United Kingdom
US	United States of America

Français

adj.	adjectif
CE	Communauté européenne économique
etc.	et caetera
f	féminin
fam.	familier
m	masculin
n	nom
opp.	opposé à
par ext.	par extension
qque	quelque
qqu'un	quelqu'un
UK	Royaume-Uni
US	États-Unis d'Amérique

Deutsch

e-e	eine
e-m	einem
e-n	einen
e-r	einer
e-s	eines
EDV	elektronische Datenverarbeitung
EG	Europäische Gemeinschaft
etw.	etwas
jd	jemand
jdm	jemandem
jdn	jemanden
jds	jemandes
od.	oder
pl.	Plural
s.	siehe
UK	Vereinigtes Königreich (Großbritannien und Nordirland)
US	Vereinigte Staaton von Amerika

English/French/German

A

ENGLISH	FRENCH	GERMAN
abandon (to)	abandonner, renoncer	abandonnieren; zurückziehen; zurücknehmen; fallenlassen
abandonment	abandon(m)	Abandon(m); Aufgabe(f); Verzicht(leistung)(f); Verlassen(n); Aussetzung(f)
abate (to)	abolir, annuler	aufheben; herabsetzen; aussetzen, einstellen
abatement	diminution(f), réduction(f)	Aufhebung(f); Nachlaß(m), Ermäßigung(f); Aussetzung(f), Einstellung(f)
– of action	action en réduction	Minderungsklage
abduction	enlèvement(m)	Entführung(f)
abet (to)	soutenir, être complice, aider	anstiften, begünstigen; Vorschub(m) leisten
abetment	incitation(f) au crime, au délit	Anstiftung(f), Begünstigung(f); Vorschub(m)
abeyance	suspension(f); vacation(f), suspension(f), interruption(f)	Schwebezustand(m); Unentschiedenheit(f)
abide by (to)	demeurer; se conformer, se soumettre	anerkennen, befolgen
abnegation (cf. waiver)	désaveu(m); renonciation(f)	Ableugnung(f), Ver–; s. Verzicht(m)
abode	demeure, résidence	Aufenthaltsort(m), Wohnsitz(m)
abolish (to)	abolir, supprimer	abschaffen, beseitigen; außer Kraft(f) setzen
abortion	avortement(m)	Abtreibung(f)
abortive	manqué, avorté, inopérant	erfolglos, ergebnislos
abridgement	diminution(f), restriction(f)	Abkürzung(f), Auszug(m), Zusammenfassung(f); Einschränkung(f), Beeinträchtigung(f)
abrogation	abrogation(f)	Abschaffung(f); Aufhebung(f), Außerkraftsetzung(f)
abscond (to)	se soustraire à la justice, fuir	flüchtig werden; (sich dem Gericht) entziehen

3

ENGLISH	FRENCH	GERMAN
absolute	absolu, irrévocable	unbeschränkt; endgültig; rechtskräftig
– power	pouvoir absolu	unbeschränkte Macht, – Gewalt
– proof	preuve(f) irréfutable	einwandfreier Beweis
absolve (to)	acquitter, absoudre	freisprechen, lossprechen, entbinden
abstract	résumé(m), abrégé(m), sommaire(m); extrait(m); analyse(f)	Auszug(m), Abriß(m); Zusammenfassung(f)
– of title	extrait du répertoire des mutations de propriété	Eigentumsnachweis
abuse	abus(m), excès(m); viol(m)	Mißbrauch(m); Beschimpfung(f); Mißhandlung(f)
abut (to)	confiner	angrenzen
accede (to)	accéder à, entrer en possession	beistimmen; beitreten; antreten
acceleration	accélération(f), réduction(f) (d'un délai), avancement(m) (d'une échéance); prise de possession anticipée	Beschleunigung(f); vorzeitige Fälligstellung(f) (Wechsel)
accept (to)	accepter, approuver, agréer	annehmen; anerkennen; akzeptieren; antreten (Amt)
acceptance	acceptation(f), consentement(m), agrément(m)	Annahme(f); Anerkennung(f); Akzept(n); Zusage(f)
– of a judgment	acquiescement à un jugement	Annahme e-s Urteils
acceptor	tiré(m), accepteur(m); intervenant(f), donneur d'aval	Annehmer(m); Akzeptant(m) (e-s Wechsels)
access	accès, abord	Zugang(m); Zutritt(m); Zugriff (EDV)(m)
accession	droit d'accession; avènement(m) au trône; assentiment(m)	Zunahme(f); Beitritt(m); Neuanschaffung(f)
act of –	acte(f) d'entrée en possession	Beitrittsakte (EG)
accessory	complice(m); accessoire(m)	Mittäter(m); Komplize(m), Mitschuldiger(m, f)
accident insurance	assurance(f) contre les accidents	Unfallversicherung(f)
accomplice	complice(m)	Komplize(m); Mittäter(m), Mitschuldiger(m, f); Helfershelfer(m)
accord	accord(m), consentement(m)	Übereinkommen, Einverständnis(n); Vergleich(m); Abmachung(f)
– and satisfaction	novation(f) éxécutée	vergleichsweise Erfüllung; außergerichtlicher Vergleich

ENGLISH	FRENCH	GERMAN
accountability	**responsabilité**(f)	**Verantwortlichkeit**(f); Rechenschaftspflicht(m), Rechnungslegungspflicht; Strafmündigkeit
accountant	**comptable**(m)	**Buchhalter**(m); Buchhaltungsfachmann(m); Buchprüfer(m)
certified public – (US)	expert(m) comptable (US)	(öffentlich zugelassener) Wirtschaftsprüfer (US)
chartered – (UK)	expert comptable (UK)	(öffentlich zugelassener) Wirtschaftsprüfer (UK)
accounting	**comptabilité**(f)	**Buchführung**(f); Rechnungslegung(f); Abrechnung(f); Rechnungswesen
– records	pièces(f) comptables	Buchungsunterlagen, Buchungsbelege
cash –	comptabilité de caisse	Kassenbuchhaltung
cost –	comptabilité de prix de revient	Kostenrechnung; Betriebskalkulation
accretion	**majoration**(f) **d'héritage**; accroissement(m) organique	**Zuwachs**(m); Zunahme(m); Anwachsen(n)
accrual	**date**(f) **de survenance**; date(f) de naissance (d'un droit); échéance(f)	**Anfall**(m); Auflauf(m) (Zinsen); Entstehung(f) (Anspruch, Recht)
accusation	**accusation**(f), incrimination(f)	**Anschuldigung**(f), Beschuldigung(f)
accuse (to)	**accuser,** incriminer	**anklagen, anschuldigen,** beschuldigen
acknowledgement	**constatation**(f), reconnaissance(f)	**Anerkennung**(f); Anerkenntnis(f); (Empfangs-)Bestätigung(f); Zugeständnis; (notarielle) Beglaubigung
– by record	aveu judiciaire	urkundliche Beglaubigung
– of complaint	récépissé d'une réclamation, d'une plainte	Anerkenntnis der Beanstandung, Beschwerde
– of debt	reconnaissance de dette	Schuldanerkenntnis
acquiescence	**acquiescement**(m), assentiment(m), consentement(m)	**(stillschweigende) Einwilligung**(f); Sichfügen(n); Duldung(f)
acquiesce (to)	**acquiescer,** consentir	**(stillschweigend) einwilligen;** sich fügen in; dulden
acquit (to)	**acquitter,** décharger	**freisprechen (von e-r Anklage);** abtragen (Schuld); entbinden von (Pflicht)
acquittal	**acquittement**(m), décharge(f), quitus(m)	**Freispruch**(m)
act	**acte**(m), action(f), mesure(f), loi(m)	**Tat**(m), Handlung(f), Akt(m); Urkunde(f); Gesetz(n)
– of God	cas(m) de force majeure	höhere Gewalt, Naturereignis
criminal –	acte relevant du droit pénal, fait pénalement punissable	Deliktshandlung, strafbare Handlung, Straftat

ENGLISH	FRENCH	GERMAN
action	**action**(f)	**Klage**(f), Verfahren(n), Rechtsstreit(m); Handlung(f), Vorgehen
– for damages	demande(m) de dommages-intérêts	Schadensersatzklage, Klage auf Entschädigung
– for declaration	demande de décision judiciaire	Feststellungsklage
– for injunction	demande d'injonction	Unterlassungsklage
to bring an –	intenter un procès à,	Klage erheben, anstrengen; jdn
against s.o.	contre, qqu'un	verklagen, gegen jdn Klage erheben
to dismiss an –	rejeter une action (en justice)	Klage abweisen
actual	**réel**, véritable, effectif, concret	**wirklich**, tatsächlich, effektiv; gegenwärtig
– loss	perte réelle	tatsächlicher Verlust
– possession	possession effective	unmittelbarer Besitz
– price	prix(m) réel; prix d'achat	Tagespreis, Marktpreis; Anschaffungskosten
– profit	profit(m) réel	echter Gewinn, tatsächlich erzielter Gewinn
– value	valeur(f) marchande	tatsächlicher od. wirklicherWert; Effektivwert Tageswert
address	**adresse**(f), allocution(f),	**Adresse**(f), Anschrift(f); Anrede(f), Ansprache(f)
– for service	domicile(m) élu	Zustellungsadresse
– to the court	plaidoirie(f)	Anrede des Gerichts
adduce (to)	**apporter**, offrir; alléguer	**erbringen**, anführen, beibringen
– an argument	invoquer une raison	Gründe anführen
– evidence	fournir une preuve	e-n Beweis erbringen
adjourn (to)	**ajourner**, différer, suspendre, remettre, renvoyer	**aufschieben;** (zeitlich od. örtlich) verlegen; vertagen
adjudge	**adjuger**, déclarer, prononcer sur	**entscheiden**, erkennen; zuerkennen, zusprechen
– damages	accorder (allouer) des dommages-intérêts	Schadensersatz zuerkennen, zusprechen
adjudgment	**jugement**(m), arrêt(m), décision(f)	**Urteil**(n) (Zivilrecht)(n); Zuerkennung(f), Zusprechung(f)
adjudicate (to)	**juger**, statuer, rendre un arrêt	**erkennen**, entscheiden, Recht(n) sprechen
– s.o. bankrupt	mettre (qqu'un) en faillite	Schuldner für zahlungsunfähig erklären; Konkurs(verfahren) über das Vermögen des Schuldners eröffnen
adjudication	**jugement**(m), décision(f), prononcé d'un jugement; adjudication(f),	**Entscheidung**(f), Urteil(n); Zuerkennung(f), Zuschlag(m)
– of bankruptcy	jugement déclaratif de faillite	Eröffnung eines Konkursverfahrens, Konkurseröffnung

ENGLISH	FRENCH	GERMAN
adjustment	ajustement(m), arrangement(m), régularisation(f), redressement(m), remaniement(m), règlement des créances	Berichtigung(f), Bereinigung(f); Angleichung(f); Schlichtung(f), Beilegung (Streit)
– of claims	règlement des indemnités	Schadensberechnung; Anspruchsregulierung
– of damages	règlement des dommages-intérêts	Schadensregulierung, Schadensfeststellung
administer (to)	administrer, gérer, appliquer	verwalten; handhaben, vollstrecken; als Nachlaßverwalter(m) tätig sein
– an oath	déférer le serment	Eid abnehmen; jdn vereidigen
– justice	rendre la justice	Recht sprechen, Recht anwenden; Gerechtigkeit walten lassen
administration	administration(f), gestion(f), régie(f)	Verwaltung(f); Führung(f), Leitung(f); Amtsperiode(f)
– (US)	le gouvernement (fédéral) (US)	Regierung (US)
administrative	administratif	verwaltungs(technisch)
– law	droit(m) administratif	Verwaltungsrecht
Admiralty court	tribunal(m) maritime	See(schiffahrt)gericht, –amt
admissible	recevable, acceptable	zulässig, erlaubt; zulassungsberechtigt
admission	admission(f), accès(m), acceptation(f), aveu(m)	Zulassung(f), Aufnahme(f), Eintritt(m); Eingeständnis(n), Anerkenntnis(n); Geständnis(n)
– of plea	aveu(m) judiciaire	Anerkenntnis der Einrede
– requirements	conditions(f) d'admission	Zulassungsbedingungen
admit (to)	admettre, concéder, avouer, laisser passer, accepter	zulassen, aufnehmen; zugeben, zugestehen; anerkennen
– a claim	reconnaître une prétention, admettre un recours	e-n Anspruch anerkennen
adoption	adoption(f)	Adoption(f), Annahme(f)
adoptive	adoptif	Adoptiv-
adulteration	altération(f)	(Ver-)Fälschung(f)
– of coinage	falsification(f) de monnaie	Münzverfälschung
– of food	fraude(f) alimentaire	Verfälschung von Nahrungsmitteln, Lebensmittelfälschung
adultery	adultère(m)	Ehebruch(m)
adversary	adversaire(m), partie(f) adverse, contradicteur(m)	Gegner(m), gegnerische Partei(f), Prozeßgegner(m)
adverse	adverse, opposé	feindlich, gegnerisch; nachteilig; entgegenstehend
– balance	balance(f) (commerciale) déficitaire	Unterbilanz; passive Bilanz
– witness	témoin(m) de la partie adverse	Zeuge der Gegenseite; feindlicher Zeuge

ENGLISH	FRENCH	GERMAN
advice	**avis**(*m*), conseil(*m*)	**Rat**(*m*)**;** Benachrichtigung(*f*), Mitteilung(*f*); Avis
legal –	avis(*m*) d'un homme de loi	juristische Beratung, Rechtsbeistand
advise (to)	**conseiller,** recommander, avertir, instruire, aviser de	**(be-)raten;** benachrichtigen, verständigen, mitteilen avisieren
advocate	**avocat**(*m*)	**Anwalt**(*m*)**,** Rechtsbeistand(*m*); Sprecher(*m*), Fürsprecher(*m*)
– general	avocat général	Generalanwalt (*am Gerichtshof der EG*)
Lord Advocate	conseiller et représentant du gouvernment en Écosse	Kronanwalt (*Schottland*)
affiant (*US*)	**auteur**(*m*) **d'un affidavit** (d'un attestation) (*US*)	**Aussteller**(*m*)**,** Abgeber(*m*) e-s Affidavit (eidesstattliche Erklärung) (*US*)
affidavit	**attestation**(*f*)**,** témoignage(*m*) écrit; déposition(*f*) de témoin sous serment	**Eidesstattliche Erklärung**(*f*) **od. Versicherung**(*f*)**,** (schriftlich) eidliche Erklärung
evidence taken on –	déposition de témoin recueillie sous serment	eidesstattliche, schriftliche Zeugenaussage entgegennehmen
to make an –	faire une déclaration sous serment	eidesstattlich erklären, eidliche schriftliche Erklärung abgeben
affiliated	**affilié**(*m*)	**angegliedert, angeschlossen**
affinity	**parenté**(*m*) **par alliance**	**Verwandtschaft**(*f*)**;** Schwägerschaft(*f*)
affirm (to)	**affirmer**	**bestätigen,** versichern; behaupten; an Eides Statt versichern
affirmation	**affirmation**(*f*) **solennelle;** confirmation(*f*); ratification(*f*)	**Bestätigung**(*f*)**,** Versicherung(*f*); Behauptung(*f*); eidliche Erklärung(*f*), eidesstattliche Versicherung(*f*)
affirmative	**affirmatif**	**bejahend,** Bejahung(*f*)
– action (*US*)	action en constatation un droit; mesures(*f*) pour favoriser les discriminés (*US*)	Rechtfeststellungsklage (Wiedergutmachung) der Folgen vergangener Diskriminierung (*US*)
– defence	moyen de défense nouveau détruisant la thèse du demandeur, même si elle était justifiée au moment où la plainte avait été déposée	Einrede des Beklagten (*US*) (*Zivilprozeß*) Behauptung(en) die der Angeklagte glaubhaft zu machen hat (*Strafprozeß*)
affix (to)	**attacher,** apposer, ajouter	**anheften,** aufkleben; aufdrücken
– a seal	sceller (un document), apposer des scellés	mit e-m Siegel versehen, siegeln

ENGLISH	FRENCH	GERMAN
agent	**agent**(*m*), représentant(*m*), préposé(*m*); mandataire(*m*), fondé de pouvoirs	**Vertreter**(*m*), Makler(*m*); Bevollmächtigter(*m*), Handlungsbeauftragter(*m*)
bank –	agent(*m*) bancaire	Bankagent; Vertreter e-r Bank
commission –	commissionnaire(*m*) en marchandises	Kommissionsvertreter, Kommissionär
export –	commissionnaire exportateur	Exportagent
sole –	agent exclusif, dépositaire exclusif	Alleinvertreter
aggravate (to)	**aggraver;** accroître	**verschlimmern;** erschweren, verschärfen
aggravating circumstances	**circonstances**(*f*) **aggravantes**	**(straf-)erschwerende, strafverschärfende Umstände**
aggravation	**aggravation**(*f*)	**Verschlimmerung**(*f*); Erschwerung(*f*), Verschärfung(*f*)
aggrieve (to)	**chagriner,** blesser, causer de la peine	**kränken,** jdn in seinem Recht verletzen
aggrieved party	**partie**(*f*) **chagrinée,** partie(*f*) perdante (dans une décision judiciaire)	**beschwerte Partei**
agreement	**accord**(*m*), convention(*f*), contrat(*m*), traité(*m*), acte(*m*), règlement(*m*), acte(*m*)	**Übereinstimmung,** Einvernehmen(*n*); Einverständnis(*n*); Abmachung(*f*); Abkommen, Vertrag(*m*); Tarifvertrag(*m*)
antenuptial –	contrat de mariage	vorehelicher Vertrag
binding –	convention(*f*) liant les parties	verbindliches Abkommen
mutual –	accord de gré à gré	gegenseitige Vereinbarung; gegenseitiges Einvernehmen
wage –	accord sur les salaires, convention salariale	Lohnabkommen; Lohnvereinbarung
aid	**aide**(*f*), assistance(*f*), secours(*m*)	**Hilfe(leistung)**(*f*), Beistand(*m*); Förderung(*f*), Beihilfe(*f*); Rechtsbeistand
aid and abet	**être le complice de**	**Beihilfe**(*f*) **leisten,** begünstigen
aider and abettor	**complice**(*m*)	**Helfershelfer**(*m*), Gehilfe(*m*)
alibi	**alibi**(*m*)	**Alibi**(*n*)
alien	**étranger,** ressortissant étranger	**Ausländer**(*m*); Fremder(*m*)
alienate (to) (rights)	**aliéner,** transférer, détourner, céder	**veräußern,** übertragen (Rechte)
alimony	**pension**(*f*) **alimentaire**	**Unterhalt(sbetrag)**(*m*)
allegation	**allégation**(*f*); chef(*m*) d'accusation; moyen(*m*) de défense	**Anführung**(*f*), Angabe(*f*); (unerwiesene) Behauptung(*f*) Parteivorbringen
allege (to)	**alléguer,** prétendre, exciper de	**anführen,** angeben; (Unerwiesenes) behaupten; (bei Gericht) vorbringen, geltend machen

ENGLISH	FRENCH	GERMAN
alleged offence	**infraction**(f) **imputée**	**zur Last gelegte Tat**(f)
allocate	**allouer,** affecter, attribuer	**zuteilen;** vergeben; aufteilen; bestimmen für
allocation	**allocation**(f), assignation(f), ventilation(f), répartition(f)	**Zuteilung**(f); Zuweisung(f); Aufteilung(f)
– of funds	affectation(f) de fonds	Mittelvergabe, Mittelzuweisung; Kapitalbewilligung, Kapitalverwendung
– of profits	répartition(f) des bénéfices	Gewinnzurechnung
– of shares	attribution(f) d'actions	Aktienzuteilung
allotment	**attribution**(f), affectation(f), répartition(f); **part**(f), portion(f)	**Zuteilung**(f); Zuweisung(f); Zuerkennung(f); Verteilung(f)
– of property	lotissement(m)	Vermögenszuteilung; Besitzverteilung
allowance	**allocation**(f), gratification(f); rabais(m), ristourne(f); pension(f), rente(f), indemnité(f); déduction(f), abattement(m)	**Anerkennung**(f), Genehmigung; ausgesetzte Summe; Beihilfe(f); Vergütung(f); Preisnachlaß(m); (Steuer-Freibetrag)
annual –	amortissement(m) linéaire	jährlicher Abschreibungsbetrag
daily –	indemnités journalières	Tagegeld(er); Diäten
expense –	indemnités pour frais	Aufwandsentschädigung
superannuation –	pension de retraite	Alterszulage
alternate	**substitut**(m)	**Stellvertreter**(m), stellvertretendes Mitglied
ambiguity	**ambiguïté**(f)	**Zweideutigkeit**(f); Ungewißheit(f), Unklarheit(f)
latent –	imprécision d'un texte légal	versteckter Dissens
amenable	**responsable**	**verantwortlich,** unterworfen; abhängig; zugänglich für
– to fines	passible d'amende(s)	e-r Geldstrafe unterliegend
amend (to)	**amender,** modifier, rectifier	**ergänzen,** abändern
– a statute	amender une loi, modifier un règlement	e-n Gesetzesentwurf, Gesetz abändern
amendment	**amendement**(m), modification(f), correction(f), rectification(f)	**Ergänzung**(f), Abänderung(f); Zusatz(m), Nachtrag(m)
amicable	**amiable**	**gütlich;** freundschaftlich
– settlement	arrangement(m) à l'amiable	gütliche Einigung, Regelung; Vergleich
ancillary	**auxiliaire**(m), subordonné(f), annexe(f) à	**ergänzend;** untergeordnet, Hilfs–, Neben–
annuity	**annuité**(f); **rente viagère**(f)	**Jahreseinkommen**(n); (jährliche) Rente(f), Annuität(f)
annul	**annuler,** abroger	**annullieren;** kündigen, aufheben; für ungültig erklären
annulment	**annulation**(f), abrogation(f), résiliation(f), cassation(f)	**Annullierung**(f); Aufhebung(f); Ungültigkeitserklärung(f); Rückgängigmachung

ENGLISH	FRENCH	GERMAN
answer	réponse(f), réplique(f)	antworten, entsprechen; Folge leisten; sich richten nach
– to a charge	réfutation(f) d'une accusation, réplique du défendeur(m)	sich wegen einer Anklage oder Beschuldigung verantworten
antagonise	contrarier	ankämpfen gegen; sich jdn zum Gegener(m) machen
antenuptial	prénuptial	vorehelich
– settlement	contrat(m) de mariage	–er güterrechtlicher Vertrag; Ehevertrag
anticipation	anticipation(f); exercice(m) anticipé d'un droit	Vorausnahme(f); Vorauszahlung(f); Vorgriff(m)
anticipatory breach	non-respect prémédité d'un contrat	antizipierter Vertragsbruch(m); vor Fälligkeit erklärte Erfüllungsverweigerung oder Verhalten, das beabsichtigten Vertragsbruch andeutet
appeal	appel(m), pourvoi(m) en cassation	Berufung(f), Revision(f), Beschwerde(f), Einspruch(m)
Court of –	cour(f) d'appel	Rechtsmittelgericht; Berufungsgericht(n)
appeal (to)	interjeter appel, faire appel d'une décision; former un recours	anrufen, sich wenden an
appeal (notice of)	déclaration(f) (avis) d'appel	Berufungsantrag; Berufungsschrift(f); Beschwerdeschrift(f)
appellant	appellant(m)	Kläger(m) (Berufungs–, Revisions–, Rechtsmittel–); Beschwerdeführer(m)
appellate court	cour(f) d'appel	Berufungsgericht(n); Gericht zweiter Instanz
appellee	intimé(f)	Beklagter(m) (Berufungs–, Beschwerde–, Revision–)
appear (to)	paraître, apparaître, comparaître	erscheinen; auftreten; den Anschein haben
– in court	ester en justice, comparaître dans un tribunal	vor Gericht erscheinen
applicant	demandeur(m), requérant(m), pétitionnaire(f, m), ayant(m) droit	Antragsteller(m); Bewerber(m); Anmelder(m)
appoint (to)	désigner, nommer, établir, choisir	anordnen, bestimmen; bestellen, ernennen zu
– a guardian	désigner un tuteur	e-n Vormund bestellen
– a trustee	désigner un trustee	e-n Treuhänder bestellen
apportion (to)	répartir, attribuer, ventiler, lotir	zuteilen, zumessen; anteilmäßig verteilen
apprehend (to)	redouter, craindre; appréhender, arrêter	festnehmen, verhaften; ergreifen, fassen; befürchten

ENGLISH	FRENCH	GERMAN
apprehension	appréhension(f), arrestation(f), prise de corps; crainte(f)	Festnahme(f), Verhaftung(f); Begriff(m), Vorstellung(f); Befürchtung(f)
appropriate (to)	approprier, allouer, répartir, doter, prélever	sich aneignen; bewilligen, bereitstellen; bestimmen, verwenden
appropriation	appropriation(f), attribution(f), dotation(f), prélèvement(m)	Aneignung(f); Bewilligung(f), Bereitstellung(f), Bestimmung(f); Verwendung(f)
– of funds	détournement(m) de fonds	Bereitstellung von Mitteln für bestimmten Zweck
– of property	appropriation(f) d'un bien	Vermögensverteilung, Besitzverwendung
approximation	approximation(f)	Angleichung(f); Annäherung(f)
– of laws and regulations (EEC)	rapprochement(m) des législations et des règlementations(f) (CEE)	Rechtsangleichung, Angleichung von Rechtsvorschriften und Verordnungen (EG)
arbitration	arbitrage(m)	Schieds(gerichts)verfahren(n); Schiedsgerichtsbarkeit(f); Arbitrage(geschäft)
– award	sentence(f) arbitrale	Schiedsspruch
– board	commission(f) arbitrale	Schiedsstelle, Schlichtungsstelle
– clause	clause(f) compromissoire	Schiedsklausel
– tribunal	tribunal(m) arbitral	Schiedsgericht(shof)
arbitrator	arbitre(m), amiable compositeur	Schiedsrichter(m)
arraign	poursuivre (traduire) en justice, mettre en accusation	vor Gericht(n) stellen; anklagen; zur Anklage(f) vernehmen
arraignment	mise en accusation	Anklage(verlesung)(f); gerichtliche Belangung
arrest	arrestation(f), prise(f) de corps, placement(m) en détention; saisie(f) (de biens); contrainte(f) par corps	festnehmen, verhaften; (Verfahren)(n) aussetzen; anhalten
warrant of –	mandat d'arrêt	Haftbefehl; Beschlagnahmeverfügung
arson	crime(m) d'incendie volontaire	Brandstiftung(f)
article(s)	article(m), clause(f), stipulation(f), élément(m), dispositions(f)	Artikel(m); Warenposten(n); Abschnitt(m), Paragraph(m); Vertragsbestimmungen (pl.)
– of association (UK)	statuts(m) d'une SARL	Gesellschaftsvertrag; Satzung
– of incorporation (US)	statuts d'une société commerciale	Gründungsurkunde; Satzung
– of marriage	contrat(m) de mariage	Heiratsvertrag
ascendancy	ascendance(f)	Überlegenheit(f), bestimmender Einfluß(m)

ENGLISH	FRENCH	GERMAN
ascertain (to)	**constater,** vérifier, déterminer	**ermitteln,** feststellen; sich vergewissern
– damages	constater les dégâts, déterminer les préjudices	Schaden feststellen
assault	**agression**(f), attaque(f), voies de fait	**tätl. Angriff**(m); Bedrohung(f); Gewaltanwendung(f)
– and battery	coups(m) et blessures	schwere tätliche Beleidigung (Mißhandlung); Körperverletzung
assault (to)	**agresser,** se livrer à des voies de fait sur	**angreifen;** tätlich bedrohen od. beleidigen
assent	**assentiment**(m), agrément(m), approbation(f)	**Zustimmung**(f), Genehmigung(f)
assert (to)	**affirmer,** revendiquer, alléguer	**behaupten,** erklären; vorbringen; geltend machen
– one's rights	revendiquer ses droits	seine Rechte geltend machen; auf seine Rechten bestehen
assessment	**évaluation**(f); estimation(f), détermination(f) du montant d'impôt	**Bewertung**(f); Festsetzung(f); (Schaden-)Feststellung(f); (Steuer-)Veranlagung
– of damages	évaluation(f) des préjudices (dégâts)	Festsetzung einer Entschädigungssumme
asset(s)	**actif**(m), avoir(m), biens(m), fonds(m), capital(m), masse(f) active	**Aktiva;** Vermögen(n)
– and liabilities	actif et (ensemble de) dettes	Aktiva und Passiva
capital –	actif immobilisé	Anlagevermögen; Vermögenswerte
current –	actif réalisable, disponible, à court terme	Umlaufvermögen; sofort realisierbare Aktiven
fixed –	immobilisations(f)	feste Anlagen; Sachanlagen; Anlagevermögen
liquid –	disponibilités(f)	flüssiges Vermögen, flüssige Mittel
assign (to)	**donner en partage,** assigner, imposer, déléguer, céder	**abtreten,** übereignen; bestimmen, ernennen
– property	attribuer des biens	Vermögen übertragen
assignee	**cessionnaire**(m); syndic(m), administrateur-séquestre(m)	**Rechtsnachfolger**(m); Zessionar(m); Erwerber(m)
assignment	**assignation**(f), affectation(f), cession(f), transfert(m)	**Abtretung**(f), Übereignung(f), Übertragung(f)
– of claim	transfert d'une créance	Forderungs–, Anspruchsabtretung
– of shares	transmission d'actions	Aktienübertragung
assignor	**cédant**(m)	**Rechtsvorgänger**(m); Zedent(m); Übertragender(m); Abtreter(m)
assize court	**cour**(f) **d'assises**	**Assisengericht**(n); Geschworenengericht(n), Schwurgericht(n)

ENGLISH	FRENCH	GERMAN
attach (to)	attacher, impliquer, imputer; saisir, contraindre par corps	anfügen; beimessen; verhaften; pfänden
– and sell	saisir et vendre	beschlagnahmen und verkaufen
attachment	attachement(m), fixation(f); saisie(f); opposition(f); mandat(m) d'amener; prise(f) de corps	Anfügung(f); Zuteilung(f); Verhaftung(f); Beschlagnahme(f), Pfändung(f)
– of property	saisie immobilière	Vermögensbeschlagnahme
– order	ordonnance(f) de saisie	Arrestbefehl; Pfändungsbefehl; Beschlagnahmeverfügung
attempt (to)	essayer, entreprendre, tâcher de	versuchen; unternehmen
attempted crime	tentative(f) de perpétration d'un crime	versuchtes Verbrechen(n); versuchte Straftat
attorney	mandataire(m), représentant dûment désigné	Anwalt(m); Rechtsbeistand(m); Bevollmächtigter(m, f)
– -at-law (US)	avocat (US)	Rechtsanwalt, –anwältin (US)
– -general	conseiller et représentant légal du gouvernement	Generalstaatsanwalt; Kronanwalt; Justizminister
letter of –	procuration	Vollmacht(surkunde); Prozeßvollmacht (US)
power of –	mandat pouvoirs	Vollmacht; Vertretungsbefugnis; Prozeßvollmacht
audit, auditing	audit(f), vérification(f), apurement(m)	Rechnungprüfung(f); Revision(f)
tax –	vérification de comptabilité par le fisc	Steuerprüfung
audit (to)	vérifier, apurer, faire un audit	(Bücher(m), Rechnungen(f)) prüfen; Revision(f) durchführen
authenticated copy	ampliation(f)	beglaubigte Abschrift
authority	autorité(f), mandat(m), pouvoir(m), compétence(f)	Behörde(f); Befugnis(n); Genehmigung(f); Vollmacht(f)
police –	la police; autorité policière	Polizeibehörde
public –	pouvoirs publics	Verwaltungs–, Staatsbehörde; öffentliche Gewalt, Staatsgewalt
autopsy	autopsie(f)	Autopsie(f), Obduktion(f)
avert (to)	prévenir, éviter	ablenken; abwenden; verhüten
– damage	prévenir des dégâts	Schaden abwenden
– violence	prévenir la violence	Gewalt abwenden
award	prix, attribution(f); jugement(m) sentence(f) arbitrale;	Belohnung(f); Zuerkennung(f); Schiedsurteil(n); Rechtsspruch
– of a judgment	prononcement d'une sentence (d'un jugement)	Urteil sprechen, (durch Urteil) zuerkennen

B

ENGLISH	FRENCH	GERMAN
back (to)	**renforcer,** épauler; endosser; financer	**unterstützen;** begünstigen; gegenzeichnen
backing	**appui**(*m*)**,** couverture(*f*); remboursement(*m*)	**Unterstützung**(*f*)**;** Deckung(*f*); Indossierung(*f*)
financial –	soutien financier	finanzielle Unterstützung
bad	**mauvais,** faux	**zweifelhaft;** unzureichend
– debt	créance(*f*) irrécouvrable	zweifelhafte Außenstände (*pl.*); uneinbringliche Forderung
– faith	mauvaise foi	böser Glaube
bail	**caution**(*f*)	**Bürgschaft**(*f*)**;** Kaution(*f*), Sicherheitsleistung(*f*)
– bond	bon de caution	Bürgschaftsschein
to grant –	admettre une caution	Sicherheitsleistung (Kaution) zulassen
to offer –	proposer une caution	Sicherheit anbieten
to release on –	mise en liberté sous caution	gegen Bürgschaft (Sicherheitsleistung) entlassen, freilassen
bailed	**admis**(*m, f*) **à caution**	**Sicherheit geleistet**(*f*)**;** Kaution gestellt
bailee	**dépositaire**(*m*)	**Übernehmer**(*m*)**;** Depositar(*m*), Verwahrer(*m*)
bailiff	**huissier**(*m*)	**Hilfsbeamter**(*m*)**;** Gerichtsdiener(*m*); Gerichtsvollzieher(*m*) Gutsverwalter
bailment	**contrat**(*m*) **de dépôt**	**Besitzübertragung**(*f*) **auf Zeit;** Verwahrung(*f*); Verpfändung(*f*); anvertrautes Gut, hinterlegte Sache
bailor	**déposant**(*m*)	**Übergeber**(*m*)**;** Hinterleger(*m*), Verpfänder(*m*)
balance sheet	**bilan**(*m*) **d'inventaire**	**Bilanz**(*f*)**,** Rechnungsabschluß(*m*)
ballot	**scrutin**(*m*)**,** tour(*m*) de scrutin	**Wahl**(*f*)**,** Abstimmung(*f*); Stimmzettel(*m*); Wahlgang(*m*)
secret –	scrutin secret	geheime Wahl, – Abstimmung
ban (to)	**interdire,** mettre hors-la-loi, prohiber	**verbieten;** Sperre verhängen über

ENGLISH	FRENCH	GERMAN
bank	**banque**(f)	**Bank**(f)
central –	banque centrale	Zentral–, Noten–
clearing –	banque de virement	Clearing–, Giro–
commercial –	banque commerciale	Geschäfts–; Handels–
credit –	banque de crédit	Kredit–
deposit –	banque de dépôt	Depositen–
industrial –	banque industrielle	Industrie–
investment – (US)	banque d'affaires (US)	Investitions– (US)
merchant –	banque d'affaires (UK)	Merchant–
banknote	**billet**(m) **de banque**	**Banknote**(f); Papiergeld(m)
bankrupt	**failli,** banqueroutier	**Konkursschuldner**(m); Zahlungsunfähiger(m); Gemeinschuldner(m)
to be declared –	être déclaré en faillite	bankrott erklärt werden
to declare s.o. –	prononcer la faillite de qqu'un	jdn für bankrott erklären
to declare oneself –	se déclarer en faillite	Konkurs (Bankrott) anmelden
to go –	faire faillite	in Konkurs gehen (geraten); bankrott machen
bankruptcy	**faillite**(f)	**Bankrott**(m), Konkurs(m); Zahlungseinstellung(f)
– court	tribunal(m) de faillite	Konkursgericht
proceedings in –	procédure(f) de faillite	Konkursverfahren
to present a –	se mettre en faillite,	e-n Antrag auf
petition	deposer son bilan	Konkurseröffnung stellen Konkurs anmelden
voluntary –	faillite volontaire	freiwilliger Konkurs
bar (to)	**empêcher,** exclure	**verbieten,** untersagen; ausschließen
– legal proceedings	retirer une plainte	Rechtsweg ausschließen
bare	**nu**	**bloß,** nackt, dürftig, arm
barrister	**avocat**(m), **avocate à la Cour**	**(plädierender)**(m) **Anwalt**(m); Barrister(m)
barter	**troc**(m)	**Tausch**(m)
– transaction	échange	Tauschgeschäft; Barter–, Kompensations–
bastard	**enfant**(m, f) **naturel**	**uneheliches Kind**
battery	**voies**(f) **de fait**	**Gewaltanwendung**(f); Körperverletzung(f), Mißhandlung(f), tätlicher Angriff
assault and –	coups(m) et blessures	schwere tätliche Beleidigung (Mißhandlung); Körperverletzung
bearer (cf. holder)	**porteur**	**Träger**(m), Überbringer(m) (s. Inhaber, Besitzer)
– bond	titre(m) au porteur	Inhaberobligation, Inhaberschuldverschreibung
– certificate	attestation au porteur	Inhaberzertifikat
– securities	titres, valeurs au porteur	Inhaberpapiere
beat (police)	**tournée**(f), ronde(m) (de police)	**(Polizei–)Runde**(f), Rundgang(m)
beguile (to)	**tromper,** duper	**hintergehen,** betrügen; verleiten

ENGLISH	FRENCH	GERMAN
bench	**banc**(*m*)	**Richterbank**(*f*); Gericht(*n*); Richterschaft(*m*)
– warrant	mandat(*m*) d'arrêt décerné sur le siège	(richterlicher) Haftbefehl
beneficial	**profitable,** avantageux	**nutznießend;** nutzbringend, vorteilhaft
– interest	titre de droit en équité	Nutzungsrecht, Nießbrauchrecht; materieller Eigentumsanspruch
beneficiary	**bénéficiaire**(*m, f*), ayant(*m*) droit	**Nutzungsberechtigter**(*m*), Begünstigter(*m*); Empfangsberechtigter Leistungsempfänger; Anspruchsberechtigter
benefit	**avantage**(*m*)	**Nutzen**(*m*), Vorteil(*m*); Hilfe(*f*), Begünstigung(*f*); Versicherungsleistung
benefits in kind	avantages en nature	Sachleistungen
sickness –	prestation(*f*) maladie	Krankengeld, –unterstützung
unemployment –	indemnité(*f*) de chômage	Arbeitslosenunterstützung
bequeath (to)	**léguer**	**testamentarisch vermachen;** vererben
bequest	**legs**(*m*)	**Vermächtnis**(*n*); Legat(*m*); Erbteil(*n*)
betrayal	**trahison**(*f*)	**Verrat**(*m*); Treubruch(*m*)
betrothal	**fiançailles**(*f*)	**Verlobung**(*f*)
beyond reasonable doubt	**quasi-certitude du jury,** conviction(*f*) dépassant la croyance en un doute raisonnable	**jeder Zweifel ausgeschlossen;** (Beweisergebnis, das jeden vernünftigen Zweifel ausschließt)
bias	**opinion**(*f*) **préconçue**	**Vorurteil**(*n*); Befangenheit(*f*), Voreingenommenheit(*f*)
personal –	parti pris personnel	persönliches Vorurteil
biased	**tendancieux,** non impartial, partial	**voreingenommen,** befangen, parteiisch
bid	**enchère,** offre	**Angebot**(*n*), Offerte(*f*); Antrag(*m*), Bewerbung(*f*); Gebot(*n*)
bidder	**enchérisseur**(*m*)	**Bietender**(*m*), Steigerer(*m*); Bewerber(*m*)
bilateral	**bilatéral,** synallagmatique	**bilateral;** gegenseitig
bill	**projet**(*m*) **de loi**	**Schriftstück**(*n*), Urkunde(*f*); Rechnung(*f*); Gesetzentwurf(*m*), –vorlage; Wechsel, Tratte; Geldschein (*US*), Banknote(*f*)
government –	projet de loi gouvernemental	Regierungsvorlage
– of exchange	lettre(*f*) de change	(gezogener) Wechsel, Tratte
– of indictment	résumé(*m*) des chefs d'accusation	Anklageschrift
– of lading	connaissement(*m*)	Konnossement, Seefrachtbrief; (Binnenschiffahrt) Ladeschein

ENGLISH	FRENCH	GERMAN
bind (to) – oneself	**obliger,** engager, lier s'engager	**binden;** verpflichten sich verpflichten (etwas zu tun)
binding commitment	**engagement**(m) **irrévocable**	**zwingende Verpflichtung**(f)
bipartite	**biparti,** bilatéral	**in doppelter Ausfertigung**(f) **(Urkunden)**(f)**;** zweiteilig
birthright	**droit de naissance,** droit d'aînesse; patrimoine	**Geburtsrecht**(n)**,** angestammtes Recht(n)
blackmail	**chantage**(m)	**Erpressung**(f)**;** Nötigung
blanket – authority	**d'application**(f) **générale** carte blanche	**generell,** alles umfassend; Gesamt– Blankovollmacht
blasphemy	**blasphème**(m)	**Blasphemie**(f)**,** Gotteslästerung(f)
board administrative – advisory – – of directors	**commission**(f)**,** conseil(m), administration(f) comité(m) administratif comité consultatif conseil d'administration	**Direktion**(f)**;** Verwaltungsstelle(f); Behörde(f); Ausschuß(m), Gremium(n); Verpflegung(f) Verwaltungsrat; –ausschuß Beratungsausschuß, –stelle (Gremium der) Direktoren; Vorstand
body administrative – – corporate	**corps**(m) instance(f) administrative personne morale, corps constitué	**Körperschaft**(f)**;** Vereinigung(f); Gremium(n), Organ(n) Verwaltungsgremium, –behörde, –stelle juristische Person; Körperschaft
bona fide – holder – offer	**bonne foi**(f) détenteur(m) de bonne foi offre(f) ferme(f)	**in gutem Glauben;** gutgläubig, redlich gutgläubiger Inhaber (Eigentümer) solides Angebot
bond bearer – government – redeemable – savings –	**obligation**(f)**,** engagement(m) titre(m) au porteur obligation d'État, rente d'État obligation amortissable bon d'épargne	**Schuldurkunde**(f)**,** –schein(m); Wertpapier(n), Obligation(f), Schuldverschreibung(f); Haftungsversprechen(n), Bürgschaft(f), Garantieerklärung(f); Zollverschluß(m) Inhaberobligation, – schuldverschreibung Staatsanleihen, –papiere, – schuldverschreibungen tilgbare Obligation, kündbare Obligation (staatl.) Sparbrief; Sparschuldverschreibung (US)
book value	**valeur comptable,** prix(m) d'inventaire	**Buchwert**(m)**;** buchmäßiger Wert(m)
border crossing	**passage**(m) **de frontière**	**Grenzübergang**(m)**;** –übertritt(m)
born in (out of) wedlock	**né dans (hors) (des liens) du mariage**	**(un-)ehelich geboren**

ENGLISH	FRENCH	GERMAN
borough	municipalité(f); circonscription(f) électorale urbaine	Stadtbezirk(m); Gemeinde, Kreis(m)
borrower	emprunteur (n.)	Entleiher(m); Kredit–, Darlehensnehmer(m)
borrowing	emprunteur (adj.)	Leihen, Borgen; Darlehens–, Kreditaufnahme(f)
boycott	boycottage(m)	Boykott(m), Sperre(f)
branch	branche(f), succursale(f), agence(f)	Zweigstelle(f), –niederlassung(f), Filiale(f), Nebenstelle(f); Branche, Sparte
breach	infraction(f), violation(f)	Verletzung(f), Übertretung(f), Verstoß(m)
– of contract	rupture de contrat	Vertragsbruch, –verletzung
– of duty	manquement(m) au devoir (aux obligations), forfaiture(f)	Pflichtverletzung, –vergehen
– of law	violation de la loi	Gesetzesverletzung, Rechtsbruch
– of rules	infraction aux règles	Ordnungswidrigkeit
– of secrecy	indiscrétion(f), violation de la confidentialité	Verletzung der Geheimhaltungspflicht
breaking and entering	effraction(f)	Einbruch(m)
bribe	pot-de-vin(m)	Bestechung(f)
bribe (to)	corrompre, acheter (qqu'un)	bestechen
brief	exposé(m), dossier(m)	schriftl. Beauftragung(f) und Information(f) (des Barrister durch den Solicitor) zur Vertretung vor Gericht; Schriftsatz; Auftrag, Mandat
briefing	exposé; constitution(f) de dossier	Information(f); Bestellung(f) eines vor Gericht(n) auftretenden Anwalts; Anweisung, Unterweisung; Einsatzbesprechung
bring (to)	apporter, amener	bringen, tragen, erheben
– an action	intenter une action en justice	Klage erheben; Prozeß anhängig machen; verklagen
broker	courtier(m), agent(m) de change	Makler(m), Vermittler(m)
burden of proof	charge de la preuve	Beweispflicht(f), – last
burglar	cambrioleur(m)	Einbrecher(m)
burglary	cambriolage(m)	Einbruch(sdiebstahl)(m)
by-laws	arrêté municipal ou communal; statuts(m) d'une société	Ortsstatuten(n); Gemeindeverordnung(f); Satzung(f); Geschäftsordnung

C

ENGLISH	FRENCH	GERMAN
cabinet	**cabinet**(*m*), conseil(*m*) des ministres	**Kabinett**(*n*); Ministerium(*n*)
– committee	commission(*f*) du conseil des ministres	Kabinetts–, Regierungsausschuß
– meeting	réunion(*f*) du cabinet, du conseil des ministres	Kabinettssitzung
cache	**cachette**(*f*)	**Aufbewahrungsort**(*f*); Versteck(*n*), geheimes Lager(*n*)
calculated	**prémédité, délibéré**	**berechnet,** er–; kalkuliert
call (to)	**appeler,** citer à comparaître	**(an-)rufen;** vorsprechen; einberufen; einfordern, auffordern
– a case	appeler une cause, une affaire	(gerichtlich) aufrufen, e-e Sache –
– a person to give evidence	appeler un témoin à faire sa déposition	jdn auffordern über etwas auszusagen
– to order	ouvrir (une séance)	zur Ordnung rufen
call option	**prime**(*f*) **à la hausse;** option(*f*) d'achat	**Kaufoption**(*f*); Vorprämie(*f*)
call price	**prix**(*m*) **de rachat**	**Vorprämienkurs**(*m*)
call-up of capital	**appel**(*m*) **de fonds**	**Kapital einfordern**(*n*); Einzahlung(*f*) verlangen
cancellation	**annulation**(*f*)	**Rückgängigmachung**(*f*), Ungültig–; Aufhebung(*f*), Widerruf(*m*); Kündigung(*f*)
– clause	clause(*f*) de résiliation, clause résolutoire	Aufhebungs–, Kündigungs–, Rücktrittsklausel
capacity	**capacité**(*f*); **qualité**(*f*)	**Fähigkeit**(*f*); Kapazität(*f*); Inhalt(*m*)
legal –	capacité légale	Rechtsfähigkeit; Geschäftsfähigkeit
official –	exercice des fonctions	dienstliche, amtliche Eigenschaft
testamentary –	capacité de tester	Testierfähigkeit
capias (*US*)	**ordre**(*m*) **d'arrestation** (*US*)	**Haftbefehl**(*m*) (*US*)
capital (*criminal law*)	**capital**(*m*)	**Kapital-**(*n*)
– crime	crime(*m*) punissable de la peine capitale	–verbrechen
– punishment	peine(*f*) capitale, peine de mort	Todesstrafe

ENGLISH	FRENCH	GERMAN
capital	**capital**(*m*)	**Kapital**(*n*); Vermögen(*n*)
– adequacy ratio	rapport(*m*) d'adéquation du capital	Eigenmittelrelation
– advance	prêt(*m*) pour constitution de capital	Kapitalvorschuß
– gain	plus(*f*)-value	(Kapital-)Veräußerungsgewinn; realisierter Kursgewinn
– holding	possession(*f*) de capital	Kapitalanteil
– interest	intérêt(*m*) du capital	Kapitalbeteiligung
– market	marché(*m*) des capitaux	Kapitalmarkt
– return	rendement(*m*), rentabilité du capital	Kapitalverzinsung
– stock	capital social	Aktienkapital; Stammkapital
paid-up –	capital versé	voll eingezahltes Kapital
share –	capital actions	Aktien-, Stamm-; Betriebskapital
captive	**captif, captive**(*m, f*)	**Gefangener**(*m*); gefangen; für den Eigenbedarf(*m*)
cardinal error	**erreur**(*f*) **fondamentale**	**Kardinalfehler**(*m*)
carrier	**transporteur**(*m*)	**Beförderer**(*m*); Spediteur(*m*); Frachtführer(*m*)
carry (to)	**porter**; adopter	**unterstützen**, durchbringen, einbringen
– a motion	faire passer une proposition	e-n Antrag annehmen
– a resolution	adopter une résolution	e-n Beschluß durchbringen
case	**cas**(*m*), **affaire**(*f*)	**Fall**(*m*); Rechts–, Streitsache(*f*); Prozeß(*m*)
– at issue	espèce	der zur Entscheidung stehende Fall; der vorliegende Fall
– on appeal	affaire dont la Cour d'Appel est saisie	Berufungssache
criminal –	affaire criminelle	Strafsache; Strafprozeß
juvenile –	affaire concernant un mineur	Jugendsache
pending –	affaire en cours d'instance, affaire pendante devant	schwebende, anhängige Streitsache
case law	**jurisprudence**(*f*), droit jurisprudentiel	**Fallrecht**(*n*); Präzedenzrecht(*n*)
casting vote	**voix**(*f*) **prépondérante**	**ausschlaggebende Stimme**(*f*)
casualty insurance	**assurance**(*f*) **contre les accidents**	**Schadenversicherung**(*f*); Unfall-Haftpflichtversicherung(*f*) (*US*)
catch (to)	**attraper**	**ergreifen**; einholen; erreichen; ertappen
causal connection	**connection causal,** relation(*f*) de causalité	**Kausalzusammenhang**(*m*)
cause	**cause**(*f*), raison(*f*)	**Ursache**(*f*), Grund(*m*); Rechtsfall(*m*), –streit, –sache
– of appeal	motif(*m*) de l'appel	Anfechtungsgrund
– of complaint	motif de la plainte	Klage-, Beschwerdegrund
– of suspicion	raison de soupçonner	Verdachtsgrund

ENGLISH	FRENCH	GERMAN
caution (to)	prévenir; informer qqu'un de ses droits (police)	(ver-)warnen
cede (to)	céder	abtreten, zedieren; überlassen
censure	réprimande(f), critique(f)	Kritik(f), Tadel(m), Rüge(f)
motion of –	motion(f) de censure	Mißtrauensantrag
certainty	certitude(f), conviction(f)	Gewißheit(f), Sicherheit(f); Rechtssicherheit(f)
degree of –	degré(m) de certitude	Sicherheits-, Gewißheitsgrad
certificate	certificat(m), attestation	Zeugnis(n), Bescheinigung(f); Urkunde(f); Anteilschein(m)
birth –	acte(m) de naissance	Geburtsurkunde
– of deposit	certificat de dépôt	Einlagezertifikat; Depot-, Hinterlegungsschein
– of origin	certificat d'origine	Ursprungszeugnis; Herkunftsbescheinigung
death –	acte de décès	Sterbeurkunde; Totenschein
health –	billet(m) de santé	Gesundheitsattest; –zeugnis
marriage –	acte de mariage	Heiratsurkunde
certiorari	requète de révision pénale	Aktenanforderung(f); Revisionsantrag(f)
cession	cession(f)	Abtretung(f); Zession(f); Überlassung(f)
deed of –	acte(m) de cession	Abtretungsurkunde
chairman	président(m)	Vorsitzender(m), Präsident(m); Obmann(m)
challenge (to)	contester, défier, interpeller	ablehnen; bestreiten; beanstanden;
– a claim	contester une réclamation, une demande	einen Anspruch in Abrede stellen
– a right	contester un droit; attaquer une décision	ein Recht bestreiten, in Frage stellen
chambers	cabinet(m) de juge, d'avocat, étude(f) d'avoué	Anwaltsbüro(n), Kanzlei(f)
hear in –	juger en chambre du conseil	unter Ausschluß der Öffentlichkeit verhandeln
in –	en référé	unter Ausschluß der Öffentlichkeit
chancellor	chancelier(m)	Kanzler(m); Richter(m) od. Vorsitzender(m) (des Court of Chancery)
Chancellor of the Exchequer	chancelier de l'Échiquier, ministre(m) des finances	Schatzkanzler; Finanzminister
Lord Chancellor	le Grand Chancelier d'Angleterre	Lordkanzler
chancery	chancellerie(f)	Rechtsprechung(f) nach equity-Recht(n); Kanzleigericht
court of –	tribunal(m) jugeant en 'equity'	Gericht(n), das nach den Grundsätzen des equity urteilt

ENGLISH	FRENCH	GERMAN
charge	acte(m) d'accusation, inculpation; chef(m) d'accusation; réquisitoire(m)	Anklage(f), Beschuldigung(f); Belastung(f), Hypothek(f); Obhut(f), Sorge(f); Gebühr(f), Unkosten
– of murder	inculpation(f) de meurtre	angeklagt wegen Mordes
– of theft	inculpation de vol	angeklagt wegen Diebstahls
– of treason	inculpation de trahison	angeklagt wegen Landesverrats, Hochverrats
charge (to)	accuser, inculper	anklagen, unter Anklage stellen
charter	charte(f), statuts(m), privilège(m)	Urkunde(f); Verfassungs–, Verleihungs–, Gründungsurkunde(f)
– of a company	acte(m), statuts d'association d'une compagnie, d'une société	Gründungsurkunde einer Gesellschaft
chattels	biens (m) meubles	Fahrnis(n), bewegliches Vermögen(n)
cheat (to)	tromper, tricher, escroquer	betrügen, beschwindeln; übervorteilen
chief justice	premier président(f) d'une cour	Oberrichter(m); Vorsitzender(m, f) e-s hohen Gerichts, Präsident des Obersten Bundesgerichtshofs
child	enfant(m, f)	Kind(n), Nachkomme(m)
children's allowance	allocation familiale	Kinderbeihilfe(f), Kindergeld(n)
chose in action	créance(f), titre de créance; droit(m) incorporel permettant une action en justice	Forderungsrecht(n); obligatorischer Anspruch(m)
CIF	CAF (coût, assurance maritime, fret)(m)	c.i.f. (s. Fracht)
circuit	circuit(m)	Kreis(m), Bezirk(m)
– court (US)	tribunal(m) de première instance (US)	erstinstanzliches Gericht für mehrere Bezirke (US)
– judge	juge(m) de la Crown Court et de la county court (Angleterre)	Strafrichter; Richter
circumstantial evidence	présomptions(f), preuve(f) indirecte	Indizienbeweis(m)
citizen	citoyen(m), ressortissant	Bürger(m); Staatsbürger(m)
citizenship	citoyenneté(f), nationalité(f)	Staatsbürgerschaft(m), Staatsangehörigkeit(f)
civic	civique, municipal	bürgerlich, staatsbürgerlich; städtisch

ENGLISH	FRENCH	GERMAN
civil	**civil, –e**	**bürgerlich,** zivilrechtlich
– action	action(f) civile	Zivilprozeß, bürgerlicher Rechtsstreit
– court	tribunal(m) civil	Zivilgericht
– law	'jus civile', droit(m) romain; droit civil	Zivilrecht; bürgerliches Recht, Privatrecht
– liability	responsabilité(f) civile	zivilrechtliche Haftung
– marriage	mariage(m) civil	Ziviltrauung, standesamtliche Trauung
– rights	droits(m) civils; droits civiques	(Staats-)Bürgerrechte
– servant	fonctionnaire(m)	(Staats-)Beamter; öffentlicher Bediensteter
claim	**créance**(f); revendication(f), requête(f); droit(m) qu'on entend faire valoir en justice	**Anspruch**(m); Forderung(f); Behauptung(f); Klagebegehren
– for damages	action(f) en dommages-intérêts	Schadensersatzanspruch, –forderung
– for relief	demande(f) de déduction	Rechtsmittelanspruch
counter- –	demande reconventionnelle	Gegenanspruch; Widerklage
declaratory –	demande déclaratoire	deklaratorischer Anspruch, Feststellungs–
claimant	**demandeur**(m), partie(f) requérante	**Anspruchsteller**(m); Antragsteller(m); Kläger(m)
class action (US)	**action**(f) **de groupe** (US)	**Gruppenklage**(f); von einer Interessengruppe angestrengte Klage(f)
classified information	**information**(f) **confidentielle**	**Verschlußsache**(f); unter Geheimschutz gestellte Information(f)
clause	**clause**(f)	**Klausel**(f); Absatz(m); Vereinbarung(f)
exemption –	clause d'exonération	Freizeichnungsklausel; Befreiungsklausel
penalty –	clause pénale, dédit	Strafklausel, Strafbestimmung
clearing bank	**banque**(f) **de virement**	**Clearingbank**(f), Giro–
clerk of court	**greffier**(m)	**Urkundsbeamter**(m) **der Geschäftsstelle**(f); Leiter der Gerichtskanzlei
close (to)	**fermer,** clore(m)	**schließen;** einstellen; beenden
– the proceedings	clôture(f) de la procédure	Verfahren einstellen
closed-end	**à capital limité,** fixe	**geschlossen**
– (investment) company	société à capital fixe	–e (Investment-)gesellschaft
closing address	**allocution**(f), plaidoirie(f) finale	**Schlußplädoyer**(m)
closure	**clôture**(f)	**Schließung**(f); Schluß(m); Abschluß(m)
– of debate	clôture des débats	Schluß der Debatte
clue	**indice**(m)	**Anhaltspunkt**(m)

ENGLISH	FRENCH	GERMAN
co-accused, co-defendant	co-défendeur(*m*), co-accusé(*m*)	**Mitbeklagter**(*m, f*), Neben–; Mitangeklagter(*m, f*)
co-insurance	coassurance(*f*)	**Mitversicherung**(*f*)
code	code(*m*)	**Code**(*m*)
codicil	codicille(*m*), avenant(*m*)	**Kodizil**(*n*); Testamentsnachtrag(*m*); Zusatz(*m*)
coercion	coercition(*f*), contrainte(*f*)	**Zwang**(*m*); Nötigung(*f*)
coercive measures	mesures(*f*) de contrainte	**Zwangsmaßnahmen**(*f*)
cognisable	du ressort de, de la compétence de	erkennbar; gerichtlich verfolgbar; der Gerichtsbarkeit unterworfen
cognisance	connaissance(*f*)	**Erkenntnis**(*n*); (gerichtliche) Kenntnisnahme; (richterliche) Zuständigkeit(*f*); Anerkenntnis(*n*)
cohabitation	cohabitation(*f*), concubinage(*m*), union(*f*) libre	**Zusammenleben;** Lebensgemeinschaft
coheir	cohéritier(*m*)	**Miterbe**(*m*), Neben–
collateral	additionnel, indirect; nantissement(*m*); parent(*m*) en ligne colatérale	**Sicherungsgegenstand**(*m*); Nebensicherheit(*f*); Verwandte(r) in der Seitenlinie
collateral proceeding(s)	procédure(*f*) connexe	**Verfahren außerhalb der Streitverhandlung**(*f*); Nebenverfahren
collection	encaissement(*m*); levée(*f*), perception(*f*); rassemblement(*f*), réunion(*f*); recouvrement(*m*)	**Einziehung**(*f*), Inkasso(*n*), Beitreibung(*f*)
– agency	agence(*f*) de recouvrement	Inkassostelle
– order	ordre(*m*) de recouvrement	Inkassoauftrag
– procedure	procédure(*f*) de mise en recouvrement	Einziehungsverfahren
collective	collectif, collective	**kollektiv**(*n*), gesamt(*f*)
– agreement, bargain	convention(*f*) collective	Tarifvertrag; Kollektivvertrag
– bargaining	négociation(*f*) pour convention collective	Tarifverhandlungen
– guilt	culpabilité(*f*) collective	Kollektivschuld
– investment company	société(*f*) de placement	gemeinsame Kapitalanlagegesellschaft, Investmentgesellschaft
– liability	responsabilité(*f*) collective	Gesamtverpflichtung, –schuld; Kollektivhaftung
collusion	collusion(*f*), connivence(*f*)	**Kollusion**(*f*); geheimes (unerlaubtes) Einverständnis(*n*)

ENGLISH	FRENCH	GERMAN
commercial	commercial	wirtschaftlich; gewerblich; geschäftlich; handelsüblich
– agency	agence(f) de renseignements commerciaux	Handelsvertretung
– bank	banque(f) commerciale	Geschäftsbank; Handels–
– court	tribunal(m) commercial	Handelsgericht
– law	droit(m) commercial	Handelsrecht; –gesetz
– register	registre(m) de commerce	Handelsregister
commissioner for oaths	officier habilité à recevoir les déclarations sous serment(m)	Urkundsperson(f); zur Abnahme(f) von Eiden berechtigter Jurist
commit (to)	commettre, perpétrer	übergeben; begehen; verüben
– a crime	commettre, perpétrer un crime	strafbare Handlung, Verbrechen begehen
commitment	engagement(m), obligation(f); renvoi(m) à une commission	Verpflichtung(f); Übergabe(f); Einlieferung(f)
– to custody, prison	incarcération(f)	Einlieferung ins Gefängnis/in (Untersuchungs-Haft) nehmen
contractual –	obligation contractuelle	vertragliche Verpflichtung
committal	délégation(f); renvoi(m); incarcération	Überweisung(f), Einlieferung(f); Verhaftung(f)
– for trial	renvoi devant la cour d'assises; mise(f) en accusation	Anordnung der Hauptverhandlung (Strafprozeß)
committee	comité(m), conseil(m)	Komitee(n), Ausschuß(m)
creditors'	délégation(f) des créanciers	Gläubigerausschuß
liquidation –	commission(f) d'enquête parlementaire	Parlaments–; Sonder–; Untersuchungsausschuß
select –	comité de direction;	
standing –	réunion des présidents	Ständiger Ausschuß
commodity	marchandise(f), denrées(f)	(Handels-)Artikel(m); Ware; Rohstoff(m)
common land	terrain(m) communal, banal	Gemeindeland(n); Allmende
common law	droit(m) coutumier et jurisprudentiel	Gewohnheitsrecht(n); (ungeschriebenes) geme in Recht
commonwealth	État(m), Commonwealth	Gemeinwesen(n); Staat(m), Nation(f)
community	collectivité(f)	Gemeinschaft(f) (EG); Gemeinde(f)
Community legislation (EC)	législation(f) communautaire (CE)	gemeinschaftliche Rechtsvorschriften (EG)
commutation	commutation(f)	Austausch(m); Umwandlung(f)
– of penalty	commutation de peine	Strafumwandlung
commute (to) a penalty	commuer une peine	Strafe(f) umwandeln

ENGLISH	FRENCH	GERMAN
company	**compagnie**(*f*), société(*f*), entreprise(*f*)	**(Kapital-)Gesellschaft**(*f*); Firma(*f*)
affiliated –	filiale(*m*)	angeschlossenes Unternehmen; Konzern–
associated	associée(*f*)	Schwestergesellschaft angegliederte Gesellschaft; Beteiligungs–
controlling –	société mère	Dachgesellschaft
holding –	holding, société de participations financières	Holding–, Dachgesellschaft
incorporated –	société constituée	eingetragene (rechtsfähige) Gesellschaft
joint-stock –	société de capitaux, par actions	Kapitalgesellschaft
private –	société à responsabilité limitée (SARL)	Gesellschaft mit beschränkter Haftung
public –	société anonyme	Aktiengesellschaft
trading –	société commerciale	Handelsgesellschaft
compel (to)	**forcer**, contraindre	**zwingen**; nötigen
competence, competency	**compétence**(*f*), capacité(*f*)	**Zuständigkeit**(*f*); Befugnis(*n*); Geschäftsfähigkeit(*f*)
competent	**compétent**	**zuständig**; befugt; maßgeblich; sachverständig geschäftsfähig
– advice	avis(*m*) qualifié	sachverständiger Rat
– authority	autorité(*f*) compétente	zuständige Behörde
– evidence	preuve(*f*) recevable	zulässiges (und schlüssiges) Beweismaterial
court of – jurisdiction	tribunal(*m*) compétent	zuständiges Gericht
competition	**concurrence**(*f*)	**Konkurrenz**(*f*); Wettbewerb
– clause	clause(*f*) de concurrence	Wettbewerbsklausel
unfair –	concurrence déloyale	unlauterer Wettbewerb
complainant	**plaignant**	**Beschwerdeführer**(*m*); Erstatter(*m*) e-r Strafanzeige(*f*); Kläger(*m*)
complaint	**plainte**(*f*)	**Klage**(*f*); Klageschrift(*f*); Beschwerde(*f*)
complicity	**complicité**(*f*)	**Mittäterschaft**(*m*) (*StrafR*); Mitschuld(*f*); Tatbeteiligung(*f*)
composition	**arrangement**(*m*) **transactionnel**, concordat(*m*)	**Beilegung**(*f*), Vergleich; Zusammensetzung
compound (to)	**composer**, transiger	**sich vergleichen**, einigen
– with one's creditors	s'arranger avec ses créanciers	mit s-n Gläubigern einen Vergleich schließen
compulsion	**contrainte**(*f*), violence(*f*)	**Zwang**(*m*); Nötigung(*f*)
compulsory	**obligatoire**, forcé(*f*)	**obligatorisch**; zwangsweise
– administration	administration(*f*) forcée	Zwangsverwaltung
– commitment	engagement(*m*) obligatoire	Zwangsverpflichtung
– joinder	jonction(*f*) d'instances obligatoire	notwendige Streitgenossenschaft (*US*)
– liquidation	liquidation(*f*) judiciaire	Zwangsliquidation

ENGLISH	FRENCH	GERMAN
conceal (to)	dissimuler, cacher	verbergen; verheimlichen; verschleiern; verschweigen
concealment	dissimulation(f); recel(m)	Verbergen(n); Verheimlichung(f); Verschleierung(f); Verschweigen
– of evidence	dissimulation de preuves	Unterdrücken von Beweismaterial
concede (to)	concéder	einräumen; zugestehen; gewähren
concession	concession(f); dégrèvement(m)	Konzession(f); Zugeständnis(n); Zulassung(f)
conciliation	conciliation(f), arbitrage(m)	Versöhnung(f), Schlichtung(f)
conciliator	conciliateur(m), arbitre(m)	Vermittler(m); Schlichter(m)
conclusive evidence	preuve(f) concluante, pertinente	schlüssiger (zwingender) Beweis
concordance	concordance(f)	Übereinstimmung(f)
concur (to)	approuver, accéder à	übereinstimmen; zusammentreffen
concurrence	approbation(f), accord(m); conflit(m), concurrence(f)	Übereinstimmung(f); Zusammentreffen
– of jurisdiction	compétence(f) simultanée de plusieurs tribunaux	Kompetenzkonflikt; konkurrierende Zuständigkeit
condemn (to)	condamner	verurteilen; für unbrauchbar erklären
condemnation	condamnation(f)	Verurteilung(f); Unbrauchbarerklärung(f)
conditional	conditionnel	bedingt (durch); abhängig(von)
– discharge	libération(f) conditionnelle	Strafaussetzung zur Bewährung; bedingte Entlassung
– limitation	héritage(m) dévolu sous condition résolutoire	auflösende Bedingung (bei Einräumung e-s zeitlich begrenzten Nutzungsrechts)
condominium	condominium(m), copropriété(f) immobilière	Kondominium; Eigentumswohnung(f) (US)
conduct (to) somebody's cause	plaider la cause de qqu'un	e-n Rechtsstreit für jdn führen
confess (to)	se confesser, avouer	gestehen; bekennen
confession	confession(f), aveu(m)	Geständnis(n); Bekenntnis(n)
confidential information	information(f) confidentielle	vertrauliche Mitteilung(f), – Information(f)
confine (to) – to prison	détenir envoyer en prison	begrenzen; inhaftieren in Gefängnishaft nehmen
confinement solitary –	emprisonnement(m) emprisonnement cellulaire (au Cecret)	Beschränkung(f); Inhaftierung(f) Einzelhaft
confiscation	confiscation(f)	Konfiszierung(f); Beschlagnahme(f)
conflicting evidence	témoignages(m) contradictoires	sich widersprechende Beweise(m), sich widersprechende Zeugenaussage(f)

ENGLISH	FRENCH	GERMAN
confront (to) – witnesses	**envisager**, confronter confronter les témoins	**gegenüberstellen**; konfrontieren Zeugen gegenüberstellen
connivance	**collusion**(f), complicité(f)	**geheimes Einverständnis**(n); stillschweigende Einwilligung(f)
consecutive sentences	**jugement**(m) **ordonnant le cumul des peines**	**zusätzliche Strafzumessung**
consensus	**consensus**	**Konsens**(m); Übereinstimmung(f)
consent by mutual –	**consentement**(m) d'un commun accord	**Einwilligung**(f); Zustimmung(f) in gegenseitigem Einvernehmen; einverständlich
consequential – damage	**conséquent**, consécutif dommage(m) indirect	**kausal bedingt** mittelbarer Schaden, Folgeschaden
consign (to)	**expédier**	**versenden**, liefern; konsignieren; hinterlegen
consignation	**consignation**(f)	**Konsignation**(f); Hinterlegung(f) (Schottland)
consignee	**destinataire**	**Konsignatar**; Empfänger
consignment	**expédition**(f) **de marchandises**	**Sendung**(f)
consolidate (to)	**consolider**, codifier	**konsolidieren**; zusammenlegen
consolidated	**consolidé**(m), unifié, capitalisé	**konsolidiert**
consolidation – of actions – of companies	**consolidation**(f), fusion(f) jonction(f) d'instances fusion de sociétés	**Konsolidierung**(f); Vereinigung(f) Prozeß–, Klagenverbindung Zusammenlegung (od. Fusion) von Gesellschaften
consols (UK)	**fonds**(m) **consolidés** (UK), rentes(f) perpétuelles	**konsolidierte Staatsanleihen**(f); Konsols (UK)
consortium	**consortium**(m); **mariage**(m) **légitime**	**Konsortium**(n); (Recht der) eheliche(n) Lebensgemeinschaft(f)
conspiracy	**conspiration**(f), complot(m)	**Verschwörung**(f); geheime Absprache(f)
conspire (to)	**conspirer**, comploter	**s. verschwören**; sich heimlich verabreden
constabulary	**gendarmerie**(f)	**Polizei**(f)
constitution	**constitution**(f)	**Verfassung**(f); Gründung(f); Beschaffenheit(f)
constitutional – court – law	**constitutionnel**(m), **constitutionelle**(f) tribunal(m) constitutionnel droit(m) constitutionnel	**verfassungsmäßig**, –rechtlich Verfassungsgericht; ordentliches Bundesgericht Verfassungsrecht
constraint to act under –	**contrainte**, obligation; privation(f) de liberté, internement(m) agir sous la contrainte	**Zwang**(m), Nötigung(f); Beschränkung(f) unter Zwang handeln
construe (to)	**interpréter**, analyser	**auslegen**

ENGLISH	FRENCH	GERMAN
consultant	**consultant**(m), conseil(m), expert(m)	**Berater**(m)
consultation	**consultation**(f), délibération	**Beratung**(f); Konsultation(f)
consultative	**consultatif**	**beratend;** konsultativ
consumer	**consommateur**(m), usager(m)	**Verbraucher**(m)
– credit	crédit(m) à la consommation	Konsumkredit; Konsumenten–
– goods	biens de consommation	Konsumgüter; Verbrauchs–
– price index	indice(m) des prix à la consommation	Index der Verbraucherpreise
– protection	protection(f) des consommateurs	Verbraucherschutz
consummation of marriage	**consommation**(f) **du mariage**	**Vollziehung**(f) **des Eheaktes**
contango	**intérêt**(m) **de report**	**(Börse)**(f) **Report**(m); Kursaufschlag(m)
– business	marché(m) des reports	Reportgeschäft
– rate	taux(m) de report	Reportsatz, Prolongationssatz
contempt	**mépris**(m), outrage(m), manque de respect	**Mißachtung**(f); Geringschätzung(f)
civil –	outrage civil	Ungehorsam gegenüber gerichtlichem Gebot
– of court	outrage à magistrat(s)	Mißachtung des Gerichts
criminal –	outrage délictueux	strafbare Mißachtung des Gerichts; Ungebühr vor Gericht
contend (to)	**affirmer,** prétendre	**behaupten;** geltend machen
contention	**contestation**(f), dispute(f)	**Behauptung**(f); Streit(m); Vorbringen
contest (to)	**contester,** disputer, attaquer	**bestreiten;** anfechten
contestant	**opposant**	**streitende Partei**(f), anfechtende–
contiguous	**contigu, contiguë**	**angrenzend;** benachbart
contingency	**contingence**(f), cas(m) imprévu	**unvorhergesehenes Ereignis**(n); Eventualfall(m)
– reserve	fonds(m) de réserve	Reserve für unvorhergesehen Ausgaben; Rückstellung für Eventualverbindlichkeiten; Sicherheitsrücklage
contingent	**éventuel,** conditionnel, fortuit	**abhängig**
– fee	honoraires éventuels	Erfolgshonorar
– liabilities	engagement(m) éventuel; tierce caution	Eventualverbindlichkeiten
continuation clause	**clause**(f) **de report**	**Verlängerungsklausel**(f); Report– (m)
contract	**contrat**(m), convention(f), pacte(m)	**Vertrag**(m); Abkommen(n)
bilateral –	contrat bilatéral	zweiseitiger Vertrag
– law	droit(m) des obligations	Vertragsrecht
unilateral –	contrat unilatéral	einseitig verpflichtender Vertrag

ENGLISH	FRENCH	GERMAN
contractor	contractant(*m*), adjudicataire(*m*), entrepreneur(*m*)	**Vertragspartei**(*f*); Lieferant(*m*); Unternehmer(*m*)
contradict (to)	contredire	widersprechen; in Abrede stellen
contradiction	contradiction(*f*), contredit(*m*)	**Widerspruch**(*m*); Widerrede(*f*)
contradictory	contradictoire	entgegengesetzt; sich widersprechend
contravention	contravention(*f*), infraction(*f*)	**Zuwiderhandlung**(*f*); Übertretung(*f*); Verstoß(*m*)
in – of	en violation de	Zuwiderhandlung in Verletzung von
contributory negligence	négligence(*f*) contributoire	**Mitverschulden**(*n*); mitwirkendes Verschulden
convene (to)	rassembler, réunir, citer	einberufen; laden; sich versammeln
– a shareholders' meeting	tenir une réunion des actionnaires	e-e Hauptversammlung, Gesellschafter einberufen
convert (to)	convertir, transformer, changer	umwandeln; –wechseln, –tauschen
convertible – securities	convertible titres(*m*) convertibles	umwandelbar; konvertierbar konvertierbare Papiere
conveyance – of property	transport(*m*), transmission(*f*) tout mode de transmission de propriété	**Übertragung**(*f*); Beförderung(*f*) Vermögens–, Eigentumsübertragung
– of real estate deed of –	transport d'immeubles acte(*m*) de cession	Grundstücksauflassung; Übertragungs–, Auflassungsurkunde
convict	forçat(*m*), déporté(*m*, *f*), bagnard(*m*); détenu(*m*) d'un pénitencier (*US*)	**Strafgefangener**(*m*); Sträfling(*m*); Verurteilter(*m*)
conviction	condamnation(*f*)	**Überführung**(*f*); Schuldspruch(*m*), Verurteilung(*f*)
cooperative society	coopérative, société(*f*) coopérative	**Genossenschaft**(*f*); Konsumverein(*m*)
coopt (to)	coopter	hinzuwählen; kooptieren
copyright	droit(*m*) d'auteur, propriété(*f*) littéraire	**Urheberrecht**(*n*)
coroner	'coroner'(*m*)	richterlicher Beamter(*m*) zur Untersuchung(*f*) der Todesursache(*f*)
corporal punishment	châtiment(*m*) corporel	körperliche Züchtigung(*f*); Prügelstrafe(*f*)
corporate	relatif à une personne morale ou sociale	körperschaftlich; korporativ
– assets	actif(*m*) social	Gesellschaftsvermögen
– body	corps(*m*) constitué, personne morale	Körperschaft, juristische Person
– stock	actions(*f*) d'une société	Aktien

ENGLISH	FRENCH	GERMAN
corporation	corporation(f), guilde(f), corps(m) constitué, corps(m) de métier	Körperschaft(f); juristische Person(f)
corporeal property	biens corporels	Sachen; körperliche Gegenstände
corpus delicti	corps(m) du délit	Korpus delicti; Tatbestand (eines Verbrechens)
correctional institution	maison(f) de correction	Straf(vollzugs)anstalt(f) (US); Gefängnis(n)
corroborating evidence	preuve(f) corroborante	bestätigende Zeugenaussage(f)
council	conseil(m), assemblée(f)	Rat(m); Versammlung(f); Ortsbehörde(n)
Council directive	directive(f) du conseil	Weisung, Verfügung, Richtlinie(des Rats)
Council decision	décision(f) du conseil	Ratsbeschluß
Council of the EEC	le Conseil de la CE	Rat der Europäischen Gemeinschaft
UN Security Council	le Conseil de sécurité des Nations Unies	Sicherheitsrat der Vereinten Nationen
counsel	avocat(m), conseil(m); avis(m)	Anwalt(m); Rechtsbeistand(m)
– for the plaintiff	avocat du plaignant	Prozeßbevollmächtigter des Klägers
– for the prosecution	représentant(m) du ministère public	Anklagevertreter
count	compte(m), calcul(m); chef(m) d'accusation	Klagepunkt(m)
of the first –	au premier chef	erster Klagepunkt
of the second –	au second chef	zweiter Klagepunkt
countercharge	contre-accusation(f)	Gegenklage(f), –beschuldigung(f)
counterclaim	demande(f) reconventionnelle	Gegenforderung(f), –anspruch(m)
counterfeit	contrefaçon, faux	Nachahmung(f); Fälschung(f)
counterfeiting	contrefaçon	Nachahmung(f); Fälschung(f)
countermand (to)	annuler, rappeler, révoquer	aufheben; widerrufen; abbestellen
counterpart	contrepartie(f); duplicata(m)	Zweitausfertigung(f); Gegenstück(n)
county	comté(m)	Grafschaft(f); Verwaltungsbezirk(m)
– council	conseil(m) général	Grafschaftsrat; Bezirksausschuß
– court	tribunal(m) de première instance	Grafschaftsgericht; Kreisgericht (US); Amtsgericht

ENGLISH	FRENCH	GERMAN
court	**cour**(*f*) **de justice,** tribunal	**Gericht**(*n*)
administrative –	tribunal administratif	Verwaltungs–
arbitration –	tribunal d'arbitrage	Schieds–
circuit –	tribunal de première instance (*US*)	erstinstanzliches – für mehrere Bezirke (*US*)
civil –	tribunal civil	– für Zivilsachen
county –	tribunal de première instance	Grafschafts–; Kreis– (*US*); Amts–
– of appeal	cour d'appel	Berufungs–
criminal –	cour(*f*) de juridiction criminelle	– für Strafsachen, Strafkammer
district – (*US*)	tribunal(*m*) fédéral de première instance (*US*)	(Bundes-)Bezirksgericht (*US*)
federal –	cour fédérale	Bundes–
inferior –	tribunal inférieure	unteres –; Instanzgericht
magistrates' –	tribunal de première instance	erstinstanzliches Gericht (ohne Geschworene); Amts–
police –	tribunal de police	Polizei–
probate – (*US*)	tribunal des successions et des tutelles (*US*)	Nachlaß–
state –	tribunal d'État	einzelstaatliches – (*US*)
superior –	tribunal supérieure	höhere Instanz; übergeordnetes –
supreme –	cour suprême	Oberster Gerichtshof; Oberstes Bundes– (*US*) *höheres Berufungs–*
trial –	tribunal de première instance	erkennendes –; – erster Instanz
court order	**injonction**(*f*)	**gerichtl. Verfügung**(*f*); Gerichtsbeschluß(*m*)
court record	**archives**(*f*) **judiciaires**	**Gerichtsakte**(*f*); Prozeßakte(*f*)
covenant	**contrat**(*m*), convention(*f*), pacte(*m*)	**Vertragsabrede**(*f*); Verpflichtung(*f*); Zusicherung(*f*)
covert	**couvert**	**geschützt;** gedeckt; heimlich
credibility	**crédibilité**(*f*)	**Glaubwürdigkeit**(*f*)
credit	**crédit**(*m*)	**Kredit**(*m*); Darlehen(*n*); Guthaben(*n*)
creditor	**créditeur**(*m*), créancier(*m*)	**Gläubiger**(*m*); Kreditgeber(*m*)
crime	**crime**(*m*)	**Verbrechen;** strafbare Handlung(*f*), Straftat(*f*)
criminal	**criminel**(*m*) (*n et adj*)	**kriminell;** strafbar; strafrechtlich
– action	action(*f*) au criminel	Strafverfahren; strafrechtliche Verfolgung;
– charge	inculpation(*f*) de crime	Anklage wegen e-s Verbrechens
– court	cour(*f*) de juridiction criminelle	Gericht für Strafsachen; Strafkammer
– law	droit(*m*) pénal, droit criminel	Strafrecht
– record	casier(*m*) judiciaire	Strafregister; Vorstrafe(nverzeichnis)

ENGLISH	FRENCH	GERMAN
cross	**contre-**, anti-	**entgegengesetzt;** wechselseitig
– -action	action(f) reconventionnelle, opposition(f)	Wider-, Gegenklage
– -appeal	appel(m) incident	Anschlußberufung
– -claim	revendication(f) dans une action reconventionelle	Gegenanspruch
– -examination	contre-interrogatoire(m)	Kreuzverhör
– -guarantee	contre-garantie(f)	beiderseitig Garantie
– -liability	contre-responsabilité(f)	beiderseitige Haftung
Crown	**Couronne (l'État)**(f)	**Krone**(f)
– Court	cour d'assises	Gericht für Strafsachen und einige Zivilsachen (*England und Wales*)
cruelty	**cruauté**(f), mauvais traitements(m)	**Grausamkeit**(f)
mental –	cruauté mentale, excès(m) et injures(f) graves	seelische Grausamkeit
culpable	**coupable;** volontaire	**schuldhaft;** strafbar
culprit	**coupable;** accusé(m), prévenu	**Angeklagter**(m); Beschuldigter(m); Täter(m)
cumulative evidence	**témoignages**(m) **concordants**	**verstärkender Beweis**(m); erdrückendes Beweismaterial(n)
currency	**circulation**(f), cours(f) de l'argent; devise(m), monnaie	**Währung**(f); Umlauf(m), Laufzeit(f)
– of a contract	devise d'un contrat	Laufzeit e-s Vertrags
– offence	infraction(f) à la réglementation des changes	Devisenvergehen
– restrictions	réglementation(f) des changes	Währungsbeschränkungen
custodian	**garde**(f); syndic(m)	**Verwahrer**(m); Vormund(m) (US); Treuhänder(m)
custody	**garde,** garde d'un enfant; détention(f), état(m) d'arrestation	**Haft**(f); Obhut(f), Sorgerecht(n); Verwahrung(f)
preventive –	détention préventive	Untersuchungshaft; Sicherungsverwahrung
protective –	détention à fins de protection	Schutzhaft
safe –	bonne(f) garde	sichere Aufbewahrung; Verwahrung
customary law	**droit**(m) **coutumier**	**Gewohnheitsrecht**(n)
customs	**douanes**(f)	**Zoll**(m); Zollbehörde(f)
– clearance	expédition(f) en douane	Zollabfertigung; Verzollung
– declaration	déclaration(f) en douane	Zollerklärung; Zollanmeldung
– duties	droits(m) de douane	Zollgebühren, –abgaben
– union	union(f) douanière	Zollunion, –verband

D

ENGLISH	FRENCH	GERMAN
damage	**dommage**(*m*), dégât(*m*)	**Schaden**(*m*); Beschädigung(*f*); Verlust(*m*)
actual –	dommage réel	tatsächlicher Schaden
consequential –	dommage indirect	mittelbarer Schaden; Folgeschaden
criminal –	dégâts criminels	strafbare Sachbeschädigung
direct –	dommage direct	unmittelbarer Schaden
general –	dommage général	Gesamtschaden; allgemeiner Schaden
partial –	dommage partiel	Teilschaden
damages	**indemnité**(*f*), dommages-intérêts(*m*)	**Schadensersatz**(*m*); Entschädigung(-ssumme)(*f*)
contingent –	dommages-intérêts conditionnels	bedingt zuerkannter Schadensersatzanspruch
incidental –	dommages-intérêts incidents	Schadenersatz für Aufwendungen bei Vertragserfüllung
liquidated –	dommages liquidés	im voraus der Höhe nach bestimmter Schadensersatz; Vertragsstrafe
nominal –	dommages-intérêts symboliques ('un franc symbolique')	nomineller Schadensersatz
unliquidated –	dommages-intérêts non liquidés	(der Höhe nach noch) unbestimmter Schadensersatz
date	**date**(*f*)	**Datum**(*n*); Zeitpunkt(*m*); Termin
closing –	date limite	Abschlußtermin; Anmeldeschluß; Abschlußstichtag
expiry –	date d'expiration	Verfallstag; Ablauftermin
redemption –	date de remboursement, date d'amortissement	Tilgungstermin; Einlösungstermin
termination –	date de cessation, date de résiliation	Ablauf-, Enddatum; Tag des Außerkrafttretens
deadline	**date limite**, date de clôture	**Stichtag**(*m*); (letzter) Termin(*m*); Anmeldeschluss(*n*)
dealer	**négociant**, marchand; courtier(*m*) de change, cambiste(*m*) (*US*); 'dealer'(*m*), trafiquant(*m*) de stupéfiant	**Händler**(*m*); Wertpapier–(*n*)
dealings	**menées**(*f*) **commerciales**, transactions boursières	**Geschäfte**(*n*); Transaktionen; Geschäftsverbindungen

35

ENGLISH	FRENCH	GERMAN
death certificate	**acte**(*m*) **de décès**, extrait(*m*) mortuaire	**Totenschein**(*m*); Sterbeurkunde(*f*)
death penalty	**peine capitale**, peine de mort	**Todesstrafe**(*f*)
debenture	**obligation**(*f*), reconnaissance(*f*) de dette	**Verbindlichkeiten** (Sammelbegriff für alle ungesicherten, langfristigen–); Rückzollschein
debt doubtful – instrument of – outstanding – preferential –	**dette**(*f*), créance(*f*) créance douteuse titre(*m*) de créance dette à recouvrer créance préférentielle	**Schuld**(*f*); Forderung(*f*) zweifelhafte Forderung Schuldurkunde (pl.) Außenstände bevorrechtigte Schuld, Forderung
debtor	**débiteur**(*m*)	**Schuldner**(*m*); Darlehens–, Kreditnehmer(*m*)
decease	**mort**, décès	**Ableben**(*n*); Tod(*m*)
deceased, decedent	**personne**(*f*) **décédée**, le défunt	**Verstorbener**(*m*); Erblasser(*m*)
deceased's estate	**succession**(*f*)	**Nachlaß**(*m*); Erbschaft(*f*)
deceit	**tromperie**(*f*), fraude(*f*)	**Täuschung**(*f*); Betrug(*m*)
deceptive	**trompeur**(*m*), mensonger, déloyal	**täuschend**; irreführend; trügerisch
decision court – (*cf. judgment*)	**décision**(*f*), résolution(*f*) décision de justice, verdict(*m*)	**Beschluß**(*m*); Entscheidung(*f*); Urteil(*n*) (Zivilprozeß)(*m*) gerichtliche Entscheidung, Urteil (s. Zivil– od. Strafurteil; Urteilsspruch)
declaration – of bankruptcy – of consent – of dissent – of intention	**déclaration**(*f*); décision(*f*) judiciaire; dispositif(*m*) de jugement déclaration de faillite déclaration de consentement déclaration de désaccord déclaration d'intention; demande(*f*) de naturalisation (*US*)	**Erklärung**(*f*); Klageschrift(*f*); (Wert-)Angabe(*f*); Zolldeklaration(*f*) Konkurserklärung, –eröffnung Einverständnis–, Zustimmungserklärung Beschwerde Willens–, Absichtserklärung
declaratory – judgment	**déclaratoire** jugement(*m*) déclaratoire	**feststellend**; (rechts-)erklärend; deklaratorisch Feststellungsurteil
decree (*cf. judgment*) – absolute – nisi divorce – final –	**décret**(*m*), décision(*f*) d'ordre judiciaire ou administratif jugement définitif jugement provisoire; jugement interlocutoire jugement de divorce jugement final	**Urteil**(*n*); Verfügung(*f*); Verordnung(*f*) (s. Urteilsspruch) rechtskräftiges Scheidungsurteil vorläufiges Scheidungsurteil Scheidungsurteil Endurteil, rechtskräftiges Urteil

ENGLISH	FRENCH	GERMAN
deed	**action**(f), acte(m); acte notarié	**Urkunde**(f), Vertrag(m); Tat(f), Handlung(f)
– of assignment	acte attributif de biens	Abtretungsurkunde
– of consent	déclaration(f) de consentement	Beitrittsurkunde; Einwilligungserklärung
– of conveyance	acte de cession	Übertragungs–, Auflassungsurkunde (bei Grundeigentum)
– of trust	acte fiduciaire	Treuhandvertrag; Sicherungsübereignung
defamation	**diffamation**(f)	**Ehrverletzung**(f); Beleidigung(f); Verleumdung(f)
defamatory	**diffamatoire**	**beleidigend**; diffamierend; verleumderisch
default	**manquement**(f), défaillance(f)	**Nichterfüllung**(f); Unterlassung(f); (Zahlungs-) Verzug(m)
– of appearance	défaut(m) de comparution	Nichterscheinen (vor Gericht); Versäumnis der Einlassung
judgment by –	jugement(m) par défaut	Versäumnisurteil
defeat (to)	**frustrer**, faire échouer, déjouer	**besiegen**; vereiteln; zu Fall(m) bringen; aufheben
defence	**défense**(f); la défense	**Einrede**(f); Einlassung(f); Klagebeantwortung(f)
– counsel	avocat(m) de la défense, défenseur	Verteidiger; Anwalt des Beklagten
statement of –	conclusions(f) de la défense	Klagebeantwortung; Verteidigungsvorbringen
witness for the –	témoin(m) de la défense	Entlastungszeuge; von der Verteidigung benannter Zeuge
defendant	**défenseur**(m), **défenderesse**(f), accusé,–e	**Beklagter**(m); Angeklagter(m)
defer (to)	**différer**, ajourner	**aufschieben**; zurückstellen
deferment	**ajournement**(m), remise(f)	**Aufschub**(m); Zurückstellung(f)
deferred	**différé**, ajourné	**aufgeschoben**; gestundet; zurückgestellt
– payment	paiement différé	hinausgeschobene Zahlung; Ratenzahlung (US)
deficiency	**découvert**(m)	**Mangel**(m); Fehlbetrag(m), Minderbetrag(m)
deficit	**déficit**(m)	**Defizit**(n); Minder–, Fehlbetrag(m); Passivsaldo(m)
defray (to)	**défrayer**	**(Kosten) bestreiten**; aufkommen für
degree (cf. murder)	**degré**(m)	**Grad**(m); Rang(m); (s. Mord)
del credere	**ducroire**(m)	**Delkredere**
delegate (to)	**déléguer**	**delegieren**; weiterübertragen
– responsibility	déléguer une responsabilité	Verantwortung übertragen
delete (to)	**effacer**, radier, supprimer	**löschen**, streichen
deletion	**effacement**, radiation	**Löschung**(f); Streichung(f)

ENGLISH	FRENCH	GERMAN
deliberate	délibéré(m), prémédité, voulu	absichtlich, vorsätzlich; (wohl-) überlegt
delinquency	délinquence(f)	Pflichtverletzung(f), Vergehen(n); Kriminalität(f)
juvenile –	délinquence juvénile	Jugendkriminalität
demand bill	traite(f) à vue	Sichtwechsel(m)
demise	cession(f) à bail; décès(m)	Übertragung(f), Verpachtung(f); Ableben(n), Tod(m)
demurrage	surestaries(f), droits(m) de surestarie; magasinage, droits(m) de magasinage	Überliegezeit(f); Überliegegeld
denial	dénégation(f), déni(m), démenti(m)	Bestreitung(f); Ableugnung(f); abschlägiger Bescheid(m)
denounce (to)	dénoncer	anzeigen; denunzieren; (Vertrag)(m) kündigen
deny (to)	nier, contester	in Abrede(f) stellen; leugnen; verweigern
departure – from statutory regulations	départ(m); écart(m) dérogation(f) aux dispositions légales	Abweichen; Klageänderung(f) Abweichen von den gesetzlichen Vorschriften
dependants	personnes(f) à charge	(Familien-)Angehörige(f); Unterhaltsberechtigte; Hinterbliebene
deponent	signataire(m) d'un affidavit, d'une attestation; témoin(m) déposant	vereidigter Zeuge(m); Aussteller(m) (e-s Affidavit)
depose (to)	déposer	eidlich bezeugen; vor Gericht(n) aussagen; absetzen
deposit	dépôt(m)	Anzahlung(f); Einlage(f); Hinterlegung(f); Sicherheitsleistung(f); Verwahrung(f)
– guarantee	dépôt de garantie	Einlagegarantie
depositary	dépositaire(m); consignation(f)	Verwahrer(m); Depositar(m); Hinterlegungsstelle
deposition	déposition(f)	Zeugenaussage(f); Beweisaufnahmeprotokoll(n); Hinterlegung(f); Absetzung(f)
– of evidence – of witness	témoignage(m) déposition d'un témoin	eidliche Zeugenaussage Zeugenaussage
depositor	déposant(m)	Hinterleger(m); Einzahler(m)
deprivation	privation(f), destitution(f)	Beraubung(f); Entziehung(f); Verlust(m)
– of liberty	privation de liberté	Freiheitsberaubung; –entziehung
deputy	vice-, -adjoint; député(m); substitut(m) (d'un juge)	Abgeordneter(m); Stellvertreter(m)
derogate (to)	déroger, porter atteinte à	beeinträchtigen; Abbruch(m) tun; (teilweise) aufheben

ENGLISH	FRENCH	GERMAN
derogation	dérogation(f), diminution(f)	Beeinträchtigung(f); Minderung(f); teilweise Außerkraftsetzung
derogative clause	clause(f) dérogatoire	Abänderungsklausel(f)
desertion	désertion(f)	Verlassen; Fahnenflucht
detain (to)	retenir, détenir, garder	in Haft nehmen; zurück-, einbehalten
detainer	détention(f), prise de possession	(widerrechtliche) Vorenthaltung(f) (Grundbesitz); Haftbefehl
detention	détention	(Untersuchungs-)Haft(f); Festnahme(f); Zurückhaltung(f), Beschlagnahme
deter (to) – s.o. from	empêcher, dissuader empêcher qqu'un de	abschrecken; verhindern jdn abhalten von
detriment	détriment(m), préjudice(m), perte(f)	Nachteil(m); Schaden(m); Beeinträchtigung(f)
deviation	déviation(f), écart(m); dérogation(f)	Abweichung(f); Deviation(f)
devise	disposition(f) testamentaire de biens immobiliers	letztwillige Verfügung(f) (Vermächtnis(n) über Grundbesitz)(m)
devisee	légataire(m, f)	Testamentserbe(m); Vermächtnisnehmer(m)
devisor	testateur(m)	Erblasser(m); Vermächtnisgeber(m)
dilatory – plea	dilatoire exception(f) dilatoire	dilatorisch; aufschiebend dilatorische (od. prozeßhindernde) Einrede
direct – cost – damage – descendant – evidence – examination	direct frais(m) spéciaux dommages(m) directs descendant(m) direct preuve(f) directe interrogatoire(m) direct	direkt; unmittelbar direkte Kosten, Einzelkosten; leistungsabhängige Kosten unmittelbarer Schaden direkter Nachkomme unmittelbarer Beweis erste Befragung des Zeugen durch die den Zeugen stellende Partei
direction	direction(f); ordre(m), prescription(f)	Anordnung(f); Leitung(f); Rechtsbelehrung(f)
directive (EC law) Council –	directive(f) directive du Conseil	Richtlinie(f); Anordnung(f) (EG) EG-Rat Richtlinie
disability – pension legal – partial – permanent –	incapacité(f); infirmité(f), invalidité(f) pension(f) d'invalidité incapacité légale incapacité partielle incapacité permanente	Unfähigkeit(f) Invaliditätsrente; (Kriegs-) Beschädigtenrente Rechts-, Prozeßunfähigkeit teilweise Erwerbs-, Arbeitsunfähigkeit dauerhafte Erwerbs-, Arbeitsunfähigkeit

ENGLISH	FRENCH	GERMAN
disagreement	désaccord(m)	Meinungsverschiedenheit(f); Widerspruch(m)
disallowance	rejet(m), réfaction(f)	Nichtanerkennung(f); Zurückweisung(f)
disbarment	radiation(f) d'un avocat du barreau	Ausschluß(m) aus der Anwaltschaft
discharge	libération(f), décharge(f)	Entlassung(f); Entlastung(f); Entladung(f), Löschen
conditional –	libération conditionnelle	Strafaussetzung zur Bewährung; bedingte Entlassung
– from an encumbrance	dégrevage	Entlastung; Entschuldung
– from prison	libération de prison	Freilassung
disclaim (to)	rejeter, renoncer à	verzichten auf; nicht anerkennen; dementieren
disclaimer	renonciation(f) explicite à un droit; refus(m) d'une charge	Verzichtleistung(f), –serklärung; Widerruf(m)
disclosure (of)	communication(f) de pièces	Offenlegung(f); Bekanntgabe(f)
discontinuance	cessation(f), abandon(m)	Unterbrechung(f); Einstellung(f)
– of an action	désistement(m) d'action	Aussetzung e-s Verfahrens; Klagerücknahme
discovery	découverte(f), divulgation(f)	Entdeckung(f), Enthüllung(f); Ermittlung(f); Offenlegung(f)
– proceedings	procédure(f) en vue d'identifier les actifs d'une succession	Entdeckungsverfahren
discredit	discrédit(m), déconsidération(f)	Mißkredit(m); schlechter Ruf(m); Unglaubwürdigkeit(f)
discrepancy	désaccord(m), contradiction(f)	Widerspruch(m); Unstimmigkeit(f); Abweichung(f)
discretion	discrétion(f), pouvoir discrétionnaire	Ermessen(n); Diskretion(f); Klugheit(f)
discretionary	discrétionnaire	beliebig; Ermessens-
discriminate (to)	pratiquer la discrimination	diskriminieren; unterscheiden
discrimination	discrimination(f)	Diskriminierung(f); Benachteiligung(f)
discriminatory	discriminatoire	diskriminierend; unterscheidend
– legislation	législation(f) d'exception	Ausnahmegesetzgebung
– measure	mesure(f) discriminatoire	diskriminierende Maßnahme
– policy	politique(f) de discrimination, de favoritisme	diskriminierende Politik
– procedure	procédure(f) d'exception	diskriminierendes Verfahren
– treatment	traitement(m) discriminatoire	unterschiedliche Behandlung
disendow (to)	retirer, ôter	e-r Pfründe berauben; Einkommen entziehen
dishonesty	malhonnêteté(f)	Unredlichkeit(f); Unehrlichkeit(f)

ENGLISH	FRENCH	GERMAN
dishonour (to) – a bill	**déshonorer** refuser le paiement d'une traite, ne pas honorer une traite	**nicht erfüllen**; zurückweisen e-n Wechsel nicht bezahlen, – einlösen
disinherit (to)	**déshériter**	**enterben**
dismiss (to) – an appeal	**renvoyer**, congédier, destituer, licencier rejeter un appel, débouter d'un appel	**entlassen**; abweisen, zurückweisen Berufung verwerfen, zurückweisen
dismissal – of an action	**renvoi**(*m*), congédiement(*m*), rejet(*m*), licenciement(*m*) classement d'une affaire	**Entlassung**(*f*); Zurückweisung(*f*); Einstellung(*f*) Klageabweisung
disobey (to)	**désobéir**	**nicht befolgen**; mißachten
disorder	**désordre**(*m*)	**Unruhe**(*f*); Störung(*f*)
disobedience	**désobéissance**(*f*)	**Ungehorsam;** Gehorsamsverweigerung
disorderly conduct	**conduite**(*f*) **contraire aux bonnes moeurs**	**ordnungswidriges Verhalten**(*n*); ärgernis(*n*) erregendes Benehmen
disown (to)	**désavouer**, renier	**(ab-, ver-)leugnen**; nichts zu tun haben mit; verstoßen
dispensation – of justice	**dispense**(*f*) exercice(*m*), pratique de la justice	**Befreiung**(*f*); Verteilung(*f*); Erlassung(*f*) Rechtsanwendung; Rechtsprechung
disposal right of –	**vente**(*f*), distribution, cession droit(*m*) de libre disposition	**Verfügung**(*f*); Erledigung(*f*); Veräußerung(*f*) Verfügungsrecht
disposing of – mind	**disposition**(*f*) de bonne disposition	**testierfähig**; verfügungs–testierfähig sein
disposition	**disposition testamentaire,** cession(*f*) (de biens)	**Verfügungsgewalt**(*f*); Anordnung(*f*); Bestimmung(*f*)
dispossess (to)	**déposséder**, dessaisir, exproprier	**(widerrechtlich) Besitz**(*m*) **entziehen**; zur Räumung(*f*) zwingen
disregard (to)	**enfreindre**, mépriser, passer outre à	**nicht beachten**; ignorieren
dissent	**dissentiment**(*m*), différence(*f*) d'opinion	**Dissens**(*m*), Meinungsverschiedenheit(*f*)
dissentient	**dissident,** opposant	**abweichend**; andersdenkend
dissenting juror	**juré en désaccord avec le reste du jury**	**nicht Zustimmende(r)**(*f, m*), widersprechende(r)(*f, m*) Geschworene(r)(*f, m*)
dissolution – of marriage	**dissolution**(*f*) dissolution du mariage	**Auflösung**(*f*); Aufhebung(*f*) Auflösung der Ehe
distrain (to)	**saisir,** opérer une saisie	**in Besitz**(*m*) **nehmen**; mit Beschlag(*m*) (Arrest)(*m*) belegen

ENGLISH	FRENCH	GERMAN
distraint	**saisie-exécution**(f); l'objet saisi	**Inbesitznahme**(f); Beschlagnahme(f)
distress	**détresse**(f), désespoir(m); saisie(f) en cas de non-paiement du loyer	**Inbesitznahme**(f); Beschlagnahme(f); Not(lage)(f)
distribution	**distribution**(f), répartition(f), partage(m)	**Verteilung**(f); Distribution(f)
– of dividends	paiement(m) des dividendes	Ausschüttung der Dividende
– of property	partage des biens	Vermögensverteilung
district	**district**(m), quartier(m)	**Bezirk**(m), Kreis(m)
– attorney (US)	procureur(m) de la République (US)	(Bezirks-)Staatsanwalt (US)
– court (US)	tribunal(m) fédéral de première instance (US)	(Bundes-)Bezirksgericht (US)
judicial –	ressort(m) territorial d'un tribunal	Gerichtsbezirk
disturbance	**dérangement**, perturbation(f), trouble	**Behinderung**(f); Störung(f)
– of public order	atteinte(f) à l'ordre public	Störung der öffentlichen Ordnung (Ruhe)
divergence	**divergence**(f)	**Abweichung**(f)
– of opinion	divergence d'opinions	Meinungsverschiedenheit
dividend	**dividende**(m)	**Dividende**(f)
divorce	**divorce**(m)	**Scheidung**(f)
– proceedings	action(f) en divorce	Ehescheidungsverfahren
dock	**banc**(m) des accusés	**Dock**(n), Kai(m); Anklagebank(f)
docket	**résumé**(m) **ou extrait du jugement**; bordereau(m) d'un dossier de procédure; registre(m) des jugements rendus; récépissé(m) de douane	**Urteilsregister**(n), –liste; Etikett(n); Inhaltsverzeichnis(n); Lieferschein; Zollquittung
doctrine	**doctrine**(f)	**Lehre**(f), Doktrin(f)
documentary credit	**crédit**(m) **documentaire**	**Dokumentenakkreditiv**(n)
domestic	**familial**(m); national(m)	**inländisch**; innerstaatlich; Familien–
– economy	économie(f) nationale	Binnenwirtschaft
– law	droit(m) interne	inländisches, innerstaatliches Recht
domicile	**domicile**(m)	**Domizil**(n); Wohnsitz(m); Firmensitz(m)
domiciliary	**domiciliaire**	**den Wohnort**(m) **betreffend**; Heimats–
dominant tenement	**fonds**(m) **dominant**	**herrschendes Grundstück**(n) **(bei Grunddienstbarkeit)**
donee	**donataire**(m), bénéficiaire(m)	**Schenkungsempfänger**(m); Begünstigter(m)
donor	**donneur**(m), donateur(m)	**Schenkungsgeber**(m); Stifter(m)
dormant	**non exercé**	**verborgen**; still

ENGLISH	FRENCH	GERMAN
double jeopardy	**double incrimination**	**Verbot**(*n*) **der doppelten Strafverfolgung**(*f*) **eines Täters wegen derselben Tat**
doubt	**doute**(*m*)	**Zweifel**(*m*); Bedenken(*n*)
beyond reasonable –	quasi-certitude du jury rendant un verdict de culpabilité, conviction(*f*) dépassant la croyance en un doute raisonnable	jeder vernünfige Zweifel ausgeschlossen
dower	**douaire**(*m*)	**Mitgift**(*f*); lebenslängliches Nießbrauchrecht des verwitweten Ehegatten an 1/3 des Grundbesitzes des verstorbenen (*US*)
down-payment	**accompte (hypothèque, vente à crédit)**	**Anzahlung**(*f*)
dowry	**dot**(*f*)	**Mitgift**(*f*); Aussteuer(*m*)
draft	**projet**(*m*) **d'acte**	**Entwurf**(*m*); Konzept(*n*)
– Bill	avant-projet de loi	Gesetzesentwurf, –vorlage
– contract	projet de contrat	Vertragsentwurf
drawee	**tiré**(*m*) **(d'un effet),** payeur(*m*) (d'une lettre de change)	**Bezogener**(*m*); Trassat(*m*)
drawer	**tireur**(*m*), souscripteur(*m*)	**Aussteller**(*m*); Trassant(*m*)
driving licence	**permis**(*m*) **de conduire**	**Führerschein**(*m*)
drop (to)	**baisser,** diminuer; renoncer à, retirer	**einstellen;** fallen lassen
– a case	abandonner des poursuites	Klage fallenlassen, zurücknehmen
drug offence (*cf. narcotics*)	**infraction**(*f*) **à la législation sur les stupéfiants**	**Drogendelikt**(*n*) (*s. Rauschgift*)(*n*)
drunken driving	**conduite**(*f*) **en état d'ivresse**	**Trunkenheit**(*f*) **am Steuer**(*m*)
due	**dû**(*m*); **légitime**	**geschuldet;** zustehend; fällig; gebührend
– consideration	réflexion(*f*) voulue, mûre réflexion	(nach) reifliche(r) Überlegung
– date	échéance(*f*), (en) temps utile	Fälligkeitsdatum; –termin
– process of law (*US*)	procédure judiciaire(*f*) de sauvegarde de la liberté individuelle	ordnungsgemäßes Verfahren; ordentliches Gerichtsverfahren
dues	**dû**(*m*), droits(*m*), frais(*m*), redevance(*f*)	**Gebühren**(*f*), Abgaben(*n*); Beitrag(*m*)
duly	**dûment,** en temps utile	**gebührend;** ordnungsmäßig; rechtzeitig
dummy	**simulacre**(*m*); mannequin(*m*); homme(*m*) de paille; factice (*adj.*)	**Strohmann**(*m*); Schein–

ENGLISH	FRENCH	GERMAN
dummy company	**société**(f) **prête-nom**	**Scheingesellschaft**(f); vorgeschobene Gesellschaft(f)
duplicity	**duplicité**(f), double jeu	**(unzulässige) Häufung**(f) **mehrerer Klagegründe**(m) **in e-r Klageschrift**(f)
duress to act under –	**violence**(f), contrainte(f) agir à son corps défendant sous la contrainte	**Zwang**(m); Nötigung(f) unter Zwang handeln
duty	**devoir**(m), obligation(f); fonction(f), responsabilité(f); service(m) commandé; droit(m), impôt(m), taxe(f)	**Pflicht**(f); Aufgabe(f); Abgabe(f)
customs –	droits de douane	Zollgebühr
dwelling	**logement**(m), résidence(f)	**Aufenthalt**(m); Wohnung(f)

E

ENGLISH	FRENCH	GERMAN
earning(s)	**gain(s)**(*m*), salaire(*m*), bénéfice(*m*)	**Ertrag**(*m*); Einkommen(*n*)
gross (net) –	bénéfice, gains bruts (nets)	Brutto– (Netto–)einkommen
easement	**servitude**(*f*), droit(*m*) d'usage	**Grunddienstbarkeit**(*f*)
economic agent	**agent**(*m*) **économique**	**Wirtschaftsbeauftragter**(*m*)
economies of scale	**économies**(*f*) **d'échelle**	**Größenvorteile**(*m*); Rationalisierung(*f*)
ecu	**ecu**	**Ecu**
EEC (European Economic Community)	**CEE (Communauté économique européenne)**	**EWG (Europäische Wirtschaftsgemeinschaft)**
– law	droit(*m*) communautaire	EG-Recht(*n*)
– legislation	directives(*f*) européennes	EG – Gesetzgebung(*f*)
effect	**effet**(*m*)	**Wirkung**(*f*); Folge(*f*); Kraft(*f*)
legal –	conséquence(*f*) légale, effet juridique	Rechtswirkung; –kraft
effective	**efficace**; frappant; solvable	**effektiv**; wirksam
– date	date(*f*) d'entrée en vigueur	Tag des Inkrafttretens
efficiency	**efficacité**(*f*), compétence(*f*)	**Leistungsfähigkeit**(*f*); Wirksamkeit(*f*)
– ratio	taux(*m*), courbe(*f*) d'efficacité de rentabilité	Leistungsverhältnis
– variance	différence(s) d'efficacité	Leistungsabweichung, Intensitätsabweichung
eject (to)	**éjecter**, évincer, expulser	**ausweisen**; entfernen; (Amt) entheben
elope (to)	**fuir**	**entlaufen**; durchgehen
embarrassed	**gêné**, embarassé; grevé(*f*) d'hypothèques	**in Geldverlegenheit**(*f*); Zahlungsschwierigkeit(*f*)
embezzle (to)	**détourner**, escroquer (des fonds)	**veruntreuen**; unterschlagen
embezzlement	**escroquerie**(*f*), détournement(*m*), abus(*m*) de confiance	**Veruntreuung**(*f*); Unterschlagung(*f*)

ENGLISH	FRENCH	GERMAN
emblements	fruits(*m*) **civils**, fruits du travail agricole	**Ernte(ertrag)**(*f*); Früchte auf dem Halm(*m*)
emergency – law – sale	**urgence**, situation(*f*) critique loi(*f*) d'exception vente(*f*) forcée	**Not(zu)stand**(*m*); Notfall(*m*) Notstandsverordnung, –gesetz Notverkauf
emolument(s)	**émoluments**(*m*), honoraires(*m*)	**Einkünfte**; Bezüge(*m*)
employer's liability insurance	**l'assurance responsabilité**(*f*) **des patrons**	**Unternehmerhaftpflichtversicherung**; Arbeitgeberversicherung
employment security	**sécurité**(*f*) **d'emplois**	**Arbeitsplatzsicherheit**(*f*)
enabling Act	**loi**(*f*) **habilitante**	**Ermächtigungsgesetz**(*n*)
enactment	**loi**, ordonnance(*f*), décret(*m*)	**Gesetzeserlaß**(*m*); Gesetzeskraftverleihung(*f*)
encroach (to) (upon)	**empiéter sur**	**übergreifen**; eingreifen
encroachment (upon s.o.'s rights)	**usurpation**(*f*) **de droits**, empiètement(*f*) sur la propriété d'autrui	**Übergriff**(*m*), Eingriff(*m*) in jds Rechte(*f*)
encumber (to)	**grever**, gêner	**belasten**; erschweren
encumbrance	**embarras**(*m*), hypothèque(*f*)	**Last**(*f*); (Grundstücks-) Belastung(*f*); Hypothekenlast(*f*)
end	**fin**(*f*), terme(*m*)	**Ende**(*n*); Ziel(*n*); Absicht(*f*)
end-product	**produit**(*m*) **fini**, résultat(*m*)	**Endprodukt**(*n*)
end-user	**utilisateur**(*m*) **final**	**Endabnehmer**(*m*); Endanwender(*m*)
endorse (to)	**endosser**, souscrire à	**indossieren**; (auf der Rückseite einer Urkunde) vermerken; zustimmen
endorsement	**endos**, endossement(*m*), approbation(*f*), visa	**Indossament**(*n*); Vermerk(*m*); Bestätigung(*f*)
endorser	**endosseur**(*m*), concessionnaire(*m*), avaliste(*m*)	**Indossant**(*m*); Girant(*m*); Begeber(*m*)
endowment – capital – insurance	**dotation**(*f*) apports(*m*) en capital assurance(*f*) à capital différé	**Ausstattung**(*f*); Stiftung(*f*) Stiftungskapital Lebensversicherung auf Todes- und Erlebensfall
enforce (to)	**appliquer**, faire exécuter	**(zwangsweise) durchführen**; gerichtlich geltend machen; vollstrecken
enforcement of a judgment	**exécution**(*f*) **d'un jugement**	**Vollstreckung**(*f*) e-s Urteils
engagement	**engagement**(*m*)	**Verpflichtung**(*f*); Abmachung(*f*); Versprechen(*n*)
enjoin (to)	**enjoindre**, prescrire	**auferlegen**; vorschreiben; (gerichtlich) untersagen

ENGLISH	FRENCH	GERMAN
enjoyment	**jouissance**(*f*), exercice(*m*) d'un droit possession(*f*)	**Genuß**(*n*); Nießbrauch(*m*)
– of property		Eigentumsausübung
enrich (to)	**enrichir**	**bereichern**
enter (to)	**entrer**, enregistrer	**eintreten**; einbringen, erheben
– into an agreement (with)	conclure un accord (avec)	e-n Vertrag mit jmd abschließen
enterprise	**entreprise**(*f*)	**Unternehmen**(*n*); Betrieb(*m*); Geschäft(*n*)
entertain (to)	**recevoir**, admettre	**(Geschäftsbeziehungen) unterhalten**; in Erwägung(*f*) ziehen
enticement	**séduction**(*f*)	**Anlockung**(*f*); Verführung(*f*), Anwerbung(*f*)
entitle (to)	**donner le droit de**	**nennen**, betiteln; berechtigen
entitled to damages	**fondé à réclamer des dommages-intérêts**	**zum Schadensersatz**(*m*) **berechtigt sein**
entrepreneur	**entrepreneur**(*m*)	**Unternehmer**(*m*)
entry	**entrée**(*f*), article(*m*); enregistrement(*m*), déclaration(*f*)	**Beitritt**(*m*); Eintrag(*m*); Buchung(*f*); Zollanmeldung(*f*)
– for dutiable goods (customs)	déclaration en douane de marchandises passibles de droits	Zolldeklaration für zollpflichtige Waren (Zoll)
illegal –	immigration(*f*) clandestine	illegale Einreise
right of –	droit(*m*) d'entrée, droit de prendre possession	Inbesitznahmerecht; Einreiserecht
to make an – (bookkeeping)	passer une écriture (comptabilité)	etw. eintragen, verbuchen (Buchhaltung)
equal	**égal**	**gleich**; gleichberechtigt
– rights	égalité(*f*) des droits	Gleichberechtigung; Rechtsgleichheit
– votes	partage(*m*) des voix	Stimmengleichheit
equilibrium	**équilibre**(*m*)	**Gleichgewicht**(*n*)
equitable	**juste**, équitable	**billig**; gerecht
– claim	réclamation(*f*) en accord avec les principes de l'équité	Billigkeitsanspruch
equity	**équité**(*f*), principes(*m*) de la justice (opp. droit formel)	**Billigkeit**(*f*); Unparteilichkeit(*f*)
court of –	tribunal(*m*) qui applique les principes de l'équité	Billigkeitsgericht
– capital	capital(*m*) effectif, fonds(*m*) propres	Eigenkapital; Beteiligungskapital
equivalence	**équivalence**(*f*)	**Gleichwertigkeit**(*f*)
erroneous	**erroné**	**irrtümlich**; unrichtig
error	**erreur**(*f*)	**Irrtum**(*m*); Fehler(*m*); Versehen(*n*)
judicial –	erreur judiciaire	Fehlspruch; Rechtsirrtum; Fehler des Gerichts
escape clause	**clause**(*f*) **de sauvegarde**	**Vorbehaltsklausel**(*f*); Rücktritts-, Schutz-;

ENGLISH	FRENCH	GERMAN
escheat	**déshérence**(f), bien(m) tombé en déshérence	**Heimfall**(m) **herrenlosen Vermögens an den Staat**(m); Staatserbrecht
escrow	**dépôt**(m) **fiduciaire,** dépôt conditionnel	**vorläufige Hinterlegung**(f) **e-r Urkunde**(f); bei e-m Treuhänder(m) hinterlegte Urkunde(f)
establish (to)	**établir**	**gründen;** nachweisen; bestätigen
establishment	**'establishment',** classes(f) dirigeantes; fondation(f), assiette(f), établissement(m)	**Gründung**(f); Unternehmen(n); Feststellung(f)
banking –	établissement bancaire	Bankinstitut
business –	maison(f) de commerce	Geschäftsbetrieb
place of –	siège(m) social	Ort der Niederlassung
estate	**état**(m), condition(f); mode(m, f) légal de possession; biens(m) immeubles; patrimoine(m); masse(f) des biens	**Vermögen**(n); Nachlaß(m); Grundeigentum(n); Anwesen(n)
deceased's –	succession(f)	Nachlaß
distribution of an –	partage(m) d'une succession	Aufteilung des Nachlasses, Erbauseinandersetzung
– agent	agent(m) immbilier	Grundstücksmakler; Immobilienhändler
personal –	bien(m) mobiliers	Mobiliarvermögen; beweglicher Nachlaß
estoppel	**exclusion**(f), empêchément(m)	**Hinderung**(f)**(sgrund)**(m); rechtshemmender(m) Einwand(m); Rechtsverwirkung
– by deed	écartement(m) du bénéfice de certains droits par acte notarié	Verwirkung des Einwands gegen den Inhalt einer gesiegelten Urkunde;
– by judgment	déchéance(f) de ses droits par jugement	Ausschluß der nochmaligen Prozeßführung über denselben Streitgegenstand
Euro-currency	**eurodevise**(m), euromonnaie(f)	**Eurowährung**(f)
European Economic Community (EEC)	**Communauté**(f) **économique européenne** (CEE)	**Europäische Wirtschaftsgemeinschaft** (EWG)
European Monetary System (EMS)	**Système**(m) **Monétaire Européen** (SME)	**Europäisches Währungssystem** (EWS)
evasion	**évasion**(f), fraude(f)	**Ausweichen;** Umgehung(f); Vermeidung(f)
tax –	fraude(f) fiscale	Steuerhinterziehung
eviction	**éviction**(f), expulsion	**Zwangsräumung**(f); Heraussetzung(f)
– order	ordre(m) d'expulsion	Räumungsbefehl, –urteil

ENGLISH	FRENCH	GERMAN
evidence	**preuve**(f) **testimoniale,** témoignages(m)	**Beweis**(m)**(material)**(n)**;** Nachweis(m); Zeugenaussage(f)
admissible –	preuve recevable	zulässiger Beweis
burden of –	charge(f) de la preuve	Beweislast, –pflicht
circumstantial –	présomptions(f), preuve indirecte	Indizienbeweis
conclusive –	preuve concluante, pertinente	schlüssiger (zwingender) Beweis
direct –	preuve directe	unmittelbarer Beweis
documentary –	preuve authentique, notoriété(f) de droit	Urkundenbeweis
false –	faux(f)témoignage	falsche Zeugenaussage
indirect –	preuve indirecte	mittelbarer Beweis
oral –	témoignage, déposition(f) orale	mündlicher Beweis; Beweis durch Zeugenaussagen
presumptive –	preuve par déduction, par présomption	Wahrscheinlichkeits–, Indizienbeweis
primary –	meilleure preuve	primäres Beweismittel; Beweismittel erster Ordnung
real –	preuve par vue des lieux	Augenscheinsbeweis; Beweis durch Augenscheinnahme
ex factory	**hors usine**	**ab Fabrik**(f)
ex quay	**à quai,** dédouané	**ab Kai**(m)
ex ship	**au débarquement,** à bord	**ab Schiff**(n)
ex store	**disponible**	**ab Lager**(n)
examination	**examen**(m), étude(f), visite(f)	**Zeugenvernehmung**(f)**;** Verhör(n)
cross––	contre-interrogatoire	Kreuzverhör
direct –	interrogatoire(m)	Hauptvernehmung (durch die benennende Partei)
– of witness	audition(f) d'un témoin	Zeugenvernehmung
post-mortem –	autopsie(f)	Leichenschau; Obduktion
excess profits	**bénéfice**(m) **actualisé net**	**Mehrgewinn**(m)**;** Übergewinn(m)
excess profits tax	**impôt**(m) **sur les bénéfices exceptionnels**	**Sondergewinnsteuer**(m)**;** Mehrgewinnsteuer(m)
exchange	**change**(m)**;** transmission(f); Bourse(f)	**Devisen;** Umtausch(m)
– control	contrôle(m) des changes	Devisenkontrolle
– loss	perte(f) de change	(Wechsel-)Kursverlust
– rate	taux(m) de change, cours du change	Wechsel–, Devisen–, Umrechnungskurs
exchequer	**fisc**(m), trésor(m) (public)	**Staatskasse**(f)**;** Fiskus(m)
Chancellor of the Exchequer	ministre(m) des finances, 'chancelier(m) de l'échiquier' (UK)	Finanzminister (UK)
excise tax	**contributions**(f) **indirectes,** impôt(m) indirect	**indirekte Steuer**(m)**;** Verbrauchsteuer(m); Gewerbesteuer(m)
exclusion clause	**clause**(m) **d'exclusion,** refus(m) d'admission	**Freizeichnungsklausel**(f)
exculpation	**disculpation**(f)	**Entschuldigung**(f)**;** Rechtfertigung(f)

ENGLISH	FRENCH	GERMAN
execution – of a will	exécution(f) exécution d'un testament	Ausfertigung(f) e-s Testaments
executor, executrix	exécuteur(m), exécutrice(f) (testamentaire)	Vollstrecker(m); Erbschaftsverwalter(in)(m, f), Testamentsvollstrecker(in)
executory decree	jugement exécutoire	Vollstreckungsurteil(n)
exemplary damages	dommages-intérêts(m) pour préjudice moral	verschärfter Schadensersatz(m)
exempt (to)	exempter, exonérer	befreien; freistellen; ausnehmen
exemption clause	clause(m) d'exonération, clause d'exemption	Freistellungsklausel(f); Haftungsausschluß-(f)
exhibit	pièce(f) à conviction	Beweisstück(n)
exonerate (to) – s.o. from guilt or liability	exonérer, dispenser disculper qqu'un, exonérer qqu'un de ses responsabilités(f)	entlasten; entbinden jdn von einer Schuld oder Haftung befreien
expatriate (to)	expatrier	ausbürgern
expel (to)	expulser	ausschließen; ausweisen
expiration, expiry – of a contract	expiration(f), cessation(f), échéance(f) expiration(f) d'un contrat	Ablauf(m); Erlöschen(n); Verfall(m) Ablauf e-s Vertrags
expropriate (to)	exproprier, déposséder	enteignen
expropriation of land	expropriation(f)	Landenteignung(f)
expulsion	expulsion(f)	Vertreibung(f); Ausweisung(f); Ausschluß(m)
extend (to) – a payment term	étendre, prolonger, proroger reculer l'échéance d'un paiement	verlängern Zahlungsfrist –
extenuating circumstances	circonstances(f) atténuantes	mildernde Umstände
extortion	extortion(f)	Erpressung(f)
extradite (to)	extrader	ausliefern
extradition	extradition(f)	Auslieferung(f)
extramarital	en dehors du mariage	außerehelich
extrajudicial	extrajudiciaire	außergerichtlich
extraterritorial	extraterritoriaux(f)	exterritorial; außerhalb des Hoheitsgebiets(n)
eyewitness	témoin(m) oculaire	Augenzeuge(m)

F

ENGLISH	FRENCH	GERMAN
fact	**fait**(m), réalité(f)	**Tatsache**(f); Umstand(m)
evidentiary –	fait brut	beweiserhebliche Tatsache; beweisbare Tatsache
– in issue	point(m) de fait	strittige Tatsachen; zu beweisende –
material –	fait pertinent, fait essentiel	wesentliche Tatsache
factoring	**service**(m) **d'affacturage;** achat(m) ferme de créances	**Factoring**(n) **(Forderungsankauf)**(m)
faculty	**faculté**(f), liberté(f), droit(m) de faire qque chose	**Lehrkörper**(m)
– of laws	faculté de droit	juristische Fakultät
fail (to)	**échouer,** manquer, faire défaut	**scheitern;** unterliegen; Zahlung(f) einstellen; in Konkurs gehen
failure	**échec**(m), manquement(m), faillite(f)	**Mißerfolg**(m); Bankrott(m); Versäumnis(n); Zahlungseinstellung
– of justice	déni(m) de justice	Justizversagen
– to appear	non-comparution(f)	Nichterscheinen (vor Gericht)
– to comply with	non-observation(f) de	Nichtbefolgung; –einhaltung; –erfüllung
– to pay	défaut(m) de paiement	Nichtzahlung; Zahlungsversäumnis
fair	**juste,** impartial	**gerecht;** billig; fair
– trade practices	libre échange dans des conditions de réciprocité loyale	Praxis der Nichtdiskriminierung im Außenhandel
– trial	procès(m) équitable	ordentliches Gerichtsverfahren; unparteiisches Verfahren
faith	**foi**(f), confiance(f)	**Glaube**(m)
in bad –	de bonne foi	in bösem Glauben, wider Treu und Glauben
in good –	de mauvaise foi	in gutem Glauben; nach Treu und Glauben
fake (to)	**truquer,** maquiller, contrefaire	**fälschen;** nachmachen
fallacy	**erreur**(f), faux raisonnement	**Trugschluß**(m); Irrtum(m)
false	**faux,** erroné	**falsch;** unwahr
– testimony	témoignage(m) faux	falsches Zeugnis
– pretence	prétextes(m) fallacieux	falsche Darstellung, Behauptung

ENGLISH	FRENCH	GERMAN
falsification	falsification(f), trucage(m), contrefaçon(f)	Verfälschung(f)
falsify (to)	falsifier, fausser, dénaturer	verfälschen
family allowance	allocation(s)(f) familiale(s)	Familienbeihilfe(f); Familienzulage(f)
family law	droit(m) de la famille	Familienrecht(n)
FAS (free alongside ship)	franco quai	f.a.s. (Frei Langseite Seeschiff)
fatal – accident – injury	fatal, mortel accident(m) mortel blessures(f) ayant entraîné la mort	tödlich –er Unfall –e Verletzung
fault – liability	faute(f), négligence(f), imperfection(f) responsabilité(f) de la faute	Schuld(f); Verschulden; Fehler(m) vom Verschulden abhängige Haftung; Fehleranfälligkeit (EDV)
federal – court – jurisdiction	fédéral cour(f) fédérale juridiction(f) fédérale	Bundes- –gericht –gerichtsbarkeit, Zuständigkeit der Bundesgerichte
Federal Reserve Bank (US)	Banque(f) Fédérale de Réserve (US)	Bundeszentralbank(f) (US)
Federal Rules of Civil Procedure (US)	Règles Fédérales de Procédure Civile (US)	Bundeszivilprozeßordnung(f) (US)
fee counsel's – court – – simple licence –	honoraire(s), cachet(m), cotisation(f); terre(f) ou droit réel transmissible honoraires d'avocat frais(m) de justice propriété inconditionelle droits de patente(f)	Gebühr(f); Vergütung(f) Anwaltshonorar Gerichtskosten, –gebühren Eigentumsrecht; bedingungsloses Eigentum(m) Lizenzgebühr
fictitious, fictive – contract	fictif, simulé contrat(m) fictif	fiktiv; Schein- Scheinvertrag
fiduciary	fiduciaire(m) (n et adj), dépositaire(m, f)	Treuhänder(m); Vermögensverwalter(m)
file (to) – an appeal – a petition	verser au dossier, classer, archiver se pourvoir en appel déposer une requête	einreichen; zu den Akten nehmen ein Rechtsmittel (Berufung, ua.) einlegen ein Gesuch (Antrag) einreichen
fill (to) – a vacancy – in a form	remplir, exécuter, suppléer à pourvoir à une vacance remplir un formulaire	füllen; bekleiden; besetzen eine freie Stelle besetzen ein Formular ausfüllen
final judgment/ decree/sentence	jugement(m) définitif, sans appel	Endurteil(n); rechtskräftiges Urteil(n)

ENGLISH	FRENCH	GERMAN
finance	**finance**(*f*)	**Finanzwesen**(*n*)
business –	gestion(*f*) financière	betriebliche Finanzwirtschaft; Unternehmensfinanzierung
– company	société(*f*) de financement	Finanzierungsgesellschaft; Kreditinstitut für Kundenfinanzierung
financial	**financier, financiére**	**finanziell**; Finanz-
– audit	audit(*m*) financier	Buchprüfung
– budget	budget(*m*) financier	Finanzplan
– futures	contrats(*m*) à terme	Finanztermingeschäfte
– guarantee	garantie(s)(*f*) financière(s)	Finanzgarantie
– institution	institution(*f*) financière	Kredit-, Finanzinstitut
– market	marché(*m*) financier	Finanz-, Kreditmarkt
– legislation	lois(*f*) de finances	Finanzgesetzgebung
– management	management(m) financier	Finanzmanagement
– statement	bilan(*m*), état(*m*) des finances	Finanzbericht; Handelsbilanz (*US*)
findings	**données**(*f*), constatations(*f*)	**Untersuchungsergebnis**(*n*); Befund(*m*)
court's –	conclusions(*f*) du tribunal, verdict	(tatsächliche) Feststellungen des Gerichts
interlocutory –	conclusions interlocutoires	Zwischenentscheidung
judicial –	conclusions d'un tribunal	Richterspruch; Gerichtsurteil; richterliche Feststellungen
fine	**amende**(*f*)	**Geldstrafe**(*f*)
under penalty of (a) –	sous peine d'amende	unter Androhung e-r Geldstrafe
fine (to) s.o.	**condamner qqu'un à une amende**	**jn zu einer Geldstrafe**(*f*) **verurteilen**; mit einer Geldstrafe belegen
fire insurance	**assurance**(*f*) **incendie**	**Feuerversicherung**(*f*)
firm name	**raison**(*f*) **sociale**	**Firmenname**(*m*); Bezeichnung(*f*) (der Firma)
first	**premier**, d'origine	**erste, erster, erstes**, an erster Stelle
-degree (murder) (*US*)	assassinat(*m*)	schwerer Mord
– lien	privilèges(*m*) privilégiées	erstrangiges Pfandrecht
– offender	délinquant(*m*) primaire	Ersttäter; Nichtvorbestrafter
fiscal	**fiscal, fiscale**	**Finanz**-; Steuer-
– authority	fisc(*m*)	–behörde(*f*)
– control	contrôle(*m*) fiscal	–kontrolle, –aufsicht
fixed	**immobilisé**(*f*), fixe	**fest**; festliegend
– assets	immobilisations(*f*)	Anlagevermögen
– costs	coûts(*m*) fixes	Fixkosten
– price	prix(*m*) fixe	Festpreis; festgesetzter Preis
fixtures and fittings	**(toutes les) installations (d'une maison)**	**Einrichtungsgegenstände**(*m*)
flat rate	**taux**(*m*) **uniforme**	**Pauschalsatz**(*m*); Pauschalgebühr(*f*)
float (to)	**flotter**; émettre, lancer	**frei schwanken**; in Umlauf(*m*) bringen
– a loan	lancer un emprunt	Anleihe auflegen od. begeben

ENGLISH	FRENCH	GERMAN
floating charge	**droit**(m) **de préférence sur tout ou partie de l'actif présent et à venir d'une société, sous réserve du droit pour la société de modifier cet actif dans le cours normal de ses affaires**	**schwebendes Sicherungsrecht**(n)
FOB (free on board)	**franco bord**	**f.o.b.** (Frei an Bord)
FOP (free on plane)	**franco avion**	**f.o.p.** (Frei an Flugzeug)(n)
FOQ (free on quay)	**franco quai**	**f.o.q.** (Frei Kai)(m)
FOR (free on rail)	**franco wagon**	**f.o.r.** (Frei Bannstation(f), Eisenbahnwaggon(m))
force by – – of law – majeure	**force**(f) de force, par force force de la loi (cas de) force majeure	**Kraft**(f) zwangsweise, mit Gewalt Gesetzes– höhere Gewalt
forced – loan – sale	**forcé** emprunt(m) forcé vente(f) forcée	**Zwangs-** –anleihe(f) –verkauf(m)
foreclose (to)	**forclore saisir**, mettre fin à un prêt	**ausschließen;** verfallen lassen; präkludieren
forego (to)	**précéder**	**vorhergehen**
foreign exchange market	**marché**(m) **des changes**	**Devisenmarkt**(m)
forensic medicine	**médecine**(m) **légale**	**Gerichtsmedizin**(f)
forfeit (to)	**être déchu de**, perdre par confiscation	**verwirken;** einbüßen
forfeiture – of a patent – of an insurance – of property	**mort**(f) **civile,** perte(f) d'un droit, perte par confiscation expiration(f) d'un brevet déchéance(f) d'une police d'assurance perte de biens par confiscation	**Verwirkung**(f); Verlust(m); Beschlagnahme(f) Patentverlust Versicherungsverfall Eigentumsverlust; Vermögenseinziehung
forger	**faussaire**(m), contrefacteur(m)	**Fälscher**(m)
forgery	**faux,** contrefaçon(f), falsification(f), supposition(f)	**Fälschung**(f)
forgo (to)	**s'abstenir de**	**verzichten auf**
formal – error	**formel,** régulier, absolu, conventionnel vice de forme	**formal;** formell Formfehler
fornication	**fornication**(f)	**außerehelicher Geschlechtsverkehr**(m); Unzucht(f)
fortuitous event	**cas**(m) **fortuit**	**Zufall**(m), zufälliges Ereignis(n)
forum	**forum**(m); tribunal(m) compétent (et son siège)	**Forum**(n); Gremium(n)

ENGLISH	FRENCH	GERMAN
forward	**en avant,** antérieur; à terme	**Termin-**(*m*)
– contract	engagement(*m*) d'acheter ou de vendre à un prix fixé, à une date ultérieure	–kontrakt
– transactions	transaction(*f*) à terme	–geschäft
FOT (free on truck)	**franco camion**	**Frei Lastwagen**(*m*)
forwarding	**transitaire**(*m*), expéditionnaire(*m*)	**Beförderung**(*f*); Versand(*m*); Spedition(*f*)
foul	**malpropre,** déloyal	**unredlich**
– play	jeu(*m*) déloyal, malveillance(*f*) (par ext., crime, meurtre)	unfaires Spiel; Verbrechen
foundation	**fondation**(*f*), institution(*f*); fondement(*m*)	**Stiftung**(*f*)
charitable –	fondation charitable	– mit gemeinnützigem Zweck
fractional	**fractionnel,** divisionnaire (*adj.*)	**Teil-**(*m*)
– certificate	titre(*m*) fractionnel	–schein
– share	action(*f*) fractionnelle	Aktienspitzen
frame (to) s.o.	**monter un coup contre qqu'un** (*fam.*), inventer	**jdn lügnerisch bezichtigen**
franchise	**liberté**(*f*), privilège(*m*); droit(*m*) électoral; minimum de couverture(*f*) (assurance)	**Konzession**(*f*)
fraud	**fraude**(*f*), tromperie(*f*), abus(*m*) de confiance	**Betrug**(*m*); Veruntreuung(*f*); arglistige Täuschung(*f*)
free	**libre,** en franchise, exempt	**frei**
– alongside ship (FAS)	franco quai	Frei Längsseite Seeschiff
– on board (FOB)	franco bord	Frei an Bord
– on plane (FOP)	franco avion	Frei an Flugzeug
– on quay (FOQ)	franco quai	Frei Kai
– on rail (FOR)	franco wagon	Frei Bahnstation, Eisenbahnwaggon
– on truck (FOT)	franco camion	Frei Lastwagen
– port	port(*m*) libre	Freihafen
– trade	libre-échange	Freihandel
freedom	**liberté**(*f*), franchise(*f*), immunité(*f*)	**Freiheit**(*f*)
– of assembly	liberté d'association	Versammlungs–
– of religion	liberté religieuse, liberté du culte	Religions–
– of speech	liberté d'expression	Rede–
– of the press	liberté de la presse	Presse–
– of trade	liberté du commerce	Handels–
freehold	**tenure**(*f*) **en propriété perpétuelle et libre**	**Grundeigentum**(*n*); (zeitl. unbeschränktes) Eigentumsrecht(*n*) (an Grundbesitz)
freeholder	**propriétaire**(*m*) **foncier**	**Grundeigentümer**(*m*)

ENGLISH	FRENCH	GERMAN
freight	**fret**(*m*), cargaison(*f*), transport(*m*) de marchandises;frais(*m*) de transport	**Fracht**(*f*)
air –	transport par avion	Luft–
ocean (sea) –	transport maritime	See–
freighter	**affréteur**(*m*); navire(*m*) marchand; wagon(*m*) de marchandises	**Frachter**(*m*); Verlader(*m*), Verfrachter(*m*)
friendly society	**amicale**(*f*), société(*f*) de recours mutuel	**Unterstützungsverein**(*m*); Versicherungsverein(*m*) auf Gegenseitigkeit(*f*)
frustration	**frustration**(*f*); anéantissement(*m*); impossibilité(*f*) d'exécuter un contrat	**Vereitelung**(*f*); Verhinderung(*f*)
fugitive from justice	**fugitif recherché par la justice**	**flüchtiger Rechtsbrecher**(*m*)
funds statement	**tableau**(*m*) **de financement**	**Kapitalflußrechnung**(*f*)
futures (forward)	**opérations**(*f*), livraisons(*f*) à terme; cotation à terme	**Termingeschäfte**(*n*); (Termin-)
financial future(s)	instruments(*m*) financiers à terme	Finanztermingeschäfte
futures business	marché(*m*) des instruments à terme	Termingeschäft
futures contract	commande(*m*) à terme, contrat à terme	Terminkontrakt
future(s) option	option(*f*) sur contrat à terme	Option auf e-n Terminkontrakt

G

ENGLISH	FRENCH	GERMAN
gain	gain(*m*), profit(*m*), bénéfice(*m*)	Gewinn(*m*); Verdienst(*m*); Erwerb(*m*)
gainful employment	emploi(*m*) rémunéré	Erwerbstätigkeit(*f*)
gallows	potence(*f*), gibet(*m*)	Galgen(*m*)
gambling	jeux(*m*) de hasard, jeux d'argent	Glücksspiel(*n*)
game law (hunting)	lois(*m*) de la chasse	Jagdgesetz(*n*), (Jagd)
gaol, also spelled jail	prison(*f*), maison(*f*) d'arrêt	Gefängnis(*n*)
garnish (to)	garnir, orner; saisir	Drittschuldnerpfändung(*f*) vornehmen; Drittschuldner(*m*) ein Zahlungsverbot zustellen
garnisher	créancier saisissant	Vollstreckungsgläubiger(*m*); (Pfändungs-)Pfandgläubiger(*m*) (*US*); Partei die Forderungspfändung(*f*) bewirkt hat
garnishment	saisie-arrêt(*f*), opposition(*f*)	Forderungspfändung(*f*); Verbot(*n*) (dem Drittschuldner)(*m*) Zahlung(*f*) zu leisten
GATT (General Agreement on Tariffs and Trade)	Accord(*m*) Général sur les Tarifs Douaniers et le Commerce	GATT (Allgemeines Zoll- und Handelsabkommen)
general	général(*m*)	General-
– agent	homme(*m*) d'affaires	–bevollmächtiger(*m*); allgemeiner Handelsvertreter(*m*)
– average	avaries(*f*) communes	Große Havarie
– contractor	entrepreneur(*m*) général	–unternehmer
– damages	dommages-intérêt(*m*) qui découlent naturellement de la plainte	Gesamtschaden; allgemeiner Schaden
– lien	privilège(*m*) général	allgemeines Pfandrecht
– meeting	assemblée(*f*) générale	Mitgliederversammlung; Hauptversammlung
– partner	associé(*m*) ordinaire	unbeschränkt (persönlich)haftender Gesellschafter
– partnership	société(*m*) en nom collectif	allgemeine offene Handelsgesellschaft; allgemeine Personengesellschaft
genocide	génocide(*m*)	Genozid(*m*); Völkermord(*m*)

ENGLISH	FRENCH	GERMAN
gift	**don**(*m*)	**Schenkung**(*f*); Zuwendung
demonstrative –	legs(*m*) à payer d'une source spécifiée	beschränkte (aus bestimmten Mitteln erfüllte) Schenkung
– in trust	don placé sous tutelle	Schenkung zu treuen Händen
– tax	impôt(*m*) sur les donations	Schenkungssteuer
giro account	**CCP** (compte courant postal)	**Girokonto**(*n*) (UK); Postgirokonto(*n*)
given name	**prénom**(*m*)	**Vorname**(*m*); Tauf-
go (to) bail for s.o.	**se porter garant de qqu'un, pour qqu'un**	**Kaution**(*f*) **stellen,** für jdn Sicherheit(*f*) leisten
good	**bon**(*m*)	**gültig;** zahlungsfähig
– debts	créance(*f*) recouvrable	sichere Forderung
– faith	bonne foi(*f*)	in gutem Glauben, nach Treu und Glauben
goods and chattels	**biens**(*m*) **mobiliers**	**bewegliche Sachen**(*f*); Hab und Gut
goodwill	**achalandage**(*m*), fonds(*m*) de commerce; profit(*m*) net	**(ideeller) Firmenwert**(*m*)
government	**gouvernement**(*m*) **de l'État**	**Regierung**(*f*)
grace	**grâce**(*f*), pardon(*m*), amnistie(*f*)	**Gnade**(*f*)
act of –	loi(*f*) d'amnistie	–nfrist, Nachfrist
graft	**concussion**(*f*), corruption(*f*) de fonctionnaires	**Schiebung**(*f*), Korruption(*f*); Bestechungsgeld(*n*)
grafter	**escroc**(*m*), chevalier(*f*) d'industrie	**Schieber**(*m*); korrupter Beamter(*m*)
grand jury (*US*)	**jury**(*m*) **d'accusation** (*US*)	**Anklagejury**(*f*) (*US*)
grant	**concession**(*f*), octroi; subvention(*f*)	**Bewilligung**(*f*); Übertragung(*f*); Schenkung(*f*); Beihilfe(*f*); Stipendium
grant (to)	**accorder,** octroyer, consentir	**bewilligen;** übertragen; zugestehen
grantee	**concessionnaire**(*m*)	**Begünstigter**(*m*) (dem etwas bewilligt, übertragen, verliehen wurde)
grantor	**concédant**(*m*), donateur(*m*)	**Bewilligender**(*m*); Übertragender(*m*)
grievance	**grief**(*m*); injustice(*f*)	**Beschwerdegrund**(*m*), Klage–; Mißstand(*m*)
– committee	commission(*f*) du contentieux administratif	Arbeiter-Beschwerdeausschuß; Schlichtungsausschuß
– procedure	procédure(*f*) de règlement des différends	Beschwerdeverfahren
to redress a –	redresser un tort	Übelstand, Mißstand abhelfen
gross	**gros**(*m*), grossier, trop fort; brut(*m*)	**schwer**
– negligence	négligence(*f*) coupable	grobe Fahrlässigkeit

ENGLISH	FRENCH	GERMAN
ground – for appeal grounds for judgment	**raison**(*f*), cause(*f*) motif(*m*) d'appel considérants	**Grund**(*m*) Rechtsmittelbegründung; Berufungsbegründung Urteilsbegründung
group (of companies)	**groupement**(*m*) **(de sociétés)**	**Firmengruppe**(*f*), Konzern(*m*)
group insurance	**assurance**(*f*) **collective**	**Gruppenversicherung**(*f*)
guarantee (*cf. surety*) absolute – collateral – conditional –	**garantie**(*f*), caution(*f*); aval(*m*), cautionnement(*m*) garantie absolue garantie collatérale garantie conditionnelle	**Bürgschaft(sleistung)**(*f*); Sicherheit(*f*); Garantie(*f*) selbstschuldnerische Bürgschaft Nebenbürgschaft Ausfallbürgschaft
guarantor	**garant**(*m*), caution(*f*), répondant(*m*), avaliste	**Bürge**(*m*); Garant(*m*)
guardian	**tuteur**(*m, f*), conseil(*m*) judiciaire, curateur(*m*)	**Vormund**(*m*); Hüter(*m*)
guardianship	**garde**(*m*), tutelle(*f*)	**Vormundschaft**(*f*); Schutz(*m*), Obhut(*f*)
guidelines	**directives**(*f*)	**Richtlinien**(*f*)
guiding idea	**idée**(*f*) **directrice**	**Leitgedanke**(*m*)
guiding principles	**principe**(*m*) **conducteur**	**Grundprinzipien**(*n*)
guilt	**culpabilité**(*f*)	**Schuld**(*f*)
guilty not – to plead – verdict of –	**coupable**(*m, f*) innocent, non coupable plaider coupable verdict(*m*) de culpabilité	**schuldig** nicht – s. – bekennen Urteil auf-

H

ENGLISH	FRENCH	GERMAN
habeas corpus	habeas corpus	**Habeas Corpus**; richterliche Haftprüfung(*f*)
habitat	habitat(*m*)	**Heimat**(*f*); Habitat(*n*)
habitual residence	domicile(*m*) habituel	gewöhnlicher Aufenthaltsort(*m*)
Hague (The) – Convention – Tribunal	La Haye Convention(*f*) de La Haye tribunal(*m*) de La Haye	Haag(*m*) –er Abkommen –er Schiedshof
hail insurance	assurance(*f*) contre la grêle	Hagelversicherung(*f*)
hallmark	poinçon(*m*), cachet	Feingehaltsstempel(*m*); Kennzeichen
handcuffs	menottes(*f*)	Handschellen(*f*)
hand (to) over (*cf. surrender*)	remmettre (qqu'un entre les mains de la justice)	übergeben, aushändigen; (s. abtreten)
handicap	handicap(*m*), inaptitude(*f*)	Hindernis(*n*); Benachteiligung(*f*); Behinderung(*f*)
handling charges	frais(*m*) de manutention	Bearbeitungsgebühren(*f*); Umschlagspesen(*n*)
harass (to)	harceler, tourmenter	belästigen
harassment	harcèlement(*m*)	Belästigung(*f*)
harm	mal(*m*), tort(*m*), préjudice(*m*)	Schaden(*m*)
bodily –	lésion(*f*) corporelle	körperlicher –; Körperverletzung
harm (to)	nuire, blesser	schädigen; verletzen
harmonise (to)	harmoniser, concilier	angleichen; harmonisieren
harmonisation (*EEC*)	harmonisation(*f*)	Angleichung(*f*) (*EG*)
hashish	haschisch(*m*)	Haschisch(*n*)
haulage	transport(*m*), charroi(*m*)	Beförderung(*f*); Transport(kosten)(*m*)
haven	refuge(*m*)	Zufluchtsort(*m*); Hafen(*m*)
havoc to wreak –	ravages(*m*), dégâts(*m*) causer des ravages	Verwüstung(*f*); Unheil(*n*) – anrichten
hazard	danger(*m*), risque(*m*); jeu(*m*) de hasard	Gefahr(*f*); Risiko(*n*)

ENGLISH	FRENCH	GERMAN
health	**santé**(f)	**Gesundheit**(f)
– centre	dispensaire(m), centre(m) de soins	medizinisches Versorgungszentrum
– certificate	certificat(m) médical	–szeugnis, –sattest
– hazard	risque(m) pour la santé	–srisiko
– insurance	assurance(f) maladie	Krankenversicherung
public –	santé(f) publique	(öffentliches) –swesen;
hear (to)	**entendre,** écouter; instruire	**verhandeln;** hören
hearing	**audience**(f), débats(m) (d'un procès); interrogatoire(m) d'un accusé	**Verhandlung**(f)
detention –	audience concernant la détention	Haftverhandlung
final –	audience de jugement	Schlußverhandlung, Schlußtermin;
– of a case	instruction(f) d'une affaire	– e-s Falls
– of witnesses	audition des témoins	Zeugenvernehmung
preliminary –	audience préliminaire	Voruntersuchung
public –	audience publique	öffentliche Verhandlung
hearsay	**ouï-dire**(f)	**Hörensagen**(n)
hedge	**couverture**(f), arbitrage(m), contrepartie(f)	**Sicherungsgeschäft**(n); Deckungsgeschäft(n)
heir	**héritier**(m), **héritière**(f)	**Erbe**(m)
intestate –	héritier ab intestat	Intestats–
legal –	héritier légal	gesetzlicher –
natural –	héritier naturel	– durch Geburtsrecht
sole –	seul héritier, héritier unique	Allein–
testamentary –	héritier désigné par disposition testamentaire	Testaments–
universal –	légataire(m, f) universel	Allein–
hereditary	**héréditaire**	**erblich**
hide (to)	**(se) cacher**	**sich verstecken**
– from justice	se soustraire à l'action de la justice	sich der Strafverfolgung entziehen
high treason	**haute trahison**	**Hochverrat**(m); Landesverrat(m)
hijacking	**détournement**(m) **(d'avion)**	**(Flugzeug-)**(n)**Entführung**(f)
hire	**location**(f), louage(m); embauchage(m); salaire(m)	**Miete**(f); Einstellung(f); Heuer(m)
– -purchase	vente(m) à tempérament	Teilzahlungs–, Abzahlungskauf (UK)
hire (to)	**louer,** embaucher	**mieten**
– out	donner en location, louer	ver–
hit-and-run driving	**délit de fuite**	**Fahrerflucht**(f)
hoard (to)	**accumuler,** thésauriser	**ansammeln;** horten
hold (to)	**tenir,** détenir; être investi; conclure, juger; obliger	**besitzen;** für Recht(n) erkennen
– in trust	avoir confiance (en)	als Treuhänder verwalten
– shares	détenir des actions	Aktien besitzen

ENGLISH	FRENCH	GERMAN
holder – in trust – of shares, shareholder	**détenteur**(m), porteur(m) détenteur(m) de bonne foi actionnaire(m)	**Inhaber**(m); Besitzer(m) Treuhänder Aktien–
holding majority –	**tenue**(f) **(d'une réunion)**; portefeuille(m), disponibilités; ferme(f), tenure(f); holding(m) participation(f) majoritaire	**Beteiligung**(f) Mehrheits–
hold-up	**hold-up**(m), braquage(m) (fam.), attaque(f) à main armée	**Überfall**(m); Hindernis(n)
home – country – member State (EEC)	**domicile**(m), foyer(m) pays (terre) natale; pays d'origine pays(m) membre permanent (CEE)	**Binnen–**; inländisch Heimat, Heimatland EG-Heimatstaat
Home Office (UK)	**ministère**(m) **de l'intérieur** (UK)	**Innenministerium**(n) (UK)
Home Secretary (UK)	**ministre**(m) **de l'intérieur** (UK)	**Innenminister**(m) (UK)
homicide (cf. murder)	**homicide**(m, f), meurtre(m)	**Tötung**(f) (s. Mord)
honour (to) – a cheque	**honorer**, respecter honorer un chèque	**honorieren**; einlösen e-n Scheck einlösen
hooligan	**voyou**(m), vandale(m, f), hooligan(m)	**Rowdy**(m)
horizontal integration	**intégration horizontale**(f)	**horizontale Integration**(f)
host country	**pays**(m) **hôte**, pays d'accueil	**Gastland**(n); Aufnahmestaat(m)
host member State (EEC)	**pays membre invité** (CEE)	**Gaststaat**(m) (EG)
hostage	**otage**(m)	**Geisel**(f)
House of Lords (UK)	**Chambre**(f) **des Lords** (UK)	**Oberhaus**(n) (UK)
housebreaking	**violation**(f) **de domicile**, effraction(f)	**Einbruchdiebstahl**(m)
householder	**chef**(m) **de famille**; locataire(m, f), propriétaire(m, f)	**Haushalt(ung)svorstand**(m)
hull insurance	**assurance**(f) **d'un navire** **hors cargaison**	**Kaskoversicherung**(f) (Schiffs–, Flugzeug–)
human rights	**droits**(m) **de l'homme**	**Menschenrecht**(n)
hurt (to)	**blesser**	**verletzen**; Schaden zufügen
hurtful	**douloureux**, pénible	**schädlich**; nachteilig

ENGLISH	FRENCH	GERMAN
husband	mari(*m*)	Ehemann(*m*); Gatte(*m*)
hush money	argent(*m*) donné à qqu'un pour prix de son silence	Schweigegeld(*n*)
hypothecary	hypothécaire	hypothekarisch; pfandrechtlich
hypothetical	hypothétique(*f*)	hypothetisch; mutmaßlich;

I

ENGLISH	FRENCH	GERMAN
identification	**identification**(f)	**Identifizierung**(f)
– card	carte(f) d'identité	Kennkarte, Personalausweis
– certificate	acte(m) de notoriété	Kennkarte, Personalausweis
– mark	signe(m) d'identification	Erkennungs–, Kennzeichen
identify (to)	**identifier**	**identifizieren**
identity	**identité**(f)	**Identität**(f)
false –	fausse(f) identité	gefälschte –
mistaken –	erreur(f) sur la personne	Personenverwechslung
ignorance	**ignorance**(f)	**Unwissenheit**(f); Unkenntnis(n)
ignorant	**ignorant**	**unwissend**; unkundig
illegal	**illégal**, illicite	**illegal**; rechtswidrig
illegality	**illégalité**	**Illegalität**(f); Rechtswidrigkeit(f)
illegitimate	**illégitime**	**unehelich**; unrechtmäßig
illicit	**illégal**, illicite	**rechtswidrig**; unzulässig
illiterate	**illettré**, analphabète	**Analphabet**(m)
imitation	**imitation**(f), factice, faux(f)	**Nachahmung**(f)
immaterial	**sans importance**, non pertinent	**unerheblich**
– evidence	témoignage(m) non pertinent	–er Beweis
immigration	**immigration**(f)	**Einwanderung**(f)
immovables	**biens**(m) **immobiliers**	**Immobilien**; Liegenschaften
immunity	**immunité**(f), exemption(f), exonération(f)	**Immunität**(f)
diplomatic –	immunité diplomatique	diplomatische –
judicial –	immunité juridique	gerichtliche –
impact	**incidence**(f), répercution(f) (de la fiscalité)	**Wirkung**(f)
impair (to)	**porter atteinte ou préjudice**, compromettre, affaiblir	**beeinträchtigen**; verschlechtern
impairment	**affaiblissement**(m), altération(f), diminution(f)	**Beeinträchtigung**(f); Verschlechterung(f)
physical –	infirmité(f)	körperliche Behinderung

ENGLISH	FRENCH	GERMAN
impanelling, alternative spelling of empanelling	désignation(*f*) des membres du jury	Aufstellung(*f*) der Geschworenenliste
impartiality	impartialité	Unparteiischkeit(*f*); Objektivität(*f*)
impeach (to)	mettre en accusation, récuser, contester	anklagen; anfechten; in Zweifel ziehen
– a witness	récuser un témoin	die Glaubwürdigkeit eines Zeugen anzweifeln (*US*)
impediment	entrave(*f*), obstacle(*m*); cause(*f*) d'incapacité de contracter	Behinderung(*f*); Hinderungsgrund(*f*)
impel (to)	forcer à faire	drängen; zwingen
implementation	mise(*f*) en oeuvre, application	Durchführung(*f*); Erfüllung(*f*)
– of a policy	mise en oeuvre d'une politique	(politisches) Programm in die Tat umsetzen
– of regulations	application(*f*) d'un règlement	Durchführung von Bestimmungen
implicate (to)	compromettre, impliquer	hineinziehen; verwickeln
implication	intention(*f*) ou état de fait présumé; incidence(*f*), répercussion(*f*)	Verwicklung(*f*); innewohnende Bedeutung(*f*); (stillschweigende) Folgerung
by –	implicitement	stillschweigend; durch sinngemäße Auslegung
the financial –(s)	incidences financières	die finanziellen Folgen, Auswirkungen
implicit, implied	implicite, tacite, absolu	stillschweigend; mit einbegriffen
– assent	consentement(*m*) tacite	stillschweigende Zustimmung
– warranty	garantie(*f*) implicite	–e Garantie, konkludente Garantie
import	importation(*f*)	Einfuhr(*f*)
– agent	importateur(*m*)	–vertreter
– licence	licence(*f*) d'importation	–lizenz
– quota	contingents(*m*) d'importation	–quote
– restrictions	restrictions(*f*) à l'importation	–beschränkungen
imposition	impôt(*m*), taxe(*f*), imposition(*f*)	Auferlegung(*f*); Verhängung(*f*); Abgabe(*f*)
impound (to)	déposer (des documents au greffe); saisir, confisquer	in Verwahrung(*f*) nehmen (gerichtlich od. behördlich)
imprint	empreinte(*f*)	Abdruck(*m*)
imprison (to)	emprisonner, mettre en prison	inhaftieren; ins Gefängnis(*n*) setzen
imprisonment	emprisonnement(*m*)	Inhaftierung(*f*); Freiheits–, Gefängnisstrafe(*f*)
improper	impropre, incorrect, irrégulier	ungehörig
– use	usage(*m*) abusif	–e, unsachgemäße Verwendung, Mißbrauch

ENGLISH	FRENCH	GERMAN
impugn (to)	**attaquer,** mettre en doute, discuter	**anfechten**
– evidence	récuser un témoignage	Beweismaterial –
impute (to)	**imputer,** attribuer, accuser	**zuschreiben;** zur Last legen
in camera	**à huis clos**	**unter Ausschluß**(*m*) **der Öffentlichkeit**(*f*)
in chambers	**(juge)**(*m*) **des référés**	**unter Ausschluß**(*m*) **der Öffentlichkeit**(*f*)
inability	**incapacité**(*f*), impuissance(*f*)	**Unfähigkeit**(*f*); Unvermögen(*n*)
inaccuracy	**inexactitude**(*f*), imprécision(*f*)	**Ungenauigkeit**(*f*); Unrichtigkeit(*f*)
inadequacy	**insuffisance**(*f*)	**Unangemessenheit**(*f*); Unzulänglichkeit(*f*)
inadmissible	**irrecevable,** illicite, inadmissible	**unzulässig**
– evidence	témoignage(*m*) irrecevable	–e Beweismittel; nicht zugelassenes Beweismaterial
inalienable	**inaliénable**	**unabdingbar**
– claim	revendication(*f*) inaliénable	–e Forderung
– right	droit(*m*) inaliénable	–es Recht
incapacitate (to)	**frapper d'incapacité légale,** interdire	**unfähig** machen; für unfähig erklären
incapacity	**incapacité**(*f*)	**Unfähigkeit**(*f*)
legal –	incapacité légale	Geschäfts-, Rechts-
incendiary	**incendiaire**	**Brandstifter**(*m*); durch Brandstiftung(*f*) verursacht
incest	**inceste**(*m*)	**Inzest**(*m*)
inchoate	**en puissance,** incomplet	**angefangen;** in Entstehung(*f*) begriffen; teilweise begründet unvollkommene Missetat
– crime	crime(*m*) non parfait	entstehendes od. im Entstehen
– right	droit(*m*) en puissance	begriffenes Recht
incident	**privilège**(*m*); incident(*m*); qui appartient	**Vorfall**(*m*); Ereignis(*n*)
incidental	**accidentel,** éventuel, accessoire	**Neben-**
– action	poursuites sur incident	–klage(*f*)
– expenses, incidentals	faux frais	–ausgaben; –kosten
incite (to) s.o.	**inciter qqu'un (à)**	**anstiften;** aufwiegeln
incitement	**incitation**(*f*), provocation(*f*) (au crime, au délit)	**Anstiftung**(*f*); Aufwiegelung(*f*)
incommunicado	**au secret**	**ohne Möglichkeit**(*f*) **der Verbindung**(*f*) **mit der Außenwelt**
incompatible	**incompatible,** inconciliable	**unvereinbar**
– interests	intérêts(*m*) inconciliables	–e Interessen

ENGLISH	FRENCH	GERMAN
incompetent	**incompétent**, non qualifié (pour)	**unfähig;** unzurechnungsfähig (US), geschäftsunfähig
– evidence	preuve(f) irrecevable	unzulässiges Beweismittel
– person	incapable, interdit (aliéné, etc.)	Geschäftsunfähiger (US)
– witness	témoin(m) récusé, non qualifié	unzulässiger Zeuge
incorporate(d)	**constitué,** autorisé, enregistré	**eingetragen (als Kapitalgesellschaft)**(f)
– body	doté de la personnalité civile, personne(f) morale	Körperschaft
– company	société(f) constituée, société enregistrée	rechtsfähige (Handels-) Gesellschaft
incorporation	**incorporation**(f), fusion(f), constitution(f); octroi(m) de la personnalité morale	**Gründung**(f) **(e-r juristischen Person**(f)**, Kapitalgesellschaft)**(f)
certificate of –	certificat(m) de constitution	–sbescheinigung;
charter of –	statut(m) de constitution de société	–urkunde
incorporeal	**incorporel**	**immateriell;** nicht körperlich
– property	biens(m) incorporels	–e Gegenstände
– rights	droits(m) incorporels	Immaterialgüterrechte
incorruptible	**incorruptible**	**unbestechlich**
increment	**d'accroissement**	**Zunahme**(f); (Wert-)Zuwachs(m)
incriminate (to) s.o.	**accuser qqu'un**	**jd belasten;** beschuldigen
incriminating	**compromettant**	**belastend**
– evidence	pièce(f) à conviction	Belastungsmaterial
incumbent	**titulaire**(m) **d'un poste**	**Amtsinhaber**(m)
incumber (to), alternative spelling of encumber	**grever,** gêner	**hypothekarisch belasten**
incur (to)	**encourir,** subir	**sich zuziehen;** erleiden; sich (e-r Gefahr) aussetzen
– damage	subir des dégâts	Schaden erleiden
– losses	subir des pertes	Verlust erleiden
indecent	**indécent,** pornographique	**ungehörig;** anstößig
indemnify (to)	**indemniser,** dédommager	**schadlos halten**
indemnity	**indemnité**(f)	**Schadloshaltung**(f); Abfindung(f); Freistellung(f)
indict (to)	**inculper,** accuser, incriminer	**anklagen**
– s.o. for a crime	poursuivre qqu'un pour un crime	jdn e-s Verbrechens –
indictment	**acte**(m) **d'accusation,** inculpation(f)	**formelle Anklageschrift**(f)
indigent	**indigent,** nécessiteux	**Bedürftiger**(m)
indispensable party	**partie**(f) **indispensable**	**notwendige Streitpartei**(f)

ENGLISH	FRENCH	GERMAN
indorsement, alternative spelling of endorsement	approbation(f) (d'un appel); visa(m); appui(m), soutien(m)	Indossament(n); Vermerk(m), Bestätigung(f)
indulgence	indulgence(f); jour(m) de grâce, délai de paiement	Stundung(f); Nachsicht(f), Milde(f)
infamy	incapacité(f) de témoigner; infamie(f)	Ehrlosigkeit(f), Schande(f); Verlust(m) der bürgerlichen Ehrenrechte
infant (cf. minor)	mineur(m)	Unmündiger(m) (s. Minderjähriger)
infer (to)	conclure	folgern, schließen
inference	supposition(f), déduction(f), inférence(f)	Folgerung(f); Rückschluß(m)
inferior court	tribunal(m) inférieur, tribunal de première instance	unteres Gericht(n); Instanzgericht(n)
infirmative fact	fait(m) réfutatif	entlastende Tatsache(f)
inflict (to)	infliger	auferlegen; zufügen
informant	dénonciateur(m), délateur(m)	Informant(m); Gewährsmann(m)
information	information(s)(f); acte(m) d'accusation émanant du ministère public; dénonciation(f), délation(f)	Nachricht(f); Mitteilung(f); Strafanzeige(f); Anklage(f)
confidential –	renseignements(m) confidentiels	vertrauliche Mitteilung
exchange of –	échange(m) de renseignements	Informationsaustausch
informer	informateur(m)	Anzeigenerstatter(m); Denunziant(m); Spitzel(m)
infraction	infraction(f), violation(f)	Verletzung(f); Verstoß(m)
infringe (to)	enfreindre, violer, empiéter sur	verletzen (Recht); verstoßen gegen
infringement	infraction, violation (d'une loi), contrefaçon	(Rechts-)Verletzung(f); Verstoß(m); Zuwiderhandlung(f)
– of copyright	contrefaçon(f) en matière de droits d'auteur	Urheberrechtsverletzung
– of patent	contrefaçon en matière de brevet	Patentverletzung
inherit (to)	hériter (de)	erben
inheritance	héritage(m), succession(f); procédure(f) en matière de succession	Erbschaft(f); Erbe(n)
– tax	droits(m) successoraux	Erbschaftssteuer
inhibition	défense(f) expresse, interdiction(f), prohibition	Verbot(n); Untersagung(f)
initial fund/capital	fonds(m) d'apport, capital(m) d'apport	Anfangs-/Einlagekapital(n); Gründungs-
initial (to)	parafer, émarger	abzeichnen, unterzeichnen; paraphieren

ENGLISH	FRENCH	GERMAN
initiate (to)	entamer (des poursuites), commencer	beginnen; einleiten
injunction	arrêt(m) de suspension, de sursis; jugement(m) avant faire droit; injonction(f), ordre	(gerichtliche) Verfügung(f), Anordnung(f)
interim –	ordonnance(f) de référé	einstweilige Verfügung (auf Unterlassung)
mandatory –	commandement(m) du tribunal	einstweilige Verfügung (zur Vornahme einer Handlung)
perpetual –	ordonnance définitive	endgültige gerichtliche Verfügung (zur Unterlassung)
preventive –	ordonnance de ne pas faire	einstweilige Verfügung (zur Unterlassung); gerichtliches Verbot
prohibitive –	ordonnance de ne pas faire	einstweilige Verfügung (zur Unterlassung);
temporary –	ordonnance temporaire	einstweilige Verfügung
injury	préjudice(m), lésion(f) (d'un droit), tort(m), dommage(m)	Verletzung(f); Schaden(m)
accidental –	blessure(f) accidentelle	Unfallverletzung
bodily –	lésion(f) corporelle	Körperverletzung
occupational –	accident(m) du travail	Betriebs–, Arbeitsunfall
permanent –	incapacité(f) permanente	Dauerschaden; lebenslängliche Körperbeschädigung
personal –	blessure	Personenschaden; Körperverletzung
Inland Revenue	fisc(m)	Finanzamt(n)
inmate	détenu(m), interné(m, f)	Insasse(m)
innings (lands reclaimed from the sea)	relais(m) de mer	aus dem Meer(n) gewonnenes Land(n); Marschen(f)
innocence	innocence(f)	Schuldlosigkeit(f); Unschuld(f)
innocent	innocent(m)	schuldlos; unschuldig
Inns of Court (UK)	les quatre sociétés du barreau	(Gebäude(n) der vier alten) Innungen(f) der Barrister(m) in London; Berufsorganisation(f) der Barrister(m)
inoperative enactment	texte(m), loi(f) inopérant(e)	unwirksame, ungültige Rechtsvorschrift(f), Verordnung(f)
inquest	enquête(f)	(gerichtliche) Untersuchung(f); Beweisaufnahme(f)
coroner's –	enquête après mort d'homme menée par un coroner(m)	amtliche Leichenschau
to hold an –	procéder à une enquête	Leichnam gerichtlich untersuchen; obduzieren
inquire (to)	enquêter, faire une enquête	nachfragen; sich erkundigen
inquiry	enquête(f), investigation(f)	Untersuchung(f)
judicial –	enquête judiciaire	gerichtliche -
official –	enquête officielle	amtliche -

ENGLISH	FRENCH	GERMAN
insolvency	insolvabilité(f), mise(f) en liquidation judiciaire	Zahlungsunfähigkeit(f); Insolvenz(f)
insolvent	insolvable	zahlungsunfähig; insolvent
inspection	contrôle(m), inspection(f), vérification(f)	Einsichtnahme(f)
– of documents (US)	remise(f) de documents à la partie adverse	– in Urkunden, Akten
instalment purchase	achat(m) à tempérament	Ratenkauf(m)
instance	instance(f), circonstance(f), preuve(f)	Instanz(f)
court of higher – court of lower –	tribunal(m) supérieur tribunal inférieur	höheres Gericht; höhere – Vorinstanz; untere –
instigate (to)	inciter, pousser, fomenter	anstiften; aufhetzen
instigator	instigateur(m), auteur(m)	Anstifter(m); Aufhetzer(m)
institute (to) – an action	instituer, fonder, établir engager une action en justice	einleiten; erheben eine Klage erheben
– legal proceedings	engager des poursuites judiciaires	gerichtliches Verfahren einleiten
instructions to jury (US)	recommandations(f) du juge aux jurés (US)	Rechtsbelehrung(f) der Geschworenen (US)
instrument	acte(m) juridique, document(m) officiel, élément(m) de preuve écrite	Mittel(n); Urkunde(f)
instrumental	utile, actif, productif, instrumental	behilflich; mitwirkend
to be – in	contribuer à	beitragen zu, mitwirken bei
insult	insulte(f), injure(f), affront(m)	Beleidigung(f)
gross –	injure grave	gröbliche –

ENGLISH	FRENCH	GERMAN
insurance	**assurance**(f)	**Versicherung**(f)
accident, casualty –	assurance contre les accidents	Unfall–, Schadens–
air passenger –	assurance sur voyage aérien	Fluggast–
all-risk –	assurance tous risques	– gegen alle Verfahren und Risiken
annuity –	assurance viagère	Renten–
automobile –	assurance automobile	Kraftfahrzeug–
burglary –	assurance contre le cambriolage	Einbruchdiebstahl–
cargo –	assurance sur faculté (de marchandises)	Fracht–; Güter–
co- –	coassurance	Mit–
collective –	assurance de groupe	Kollektiv–; Gruppen–
credit –	assurance contre les risques de crédit	Kredit–
disablement –	assurance invalidité	Invaliditäts–
employers' liability –	assurance contre les accidents du travail	Betriebshaftpflicht–; Arbeitgeberhaftpflicht–
export credit –	assurance contre les risques de crédit à l'exportation	Ausfuhrkredit–;
fire –	assurance incendie	Feuer–
freight –	assurance du fret	Fracht–
full value –	assurance pour la totalité de la valeur déclarée	Gesamtwert–
goods –	assurance marchandises	Waren–
hail –	assurance contre la grêle	Hagel–
health –	assurance maladie	Kranken–
legal expenses –	assurance sur les frais de justice	Rechtsschutz–
liability –	assurance responsabilité civile	Haftpflicht–
life –	assurance sur la vie	Lebens–
life annuity –	assurance de rente viagère	Leibrenten–
loss of profit –	assurance sur le manque à gagner	Betriebsunterbrechungs–
luggage –	assurance sur les bagages	(Reise-)Gepäck–
marine –	assurance maritime	See(transport)–
mutual –	assurance mutuelle	– auf Gegenseitigkeit
old age pension –	assurance de rente vieillesse	Alters–
pluvious –	assurance contre les dégâts causés par la pluie	Regen–
property –	assurance immobilière	Sach–; Vermögens–
social –	assurance(s) sociale(s)	Sozial–
transport –	assurance transports	Transport–
travel –	assurance voyages	Reise–
unemployment –	assurance chômage	Arbeitslosen–
water-damage –	assurance contre les dégâts d'eau	Wasserschaden–
insured person (cf. policyholder)	**assuré (–e)**	**Versicherter**(m) (s. Versicherungsnehmer)(m)
insurer	**assureur**	**Versicherer**(m); Versicherungsträger(m)

ENGLISH	FRENCH	GERMAN
intangible assets	actif incorporel	immaterielle Vermögenswerte(*m*)
intellectual property	propriété(*f*) intellectuelle	geistiges Eigentum(*n*)
intent	dessein(*m*), motif(*m*), but(*m*), intention(*f*)	Vorsatz(*m*)
criminal –	intention malveillante	strafrechtlicher –
evil –	intention criminelle	böswillige Absicht
fraudulent –	intention frauduleuse	betrügerische Absicht
intentional	prémédité, intentionnel	vorsätzlich; absichtlich
interdiction	interdiction(*f*), interdit(*m*), défense(*f*)	Verbot(*n*)
interest	intérêt(s)(*m*); titre(*m*), droit(*m*); parti(*m*), groupe(*m*)	Anrecht(*n*); Beteiligung(*f*); Zins(*m*)
compound –	intérêts composés	Zinseszins
controlling –	participation(*f*) de contrôle	ausschlaggebender Kapitalanteil
– on overdue payment	intérêts moratoires	Verzugszinsen
majority –	participation majoritaire	Mehrheitsbeteiligung
simple –	intérêts simples	einfache, gewöhnliche Zinsen
vested –	droit acquis	wohlerworbenes, sicher begründetes Anrecht
interim	provisoire, transitoire, intérimaire; intérim(*m*)	Zwischen-
– decree	décret(*m*) intérimaire	–urteil(*n*)
– report	rapport(*m*) provisoire	–bericht(*m*)
Interior (*US*)	environnement(*m*) (*US*)	Innen-
Department of the – (*US*)	ministère(*m*) de l'environnement (*US*)	–ministerium(*n*) (*US*)
Secretary of the – (*US*)	ministre(*m*) de l'environnement (*US*)	–minister(*m*) (*US*)
interlocutory	interlocutoire	einstweilig; vorläufig
– judgment	jugement(*m*) interlocutoire	Zwischenurteil
intermediary	intermédiaire(*m*), personne(*m*) interposée	Vermittler(*m*)
intern (to)	interner	internieren
internal	interne, intérieur	intern; inländisch, Binnen-
international	international	international; zwischenstaatlich
interpleader (*US*)	mise(*f*) en cause (*US*)	Streitverkündung(*f*) (*US*)
interpretation	interprétation(*f*)	Auslegung(*f*); Erklärung(*f*)
interrogation	interrogatoire(*m*), interrogation(*f*)	Befragung(*f*); Verhör(*n*), Vernehmung(*f*)
intervene	intervenir	eingreifen; Prozeß(*m*) beitreten
intervention	intervention(*f*)	Eingriff(*m*); Prozeßbeitritt(*m*)
intestacy	fait(*m*) de mourir intestat, sans testament	Sterben ohne Hinterlassung(*f*) eines Testaments
intestate	intestat	ohne Testament verstorben

ENGLISH	FRENCH	GERMAN
intimidation	subornation(f) (de témoins), intimidation(f), menaces(f)	Einschüchterung(f)
intoxication	ivresse(f); empoisonnement(m)	(Be-)Trunkenheit(f)
intrusion	usurpation(f), intrusion(f), empiètement(m)	Eindringen; Besitzstörung(f)
invalid	non-valable, sans effet légal	(rechts-)ungültig
invalidate (to)	casser, abroger, invalider, annuler	ungültig machen; für ungültig erklären
inventory	inventaire(m), stock(m); bilan(m) de faillite (US)	(Lager-)Bestand(m); Inventar(n); Inventur(f)
investigate (to)	faire une enquête, vérifier	ermitteln; untersuchen
investigation – officer	enquête(f), investigation(f) officier(m) chargé de l'enquête	Ermittlung(f); Untersuchung –sbeamter
preliminary –	enquête préliminaire	Voruntersuchung
investment	investissement(m), placement de fonds	Investition(f); (Kapital-)Anlage, Beteiligung(f)
– bank (US) – company	banque(f) d'affaires (US) société(m) de placement (de portefeuill(e)	Investitionsbank; Emissions– Investment–, Kapitalanlagegesellschaft
– fund – trust	fonds(m) de placement société d'investissement	Investitionsfonds Kapitalanlagegesellschaft
inviolate	inviolé	unverletzlich; unversehrt
invoke (to) – an enactment	invoquer invoquer la loi	sich berufen auf – eine Rechtsvorschrift, e-n Gesetzeserlaß
irrebuttable – presumption	irréfragable présomption(f) absolue	unwiderlegbar –e Rechtsvermutung
irrefutable	irréfutable	unwiderlegbar
irrelevance	non pertinent, inconsistant	Unerheblichkeit(f)
irrelevant	non pertinent, sans effet	unerheblich; nicht zur Sache gehörig
irresponsible	irresponsable, insolvable	unverantwortlich; nicht haftbar
irrevocable	irrévocable, non recouvrable	unwiderruflich
– letter of credit	lettre(f) de crédit irrévocable	–es Akkreditiv
issue	question(f), point(m) litigieux, objet(m) du litige; émission(f); conséquence(f)	Streitfrage(f)
– of fact – of law ultimate –	question de fait question de droit question finale	strittige Tatfrage; Tatbestand strittige Rechtsfrage entscheidungs-, rechtserhebliche Streitfrage

ENGLISH	FRENCH	GERMAN
issue (to)	**lancer (un mandat d'arrêt),** émettre, publier	**erlassen;** ausstellen
– a court order	rendre un arrêt de justice	e-n Gerichtsbeschluß erlassen
– a writ of summons	délivrer une citation à comparaître	Prozeßladung (mit Klageschrift) ergehen lassen
– instructions	donner des instructions	Vorschriften erlassen
– securities *(cf. share)*	émettre des actions	Wertpapiere ausgeben *(s. Aktien)*
itinerant	**en tournée,** itinérant, ambulant	**reisend**
– judge	juge*(m)* en tournée	Reiserichter

J

ENGLISH	FRENCH	GERMAN
jactitation of marriage	**fait de prétendre faussement que l'on est marié à une certaine personne**	**Vorspiegelung**(f) **des Bestehens e-r Ehe**(f)
jail	**prison**(f), maison(f) d'arrêt	**Gefängnis**(n)
jeopardise (to)	**mettre en danger,** compromettre	**gefährden**
jeopardy	**danger**(m), risque(m)	**Gefährdung**(f)
double –	être traduit en justice pour un crime ou un délit dont on a déjà eu à répondre	Verbot der doppelten Strafverfolgung eines Täters wegen derselben Tat
join (to)	**intervenir (dans un procès)**; accepter (un arbitrage); s'affilier, adhérer à	**verbinden**
– in matrimony	unir par les liens du mariage	jdn trauen
joinder	**réunion**(f)**, union**(f)	**Beitritt**(m)**;** Verbindung(f)
– of actions/claims	jonction(f) d'instances	Klagehäufung; Anspruchshäufung
– of defendants	jonction d'instance des défendeur	Mitverklagen (weiterer Parteien)
– of issue	acceptation(f) d'un arbitrage	Festlegung der zu entscheidenden streitigen Fragen
– of parties	jonction d'instances	Bildung e-r Streitgenossenschaft; Nebenintervention
– of remedies	jonction des appels	Rechtsmittelverbindung

ENGLISH	FRENCH	GERMAN
joint	**solidaire,** collectif, conjoint	**gemeinsam**
– action	action(f) collective	–es Vorgehen
– custody	garde(m, f) conjointe d'un enfant	–es Sorgerecht
– defendant	codéfendeur(m)	Mitbeklagter
– interest	intérêt(m) commun	–es Interesse
– liability	responsabilité(f) conjointe	–e Haftung; Gesamthaftung
– ownership	copropriété(f)	–es Eigentum; Miteigentum
– plaintiff	codemandeur(m)	Mit–, Nebenkläger
– responsibility	responsabilité solidaire	–e Verantwortung; Solidarhaftung
– venture	coentreprise(f), opération(f) conjointe, association(f) en participation	Joint Venture; Gemeinschaftsuntenehmen
joint-stock company	**société**(f) **par actions**	**Kapitalgesellschaft**(f)
jointly and severally	**conjointement et solidairement**	**gesamtschuldnerisch;** solidarisch
– liable	solidairement et conjointement responsable	gesamtschuldnerisch haftbar
judge	**juge**(m), magistrat(m)	**Richter**(m)
appellate –	juge de cour d'appel	Berufungs–
assistant –	magistrat assesseur	Hilfs–
– in chambers	juge du siège	Einzelrichter, im Büroweg entscheidender Richter
presiding –	président(m) du tribunal	Gerichtspräsident; vorsitzender Richter
judgment	**jugement**(m), décision(f) judiciaire	**Urteil**(n)
declaratory –	jugement déclaratoire	Feststellungs–
definitive –	jugement définitif	End–
final –	jugement définitif	rechtskräftiges –; End–
interlocutory –	jugement interlocutoire	Zwischen–
– by consent	jugement rendu à l'unanimité	Anerkenntnis–
– by default	jugement par défaut	Versäumnis–
– creditor	créancier dont la dette est ajugée due par le cour	Vollstreckungsgläubiger
– debtor	débiteur(m) dont la dette est ajugée due par le cour	Urteilsschuldner
summary –	jugement sommaire	– im abgekürzten, summarischen Verfahren
to award –	prononcer une sentence	– erlassen, verkünden
to deliver –	rendre un jugement	– erlassen
judicature	**magistrature**(f); période(f) d'exercice d'un juge	**Gerichtsbarkeit**(f); Rechtsprechung(f)
judicial	**judiciaire,** juridique	**gerichtlich;** richterlich
– act	acte(m) judiciaire	richterliche Handlung
– district	ressort(m) territorial d'un tribunal	Gerichtsbezirk
– notice	reconnaissance(f) d'un fait par la justice	Kenntnisnahme des Gerichts
– power	pouvoir judiciaire	richterliche Gewalt; Justizgewalt
– proceeding	procédure(f) judiciaire	Gerichtsverhandlung
– review	révision(f) judiciaire	gerichtliche Überprüfung
– system	système(m) judiciaire	Gerichtswesen

ENGLISH	FRENCH	GERMAN
judiciary	**judiciaire** *(adj.)*; **magistrature**(*f*) (*n.*)	**Gerichtswesen**(*n*); Rechts–; Richterstand(*m*)
juridical	**judiciaire**, juridique, légal	**juristisch**; Rechts-
jurisdiction	**droit**(*m*); compétence(*f*) judiciaire	**Gerichtsbarkeit**(*f*); Gerichtshoheit(*f*); Gerichtsstand(*m*); Rechtsprechung(*f*)
general –	toutes matières contentieuses, compétence générale	allgemeine Zuständigkeit
special –	compétence d'exception	besondere Zuständigkeit
jurisprudence	**philosophie**(*f*) **du droit**	**Rechtswissenschaft**(*f*)
comparative –	droit(*m*) comparé	vergleichende –
medical –	médecine(*f*) légale	Gerichtsmedizin
jurist	**juriste**(*m*), légiste(*m*); homme(*m*) de loi (*US*), avocat	**Jurist**(*m*); Rechtsgelehrter(*m*)
juror	**juré,** membre(*m*) du jury	**Geschworener**(*m*)
jury	**jury**(*m*)	**Schwurgericht**(*n*); Geschworene
advisory –	jury de conseil	beratende Jury
grand – (*US*)	jury d'accusation (*US*)	Anklagejury (*US*)
petty – (*US*)	jury de jugement (*US*)	Urteilsjury (*US*)
trial by –	procès(*m*) conduit devant un jury	Schwurgerichtsverfahren
trial –	jury du procès	Geschworene in e-m Prozeß; Urteilsjury
just	**conforme à la loi,** juste, équitable	**gerecht**; rechtmäßig
justice	**justice**(*f*), équité(*f*); administration(*f*) de la justice; titre(*m*) donné aux magistrats	**Gerechtigkeit**(*f*); Rechtspflege(*f*); Richter(*m*) (Titel)
justify (to)	**légitimer,** justifier	**rechtfertigen**
juvenile	**juvénile**	**Jugend-**
– court	tribunal(*m*) pour enfants	–gericht(*n*)
– crime	crime(*m*) ou délit commis par un mineur	–verbrechen
– delinquency	délinquance(*f*) juvénile	–kriminalität(*f*)
– delinquent, offender	délinquant(*m, f*) juvénile, accusé(*m*) mineur	jugendlicher Straftäter(*m*)

K

ENGLISH	FRENCH	GERMAN
kidnapping	**enlèvement**(*m*), kidnapping(*m*), rapt(*m*) (s'emploie plutôt quand la victime est un enfant)	**Entführung**(*f*)
killing	**meurtre**(*m*), tuerie(*f*)	**Tötung**(*f*)
mercy –	euthanasie(*f*)	Gnadentod, Euthanasie
kin	**parent**(*m, f*), allié(*m, f*)	**(Bluts-)Verwandtschaft**(*m*); Angehörige(r)(*m*)
next of –	parent le plus proche	der (die) nächste(r) Verwandte(r)
kind	**espèce**(*f*), genre(*m*), nature(*f*)	**Art**(*f*); Gattung(*f*)
in –	(paiement, règlement) en nature	in natura; – Waren
King's Bench (*UK*)	**Cour**(*f*) **du Banc du Roi** (*UK*)	**Abteilung**(*f*) **des High Court** (*UK*); Gerichtshof(*m*) erster Instanz(*f*)
knowingly	**sciemment**	**wissentlich**
known	**connu**, constaté, avéré	**bekannt**
make –	faire savoir	bekanntmachen; zur Kenntnis bringen

L

ENGLISH	FRENCH	GERMAN
Labor *(US)*, labour	**main***(f)* **d'oeuvre,** salariés*(m)*; travail*(m)*, labeur*(m)*	**Arbeit***(f)*(skräfte*(f)*, –nehmer)*(m)*
Department of –	Ministère*(m)* du Travail	–sministerium *(US)*
forced –	travaux*(m)* forcés	Zwangs–
– conflict, dispute	conflit*(m)* du travail	–skampf
– law	droit*(m)* du travail	–srecht
– permit	permis*(m)* de travail	–sgenehmigung
organised –	organisations*(f)* ouvrières, ouvriers*(m)* syndiqués	gewerkschaftlich organisierte Arbeitnehmer
International – Organisation (ILO)	Bureau*(m)* International du travail (BIT)	Internationales –samt, IAA
laches	**négligence***(f)*, délai*(m)* tardif pour faire valoir un droit	**(schuldhafte) Unterlassung;** Versäumnis*(n)* (in der Geltendmachung*(f)* e-s Anspruchs; Verwirkung*(f)*
landed property	**propriété***(f)* **foncière,** biens*(m)* immobiliers	**Grundvermögen***(n)*; Liegenschaften*(n)*
land register	**cadastre***(m)*, registre*(m)* du cadastre	**Grundbuch***(n)*; Kataster*(m)*
lapse	**défaillance***(f)*, erreur*(f)*; caducité*(f)*, extinction; laps*(m)* (de temps)	**Erlöschen**
– of patent	déchéance*(f)* d'un brevet	– e-s Patents
– of rights	déchéance de droits	– e-s Rechts
– of time	laps de temps	Fristablauf; Verjährung
lapse (to)	**périmer,** se périmer, tomber en désuétude; devenir disponible	**erlöschen;** außer Kraft treten
lapsed	**déchu,** périmé, caduc	**erloschen;** verfallen; hinfällig geworden
– copyright	droit*(m)* d'auteur périmé	erloschenes Urheberrecht
– insurance	assurance*(f)* périmée	verfallene Versicherung
larceny	**vol***(m)*	**Diebstahl***(m)*
grand –	vol important	schwerer –
petty –	larcin*(m)*	leichter –
latent	**latent,** caché*(m)*	**verborgen;** heimlich

ENGLISH	FRENCH	GERMAN
law	droit(m); science(f) juridique; législation(f), loi(f)	Recht(n)
adjective –	procédure(f)	formelles –, Prozeß–
administrative –	droit administratif	Verwaltungs–
air –	droit aérien	Luft–
banking –	droit bancaire	Bank–
bankruptcy –	droit des faillites	Konkurs–
case –	droit des précédents	Fall–
civil –	droit civil	Zivil–
common –	droit coutumier, droit commun	Gewohnheits–
Community –	droit communautaire	Gemeinschaftsrecht (EG)
company –	droit des sociétés	Gesellschafts–; Aktien–
constitutional –	droit constitutionnel	Verfassungs–
contract –	droit des obligations	Vertrags–; Schuld–
corporation – (US)	droit des sociétés (US)	Gesellschafts–; Aktien– (US)
criminal –	droit criminel	Straf–
electoral –	droit électoral	Wahl–; Wahlgesetz
EEC –	droit communautaire	EG-Recht
employment –	droit du travail	Arbeitsrecht
environmental –	droit de l'environnement	Recht zum Schutz der Umwelt
family –	droit de la famille	Familien–
federal –	droit fédéral	Bundes–; Bundesgesetz
financial –	droit financier	Finanzgesetz
fiscal –	droit fiscal	Steuer–
insurance –	droit des assurances	Versicherungs–
international –	droit international	internationales –
labour –	droit du travail	Arbeits–
maritime –	droit maritime	See–
martial –	loi martiale, état de siège	Stand–;Kriegs–
matrimonial –	droit du mariage	Ehe–
mercantile –	droit commercial	Handels–
military –	droit militaire, code de justice militaire	Militär(straf)–; Wehr(straf)–
penal –	droit pénal	Straf–; Strafgesetz
positive –	droit positif	positives Recht
private–	droit privé	Privat–
procedural –	droit de la procédure	Verfahrens–
property –	droit de la propriété	Liegenschafts–; Sachen–
public –	droit public	öffentliches –
Roman –	droit romain	Römisches –
tax –	loi fiscale	Steuer–; Steuergesetz
law-abiding	respectueux des lois	gesetzestreu
law-breaker	transgresseur(m) de la loi	Rechtsbrecher(m); Gesetzesübertreter(m)
law enforcement	application(f) de la loi	Gesetzesvollzug(m)
law of torts	droit(m) de la responsabilité	Recht(n) der unerlaubten Handlungen(f)
law office (US)	étude(f) d'avocat, d'avoué (US)	Rechtsanwaltsbüro(n) (US)
lawful	légal, licite, légitime	gesetzlich; rechtmäßig; rechtsgültig
– age	majorité(f) (légale)	Volljährigkeit
– heir	héritier(m) légitime	gesetzlicher, rechtmäßiger Erbe

ENGLISH	FRENCH	GERMAN
lawsuit	procès(m)	(Zivil-)Prozeß(m); Rechtsstreit(m); Klage(f)
lawyer	homme(m) de loi, juriste(m); avocat(m) (surtout US)	(Rechts-)Anwalt(m)
lay judge	juge(m) non-professionel	Laienrichter(m)
lease	bail(m), concession(f)	Miet(e)(f); Pacht(f)
agricultural (farm) –	bail à ferme	Pachtvertrag (landwirtschaftliche Grundstücke, Betrieb)
land –	bail à ferme	Pachtvertrag (Pachtland)
– agreement	contrat(m) de bail	Mietvertrag
leasehold	tenure(f) à bail, propriété(f) louée à bail	Mietbesitz(m); Pachtbesitz(m); Mietgrundstück(n); Pachtland(n)
leaseholder	locataire(m) à bail, emphytéote(m)	Mieter(m); Pächter(m)
leasing	location-vente(f), crédit-bail(m), leasing(m)	(ver-)mieten; (ver-)pachten;
legacy	legs(m)	Vermächtnis(n); Erbe(m)
demonstrative –	legs à payer d'une source spécifiée	beschränktes Gattungsvermächtnis
general –	legs universel	Gattungsvermächtnis; Geldsummenvermächtnis
legal	légal, licite, légitime, judiciaire, juridique	gesetzmäßig; rechtmäßig; rechtsgültig; juristisch
– age	âge(m) de la majorité légale	Volljährig-, Mündigkeit
– aid	assistance(f) judiciaire	Armenrecht, Prozeßkostenhilfe (UK); unentgeltliche Beratungshilfe (US)
– capacity	capacité(f) judiciaire	Rechts-, Geschäftsfähigkeit
– competence	compétence judiciaire	Geschäftsfähigkeit
– disability	incapacité(f) légale	Geschäftsunfähigkeit; Prozeßunfähigkeit (US)
– excuse	excuse(f) légale	Schuldausschließungsgrund; rechtliche erhebliche Einwendung(f)
– incapacity	incapacité légale	Geschäftsunfähigkeit
– liability	responsabilité(f) légale	gesetzlicher Haftpflicht; – Haftung
– person	personne(f) morale	juristische (rechtsfähige) Person
– proceedings	poursuites(f) judicaires	Gerichtsverfahren; Prozeß
– representative	représentant(m, f) légal	Vertreter in Rechtssachen; gesetzlicher Vertreter; Nachlaßverwalter(m)
– status	statut(m) légal	Rechtsstellung; –position
legalise (to)	légaliser, authentifier, certifier	legalisieren; beglaubigen
legatee	légataire(m, f)	Vermächtnisnehmer(m); Erbe(m)
legator	testateur(m)	Vermächtnisgeber(m); Erblasser(m)

ENGLISH	FRENCH	GERMAN
legislate (to)	légiférer	Gesetze geben(n), – machen, – erlassen
legislation	législation(f)	Gesetzgebung(f); Gesetze(n)
legislative – assembly – power	législatif, législative assemblée(f) législative pouvoir(m) législatif	gesetzgebend –e Versammlung –e Gewalt; Legislative
legislature	corps(m) législatif, législature(f)	Legislative(f); gesetzgebende Körperschaft(f)
legitimate	légitime, justifié	legitim; rechtmäßig, gesetzmäßig; ehelich
lend (to)	prêter	(ver-, aus-)leihen; leisten
lender	prêteur(m)	Darlehensgeber(m); Kredit–; Verleiher(m)
lessee	locataire(m, f), tenancier(m), concessionnaire(m, f)	Mieter(m); Pächter(m); Leasingnehmer(m)
lessor	bailleur(m), loueur(m) à bail	Vermieter(m); Verpächter(m); Leasinggeber(m)
let (to)	louer; adjuger un contrat de travaux publics	vermieten; verpachten; zulassen
lethal	mortel, léthal	tödlich
letter – of attorney – of credit – of intent	lettre(f) procuration(f) lettre(f) de crédit déclaration(f) d'intention	Brief(m); Schreiben (schriftlicher) Vollmacht Akkreditiv Absichtserklärung
letters rogatory	commission(f) rogatoire	Rechtshilfeersuchen
levy (to) – a tax – distress	imposer, prélever, frapper de, saisir lever un impôt, percevoir une taxe faire une saisie-exécution	erheben Steuer – beschlagnahmen; in Besitz nehmen
liability contingent – current – joint – limited – personal – strict –	responsabilité(f), obligation(f), passif obligation future; dépenses(f) imprévues passif exigible à court terme responsabilité conjointe responsabilité limitée responsabilité personnelle responsabilité inconditionnelle	Haftung(f); Verbindlichkeit(f) Eventual- kurzfristige Verbindlichkeiten (pl.) gemeinsame Haftung; Gesamthaftung beschränkte Haftung persönliche Haftung Gefährdungshaftung; verschuldensunabhängige Haftung
liable	responsable (de); assujetti à, tenu de; passible de, sujet à	haftbar; verantwortlich
libel	diffamation(f), libelle(m), écrit diffamatoire	Beleidigung(f); Verleumdung(f); Klage(f)
libellous	diffamatoire	beleidigend; verleumderisch

ENGLISH	FRENCH	GERMAN
liberty (*cf. freedom*)	**liberté**(*f*)	**Freiheit**(*f*)
licence, license (*US*)	**permis**(*m*), autorisation(*f*), concession(*f*), brevet(*m*)	**Genehmigung**(*f*); Konzession(*f*); Lizenz(*f*)
driving –	permis de conduire	Führerschein
– plate	plaque(*f*) d'immatriculation	Nummernschild; Kraftfahrzeug-Zulassungsnummer
marriage –	certificat(*m*) de extrait (d'acte) de mariage	Heiratserlaubnis, –genehmigung
licensee	**concessionnaire**(*m, f*)	**Lizenznehmer**(*m*); Konzessionsinhaber(*m*)
licensor	**concédant**	**Lizenzgeber**(*m*); Konzessionserteiler(*m*)
lien	**privilège**(*m*), droit(*m*) de rétention, nantissement	**Pfandrecht**(*n*); Zurückbehaltungsrecht(*n*)
general –	privilège général	allgemeines Pfandrecht
– on assets	privilège sur les biens	Zurückbehaltungsrecht an Vermögen(swerten)
particular –	privilège particulier	Pfandrecht an e-r bestimmten Sache
possessory –	droit de rétention	Zurückbehaltungsrecht (das Besitz der Sache voraussetzt)
life	**vie**(*f*)	**Leben**(*n*)
imprisonment for –	prison(*f*) à perpétuité, emprisonnement(*m*) à vie	–slängliche Freiheitsstrafe
– assurance/ insurance	assurance(*f*) vie, assurance sur la vie	–sversicherung
limitation	**limitation**(*f*), prescription(*f*), restriction(*f*)	**Verjährung**(*f*)
– of actions	prescription d'action	Klage–
– period	période(*f*) de prescription	–sfrist
statute of –	droit(*m*) de prescription	–sgesetz
limited	**limité**, restreint	**beschränkt**; begrenzt
– company	société(*f*) dans laquelle la responsabilité des associés est limitée (société anonyme, société à responsabilité(*f*) limitée)	Kapitalgesellschaft mit (Haftungsbeschränkung)
– liability	responsabilité limitée	beschränkte Haftung
– partner	commanditaire(*m*)	beschränkt haftender Gesellschafter; Kommanditist
– partnership	société(*f*) en commandite simple	Kommanditgesellschaft
liquid	**disponible**, liquide	**flüssig**; liquid(e)
– assets	liquidités(*f*)	Umlaufkapital
– funds	disponibilités(*f*)	flüssige Mittel; Bargeld
liquidate (to)	**liquider**	**abwickeln**; in Liquidation gehen
– a company	liquider une société	Liquidation e-r Gesellschaft durchführen
liquidated	**liquidé**, certain	**beziffert**
– claim	créance(*f*) liquide	auf eine bestimmte Summe –e Forderung
– damages	dommages-intérêts(*m*) par contrat	–er Schadensersatz; vereinbarte Vertragsstrafe

ENGLISH	FRENCH	GERMAN
liquidation to go into – voluntary –	**liquidation**(f) entrer en liquidation liquidation volontaire	**Liquidation**(f) in – gehen –aufgrund Gesellschaftsbeschlusses; freiwillige –
liquidator	**liquidateur**(m)	**Konkursverwalter**(m); Liquidator(m)
liquidity – ratio	**disponibilité**(f), liquidité(f) taux(m) de liquidité	**Liquidität**(f) –sgrad
list of shareholders	**liste**(f) **des actionnaires**	**Gesellschaftsverzeichnis**(n); Liste der Aktionäre
list price	**prix**(m) **du catalogue**	**Listenpreis**(m); Katalogpreis(m)
list (to)	**coter en Bourse,** cataloguer, enregistrer	**an der Börse**(m) **notieren;** listenmäßig erfassen
listed – company – securities	**coté,** énuméré société(f) bourse cotée valeurs(f) cotées	**börsennotiert** –es Unternehmen –e Wertpapiere
listing – particulars (cf. prospectus)	**cotation**(f) prospectus(m) d'émission d'action, appel(m) à la souscription	**Börsennotierung**(f); Zulassung(f) Zulassungseinzelheiten (s. Prospekt)
litigant	**plaideur**(m)	**Prozeßpartei**(f); prozeßführende Partei(f)
litigate (to)	**mettre en litige,** contester	**prozessieren**
litigation	**litige**(m), procès(m)	**Prozeß**(m); Rechtsstreit(m)
litigious	**litigieux**	**strittig**
LLB	**licencié**(f) **en droit**	**niedrigster akademicher Grad**(m) **der jurist. Fakultät**(f)
LLD	**docteur**(m) **endroit**	**Doktortitel**(m) **der juristischen** **Fakultät**(f)
LLM	**maître**(m) **en droit**	**höherer akademischer Grad der** **jurist. Fakultät**(f)
Lloyd's Register	**registre**(m) **de la Lloyd**	**Lloyd's Register**(m)
loan – against a guarantee – agreement – at call – at interest – capital – interest mortage – secured –	**prêt**(m), emprunt(m) prêt sur garantie accord(m) de prêt, d'emprunt prêt remboursable sur demande, argent à vue prêt à intérêt(s) capital(m) d'emprunt intérêt(m) sur emprunt prêt hypothécaire emprunt garanti	**Darlehen**(n) besichertes –; Bürgschaftskredit –svertrag; Kreditvertrag kurzfristiges – verzinsliches – –skapital; Anleihekapital –szinsen; Anleihezinsen Hypotheken- gesichertes –
loco	**sur place,** 'loco'	**Loco-Konto**(n)
lodge (to) – a claim – an appeal	**interjeter,** confier (des valeurs), placer, remettre déposer une réclamation interjeter appel	**einreichen;** vorbringen Anspruch geltend machen Berufung einlegen

ENGLISH	FRENCH	GERMAN
logistics	**logistique**	**Logistik**(*f*)
long-term – credit – debt	**à long terme** crédit(*m*) à long terme créance(*f*) à long terme	**langfristig** –er Kredit –e Verbindlichkeit
Lord High Chancellor	**Grand Chancelier d'Angleterre**	**Lordkanzler**(*m*)
loss – carried (brought) forward – for the year – of capital – of interest total –	**perte**(*f*)**, déficit**(*m*)**, déperdition**(*f*) pertes reportées sur les années futures déficit annuel, pertes annuelles perte, déperdition du capital perte d'intérêt(s) perte totale	**Verlust**(*m*)**; Schaden**(*m*) Verlustvortrag Verlust für das betreffende Jahr Kapitalverlust Zinsverlust Totalschaden; Totalverlust
lower court	**juridiction**(*f*) **du premier degré**	**Vorinstanz**(*f*)**; unteres Gericht**(*n*)
lump sum	**somme**(*f*) **globale,** somme forfaitaire	**Pauschalbetrag**(*m*)**;** Abfindungsbetrag(*m*)

M

ENGLISH	FRENCH	GERMAN
macroeconomics	macro-économie(f)	Makroökonomie(f)
magistrate	magistrat(m), juge(m)	Ehrenamtlicherichter(m)
magistrates' court	tribunal(m) de police	Amtsgericht(n); erstinstanzliches Gericht(n)
maintenance	pension(f) alimentaire; défense(f) de ses droits; maintien(m), conservation(f)	Unterhalt
– contribution	contribution(f) à l'entretien	–sbeitrag(m)
– liability	responsabilité(f) en matière d'aliments	–sverpflichtung(f)
majority	majorité(f) (n), majoritaire (adj.)	Mehrheit(f)
absolute –	majorité absolue	absolute –
– vote	vote(m) majoritaire	–sbeschluß; –swahl
qualified –	majorité requise	qualifizierte –
make out	dresser, faire établir, rédiger	ausstellen
– a cheque	tirer un cheque	e-n Scheck –
– an invoice	dresser une facture	e-e Rechnung –
malefactor	malfaiteur(m)	Täter(m); Verbrecher(m)
malfeasance	méfait(m); prévarication(f)	rechts, gesetzwidrige Handlung(f), –s Verhalten
malice	préméditation(f), malveillance(f)	böse Absicht(f)
malicious	criminel, fait avec intention de nuire, malveillant	böswillig
– act	acte(m) criminel	–e Handlung; vorsätzlich rechtswidrige Handlung
– intent	but(m) délictueux	–e Absicht
malingerer	simulateur(m)	Simulant(f)
malingering	simulation(f), absentéisme(m)	simulieren
malpractice	négligence(f) professionnelle, faute(f)	gesetzeswidrige Handlung(f); standeswidriges Verhalten
maltreatment	mauvais traitement	Mißhandlung(f)

ENGLISH	FRENCH	GERMAN
management	direction(f), administration(f), gestion(f), gérance(f), exploitation(f); management(m), technique de gestion	Management(n)
company –	gestion de société	Unternehmensführung; Geschäftsleitung
– committee	comité(m) chargé des comptes de gestion	Abrechnungsausschuß
– company	société(f) de gérance	Verwaltungsgesellschaft
manager	directeur(m), gérant(m), gestionnaire(m)	Manager(m); Geschäftsführer(m)
managing director	administrateur(m) délégué(m), administrateur(m) gérant	geschäftsführender Direktor(m); Generaldirektor(m)
mandate	mandat(m), procuration(f)	Auftrag(m); Mandat(n)
mandatory	obligatoire, impératif	obligatorisch; zwingend
manslaughter	homicide(m, f)	Totschlag(m)
marginal cost	coût(m) marginal	Grenzkosten
marginal revenue	recette(m) marginale	Grenzeinnahmen
marine	maritime, marin	See(schiffahrt)(f)
– insurance	assurance(f) maritime	–(transport)versicherung
marital status	état(m) matrimonial	Familienstand(m)
maritime law	droit(m) maritime	See(schiffahrts)recht(n)
market	marché	Markt(m)
– place	place(f) du marché	Marktplatz
– price	prix(m) courant du marché	–preis; Kurswert
– share	part(f) du marché	–anteil
– value	valeur(f) marchande	–wert; Kurswert; Verkehrswert
marriage	mariage(m)	Heirat(f); Ehe(f)
– articles	contrat(m) de mariage	Ehevertrag
– licence	dispense(f) de bans	Heiratserlaubnis
– settlement	contrat de mariage	Ehevertrag
sham –	mariage simulé	Scheinehe
marshal (US)	shérif(m) (US)	Polizeihauptmann(m) (US); Vollstreckungsbeamter(m)
martial law	loi(f) martiale	Kriegsrecht(n); Standrecht(n)
mass arrest	arrestation(f) massive	Massenverhaftung(f)
material	matériel(m), réel, essentiel	wesentlich
– evidence	preuve(f) matérielle	beweiserhebliche Zeugenaussage
– fact	fait(m) essentiel	–e Tatsache
maternity benefit	allocation(f) de maternité	Mutterschaftsgeld(n); –leistungen(f)
matricide	matricide(m, f)	Muttermord(m)
matrimonial law	droit(m) du mariage	Eherecht(n)

ENGLISH	FRENCH	GERMAN
matrimony	mariage(m)	Ehe(f)(stand)(m)
maturity date of –	échéance(f) date(f) d'échéance	Fälligkeit(f)(stermin)(m) –stag; Verfalltag
mayor	maire(m)	Bürgermeister(m)
means – of coercion – of evidence – of payment	moyens(m), façons(f); ressources(f) financières moyens de pression moyens de preuve moyen de paiement, méthode de paiement	Mittel(n) Zwangs– Beweis– Zahlungs–
measure coercive – lawful – precautionary – preventive –	mesure(f), démarches mesure coercitive mesure licite mesure de précaution mesures préventives	Maßnahme(f) Zwangs– rechtmäßige – Vorsichts– vorbeugende –
mediation	conciliation(f), médiation(f), intervention(f) amicale	Schlichtung(f); Vermittlung(f)
mediator	conciliateur(m), médiateur(m)	Schlichter(m); Vermittler(m)
medical – certificate – evidence	médical(m) certificat(m) médical expertise(f) médicale	ärztlich; medizinisch ärztliches Attest medizinischer Sachverständigenbeweis
meeting general – – of creditors	rencontre, réunion(f), assemblée(f), meeting(m) assemblée générale assemblée générale des créanciers	Versammlung(f); Besprechung(f) Jahreshauptversammlung Gläubigerversammlung
member State	pays(m) membre	Mitgliedsstaat(m)
memorandum of association (UK)	acte(m) constitutif d'une société (UK)	Satzung(f) (UK); Statut(n) (e-r Kapitalgesellschaft)(f), Gründungsvertrag(m)
menace	menace(f)	(Be)Drohung(f)
mental – cruelty – disorder – hospital, home – incapacity – nursing	mental(m) cruauté(f) mentale aberration(f) mentale hôpital(m) psychiatrique incapacité(f) mental soins(m) psychiatriques	geistig seelische Grausamkeit Geistesstörung psychiatrisches Krankenhaus; –e Anstalt Geisteskrankheit Pflege der Geisteskranken
mercantile law	droit(m) commercial	Handelsrecht(n)
mercy – killing petition for –	grâce(f), clémence(f), pitié(f) euthanasie(f) recours(m) en grâce	Gnade(f) Euthanasie; Tötung auf Verlangen –ngesuch
merger – clause	extinction(f) d'un droit; confusion(f); fusion(f), unification(f) clause(f) de fusion	Zusammenschluß(m); Fusion(f) Zusammenschlußklausel

ENGLISH	FRENCH	GERMAN
merits	**fond**(*m*), substance(*f*); mérite(*m*)	**Tatsachen**(*f*) **und Rechtspunkte**(*m*); materielle Umstände(*m*)
decision on the –	jugement(*m*) au fond	Entscheidung in der Sache selbst, Entscheidung nach materiellem Recht
dismissal on the –	rejet(*m*) (d'une plainte) pour manque de fondement	Klageabweisung aufgrund e-r Sachentscheidung
mesne process	**instance**(*f*) **en cours**	**Nebenprozess**(*m*); Zwischenverfahren
mete (to) out	**assigner**, décerner	**zumessen**
microeconomics	**micro-économie**(*f*)	**Mikroökonomie**(*f*)
middleman	**intermédiaire**, revendeur(*m*)	**Zwischenhändler**(*m*); Vermittler(*m*)
military	**militaire**	**Militär-**(*n*)
– law	code(*m*) de justice militaire, droit(*m*) militaire	–(straf)recht(*n*); Wehr(straf)recht(*n*);
– police	police(*m*) militaire	–polizei(*f*)
– tribunal	tribunal(*m*) militaire	–gericht(*n*)
minor (*cf. infant*)	**mineur**(*m*)	**Minderjähriger**(*m*), (s. Unmündiger)
minority	**minorité**(*f*)	**Minderheit**(*f*)
– interest	participation(*f*) minoritaire	–sbeteilung; Anteile in Fremdbesitz
– share	participation minoritaire	Fremdanteil
minutes	**procès-verbal**(*m*), compte-rendu(*m*)	**Protokoll**(*n*); Niederschrift(*f*)
misappropriation	**abus**(*m*) **de confiance**	**widerrechtliche Aneignung**(*f*)/ **Verwendung**(*f*); Veruntreuung(*f*)
miscarriage of justice	**erreur**(*f*) **judiciaire**, déni(*m*) de justice	**Fehlurteil**(*n*); Justizirrtum(*m*)
mischief	**dégâts**(*m*), dommages(*m*), méfait(*m*)	**Mißstand**(*m*); Schaden(*m*); Unheil(*n*)
misconduct	**adultère**(*m*); mauvaise gestion, inconduite(*f*)	**schlechtes (ordnungswidriges) Verhalten**; Verletzung(*f*) der Amtspflich
misfeasance	**accomplissement**(*m*) **incorrect d'un acte licite**	**Delikt**(*n*); unerlaubte Ausführung(*f*) e-r an sich rechtmäßigen Handlung
misjoinder	**fausse**(*f*) **constitution des parties**	**unzulässige Klageverbindung**(*f*)
misnomer	**erreur**(*f*) **sur le nom d'une partie**	**falsche Benennung**(*f*); Namensirrtum(*m*)
misprision	**non-dénonciation**(*f*), recel(*m*); forfaiture(*f*)	**(pflichtwidrige) Nichtanzeige e-r strafbaren Handlung**(*f*)

ENGLISH	FRENCH	GERMAN
misrepresentation	conduite(f) visant à induire en erreur	falsche Darstellung(f)
fraudulent –	fraude(f) pénale	arglistige Täuschung; wissentlich falsche Angaben
– of facts	déformation(f) des faits	Irreführung durch Vorspiegelung falscher Tatsachen
mistake	erreur(f), méprise(f)	Irrtum(m); Fehler(m)
– of fact	erreur sur les faits	Tatsachenirrtum
– of law	faute(f) de droit	Rechtsirrtum
mistrial	erreur(f) judiciaire	fehlerhaftes Gerichtsverfahren
misuse	abus(m), mauvais usage(m)	Mißbrauch(m)
mitigate (to)	atténuer	mildern; herabsetzen
mitigating circumstances	circonstances(f) atténuantes	mildernde Umstände(m)
mitigation	adoucissement(m)	Milderung(f)
– of damages	réduction(f) de dommages-intérêts	Herabsetzung des Schadensersatzes
– of penalty	réduction de peine	Strafmilderung
mock trial	simulacre(m) de procès	Scheinprozeß(m)
monetary	monétaire	Währungs-
– system	système(m) monétaire	–system(n)
– unit	unité(f) monétaire	–einheit(f)
money market	marché(m) monétaire	Geldmarkt(m)
monitor (to)	surveiller, vérifier, contrôler	überwachen; kontrollieren
monogamy	monogamie	Monogamie(f)
monopolise (to)	monopoliser	monopolisieren; für sich allein in Anspruch nehmen
monopoly	monopole(m), droit(m) d'exclusivité	Monopol(n)
moratorium	moratoire(m)	Moratorium(n), Stillhalteabkommen(n)
mortality	mortalité(f)	Sterblichkeit(f)
– rate	taux(m) de mortalité	–ziffer
– statistics	statistiques(m) de mortalité	–sstatistik
mortgage	hypothèque(f)	Grundpfandrecht(n); Hypothek(f)
chattel –	hypothèque sur biens mobiliers	Mobiliarhypothek
– bond	obligation(f) hypothécaire	Hypothekenpfandbrief, –urkunde
– deed	contrat(m) d'hypothèque, acte hypothécaire	Hypothekenbrief
– loan	emprunt(m), prêt(m) hypothécaire	Hypothekendarlehen; –anleihe
mortgage (to)	hypothéquer	hypothekarisch belasten; verpfänden
mortgagee	créancier hypothécaire	Hypothekengläubiger(m); Pfandgläubiger(m)

ENGLISH	FRENCH	GERMAN
mortgagor	**débiteur**(m) **hypothécaire**	**Hypothekenschuldner**(m); Verpfänder(m)
mortuary	**morgue**(f), institut(m) médico-légal	**Leichenhalle**(f)
motion	**motion**(f), requête(f), demande(f)	**Antrag**(m)
– for adjournment	demande d'ajournement	Vertagungs–
– for new trial	demande tendant à juger à nouveau la même affaire	– auf Wiederaufnahme des Verfahrens
motive	**mobile**(m), ressort(m), raison(f), motif(m)	**Beweggrund**(f); Motiv(n)
main/principal –	raison(f), mobile principal(e)	Haupt–
mounted police	**police**(m) **montée**, police à cheval	**berittene Polizei**(f)
movables	**biens**(m) **mobiliers**	**bewegliches Vermögen**(n)
multilateral	**multilatéral**, plurilatéral	**multilateral**
murder	**meurtre**(m), assassinat(m)	**Mord**(m)
attempted –	tentative(f) de meurtre	–versuch
first-degree – (US)	assassinat (US)	schwerer –
second-degree – (US)	homicide(m, f) par imprudence, involontaire (US)	leichter –
mutiny	**mutinerie**(f)	**Meuterei**(f)
mutual	**mutuel**	**gegenseitig**
– insurance	assurance(f) mutuelle	Versicherung auf Gegenseitigkeit
– insurance company	société(f) d'assurances mutuelles	Versicherungsverein auf Gegenseitigkeit
– will	donation(f) au dernier survivant	–es Testament

N

ENGLISH	FRENCH	GERMAN
narcotics crime	infraction(f) à la législation sur les stupéfiants	Rauschgiftverbrechen(m)
national	national	National-
– assembly	assemblée(f) nationale	–versammlung(f)
– currency	monnaie(f) nationale	Landeswährung
– debt	dette(f) publique	Staatsschuld
– income	revenu(m) national	Volkseinkommen
– insurance	sécurité(f) sociale	Sozialversicherung (UK)
– law	droit(m) interne, droit national	Landesrecht, innerstaatliches –, einzelstaatliches(EG) Recht
– territory	territoire(m) national	Staats–, Hoheitsgebiet
nationalisation	nationalisation(f)	Verstaatlichung(f)
natural	naturel	natürlich-
– heir	héritier(m) naturel	Erbe durch Geburtsrecht
– person	personne physique, individu(m)	natürliche Person
naturalisation	naturalisation	Einbürgerung(f)
application for –	demande(f) de naturalisation	–santrag
certificate of –	décret(m) de naturalisation	–surkunde
nautical mile	mille(m) marin	Seemeile(f)
necessity	nécessité(f)	Notwendigkeit(f); Bedürfnis(n)
neglect	négligence(f)	Vernachlässigung(f); Unterlassung(f)
gross –	négligence, faute(f) de nature délictuelle	grobe Fahrlässigkeit
negligence	négligence(f), incurie(f), imprudence(f)	Fahrlässigkeit(f); Verschulden
contributory –	part(f) de responsabilité de la victime dans un accident	Mitverschulden
criminal –	négligence criminelle	strafbare Fahrlässigkeit
gross –	négligence, faute(f) de nature délictuelle	grobe Fahrlässigkeit
negotiable	négociable	begebbar; umlauffähig
– instrument	instrument(m) (commercial) négociable	–es Wertpapier
– security	titre(m) négociable	–es Wertpapier

ENGLISH	FRENCH	GERMAN
net	**net**	**netto;** rein
– assets	actif(*m*) net	Reinvermögen
– income	revenu(*m*) net	Nettoeinkommen; Reinertrag
– result	résultat(*m*) net	Endergebnis
– worth	valeur(*f*) nette	Reinvermögen; Eigenkapital
neutrality	**neutralité**(*f*)	**Neutralität**(*f*)
– legislation	législation(*f*) de neutralité	–sgesetzgebung
– policy	politique(*f*) de neutralité	–spolitik
next of kin	**parent**(*m, f*) **le plus proche**	**Verwandte**(*m, f*); nächste Familienangehörige(*m, f*)
nominal value	**valeur**(*f*) **nominale**	**Nennwert**(*m*)
nominate (to)	**nommer,** désigner	**ernennen;** nominieren
non-	**non-**	**Nicht-**
-acceptance	-acceptation(*f*)	–annahme; Annaheverweigerung
-appearance	-comparution(*f*)	–erscheinen
-compliance	-conformité(*f*), insoumission(*f*), refus(*m*) de se conformer	–befolgung, –efüllung
-contentious	-litigieux	–streitig; kontradiktorisch
-existent	inexistant	– vorhanden
-feasance	négligence(*f*) simple	(pflichtwidrige) Unterlassung, Nichterfüllung
-observance	-observation(*f*)	–befolgung, –beachtung
-member country (*EEC*)	pays(*m*) non-membre de la CEE	Drittländer(*pl.*) (*EG*)
-performance	inexécution(*f*)	–erfüllung, –leistung
-resident	-résident(*m*)	– ansässig; im Ausland ansässig
non sequitur	il ne s'en suit pas	irrige Folgerung; unschlüssig
not guilty	**innocent**(*m*)	**unschuldig**
notary public	**notaire**(*m*)	**Notar**(*m*)
note	**billet**(*m*)**,** bordereau(*m*), facture(*f*), bulletin(*m*)	**Note**(*f*)**;** Schein(*m*)
consignment –	lettre(*f*) de voiture	(Luft-)Frachtbrief
credit –	facture d'avoir, bordereau de crédit	Gutschriftanzeige
discount –	bordereau d'escompte	Diskontabrechnung
promissory –	billet à ordre	Eigenwechsel; Schuldschein
shipping –	permis(*m*) d'embarquement	Versandanzeige; Schiffszettel
notice	**avis**(*m*)**,** préavis(*m*), notification(*f*), convocation(*f*)	**Benachrichtigung**(*f*)**;** Anzeige(*f*)
– by publication	notification par voie de presse	öffentliche Bekanntmachung
– of appeal	déclaration(*f*) d'appel	Berufungsschrift
– of assessment (tax)	avis d'imposition, avertissement(*m*) du fisc	Steuerbescheid
– of delivery	accusé de réception	Andienung; Empfangsbestätigung
– of termination	congé(*m*)	Kündigungsschreiben
to give –	donner un préavis; signifier son congé (à qqu'un); donner sa démission	kündigen

ENGLISH	FRENCH	GERMAN
notification of an act	**notification**(*f*) **d'un acte,** d'une mesure	**Handlungsanzeige**(*f*)
notify (to)	**aviser,** signifier, avertir	**melden;** mitteilen
nugatory	**non valable,** inopérant	**unwirksam;** wertlos
nuisance	**acte**(*m*) **dommageable,** désagrément	**Störung**(*f*)
private –	atteinte(*f*) aux droits privés, trouble(*m*) de jouissance	Besitz– od. Eigentums– (der Einzelnen)
public –	atteinte aux droits du public	– der Allgemeinheit; öffentliches ärgernis
null and void	**nul et non avenu**	**(null und) nichtig**
nullify (to)	**annuler**	**ungültig machen;** annullieren
nullity	**nullité**(*f*)	**Nichtigkeit**(*f*)**;** Ungültigkeit(*f*)
– action	action(*f*) en nullité	Nichtigkeitsklage
– of marriage	nullité de mariage	absolute Nichtigkeit der Ehe

O

ENGLISH	FRENCH	GERMAN
oath	**serment**(*m*)	**Eid**(*m*)
administer the – to s.o.	déférer le serment à qqu'un	jdn e-n Eid abnehmen; vereidigen
under –	sous serment	unter –
obedience to the law	**respect**(*m*) **de la loi**	**Gesetzestreue**(*f*)
object (to)	**objecter**, récuser (un témoin)	**einwenden**; beanstanden
objection	**objection**(*f*), récusation(*f*) (d'un témoin)	**Einwand**(*m*); Beanstandung(*f*)
overrule an –	rejeter une objection	e-n Einspruch zurückweisen
sustain an –	admettre une objection	e-r Einwendung stattgeben
objectionable	**répréhensible**	**zu beanstanden**; unzulässig
obligate (to)	**imposer à**, obliger à	**verpflichten**; zwingen
obligation	**obligation**(*f*), devoir(*m*), engagement(*m*)	**Verpflichtung**(*f*); Schuldverhältnis(*n*); Auflage(*f*)
accessory –	obligation accessoire	akzessorische Verpflichtung; Nebenpflicht
joint –	devoir de secret	gemeinsame Verpflichtung; Gesamtverpflichtung
– of secrecy	obligation conjointe	Verpflichtung zur Geheimhaltung
principal –	obligation à titre principal	Hauptpflicht; Hauptverbindlichkeit
obligatory	**obligatoire**	**verpflichtend**; obligatorisch
obliterate (to)	**oblitérer**, effacer	**(aus)löschen**; unkenntlich machen
obnoxious	**odieux**, abominable	**anstößig**; belästigend
observance – of the law	**respect**(*m*) respect de la loi	**Einhaltung**(*f*) – der Gesetze
obsolescence	**désuétude**(*f*), obsolescence(*f*), caducité(*m*); amortissement(*m*) industriel	**Überalterung**(*f*) (technisch oder wirtschaftlich); Wertminderung(*f*) wegen –
obstruct (to)	**faire de l'obstruction**, entraver	**behindern**; hemmen
– legal procedure	entraver l'action de la justice	Gerichtsverfahren behindern
occupancy	**occupation**(*f*), possession(*f*)	**Besitz**(*m*)(**-ergreifung**)(*f*)

ENGLISH	FRENCH	GERMAN
occupant	occupant(m), locataire(m, f), usufruitier(m, f)	Besitzer(m); Inhaber(m); Bewohner(m)
occupational	professionnel (adj.)	beruflich
– accident	accident(m) du travail	Betriebs–, Berufsunfall
– disease	maladie(f) professionnelle	Berufskrankheit
offence	crime(m), délit(m), acte(m) délictueux, toute violation(f) de la loi	Straftat(f); Delikt(n)
criminal –	crime, infraction(f) pénale	strafbare Handlung
indictable –	acte délictueux, crime, délit	Verbrechen, schweres Vergehen
juvenile –	délit commis par un mineur	Jugendstraftat
offender	criminel, délinquant(m), contrevenant	Täter(m)
first –	délinquant primaire	Erst–, Nichtvorbestrafter
habitual –	récidiviste(m)	Gewohnheits–
juvenile –	délinquant juvénile	jugendlicher –
offer	offre(f), proposition(f)	Angebot(n); Offerte(f)
– price	cours(m) d'offre	Angebotspreis; Briefkurs
official	officiel (adj.); fonctionnaire(m) (n), représentant(m) officiel	amtlich
– act	acte(m) officiel	Amtshandlung
– administrator	administrateur(m) officiel	Konkursverwalter; – bestellter Nachlaßverwalter
– authorisation	autorisation(f) officielle	–e Genehmigung
– journal	publication(f) officielle	Amtsblatt
– receiver	liquidateur(m) judiciaire	Konkursverwalter
– seal	cachet(m) réglementaire	Amts–, Dienstsiegel
– secrecy	secret(m) d'État	Amts–, Dienstverschwiegenheit
officiate (to)	officier, célébrer	amtieren
offspring	descendance(f)	Nachkommenschaft(f); Abkomme(m)
offprint	tirage(m), tiré à part	(Sonder-)Abdruck(m)
oligopoly	oligopole(m)	Oligopol(n)
ombudsman	médiateur(m)	Ombudsmann(m); Beschwerdekommissar(m)
omission	omission(f), négligence(f)	Auslassung(f); Unterlassung(f)
omit (to)	omettre	auslassen; unterlassen
one-sided	unilatéral	einseitig; voreingenommen
onerous property	biens(m) onéreux	Vermögen(n) mit Belastungen(f) od. Auflagen
onus of proof	charge(f) de la preuve	Beweislast
open	ouvert, public(m), libre, accessible	öffentlich; zugänglich für
– court	tribunal(m) siégeant en public	in öffentlicher Verhandlung;
– end credit	crédit(m) à capital variable	revolvierender Kredit

ENGLISH	FRENCH	GERMAN
operating	**d'exploitation**	**Betriebs-**
– capital	capital(*m*) d'exploitation	–kapital(*n*)
– expenses	frais(*m*) d'exploitation, dépenses(*f*) de fonctionnement	–aufwendungen(*f*)
– result	résultat(*m*) d'exploitation	–ergebnis(*n*)
operative fact	**état(*m*) de fait**	**Tatbestand(smerkmale)**
opinion	**opinion(*f*)**	**Meinung(*f*)**; Urteilsbegründung(*f*)
concurring –	avis(*m*) en accord	zustimmendes Votum mit v.d. Mehrheit abweichender Begründung
dissenting –	avis de la minorité	mit der Mehrheitsentscheidung nicht übereinstimmende Stellungnahme e-s Richters
public –	opinion publique	öffentliche Meinung
opponent	**opposant**	**(Prozeß-)Gegner(*m*)**
opposing (opposite) party	**partie(*f*) opposée**, partie adverse	**Gegenpartei(*f*)**
oppression	**oppression(*f*)**	**Unterdrückung(*f*)**
option	**faculté(*f*)**, option(*f*); droit(*m*) de souscription	**Option(*f*)**
oral testimony	**témoignage(*m*) oral**	**mündliche Zeugenaussage(*f*)**
order	**mandat(*m*)**, décret(*m*), ordre(*m*), arrêté(*m*)	**Befehl(*m*)**; Verfügung(*f*)
court –	injonction(*f*)	gerichtliche Verfügung; Gerichtsbeschluß
detention –	ordonnance(*f*) de mise en détention	Haftbefehl
extradition –	ordonnance d'extradition	Auslieferungsbefehl; –beschluß
interlocutory –	ordonnance interlocutoire	Zwischenverfügung; einstweilige Verfügung
restraining –	ordonnance de ne pas faire	richterlicher Verbot; einstweilige Verfügung
ordinance	**ordonnance(*f*)**, décret(*m*), règlement(*m*)	**Verordnung(*f*)**; Erlaß(*m*)
ordinary	**ordinaire**	**ordentlich**
– general meeting	assemblée(*f*) générale ordinaire	–e Hauptversammlung
origin	**origine(*f*)**, provenance(*f*)	**Ursprung(*f*)**; Herkunft(*f*)
certificate of –	certificat(*m*) d'origine	–szeugnis
country of –	pays(*m*) d'origine	–sland
original	**original**, initial, primitif (*adj.*); original(*m, f*) (*n*)	**ursprünglich**;
– acquisition cost	prix(*m*) d'achat d'origine	Anschaffungskosten
– document	acte(*m*) primordial	Originalurkunde
– jurisdiction	juridiction(*f*) de première instance	erstinstanzliche Zuständigkeit; Gericht erster Instanz
originator	**créateur(*m*)**, promoteur(*m*)	**Urheber(*m*)**; Begründer(*m*)
orphan	**orphelin(*m*)**	**Waise(*f*)**
outlaw (to)	**mettre hors-la-loi**, proscrire, prohiber	**ächten**; für unrechtmäßig erklären

ENGLISH	FRENCH	GERMAN
out-of-court settlement	règlement(*m*) à l'amiable	außergerichtliche od. gütliche Einigung(*f*)
outrage	outrage(*m*); atrocité(*f*)	Gewalttätigkeit(*f*); Ausschreitung(*f*); grobe Beleidigung(*f*)
outstanding	échu, arriéré, en souffrance	hervorragend; offenstehend, ausstehend
overdue	arriéré, impayé, en souffrance	überfällig; rückständig
override (to)	passer outre, outrepasser	sich hinwegsetzen über; außer Kraft(*f*) setzen
overriding clause	clause(*f*) dérogatoire	maßgebliche Klausel(*f*)
overriding principle	principe(*m*) auquel on ne peut déroger	maßgebliches Prinzip(*n*)
overrule (to)	annuler, passer outre, décider contre	aufheben, verwerfen
oversight	omission(*f*), oubli(*m*), bévue(*f*)	Versehen
overt act	acte(*m*) manifeste	offenkundige Handlung(*f*)
own (to)	posséder	besitzen; zugeben
owner	propriétaire(*m, f*), possesseur(*m*)	Eigentümer(*m*); Eigner(*m*)
ownership	propriété(*f*), possession(*f*)	Eigentum(srecht)(*n*); Besitz(*m*)
bare –	nue-propriété(*f*)	bloßes Eigentumsrecht (ohne Nutzungen)
joint –	propriété(*f*) dans l'indivision	Miteigentum; gemeinsames Eigentum

P

ENGLISH	FRENCH	GERMAN
paid	payé, acquitté, versé, rémunéré	bezahlt
– -in capital	capital(*m*) versé	eingezahltes Kapital
– -up policy	police(*f*) d'assurances libérée	prämien-, beitragsfreie Police
– -up shares/stock	actions(*f*) libérées	(v.d. Aktionären) voll eingezahltes Kapital
pain and suffering	blessures(*f*) et souffrances(*f*)	psychische Leiden(*n*)
palmprint	empreinte(*f*) de la main	Handballenabdruck(*m*)
pander (to)	proxénétisme (*m*) commettre	Kuppelei betreiben; Vorschub(*m*) leisten
panel	groupe(*m*), réunion(*f*) (de spécialistes); panneau(*m*), tableau(*m*)	Gremium(*n*); Ausschuß(*m*)
jury –	jury(*m*)	Geschworene(nliste)
par value	valeur(*f*) au pair	Nennwert(*m*); Nominalwert(*m*)
paragraph	paragraphe(*m*)	Absatz(*m*); Abschnitt(*m*)
pardon	grâce(*f*), amnistie(*f*)	Begnadigung(*f*); Straferlaß(*m*)
pardoning	action(*f*) de gracier, d'amnistier	Begnadigung(*f*); Straferlaß(*m*)
parent company	société(*f*) mère	Dachgesellschaft(*f*); Muttergesellschaft(*f*)
parentage	lignée(*f*), origine(*f*)	Abstammung(*f*); Herkunft
parish	paroisse(*f*)	(Kirchen-)Gemeinde(*f*)
parity of votes	égalité(*f*) de voix	Stimmengleichheit(*f*)
Parliament	parlement(*m*)	Parlament(*n*)
Act of –	loi(*f*)	Gesetz
parole	liberté surveillée; liberté conditionnelle	Entlassung(*f*) auf Bewährung(*f*); bedingter Straferlaß(*m*)
on –	en liberté(*f*) surveillée	gegen Ehrenwort freigelassen
– officer	contrôleur(*m*) judiciaire	Bewährungsbeamter
parolee	délinquant(*m*) en liberté surveillée	bedingt Entlassener
part	partie(*f*), fraction(*f*)	Teil(*n*); Partei(*f*)

ENGLISH	FRENCH	GERMAN
participating interest	intéressement(m) sur les bénéfices	Beteiligungen(f) (pl.)
participation – certificate – loan	participation(f) certificat(m) de participation prêt(m) en participation	Beteiligung(f); Teilhabe(f) Anteilschein Konsortialkredit; Gemeinschaftsdarlehen
particular lien	privilège(m) spécial	Pfandrecht(n) an e-r bestimmten Sache(f)
partition – of an estate	partage(m), répartition(f), morcellement(m) répartition d'un héritage	Teilung(f) Erb(schafts)–; Erbauseinandersetzung
partner general – limited –	associé(m) commandité(m) commanditaire(m)	Gesellschafter(m) persönlich (unbeschränkt) haftender – Kommanditist; beschränkt haftender –
partnership limited –	association(f), société(f), participation(f) société en commandite simple	Personengesellschaft(f) Kommanditgesellschaft
party adverse – indispensable – injured – opposite – third –	partie(f); parti(m) (politique) partie opposée, partie adverse partie indispensable partie lésée partie opposée, partie adverse tiers(m), tierce personne	(Prozeß–)Partei(f) Gegen–; Prozeßgegner notwendiger Streitgenosse Verletzte(r); Geschädigte(r) Gegen– Dritte(r); Nebenintervenient
pass (to) – a Bill – a resolution – sentence	adopter, passer adopter un projet de loi prendre, adopter une résolution prononcer une condamnation	annehmen; verabschieden ein Gesetz verabschieden e-n Beschluß fassen (Straf)Urteil fällen, verkünden
passive debt	dette(f) passive	unverzinsliche Schuld(f); nicht-zinstragende Forderung(f)
patent – infringement – law – rights	brevet d'invention (n); breveté (adj.), patenté (adj.) contrefaçon(f) droit(m) des brevets propriété(f) industrielle	Patent(n) –verletzung –recht; –gesetz –rechte
patentee	breveté(m), titulaire(m) d'un brevet d'invention	Patentinhaber(m)
paternity acknowledgement of –	paternité(f) reconnaissance(f) de paternité	Vaterschaft(f) –sanerkenntnis
pauper	indigent(m), économiquement faible	Bedürftiger(m); Unterstützungsempfänger(m)
pawn (to)	mettre en gage, gager	verpfänden

ENGLISH	FRENCH	GERMAN
pawnee	prêteur(m) sur gages	Pfandgläubiger(m)
pay (to)	payer, acquitter, régler; rétribuer, rémunérer	(be-)zahlen
payable	payable, exigible	zahlbar; fällig
accounts –	dettes(f) passives	Verbindlichkeiten; Passiva
payee	bénéficiaire(m), porteur(m) d'un effet	Zahlungsempfänger(m)
payer	payeur(m), tiré (d'un effet)	Zahler(m)
paying	rémunérateur, payant; paiement(m)	zahlend
– agent	agent(m) payant	Zahlstelle
– banker	banquier(m) payant	zweitbeauftragte Bank
payment	paiement(m), règlement(m), versement(m); paye(f), rémunération(f)	Zahlung(f)
advance –	paiement d'avance, paiement par anticipation	Voraus–, An–
deferred –	paiement différé	aufgeschobene –; Raten–
part –	paiement partiel	Teil–, Raten–
– in full	paiement intégral	volle (Ein)–
– in kind	paiement en nature	Naturalleistung
terms of –	conditions(f) de paiement	–sbedingungen
payroll tax	impôt(m) sur les salaires	Sozialversicherungsbeitrag(m)
peace officer	gardien(m) de la paix	Sicherheitsbeamter(m)
peddling	colportage(m)	Hausieren
peer	pair(m); pair du royaume (UK)	Ebenbürtige(r)(m); Adlige(r)(m)
penal	pénal	straf-(rechtlich)
– action	action(f) pénale	–klage
– law	droit(m) pénal	–recht
– servitude	travaux(m) forcés	Zuchthaus(strafe); Zwangsarbeit
penalty	peine(f), amende(f), forfait(m) d'indemenité	Strafe(f)
death –	peine capitale, peine de mort	Todes–
– clause	dédit(m), clause(f) pénale	Vertragsstrafeklausel
under – of	sous peine de	bei e-r Strafe von
pending	en instance, en cours	anhängig; schwebend
– action	action(f) en cours	–er Rechtsstreit
pendency of action	en cours d'action	Anhängigkeit(f) des Verfahrens
penitentiary	pénitencier(m)	Strafgefängnis(n)
pension	retraite(f), pension(f)	Pension(f); Rente(f)
disability –	pension d'invalidité	Invalidenrente
old age –	pension de vieillesse, retraite vieillesse	Altersrente
– benefits	allocation(f) de retraite	Pensionsleistungen
– fund	caisse(f) de retraite	Pensionsfonds
– insurance	assurance(f) retraite	Rentenversicherung; Pensionsversicherung
per capita	par tête	pro(m) kopf

ENGLISH	FRENCH	GERMAN
percentage share	part(f) de participation	prozentualer Anteil(m)
peremptory – argument – challenge – defence	décisif, absolu, péremptoire argument(m) décisif exception(f) péremptoire, récusation(f) de jurés défense(f) au fond	peremptorisch; zwingend zwingendes Argument Ablehnung der Geschworenen ohne Angabe von Gründen peremptorischer Einwand
performance part – of an agreement	accomplissement(m), résultats(m); prestation(f) éxécution(f) partielle d'une convention	Leistung(f); Erfüllung(f) Teilerfüllung eines Abkommens
peril – of the sea – of transportation	péril(m), danger(m) fortune(f) de mer danger(m) encouru pendant le transport	Gefahr(f); Risiko(n) Seerisiken, Gefahren auf See (pl.) Transportgefahr
perjure (to)	se parjurer, faire un faux serment, un faux témoignage	Meineid(m) leisten
perjury	parjure(m), faux serment(m), faux témoignage(m)	Meineid(m)
permanent residence	résidence(f) habituelle	ständiger Aufenthaltsort(m); – Wohnsitz(m)
permissible	permissible, tolérable	zulässig; erlaubt
permissive legislation	législation(f) facultative, non impérative	Kannbestimmungen(f)
permit building – export (import) – labour –	permis(m), licence(f), autorisation(f) permis de construire autorisation d'exporter (d'importer) permis de travail	Genehmigung(f) Bau– Export– (Import–) Arbeits–
perpetuate (to) evidence	préserver les preuves	Beweissicherung(f)
perpetuating testimony (US)	la conservation des preuves (US)	Beweissicherung(f) (US)
perpetuity	perpétuité(f)	unbegrenzte Dauer(f)
perquisites	avantages(m) accessoires, gratifications(f)	Nebeneinkünfte
persecute (to)	persécuter, harceler	verfolgen; belästigen
persecution	persécution(f), harcèlement(m)	Verfolgung(f); Belästigung(f)
person artificial – legal – natural –	personne(f), individu(m) personne morale personne morale personne physique	Person(f) juristische – juristische – natürliche –

ENGLISH	FRENCH	GERMAN
personal	**personnel**	**persönlich**
– attendance	présence(*f*) en personne	–e Anwesenheit
– description	signalement(*m*)	–e Beschreibung
– property,	biens(*m*) personnels, biens	bewegliches Vermögen
personalty	propres	
– surety	caution(*f*) personnelle	–e Bürgschaft
persuade (to)	**persuader,** convaincre	**überzeugen;** überreden
persuasion	**persuasion**(*f*); conviction(*f*);	**Überzeugung**(*f*); Überredung(*f*)
	confession(*f*) religieuse	
petition	**requête**(*f*), appel(*m*),	**Antrag**(*m*)
	pétition(*f*)	
appeal –	recours en droit	Berufungs–
– for pardon or	recours(*m*) en grâce	Gnadengesuch
commutation of		
penalty		
petitioner	**requérant**(*m*)	**Antragsteller**(*m*); Kläger(*m*)
petty	**mineur**(*m*), peu important	**geringfügig;** unbedeutend
– larceny	vol(*m*) simple	Bagatelldiebstahl
– offence	infraction(*f*) mineure,	Übertretung; Bagatelldelikt
	contravention(*f*)	
– theft	larcin(*m*)	Bagatelldiebstahl
physical	**physique**	**physisch;** körperlich
– disability	handicap(*m*) physique,	Körperbehinderung
	invalidité(*f*)	
– duress	constrainte(*f*) physique	physicher Zwang
– harm	lésion(*f*) corporelle	Körperverletzung
– incapacity	invalidité	unheilbare Impotenz
– injury	préjudice(*m*) corporel	Körperverletzung
– inventory	inventaire(*m*) détaillé	körperliche Bestandsaufnahme;
		Inventur
pickpocket	**pickpocket**(*m*)	**Taschendieb**(*m*)
piecework	**travail**(*m*) **à la pièce,** travail	**Akkordarbeit**(*f*)
	à la tâche	
pilfer (to)	**chaparder,** commettre de	**entwenden;** stehlen
	menus larcins	
pilfering, pilferage	**chapardage**(*m*), larcins(*m*)	**Entwendung**(*f*); geringfügiger
		Diebstahl(*m*)
pillage (to)	**piller,** saccager	**plündern**
place	**lieu**(*m*), endroit(*m*), place(*f*)	**Ort**(*m*)
– of business	siège(*m*) d'une société	Geschäftssitz; geschäftliche
		Niederlassung
– of delivery	lieu de livraison	Liefer–
– of performance	lieu d'accomplissement	Erfüllungs–
	(d'un contrat)	
– of residence	lieu de résidence	Wohn–, Aufenthalts–
placement of	**placement**(*m*) **de valeurs**	**Plazierung**(*f*) **von Wertpapieren;**
securities (*US*),		Unterbringung –(*f*)
placing of securities		
(*UK*)		
plaint	**plainte**(*f*)	**Klage**(*f*); Beschwerde(*f*)
plaintiff	**plaignant**(*m*), requérant(*m*),	**Kläger**(*m*)
	demandeur(*m*)	

ENGLISH	FRENCH	GERMAN
plea	**défense**(f), moyens(m) de défense; cause(f) (US), procès(m)	**Einrede**; Vorbringen
defendant's –	– conclusion(f) de le défense	Klageerwiderung
dilatory –	exception(f) dilatoir	dilatorische, aufschiebende Einrede
– of guilty	aveu(m) de culpabilité fait à l'audience	Schuldbekenntnis; Schuldigerklärung
– of nullity	exception de nullité	Nichtigkeitsbeschwerde; – der Rechtsunwirksamkeit
– for mercy	appel(m) à la clémence, recours(m) en grâce	Gnadengesuch
plead (to)	**plaider**	**plädieren**; vor Gericht vorbringen
– guilty (not guilty)	plaider coupable (non coupable)	sich schuldig (nicht schuldig) bekennen
pleadings	**(les) débats**(m)	**Schriftsätze**(m)
pledge	**gage**(m), promesse(f), nantissement(m), voeu(m)	**Pfand**(n); Versprechen
pledge (to)	**gager**, mettre en gage	**verpfänden**; geloben
pledgee	**créancier**(m) **gagiste**(m), prêteur(m) sur gages	**Pfandnehmer**(m); –gläubiger(m)
pledgor	**emprunteur**(m), débiteur(m) sur gages, gageur(m)	**Pfandgeber**(m); –schuldner(m)
plenary session	**session**(f) **plénière**	**Plenarsitzung**(f)
plot	**complot**(m), intrigue(f), conspiration(f); parcelle(f) de terrain	**Anschlag**(m); Verschwörung(f)
poacher	**chasseur**(m) **de têtes** (fam.); braconnier(m)	**Wilddieb**(m)
poaching	**recrutement**(m) **par un 'chasseur de têtes'**; braconnage(m)	**Wildern**
poison	**poison**(m)	**Gift**
poison (to)	**empoisonner**	**vergiften**
police	**police**(f)	**Polizei**(f)
– authority	la police	–behörde
– constable	officier(m) de police	Polizist
– court	tribunal(m) de police	–gericht
– force	forces(f) de police, corps(m) de police	–(truppe)
– inspector	inspecteur(m) de police	–kommissar
– officer	policier	–beamter
– station	poste(f) de police	–revier; –wache
policy	**police**(f) **(d'assurance)**; politique, ligne(f) de conduite	**(Versicherungs-)Police**(f)
– holder	assuré, détenteur(m) d'une police d'assurance	Versicherungsnehmer
to take out a –	prendre, contracter une police d'assurance	e-e Versicherung abschließen

ENGLISH	FRENCH	GERMAN
population	population(f)	Bevölkerung(f); Einwohner(zahl)(m)
port – authority – charges	port(m) (les) autorités(f) portuaires droits(m) portuaires	Hafen(m) –behörde –gebühren
portfolio	portefeuille(m) (d'actions, de valeurs)	Portefeuille(n)
portion (of an estate) reserved by law for an heir	part(m) d'héritage réserve(f) légale	Erbteil(n) gesetzliche Rücklagen
possession actual – adverse – date of taking –	possession(f) possession effective possession de fait date(f) d'entrée en possession	Besitz(m) tatsächlicher, unmittelbarer - unberechtigter –; Ersitzung Datum der Inbesitznahme, der – ergreifung
possessor	possesseur(m), détenteur(m)	Besitzer(m); Inhaber(m)
possessory action	action(f) possessoire	Besitz(schuld)klage(f)
post-mortem	autopsie(f)	Obduktion(f)
post-nuptial	post-nuptial(f)	nachehelich
postpone (to)	ajourner, repousser, différer	aufschieben
postponement	ajournement(m), report(m), renvoi(m)	Aufschub(m)
power – of appointment – of attorney to act with special –(s)	pouvoir; énergie(f), puissance(f) pouvoir de désignation procuration(f) (écrite), mandat(m) (de faire) agir investi de pouvoirs spéciaux	Vollmacht(f); Befugnis(n) Ernennungsrecht Vollmacht mit Spezialvollmacht handeln; mit besonderer Befugnis handeln
practice legal – civil – trade –(s)	procédure(f); cabinet(m), clientèle(f); pratique(f), méthode(f) manoeuvre(f), procédure(f) légale procédure civile usages(m) commerciaux	Praxis(f); Verfahren Anwaltspraxis Zivilverfahren Handelspraktikten
preamble	exposé des motifs d'une loi, attendus d'un arrêt; préambule(m)	Präambel(f); Eingangsformel(f)
precarious – posession – right	précaire possession(f) précaire droit(m) accordé à titre précaire	widerruflich; kündbar jederzeit entziehbarer Besitz widerruflich gewährtes Recht
precautionary – measures	préventif, préventive; de précaution mesures(f) de précaution, mesures préventives	Vorsichts-; vorbeugend –maßregeln treffen
precedent	décision(f) judiciaire faisant jurisprudence; précédent(m)	Präzedenzfall(m)

ENGLISH	FRENCH	GERMAN
precept	mandat(*m*) d'un magistrat; feuille(*f*) de contributions; précepte(*m*), principe(*m*)	(gerichtliche) Anweisung(*f*); Regel(*f*)
precinct (*US*)	circonscription(*f*) électorale (*US*)	Bezirk(*m*) (*US*)
preclude (to)	empêcher, prévenir, exclure	ausschließen
preclusion	exclusion(*f*), prévention(*f*)	Ausschluß(*m*)
preconceived conclusion	conclusions(*f*) préconçues	vorgefaßte Schlußfolgerung(*f*)
predecease	prédécès(*m*)	vorher erfolgter Tod(*m*); vorzeitiger erfolgter Tod(*m*)
predecessor	prédécesseur(*m*)	Vorgänger(*m*)
predetermine (to)	fixer d'avance, prédéterminer	vorherbestimmen
preemptive right	droit(*m*) de préemption	Vorkaufsrecht(*n*); Bezugsrecht(*n*)
preference share (*UK*)	action(*f*) privilégiée (*UK*), action de priorité	Vorzugsaktie(*f*) (*UK*)
preferential right	privilège(*m*), droit(*m*) préférentiel	Vorzugsrecht(*n*)
preferred stock (*US*)	titre(*m*) privilégié (*US*)	Vorzugsaktie(*f*) (*US*)
prejudice	préjudice(*m*), tort(*m*); préjugé(*m*)	Vorurteil(*n*); Beeinträchtigung(*f*); Schaden
without – to	sans préjudice de	unbeschadet; unter Vorbehalt; ohne Verbindlichkeit
preliminary	préliminaire, préalable(*m*)	vorläufig
– evidence	témoignage(*m*) préliminaire	vorläufige Beweisaufnahme
– hearing	audience(*f*) préliminaire	gerichtl. Voruntersuchung
– investigation	instruction(*f*) (d'une affaire), enquête(*f*) préliminaire	Voruntersuchung
premeditated	prémédité	vorsätzlich
premeditation	préméditation(*f*)	Vorbedacht(*m*)
premises	intitulé(*m*); prémisses(*f*); local(*m*), (les) lieux(*m*), (l')immeuble(*m*)	Geschäftsräume(*m*); Betriebsräume(*m*)
premium	prime(*f*), agio(*m*); récompense(*f*); prix convenu(*m*); profit net(*m*); reprise(*f*) (en cas de location)	Prämie(*f*)
insurance –	prime d'assurance	Versicherungs–
– bonds	obligations(*f*) à primes	Sparprämienanleihen
– wage	salaire(*m*) supplémentaire (exceptionnel)	–nlohn
prepense	prémédité	Vorbedacht(*m*) in böswilliger Absicht

ENGLISH	FRENCH	GERMAN
preponderance	supériorité(f), prépondérance(f), supériorité(f) numérique	Übergewicht(n); Überwiegen
– of evidence	supériorité des preuves du demandeur	überzeugender Beweis
prerequisite (condition)	condition(f) préalable(m), prérequis	Vorbedingung(f)
prerogative	prérogative(f), privilège(m)	Vorrecht(n); Prärogativ(n)
prescribe (to)	prescrire, ordonner	verjähren; vorschreiben
prescription	prescription(f)	Verjährung(f); Vorschrift(f)
present (to) – evidence	présenter porter témoignage	einreichen; vorbringen Beweismittel beibringen
presiding judge	président(m) du tribunal	Vorsitzender(m); Vorsitz(m) führender Richter(m)
press libel	diffamation(m) publiée dans un journal	Verleumdung(f) durch die Presse
presume (to)	présumer	vermuten; annehmen
presumption – of death – of fact – of innocence – of intent – of title	présomption(f) décès(m) présumé présomption de fait présomption d'innocence intention(f) présumée présomption de titre	Vermutung(f) Todes– Tatsachen– Unschulds– Folgerung daß Vorsatz vorlag Eigentums–
presumptive – evidence	présomptif preuve(f) par déduction, par présomption	mutmaßlich Wahrscheinlichkeits–, Indizienbeweis
pretence false –	simulation(f), faux(f) semblant fausses allégations, moyens(m) frauduleux	Vorwand(m) Vorspiegelung falscher Tatsachen
pretend (to)	prétendre, faire semblant de	vorspiegeln; vortäuschen
pretender	prétendant(m)	Heuchler(m); Prätendent(m)
pretest	essai(m) préliminaire, vérification(f) préalable	Vortest(m)
pre-trial procedure	procédures(f) d'avant-procès, procédure gracieuse	Vorverfahren(n)
prevent (to)	empêcher, prévenir	verhindern; verhüten
preventive – detention	préventif détention(f) préventive	vorbeugend; verhütend Sicherungsverwahrung
price – cartel – control – discrimination – index – limit	prix(m), cours(f), cote(f) cartel(m) des prix contrôle(m) des prix discrimination(f) des prix indice(m) des prix limite(f) de prix	Preis(m) –kartell –kontrolle –diskriminierung –index –grenze
prima facie evidence	commencement(m) de preuve	Anscheinsbeweis(m); Glaubhaftmachung(f)
prime cost	prix(m) de revient, prix de fabrication	Gestehungskosten; Einzelkosten

ENGLISH	FRENCH	GERMAN
principal	auteur(m) d'un crime ou délit; débiteur(m) principal	Auftraggeber(m); Vorgesetzter(m); Hauptschuldner(m); Kapital(n)
– and interest	capital(m) et intérêt(s)	Kapital und Zinsen
– in the first degree	auteur(m) principal d'un crime	Haupttäter
– in the second degree	complice	Mittäter; Tatgehilfe
priority	priorité(f), privilège(m); hypothèque(f)	Vorrang(m); Priorität(f)
order of –	clause(f) de priorité	Rangfolge, Reihenfolge
– clause	ordonnance(f) de priorité	Prioritätsklausel
prison	prison(f)	Gefängnis(n)
prisoner	prisonnier(m), prisonnière(m)	Gefangener(m); Häftling
private	privé, particulier(m)	privat; nicht öffentlich
– company	société(f) à responsabilité limitée (SARL), société privée	personenbezogene Kapitalgesellschaft; (etwa: Gesellschaft mit beschränkter Haftung)
– enterprise	entreprise(f) privée	Privatunternehmen; freie Marktwirtschaft
– international law	international droit privé	internationales Privatrecht
– law	droit(m) privé	Privat-, Zivilrecht
– prosecution	action(f) en justice privée	Privatklage
– sale	vente(f) de gré à gré	Privatverkauf; freihändiger Verkauf
– sector	secteur(m) privé	Privatsektor; Privatwirtschaft
privileged information	renseignements(m) privilégiés	durch Aussageverweigerungsrecht(n) geschützte Mitteilung(f)
privity in contract	obligation(f) contractuelle	Vertragsbeziehung(f); Rechtsbeziehung(f) zwischen den unmittelbaren Vertragsparteien
pro forma invoice	facture(f) pro forma, facture pour la forme	Proformarechnung(f)
probability	probabilité(f)	Wahrscheinlichkeit(f)
probate	preuve(f); homologation(f) (d'un testament); vérification(f)	Testamentsbestätigung(f)
probate court	tribunal(m) des successions et des tutelles	Nachlaßgericht(n)
probation	liberté surveillée(f), mise(f) à l'épreuve; essai	Bewährung(f)
on –	à l'épreuve, à l'essai	auf –
– officer	contrôleur(m) judiciaire	–sbeamter
probationer	stagiaire(m)	auf – Freigelassener(m); auf Probe(f) Eingestellter(m)
probative	probant	beweisrechtlich
– fact	fait(m) probant	beweiserhebliche Tatsache
– value	force(f) probante	Beweiswert; Beweiskraft
procedural law	code(m) de procédure	Prozeßrecht(n); Verfahrens-(n)

108

ENGLISH	FRENCH	GERMAN
proceedings	acte(m) de procédure, procès(m); délibérations(f); marche(f) à suivre	Verfahren(n); Prozeß(m)
arbitration –	procédure(f) d'arbitrage	Schieds(gerichts)verfahren
court –	procès(m)	Gerichtsverfahren
divorce –	instance(f) en divorce	Ehescheidungsverfahren
– in bankruptcy	procédure en faillite	Konkursverfahren
summary –	procédure sommaire	Schnellverfahren; summarisches Verfahren
process	processus(m), procédé(m), méthode(f)	gerichtliche Verfügung(f); Verfahren(n)
juridical –	action(f) en justice, procès	gerichtliches Verfahren
– server	huissier	Zusteller (e-r gerichtlichen Verfügung)
procuration	procuration,(f) mandat(m)	Vollmacht(f); Besorgung(n)
procurator	procurateur(m); fondé(m) de pouvoir; agent(m) d'affaires	Bevollmächtigter(m); Anwalt(m)
product liability insurance	assurance(f) contre les défauts de fabrication	Produkthaftpflichtversicherung(f)
production	production(f), fabrication(f), présentation(f)	Produktion(f); Herstellung(f)
– licence	droits(m) de licence	Herstellungslizenz
– rights	droits de fabrication	Herstellungsrecht
profit	profit(m), bénéfice(m), boni(m), gain(m), prime(f)	Gewinn(m); Ertrag(m); Nutzen(m)
profitability	rentabilité(f)	Rentabilität(f); Wirtschaftlichkeit(f)
profiteering	mercantilisme(m)	Geschäftemacher(m); Schieber(m)
prohibit (to)	prohiber, interdire	verbieten
prohibited	interdit(m), prohibé	verboten
prohibition	prohibition(f), défense(f), interdiction(f)	Verbot(n); Prohibition(f)
prohibitory injunction	ordonnance(f) prohibitoire, ordonnance prononçant une interdiction	einstweilige Verfügung(f) (zur Unterlassung)(f)
promise	promesse(f)	Versprechen(n); Zusage(f)
promise (to)	promettre	versprechen
promissory note	billet(m) à ordre, promesse écrite de payer sa dette	Schuldanerkenntnis(n); Eigenwechsel(m)
promulgation	promulgation(f), proclamation(f)	Bekanntmachung(f); Veröffentlichung(f)
pronounce (to)	rendre, déclarer	verkünden
– a decree	rendre un arrêt	ein (Scheidungs-) Urteil –, erlassen
– a judgment	prononcer un jugement	ein Urteil –

ENGLISH	FRENCH	GERMAN
proof	**preuve**(f); épreuve(f)	**Nachweis**(m), Beleg(m); Beweis(m)
burden of –	charge(f) de la preuve	Beweislast
positive –	preuve manifeste	eindeutiger Beweis
– of claim	preuve de créance	Forderungsnachweis
– of guilt	preuve de culpabilité	Schuldbeweis
– of identity	justification(f) d'identité	Identitätsnachweis
written –	preuve littérale	schriftlicher Beweis
property	**biens**(m), propriété(f), avoirs(m), possessions(f)	**Eigentum**(f); Vermögen(n)
fixed –	biens immobiliers, immeubles	Grundstücke und Gebäude
intangible –	biens incorporels	immaterielle Vermögenswerte
landed –	biens-fonds, propriété foncière	Grundvermögen; Liegenschaften
law of –	droit(m) de la propriété	Sachenrecht
leasehold –	propriété affermée, louée à bail	Pachtgrundstücke
movable –	biens mobiliers	bewegliches Vermögen
personal –	biens mobiliers	persönliches Eigentum; bewegliches Vermögen
public –	propriété publique	Staatseigentum; Eigentum der öffentlichen Hand
propound (to) a will	**demander l'homologation d'un testament**	**klagen auf Testamentsanerkennung**(f)
proprietary	**de propriété**, de propriétaire	**Eigentums-**
– rights	droits(m) de propriété	–rechte(n)
proprietor	**propriétaire**(m, f)	**Eigentümer**(m)
prosecute (to)	**poursuivre en justice**	**anklagen**; strafrechtlich verfolgen
an action	intenter une action	Prozeß betreiben, – führen
prosecution	**poursuite**(f), accusation(f), action(f) publique; ministère(m) public; plaignant(m)	**Strafverfolgung**(f); Anklageerhebung(f)
prosecutor	**accusateur**(m), plaignant	**Ankläger**(m); Vertreter(m) der Anklage(f)
public –	ministère(m) public	Staatsanwalt
prospectus	**prospectus**(m), appel(m) à souscription publique	**Prospekt**(m); Einführungs-(m); Werbeschrift(f)
protect (to)	**protéger**, sauvegarder	**schützen**
protective	**protecteur**(m)	**schützend**
prove (to)	**prouver**, établir, justifier, attester	**beweisen**; belegen
proved, proven	**prouvé**, qui a fait ses preuves, attesté	**erwiesen**
provide (to)	**fournir**, prévoir, stipuler	**bestimmen**; beschaffen
provision(s)	**disposition(s)**(f), clause(s)(f), stipulation(s)(f)	**Bestimmung(en)**(f); Vorschrift(en)(f)
restrictive –	clause(s) restrictive(s)	einschränkende –
statutory –	disposition(s) statutaire(s)	gesetzliche –

ENGLISH	FRENCH	GERMAN
provisional	provisoire, temporaire, conservatoire	vorläufig
– injunction	ordonnance(f) de référé	einstweilige Verfügung
– remedy	mesure(f) provisoire, recours(m) dans le cadre d'un jugement(m) avant dire droit	–er Rechtsbehelf; einstweilige Anordnung
provocation	provocation(f)	Herausforderung(f)
provoke (to)	provoquer, inciter	herausfordern
proximate cause	cause(f) immédiate	unmittelbare Ursache(f)
proxy	mandataire(m), fondé de pouvoir; procuration(f), mandat(m)	(Stimmrechts-)Vollmacht(f); (Stimmrechts-)Vertreter(m)
psychopath	psychopathe(m, f)	Psychopath(m)
public	public (adj.); public(m) (n)	öffentlich
– auction	vente(f) aux enchères publiques	–e Versteigerung; Zwangsversteigerung
– authority	pouvoirs(m) publics	–e Behörde
– company	société(f) anonyme	Kapitalgesellschaft
– expenditure	dépenses(f) publiques	–e Ausgaben; Ausgaben der –en Hand
– funds	fonds(m) publics	–e Mittel
– health system	système(m) de santé publique	staatlicher Gesundheitsdienst
– hearing	audience(f) publique	–e Verhandlung
– holiday	jour(m) férié, fête légale	gesetzlicher Feiertag
– notice	avis(m) au public	–e Bekanntmachung
– property	propriété(f) publique	Staatseigentum; Eigentum der –en Hand
– prosecutor	ministère(f) public	Staatsanwalt
– sector	secteur(m) public	–er Sektor; –e Hand
– utilities	services(m) publics	Versorgungsunternehmen (Elektrizität, Gas, Wasser)
publication	publication(f), avis(m) public	Veröffentlichung(f)
publish (to)	faire connaître, publier, rendre public	veröffentlichen
punishment	châtiment(m), peine(f), sanction(f), punition(f)	Strafe(f)
collective –	peine collective	Kollektiv–
purchase	achat(m)	Kauf(m); Erwerb(m)
punitive	répressif	Straf-(f)
– justice	justice(f) répressive, justice pénale	–justiz
purpose	but(m), objet(m), dessein(m), affectation(f)	Zweck(m); Absicht(f)
pursue (to)	poursuivre (une enquête), suivre, continuer	verfolgen; betreiben
putative	putatif	vermeintlich; mutmaßlich

Q

ENGLISH	FRENCH	GERMAN
qualify (to) a statement	limiter la portée d'une déclaration	Erklärung(*f*) unter Einschränkungen(*f*) abgeben
quality	qualité(*f*); statut(*m*), condition(*f*)	Qualität(*f*)
– approval	contrôle(*m*), agrément(*m*) de la qualité	–sabnahme(prüfung)
– complaint	plainte portant sur la qualité	–sbeanstandung
quarantine	quarantaine(*f*)	Quarantäne(*f*)
quash	casser, infirmer, annuler	aufheben; für ungültig erklären
Queen's Bench Division (*UK*)	Cour(*f*) du Banc de la Reine (*UK*)	Abteilung(*f*) des High Court (*UK*); Gerichtshof erster Instanz
query	question(*f*), interrogation(*f*)	Frage(*f*); Beanstandung(*f*)
question (to)	interroger, mettre en doute	verhören; in Zweifel(*m*) ziehen
questioning	interrogatoire(*m*)	Verhör(*n*); Befragung(*f*)
questionnaire	questionnaire(*m*)	Fragebogen(*m*)
quitclaim deed	acte(*m*) de transfert d'un droit ou d'un titre par voie de renonciation(*f*), mais sans garantie de validité	Grundstücksauflassungsurkunde(*f*); Verzichtsurkunde(*f*)
quittance	quittance(*f*), quitus(*m*), acquit(*m*)	Abfindung(*f*); Entlastung(*f*); Quittung(*f*)
quorum (to be a)	qui a un quorum	beschlußfähig
quorum	quorum(*m*), quantum(*m*)	Quorum(*n*); Beschlußfähigkeit(*f*)
quota	quota(*f*), contingent; quote-part(*f*); cotisation(*f*)	Quote(*f*); Kontingent(*n*)
quotation	cotation(*f*), cours(*m*); référence(*f*)	Preisangabe(*f*); –angebot(*n*); Notierung(*f*)
quote (to)	coter (une valeur); faire un devis; se référer à, rappeler	(Preis) angaben(*f*); notieren

R

ENGLISH	FRENCH	GERMAN
raid	descente(f), rafle(f) de police, raid	Überfall(m); Razzia(f)
raise (to)	augmenter; se procurer, réunir	aufnehmen; aufbringen
– funds	se procurer des fonds, réunir des fonds	Geldmittel –
random sampling	échantillonnage(m) au hasard	Stichprobenerhebung(f)
range of application	champ(m) d'application	Anwendungsbereich(m)
ransack (to)	saccager, piller	durchwühlen; plündern
ransom	rançon(f)	Lösegeld(n)
demand (to) a – from s.o.	exiger une rançon de qqu'un	– von jdm fordern
rapist	violeur(m)	Vergewaltiger(m)
rate	taux(m), cours(m), tarif(m)	Satz(m); Kurs(m)
conversion –	taux de conversion	Umrechnungskurs
discount –	taux d'escompte	Diskontsatz
exchange –	taux de change	Wechselkurs
– of interest	taux d'intérêt	Zinssatz
– of return	taux de rendement	Ertragsrate; Rentabilität
rates (UK)	impôts(m) locaux (UK)	Gemeindesteuer(m) (UK)
ratification	homologation(f), ratification(f), entérinement(m)	Ratifizierung(f); Bestätigung(f)
ratio	rapport(m), proportion(f), raison(f), quotient(m), coefficient(m)	Verhältnis(n); Koeffizient(m)
debt-equity –	ratio(f) d'autonomie financière	Verschuldungsgrad; –koeffizient
liquidity –	coefficient de trésorerie	Liquiditätsquote; Deckungsgrad
rationalise (to)	rationaliser	rationalisieren
rationalisation	rationalisation(f)	Rationalisierung(f)
rationing	rationnement(m)	Rationierung(f); Bewirtschaftung(f)

113

ENGLISH	FRENCH	GERMAN
real	**réel,** vrai	**dinglich;** unbeweglich; effektiv
– estate	**biens**(m) **immobiliers**	Grundeigentum; unbewegliches Vermögen
– evidence	**preuve**(f) par vue des lieux	Augenscheinsbeweis; Beweis durch Augenscheinnahme
– income	**revenu**(m) réel	Realeinkommen
– property	biens immobiliers	Immobiliarvermögen
realise (to)	**réaliser;** convertir en espèces; se rendre compte de qque chose	**realisieren;** veräußern
– property	vendre des biens	Eigentum veräußern
realtor (US)	**agent**(m) **immobilier** (US)	**Grundstücksmakler**(m) (US); Immobilien–
realty	**biens**(m) **immobiliers**	**Grundstücke**(n); Immobilien
reasonable	**raisonnable**	**vernünftig;** angemessen; zumutbar; gerechtfertigt
beyond – doubt	quasi-certitude du jury rendant un verdict, conviction(f) dépassant la croyance en un doute raisonnable	jeder vernünftige Zweifel ausgeschlossen
reassess (to)	**réévaluer,** réviser la cote de, réimposer	**neu veranlagen;** – festsetzen
reassessment	**réévaluation**(f), réimposition(f)	**Neuveranlagung**(f); Neufestsetzung(f)
reassign (to)	**réaffecter;** opérer une nouvelle cession	**rückübertragen;** –abtreten
rebate	**rabais**(m), remise(f), réduction(f)	**Nachlaß**(m); Rabatt(m)
rebut (to)	**réfuter une preuve,** une présomption	**widerlegen;** entkräften
receipt	**reçu**(m), récépissé(m)	**Quittung**(f); Empfangsschein
receipt (to)	**acquitter**	**quittieren;** Empfang(m) bescheinigen
receiver	**receleur**(m); destinataire(m), réceptionnaire(m); liquidateur(m)	**Konkursverwalter**(m)
official –	administrateur(m) judiciaire (pour faillite)	(vorläufiger) –; Zwangsverwalter
receivable	**recevable,** plausible	**ausstehend**
accounts –	sommes à encaisser, dettes actives	Außenstände
receiving of stolen goods	**recel**(m) **de marchandises volées**	**Hehlerei**(f)
recess	**vacances**(f) **judiciaires,** suspension(f) d'audience; intersession(f) parlementaire	**(Sitzungs)**(f)**Unterbrechung**(f); Pause(f)
recipient	**bénéficiaire**(m), destinataire(m), allocataire(m)	**Empfänger**(m)

ENGLISH	FRENCH	GERMAN
reciprocal	réciproque, bilatéral	gegenseitig
reciprocity	réciprocité(f)	Gegenseitigkeit(f)
recitals	introduction(f) d'un texte juridique	einleitende Erklärung(f); Präambel(f); Darstellung(f)
reclaim (to)	récupérer; mettre en valeur	zurückfordern; urbar machen
recognisance	caution(f) juridique	Sicherheitsversprechen(n); Kautions–
recompense	récompense(f), dédommagement(m)	Belohnung(f); Entschädigung(f)
reconcile (to)	ajuster, apurer; concilier, réconcilier	versöhnen; in Einklang bringen
reconciliation	accord(m), réconciliation(f)	Versöhnung(f); (Konten)Abstimmung(f)
reconsider (to)	réexaminer, reconsidérer	neu erwägen; nachprüfen
reconstruction	reconstitution(f), reconstruction(f)	Wideraufbau(m); Reorganisation(f)
record	document(m), dossier(m)	Niederschrift(f); Urkunde(f); Protokoll
court –	dossier du tribunal	Gerichtsakte
criminal –	casier(m) judiciaire	Vorstrafenregister
– of evidence	procès-verbal(m) de témoignage	Beweisaufnahme
recourse	recours(m)	Regreß(m); Rückgriff(m)
– against a third party	recours contre un tiers	gegen Dritte Regreß nehmen
recovery	réintégrande(f); montant(m) alloué par jugement; recouvrement(m), récupération; reprise(f); redressement(m)	(Wieder)Erlangung(f); Beitreibung(f)
– of damages	obtention(f) de dommages-intérêts	Erlangung von Schadensersatz
rectification	rectification(f), redressement(m)	Richtigstellung(f); Berichtigung(f)
redeem (to)	amortir, racheter, rembourser	zurückkaufen; einlösen; tilgen
redemption	amortissement(m), rachat(m), remboursement(m), faculté(f) de réméré	Rückkauf(m); Einlösung(f); Tilgung(f)
– of a mortgage	purge(f) d'hypothèque	Tilgung e-r Hypothek
– of securities	amortissement de titres	Rückkauf von Wertpapieren
– rate	taux(m) de remboursement, d'amortissement	Tilgungskurs
– right	droit(m) de rachat	gesetzliches Rückkaufsrecht
redress (to)	redresser, rétablir, réparer un tort	Abhilfe(f) schaffen; wiedergutmachen
redundancy	licenciement(m) économique	(betriebsbedingte) Entlassung(f)

ENGLISH	FRENCH	GERMAN
redundant	**superflu,** au chômage, licencié économique	**entlassen;** überflüssig
re-examine (to)	**procéder à un nouvel interrogatoire,** réexaminer	**nochmals vernehmen;** erneut überprüfen
re-exportation	**ré-exportation**(*f*)	**Wiederausfuhr**(*f*)
referee	**arbitre**(*m*), amiable compositeur	**Schiedsrichter**(*m*); Sachverständiger(*m*)
reference	**référence**(*f*), renvoi(*m*), mention	**Bezugnahme**(*f*); Betreff(*m*)
by –	en fonction (de)	unter Bezugnahme
refinancing	**refinancement**(*m*)	**Refinanzierung**(*f*)
reformatory (*US*)	**prison**(*f*) **pour jeunes détenus** (*US*), maison de correction(*f*)	**Jugendhaftanstalt**(*f*) (*US*)
refrain (to)	**se retenir,** s'abstenir	**Abstand**(*m*) **nehmen von**
refuge	**refuge**(*m*), asile(*m*)	**Zuflucht**(*f*)
refugee	**réfugié**(*m*)	**Flüchtling;** Heimatvertriebener(*m*)
refund (to)	**rembourser,** restituer, ristourner	**rückvergüten**
refusal	**refus**(*m*), déni(*m*)	**Weigerung**(*f*); Absage(*f*)
refuse (to)	**refuser**	**verweigern;** absagen
refutable	**réfutable**	**widerlegbar**
register	**registre**(*m*), livre(*m*); teneur(*f*) de registre (*US*), greffier(*m*), archiviste(*m*)	**Register**(*n*); Verzeichnis(*n*); Registerführer(*m*) (*US*); Gerichts–, Standesbeamter(M)
registered	**enregistré,** inscrit, immatriculé	**eingetragen**
– letter	lettre(*f*) recommandée	eingeschriebener Brief
– mail	courrier(*m*) recommandé	Einschreiben
– office	siège(*m*) social	–er Sitz
registrar	**teneur**(*m*) **de registre,** greffier(*m*), archiviste(*m*)	**Registerführer**(*m*); Gerichts–(*m*), Standesbeamter(*m*)
the – of companies	directeur(*m*) de l'enregistrement de sociétés	Führer des Gesellschaftsregisters
registration	**enregistrement**(*m*), immatriculation(*f*), inscription(*f*)	**Eintragung**(*f*); Zulassung(*f*)
patent –	dépôt(*m*) d'un brevet	Eintragung in die Patentrolle
– plate	plaque(*f*) d'immatriculation	Nummernschild; polizeil. Kennzeichen
trade mark –	dépôt d'une marque de fabrique	Eintragung e-s Warenzeichens
regress	**rentrée**(*f*), rentrée en possession d'un bien-fonds (*US*)	**Wiederinbesitznahme**(*f*); Rückgriff(*m*)
regulations (*EEC*)	**réglements**(*m*) (*CEE*)	**Verordnungen**(*f*) (*EG*)

ENGLISH	FRENCH	GERMAN
rehabilitation	réhabilitation(f), redressement(m), rétablissement(m)	Rehabilitierung(f)
rehearing	nouvelle audition(f)	erneute Verhandlung(f); Berufung(f)(sverfahren)(n)
reinstate (to) a court matter	réinscrire une affaire au rôle	wiedereinsetzen in den vorigen Stand(m); klageabweisendes Urteil aufheben
reinsurance	réassurance(f), contre-assurance(f)	Rückversicherung(f)
reject (to)	rejeter, refuser	ablehnen; zurückweisen
rejoinder	répartie(f)	Erwiderung(f); Duplik(f)
release	mise(f) en liberté, élargissement; cession(f) de propriété; décharge(f); mise(f) en vente; libération(f)de capitaux	Freilassung(f); Erlösung; Entlastung
– from custody	relaxe, mise en liberté	Haftentlassung
release (to)	libérer, relaxer, élargir, renoncer, délier, décharger	freilassen; entlassen
relevancy	pertinence(f)	Relevanz(f); Wichtigkeit(f)
relevant	pertinent, applicable, approprié, utile	relevant; erheblich
reliance	confiance(f)	Vertrauen; Verlaß(m)
relief	réparation(f), redressement(m); secours(m), aide(f)	Rechtshilfe(f)
affirmative –	conclusions(f) acceptées	beantragte –; Gegenstand der Leistungsklage
claim for –	demande(m) d'assistance	Klageantrag; Sachantrag
declaratory –	jugement(m) déclaratif	deklaratorischer Rechtsschutz
relinquishment	répudiation(f), abandon(m)	Aufgabe(f); Verzicht
remand	ajournement(m), renvoi(m)	Untersuchungshaft(f); Anordnung der Haftfortdauer
remedial action	action(f) en recours	Schadensersatzklage(f)
remedy	voie(f) de recours, moyen(m) de droit, dédommagement(m)	Rechtsbehelf(m)
provisional –	ordonnance(f) de référé, mesure(f) provisoire	vorläufiger -
reminder	mémento(m), rappel(m) pour mémoire	Mahnung(f); Beanstandung(f)
remission of charges	détaxe(f)	Gebührenerlaß(m)
remittance	envoi(m) de fonds, versement(m), traite(f), chèque(m)	Überweisung(f)

ENGLISH	FRENCH	GERMAN
remoteness – of damage	éloignement(m) dommage(m) indirect	Entlegenheit(f); Ferne(f) Nichtzurechenbarkeit e-s Schadens
– of evidence	non-pertinence d'un témoignage	Beweisunerheblichkeit
remuneration	rémunération(f), allocation(f), indemnité(f)	Vergütung(f); Honorar(n)
renounce (to)	abandonner, renoncer à, se démettre de, répudier	verzichten; aufgeben
rent	loyer(m); prix(m) de location	Miete(f); Pacht(f)
rental income	revenu(m) locatif	Mieteinnahmen(f); Pacht-(f)
renunciation	répudiation(f) (d'une succession), renoncement(m), abandon(m)	Verzicht(m)(leistung)(f); Aufgabe(f)
repeal	abrogation(f), révocation(f)	Aufhebung(f); Außerkraftsetzung(f)
repossess (to)	faire saisir un article non payé	wieder in Besitz(m) nehmen; zurücknehmen
reprieve	sursis(m), commutation(f) de peine de mort	Strafvollstreckungsaufschub(m)
rescind (to)	casser, annuler, rescinder	aufheben; rückgängig machen
research and development (R & D)	recherche(f) et développement (R & D)	Forschung(f) und Entwicklung(f) (F & E)
reservation of title	clause(f) de restriction d'un titre	Eigentumsvorbehalt(m)
reserve	réserve(f), provision(f), couverture(f)	Rücklage(f); Reserve(f)
contingency –	fonds(m) de réserve	Rückstellung für Eventualverbindlichkeiten
legal –	réserve légale	gesetzliche Mindestreserven; – Rücklagen;
revaluation –	réserve de réévaluation	Neubewertungsrücklage
residence official – permanent –	résidence(f), domicile(m) résidence officielle domicile habituel	Wohnsitz(m); Domizil(n) Amtssitz ständiger Wohnsitz
residuary legatee	légataire(m) universel	Restnachlaßempfänger(m)
resist (to) arrest	résister lors de son arrestation	sich der Verhaftung(f) widersetzen
resolution	résolution(f), délibération(f), ordre(m) du jour	Beschluß; Resolution(f)
resort (to) to violence	avoir recours à la violence	Gewalt(f) anwenden
respite	sursis(m), délai(m), répit(m)	Fristverlängerung(f); Vollstreckungsaufschub(m)
respond (to)	répondre; réagir; être l'intimé	erwidern; Klageerwiderung(f) einreichen

ENGLISH	FRENCH	GERMAN
respondent	défendeur(*m*); intimé	Beklagter(*m*); Antragsgegner(*m*); (siehe(*m*) Berufungsbeklagter)
response	réaction(*f*), réponse(*f*)	(Klage)Beantwortung(*f*); Erwiderung(*f*)
responsible	responsable; compétent	haftbar; haftpflichtig
restitution	restitution(*f*), réparation(*f*), dommages-intérêt(s)(*m*)	Rückerstattung(*f*); Wiederherstellung(*f*) des früheren Rechtszustands
restoration	restitution	Rückgabe(*f*); Wiederherstellung(*f*)
restraining order	ordonnance(*f*) de ne pas faire	einstweilige Verfügung(*f*); richterliches Verbot(*n*)
restraint	contrainte(*f*) par corps, emprisonnement(*m*), séquestration(*f*)	Beschränkung(*f*); Verhinderung(*f*); Zurückbehaltung(*f*)
restrict (to)	restreindre, limiter, réduire	beschränken; ein–
restrictive trade practices	pratiques(*f*) commerciales restrictives	Wettbewerbsbeschränkungen(*f*); Kartelle(*n*)
retain (to)	choisir, retenir, conserver	beibehalten; beauftragen
retainer	provision(*f*) sur honoraires d'avocat; arrhes(*f*); cachet(*m*)	Anwaltsbestellung(*f*); Gebührenvorschuß(*m*)
retaliation	représaille(s)(*f*), mesure(*f*) de rétorsion; remboursement(*m*)	Vergeltung(*f*)(smaßnahmen)
retirement	retraite(*f*)	Ruhestand(*m*); Rücktritt(*m*)
retraction	rétractation(*f*)	Widerruf(*m*)
retrial	nouveau procès(*m*)	Wiederaufnahmeverfahren(*n*); erneute Verhandlung(*f*)
retrieve (to)	récupérer	wiedererlangen; –gutmachen
retrocession	rétrocession(*f*)	Wiederabtretung(*f*); Retrozession(*f*)
return	revenu(*m*), rendement(*m*); remboursement(*m*), ristourne; renvoi(*m*), réexpédition(*f*)	Rückerstattung(*f*); Steuererklärung(*f*); Ertrag(*m*) Vermögensangabe
– on assets	rendement(*m*) d'un actif	Gesamtkapitalrentabilität
– on capital	rentabilité(*f*) du capital (investi)	Kapitalertrag
– on investment (ROI)	rendement sur investissement (RSI)	Ertrag aus Kapitalanlage; Kapitalrendite
returns	recettes(*f*), rendement(*m*); retour(*m*) des invendus; statistiques(*m*), résultats	(Kapital)ertrag(*m*); Gewinn(*m*); Rendite(*f*)
revaluation	réévaluation(*f*)	Aufwertung(*f*); Neubewertung(*f*)
reveal (to)	révéler	enthüllen; offenbaren
revenge	vengeance(*f*)	Rache(*f*)
revenue	revenu(*m*), rapport(*m*), rentes(*f*)	(Staats)Einkommen(*n*); Steuereinnahmen(*m*)

ENGLISH	FRENCH	GERMAN
reversal	**arrêt**(*m*) **d'annulation,** réforme(*f*) d'un jugement en appel	**Aufhebung**(*f*); Stornierung(*f*); Rückbuchung(*f*)
reverse (to) – a judgment	**réformer,** révoquer, casser casser, révoquer un jugement, une sentence	**aufheben;** stornieren; rückbuchen Urteil aufheben
review on appeal	**révision**(*f*) **en appel**	**Überprüfung**(*f*) **e-s Urteils (durch Rechtsmittelgericht)**
revocation	**révocation**(*f*), abrogation(*f*), annulation(*f*)	**Widerruf**(*m*)
– of a tender	annulation d'un appel d'offres	Zurücknahme e-s Angebots
– of a will	annulation d'un testament	– des Testaments
revoke (to)	**révoquer,** abroger, revenir sur une promesse	**widerrufen;** aufheben
reward	**récompense**(*f*)	**Belohnung**(*f*); Vergütung(*f*)
right	**le droit,** la justice, le bien; droit(*m*), titre(*m*), privilège(*m*)	**Recht(sanspruch)**(*m*)
civil –(s)	droits civils	Grundrechte; bürgerliche Ehrenrechte
human –(s) intangible –(s) – of appeal – of redress – of way vested –	droits de l'homme propriété(*f*) intellectuelle droit d'appel droit(*m*) de recours droit de passage droits acquis en vertu de la constitution	Menschenrechte immaterielle Rechte Berufungsrecht; Rechtsmittel Entschädigungsrecht Vorfahrtsrecht; Wegerecht wohlerworbene, wohlbegründete Rechte
riot	**émeute**	**Aufruhr**(*f*)
risk – management – margin	**risque**(*m*), aléa(*m*), péril(*m*) contrôle(*m*) des pertes marge(*f*) de risque	**Risiko**(*n*) –management –spanne
robbery armed – – with violence	**vol**(*m*) **qualifié** vol à main armée vol qualifié avec violences	**Raub**(*m*); Beraubung(*f*) bewaffneter Raubüberfall gewalttätige(r) –
royalty	**royauté**(*f*), princes(*m*) du sang	**Königtum**(*n*); Lizenzgebühr(*f*)
rule	**règle**(*f*) **de procédure,** règle de droit immuable; disposition(*f*)	**Regel**(*f*); Bestimmung(*f*); Verordnung(*f*)
rule (to) 'the court rules that'	**décider,** régir, gouverner 'le tribunal a décidé que'	**entscheiden;** beschließen 'das Gericht verfügt, daß'
ruling	**ordonnance**(*f*), décision(*f*) d'un juge sur un point de droit	**(amtliche oder gerichtliche) Enscheidung**(*f*); Anordnung(*f*)

S

ENGLISH	FRENCH	GERMAN
sabotage	sabotage(m)	Sabotage(f)
sacrilege	sacrilège(m)	Sakrileg(n); Kirchenschändung(f)
safe – custody – deposit	sain, sûr dépôt(m) en garde dépôt en coffre-fort	sicher –e Verwahrung; Depot Tresor; Aufbewahrung (im Tresor)
safeguard (to) – a person's interests	sauvegarder, prendre des mesures de protection protéger les intérêts de qqu'un	sichern; wahrnehmen jds Interessen wahren
safety	sécurité(f), sûreté(f)	Sicherheit(f)
salary	traitement(m), appointement(m), salaire(m)	Gehalt(m); Besoldung(f)
sales contract	contrat(m) de vente	Kaufvertrag(m)
salvage	prime(f) de sauvetage, indemnité de remorquage; sauvetage(m), renflouement(m); récupération de matériels et marchandises après sauvetage(m)	Bergung(f); Altmaterialverwertung(f)
– company – contract – costs	société(f) de sauvetage contrat(m) de sauvetage frais(m) de sauvetage	Bergungsgesellschaft Bergungsvertrag Bergungskosten
sample	échantillon(m); sondage(m)	(Stich-)Probe(f); (Waren-)Probe(f), Muster(n)
sampling random –	échantillonnage(m) échantillonage au hasard	(Auswahl(f) nach dem) Stichprobenverfahren(m); Zufallsstichprobenerhebung
sanction punitive –	sanction(f), ratification(f), approbation(f) sanction pénale	Sanktion(f); Bestätigung(f) Strafmaßnahmen
sanction (to)	sanctionner, ratifier	(offiziell) genehmigen; sanktionieren
sanctuary	asile(m), refuge(m), sanctuaire(m)	Asyl(n); Freistatt(f)
sanitary	sanitaire	sanitär; hygienisch

ENGLISH	FRENCH	GERMAN
satisfaction	satisfaction(f), réparation(f), purge(f)	Befriedigung(f); Bezahlung(f); Erfüllung(f)
savage	brutal(m), féroce	wild; unzivilisiert
save (to)	sauver; économiser, épargner	retten
– a person's life	sauver la vie de qqu'un	jdm das Leben retten
savings bank	caisse(f) d'épargne	Sparkasse(f)
scaffold	gibet(m), potence(f)	Gerüst(n); Schafott(n)
scandalise (to)	scandaliser, indigner	Anstoß(m) erregen; empören
scapegoat	bouc(m) émissaire	Sündenbock(m)
scar	cicatrice(f)	Narbe(f)
scars and bruises	cicatrices et contusions	-n und blaue Flecken
scene of crime	lieu(m) du crime	Tatort(m)
schedule	annexe(f), avenant(m); cédule(f); programme(m), horaire(m)	Liste(f); Aufstellung(f); Anhang(m); Zeitplan(m)
scheming and planning	machinations(f) et intrigues(f)	planen und Ränke schmieden
science	science(f)	(Natur)wissenschaft(f)
scope	portée(f), champ(m) d'action, compétence(f)	Bereich(m); Rahmen(m)
within the – of	qui sont du ressort de, qui relève de	im Rahmen von
screen (to)	interroger un suspect; filtrer, trier; masquer, protéger	überprüfen; untersuchen
– security risks	étudier les risques de sécurité	Sicherheitsrisiken überprüfen
scrip	bon(m), document(m), titre(m), certificat(m)	Scrip(m); Zwischenschein(m)
– -holder	porteur(m) de titre, détenteur(m) de documents	–inhaber
scrutinise (to)	examiner de très près, enquêter minutieusement	genau prüfen; (Stimmen) nachzählen
scuffle	rixe(f), bagarre(f), échaufourrée(f)	Handgemenge(n); Prügelei(f)
seaborne trade	commerce(m) maritime	Seehandel(m)
seal	cachet(m), sceau(m)	(Amts)Siegel(n); Plombe(f), Verschluß(m)
to affix one's –	apposer son cachet	seinen Siegel anbringen, beidrücken
under the – of	sous le sceau de	unter dem Siegel von; gesiegelt
search	perquisition(f), fouille, recherche(f)	Suche(f); Fahndung(f)
– warrant	mandat(m) de perquisition	Durchsuchungsbefehl

ENGLISH	FRENCH	GERMAN
seat	**siège**(m), charge(f), office(m)	**Sitz**(m)
– of government	siège du gouvernement	Regierungssitz;
the company's –	le siège social de la société	Firmen–
secrecy	**secret**(m)	**Geheimhaltung**(f); Verschwiegenheit(f)
– clause	clause(f) de secret	Geheimhaltungsklausel
secret	**secret**	**Geheimnis**(n)
Official Secrets Act	Loi(f) relative aux secrets d'État	Gesetz zum Schutz von Staatsgeheimnissen
section	**section**(f), article(m) (d'une loi)	**Paragraph**(m); Abschnitt(m)
secure (to)	**réussir à avoir,** obtenir, se procurer; garantir	**sichern;** sicherstellen
– a loan (debt)	garantir un prêt (une créance)	Sicherheit für ein Darlehen leisten
– evidence	obtenir un témoignage	Beweise sicherstellen
securities	**titres**(m), fonds(m), valeurs(f) boursières	**Wertpapiere**(n); Effekten
listed –	valeurs cotées	börsenfähige –
redeemable –	titres remboursables	einlösbare Wertpapiere
transferrable –	valeurs mobilières librement cessibles	übertragbare –
security	**sécurité**(f), sûreté(f)	**Bürgschaft**(f); Sicherheit(f)
collateral –	nantissement(m)	Nebensicherheit; Deckung durch Hinterlegung von Effekten
– by mortgage	garantie(f) hypothécaire	hypothekarische Sicherheit
– interest	intérêt(s)(m) garanti(s)	Sicherungsrecht an beweglichen oder unbeweglichen Sachen
– police	forces(f) de sécurité	Sicherheitspolizei
– risk	risque(m) sécuritaire	Sicherheitsrisiko
seduction	**corruption**(f), séduction(f)	**Verführung**(f)
segment	**branche**(f), segment(m)	**Segment**(n); Sparte(f)
market –	secteur(m) du marché	Marktsegment
seize (to)	**saisir,** confisquer	**ergreifen;** beschlagnahmen
seizure	**saisie**(f), confiscation(f)	**Beschlagnahme**(m)
– of chattels	saisie des biens et effets	– bewegliches Vermögens
– of real estate	saisie immobilière	– unbewegliches Vermögens; – von Grundbesitz
self-defence	**légitime défense**(f), autodéfense	**Notwehr**(f); Selbstverteidigung(f)
self-employed person	**travailleur**(m) **indépendant**	**Selbständiger**(m)
self-financing	**autofinancement**(m)	**Selbstfinanzierung**(f)
self-incrimination	**incrimination**(f) **de soi-même**	**Selbstbezichtigung**(f)
self-supporting	**autosuffisant**	**finanziell unabhängig;** nicht auf fremde Hilfe angewiesen
seller	**vendeur**(m)	**Verkäufer**(m)
semifinished goods	**produits**(m) **semi-finis**	**Halbfabrikate**(n)

ENGLISH	FRENCH	GERMAN
sentence	**sentence**(*f*), condamnation(*f*), jugement(*m*)	**(Straf)Urteil**(*n*); Strafe(*f*)
death –	arrêt(*m*) de mort, condamnation à mort, peine(*f*) de mort	Todesurteil
life –	condamnation à perpétuité	lebenslängliche Freiheitsstrafe
prison –	condamnation à une peine de prison	Gefängnisstrafe
suspended –	condamnation avec sursis	Strafaussetzung (zur Bewährung)
to pass – on s.o.	prononcer une condamnation à l'encontre de qqu'un	Strafurteil fällen, verkünden
separation	**séparation**(*f*) **(des époux)**	**Gerichtliche Trennung**(*f*)
judicial –	séparation(*f*) juciciaire (des époux)	Ehetrennung; Aufhebung der ehelichen Gemeinschaft
sequestration	**séquestration**(*f*), mise(*f*) sous séquestre	**Zwangsverwaltung**(*f*); Sequestration(*f*)
service	**assignation**(*f*), signification(*f*); service(*m*)	**Zustellung**(*f*)
– by bailiff	signification par huissier	– durch Hilfsbeamten
– of summons	signification de convocation	– e-r Vorladung
servitude	**servitude**(*f*)	**Dienstbarkeit**(*f*)
penal –	travaux forcés	Zuchthaus (strafe); Zwangsarbeit
session	**audience**(*f*), session(*f*), séance(*f*)	**Sitzung**(*f*)
court in –	tribunal(*m*) en session, en séance	Gericht tagt
open –	audience publique	öffentliche –
settlement	**arrangement**(*m*), règlement(*m*), transaction(*f*); disposition(*f*) de biens, liquidation(*f*)	**Regelung**(*f*); Beilegung(*f*); Abfindung(*f*)
out-of-court –	arrangement à l'amiable	außergerichtliche Regelung
– by arbitration	règlement arbitral	Regelung auf schiedsgerichtlichem Weg
several	**individuel,** indivis; séparé; plusieurs	**einzeln;** gesondert
severance	**rupture**(*f*) **(de contrat),** séparation(*f*)	**Trennung**(*f*)
– of legal actions	cessation(*f*) d'actions en justice	Klagen–
– pay	indemnité(*f*) de licenciement, de rupture de contrat	Entlassungsabfindung; Härteausgleich
severity	**sévérité**(*f*), rigueur(*f*); violence(*f*)	**Härte**(*f*); Strenge(*f*)
– of an offence	gravité(*f*) d'un crime, d'un délit	Schwere e-r Straftat, e-s Delikts
sex crime	**crime**(*m*) **d'ordre sexuel**	**Sexualverbrechen**
sexual offence	**délit**(*m*) **d'ordre sexuel**	**Sittlichkeitsvergehen**

124

ENGLISH	FRENCH	GERMAN
sham pleading	usage(m) de moyens dilatoires	mutwilliges (dilatorisches) Parteivorbringen
share bonus – common – (US) listed –	action(f), valeur(f), part(f) action gratuite action(f) ordinaire (US) action cotée (officiellement)	Aktie(f); Gesellschaftsanteil(m) Gratisaktie Stammaktie börsennotierte Aktie
ordinary – preference –	action ordinaire action privilégiée, de priorité	Stammaktie Vorzugsaktie
registered – restricted (non- restricted) –	action nominative valeur sujette (non sujette) à restriction	Namensaktie Stammaktie mit bedingter (keine Bedingung unterliegemer) Dividendenzahlung
– dividend	dividende(m) de l'action	(Dividendein Form von) Gratisaktien
– issue unlisted –	émission(f) d'actions action non cotée	Aktienausgabe; Emission nicht notierte Aktie
shareholder	actionnaire(m), détenteur(m) d'actions	Aktionär(f); Antelseigner(m)
shareholding	actionnariat(m)	Aktienbesitz(m); Anteils–(m)
sheriff	shérif(m)	(oberster)(m) Verwaltungsbeamter
– (England) – (US)	préfet(m) (Angleterre) capitaine(m) de gendarmerie (US)	Vollstreckungsbeamter (England) Vollstreckungsbeamter; Polizeichef (US)
shipbroker	courtier(m) maritime	Schiffsmakler(m)
shipping agency	agence(f) maritime, agence(f) d'affrètement	Schiffsagentur(f)
shipping agent	agent maritime, commissionnaire(m) chargeur	Schiffsmakler(m); Seehafenspediteur(m)
shipowner	armateur(m)	Schiffseigner(m); Reeder(m)
shoplifting	vol(m) à l'étalage	Ladendiebstahl(m)
short delivery	livraison(f) à court terme	Minderlieferung(f); unvollständige Lieferung(f)
shut-down	immobilisation(f), fermeture(f)	Betriebseinstellung(f); Stillegung(f)
sight bill	effet(m) payable à vue, traite(f) à vue	Sichtwechsel(m)
signatory	signataire(m), souscripteur(m)	Unterzeichner(m)
signature personal – witnessed	signature(m), visa(m) signature personnelle devant témoin	Unterschrift(f) eigenhändige – bestätigt
simple contract	convention(f) verbale, contrat(m) tacite, contrat sous seing privé	formloser Vertrag(m)
single (marital status)	célibataire(m, f)	ledig (Familienstand)(m)

ENGLISH	FRENCH	GERMAN
Single European Act *(EC)*	**Acte***(m)* **Unique Européen** *(CE)*	**Einheitliche Europäische Akte** *(EG)*
site	**site***(m)*, terrain*(m)* (à bâtir), *par ext.* chantier	**Lage***(f)*; Standort*(m)*; Bauplatz*(m)*
slander	**diffamation***(f)* **verbale**	**üble Nachrede***(f)*; (mündliche Beleidigung)*(f)*
smuggling	**contrebande***(f)*	**Schmuggel***(m)*
social	social	sozial
– administration	les services sociaux	–verwaltung
– insurance	assurance*(f)* sociale	–versicherung
– security system	système*(m)* de sécurité sociale	–versicherungssystem
– welfare	bien-être*(m)* social	–fürsorge; Wohlfahrt
– worker	assistant(e)*(m, f)* social(e)	–fürsorger; Wohlfahrtsbeamter
society	**société***(f)*, association*(f)*	**Gesellschaft***(f)*
building –	établissement*(m)* de crédit foncier	Bausparkasse
cooperative –	coopérative*(f)*	Genossenschaft; Konsumverein
incorporated –	société constituée	rechtsfähige Gesellschaft; eingetragene –
sole	**seul,** unique	**allein;** einzig
– beneficiary	seul bénéficiaire	Alleinbegünstigter
solicitation	**sollicitation***(f)*	**Bitte***(f)*, Ersuchen
solicitor	**conseiller juridique,** avocat*(m)* non plaidant, avoué	**Anwalt***(m)*; Rechtsbeistand*(m)*
solitary confinement	**régime***(m)* **cellulaire,** isolement carcéral	**Einzelhaft***(f)*
solvency	**solvabilité***(f)*	**Zahlungsfähigkeit***(f)*; Solvenz*(f)*
– margin	marge*(f)* de solvabilité	Liquiditätsmarge
– ratio	taux*(m)* de solvabilité	Solvenzkennzahl
specialty	**contrat***(m)* **formel**	**Besonderheit***(f)*; Spezialität*(f)*
specific performance	**exécution***(f)* **d'un contrat ordonnée par le cour**	**vertragserfallung nach gerichtsurteil**
speculation	**spéculation***(f)*	**Spekulation***(f)*; Vermutung*(f)*
sponsor	**caution***(f)*, garant*(m)*; caution personnelle d'un immigrant *(US)*; parrain*(m)*, commanditaire*(m)*, 'sponsor'	**Sponsor***(m)*; Geldgeber*(m)*
spot	**disponible;** lieu*(m)* précis, point; message*(m)* publicitaire	**Spot***(m)*
– market	march*(m)*é au comptant	–markt
– rate	cours*(f)* du disponible	–kurs; Kassakurs
– transaction	opération*(f)* au comptant	–geschäft; Kassageschäft
spy	**espion***(m)*	**Spion***(m)*
squander (to)	**gaspiller**	**verschwenden;** vergeuden
stamp duty	**droit***(m)* **de timbre**	**Gebührenstempel***(m)*; –marke
state (to)	**déclarer,** énoncer, fixer	**erklären;** aussagen

ENGLISH	FRENCH	GERMAN
statement	**déclaration**(*f*), exposé(*m*), rapport(*m*), relevé(*m*)	**Bericht**(*m*); Aufstellung(*f*); Auszug(*f*)
closing –	plaidoierie(*f*) finale	Schlußbericht; –plädoyer
financial –	compte(*m*) de recettes	Finanzbericht; Rechnungsabschluß
income –	déclaration de revenus	Erfolgsrechnung; Ertragsbilanz
opening –	plaidoierie inaugurale	Eröffnungsplädoyer
– of account	relevé de compte	Kontoauszug; Abrechnung
– of claim	demande(*m*) introductive d'instance; conclusion(*f*) en matière de dommages-intérêts	Klagebegründung
– of defence	conclusions de la défense	Klagebeantwortung
sworn –	déposition(*f*) sous serment	eidliche (Zeugen)Erklärung
status	**statut**(*m*), capacité(*f*) juridique	**Status**(*m*)
legal –	état(*m*) statut légal, union(*f*)	Personenstand; Rechtsposition(*f*)
marital –	état(*m*) matrimonial, état de mariage	Familienstand
statute	**acte**(*m*) **législatif**, loi(*f*) écrite (*opp.* 'common law')	**Gesetz**(*n*); Statut(en)(*n*); Satzung(*f*)
statutory	**prévu**(*f*) **par la loi**, légal, statutaire, réglementaire	**gesetzlich**
stay (to)	**surseoir**, suspendre	**aufhalten**; einstellen; aussetzen
– execution	surseoir à l'exécution	(Zwangs)Vollstreckung einstellen, aufschieben
– proceedings	suspendre l'audience	Verfahren aussetzen
steal (to)	**voler**, dérober	**stehlen**
stirpes	**souches**(*f*), familles(*f*), lignées(*f*)	**Stämmen**; (Parentelen)
per –	par souches	(Erbfolge) nach Stämmen
stock exchange	**Bourse**(*f*)	**Börse**
stockholder	**porteur**(*m*) **de titres**, actionnaire(*m*)	**Aktieninhaber**(*m*); Anteilseigner(*m*)
stockbroker	**agent**(*m*) **de change**, courtier(*m*) en valeurs mobilières	**Börsenmakler**(*m*)
strangle (to)	**étrangler**	**erwürgen**; strangulieren
strangulation	**strangulation**(*f*)	**Erwürgung**(*f*)
strength	**force**(*f*), vigueur(*f*), résistance(*f*)	**Kraft**(*f*); Macht(*f*)
on the – of	en vertu de, au regard de	aufgrund von; unter Berufung auf
– of law	force(*f*) de la loi	Gesetzeskraft
strict liability	**responsabilité**(*f*) **stricte**	**strenge (verschuldensunabhängige) Haftung**(*f*) Gefährdungshaftung
subcontractor	**sous-entrepreneur**(*m*), sous-traitant	**Subunternehmer**(*m*); Nach–; Unterlieferant(*m*)

ENGLISH	FRENCH	GERMAN
subject	**sujet**(*m*) **(à)**, soumis (à), sous réserve (de), redevable (de)	**abhängig von**; vorbehaltlich
– to current law – to the provisions of	soumis au droit coutumier asujetti aux stipulations	nach derzeit gültigem Recht vorbehaltlich der Bestimmungen von
subject (to) – s.o. to maltreatment	**soumettre**, asujettir faire subir de mauvais traitements à qqu'un	**unterwerfen**; aussetzen Mißhandlung aussetzen
subjective	**subjectif**	**subjektiv**; unsachlich
sublease	**sous-location**(*f*)	**Untervermietung**(*f*); –pacht(*f*)
submit (to) – an application for approval – that the court declare	**plaider**, soumettre soumettre une demande d'agrément demander à la cour de dire que	**vorlegen**; beantragen Genehmigungsantrag einreichen dem Gericht zur Entscheidung stellen
subpoena (to) – a witness	**assigner à comparaître** assigner un témoin à comparaître	**unter Strafandrohung**(*f*) **laden** einen Zeugen -
subrogation	**subrogation**(*f*)	**Subrogation**(*f*); Rechtsübergang(*m*)
subscribe (to)	**souscrire**	**unterzeichnen**; – schreiben
subsection	**paragraphe**(*m*), sous-section(*f*)	**Unterabschnitt**(*m*)
subsidiary company	**filiale**(*f*)	**Tochtergesellschaft**(*f*)
substantial evidence	**preuve**(*f*) **suffisante**	**hinreichender Beweis**(*m*); Glaubhaftmachung(*f*)
substantiate (to)	**établir**, prouver le bien-fondé	**substantiieren**; begründen
substantive law	**droit**(*m*) **matériel**	**materielles Recht**(*n*)
subversive	**subversif**	**subversiv**; staatsgefährdend
succession intestate – right of –	**succession**(*f*), descendance(*f*), héritiers(*m*) succession ab intestat droits(*m*) de succession, droits successifs	**Erbfolge**(*f*) Intestat–; gesetzliche – –recht; Erbberechtigung
sue (to) – for damages – for malicious slander	**intenter un procès à,** poursuivre qqu'un en justice poursuivre qqu'un en dommages-intérêts poursuivre qqu'un en diffamation	**verklagen**; Klage einreichen auf Schadenersatz verklagen wegen übler Nachrede verklagen
suicide	**suicide**(*m*)	**Suizid**(*m*); Selbstmord(*m*)
suit	**action**(*f*) **civile**, poursuite(*f*), procès(*m*)	**Prozeß**(*m*); Klage(*f*)
summary – judgment – proceedings	**sommaire** jugement(*m*) sommaire procédure(*f*) sommaire	**summarisch**; kurz Urteil im abgekürzten (beschleunigten) Verfahren summarisches (abgekürztes) Verfahren

ENGLISH	FRENCH	GERMAN
summing-up	résumé(m) du juge à l'intention des jurés	Schlußplädoyer(m); Rechtsbelehrung(f) d. Geschworenen Zusammenfassung
summon (to) – s.o. before the court	convoquer, mander, citer citer qqu'un à comparaître devant le tribunal	laden; auffordern, zu erscheinen jdn vor Gericht laden
summons to serve a – on s.o.	citation(f) à comparaître, assignation(f) assigner qqu'un (à comparaître)	gerichtliche Vorladung(f) jdn eine Ladung zustellen
superior court	tribunal(m) supérieure	höhere Instanz(f); übergeordnetes Gericht
supersede (to)	annuler, remplacer, supplanter	außer Kraft(f) setzen; ersetzen
supervisory authority	autorités(f) de contrôle, de surveillance	Aufsichtsbehörde(f)
supplier	fournisseur(m)	Lieferant(m)
support (cf. alimony)	pension(f) alimentaire	Unterstützung(f); (s. Unterhalt)
suppression – of evidence	suppression(f) dissimulation(f), destruction(f) de preuves	Unterdrückung(f); Verheimlichung(f) Unterdrückung von Beweismaterial
supreme court	cour(f) suprême	Oberster(m) Gerichtshof(m); Oberstes Bundesgericht (US); höheres Berufungsgericht
surety	garantie(f), caution(f), garant(m); sûreté(f), certitude(f)	Bürge(m); Garant(m); Sicherheitsleistung(f)
surrender	reddition(f); abandon(m), abdication(f)	Abtretung(f); Aufgabe(f)
surrender (to) – a deceased's estate	se rendre; renoncer à renoncer à une succession	ausliefern; übergeben Besitzrecht am Nachlaß e-s Verstorbenen aufgeben
surveillance	surveillance(f)	Überwachung(f); Kontrolle(f)
surveyor	contrôleur(m), inspecteur(m), expert(m)	Gutachter(m); Sachverständiger(m); Havariekommissar(m)
surviving spouse	époux(m) survivant	überlebender Ehegatte
survivor	survivant	Überlebende(r)(m); Hinterbliebene(r)(m)
suspended sentence	condamnation(f) avec sursis	Strafaussetzung(f) zur Bewährung(f)
suspension – of payments – of sentence	suspension(f), surséance(f) arrêt(m) de paiement surséance de jugement	Einstellung(f); Aufhebung(f) Zahlungseinstellung Aussetzen der Strafe zur Bewährung
suspicion	suspicion, soupçon(m)	Verdacht(m); Argwohn(m)

ENGLISH	FRENCH	GERMAN
sustain (to) – an appeal – an objection	**soutenir,** supporter accepter un pourvoi accorder une objection	**stattgeben;** aufrechterhalten e-m Berufungsantrag stattgeben e-r Einwendung stattgeben
swindle	**escroquerie**(*f*)	**Schwindel**(*m*)**;** Betrug(*m*)
swindler	**escroc**(*m*)	**Schwindler**(*m*)**;** Betrüger(*m*)
sworn statement witness	**assermenté** déposition(*f*) sous serment témoin(*m*) sous serment	**be–, vereidigt** eidliche Erklärung vereidigter Zeuge

T

ENGLISH	FRENCH	GERMAN
tacit – consent	**tacite** consentement(m) tacite	**stillschweigend** –e Zustimmung
tag (to)	**étiqueter,** munir d'une fiche	**Anhängezettel**(m), – versehen
take (to) – evidence	**prendre** recueillir des témoignages	**nehmen** Beweis aufnehmen, erheben; Zeugenaussage hören
– over	prendre en charge, reprendre	übernehmen
– the oath of s.o.	recueillir le serment de qqu'un	jdn vereidigen
tamper (to)	**altérer,** falsifier	**(betrügerisch) Veränderungen**(f) **vornehmen an etw.;** beeinflussen
– with evidence	falsifier une preuve	Beweis fälschen
tangible – assets	**réel,** tangible actif corporel, biens tangibles	**materiell;** erheblich materielle Vermögenswerte; Sachvermögen
tariff protective – – legislation	**tarif**(m), barème(m) tarif protecteur législation(f) douanière	**(Zoll**(m)**)Tarif**(m); Satz(m) Schutzzoll Zollgesetzgebung
tax	**impôt**(m), taxe(f), contribution(f)	**Steuer**(m)
gift – income – indirect – inheritance – municipal –	impôt surles donations impôt sur le revenu impôt indirect impôt sur les successions impôt municipal, impôt local	Schenkungs– Einkommens– indirekte – Erschafts– Kommunal–
poll – – assessment	'poll tax', capitation(f) calcul(m) d'imposition, assiette(f) de l'impôt	Kopf–, Kommunal– –veranlagung
– authority – evasion – fraud – law – return value added – (VAT) withholding –	le fisc fraude(f) fiscale fraude fiscale loi(f) fiscale déclaration(f) d'impôts taxe sur la valeur ajoutée (TVA) impôt retenu à la source	–behörde –hinterziehung; –vermeidung –betrug –gesetz; –recht –erklärung Mehrwert– (MwSt) Abzug– Quellen–

ENGLISH	FRENCH	GERMAN
taxation	imposition(f), charges(f) fiscales, fiscalité(f)	Besteuerung(f); Kostenfestsetzung(f)
double – agreement	convention(f) relative à la double imposition	Doppelbesteuerungsabkommen
technical reserve	réserve(f) technique	versicherungstechnische Rücklagen(f)
tenancy	location(f), usufruit(m), droits(m) du tenant	Mietverhältnis(n); Pacht–(f)
tenant	locataire(m), tenancier(m), usufruitier(m)	Mieter(m); Pächter(m)
tender	offre(f), soumission(f)	(Leistungs-/Zahlungs-/ Lieferungs-/Submissions-) Angebot(n) Andienung
tentative	expérimental, provisoire	versuchsweise
tenure	période(f) de jouissance, période d'occupation d'un emploi	(Land)Besitzrecht(n); Amtsinnehabung(f)
term	limite(f), période(f), durée(f), terme(m), fin(f)	Zeitdauer(m); Fachausdruck(m)
– of a lease	durée d'un bail	Miet-, Pachtzeit
– of notice	délai(m) de congé	Kündigungsfrist
– of office	durée des fonctions	Amtszeit
terminable	réalisable, résoluble, résiliable	kündbar; befristet
terms	clauses(f), conditions(f); prix(m)	Bedingungen
– of payment	conditions de paiement	Zahlungs–
– of sale	conditions de vente	Verkaufs–
– of tender	conditions(f) d'offre	Ausschreibungs–, Submissions–
termination	résiliation(f), extinction(f), cessation(f), expiration(f)	Beendigung(f)
notice of –	congé(m)	– des Arbeitsverhältnisses durch Kündigung
– of a contract	résiliation, expiration d'un contrat	Vertrags–
territory	territoire(m)	(Staats-, Hoheits-)Gebiet(n); Territorium(f)
member State – (EEC)	territoire d'un état membre (de la CEE)	Mietgliedsstaat-Gebiet (EG)
testacy	le fait de mourir en laissant un testament	Testierfähigkeit(f)
testament	testament(m)	Testament(n)
last will and –	dernières volontés et testament	–; letzwillige Verfügung
testator, testatrix	testateur(m), testatrice(f)	Erblasser(in)(m, f); Testator(m)
testimony	déposition(f) d'un témoin, attestation(f), témoignage(m)	Zeugenaussage(f)
theft	vol(m)	Diebstahl(m)

ENGLISH	FRENCH	GERMAN

third party
  third-party action
  third-party
  insurance
  third-party liability
	tiers(*m*), tierce personne(*m*)
	mise(*f*) en cause
	assurance(*f*) de
	responsabilité civile
	responsabilité(*f*) civile
		Dritte(r)(*m, f*)
		Streitverkündung
		Haftpflichtversicherung;
		Fremdversicherung
		Haftpflicht

threat	**menace**(*f*)	**Drohung**(*f*)
threaten (to)	**menacer**, proférer des menaces	**drohen**
time-limit	**délai**(*m*), limite(*f*) de temps	**Frist**(*f*); Zeitbeschränkung(*f*)

title
 	
  assignment of –
 	
  exclusive –
  – -holder
	titre(*m*) de propriété; titre
	nobiliaire; intitulé(*m*) (d'une
	action)
	  transfert de droit
	
	  de propriété exclusive
	  détenteur(*m*) d'un titre
	  (de propriété)
		Eigentum(srecht)(*n*); Titel(*m*)
		
		  Rechtsübertragung;
		  Forderungsabtretung
		  ausschließliches Besitzrecht
		  Titelinhaber

tontine	**tontine**(*f*)	**Tontine**(*f*); lotterieähnliche Rentenversicherung(*f*) auf den Erlebensfall

tort
 	
  law of –
	tort(*m*)
	
	  droit(*m*) de la
	  responsabilité
		unerlaubte Handlung(*f*);
		zivilrechtliches Delikt(*n*)
		  Recht der unerlaubten
		  Handlungen; Deliktsrecht

torture	**torture**(*f*)	**Folterung**(*f*)
trace	**filière**(*f*); vestige(*m*), trace(*f*)	**Spur**(*f*); Anzeichen(*n*)

trade mark
 	
  registered –
	marque(*f*) **(de fabrique et
	de commerce)**
	  marque déposée
		Warenzeichen(*n*);
		Handelsmarke(*f*)
		  eingetragenes Warenzeichen

trade name	**nom**(*m*) **commercial**, raison(*f*) sociale, enseigne(*f*)	**Handelsname**(*m*) Firmenname(*m*);
trade union	**syndicat**(*m*)	**Gewerkschaft**(*f*)
trading company	**société**(*f*) **commerciale**	**Handelsgesellschaft**(*f*)

traffic
 	
  – accident
 	
  – offence
 	
  – offender
 	
  – violation
	trafic(*m*), circulation(*f*),
	transport(*m*)
	  accident(*m*) de la
	  circulation
	  infraction(*f*) au code de la
	  route
	  contrevenant(*m*) au code
	  de la route
	  infraction au code de la
	  route
		Verkehr(*m*)
		
		  –sunfall
		
		  –sdelikt
		
		  –ssünder
		
		  Verletzung der –svorschriften

traitor	**traître**	**Verräter**(*m*)
tranche	**tranche**(*f*)	**Tranche**(*f*)
transaction	**transaction**(*f*), compromis(*m*), arrangement(*m*); gestion(*f*), conduite d'une affaire	**Geschäft(svorgang)**(*n*); Durchführung(*f*)

ENGLISH	FRENCH	GERMAN
transcript	copie(f) conforme d'un acte judiciaire, transcription(f)	Abschrift(f); Ausfertigung(f) des Gerichtsprotokolls
transfer	transfert(m), mutation(f), transmission(f), virement(m)	Übertragung(f)
– of property	transmission de propriété	Vermögens–; Eigentums–
– of shares	cession(f) d'actions	Aktien–
– of title	transmission de titre constitutif propriété	Forderungs–; Eigentums–
transferable securities	valeurs(f) mobilières librement cessibles	übertragbare Wertpapiere(f)
transferee	cessionnaire(m)	(Übertragungs-)(f)Empfänger(m); Zessionar(m)
transferor	cédant(m), endosseur(m)	Übertragender(m); Zedent(m)
transgression	transgression(f), infraction(f), violation(f)	Übertretung(f); Verletzung(f)
– of a law	violation d'une loi	Gesetzesübertretung
transgressor	transgresseur(m)	Übertreter(m); Missetäter(m)
transit	transit(m), passage(m), trajet(m), route(f)	Transit(m); Transport(m)
damage in –	dommages(m) causés au cours du transport	Schaden auf dem Transport
– goods	marchandises(f) en transit	Transitgüter, –waren
– port	port(m) de transit	Transithafen
transitory	transitoire, passager	vorübergehend
travel insurance	assurance(f) voyage	Reiseversicherung(f)
traverse (CL)	passage(m) au travers	Leugnen; Bestreiten (des klägerischen Vorbringens)
treason	trahison(f)	Landesverrat(m); Hochverrat(m)
treasury bond	bon du trésor (à long terme)	Staatsschuldverschreibung (US), firmeneigene –; Schatzanweisung (UK)
treaty	traité(m), pacte(m), convention(f)	(Staats)Vertrag(m)
Treaty of Rome (EEC)	Traité(m) de Rome (CEE)	(Die Römischen) Verträge (EG)
trespasser	intrus (dans une propriété privée)	Besitzstörer; Rechtsverletzer
trespassing	violation(f) de propriété	widerrechtliches Betreten
trial	procès(m); essai(m)	Gerichtsverhandlung(f); Verfahren(n)
civil –	action(f) civile	Zivilverfahren
summary –	jugement(m) sommaire	Hauptverhandlung ohne Geschworene
– by jury	procés conduit devant un jury première instance	Schwurgerichtsverfahren
– court	cour(f) jugeant en	Prozeßgericht; Instanz
– judge	juge(m) du fond	Tatrichter; Richter der ersten Instanz

ENGLISH	FRENCH	GERMAN
tribunal	**tribunal**(*m*), cour(*f*) de justice	**Gericht(shof)**(*m*); Tribunal(*n*)
– for tax and other financial matters (Germany)	tribunal traitant les affaires financiéres (Allemagne)	Finanzgericht
trust	**fidéicommis**(*m*), tutelle(*f*); garde(*m*), dépôt(*m*); 'trust'(*m*), concentration(*f*) verticale d'entreprises; confiance(*f*)	**Treuhandverhältnis**(*n*); – vermögen(*n*)
– beneficiary	bénéficiaire(*m*) de la tutelle	Treuhandsbegünstigter
– deed	acte(*m*) fiduciaire	Treuhandvertrag;
– property	biens(*m*) placés sous tutelle	Treuhandvermögen
trustee in bankruptcy	**syndic**(*m*) **de faillite**	**Konkursverwalter**(*m*)
trust fund	**fond**(*m*) **de tutelle**	**Treuhandfonds**(*m*)
try (to)	**juger,** mettre en jugement; essayer	**(gerichtlich) verhandeln,** untersuchen
– a case	juger une affaire (au tribunal)	Prozeß führen; über eine Sache verhandeln

U

ENGLISH	FRENCH	GERMAN
unabated	d'égale intensité	unvermindert
unadulterated	pur, non édulcoré	unverfälscht; echt
unappropriated profits	bénéfices(m) non distribués	unverteilter Reingewinn(m); Bilanzgewinn(m)
unarmed	non armé, sans armes	unbewaffnet
unascertainable	impossible à vérifier	nicht zu ermitteln; nicht feststellbar
unassailable	inattaquable	unangreifbar; nicht zu widerlegen
unauthorised	non autorisé, illégal, illicite	nicht ermächtigt; unbefugt
unattested	non attesté, non certifié	unbeglaubigt; unbestätigt
unavailable	indisponible	nicht verfügbar
unavoidable	inévitable, incontournable	unvermeidbar
unbiased	objectif, sans parti-pris	unvoreingenommen; unparteiisch
uncertainty	passage(m) obscur dans la rédaction d'un jugement, incertitude(f)	Unbestimmtheit(f); Unsicherheit(f)
unchallenged	incontesté, sans rival	unbestritten; unangefochten
uncommitted	non engagé, libre, neutraliste	nicht gebunden, blockfrei
unconditional	inconditionnel, sans condition	bedingungslos; uneingeschränkt
unconfirmed	non confirmé; léonin	unbestätigt
unconscionability	absence de scrupules	sittenwidrig; gegen Treu und Glauben verstoßend
unconstitutional	anticonstitutionnel	verfassungswidrig
uncontested	incontesté; remporté sans opposition (scrutin, élection)	unbestritten; unbestreitbar
uncontrovertible	non convertible	unwiderlegbar
uncover (to)	découvrir	aufdecken; enthüllen
undecipherable	indéchiffrable, incompréhensible	unleserlich; nicht zu entziffern
undeniable	indéniable	unbestreitbar; unleugbar

ENGLISH	FRENCH	GERMAN
under par	sous pair	unter pari; unter dem Nennwert
underbid	offre(f) de conditions plus avantageuses	Minderangebot(n); Unter–
underlying – motives	sous-jacent, fondamental raisons(f) cachées	zugrundeliegend –e Ursachen, –e Beweggründe
underrate (to)	sous-estimer	unterbewerten; underschätzen
undersigned (the)	le soussigné	Unterzeichnete(r)(m)
understatement	'understatement', litote(f)	Untertreibung(f); Unterbewertung(f)

undertaking	soumission(f);
	engagement(m), promesse(f);
	entreprise(f) commerciale
		Verpflichtung(serklärung)(f);
		Unternehmen(n)

underwriter	assureur(m), souscripteur(m)	Versicherer(m); Garant(m)
underwriting syndicate	syndicat(m) de garantie, groupe(m) de souscription	Versicherungskonsortium(f); Emissions–(f)
undistributed profits (cf. unappropriated)	bénéfices(m) non distribués	unverteilter Gewinn(m); nicht ausgeschütteter –; s. unverteilter Reingewinn
undivided property	propriété(f) indivise, bien(m) indivis	ungeteiltes Vermögen(n)
undue – allegation	illégitime, indu allégation(f) sans fondement	ungebührlich; ungehörig –e Behauptung
unduly	illégalement, à tort	unangemessen; übermäßig
unemployment	chômage(m)	Arbeitslosigkeit(f)
unencumbered	libre d'hypothèques	unbelastet; hypothekenfrei
unenforceable	innapplicable	nicht (ein-)klagbar; nicht vollstreckbar
unfair – competition – market practices	injuste, déloyal, inéquitable concurrence(f) déloyale pratiques(f) commerciales déloyales	unredlich; ungerecht unlauterer Wettbewerb unlautere Marktmethoden
unfounded – accusation	non fondé, sans fondement(m) accusation(f) sans fondement	unbegründet; grundlos –e Beschuldigung
unharmed	sain et sauf, indemne	unversehrt; unbeschädigt
unimpeachable	irréprochable	zuverlässig; nicht widerlegbar
unintentional	non intentionnel, involontaire	unbeabsichtigt; ungewollt
unit trust	SICAV	offener Investmentfonds
unjust – enrichment	injuste enrichissement(m) sans cause	ungerecht; unbillig ungerechtfertigte Bereicherung
unjustified	injustifié, non motivé	ungerechtfertigt
unlawful	contraire à la loi, séditieux, illégal, illicite	ungesetzlich; rechtswidrig

ENGLISH	FRENCH	GERMAN
unlimited company	société(f) à responsabilité non limitée	(Kapital-)Gesellschaft(f) mit unbeschränkter Haftung(f)
unliquidated damages	dommages-intérêts(m) non liquidés	(der Höhe nach) unbestimmter Schadensersatz(m); unbezifferte Schadensforderung
unlisted securities	valeurs(f) non cotées	nicht notierte Wertpapiere(f)
unmatured	non échu	noch nicht fällig
unobjectionable	acceptable, à qui on ne peut rien reprocher	einwandfrei
unprecedented	sans précédent	ohne Präzedenzfall(m); beispiellos
unprotected	sans protection(f), sans emballage(m)	ungeschützt; ungedeckt
unpunished	impuni	unbestraft; ungeahndet
unqualified	non qualifié; sans réserves(f)	unzuständig; uneingeschränkt
unsafe	hasardeux, risqué, dangereux	gefährlich; nicht verkehrssicher
unscrupulous	sans scrupules(m)	skrupellos
unsecured	à découvert(m), sans garantie, sur notoriété(f)	ungesichert; ungedeckt
unverified	non vérifié	nicht bestätigt
uphold (to)	soutenir	aufrecht erhalten; bestätigen
urban	urbain	städtisch
urgent	urgent	dringend; eilig
usher	huissier	Gerichtsdiener(m); Justizwachtmeister(m)
usufruct	usufruit(m)	Nutzungsrecht(n); Nießbrauch(m)
usurer	usurier	Wucherer(m)
usury	usure(f)	Wucher(zinsen)(m)
utilities	services(m) publics; commodités(f)	Versorgungsunternehmen(n); –werte(m)

V

ENGLISH	FRENCH	GERMAN
vacancy	vacance(f), emploi(m) vacant, poste(f) à pourvoir	freie, unbesetzte Stelle
vacant	vacant, libre	frei, unbesetzt
vacate (to)	annuler, résilier, évacuer, démissionner	räumen; ausziehen; aufgeben
vagrancy	vagabondage(m)	Landstreicherei
vagrant	vagabond(m), clochard(m)	Landstreicher
valid	valide, régulier, valable, recevable	(rechts)gültig; in Kraft(f); stichhaltig
validate (to)	valider	für (rechts)gültig erklären; bestätigen
validity	validité(f)	(Rechts)Gültigkeit(f); Laufzeit(f)
valuation	prisée(f) et estimation, expertise(f), évaluation, inventaire(m)	Bewertung(f); Schätzwert(m)
value book – market – surrender –	valeur(f) valeur comptable valeur marchande valeur de rachat	Wert(m); Valuta(f) Buchwert; buchmäßiger Wert Marktwert Rückkaufswert
vandalism	vandalisme(m)	Vandalismus(m); böswillige Sachbeschädigung(f)
vandalise	vandaliser	böswillig zerstören
VAT (value added tax)	TVA (taxe sur la valeur ajoutée)	MwSt (Mehrwertsteuer)(m)
vendor	vendeur(m) de biens immobiliers, vendeur, apporteur	Verkäufer(m)
vengeance	vengeance(f)	Rache(f)
venture joint –	entreprise(f), spéculation(f), risque(m) association(f), entreprise en participation	Wagnis(n); Unternehmen(n); Risiko(n) Joint Venture; Gemeinschaftsunternehmen
venue	juridiction(f), lieu(m) du jugement	Gerichtsstand(m); Zuständigkeit(f)

ENGLISH	FRENCH	GERMAN
verdict	**verdict**(*m*)	**(Urteils-)Spruch**(*m*); Entscheidung(*f*)
general –	verdict pour démandeur ou défendeur (*procédure civile*); verdict de culpabilité ou d'acquittement (*procédure criminelle*)	Entscheidung (für Kläger od. Beklagten) (Zivilprozeß); Schuld– od. Freispruch (Strafprozeß)
special –	détermination(*f*) des faits de procédure	Feststellung des Tatbestandes
– of guilty	verdict de culpabilité	Schuldspruch; Erkennen auf 'schuldig'
– of not guilty	verdict d'acquittement	Freispruch; Erkennen auf 'nicht schuldig'
verifiable	**vérifiable**, contrôlable	**verifizierbar**; nachprüfbar
verify (to)	**vérifier**, contrôler	**verifizieren**; beglaubigen, nachprüfen
vested interest	**droit**(*m*), intérêt(*m*) acquis	**sicher begründetes Anrecht**(*n*); berechtigte Interesse
vice squad	**brigade**(*f*) **mondaine**, brigade des moeurs	**Sittenpolizei**(*f*)
victim	**victime**(*f*)	**Opfer**(*m*); Geschädigter(*m*); Verletzter(*m*)
vindicate (to)	**justifier**, soutenir	**rechtfertigen**; verteidigen; beanspruchen
vindictive	**punitif**, vindicatif	**nachtragend**; strafend
violate (to)	**enfreindre**, violer	**verletzen**; verstoßen; übertreten
violation	**infraction**(*f*), violation(*f*)	**Verletzung**(*f*); Verstoß(*m*); Übertretung(*f*)
in – of the law	en contravention de la loi	ein Gesetz übertreten
– of privacy	atteinte(*f*) à la vie privée	Verletzung der Privatsphäre; – der Intimspäre
violence	**violence**(*f*), voies(*f*) de fait	**Gewalt**(*m*)**(-tätigkeit)**(*f*)
virtue	**qualité**(*f*), vertu	**Tugend**(*f*); Wert(*m*)
by – of	en vertu de	kraft; aufgrund von
visit and search	**perquisition**(*f*)	**Durchsuchung**(*f*)
– right	droit(*m*) d'effectuer une perquisition	Durchsuchungsrecht
visiting right	**droit**(*m*) **de visite**	**Besuchsrecht**(*n*); Verkehrsrecht(*n*) (zu e-m Kinde)
vital statistics	**statistiques**(*m*) **démographiques**	**Personenstandsstatistik**(*f*); Bevölkerungsstatistik
void	**nul et de nul effet**, vide	**nichtig**; unwirksam
null and –	nul et non avenu	(null und) nichtig; ungültig
volition	**volonté (délibérée)**	**Wille**(*m*); -nsäußerung(*f*)

ENGLISH	FRENCH	GERMAN
voluntary	**volontaire**	**freiwillig;** unentgeltlich
– composition	concordat préventif de la faillite	freiwilliger Vergleich
– confession	aveu(*m*) spontané	freiwilliges Geständnis
voting power	**droit**(*m*) **de vote**	**Stimmrecht**(*n*)
voting rights (of shareholders)	**droits de vote (des actionnaires)**	**Stimmrecht**(*n*) **(der Aktieninhaber)**(*m*)
vouch (to) for	**répondre de,** garantir	**einstehen für;** sich verbürgen für

W

ENGLISH	FRENCH	GERMAN
waive (to)	**renoncer à,** abandonner un droit; se déroger	**aufgeben;** Verzicht(m) leisten
waiver	**renonciation**(f), désistement(m), abandon(m)	**Aufgabe**(f); (Verzicht-)Leistung(f)
express (or implied) –	renonciation tacite	ausdrücklicher (od. stillschweigender) Verzicht(m)
– of claim	désistement de revendication, d'instance, d'action	Anspruchsaufgabe
– of rights	renonciation à un (des) droit (s)	Rechtsverzicht
– of title	abandon d'un droit de propriété	Rechtsverzicht
wanton	**capricieux,** absurde, dévergondé	**rücksichtslos;** böswillig
– injury	blessure(f) accidentelle	mutwillige Verletzung
war risk insurance	**assurance**(f) **sur les risques de guerre**	**Kriegsrisikoversicherung**(f)
ward	**tutelle**(f); pupille(m, f); service(m), salle(f) d'hôpital; surveillance(f)	**Mündel**(n); Stadtbezirk(m)
warden	**gardien**(m)	**Vorsteher**(m); Aufsichtsbeamter(m)
warrant	**mandat**(m), pouvoir(m), certificat(m), bon(m) de souscription	**Ermächtigung**(f); Bescheinigung(f); Haftbefehl(m)
distress –	ordonnance de saisie-exécution	Arrestbefehl; Pfändungsbeschluf
search –	mandat de perquisition	Durchsuchungsbefehl
– of arrest	ordre d'arrestation	Haftbefehl
– of attachment	ordonnance de saisie	Beschlagnahmeverfügung
– of attorney	procuration(f), pouvoir	Prozeßvollmacht e-s Anwalts (zur Erklärung e-s Anerkenntnisses vor Geicht)
warranty	**clause**(f) **pénale du contrat,** garantie(f); autorisation(f), justification(f)	**Garantie**(f); Gewährleistung(f)
waste	**gaspillage**(m), déchets(m)	**Verschwendung**(f); Abfall(m); Wertminderung(f)

142

ENGLISH	FRENCH	GERMAN
water damage insurance	assurance(f) sur les dégâts des eaux	Wasserschadenversicherung(f)
water pollution	pollution(f) des eaux	Wasserverunreinigung(f); Gewässerverschmutzung(f)
wedlock	mariage(m)	Ehe(stand)(m)
born in –	né dans le mariage, filiation(f) légitime	ehelich geboren
born out of –	né hors du mariage, filiation naturelle	nichtehelich geboren
welfare (social)	bien-être social, prévoyance(f) sociale, service(m) social	Fürsorge(f) (soziale)
– committee	comité(m) de bienfaisance	Wohlfahrtsausschuß
– officer	assistant(e)(m) social(e)	Sozialarbeiter(in)
wholesaler	grossiste	Großhändler(m)
wife	épouse(f), femme(f)	Ehefrau(f)
wilful	prémédité, volontaire	vorsätzlich; absichtlich
– murder	assassinat(m), homicide(m, f) volontaire	Mord; Totschlag
– waste	abus(m) de jouissance, dégâts commis intentionnellement	vorsätzliche Substanzschädigung; – Wertminderung
will (cf. testament)	testament(m)	letztwillige Verfügung; s. Testament(n)
joint (mutual) –	donation(f) au dernier survivant, testament mutuel	gemeinschaftliche(s) (wechselbezügliche(s)) –
last – and testament	acte de dernières volontés	Testament
probate of –	homologation(f) d'un testament	Testamentsbestätigung
to prove a –	établir un testament	Testament als gültig bestätigen
winding up	dissolution(f), liquidation(f)	Abwicklung(f)
– of a company	liquidation d'une société	– e-r Gesellschaft
withdraw (to)	retirer, se retirer	zurückziehen; widerrufen; zurücktreten
withdrawal	retrait(m)	Rücknahme(f); Abhebung(f); Rücktritt(m)
– of money	retrait d'argent	Geldabhebung
withholding	détention(f), dissimulation(f), refus(m)	Zurückbehaltung(f); Ein-
– of evidence	dissimulation de preuve	Verschweigen von Beweisen
– tax	impôt(m) retenu à la source	Abzugssteuer; Quellensteuer
witness	témoin(m)	Zeuge(m)
– for the defence	témoin à décharge	Entlastungs–; vom Beklagten/ Angeklagten benannter –
– for the prosecution	témoin à charge	Belastungs–; – der Anklage
– to a will	témoin instrumentaire du testament	Testaments–
work permit	permis(m) de travail	Arbeitsgenehmigung(f); – erlaubnis(n)

ENGLISH	FRENCH	GERMAN
working capital	capital(m) de roulement	Betriebskapital(n); Nettoumlaufvermögen(n)
work in progress	travail(m) (travaux) en cours	unfertige Erzeugnisse(n); in Gang befindliche Arbeit(f)
worth	valeur(f)	Wert(m)
writ	exploit(m), ordonnance(f), acte(m) judiciaire	gerichtliche Anweisung(f)/ Verfügung(f); Klageschrift(f); Schriftstück
– of attachment	ordonnance de saisie-arrêt	Beschlagnahme Pfändungsbefehl
– of enforcement	ordonnance d'exécution	Zwangsvollstreckung
– of execution	exploit de saisie-exécution	Vollstreckungsbefehl
– of habeas corpus	injonction(f) de déférer un accusé devant le tribunal	Vorführungsbefehl
– of sequestration	séquestre judiciaire	Beschlagnahmeverfügung; gerichtliche Einsetzung e-s Zwangsverwalters
– of summons	assignation(f), citation (à comparaître)	Prozeßladung mit Klageschrift
write (to) off	amortir, défalquer, annuler	abschreiben; abbuchen
write (to) up	rédiger, mettre à jour; fausser un bilan, gonfler les comptes	auf den neuesten Stand(m) bringen; höher bewerten; zuschreiben
writing	écrit(m), écriture(f), souscription(f)	Schreiben; Schriftform(f)
wrong	infraction(f) à la loi, tort(m) fait à qqu'un	Unrecht(n); Rechtsverletzung(f); Delikt(n)
wrongdoer	auteur(m) d'un méfait, délinquant(m)	Übeltäter(m); Rechtsverletzer(m)
wrongful act	acte(m) illégal	unrechtmäßige Handlung(f)

X

ENGLISH	FRENCH	GERMAN
X-ray examination	**examen**(*m*) **radioscopique**	**Roentgenuntersuchung**(*f*)

Y

ENGLISH	FRENCH	GERMAN
yard	**chantier**(*m*); cour(*f*); unité de mesure: 1 yard = 3 pieds = 91,44 cm	**Yard**(*n*), Elle(*f*); Hof(*m*); Scotland Yard (Langenmaß = 91,44 cm)
year calendar – financial – fiscal – – of birth	**année**(*f*), exercice(*m*) année civile année budgétaire, exercice financier année fiscale année de naissance	**Jahr**(*n*) Kalender– Geschäfts–; Rechnungs– Steuer– (*UK*); Haushalts–, Rechnungs– Geburts–
yield	**rapport**(*m*), rendement(*m*), production(*f*)	**Ertrag**(*m*); Rendite(*f*); Effektivverzinsung(*f*)

Z

ENGLISH	FRENCH	GERMAN
zero	**zéro**(*m*)	**null**
– -base budgeting (ZBB)	'zero-base budgeting' (ZBB)	Budgetierung auf –basis
– coupon	coupon(*m*) zéro (sans intérêt)	–kupon
– value	valeur(*m*) nulle	–wert
zipcode *(US)*	**code**(*m*) **postal** *(US)*	**Postleitzahl**(*f*) *(US)*
zone	**zone**(*m*), district(*m*), quartier(*m*)	**Zone**(*f*); Gebiet(*n*)
border –	zone frontière	Grenzgebiet
danger –	zone dangereuse	Gefahrenzone
free –	zone franche, zone libre	Frei(hafen)zone
military –	zone militaire	Militärgebiet
– tariff	tarif(*m*) de zone	Zonentarif

French/German/English

A

FRENCH	GERMAN	ENGLISH
à capital limité, fixe société à capital fixe	**geschlossen** –e (Investment-)gesellschaft	**closed-end** – (investment) company
à découvert(*m*)**,** sans garantie, sur notoriété(*f*)	**ungesichert;** ungedeckt	**unsecured**
à huis clos	**unter Ausschluß**(*m*) **der Öffentlichkeit**(*f*)	**in camera**
à long terme crédit(*m*) à long terme créance(*f*) à long terme	**langfristig** –er Kredit –e Verbindlichkeit	**long-term** – credit – debt
à quai, dédouané	**ab Kai**(*m*)	**ex quay**
abandon(*m*)	**Abandon**(*m*)**;** Aufgabe(*f*); Verzicht(leistung)(*f*); Verlassen(*n*); Aussetzung(*f*)	**abandonment**
abandonner, renoncer	**abandonnieren;** zurückziehen; zurücknehmen; fallenlassen	**abandon (to)**
abandonner, renoncer à, se démettre de, répudier	**verzichten;** aufgeben	**renounce (to)**
abolir, annuler	**aufheben;** herabsetzen; aussetzen, einstellen	**abate (to)**
abolir, supprimer	**abschaffen,** beseitigen; außer Kraft(*f*) setzen	**abolish (to)**
abrogation(*f*)	**Abschaffung**(*f*)**;** Aufhebung(*f*), Außerkraftsetzung(*f*)	**abrogation**
abrogation(*f*)**,** révocation(*f*)	**Aufhebung**(*f*)**;** Außerkraftsetzung(*f*)	**repeal**
absence de scrupules	**sittenwidrig;** gegen Treu und Glauben verstoßend	**unconscionability**
absolu, irrévocable	**unbeschränkt;** endgültig; rechtskräftig	**absolute**
pouvoir absolu preuve(*f*) irréfutable	unbeschränkte Macht, – Gewalt einwandfreier Beweis	– power – proof
abus(*m*)**,** excès(*m*); viol(*m*)	**Mißbrauch**(*m*)**;** Beschimpfung(*f*); Mißhandlung(*f*)	**abuse**
abus(*m*)**,** mauvais usage(*m*)	**Mißbrauch**(*m*)	**misuse**

FRENCH	GERMAN	ENGLISH
abus(*m*) **de confiance**	**widerrechtliche Aneignung**(*f*)**/ Verwendung**(*f*); Veruntreuung(*f*)	**misappropriation**
accéder à, entrer en possession	**beistimmen;** beitreten; antreten	**accede (to)**
accélération(*f*), réduction(*f*) (d'un délai), avancement(*m*) (d'une échéance); prise de possession anticipée	**Beschleunigung**(*f*); vorzeitige Fälligstellung(*f*) (Wechsel)	**acceleration**
acceptable, à qui on ne peut rien reprocher	**einwandfrei**	**unobjectionable**
acceptation(*f*), consentement(*m*), agrément(*m*)	**Annahme**(*f*); Anerkennung(*f*); Akzept(*n*); Zusage(*f*)	**acceptance**
acquiescement à un jugement	Annahme e-s Urteils	– of a judgment
accepter, approuver, agréer	**annehmen;** anerkennen; akzeptieren; antreten (Amt)	**accept (to)**
accès, abord	**Zugang**(*m*); Zutritt(*m*); Zugriff (*EDV*)(*m*)	**access**
accidentel, éventuel, accessoire	**Neben-**	**incidental**
poursuites sur incident	–klage(*f*)	– action
faux frais	–ausgaben; –kosten	– expenses, incidentals
accomplissement(*m*) **incorrect d'un acte licite**	**Delikt**(*n*); unerlaubte Ausführung(*f*) e-r an sich rechtmäßigen Handlung	**misfeasance**
accomplissement(*m*), résultats(*m*); prestation(*f*)	**Leistung**(*f*); Erfüllung(*f*)	**performance**
éxécution(*f*) partielle d'une convention	Teilerfüllung eines Abkommens	part – of an agreement
accompte (hypothèque, vente à crédit)	**Anzahlung**(*f*)	**down-payment**
accord(*m*), consentement(*m*)	**Übereinkommen,** Einverständnis(*n*); Vergleich(*m*); Abmachung(*f*)	**accord**
novation(*f*) éxécutée	vergleichsweise Erfüllung; außergerichtlicher Vergleich	– and satisfaction
accord(*m*), convention(*f*), contrat(*m*), traité(*m*), acte(*m*), règlement(*m*), acte(*m*)	**Übereinstimmung,** Einvernehmen(*n*); Einverständnis(*n*); Abmachung(*f*); Abkommen, Vertrag(*m*); Tarifvertrag(*m*)	**agreement**
contrat de mariage convention(*f*) liant les parties	vorehelicher Vertrag verbindliches Abkommen	antenuptial – binding –
accord de gré à gré	gegenseitige Vereinbarung; gegenseitiges Einvernehmen	mutual –
accord sur les salaires, convention salariale	Lohnabkommen; Lohnvereinbarung	wage –
accord(*m*), réconciliation(*f*)	**Versöhnung**(*f*); (Konten)Abstimmung(*f*)	**reconciliation**

FRENCH	GERMAN	ENGLISH
Accord(m) **Général sur les Tarifs Douaniers et le Commerce**	**GATT** (Allgemeines Zoll- und Handelsabkommen)	**GATT** (General Agreement on Tariffs and Trade)
accorder, octroyer, consentir	**bewilligen;** übertragen; zugestehen	**grant** (to)
accumuler, thésauriser	**ansammeln;** horten	**hoard** (to)
accusateur(m), plaignant	**Ankläger**(m); Vertreter(m) der Anklage(f)	**prosecutor**
ministère(m) public	Staatsanwalt	public –
accusation(f), incrimination(f)	**Anschuldigung**(f), Beschuldigung(f)	**accusation**
accuser, incriminer	**anklagen, anschuldigen,** beschuldigen	**accuse** (to)
accuser, inculper	**anklagen,** unter Anklage stellen	**charge** (to)
accuser qqu'un	**jd belasten;** beschuldigen	**incriminate** (to) s.o.
achalandage(m), fonds(m) de commerce; profit(m) net	**(ideeller) Firmenwert**(m)	**goodwill**
achat(m)	**Kauf**(m); Erwerb(m)	**purchase**
achat(m) **à tempérament**	**Ratenkauf**(m)	**instalment purchase**
acquiescement(m), assentiment(m), consentement(m)	**(stillschweigende) Einwilligung**(f); **Sichfügen**(n); Duldung(f)	**acquiescence**
acquiescer, consentir	**(stillschweigend) einwilligen;** sich fügen in; dulden	**acquiesce** (to)
acquittement(m), décharge(f), quitus(m)	**Freispruch**(m)	**acquittal**
acquitter	**quittieren;** Empfang(m) bescheinigen	**receipt** (to)
acquitter, absoudre	**freisprechen,** lossprechen, entbinden	**absolve** (to)
acquitter, décharger	**freisprechen (von e-r Anklage);** abtragen (Schuld); entbinden von (Pflicht)	**acquit** (to)
acte(m), action(f), mesure(f), loi(m)	**Tat**(m), Handlung(f), Akt(m); Urkunde(f); Gesetz(n)	**act**
cas(m) de force majeure acte relevant du droit pénal, fait pénalement punissable	höhere Gewalt, Naturereignis Deliktshandlung, strafbare Handlung, Straftat	– of God criminal –
acte(m) **constitutif d'une société** (UK)	**Satzung**(f) (UK); Statut(n) (e-r Kapitalgesellschaft)(f), Gründungsvertrag(m)	**memorandum of association** (UK)

FRENCH	GERMAN	ENGLISH
acte(*m*) **d'accusation,** inculpation; chef(*m*) d'accusation; **réquisitoire**(*m*)	**Anklage**(*f*)**,** Beschuldigung(*f*); Belastung(*f*), Hypothek(*f*); Obhut(*f*), Sorge(*f*); Gebühr(*f*), Unkosten	**charge**
inculpation(*f*) de meurtre inculpation de vol inculpation de trahison	angeklagt wegen Mordes angeklagt wegen Diebstahls angeklagt wegen Landesverrats, Hochverrats	– of murder – of theft – of treason
acte(*m*) **d'accusation,** inculpation(*f*)	**formelle Anklageschrift**(*f*)	**indictment**
acte(*m*) **de décès,** extrait(*m*) mortuaire	**Totenschein**(*m*)**;** Sterbeurkunde(*f*)	**death certificate**
acte(*m*) **de procédure,** procès(*m*); délibérations(*f*); marche(*f*) à suivre	**Verfahren**(*n*)**;** Prozeß(*m*)	**proceedings**
procédure(*f*) d'arbitrage procès(*m*) instance(*f*) en divorce procédure en faillite procédure sommaire	Schieds(gerichts)verfahren Gerichtsverfahren Ehescheidungsverfahren Konkursverfahren Schnellverfahren; summarisches Verfahren	arbitration – court – divorce – – in bankruptcy summary –
acte(*m*) **de transfert d'un droit ou d'un titre par voie de reconciliation**(*f*)**, mais sans garantie de validité**	**Grundstücksauflassungsurkunde**(*f*)**;** Verzichtsurkunde(*f*)	**quitclaim deed**
acte(*m*) **dommageable,** désagrément	**Störung**(*f*)	**nuisance**
atteinte(*f*) aux droits privés, trouble(*m*) de jouissance atteinte aux droits du public	Besitz– od. Eigentums– (der Einzelnen) – der Allgemeinheit; öffentliches ärgernis	private – public –
acte(*m*) **illégal**	**unrechtmäßige Handlung**(*f*)	**wrongful act**
acte(*m*) **juridique,** document(*m*) officiel, élément(*m*) de preuve écrite	**Mittel**(*n*)**;** Urkunde(*f*)	**instrument**
acte(*m*) **législatif,** loi(*f*) écrite (*opp.* 'common law')	**Gesetz**(*n*)**;** Statut(en)(*n*); Satzung(*f*)	**statute**
acte(*m*) **manifeste**	**offenkundige Handlung**(*f*)	**overt act**
Acte(*m*) **Unique Européen** (*CE*)	**Einheitliche Europäische Akte** (*EG*)	**Single European Act** (*EC*)

FRENCH	GERMAN	ENGLISH
actif(*m*), avoir(*m*), biens(*m*), fonds(*m*), capital(*m*), masse(*f*) active	**Aktiva;** Vermögen(*n*)	**asset(s)**
actif et (ensemble de) dettes	Aktiva und Passiva	– and liabilities
actif immobilisé	Anlagevermögen; Vermögenswerte	capital –
actif réalisable, disponible, à court terme	Umlaufvermögen; sofort realisierbare Aktiven	current –
immobilisations(*f*)	feste Anlagen; Sachanlagen; Anlagevermögen	fixed –
disponibilités(*f*)	flüssiges Vermögen, flüssige Mittel	liquid –
actif incorporel	**immaterielle Vermögenswerte**(*m*)	**intangible assets**
action(*f*), acte(*m*); acte notarié	**Urkunde**(*f*), Vertrag(*m*); Tat(*f*), Handlung(*f*)	**deed**
acte attributif de biens	Abtretungsurkunde	– of assignment
déclaration(*f*) de consentement	Beitrittsurkunde; Einwilligungserklärung	– of consent
acte de cession	Übertragungs-, Auflassungsurkunde (bei Grundeigentum)	– of conveyance
acte fiduciaire	Treuhandvertrag; Sicherungsübereignung	– of trust
action(*f*), valeur(*f*), part(*f*)	**Aktie**(*f*); Gesellschaftsanteil(*m*)	**share**
action gratuite	Gratisaktie	bonus –
action(*f*) ordinaire (*US*)	Stammaktie	common – (*US*)
action cotée (officiellement)	börsennotierte Aktie	listed –
action ordinaire	Stammaktie	ordinary –
action privilégiée, de priorité	Vorzugsaktie	preference –
action nominative	Namensaktie	registered –
valeur sujette (non sujette) à restriction	Stammaktie mit bedingter (keine Bedingung unterliegemer) Dividendenzahlung	restricted (non-restricted) –
dividende(*m*) de l'action	(Dividendein Form von) Gratisaktien	– dividend
émission(*f*) d'actions	Aktienausgabe; Emission	– issue
action non cotée	nicht notierte Aktie	unlisted –
action(*f*)	**Klage**(*f*), Verfahren(*n*), Rechtsstreit(*m*); Handlung(*f*), Vorgehen	**action**
demande(*m*) de dommages-intérêts	Schadensersatzklage, Klage auf Entschädigung	– for damages
demande de décision judiciaire	Feststellungsklage	– for declaration
demande d'injonction	Unterlassungsklage	– for injunction
intenter un procès à, contre, qqu'un	Klage erheben, anstrengen; jdn verklagen, gegen jdn Klage erheben	to bring an – against s.o.
rejeter une action (en justice)	Klage abweisen	to dismiss an –
action(*f*) **civile,** poursuite(*f*), procès(*m*)	**Prozeß**(*m*); Klage(*f*)	**suit**

FRENCH	GERMAN	ENGLISH
action(f) de groupe (US)	Gruppenklage(f); von einer Interessengruppe angestrengte Klage(f)	class action (US)
action(f) de gracier, d'amnistier	Begnadigung(f); Straferlaß(m)	pardoning
action(f) en recours	Schadensersatzklage(f)	remedial action
action(f) possessoire	Besitz(schuld)klage(f)	possessory action
action(f) privilégiée (UK), action de priorité	Vorzugsaktie(f) (UK)	preference share (UK)
actionnaire(m), détenteur(m) d'actions	Aktionär(f); Antelseigner(m)	shareholder
actionnariat(m)	Aktienbesitz(m); Anteils-(m)	shareholding
additionnel, indirect; nantissement(m); parent(m) en ligne colatérale	Sicherungsgegenstand(m); Nebensicherheit(f); Verwandte(r) in der Seitenlinie	collateral
adjuger, déclarer, prononcer sur accorder (allouer) des dommages-intérêts	entscheiden, erkennen; zuerkennen, zusprechen Schadensersatz zuerkennen, zusprechen	adjudge – damages
admettre, concéder, avouer, laisser passer, accepter reconnaître une prétention, admettre un recours	zulassen, aufnehmen; zugeben, zugestehen; anerkennen e-n Anspruch anerkennen	admit (to) – a claim
administration(f), gestion(f), régie(f) le gouvernement (fédéral) (US)	Verwaltung(f); Führung(f), Leitung(f); Amtsperiode(f) Regierung (US)	administration – (US)
administratif droit(m) administratif	verwaltungs(technisch) Verwaltungsrecht	administrative – law
administrateur(m) délégué(m), administrateur(m) gérant	geschäftsführender Direktor(m); Generaldirektor(m)	managing director
administrer, gérer, appliquer déférer le serment rendre la justice	verwalten; handhaben, vollstrecken; als Nachlaßverwalter(m) tätig sein Eid abnehmen; jdn vereidigen Recht sprechen, Recht anwenden; Gerechtigkeit walten lassen	administer (to) – an oath – justice
admis(m, f) à caution	Sicherheit geleistet(f); Kaution gestellt	bailed
admission(f), accès(m), acceptation(f), aveu(m) aveu(m) judiciaire conditions(f) d'admission	Zulassung(f), Aufnahme(f), Eintritt(m); Eingeständnis(n), Anerkenntnis(n); Geständnis(n) Anerkenntnis der Einrede Zulassungsbedingungen	admission – of plea – requirements

FRENCH	GERMAN	ENGLISH
adopter, passer adopter un projet de loi prendre, adopter une résolution prononcer une condamnation	**annehmen;** verabschieden ein Gesetz verabschieden e-n Beschluß fassen (Straf)Urteil fällen, verkünden	**pass (to)** – a Bill – a resolution – sentence
adoptif	**Adoptiv-**	**adoptive**
adoption(*f*)	**Adoption**(*f*), Annahme(*f*)	**adoption**
adoucissement(*m*) réduction(*f*) de dommages-intérêts réduction de peine	**Milderung**(*f*) Herabsetzung des Schadensersatzes Strafmilderung	**mitigation** – of damages – of penalty
adresse(*f*), allocution(*f*), domicile(*m*) élu plaidoirie(*f*)	**Adresse**(*f*), Anschrift(*f*); Anrede(*f*), Ansprache(*f*) Zustellungsadresse Anrede des Gerichts	**address** – for service – to the court
adultère(*m*)	**Ehebruch**(*m*)	**adultery**
adultère(*m*); mauvaise gestion, inconduite(*f*)	**schlechtes (ordnungswidriges) Verhalten;** Verletzung(*f*) der Amtspflich	**misconduct**
adversaire(*m*), partie(*f*) adverse, contradicteur(*m*)	**Gegner**(*m*), gegnerische Partei(*f*), Prozeßgegner(*m*)	**adversary**
adverse, opposé balance(*f*) (commerciale) déficitaire témoin(*m*) de la partie adverse	**feindlich,** gegnerisch; nachteilig; entgegenstehend Unterbilanz; passive Bilanz Zeuge der Gegenseite; feindlicher Zeuge	**adverse** – balance – witness
affaiblissement(*m*), altération(*f*), diminution(*f*) infirmité(*f*)	**Beeinträchtigung**(*f*); Verschlechterung(*f*) körperliche Behinderung	**impairment** physical –
affilié(*m*)	**angegliedert, angeschlossen**	**affiliated**
affirmatif action en constatation un droit; mesures(*f*) pour favoriser les discriminés (*US*) moyen de défense nouveau détruisant la thèse du demandeur, même si elle était justifiée au moment où la plainte avait été déposée	**bejahend,** Bejahung(*f*) Rechtfeststellungsklage (Wiedergutmachung) der Folgen vergangener Diskriminierung (*US*) Einrede des Beklagten (*US*) (*Zivilprozeß*) Behauptung(en) die der Angeklagte glaubhaft zu machen hat (*Strafprozeß*)	**affirmative** – action (*US*) – defence
affirmation(*f*) **solennelle;** confirmation(*f*); ratification(*f*)	**Bestätigung**(*f*), Versicherung(*f*); Behauptung(*f*); eidliche Erklärung(*f*), eidesstattliche Versicherung(*f*)	**affirmation**
affirmer	**bestätigen,** versichern; behaupten; an Eides Statt versichern	**affirm (to)**
affirmer, prétendre	**behaupten;** geltend machen	**contend (to)**

FRENCH	GERMAN	ENGLISH
affirmer, revendiquer, alléguer revendiquer ses droits	**behaupten,** erklären; vorbringen; geltend machen seine Rechte geltend machen; auf seine Rechten bestehen	**assert (to)** – one's rights
affréteur(m); navire(m) marchand; wagon(m) de marchandises	**Frachter**(m); Verlader(m), Verfrachter(m)	**freighter**
agence(f) **maritime,** agence(f) d'affrètement	**Schiffsagentur**(f)	**shipping agency**
agent(m)**,** représentant(m), préposé(m); mandataire(m), fondé de pouvoirs agent(m) bancaire commissionnaire(m) en marchandises commissionnaire exportateur agent exclusif, dépositaire exclusif	**Vertreter**(m), Makler(m); Bevollmächtigter(m), Handlungsbeauftragter(m) Bankagent; Vertreter e-r Bank Kommissionsvertreter, Kommissionär Exportagent Alleinvertreter	**agent** bank – commission – export – sole –
agent(m) **de change,** courtier(m) en valeurs mobilières	**Börsenmakler**(m)	**stockbroker**
agent(m) **économique**	**Wirtschaftsbeauftragter**(m)	**economic agent**
agent(m) **immobilier** *(US)*	**Grundstücksmakler**(m) *(US)*; Immobilien–	**realtor** *(US)*
agent maritime, commissionnaire(m) chargeur	**Schiffsmakler**(m); Seehafenspediteur(m)	**shipping agent**
aggravation(f)	**Verschlimmerung**(f); Erschwerung(f), Verschärfung(f)	**aggravation**
aggraver; accroître	**verschlimmern;** erschweren, verschärfen	**aggravate (to)**
agresser, se livrer à des voies de fait sur	**angreifen;** tätlich bedrohen od. beleidigen	**assault (to)**
agression(f)**,** attaque(f), voies de fait coups(m) et blessures	**tätl. Angriff**(m); Bedrohung(f); Gewaltanwendung(f) schwere tätliche Beleidigung (Mißhandlung); Körperverletzung	**assault** – and battery
aide(f)**,** assistance(f), secours(m)	**Hilfe(leistung)**(f)**,** Beistand(m); Förderung(f), Beihilfe(f); Rechtsbeistand	**aid**
ajournement(m)**,** remise(f)	**Aufschub**(m); Zurückstellung(f)	**deferment**
ajournement(m)**,** report(m), renvoi(m)	**Aufschub**(m)	**postponement**
ajournement(m)**,** renvoi(m)	**Untersuchungshaft**(f); Anordnung der Haftfortdauer	**remand**
ajourner, différer, suspendre, remettre, renvoyer	**aufschieben;** (zeitlich od. örtlich) verlegen; vertagen	**adjourn (to)**
ajourner, repousser, différer	**aufschieben**	**postpone (to)**

FRENCH	GERMAN	ENGLISH
ajustement(m), arrangement(m), régularisation(f), redressement(m), remaniement(m), règlement des créances	**Berichtigung**(f), Bereinigung(f); Angleichung(f); Schlichtung(f), Beilegung (Streit)	**adjustment**
règlement des indemnités	Schadensberechnung; Anspruchsregulierung	– of claims
règlement des dommages-intérêts	Schadensregulierung, Schadensfeststellung	– of damages
ajuster, apurer; concilier, réconcilier	**versöhnen;** in Einklang bringen	**reconcile (to)**
alibi(m)	**Alibi**(n)	**alibi**
aliéner, transférer, détourner, céder	**veräußern,** übertragen (Rechte)	**alienate (to) (rights)**
allégation(f); chef(m) d'accusation; moyen(m) de défense	**Anführung**(f), Angabe(f); (unerwiesene) Behauptung(f) Parteivorbringen	**allegation**
alléguer, prétendre, exciper de	**anführen,** angeben; (Unerwiesenes) behaupten; (bei Gericht) vorbringen, geltend machen	**allege (to)**
allocation(f), assignation(f), ventilation(f), répartition(f)	**Zuteilung**(f); Zuweisung(f); Aufteilung(f)	**allocation**
affectation(f) de fonds	Mittelvergabe, Mittelzuweisung; Kapitalbewilligung, Kapitalverwendung	– of funds
répartition(f) des bénéfices attribution(f) d'actions	Gewinnzurechnung Aktienzuteilung	– of profits – of shares
allocation(f), gratification(f); rabais(m), ristourne(f); pension(f), rente(f), indemnité(f); déduction(f), abattement(m)	**Anerkennung**(f), Genehmigung; ausgesetzte Summe; Beihilfe(f); Vergütung(f); Preisnachlaß(m); (Steuer-Freibetrag)	**allowance**
amortissement(m) linéaire indemnités journalières indemnités pour frais pension de retraite	jährlicher Abschreibungsbetrag Tagegeld(er); Diäten Aufwandsentschädigung Alterszulage	annual – daily – expense – superannuation –
allocation(f) **de maternité**	**Mutterschaftsgeld**(n); –leistungen(f)	**maternity benefit**
allocation familiale	**Kinderbeihilfe**(f), Kindergeld(n)	**children's allowance**
allocation(s)(f) **familiale(s)**	**Familienbeihilfe**(f); Familienzulage(f)	**family allowance**
allocution(f), plaidoirie(f) finale	**Schlußplädoyer**(m)	**closing address**
allouer, affecter, attribuer	**zuteilen;** vergeben; aufteilen; bestimmen für	**allocate**
altération(f) falsification(f) de monnaie fraude(f) alimentaire	**(Ver-)Fälschung**(f) Münzverfälschung Verfälschung von Nahrungsmitteln, Lebensmittelfälschung	**adulteration** – of coinage – of food

FRENCH	GERMAN	ENGLISH
altérer, falsifier	**(betrügerisch) Veränderungen**(f) **vornehmen an etw.**; beeinflussen	**tamper (to)**
falsifier une preuve	Beweis fälschen	– with evidence
ambiguïté(f)	**Zweideutigkeit**(f); Ungewißheit(f), Unklarheit(f)	**ambiguity**
imprécision d'un texte légal	versteckter Dissens	latent –
amende(f)	**Geldstrafe**(f)	**fine**
sous peine d'amende	unter Androhung e-r Geldstrafe	under penalty of (a) –
amendement(m), modification(f), correction(f), rectification(f)	**Ergänzung**(f), Abänderung(f); Zusatz(m), Nachtrag(m)	**amendment**
amender, modifier, rectifier amender une loi, modifier un règlement	**ergänzen,** abändern e-n Gesetzesentwurf, Gesetz abändern	**amend (to)** – a statute
amiable arrangement(m) à l'amiable	**gütlich;** freundschaftlich gütliche Einigung, Regelung; Vergleich	**amicable** – settlement
amicale(f), société(f) de recours mutuel	**Unterstützungsverein**(m); Versicherungsverein(m) auf Gegenseitigkeit(f)	**friendly society**
amortir, défalquer, annuler	**abschreiben;** abbuchen	**write (to) off**
amortir, racheter, rembourser	**zurückkaufen;** einlösen; tilgen	**redeem (to)**
amortissement(m), rachat(m), remboursement(m), faculté(f) de réméré	**Rückkauf**(m); Einlösung(f); Tilgung(f)	**redemption**
purge(f) d'hypothèque amortissement de titres taux(m) de remboursement, d'amortissement	Tilgung e-r Hypothek Rückkauf von Wertpapieren Tilgungskurs	– of a mortgage – of securities – rate
droit(m) de rachat	gesetzliches Rückkaufsrecht	– right
ampliation(f)	**beglaubigte Abschrift**	**authenticated copy**
année(f), exercice(m) année civile année budgétaire, exercice financier année fiscale	**Jahr**(n) Kalender– Geschäfts–; Rechnungs– Steuer– (UK); Haushalts–, Rechnungs–	**year** calendar – financial – fiscal –
année de naissance	Geburts–	– of birth
annexe(f), avenant(m); cédule(f); programme(m), horaire(m)	**Liste**(f); Aufstellung(f); Anhang(m); Zeitplan(m)	**schedule**
annuité(f); rente viagière(f)	**Jahreseinkommen**(n); (jährliche) Rente(f), Annuität(f)	**annuity**
annulation(f), abrogation(f), résiliation(f), cassation(f)	**Annullierung**(f); Aufhebung(f); Ungültigkeitserklärung(f); Rückgängigmachung	**annulment**

FRENCH	GERMAN	ENGLISH
annulation(f)	Rückgängigmachung(f), Ungültig-; Aufhebung(f), Widerruf(m); Kündigung(f)	cancellation
clause(f) de résiliation, clause résolutoire	Aufhebungs-, Kündigungs-, Rücktrittsklausel	– clause
annuler	ungültig machen; annullieren	nullify (to)
annuler, abroger	annullieren; kündigen, aufheben; für ungültig erklären	annul
annuler, passer outre, décider contre	aufheben, verwerfen	overrule (to)
annuler, rappeler, révoquer	aufheben; widerrufen; abbestellen	countermand (to)
annuler, remplacer, supplanter	außer Kraft(f) setzen; ersetzen	supersede (to)
annuler, résilier, évacuer, démissionner	räumen; ausziehen; aufgeben	vacate (to)
anticipation(f); exercice(m) anticipé d'un droit	Vorausnahme(f); Vorauszahlung(f); Vorgriff(m)	anticipation
anticonstitutionnel	verfassungswidrig	unconstitutional
appel(m), pourvoi(m) en cassation	Berufung(f), Revision(f), Beschwerde(f), Einspruch(m)	appeal
cour(f) d'appel	Rechtsmittelgericht; Berufungsgericht(n)	Court of –
appel(m) de fonds	Kapital einfordern(n); Einzahlung(f) verlangen	call-up of capital
appeler, citer à comparaître	(an-)rufen; vorsprechen; einberufen; einfordern, auffordern	call (to)
appeler une cause, une affaire	(gerichtlich) aufrufen, e-e Sache –	– a case
appeler un témoin à faire sa déposition	jdn auffordern über etwas auszusagen	– a person to give evidence
ouvrir (une séance)	zur Ordnung rufen	– to order
appellant(m)	Kläger(m) (Berufungs-, Revisions-, Rechtsmittel-); Beschwerdeführer(m)	appellant
application(f) de la loi	Gesetzesvollzug(m)	law enforcement
appliquer, faire exécuter	(zwangsweise) durchführen; gerichtlich geltend machen; vollstrecken	enforce (to)
apporter, amener	bringen, tragen, erheben	bring (to)
intenter une action en justice	Klage erheben; Prozeß anhängig machen; verklagen	– an action
apporter, offrir; alléguer	erbringen, anführen, beibringen	adduce (to)
invoquer une raison	Gründe anführen	– an argument
fournir une preuve	e-n Beweis erbringen	– evidence
appréhension(f), arrestation(f), prise de corps; crainte(f)	Festnahme(f), Verhaftung(f); Begriff(m), Vorstellung(f); Befürchtung(f)	apprehension

FRENCH	GERMAN	ENGLISH
approbation(f), accord(m); conflit(m), concurrence(f) compétence(f) simultanée de plusieurs tribunaux	**Übereinstimmung**(f); Zusammentreffen Kompetenzkonflikt; konkurrierende Zuständigkeit	**concurrence** – of jurisdiction
approbation(f) **(d'un appel)**; visa(m); appui(m), soutien(m)	**Indossament**(n); Vermerk(m), Bestätigung(f)	**indorsement,** alternative spelling of endorsement
appropriation(f), attribution(f), dotation(f), prélèvement(m) détournement(m) de fonds	**Aneignung**(f); Bewilligung(f), Bereitstellung(f), Bestimmung(f); Verwendung(f) Bereitstellung von Mitteln für bestimmten Zweck	**appropriation** – of funds
appropriation(f) d'un bien	Vermögensverteilung, Besitzverwendung	– of property
approprier, allouer, répartir, doter, prélever	**sich aneignen;** bewilligen, bereitstellen; bestimmen, verwenden	**appropriate (to)**
approuver, accéder à	**übereinstimmen;** zusammentreffen	**concur (to)**
approximation(f) rapprochement(m) des législations et des règlementations(f) (CEE)	**Angleichung**(f); Annäherung(f) Rechtsangleichung, Angleichung von Rechtsvorschriften und Verordnungen (EG)	**approximation** – of laws and regulations (EEC)
appui(m), couverture(f); remboursement(m) soutien financier	**Unterstützung**(f); Deckung(f); Indossierung(f) finanzielle Unterstützung	**backing** financial –
arbitrage(m)	**Schieds(gerichts)verfahren**(n); Schiedsgerichtsbarkeit(f); Arbitrage(geschäft)	**arbitration**
sentence(f) arbitrale commission(f) arbitrale clause(f) compromissoire tribunal(m) arbitral	Schiedsspruch Schiedsstelle, Schlichtungsstelle Schiedsklausel Schiedsgericht(shof)	– award – board – clause – tribunal
arbitre(m), amiable compositeur	**Schiedsrichter**(m)	**arbitrator**
arbitre(m), amiable compositeur	**Schiedsrichter**(m); Sachverständiger(m)	**referee**
archives(f) **judiciaires**	**Gerichtsakte**(f); Prozeßakte(f)	**court record**
argent(m) **donné à qqu'un pour prix de son silence**	**Schweigegeld**(n)	**hush money**
armateur(m)	**Schiffseigner**(m); Reeder(m)	**shipowner**
arrangement(m) **transactionnel,** concordat(m)	**Beilegung**(f), Vergleich; Zusammensetzung	**composition**
arrangement(m), règlement(m), transaction(f); disposition(f) de biens, liquidation(f) arrangement à l'amiable règlement arbitral	**Regelung**(f); Beilegung(f); Abfindung(f) außergerichtliche Regelung Regelung auf schiedsgerichtlichem Weg	**settlement** out-of-court – – by arbitration

FRENCH	GERMAN	ENGLISH
arrestation(f), prise(f) de corps, placement(m) en détention; saisie(f) (de biens); contrainte(f) par corps	**festnehmen**, verhaften; (Verfahren)(n) aussetzen; anhalten	**arrest**
mandat d'arrêt	Haftbefehl; Beschlagnahmeverfügung	warrant of –
arrestation(f) **massive**	**Massenverhaftung**(f)	**mass arrest**
arrêt(m) **d'annulation,** réforme(f) d'un jugement en appel	**Aufhebung**(f); Stornierung(f); Rückbuchung(f)	**reversal**
arrêt(m) **de suspension,** de sursis; jugement(m) avant faire droit; injonction(f), ordre	**(gerichtliche) Verfügung**(f), Anordnung(f)	**injunction**
ordonnance(f) de référé	einstweilige Verfügung (auf Unterlassung)	interim –
commandement(m) du tribunal	einstweilige Verfügung (zur Vornahme einer Handlung)	mandatory –
ordonnance définitive	endgültige gerichtliche Verfügung (zur Unterlassung)	perpetual –
ordonnance de ne pas faire	einstweilige Verfügung (zur Unterlassung); gerichtliches Verbot	preventive –
ordonnance de ne pas faire	einstweilige Verfügung (zur Unterlassung);	prohibitive –
ordonnance temporaire	einstweilige Verfügung	temporary –
arrêté municipal ou communal; statuts(m) d'une société	**Ortsstatuten**(n); Gemeindeverordnung(f); Satzung(f); Geschäftsordnung	**by-laws**
arriéré, impayé, en souffrance	**überfällig;** rückständig	**overdue**
article(m), clause(f), stipulation(f), élément(m), dispositions(f)	**Artikel**(m); Warenposten(n); Abschnitt(m), Paragraph(m); Vertragsbestimmungen (pl.)	**article(s)**
statuts(m) d'une SARL	Gesellschaftsvertrag; Satzung	– of association (UK)
statuts d'une société commerciale	Gründungsurkunde; Satzung	– of incorporation (US)
contrat(m) de mariage	Heiratsvertrag	– of marriage
ascendance(f)	**Überlegenheit**(f), bestimmender Einfluß(m)	**ascendancy**
asile(m), refuge(m), sanctuaire(m)	**Asyl**(n); Freistatt(f)	**sanctuary**
assentiment(m), agrément(m), approbation(f)	**Zustimmung**(f), Genehmigung(f)	**assent**
assermenté	**be—, vereidigt**	**sworn**
déposition(f) sous serment	eidliche Erklärung	statement
témoin(m) sous serment	vereidigter Zeuge	witness
assignation(f), affectation(f), cession(f), transfert(m)	**Abtretung**(f), Übereignung(f), Übertragung(f)	**assignment**
transfert d'une créance	Forderungs–, Anspruchsabtretung	– of claim
transmission d'actions	Aktienübertragung	– of shares

FRENCH	GERMAN	ENGLISH
assignation(f), signification(f); service(m) signification par huissier signification de convocation	**Zustellung**(f) – durch Hilfsbeamten – e-r Vorladung	**service** – by bailiff – of summons
assigner, décerner	**zumessen**	**mete (to) out**
assigner à comparaître assigner un témoin à comparaître	**unter Strafandrohung**(f) **laden** einen Zeugen -	**subpoena (to)** – a witness
association(f), société(f), participation(f) société en commandite simple	**Personengesellschaft**(f) Kommanditgesellschaft	**partnership** limited –
associé(m) commandité(m) commanditaire(m)	**Gesellschafter**(m) persönlich (unbeschränkt) haftender – Kommanditist; beschränkt haftender –	**partner** general – limited –

FRENCH	GERMAN	ENGLISH
assurance(*f*)	**Versicherung**(*f*)	**insurance**
assurance contre les accident	Unfall–, Schadens–	accident, casualty –
assurance sur voyage aérien	Fluggast–	air passenger –
assurance tous risques	– gegen alle Verfahren und Risiken	all-risk –
assurance viagère	Renten–	annuity –
assurance automobile	Kraftfahrzeug–	automobile –
assurance contre le cambriolage	Einbruchdiebstahl–	burglary –
assurance sur faculté (de marchandises)	Fracht–; Güter–	cargo –
coassurance	Mit–	co– –
assurance de groupe	Kollektiv–; Gruppen–	collective –
assurance contre les risques de crédit	Kredit–	credit –
assurance invalidité	Invaliditäts–	disablement –
assurance contre les accidents du travail	Betriebshaftpflicht–; Arbeitgeberhaftpflicht–	employers' liability –
assurance contre les risques de crédit à l'exportation	Ausfuhrkredit–;	export credit –
assurance incendie	Feuer–	fire –
assurance du fret	Fracht–	freight –
assurance pourla totalité de la valeur déclarée	Gesamtwert–	full value –
assurance marchandises	Waren–	goods –
assurance contre la grêle	Hagel–	hail –
assurance maladie	Kranken–	health –
assurance sur les frais de justice	Rechtsschutz–	legal expenses –
assurance responsabilité civile	Haftpflicht–	liability –
assurance sur la vie	Lebens–	life –
assurance de rente viagère	Leibrenten–	life annuity –
assurance sur le manque à gagner	Betriebsunterbrechungs–	loss of profit –
assurance sur les bagages	(Reise-)Gepäck–	luggage –
assurance maritime	See(transport)–	marine –
assurance mutuelle	– auf Gegenseitigkeit	mutual –
assurance de rente vieillesse	Alters–	old age pension 2—
assurance contre les dégâts causés par la pluie	Regen–	pluvious –
assurance immobilière	Sach–; Vermögens–	property –
assurance(s) sociale(s)	Sozial–	social –
assurance transports	Transport–	transport –
assurance voyages	Reise–	travel –
assurance chômage	Arbeitslosen–	unemployment –
assurance contre les dégâts d'eau	Wasserschaden–	water-damage –
assurance(*f*) **collective**	**Gruppenversicherung**(*f*)	**group insurance**
assurance(*f*) **contre les accidents**	**Unfallversicherung**(*f*)	**accident insurance**
assurance(*f*) **contre les accidents**	**Schadenversicherung**(*f*); Unfall-Haftpflichtversicherung(*f*) (*US*)	**casualty insurance**

FRENCH	GERMAN	ENGLISH
assurance(f) contre la grêle	Hagelversicherung(f)	hail insurance
assurance(f) contre les défauts de fabrication	Produkthaftpflichtversicherung(f)	product liability insurance
assurance(f) d'un navire hors cargaison	Kaskoversicherung(f) (Schiffs–, Flugzeug–)	hull insurance
assurance(f) incendie	Feuerversicherung(f)	fire insurance
assurance responsabilité(f) des patrons	Unternehmerhaftpflichtversich-erung(f), Arbeitgeberversicherung	employer's liability insurance
assurance(f) sur les dégâts des eaux	Wasserschadenversicherung(f)	water damage insurance
assurance(f) sur les risques de guerre	Kriegsrisikoversicherung(f)	war risk insurance
assurance(f) voyage	Reiseversicherung(f)	travel insurance
assuré (–e)	Versicherter(m) (s. Versicherungsnehmer)(m)	insured person (cf. policyholder)
assureur	Versicherer(m); Versicherungsträger(m)	insurer
assureur(m), souscripteur(m)	Versicherer(m); Garant(m)	underwriter
attachement(m), fixation(f); saisie(f); opposition(f); mandat(m) d'amener; prise(f) de corps	Anfügung(f); Zuteilung(f); Verhaftung(f); Beschlagnahme(f), Pfändung(f)	attachment
saisie immobilière ordonnance(f) de saisie	Vermögensbeschlagnahme Arrestbefehl; Pfändungsbefehl; Beschlagnahmeverfügung	– of property – order
attacher, apposer, ajouter sceller (un document), apposer des scellés	anheften, aufkleben; aufdrücken mit e-m Siegel versehen, siegeln	affix (to) – a seal
attacher, impliquer, imputer; saisir, contraindre par corps saisir et vendre	anfügen; beimessen; verhaften; pfänden beschlagnahmen und verkaufen	attach (to) – and sell
attaquer, mettre en doute, discuter récuser un témoignage	anfechten Beweismaterial –	impugn (to) – evidence
atténuer	mildern; herabsetzen	mitigate (to)
attestation(f), témoignage(m) écrit; déposition(f) de témoin sous serment déposition de témoin recueillie sous serment faire une déclaration sous serment	Eidesstattliche Erklärung(f) od. Versicherung(f), (schriftlich) eidliche Erklärung eidesstattliche, schriftliche Zeugenaussage entgegennehmen eidesstattlich erklären, eidliche schriftliche Erklärung abgeben	affidavit evidence taken on – to make an –
attraper	ergreifen; einholen; erreichen; ertappen	catch (to)

FRENCH	GERMAN	ENGLISH
attribution(f), affectation(f), répartition(f); part(f), portion(f)	**Zuteilung**(f); Zuweisung(f); Zuerkennung(f); Verteilung(f)	**allotment**
lotissement(m)	Vermögenszuteilung; Besitzverteilung	– of property
au débarquement, à bord	**ab Schiff**(n)	**ex ship**
au secret	**ohne Möglichkeit**(f) **der Verbindung**(f) **mit der Außenwelt**	**incommunicado**
audience(f), débats(m) (d'un procès); interrogatoire(m) d'un accusé	**Verhandlung**(f)	**hearing**
audience concernant la détention	Haftverhandlung	detention –
audience de jugement	Schlußverhandlung, Schlußtermin;	final –
instruction(f) d'une affaire	– e-s Falls	– of a case
audition des témoins	Zeugenvernehmung	– of witnesses
audience préliminaire	Voruntersuchung	preliminary –
audience publique	öffentliche Verhandlung	public –
audience(f), session(f), séance(f)	**Sitzung**(f)	**session**
tribunal(m) en session, en séance	Gericht tagt	court in –
audience publique	öffentliche –	open –
audit(f), vérification(f), apurement(m)	**Rechnungsprüfung**(f); Revision(f)	**audit, auditing**
vérification de comptabilité par le fisc	Steuerprüfung	tax –
augmenter; se procurer, réunir	**aufnehmen**; aufbringen	**raise (to)**
se procurer des fonds, réunir des fonds	Geldmittel –	– funds
auteur(m) **d'un affidavit** (d'un attestation) (US)	**Aussteller**(m), Abgeber(m) e-s Affidavit (eidesstattliche Erklärung) (US)	**affiant** (US)
auteur(m) **d'un crime ou délit**; débiteur(m) principal	**Auftraggeber**(m); Vorgesetzter(m); Hauptschuldner(m); Kapital(n)	**principal**
capital(m) et intérêt(s)	Kapital und Zinsen	– and interest
auteur(m) principal d'un crime	Haupttäter	– in the first degree
complice	Mittäter; Tatgehilfe	– in the second degree
auteur(m) **d'un méfait,** délinquant(m)	**Übeltäter**(m); Rechtsverletzer(m)	**wrongdoer**
autofinancement(m)	**Selbstfinanzierung**(f)	**self-financing**
autopsie(f)	**Autopsie**(f), Obduktion(f)	**autopsy**
autopsie(f)	**Obduktion**(f)	**post-mortem**

FRENCH	GERMAN	ENGLISH
autorité(f), mandat(m), pouvoir(m), compétence(f) la police; autorité policière pouvoirs publics	**Behörde**(f); Befugnis(n); Genehmigung(f); Vollmacht(f) Polizeibehörde Verwaltungs–, Staatsbehörde; öffentliche Gewalt, Staatsgewalt	**authority** police – public –
autorités(f) **de contrôle, de surveillance**	**Aufsichtsbehörde**(f)	**supervisory authority**
autosuffisant	**finanziell unabhängig**; nicht auf fremde Hilfe angewiesen	**self-supporting**
auxiliaire(m), subordonné(f), annexe(f) à	**ergänzend**; untergeordnet, Hilfs–, Neben–	**ancillary**
avantage(m) avantages en nature prestation(f) maladie indemnité(f) de chômage	**Nutzen**(m), Vorteil(m); Hilfe(f), Begünstigung(f); Versicherungsleistung Sachleistungen Krankengeld, –unterstützung Arbeitslosenunterstützung	**benefit** benefits in kind sickness – unemployment –
avantages(m) **accessoires**, gratifications(f)	**Nebeneinkünfte**	**perquisites**
avis(m), conseil(m) avis(m) d'un homme de loi	**Rat**(m); Benachrichtigung(f), Mitteilung(f); Avis juristische Beratung, Rechtsbeistand	**advice** legal –
avis(m), préavis(m), notification(f), convocation(f) notification par voie de presse déclaration(f) d'appel avis d'imposition, avertissement(m) du fisc accusé de réception congé(m) donner un préavis; signifier son congé (à qqu'un); donner sa démission	**Benachrichtigung**(f); Anzeige(f) öffentliche Bekanntmachung Berufungsschrift Steuerbescheid Andienung; Empfangsbestätigung Kündigungsschreiben kündigen	**notice** – by publication – of appeal – of assessment (tax) – of delivery – of termination to give –
aviser, signifier, avertir	**melden**; mitteilen	**notify (to)**
avocat(m), avocate à la Cour	**(plädierender)**(m) **Anwalt**(m); Barrister(m)	**barrister**
avocat(m), conseil(m); avis(m) avocat du plaignant représentant(m) du ministère public	**Anwalt**(m); Rechtsbeistand(m) Prozeßbevollmächtigter des Klägers Anklagevertreter	**counsel** – for the plaintiff – for the prosecution

FRENCH	GERMAN	ENGLISH
avocat(*m*)	**Anwalt**(*m*), Rechtsbeistand(*m*); Sprecher(*m*), Fürsprecher(*m*)	**advocate**
avocat général	Generalanwalt *(am Gerichtshof der EG)*	– general
conseiller et représentant du gouvernment en Écosse	Kronanwalt *(Schottland)*	Lord Advocate
avoir recours à la violence	**Gewalt**(*f*) **anwenden**	**resort (to) to violence**
avortement(*m*)	**Abtreibung**(*f*)	**abortion**

B

FRENCH	GERMAN	ENGLISH
bail(*m*), concession(*f*) bail à ferme bail à ferme contrat(*m*) de bail	**Miet(e)**(*f*); Pacht(*f*) Pachtvertrag (landwirtschaftliche Grundstücke, Betrieb) Pachtvertrag (Pachtland) Mietvertrag	**lease** agricultural (farm) – land – – agreement
bailleur(*m*), loueur(*m*) à bail	**Vermieter**(*m*); Verpächter(*m*); Leasinggeber(*m*)	**lessor**
baisser, diminuer; renoncer à, retirer abandonner des poursuites	**einstellen;** fallen lassen Klage fallenlassen, zurücknehmen	**drop (to)** – a case
banc(*m*) mandat(*m*) d'arrêt décerné sur le siège	**Richterbank**(*f*); Gericht(*n*); Richterschaft(*m*) (richterlicher) Haftbefehl	**bench** – warrant
banc(*m*) **des accusés**	**Dock**(*n*), Kai(*m*); Anklagebank(*f*)	**dock**
banque(*f*) banque centrale banque de virement banque commerciale banque de crédit banque de dépôt banque industrielle banque d'affaires *(US)* banque d'affaires *(UK)*	**Bank**(*f*) Zentral–, Noten– Clearing–, Giro– Geschäfts–; Handels– Kredit– Depositen– Industrie– Investitions– *(US)* Merchant–	**bank** central – clearing – commercial – credit – deposit – industrial – investment – *(US)* merchant –
banque(*f*) **de virement**	**Clearingbank**(*f*), Giro–	**clearing bank**
Banque(*f*) **Fédérale de** **Réserve** *(US)*	**Bundeszentralbank**(*f*) *(US)*	**Federal Reserve** **Bank** *(US)*
bénéfice(*m*) **actualisé net**	**Mehrgewinn**(*m*); Übergewinn(*m*)	**excess profits**
bénéfices(*m*) **non distribués**	**unverteilter Reingewinn**(*m*); Bilanzgewinn(*m*)	**unappropriated** **profits**
bénéfices(*m*) **non distribués**	**unverteilter Gewinn**(*m*); nicht ausgeschütteter –; s. unverteilter Reingewinn	**undistributed profits** *(cf. unappropriated)*

FRENCH	GERMAN	ENGLISH
bénéficiaire(m, f), ayant(m) droit	**Nutzungsberechtigter**(m), Begünstigter(m); Empfangsberechtigter Leistungsempfänger; Anspruchsberechtigter	**beneficiary**
bénéficiaire(m), porteur(m) d'un effet	**Zahlungsempfänger**(m)	**payee**
bénéficiaire(m), destinataire(m), allocataire(m)	**Empfänger**(m)	**recipient**
bien-être social, prévoyance(f) sociale, service(m) social	**Fürsorge**(f) **(soziale)**	**welfare (social)**
comité(m) de bienfaisance assistant(e)(m) social(e)	Wohlfahrtsausschuß Sozialarbeiter(in)	– committee – officer
biens(m), propriété(f), avoirs(m), possessions(f)	**Eigentum**(f); Vermögen(n)	**property**
biens immobiliers, immeubles	Grundstücke und Gebäude	fixed –
biens incorporels	immaterielle Vermögenswerte	intangible –
biens-fonds, propriété foncière	Grundvermögen; Liegenschaften	landed –
droit(m) de la propriété	Sachenrecht	law of –
propriété affermée, louée à bail	Pachtgrundstücke	leasehold –
biens mobiliers	bewegliches Vermögen	movable –
biens mobiliers	persönliches Eigentum; bewegliches Vermögen	personal –
propriété publique	Staatseigentum; Eigentum der öffentlichen Hand	public –
biens corporels	**Sachen;** körperliche Gegenstände	**corporeal property**
biens(m) **immobiliers**	**Immobilien;** Liegenschaften	**immovables**
biens(m) **immobiliers**	**Grundstücke**(n); Immobilien	**realty**
biens(m) **meubles**	**Fahrnis**(n), bewegliches Vermögen(n)	**chattels**
biens(m) **mobiliers**	**bewegliche Sachen**(f); Hab und Gut	**goods and chattels**
biens(m) **mobiliers**	**bewegliches Vermögen**(n)	**movables**
biens(m) **onéreux**	**Vermögen**(n) **mit Belastungen**(f) **od. Auflagen**	**onerous property**
bilan(m) **d'inventaire**	**Bilanz**(f), Rechnungsabschluß(m)	**balance sheet**
bilatéral, synallagmatique	**bilateral;** gegenseitig	**bilateral**
billet(m), bordereau(m), facture(f), bulletin(m)	**Note**(f); Schein(m)	**note**
lettre(f) de voiture	(Luft-)Frachtbrief	consignment –
facture d'avoir, bordereau de crédit	Gutschriftanzeige	credit –
bordereau d'escompte	Diskontabrechnung	discount –
billet à ordre	Eigenwechsel; Schuldschein	promissory –
permis(m) d'embarquement	Versandanzeige; Schiffszettel	shipping –

FRENCH	GERMAN	ENGLISH
billet(*m*) **à ordre,** promesse écrite de payer sa dette	**Schuldanerkenntnis**(*n*); Eigenwechsel(*m*)	**promissory note**
billet(*m*) **de banque**	**Banknote**(*f*); Papiergeld(*m*)	**banknote**
biparti, bilatéral	**in doppelter Ausfertigung**(*f*) **(Urkunden)**(*f*); zweiteilig	**bipartite**
blasphème(*m*)	**Blasphemie**(*f*), Gotteslästerung(*f*)	**blasphemy**
blesser	**verletzen;** Schaden zufügen	**hurt (to)**
blessures(*f*) **et souffrances**(*f*)	**psychische Leiden**(*n*)	**pain and suffering**
bon(*m*), document(*m*), titre(*m*), certificat(*m*) porteur(*m*) de titre, détenteur(*m*) de documents	**Scrip**(*m*); Zwischenschein(*m*) –inhaber	**scrip** --holder
bon(*m*) créance(*f*) recouvrable bonne foi(*f*)	**gültig;** zahlungsfähig sichere Forderung in gutem Glauben, nach Treu und Glauben	**good** – debts – faith
bon du trésor (à long terme)	**Staatsschuldverschreibung** (*US*), firmeneigene –; Schatzanweisung (*UK*)	**treasury bond**
bonne foi(*f*) détenteur(*m*) de bonne foi offre(*f*) ferme(*f*)	**in gutem Glauben;** gutgläubig, redlich gutgläubiger Inhaber (Eigentümer) solides Angebot	**bona fide** – holder – offer
bouc(*m*) **émissaire**	**Sündenbock**(*m*)	**scapegoat**
Bourse(*f*)	**Börse**	**stock exchange**
boycottage(*m*)	**Boykott**(*m*), Sperre(*f*)	**boycott**
branche(*f*), succursale(*f*), agence(*f*)	**Zweigstelle**(*f*), –niederlassung(*f*), Filiale(*f*), Nebenstelle(*f*); Branche, Sparte	**branch**
branche(*f*), segment(*m*) secteur(*m*) du marché	**Segment**(*n*); Sparte(*f*) Marktsegment	**segment** market –
brevet d'invention (*n*); breveté (*adj.*), patenté (*adj.*) contrefaçon(*f*) droit(*m*) des brevets propriété(*f*) industrielle	**Patent**(*n*) –verletzung –recht; –gesetz –rechte	**patent** – infringement – law – rights
Breveté(*m*), titulaire(*m*) d'un brevet d'invention	**Patentinhaber**(*m*)	**patentee**
brigade(*f*) **mondaine,** brigade des moeurs	**Sittenpolizei**(*f*)	**vice squad**
brutal(*m*), féroce	**wild;** unzivilisiert	**savage**
but(*m*), objet(*m*), dessein(*m*), affectation(*f*)	**Zweck**(*m*); Absicht(*f*)	**purpose**

C

FRENCH	GERMAN	ENGLISH
cabinet(*m*), conseil(*m*) des ministres	**Kabinett**(*n*); Ministerium(*n*)	**cabinet**
commission(*f*) du conseil des ministres	Kabinetts–, Regierungsausschuß	– committee
réunion(*f*) du cabinet, du conseil des ministres	Kabinettssitzung	– meeting
cabinet(*m*) **de juge,** d'avocat, étude(*f*) d'avoué	**Anwaltsbüro**(*n*), Kanzlei(*f*)	**chambers**
juger en chambre du conseil	unter Ausschluß der Öffentlichkeit verhandeln	hear in –
en référé	unter Ausschluß der Öffentlichkeit	in –
cachet(*m*), sceau(*m*)	**(Amts)Siegel**(*n*); Plombe(*f*), Verschluß(*m*)	**seal**
apposer son cachet	seinen Siegel anbringen, beidrücken	to affix one's –
sous le sceau de	unter dem Siegel von; gesiegelt	under the – of
cachette(*f*)	**Aufbewahrungsort**(*f*); Versteck(*n*), geheimes Lager(*n*)	**cache**
cadastre(*m*), registre(*m*) du cadastre	**Grundbuch**(*n*); Kataster(*m*)	**land register**
CAF (coût, assurance maritime, fret)(*m*)	**c.i.f.** (*s. Fracht*)	**CIF**
caisse(*f*) **d'épargne**	**Sparkasse**(*f*)	**savings bank**
cambriolage(*m*)	**Einbruch(sdiebstahl)**(*m*)	**burglary**
cambrioleur(*m*)	**Einbrecher**(*m*)	**burglar**
capacité(*f*); qualité(*f*)	**Fähigkeit**(*f*); Kapazität(*f*); Inhalt(*m*)	**capacity**
capacité légale	Rechtsfähigkeit; Geschäftsfähigkeit	legal –
exercice des fonctions	dienstliche, amtliche Eigenschaft	official –
capacité de tester	Testierfähigkeit	testamentary –
capital(*m*)	**Kapital-**(*n*)	**capital** (*criminal law*)
crime(*m*) punissable de la peine capitale	–verbrechen	– crime
peine(*f*) capitale, peine de mort	Todesstrafe	– punishment

FRENCH	GERMAN	ENGLISH
capital(*m*) rapport(*m*) d'adéquation du capital prêt(*m*) pour constitution de capital plus(*f*)-value possession(*f*) de capital intérêt(*m*) du capital marché(*m*) des capitaux rendement(*m*), rentabilité du capital capital social capital versé capital actions	**Kapital**(*n*); Vermögen(*n*) Eigenmittelrelation Kapitalvorschuß (Kapital-)Veräußerungsgewinn; realisierter Kursgewinn Kapitalanteil Kapitalbeteiligung Kapitalmarkt Kapitalverzinsung Aktienkapital; Stammkapital voll eingezahltes Kapital Aktien-, Stamm-; Betriebskapital	**capital** – adequacy ratio – advance – gain – holding – interest – market – return – stock paid-up – share –
capital(*m*) **d'exploitation**	**Betriebskapital**(*n*); Nettoumlaufvermögen(*n*)	**working capital**
capital(*m*) **de roulement**	**Betriebskapital**(*n*); Nettoumlaufvermögen(*n*)	**working capital**
capricieux, absurde, dévergondé blessure(*f*) accidentelle	**rücksichtslos;** böswillig mutwillige Verletzung	**wanton** – injury
captif, captive(*m, f*)	**Gefangener**(*m*); gefangen; für den Eigenbedarf(*m*)	**captive**
cas(*m*), affaire(*f*) espèce affaire dont la Cour d'Appel est saisie affaire criminelle affaire concernant un mineur affaire en cours d'instance, affaire pendante devant	**Fall**(*m*); Rechts-, Streitsache(*f*); Prozeß(*m*) der zur Entscheidung stehende Fall; der vorliegende Fall Berufungssache Strafsache; Strafprozeß Jugendsache schwebende, anhängige Streitsache	**case** – at issue – on appeal criminal – juvenile – pending –
cas(*m*) **fortuit**	**Zufall**(*m*), zufälliges Ereignis(*n*)	**fortuitous event**
casser, abroger, invalider, annuler	**ungültig machen;** für ungültig erklären	**invalidate (to)**
casser, annuler, rescinder	**aufheben;** rückgängig machen	**rescind (to)**
casser, infirmer, annuler	**aufheben;** für ungültig erklären	**quash**
cause(*f*), raison(*f*) motif(*m*) de l'appel motif de la plainte raison de soupçonner	**Ursache**(*f*), Grund(*m*); Rechtsfall(*m*), -streit, -sache Anfechtungsgrund Klage-, Beschwerdegrund Verdachtsgrund	**cause** – of appeal – of complaint – of suspicion
cause(*f*) **immédiate**	**unmittelbare Ursache**(*f*)	**proximate cause**
caution(*f*), garant(*m*); caution personnelle d'un immigrant (*US*); parrain(*m*), commanditaire(*m*), 'sponsor'	**Sponsor**(*m*); Geldgeber(*m*)	**sponsor**

FRENCH	GERMAN	ENGLISH
caution(*f*)	**Bürgschaft**(*f*)**;** Kaution(*f*), Sicherheitsleistung(*f*)	**bail**
bon de caution	Bürgschaftsschein	– bond
admettre une caution	Sicherheitsleistung (Kaution) zulassen	to grant –
proposer une caution	Sicherheit anbieten	to offer –
mise en liberté sous caution	gegen Bürgschaft (Sicherheitsleistung) entlassen, freilassen	to release on –
caution(*f*) **juridique**	**Sicherheitsversprechen**(*n*)**;** Kautions–	**recognisance**
CCP (compte courant postal)	**Girokonto**(*n*) (*UK*); Postgirokonto(*n*)	**giro account**
cédant(*m*)	**Rechtsvorgänger**(*m*)**;** Zedent(*m*); Übertragender(*m*); Abtreter(*m*)	**assignor**
cédant(*m*)**,** endosseur(*m*)	**Übertragender**(*m*)**;** Zedent(*m*)	**transferor**
céder	**abtreten,** zedieren; überlassen	**cede (to)**
CEE (Communauté économique européenne)	**EWG (Europäische Wirtschaftsgemeinschaft)**	**EEC (European Economic Community)**
droit(*m*) communautaire	EG-Recht(*n*)	– law
directives(*f*) européennes	EG – Gesetzgebung(*f*)	– legislation
célibataire(*m, f*)	**ledig (Familienstand)**(*m*)	**single (marital status)**
certificat(*m*)**,** attestation	**Zeugnis**(*n*)**,** Bescheinigung(*f*); Urkunde(*f*); Anteilschein(*m*)	**certificate**
acte(*m*) de naissance	Geburtsurkunde	birth –
certificat de dépôt	Einlagezertifikat; Depot–, Hinterlegungsschein	– of deposit
certificat d'origine	Ursprungszeugnis; Herkunftsbescheinigung	– of origin
acte de décès	Sterbeurkunde; Totenschein	death –
billet(*m*) de santé	Gesundheitsattest; –zeugnis	health –
acte de mariage	Heiratsurkunde	marriage –
certitude(*f*)**,** conviction(*f*)	**Gewißheit**(*f*)**,** Sicherheit(*f*); Rechtssicherheit(*f*)	**certainty**
degré(*m*) de certitude	Sicherheits–, Gewißheitsgrad	degree of –
cessation(*f*)**,** abandon(*m*) désistement(*m*) d'action	**Unterbrechung**(*f*)**;** Einstellung(*f*) Aussetzung e-s Verfahrens; Klagerücknahme	**discontinuance** – of an action
cession(*f*)	**Abtretung**(*f*)**;** Zession(*f*); Überlassung(*f*)	**cession**
acte(*m*) de cession	Abtretungsurkunde	deed of –
cession(*f*) **à bail**; décès(*m*)	**Übertragung**(*f*)**,** Verpachtung(*f*); Ableben(*n*), Tod(*m*)	**demise**
cessionnaire(*m*)**;** syndic(*m*), administrateur-séquestre(*m*)	**Rechtsnachfolger**(*m*)**;** Zessionar(*m*); Erwerber(*m*)	**assignee**
cessionnaire(*m*)	**(Übertragungs-)**(*f*)**Empfänger**(*m*)**;** Zessionar(*m*)	**transferee**
chagriner, blesser, causer de la peine	**kränken,** jdn in seinem Recht verletzen	**aggrieve (to)**

FRENCH	GERMAN	ENGLISH
Chambre(f) **des Lords** (UK)	**Oberhaus**(n) (UK)	**House of Lords** (UK)
champ(m) **d'application**	**Anwendungsbereich**(m)	**range of application**
chancelier(m)	**Kanzler**(m); Richter(m) od. Vorsitzender(m) (des Court of Chancery)	**chancellor**
chancelier de l'Échiquier, ministre(m) des finances	Schatzkanzler; Finanzminister	Chancellor of the Exchequer
le Grand Chancelier d'Angleterre	Lordkanzler	Lord Chancellor
chancellerie(f)	**Rechtsprechung**(f) **nach equity-Recht**(n); Kanzleigericht	**chancery**
tribunal(m) jugeant en 'equity'	Gericht(n), das nach den Grundsätzen des equity urteilt	court of –
change(m); **transmission**(f); **Bourse**(f)	**Devisen; Umtausch**(m)	**exchange**
contrôle(m) des changes	Devisenkontrolle	– control
perte(f) de change	(Wechsel-)Kursverlust	– loss
taux(m) de change, cours du change	Wechsel-, Devisen-, Umrechnungskurs	– rate
chantage(m)	**Erpressung**(f); Nötigung	**blackmail**
chantier(m); **cour**(f); unité de mesure: 1 yard = 3 pieds = 91,44 cm	**Yard**(n), Elle(f); Hof(m); Scotland Yard (Langenmaß = 91,44 cm)	**yard**
chapardage(m), **larcins**(m)	**Entwendung**(f); geringfügiger Diebstahl(m)	**pilfering, pilferage**
chaparder, commettre de menus larcins	**entwenden; stehlen**	**pilfer (to)**
charge de la preuve	**Beweispflicht**(f), – last	**burden of proof**
charge(f) **de la preuve**	**Beweislast**	**onus of proof**
charte(f), **statuts**(m), **privilège**(m)	**Urkunde**(f); Verfassungs-, Verleihungs-, Gründungsurkunde(f)	**charter**
acte(m), statuts d'association d'une compagnie, d'une société	Gründungsurkunde einer Gesellschaft	– of a company
chasseur(m) **de têtes** (fam.); braconnier(m)	**Wilddieb**(m)	**poacher**
châtiment(m), **peine**(f), **sanction**(f), **punition**(f)	**Strafe**(f)	**punishment**
peine collective	Kollektiv-	collective –
châtiment(m) **corporel**	**körperliche Züchtigung**(f); Prügelstrafe(f)	**corporal punishment**
chef(m) **de famille**; locataire(m, f), propriétaire(m, f)	**Haushalt(ung)svorstand**(m)	**householder**
choisir, retenir, conserver	**beibehalten;** beauftragen	**retain (to)**
chômage(m)	**Arbeitslosigkeit**(f)	**unemployment**
cicatrice(f) cicatrices et contusions	**Narbe**(f) -n und blaue Flecken	**scar** scars and bruises

FRENCH	GERMAN	ENGLISH
circonscription(f) électorale (US)	Bezirk(m) (US)	precinct (US)
circonstances(f) aggravantes	(straf-)erschwerende, strafverschärfende Umstände	aggravating circumstances
circonstances(f) atténuantes	mildernde Umstände	extenuating circumstances
circonstances(f) atténuantes	mildernde Umstände(m)	mitigating circumstances

circuit(m)
  tribunal(m) de première instance (US)
  juge(m) de la Crown Court et de la county court (Angleterre)
	Kreis(m), Bezirk(m)
	  erstinstanzliches Gericht für mehrere Bezirke (US)
	  Strafrichter; Richter
		circuit
		  – court (US)
		  – judge

circulation(f), cours(f) de l'argent; devise(m), monnaie
  devise d'un contrat
  infraction(f) à la réglementation des changes
  réglementation(f) des changes
	Währung(f); Umlauf(m), Laufzeit(f)
	  Laufzeit e-s Vertrags
	  Devisenvergehen
	
	  Währungsbeschränkungen
		currency
		
		  – of a contract
		  – offence
		
		  – restrictions

citation(f) à comparaître, assignation(f)
  assigner qqu'un (à comparaître)
	gerichtliche Vorladung(f)
	
	  jdn eine Ladung zustellen
		summons
		
		  to serve a – on s.o.

citoyen(m), ressortissant	Bürger(m); Staatsbürger(m)	citizen
citoyenneté(f), nationalité(f)	Staatsbürgerschaft(m), Staatsangehörigkeit(f)	citizenship

civil, –e
  action(f) civile
 	
  tribunal(m) civil
  'jus civile', droit(m) romain; droit civil
  responsabilité(f) civile
  mariage(m) civil
 	
  droits(m) civils; droits civiques
  fonctionnaire(m)
	bürgerlich, zivilrechtlich
	  Zivilprozeß, bürgerlicher Rechtsstreit
	  Zivilgericht
	  Zivilrecht; bürgerliches Recht, Privatrecht
	  zivilrechtliche Haftung
	  Ziviltrauung, standesamtliche Trauung
	  (Staats-)Bürgerrechte
	
	  (Staats-)Beamter; öffentlicher Bediensteter
		civil
		  – action
		
		  – court
		  – law
		
		  – liability
		  – marriage
		
		  – rights
		
		  – servant

civique, municipal	bürgerlich, staatsbürgerlich; städtisch	civic

clause(f)
 	
  clause d'exonération
 	
  clause pénale, dédit
	Klausel(f); Absatz(m); Vereinbarung(f)
	  Freizeichnungsklausel; Befreiungsklausel
	  Strafklausel, Strafbestimmung
		clause
		
		  exemption –
		
		  penalty –

clause(f) de report	Verlängerungsklausel(f); Report–(m)	continuation clause
clause(f) de sauvegarde	Vorbehaltsklausel(f); Rücktritts–, Schutz–	escape clause

FRENCH	GERMAN	ENGLISH
clause(*f*) **de restriction d'un titre**	**Eigentumsvorbehalt**(*m*)	**reservation of title**
clause(*f*) **dérogatoire**	**Abänderungsklausel**(*f*)	**derogative clause**
clause(*f*) **dérogatoire**	**maßgebliche Klausel**(*f*)	**overriding clause**
clause(*m*) **d'exclusion,** refus(*m*) d'admission	**Freizeichnungsklausel**(*f*)	**exclusion clause**
clause(*m*) **d'exonération,** clause d'exemption	**Freistellungsklausel**(*f*); Haftungsausschluß–(*f*)	**exemption clause**
clause(*f*) **pénale du contrat,** garantie(*f*); autorisation(*f*), justification(*f*)	**Garantie**(*f*); Gewährleistung(*f*)	**warranty**
clauses(*f*), conditions(*f*); prix(*m*)	**Bedingungen**	**terms**
conditions de paiement	Zahlungs–	– of payment
conditions de vente	Verkaufs–	– of sale
conditions(*f*) d'offre	Ausschreibungs–, Submissions–	– of tender
clôture(*f*)	**Schließung**(*f*); Schluß(*m*); Abschluß(*m*)	**closure**
clôture des débats	Schluß der Debatte	– of debate
coassurance(*f*)	**Mitversicherung**(*f*)	**co-insurance**
code(*m*)	**Code**(*m*)	**code**
code(*m*) **de procédure**	**Prozeßrecht**(*n*); Verfahrens–(*n*)	**procedural law**
code(*m*) **postal** (*US*)	**Postleitzahl**(*f*) (*US*)	**zipcode** (*US*)
co-défendeur(*m*), co-accusé(*m*)	**Mitbeklagter**(*m, f*), Neben–; Mitangeklagter(*m, f*)	**co-accused, co-defendant**
codicille(*m*), avenant(*m*)	**Kodizil**(*n*); Testamentsnachtrag(*m*); Zusatz(*m*)	**codicil**
coercition(*f*), contrainte(*f*)	**Zwang**(*m*); Nötigung(*f*)	**coercion**
cohabitation(*f*), concubinage(*m*), union(*f*) libre	**Zusammenleben;** Lebensgemeinschaft	**cohabitation**
cohéritier(*m*)	**Miterbe**(*m*), Neben–	**coheir**
collectif, collective	**kollektiv**(*n*), gesamt(*f*)	**collective**
convention(*f*) collective	Tarifvertrag; Kollektivvertrag	– agreement, bargain
négociation(*f*) pour convention collective	Tarifverhandlungen	– bargaining
culpabilité(*f*) collective	Kollektivschuld	– guilt
société(*f*) de placement	gemeinsame Kapitalanlagegesellschaft, Investmentgesellschaft	– investment company
responsabilité(*f*) collective	Gesamtverpflichtung, –schuld; Kollektivhaftung	– liability
collectivité(*f*)	**Gemeinschaft**(*f*) (*EG*); Gemeinde(*f*)	**community**
législation(*f*) communautaire (*CE*)	gemeinschaftliche Rechtsvorschriften (*EG*)	Community legislation (*EC*)
collusion(*f*), connivence(*f*)	**Kollusion**(*f*); geheimes (unerlaubtes) Einverständnis(*n*)	**collusion**

FRENCH	GERMAN	ENGLISH
collusion(f), complicité(f)	geheimes Einverständnis(n); stillschweigende Einwilligung(f)	connivance
colportage(m)	Hausieren	peddling
comité(m), conseil(m) délégation(f) des créanciers commission(f) d'enquête parlementaire comité de direction; réunion des présidents	Komitee(n), Ausschuß(m) Gläubigerausschuß Parlaments-; Sonder-; Untersuchungsausschuß Ständiger Ausschuß	committee creditors', liquidation – select – standing –
commencement(m) de preuve	Anscheinsbeweis(m); Glaubhaftmachung(f)	prima facie evidence
commerce(m) maritime	Seehandel(m)	seaborne trade
commercial	wirtschaftlich; gewerblich; geschäftlich; handelsüblich	commercial
agence(f) de renseignements commerciaux	Handelsvertretung;	– agency
banque(f) commerciale tribunal(m) commercial droit(m) commercial registre(m) de commerce	Geschäftsbank; Handels- Handelsgericht Handelsrecht; -gesetz Handelsregister	– bank – court – law – register
commettre, perpétrer commettre, perpétrer un crime	übergeben; begehen; verüben strafbare Handlung, Verbrechen begehen	commit (to) – a crime
commission(f), conseil(m), administration(f)	Direktion(f); Verwaltungsstelle(f); Behörde(f); Ausschuß(m), Gremium(n); Verpflegung(f)	board
comité(m) administratif comité consultatif conseil d'administration	Verwaltungsrat; -ausschuß Beratungsausschuß, -stelle (Gremium der) Direktoren; Vorstand	administrative – advisory – – of directors
commission(f) rogatoire	Rechtshilfeersuchen	letters rogatory
commuer une peine	Strafe(f) umwandeln	commute (to) a penalty
Communauté(f) économique européenne (CEE)	Europäische Wirtschafts- gemeinschaft (EWG)	European Economic Community (EEC)
communication(f) de pièces	Offenlegung(f); Bekanntgabe(f)	disclosure (of)
commutation(f) commutation de peine	Austausch(m); Umwandlung(f) Strafumwandlung	commutation – of penalty

FRENCH	GERMAN	ENGLISH
compagnie(*f*), société(*f*), entreprise(*f*)	**(Kapital-)Gesellschaft**(*f*); Firma(*f*)	**company**
filiale(*m*)	angeschlossenes Unternehmen; Konzern–,	affiliated –
associée(*f*)	Schwestergesellschaft angegliederte Gesellschaft; Beteiligungs–	associated
société mère	Dachgesellschaft	– controlling
holding, société de participations financières	Holding–, Dachgesellschaft	– holding –
société constituée	eingetragene (rechtsfähige) Gesellschaft;	incorporated –
société de capitaux, par actions	Kapitalgesellschaft	joint-stock –
société à responsabilité limitée (SARL)	Gesellschaft mit beschränkter Haftung	private –
société anonyme	Aktiengesellschaft	public –
société commerciale	Handelsgesellschaft	trading –
compétence(*f*), capacité(*f*)	**Zuständigkeit**(*f*); Befugnis(*n*); Geschäftsfähigkeit(*f*)	**competence, competency**
compétent	**zuständig;** befugt; maßgeblich; sachverständig geschäftsfähig	**competent**
avis(*m*) qualifié	sachverständiger Rat	– advice
autorité(*f*) compétente	zuständige Behörde	– authority
preuve(*f*) recevable	zulässiges (und schlüssiges) Beweismaterial	– evidence
tribunal(*m*) compétent	zuständiges Gericht	court of – jurisdiction
complice(*m*)	**Komplize**(*m*); Mittäter(*m*), Mitschuldiger(*m, f*); Helfershelfer(*m*)	**accomplice**
complice(*m*)	**Helfershelfer**(*m*), Gehilfe(*m*)	**aider and abettor**
complice(*m*); accessoire(*m*)	**Mittäter**(*m*); Komplize(*m*), Mitschuldiger(*m, f*)	**accessory**
complicité(*f*)	**Mittäterschaft**(*m*) *(StrafR);* Mitschuld(*f*); Tatbeteiligung(*f*)	**complicity**
complot(*m*), intrigue(*f*), conspiration(*f*); parcelle(*f*) de terrain	**Anschlag**(*m*); Verschwörung(*f*)	**plot**
composer, transiger s'arranger avec ses créanciers	**sich vergleichen,** einigen mit s-n Gläubigern einen Vergleich schließen	**compound (to)** – with one's creditors
compromettre, impliquer	**hineinziehen;** verwickeln	**implicate (to)**
compromettant	**belastend**	**incriminating**
pièce(*f*) à conviction	Belastungsmaterial	– evidence
comptabilité(*f*)	**Buchführung**(*f*); Rechnungslegung(*f*); Abrechnung(*f*); Rechnungswesen	**accounting**
pièces(*f*) comptables	Buchungsunterlagen, Buchungsbelege	– records
comptabilité de caisse	Kassenbuchhaltung	cash –
comptabilité de prix de revient	Kostenrechnung; Betriebskalkulation	cost –

FRENCH	GERMAN	ENGLISH
comptable(*m*)	**Buchhalter**(*m*); Buchhaltungsfachmann(*m*); Buchprüfer(*m*)	**accountant**
expert(*m*) comptable *(US)*	(öffentlich zugelassener) Wirtschaftsprüfer *(US)*	certified public – *(US)*
expert comptable *(UK)*	(öffentlich zugelassener) Wirtschaftsprüfer *(UK)*	chartered – *(UK)*
compte(*m*), calcul(*m*); chef(*m*) d'accusation	**Klagepunkt**(*m*)	**count**
au premier chef	erster Klagepunkt	of the first –
au second chef	zweiter Klagepunkt	of the second –
comté(*m*)	**Grafschaft**(*f*); Verwaltungsbezirk(*m*)	**county**
conseil(*m*) général	Grafschaftsrat; Bezirksausschuß	– council
tribunal(*m*) de première instance	Grafschaftsgericht; Kreisgericht *(US); Amtsgericht*	– court
concédant	**Lizenzgeber**(*m*); Konzessionserteiler(*m*)	**licensor**
concédant(*m*), donateur(*m*)	**Bewilligender**(*m*); Übertragender(*m*)	**grantor**
concéder	**einräumen**; zugestehen; gewähren	**concede (to)**
concession(*f*); dégrèvement(*m*)	**Konzession**(*f*); Zugeständnis(*n*); Zulassung(*f*)	**concession**
concession(*f*), octroi; subvention(*f*)	**Bewilligung**(*f*); Übertragung(*f*); Schenkung(*f*); Beihilfe(*f*); Stipendium	**grant**
concessionnaire(*m*)	**Begünstigter**(*m*) (dem etwas bewilligt, übertragen, verliehen wurde)	**grantee**
concessionnaire(*m, f*)	**Lizenznehmer**(*m*); Konzessionsinhaber(*m*)	**licensee**
conciliateur(*m*), arbitre(*m*)	**Vermittler**(*m*); Schlichter(*m*)	**conciliator**
conciliateur(*m*), médiateur(*m*)	**Schlichter**(*m*); Vermittler(*m*)	**mediator**
conciliation(*f*), arbitrage(*m*)	**Versöhnung**(*f*), Schlichtung(*f*)	**conciliation**
conciliation(*f*), médiation(*f*), intervention(*f*) amicale	**Schlichtung**(*f*); Vermittlung(*f*)	**mediation**
conclure	**folgern**, schließen aus	**infer (to)**
conclusions(*f*) **préconçues**	**vorgefaßte Schlußfolgerung**(*f*)	**preconceived conclusion**
concordance(*f*)	**Übereinstimmung**(*f*)	**concordance**
concurrence(*f*)	**Konkurrenz**(*f*); Wettbewerb	**competition**
clause(*f*) de concurrence	Wettbewerbsklausel	– clause
concurrence déloyale	unlauterer Wettbewerb	unfair –
concussion(*f*), corruption(*f*) de fonctionnaires	**Schiebung**(*f*), Korruption(*f*); Bestechungsgeld(*n*)	**graft**
condamnation(*f*)	**Verurteilung**(*f*); Unbrauchbarerklärung(*f*)	**condemnation**

FRENCH	GERMAN	ENGLISH
condamnation(f)	Überführung(f); Schuldspruch(m), Verurteilung(f)	conviction
condamnation(f) avec sursis	Strafaussetzung(f) zur Bewährung(f)	suspended sentence
condamner	verurteilen; für unbrauchbar erklären	condemn (to)
condamner qqu'un à une amende	jn zu einer Geldstrafe(f) verurteilen; mit einer Geldstrafe belegen	fine (to) s.o.
condition(f) préalable(m), prérequis	Vorbedingung(f)	prerequisite (condition)
conditionnel	bedingt (durch); abhängig(von)	conditional
libération(f) conditionnelle	Strafaussetzung zur Bewährung; bedingte Entlassung	– discharge
héritage(m) dévolu sous condition résolutoire	auflösende Bedingung (bei Einräumung e-s zeitlich begrenzten Nutzungsrechts)	– limitation
condominium(m), copropriété(f) immobilière	Kondominium; Eigentumswohnung(f) (US)	condominium
conduite(f) contraire aux bonnes moeurs	ordnungswidriges Verhalten(n); ärgernis(n) erregendes Benehmen	disorderly conduct
conduite(f) en état d'ivresse	Trunkenheit(f) am Steuer(m)	drunken driving
conduite(f) visant à induire en erreur	falsche Darstellung(f)	misrepresentation
fraude(f) pénale	arglistige Täuschung; wissentlich falsche Angaben	fraudulent –
déformation(f) des faits	Irreführung durch Vorspiegelung falscher Tatsachen	– of facts
confession(f), aveu(m)	Geständnis(n); Bekenntnis(n)	confession
confiance(f)	Vertrauen; Verlaß(m)	reliance
confiner	angrenzen	abut (to)
confiscation(f)	Konfiszierung(f); Beschlagnahme(f)	confiscation
conforme à la loi, juste, équitable	gerecht; rechtmäßig	just
conjointement et solidairement	gesamtschuldnerisch; solidarisch	jointly and severally
solidairement et conjointement responsable	gesamtschuldnerisch haftbar	– liable
connaissance(f)	Erkenntnis(n); (gerichtliche) Kenntnisnahme; (richterliche) Zuständigkeit(f); Anerkenntnis(n)	cognisance
connection causal, relation(f) de causalité	Kausalzusammenhang(m)	causal connection
connu, constaté, avéré	bekannt	known
faire savoir	bekanntmachen; zur Kenntnis bringen	make –

FRENCH	GERMAN	ENGLISH
conseil(*m*), assemblée(*f*)	**Rat**(*m*); Versammlung(*f*); Ortsbehörde(*n*)	**council**
directive(*f*) du conseil	Weisung, Verfügung, Richtlinie(des Rats)	Council directive
décision(*f*) du conseil	Ratsbeschluß	Council decision
le Conseil de la CE	Rat der Europäischen Gemeinschaft	Council of the EEC
le Conseil de sécurité des Nations Unies	Sicherheitsrat der Vereinten Nationen	UN Security Council
conseiller, recommander, avertir, instruire, aviser de	**(be-)raten;** benachrichtigen, verständigen, mitteilen avisieren	**advise (to)**
conseiller juridique, avocat(*m*) non plaidant, avoué	**Anwalt**(*m*); Rechtsbeistand(*m*)	**solicitor**
consensus	**Konsens**(*m*); Übereinstimmung(*f*)	**consensus**
consentement(*m*) d'un commun accord	**Einwilligung**(*f*); Zustimmung(*f*) in gegenseitigem Einvernehmen; einverständlich	**consent** by mutual –
conséquent, consécutif dommage(*m*) indirect	**kausal bedingt** mittelbarer Schaden, Folgeschaden	**consequential** – damage
conservation(*f*) **des preuves** (US)	**Beweissicherung**(*f*) (US)	**perpetuating testimony** (US)
consignation(*f*)	**Konsignation**(*f*); Hinterlegung(*f*) (Schottland)	**consignation**
consolidation(*f*), fusion(*f*) jonction(*f*) d'instances fusion de sociétés	**Konsolidierung**(*f*); Vereinigung(*f*) Prozeß-, Klagenverbindung Zusammenlegung (od. Fusion) von Gesellschaften	**consolidation** – of actions – of companies
consolidé(*m*), unifié, capitalisé	**konsolidiert**	**consolidated**
consolider, codifier	**konsolidieren;** zusammenlegen	**consolidate (to)**
consommateur(*m*), usager(*m*) crédit(*m*) à la consommation biens de consommation indice(*m*) des prix à la consommation protection(*f*) des consommateurs	**Verbraucher**(*m*) Konsumkredit; Konsumenten- Konsumgüter; Verbrauchs- Index der Verbraucherpreise Verbraucherschutz	**consumer** – credit – goods – price index – protection
consommation(*f*) **du mariage**	**Vollziehung**(*f*) **des Eheaktes**	**consummation of marriage**
consortium(*m*); mariage(*m*) légitime	**Konsortium**(*n*); (Recht der) eheliche(*n*) Lebensgemeinschaft(*f*)	**consortium**
conspiration(*f*), complot(*m*)	**Verschwörung**(*f*); geheime Absprache(*f*)	**conspiracy**
conspirer, comploter	**s. verschwören;** sich heimlich verabreden	**conspire (to)**

FRENCH	GERMAN	ENGLISH
constatation(*f*), reconnaissance(*f*)	**Anerkennung**(*f*); Anerkenntnis(*f*); (Empfangs-)Bestätigung(*f*); Zugeständnis; (notarielle) Beglaubigung	**acknowledgement**
aveu judiciaire	urkundliche Beglaubigung	– by record
récépissé d'une réclamation, d'une plainte	Anerkenntnis der Beanstandung, Beschwerde	– of complaint
reconnaissance de dette	Schuldanerkenntnis	– of debt
constater, vérifier, déterminer	**ermitteln**, feststellen; sich vergewissern	**ascertain (to)**
constater les dégâts, déterminer les préjudices	Schaden feststellen	– damages
constitué, autorisé, enregistré	**eingetragen (als Kapitalgesellschaft)**(*f*)	**incorporate(d)**
doté de la personnalité civile, personne(*f*) morale	Körperschaft	– body
société(*f*) constituée, société enregistrée	rechtsfähige (Handels-) Gesellschaft	– company
constitution(*f*)	**Verfassung**(*f*); Gründung(*f*); Beschaffenheit(*f*)	**constitution**
constitutionnel(*m*), constitutionelle(*f*)	**verfassungsmäßig**, –rechtlich	**constitutional**
tribunal(*m*) constitutionnel	Verfassungsgericht; ordentliches Bundesgericht	– court
droit(*m*) constitutionnel	Verfassungsrecht	– law
consultant(*m*), conseil(*m*), expert(*m*)	**Berater**(*m*)	**consultant**
consultatif	**beratend**; konsultativ	**consultative**
consultation(*f*), délibération	**Beratung**(*f*); Konsultation(*f*)	**consultation**
contestation(*f*), dispute(*f*)	**Behauptung**(*f*); Streit(*m*); Vorbringen	**contention**
contester, défier, interpeller	**ablehnen**; bestreiten; beanstanden; einen Anspruch in Abrede stellen	**challenge (to)**
contester une réclamation, une demande		– a claim
contester un droit; attaquer une décision	ein Recht bestreiten, in Frage stellen	– a right
contester, disputer, attaquer	**bestreiten**; anfechten	**contest (to)**
contigu, contiguë	**angrenzend**; benachbart	**contiguous**
contingence(*f*), cas(*m*) imprévu	**unvorhergesehenes Ereignis**(*n*); Eventualfall(*m*)	**contingency**
fonds(*m*) de réserve	Reserve für unvorhergesehen Ausgaben; Rückstellung für Eventualverbindlichkeiten; Sicherheitsrücklage	– reserve
contractant(*m*), adjudicataire(*m*), entrepreneur(*m*)	**Vertragspartei**(*f*); Lieferant(*m*); Unternehmer(*m*)	**contractor**
contradiction(*f*), contredit(*m*)	**Widerspruch**(*m*); Widerrede(*f*)	**contradiction**
contradictoire	**entgegengesetzt**; sich widersprechend	**contradictory**

FRENCH	GERMAN	ENGLISH
contrainte(f), violence(f)	Zwang(m); Nötigung(f)	compulsion
contrainte, obligation; privation(f) de liberté, internement(m)	Zwang(m), Nötigung(f); Beschränkung(f)	constraint
agir sous la contrainte	unter Zwang handeln	to act under –
contrainte(f) par corps, emprisonnement(m), séquestration(f)	Beschränkung(f); Verhinderung(f); Zurückbehaltung(f)	restraint
contraire à la loi, séditieux, illégal, illicite	ungesetzlich; rechtswidrig	unlawful
contrarier	ankämpfen gegen; sich jdn zum Gegener(m) machen	antagonise
contrat(m), convention(f), pacte(m)	Vertrag(m); Abkommen(n)	contract
contrat bilatéral	zweiseitiger Vertrag	bilateral –
droit(m) des obligations	Vertragsrecht	– law
contrat unilatéral	einseitig verpflichtender Vertrag	unilateral –
contrat(m), convention(f), pacte(m)	Vertragsabrede(f); Verpflichtung(f); Zusicherung(f)	covenant
contrat(m) de dépôt	Besitzübertragung(f) auf Zeit; Verwahrung(f); Verpfändung(f); anvertrautes Gut, hinterlegte Sache	bailment
contrat(m) de vente	Kaufvertrag(m)	sales contract
contrat(m) formel	Besonderheit(f); Spezialität(f)	specialty
contravention(f), infraction(f)	Zuwiderhandlung(f); Übertretung(f); Verstoß(m)	contravention
en violation de	Zuwiderhandlung in verletzung von	in – of
contre-, anti-	entgegengesetzt; wechselseitig	cross
action(f) reconventionnelle, opposition(f)	Wider-, Gegenklage	--action
appel(m) incident	Anschlußberufung	--appeal
revendication(f) dans une action reconventionelle	Gegenanspruch	--claim
contre-interrogatoire(m)	Kreuzverhör	--examination
contre-garantie(f)	beiderseitig Garantie	--guarantee
contre-responsabilité(f)	beiderseitige Haftung	--liability
contre-accusation(f)	Gegenklage(f), –beschuldigung(f)	countercharge
contrebande(f)	Schmuggel(m)	smuggling
contredire	widersprechen; in Abrede stellen	contradict (to)
contrefaçon, faux	Nachahmung(f); Fälschung(f)	counterfeit
contrefaçon	Nachahmung(f); Fälschung(f)	counterfeiting
contrepartie(f); duplicata(m)	Zweitausfertigung(f); Gegenstück(n)	counterpart
contributions(f) indirectes, impôt(m) indirect	indirekte Steuer(m); Verbrauchssteuer(m); Gewerbesteuer(m)	excise tax

FRENCH	GERMAN	ENGLISH
contrôle(*m*), inspection(*f*), vérification(*f*) remise(*f*) de documents à la partie adverse	**Einsichtnahme**(*f*) – in Urkunden, Akten	**inspection** – of documents (*US*)
contrôleur(*m*), inspecteur(*m*), expert(*m*)	**Gutachter**(*m*); Sachverständiger(*m*); Havariekommissar(*m*)	**surveyor**
convention(*f*) **verbale,** contrat(*m*) tacite, contrat sous seing privé	**formloser Vertrag**(*m*)	**simple contract**
convertible titres(*m*) convertibles	**umwandelbar;** konvertierbar konvertierbare Papiere	**convertible** – securities
convertir, transformer, changer	**umwandeln;** –wechseln, –tauschen	**convert (to)**
convoquer, mander, citer citer qqu'un à comparaître devant le tribunal	**laden;** auffordern, zu erscheinen jdn vor Gericht laden	**summon (to)** – s.o. before the court
coopérative, société(*f*) coopérative	**Genossenschaft**(*f*); Konsumverein(*m*)	**cooperative society**
coopter	**hinzuwählen;** kooptieren	**coopt (to)**
copie(*f*) **conforme d'un acte judiciaire,** transcription(*f*)	**Abschrift**(*f*); Ausfertigung(*f*) des Gerichtsprotokolls	**transcript**
'coroner'(*m*)	**richterlicher Beamter**(*m*) **zur Untersuchung**(*f*) **der Todesursache**(*f*)	**coroner**
corporation(*f*), guilde(*f*), corps(*m*) constitué, corps(*m*) de métier	**Körperschaft**(*f*); juristische Person(*f*)	**corporation**
corps(*m*) instance(*f*) administrative personne morale, corps constitué	**Körperschaft**(*f*); Vereinigung(*f*); Gremium(*n*), Organ(*n*) Verwaltungsgremium, –behörde, –stelle juristische Person; Körperschaft	**body** administrative – – corporate
corps(*m*) **du délit**	**Korpus delicti;** Tatbestand (eines Verbrechens)	**corpus delicti**
corps(*m*) **législatif,** législature(*f*)	**Legislative**(*f*); gesetzgebende Körperschaft(*f*)	**legislature**
corrompre, acheter (qqu'un)	**bestechen**	**bribe (to)**
corruption(*f*), séduction(*f*)	**Verführung**(*f*)	**seduction**
cotation(*f*), cours(*m*); référence(*f*)	**Preisangabe**(*f*); –angebot(*n*); Notierung(*f*)	**quotation**
cotation(*f*) prospectus(*m*) d'émission d'action, appel(*m*) à la souscription	**Börsennotierung**(*f*); Zulassung(*f*) Zulassungseinzelheiten (*s. Prospekt*)	**listing** – particulars (*cf. prospectus*)

FRENCH	GERMAN	ENGLISH
coté, énuméré société*(f)* bourse cotée valeurs*(f)* cotées	**börsennotiert** –es Unternehmen –e Wertpapiere	**listed** – company – securities
coter en Bourse, cataloguer, enregistrer	**an der Börse***(m)* **notieren;** listenmäßig erfassen	**list (to)**
coter (une valeur); faire un devis; se référer à, rappeler	**(Preis) angaben***(f)*; notieren	**quote (to)**
coupable; accusé*(m)*, prévenu	**Angeklagter***(m)*; Beschuldigter*(m)*; Täter*(m)*	**culprit**
coupable; volontaire	**schuldhaft;** strafbar	**culpable**
coupable*(m, f)* innocent, non coupable plaider coupable verdict*(m)* de culpabilité	**schuldig** nicht – s. – bekennen Urteil auf-	**guilty** not – to plead – verdict of –
cour*(f)* **d'appel**	**Berufungsgericht***(n)*; Gericht zweiter Instanz	**appellate court**
cour*(f)* **d'assises**	**Assisengericht***(n)*; Geschworenengericht*(n)*, Schwurgericht*(n)*	**assize court**
cour*(f)* **de justice,** tribunal tribunal administratif tribunal d'arbitrage tribunal de première instance *(US)* tribunal civil tribunal de première instance cour d'appel cour*(f)* de juridiction criminelle tribunal*(m)* fédéral de première instance *(US)* cour fédérale tribunal inférieure tribunal de première instance tribunal de police tribunal des successions et des tutelles *(US)* tribunal d'État tribunal supérieure cour suprême tribunal de première instance	**Gericht***(n)* Verwaltungs– Schieds– erstinstanzliches – für mehrere Bezirke *(US)* – für Zivilsachen Grafschafts–; Kreis- *(US)*; *Amts-* Berufungs– – für Strafsachen, Strafkammer (Bundes-)Bezirksgericht *(US)* Bundes– unteres –; Instanzgericht erstinstanzliches Gericht (ohne Geschworene); Amts– Polizei– Nachlaß– einzelstaatliches – *(US)* höhere Instanz; übergeordnetes – Oberster Gerichtshof; Oberstes Bundes- *(US) höheres Berufungs-* *erkennendes –; – erster Instanz*	**court** administrative – arbitration – circuit – civil – county – – of appeal criminal – district – *(US)* federal – inferior – magistrates' – police – probate – *(US)* state – superior – supreme – trial –
Cour*(f)* **du Banc du Roi** *(UK)*	**Abteilung***(f)* **des High Court** *(UK);* Gerichtshof*(m)* erster Instanz*(f)*	**King's Bench** *(UK)*
Cour*(f)* **du Banc de la** **Reine** *(UK)*	**Abteilung***(f)* **des High Court** *(UK);* Gerichtshof erster Instanz	**Queen's Bench** **Division** *(UK)*
cour*(f)* **suprême**	**Oberster***(m)* **Gerichtshof***(m)*; Oberstes Bundesgericht *(US);* *höheres Berufungsgericht*	**supreme court**

FRENCH	GERMAN	ENGLISH
Couronne(*f*) **(l'État)**	**Krone**(*f*)	**Crown**
cour d'assises	Gericht für Strafsachen und einige Zivilsachen (*England und Wales*)	– Court
courtier(*m*)**,** agent(*m*) de change	**Makler**(*m*)**,** Vermittler(*m*)	**broker**
courtier(*m*) **maritime**	**Schiffsmakler**(*m*)	**shipbroker**
coût(*m*) **marginal**	**Grenzkosten**	**marginal cost**
couvert	**geschützt;** gedeckt; heimlich	**covert**
couverture(*f*)**,** arbitrage(*m*)**,** contrepartie(*f*)	**Sicherungsgeschäft**(*n*)**;** Deckungsgeschäft(*n*)	**hedge**
créance(*f*)**,** titre de créance; droit(*m*) incorporel permettant une action en justice	**Forderungsrecht**(*n*)**;** obligatorischer Anspruch(*m*)	**chose in action**
créance(*f*)**;** revendication(*f*)**,** requête(*f*); droit(*m*) qu'on entend faire valoir en justice	**Anspruch**(*m*)**;** Forderung(*f*)**;** Behauptung(*f*); Klagebegehren	**claim**
action(*f*) en dommages-intérêts	Schadensersatzanspruch, – forderung	– for damages
demande(*f*) de déduction	Rechtsmittelanspruch	– for relief
demande reconventionnelle	Gegenanspruch; Widerklage	counter-
demande déclaratoire	deklaratorischer Anspruch, Feststellungs–	declaratory –
créancier(*m*) **gagiste**(*m*)**,** prêteur(*m*) sur gages	**Pfandnehmer**(*m*)**;** –gläubiger(*m*)	**pledgee**
créancier hypothécaire	**Hypothekengläubiger**(*m*)**;** Pfandgläubiger(*m*)	**mortgagee**
créancier saisissant	**Vollstreckungsgläubiger**(*m*)**;** (Pfändungs-)Pfandgläubiger(*m*) (*US*); Partei die Forderungspfändung(*f*) bewirkt hat	**garnisher**
créateur(*m*)**,** promoteur(*m*)	**Urheber**(*m*)**;** Begründer(*m*)	**originator**
crédibilité(*f*)	**Glaubwürdigkeit**(*f*)	**credibility**
crédit(*m*)	**Kredit**(*m*)**;** Darlehen(*n*)**;** Guthaben(*n*)	**credit**
crédit(*m*) **documentaire**	**Dokumentenakkreditiv**(*n*)	**documentary credit**
créditeur(*m*)**,** créancier(*m*)	**Gläubiger**(*m*)**;** Kreditgeber(*m*)	**creditor**
crime(*m*)	**Verbrechen;** strafbare Handlung(*f*), Straftat(*f*)	**crime**
crime(*m*)**,** délit(*m*), acte(*m*) délictueux, toute violation(*f*) de la loi	**Straftat**(*f*)**;** Delikt(*n*)	**offence**
crime, infraction(*f*) pénale	strafbare Handlung	criminal –
acte délictueux, crime, délit	Verbrechen, schweres Vergehen	indictable –
délit commis par un mineur	Jugendstraftat	juvenile –

FRENCH	GERMAN	ENGLISH
crime(m) **d'incendie volontaire**	**Brandstiftung**(f)	**arson**
crime(m) **d'ordre sexuel**	**Sexualverbrechen**	**sex crime**
criminel, délinquant(m), contrevenant	**Täter**(m)	**offender**
délinquant primaire récidiviste(m) délinquant juvénile	Erst-, Nichtvorbestrafter Gewohnheits– jugendlicher –	first – habitual – juvenile –
criminel, fait avec intention de nuire, malveillant	**böswillig**	**malicious**
acte(m) criminel	–e Handlung; vorsätzlich rechtswidrige Handlung	– act
but(m) délictueux	–e Absicht	– intent
criminel(m) (n et adj.) action(f) au criminel	**kriminell; strafbar; strafrechtlich** Strafverfahren; strafrechtliche Verfolgung;	**criminal** – action
inculpation(f) de crime cour(f) de juridiction criminelle droit(m) pénal, droit criminel	Anklage wegen e-s Verbrechens Gericht für Strafsachen; Strafkammer Strafrecht	– charge – court – law
casier(m) judiciaire	Strafregister; Vorstrafe(nverzeichnis)	– record
cruauté(f), **mauvais traitements**(m)	**Grausamkeit**(f)	**cruelty**
cruauté mentale, excès(m) et injures(f) graves	seelische Grausamkeit	mental –
culpabilité(f)	**Schuld**(f)	**guilt**

D

FRENCH	GERMAN	ENGLISH
d'accroissement	**Zunahme**(*f*)**;** (Wert-)Zuwachs(*m*)	**increment**
danger(*m*)**,** risque(*m*); jeu(*m*) de hasard	**Gefahr**(*f*)**;** Risiko(*n*)	**hazard**
danger(*m*)**,** risque(*m*) être traduit en justice pour un crime ou un délit dont on a déjà eu à répondre	**Gefährdung**(*f*) Verbot der doppelten Strafverfolgung eines Täters wegen derselben Tat	**jeopardy** double –
d'application(*f*) **générale** carte blanche	**generell,** alles umfassend; Gesamt–Blankovollmacht	**blanket** – authority
date(*f*) date limite	**Datum**(*n*)**;** Zeitpunkt(*m*); Termin Abschlußtermin; Anmeldeschluß; Abschlußstichtag	**date** closing –
date d'expiration date de remboursement, date d'amortissement date de cessation, date de résiliation	Verfallstag; Ablauftermin Tilgungstermin; Einlösungstermin Ablauf–, Enddatum; Tag des Außerkrafttretens	expiry – redemption – termination –
date(*f*) **de survenance;** date(*f*) de naissance (d'un droit); échéance(*f*)	**Anfall**(*m*)**;** Auflauf(*m*) (Zinsen); Entstehung(*f*) (Anspruch, Recht)	**accrual**
date limite, date de clôture	**Stichtag**(*m*)**;** (letzter) Termin(*m*); Anmeldeschluss(*n*)	**deadline**
de propriété, de propriétaire droits(*m*) de propriété	**Eigentums-** –rechte(*n*)	**proprietary** – rights
débats (les)(*m*)	**Schriftsätze**(*m*)	**pleadings**
débiteur(*m*)	**Schuldner**(*m*)**;** Darlehens–, Kreditnehmer(*m*)	**debtor**
débiteur(*m*) **hypothécaire**	**Hypothekenschuldner**(*m*)**;** Verpfänder(*m*)	**mortgagor**
décernement, attribution(*f*); jugement(*m*) irrévocable (définitif); sentence(*f*) arbitrale; adjudication(*f*); dommages-intérêts(*m*) prononcement d'une sentence (d'un jugement)	**Belohnung**(*f*)**;** Zuerkennung(*f*); Schiedsurteil(*n*); Rechtsspruch Urteil sprechen, (durch Urteil) zuerkennen	**award** – of a judgment

FRENCH	GERMAN	ENGLISH
déchu, périmé, caduc	**erloschen;** verfallen; hinfällig geworden	**lapsed**
droit(*m*) d'auteur périmé assurance(*f*) périmée	erloschenes Urheberrecht verfallene Versicherung	– copyright – insurance
décider, régir, gouverner 'le tribunal a décidé que'	**entscheiden;** beschließen 'das Gericht verfügt, daß'	**rule (to)** 'the court rules that'
décisif, absolu, péremptoire argument(*m*) décisif exception(*f*) péremptoire, récusation(*f*) de jurés défense(*f*) au fond	**peremptorisch;** zwingend zwingendes Argument Ablehnung der Geschworenen ohne Angabe von Gründen peremptorischer Einwand	**peremptory** – argument – challenge – defence
décision(*f*), résolution(*f*) décision de justice, verdict(*m*)	**Beschluß(*m*);** Entscheidung(*f*); Urteil(*n*) (Zivilprozeß)(*m*) gerichtliche Entscheidung, Urteil (s. Zivil– od. Strafurteil; Urteilsspruch)	**decision** court – (*cf. judgment*)
décision(*f*) judiciaire faisant jurisprudence; précédent(*m*)	**Präzedenzfall(*m*)**	**precedent**
déclaration(*f*); décision(*f*) judiciaire; dispositif(*m*) de jugement déclaration de faillite déclaration de consentement déclaration de désaccord déclaration d'intention; demande(*f*) de naturalisation (*US*)	**Erklärung(*f*);** Klageschrift(*f*); (Wert-)Angabe(*f*); Zolldeklaration(*f*) Konkurserklärung, –eröffnung Einverständnis–, Zustimmungserklärung Beschwerde Willens–, Absichtserklärung	**declaration** – of bankruptcy – of consent – of dissent – of intention
déclaration(*f*), exposé(*m*), rapport(*m*), relevé(*m*) plaidoirie(*f*) finale compte(*m*) de recettes déclaration de revenus plaidoirie inaugurale relevé de compte demande(*m*) introductive d'instance; conclusion(*f*) en matière de dommages-intérêts conclusions de la défense déposition(*f*) sous serment	**Bericht(*m*);** Aufstellung(*f*); Auszug(*f*) Schlußbericht; –plädoyer Finanzbericht; Rechnungsabschluß Erfolgsrechnung; Ertragsbilanz Eröffnungsplädoyer Kontoauszug; Abrechnung Klagebegründung Klagebeantwortung eidliche (Zeugen)Erklärung	**statement** closing – financial – income – opening – – of account – of claim – of defence sworn –
déclaration(*f*) (avis) d'appel	**Berufungsantrag;** Berufungsschrift(*f*); Beschwerdeschrift(*f*)	**appeal (notice of)**
déclaratoire jugement(*m*) déclaratoire	**feststellend;** (rechts-)erklärend; deklaratorisch Feststellungsurteil	**declaratory** – judgment
déclarer, énoncer, fixer	**erklären;** aussagen	**state (to)**
découvert(*m*)	**Mangel(*m*);** Fehlbetrag(*m*), Minderbetrag(*m*)	**deficiency**

191

FRENCH	GERMAN	ENGLISH
découverte(f), divulgation(f)	**Entdeckung**(f), Enthüllung(f); Ermittlung(f); Offenlegung(f)	**discovery**
procédure(f) en vue d'identifier les actifs d'une succession	Entdeckungsverfahren	– proceedings
découvrir	**aufdecken;** enthüllen	**uncover (to)**
décret(m), décision(f) d'ordre judiciaire ou administratif	**Urteil**(n); Verfügung(f); Verordnung(f) (s. *Urteilsspruch*)	**decree** (cf. *judgment*)
jugement définitif	rechtskräftiges Scheidungsurteil	– absolute
jugement provisoire; jugement interlocutoire	vorläufiges Scheidungsurteil	– nisi
jugement de divorce	Scheidungsurteil	divorce –
jugement final	Endurteil, rechtskräftiges Urteil	final –
défaillance(f), erreur(f); caducité(f), extinction; laps(m) (de temps)	**Erlöschen**	**lapse**
déchéance(f) d'un brevet	– e-s Patents	– of patent
déchéance de droits	– e-s Rechts	– of rights
laps de temps	Fristablauf; Verjährung	– of time
défendeur(m); intimé	**Beklagter**(m); Antragsgegner(m); (siehe(m) Berufungsbeklagter)	**respondent**
défense(f), moyens(m) de défense; cause(f) (US), procès(m)	**Einrede;** Vorbringen	**plea**
– conclusion(f) de le défense	Klageerwiderung	defendant's –
exception(f) dilatoir	dilatorische, aufschiebende Einrede	dilatory –
aveu(m) de culpabilité fait à l'audience	Schuldbekenntnis; Schuldigerklärung	– of guilty
exception de nullité	Nichtigkeitsbeschwerde; – der Rechtsunwirksamkeit	– of nullity
appel(m) à la clémence, recours(m) en grâce	Gnadengesuch	– for mercy
défense(f); la défense	**Einrede**(f); Einlassung(f); Klagebeantwortung(f)	**defence**
avocat(m) de la défense, défenseur	Verteidiger; Anwalt des Beklagten	– counsel
conclusions(f) de la défense	Klagebeantwortung; Verteidigungsvorbringen	statement of –
témoin(m) de la défense	Entlastungszeuge; von der Verteidigung benannter Zeuge	witness for the –
défense(f) expresse, interdiction(f), prohibition	**Verbot**(n); Untersagung(f)	**inhibition**
défenseur(m), défenderesse(f), accusé,-e	**Beklagter**(m); Angeklagter(m)	**defendant**
déficit(m)	**Defizit**(n); Minder–, Fehlbetrag(m); Passivsaldo(m)	**deficit**
défrayer	**(Kosten) bestreiten;** aufkommen für	**defray (to)**
d'égale intensité	**unvermindert**	**unabated**

FRENCH	GERMAN	ENGLISH
dégâts(m), dommages(m), méfait(m)	**Mißstand**(m); Schaden(m); Unheil(n)	**mischief**
degré(m)	**Grad**(m); Rang(m); (s. Mord)	**degree** (cf. murder)
délai(m), limite(f) de temps	**Frist**(f); Zeitbeschränkung(f)	**time-limit**
délégation(f); renvoi(m); incarcération renvoi devant la cour d'assises; mise(f) en accusation	**Überweisung**(f), Einlieferung(f); Verhaftung(f) Anordnung der Hauptverhandlung (Strafprozeß)	**committal** – for trial
déléguer déléguer une responsabilité	**delegieren**; weiterübertragen Verantwortung übertragen	**delegate (to)** – responsibility
délibéré(m), prémédité, voulu	**absichtlich**, vorsätzlich; (wohl-) überlegt	**deliberate**
délinquant(m) **en liberté surveillée**	**bedingt Entlassener**	**parolee**
délinquence(f) délinquence juvénile	**Pflichtverletzung**(f), Vergehen(n); Kriminalität(f) Jugendkriminalität	**delinquency** juvenile –
délit de fuite	**Fahrerflucht**(f)	**hit-and-run driving**
délit(m) **d'ordre sexuel**	**Sittlichkeitsvergehen**	**sexual offence**
demande(f) **reconventionnelle**	**Gegenforderung**(f), –anspruch(m)	**counterclaim**
demander l'homologation d'un testament	**klagen auf Testamentsanerkennung**(f)	**propound (to) a will**
demandeur(m), requérant(m), pétitionnaire(f, m), ayant(m) droit	**Antragsteller**(m); Bewerber(m); Anmelder(m)	**applicant**
demandeur(m), partie(f) requérante	**Anspruchsteller**(m); Antragsteller(m); Kläger(m)	**claimant**
demeure, résidence	**Aufenthaltsort**(m), Wohnsitz(m)	**abode**
demeurer; se conformer, se soumettre	**anerkennen**, befolgen	**abide by (to)**
dénégation(f), déni(m), démenti(m)	**Bestreitung**(f); Ableugnung(f); abschlägiger Bescheid(m)	**denial**
dénoncer	**anzeigen**; denunzieren; (Vertrag)(m) kündigen	**denounce (to)**
dénonciateur(m), délateur(m)	**Informant**(m); Gewährsmann(m)	**informant**
départ(m); écart(m) dérogation(f) aux dispositions légales	**Abweichen**; Klageänderung(f) Abweichen von den gesetzlichen Vorschriften	**departure** – from statutory regulations
déposant(m)	**Übergeber**(m); Hinterleger(m), Verpfänder(m)	**bailor**
déposant(m)	**Hinterleger**(m); Einzahler(m)	**depositor**
déposer	**eidlich** bezeugen; vor Gericht(n) aussagen; absetzen	**depose (to)**

FRENCH	GERMAN	ENGLISH
déposer (des documents au greffe); saisir, confisquer	**in Verwahrung**(f) **nehmen** (gerichtlich od. behördlich)	**impound (to)**
dépositaire(m)	**Übernehmer**(m); Depositar(m), Verwahrer(m)	**bailee**
dépositaire(m); consignation(f)	**Verwahrer**(m); Depositar(m); Hinterlegungsstelle	**depositary**
déposition(f)	**Zeugenaussage**(f); Beweisaufnahmeprotokoll(n); Hinterlegung(f); Absetzung(f)	**deposition**
témoignage(m) déposition d'un témoin	eidliche Zeugenaussage Zeugenaussage	– of evidence – of witness
déposition(f) **d'un témoin,** attestation(f), témoignage(m)	**Zeugenaussage**(f)	**testimony**
déposséder, dessaisir, exproprier	**(widerrechtlich) Besitz**(m) **entziehen;** zur Räumung(f) zwingen	**dispossess (to)**
dépôt(m)	**Anzahlung**(f); Einlage(f); Hinterlegung(f); Sicherheitsleistung(f); Verwahrung(f)	**deposit**
dépôt de garantie	Einlagegarantie	– guarantee
dépôt(m) **fiduciaire,** dépôt conditionnel	**vorläufige Hinterlegung**(f) **e-r Urkunde**(f)**;** bei e-m Treuhänder(m) hinterlegte Urkunde(f)	**escrow**
dérangement, perturbation(f), trouble	**Behinderung**(f); Störung(f)	**disturbance**
atteinte(f) à l'ordre public	Störung der öffentlichen Ordnung (Ruhe)	– of public order
dérogation(f), diminution(f)	**Beeinträchtigung**(f); Minderung(f); teilweise Außerkraftsetzung	**derogation**
déroger, porter atteinte à	**beeinträchtigen;** Abbruch(m) tun; (teilweise) aufheben	**derogate (to)**
désaccord(m)	**Meinungsverschiedenheit**(f); Widerspruch(m)	**disagreement**
désaccord(m), contradiction(f)	**Widerspruch**(m); Unstimmigkeit(f); Abweichung(f)	**discrepancy**
désaveu(m); renonciation(f)	**Ableugnung**(f), Ver–; s. Verzicht(m)	**abnegation** (cf. waiver)
désavouer, renier	**(ab-, ver-)leugnen;** nichts zu tun haben mit; verstoßen	**disown (to)**
descendance(f)	**Nachkommenschaft**(f); Abkomme(m)	**offspring**
descente(f), rafle(f) de police, raid	**Überfall**(m); Razzia(f)	**raid**
désertion(f)	**Verlassen;** Fahnenflucht	**desertion**
déshérence(f), bien(m) tombé en déshérence	**Heimfall**(m) **herrenlosen Vermögens an den Staat**(m); Staatserbrecht	**escheat**

FRENCH	GERMAN	ENGLISH
déshériter	**enterben**	**disinherit (to)**
déshonorer refuser le paiement d'une traite, ne pas honorer une traite	**nicht erfüllen**; zurückweisen e-n Wechsel nicht bezahlen, – einlösen	**dishonour (to)** – a bill
désignation(f) **des membres du jury**	**Aufstellung**(f) **der Geschworenenliste**	**impanelling,** alternative spelling of empanelling
désigner, nommer, établir, choisir désigner un tuteur désigner un trustee	**anordnen,** bestimmen; bestellen, ernennen zu e-n Vormund bestellen e-n Treuhänder bestellen	**appoint (to)** – a guardian – a trustee
désobéir	**nicht befolgen**; mißachten	**disobey (to)**
désobéissance(f)	**Ungehorsam;** Gehorsamsverweigerung	**disobedience**
désordre(m)	**Unruhe**(f); Störung(f)	**disorder**
dessein(m)**,** motif(m)**,** but(m)**,** intention(f) intention malveillante intention criminelle intention frauduleuse	**Vorsatz**(m) strafrechtlicher – böswillige Absicht betrügerische Absicht	**intent** criminal – evil – fraudulent –
destinataire	**Konsignatar;** Empfänger	**consignee**
désuétude(f)**,** obsolescence(f), caducité(m); amortissement(m) industriel	**Überalterung**(f) (technisch oder wirtschaftlich); Wertminderung(f) wegen –	**obsolescence**
détaxe(f)	**Gebührenerlaß**(m)	**remission of charges**
détenir envoyer en prison	**begrenzen;** inhaftieren in Gefängnishaft nehmen	**confine (to)** – to prison
détenteur(m)**,** porteur(m) détenteur(m) de bonne foi actionnaire(m)	**Inhaber**(m); Besitzer(m) Treuhänder Aktien–	**holder** – in trust – of shares, shareholder
détention	**(Untersuchungs-)Haft**(f); Festnahme(f); Zurückhaltung(f), Beschlagnahme	**detention**
détention(f)**,** prise de possession	**(widerrechtliche) Vorenthaltung**(f) **(Grundbesitz);** Haftbefehl	**detainer**
détention(f)**,** dissimulation(f), refus(m) dissimulation de preuve impôt(m) retenu à la source	**Zurückbehaltung**(f); Ein– Verschweigen von Beweisen Abzugssteuer; Quellensteuer	**withholding** – of evidence – tax
détenu(m)**,** interné(m, f)	**Insasse**(m)	**inmate**
détournement(m) **(d'avion)**	**(Flugzeug-)**(n)**Entführung**(f)	**hijacking**
détourner, escroquer (des fonds)	**veruntreuen;** unterschlagen	**embezzle (to)**

FRENCH	GERMAN	ENGLISH
détresse(f), désespoir(m); saisie(f) en cas de non-paiement du loyer	**Inbesitznahme**(f); Beschlagnahme(f); Not(lage)(f)	**distress**
détriment(m), préjudice(m), perte(f)	**Nachteil**(m); Schaden(m); Beeinträchtigung(f)	**detriment**
dette(f), créance(f) créance douteuse titre(m) de créance dette à recouvrer créance préférentielle	**Schuld**(f); Forderung(f) zweifelhafte Forderung Schuldurkunde (pl.) Außenstände bevorrechtigte Schuld, Forderung	**debt** doubtful – instrument of – outstanding – preferential –
dette(f) **passive**	**unverzinsliche Schuld**(f); nicht-zinstragende Forderung(f)	**passive debt**
déviation(f), écart(m); dérogation(f)	**Abweichung**(f); Deviation(f)	**deviation**
devoir(m), obligation(f); fonction(f), responsabilité(f); service(m) commandé; droit(m), impôt(m), taxe(f) droits de douane	**Pflicht**(f); Aufgabe(f); Abgabe(f) Zollgebühr	**duty** customs –
d'exploitation capital(m) d'exploitation frais(m) d'exploitation, dépenses(f) de fonctionnement résultat(m) d'exploitation	**Betriebs-** –kapital(n) –aufwendungen(f) –ergebnis(n)	**operating** – capital – expenses – result
diffamation(f)	**Ehrverletzung**(f); Beleidigung(f); Verleumdung(f)	**defamation**
diffamation(f), libelle(m), écrit diffamatoire	**Beleidigung**(f); Verleumdung(f); Klage(f)	**libel**
diffamation(m) **publiée dans un journal**	**Verleumdung**(f) **durch die Presse**	**press libel**
diffamation(f) **verbale**	**üble Nachrede**(f); (mündliche Beleidigung)(f)	**slander**
diffamatoire	**beleidigend**; diffamierend; verleumderisch	**defamatory**
diffamatoire	**beleidigend**; verleumderisch	**libellous**
différé, ajourné paiement différé	**aufgeschoben**; gestundet; zurückgestellt hinausgeschobene Zahlung; Ratenzahlung (US)	**deferred** – payment
différer, ajourner	**aufschieben**; zurückstellen	**defer (to)**
dilatoire exception(f) dilatoire	**dilatorisch**; aufschiebend dilatorische (od. prozeßhindernde) Einrede	**dilatory** – plea
diminution(f), réduction(f) action en réduction	**Aufhebung**(f); Nachlaß(m), Ermäßigung(f); Aussetzung(f), Einstellung(f) Minderungsklage	**abatement** – of action

FRENCH	GERMAN	ENGLISH
diminution(f), restriction(f)	**Abkürzung**(f), Auszug(m), Zusammenfassung(f); Einschränkung(f), Beeinträchtigung(f)	**abridgement**
direct	**direkt;** unmittelbar	**direct**
frais(m) spéciaux	direkte Kosten, Einzelkosten; leistungsabhängige Kosten	– cost
dommages(m) directs	unmittelbarer Schaden	– damage
descendant(m) direct	direkter Nachkomme	– descendant
preuve(f) directe	unmittelbarer Beweis	– evidence
interrogatoire(m) direct	erste Befragung des Zeugen durch die den Zeugen stellende Partei	– examination
directeur(m), gérant(m), gestionnaire(m)	**Manager**(m); Geschäftsführer(m)	**manager**
direction(f), administration(f), gestion(f), gérance(f), exploitation(f); management(m), technique de gestion	**Management**(n)	**management**
gestion de société	Unternehmensführung; Geschäftsleitung	company –
comité(m) chargé des comptes de gestion	Abrechnungsausschuß	– committee
société(f) de gérance	Verwaltungsgesellschaft	– company
direction(f); ordre(m), prescription(f)	**Anordnung**(f); Leitung(f); Rechtsbelehrung(f)	**direction**
directive(f)	**Richtlinie**(f); Anordnung(f) (EG)	**directive** (EC law)
directive du Conseil	EG-Rat Richtlinie	Council –
directives(f)	**Richtlinien**(f)	**guidelines**
discrédit(m), déconsidération(f)	**Mißkredit**(m); schlechter Ruf(m); Unglaubwürdigkeit(f)	**discredit**
discrétion(f), pouvoir discrétionnaire	**Ermessen**(n); Diskretion(f); Klugheit(f)	**discretion**
discrétionnaire	**beliebig;** Ermessens-	**discretionary**
discrimination(f)	**Diskriminierung**(f); Benachteiligung(f)	**discrimination**
discriminatoire	**diskriminierend;** unterscheidend	**discriminatory**
législation(f) d'exception	Ausnahmegesetzgebung	– legislation
mesure(f) discriminatoire	diskriminierende Maßnahme	– measure
politique(f) de discrimination, de favoritisme	diskriminierende Politik	– policy
procédure(f) d'exception	diskriminierendes Verfahren	– procedure
traitement(m) discriminatoire	unterschiedliche Behandlung	– treatment
disculpation(f)	**Entschuldigung**(f); Rechtfertigung(f)	**exculpation**
dispense(f)	**Befreiung**(f); Verteilung(f); Erlassung(f)	**dispensation**
exercice(m), pratique de la justice	Rechtsanwendung; Rechtsprechung	– of justice

FRENCH	GERMAN	ENGLISH
disponibilité(f), liquidité(f) taux(m) de liquidité	**Liquidität**(f) –sgrad	**liquidity** – ratio
disponible	**ab Lager**(n)	**ex store**
disponible, liquide liquidités(f) disponibilités(f)	**flüssig;** liquid(e) Umlaufkapital flüssige Mittel; Bargeld	**liquid** – assets – funds
disponible; lieu(m) précis, point; message(m) publicitaire march(m)é au comptant cours(f) du disponible opération(f) au comptant	**Spot**(m) –markt –kurs; Kassakurs –geschäft; Kassageschäft	**spot** – market – rate – transaction
disposition(f) de bonne disposition	**testierfähig;** verfügungs– testierfähig sein	**disposing** of – mind
disposition(s)(f), clause(s)(f), stipulation(s)(f) clause(s) restrictive(s) disposition(s) statutaire(s)	**Bestimmung(en)**(f); Vorschrift(en)(f) einschränkende – gesetzliche –	**provision(s)** restrictive – statutory –
disposition testamentaire, cession(f) (de biens)	**Verfügungsgewalt**(f); Anordnung(f); Bestimmung(f)	**disposition**
disposition(f) **testamentaire de biens immobiliers**	**letztwillige Verfügung**(f) **(Vermächtnis**(n) **über Grundbesitz)**(m)	**devise**
dissentiment(m), différence(f) d'opinion	**Dissens**(m), Meinungsverschiedenheit(f)	**dissent**
dissident, opposant	**abweichend;** andersdenkend	**dissentient**
dissimulation(f); recel(m) dissimulation de preuves	**Verbergen**(n); Verheimlichung(f); Verschleierung(f); Verschweigen Unterdrücken von Beweismaterial	**concealment** – of evidence
dissimuler, cacher	**verbergen;** verheimlichen; verschleiern; verschweigen	**conceal (to)**
dissolution(f) dissolution du mariage	**Auflösung**(f); Aufhebung(f) Auflösung der Ehe	**dissolution** – of marriage
dissolution(f), liquidation(f) liquidation d'une société	**Abwicklung**(f) – e-r Gesellschaft	**winding up** – of a company
distribution(f), répartition(f), partage(m) paiement(m) des dividendes partage des biens	**Verteilung**(f); Distribution(f) Ausschüttung der Dividende Vermögensverteilung	**distribution** – of dividends – of property
district(m), quartier(m) procureur(m) de la République (US) tribunal(m) fédéral de première instance (US) ressort(m) territorial d'un tribunal	**Bezirk**(m), Kreis(m) (Bezirks-)Staatsanwalt (US) (Bundes-)Bezirksgericht (US) Gerichtsbezirk	**district** – attorney (US) – court (US) judicial –
divergence(f) divergence d'opinions	**Abweichung**(f) Meinungsverschiedenheit	**divergence** – of opinion
dividende(m)	**Dividende**(f)	**dividend**

FRENCH	GERMAN	ENGLISH
divorce(*m*)	**Scheidung**(*f*)	**divorce**
action(*f*) en divorce	Ehescheidungsverfahren	– proceedings
docteur(*m*) **endroit**	**Doktortitel**(*m*) **der juristischen Fakultät**(*f*)	**LLD**
doctrine(*f*)	**Lehre**(*f*), Doktrin(*f*)	**doctrine**
document(*m*), dossier(*m*)	**Niederschrift**(*f*); Urkunde(*f*); Protokoll	**record**
dossier du tribunal	Gerichtsakte	court –
casier(*m*) judiciaire	Vorstrafenregister	criminal –
procès-verbal(*m*) de témoignage	Beweisaufnahme	– of evidence
domicile(*m*)	**Domizil**(*n*); Wohnsitz(*m*); Firmensitz(*m*)	**domicile**
domicile(*m*), foyer(*m*)	**Binnen-;** inländisch	**home**
pays (terre) natale; pays d'origine	Heimat, Heimatland	– country
pays(*m*) membre permanent (*CEE*)	EG-Heimatstaat	– member State (*EEC*)
domicile(*m*) **habituel**	**gewöhnlicher Aufenthaltsort**(*m*)	**habitual residence**
domiciliaire	**den Wohnort**(*m*) **betreffend;** Heimats–	**domiciliary**
dommage(*m*), dégât(*m*)	**Schaden**(*m*); Beschädigung(*f*); Verlust(*m*)	**damage**
dommage réel	tatsächlicher Schaden	actual –
dommage indirect	mittelbarer Schaden; Folgeschaden	consequential –
dégâts criminels	strafbare Sachbeschädigung	criminal –
dommage direct	unmittelbarer Schaden	direct –
dommage général	Gesamtschaden; allgemeiner Schaden	general –
dommage partiel	Teilschaden	partial –
dommages-intérêts(*m*) **non liquidés**	**(der Höhe nach) unbestimmter Schadensersatz**(*m*); unbezifferte Schadensforderung	**unliquidated damages**
dommages-intérêts(*m*) **pour préjudice moral**	**verschärfter Schadensersatz**(*m*)	**exemplary damages**
don(*m*)	**Schenkung**(*f*); Zuwendung	**gift**
legs(*m*) à payer d'une source spécifiée	beschränkte (aus bestimmten Mitteln erfüllte) Schenkung	demonstrative –
don placé sous tutelle	Schenkung zu treuen Händen	– in trust
impôt(*m*) sur les donations	Schenkungssteuer	– tax
donataire(*m*), bénéficiaire(*m*)	**Schenkungsempfänger**(*m*); Begünstigter(*m*)	**donee**
données(*f*), constatations(*f*)	**Untersuchungsergebnis**(*n*); Befund(*m*)	**findings**
conclusions(*f*) du tribunal, verdict	(tatsächliche) Feststellungen des Gerichts	court's –
conclusions interlocutoires	Zwischenentscheidung	interlocutory –
conclusions d'un tribunal	Richterspruch; Gerichtsurteil; richterliche Feststellungen	judicial –

FRENCH	GERMAN	ENGLISH
donner en partage, assigner, imposer, déléguer, céder	**abtreten,** übereignen; bestimmen, ernennen	**assign (to)**
attribuer des biens	Vermögen übertragen	– property
donner le droit de	**nennen,** betiteln; berechtigen	**entitle (to)**
donneur(*m*), donateur(*m*)	**Schenkungsgeber**(*m*); Stifter(*m*)	**donor**
dot(*f*)	**Mitgift**(*f*); Aussteuer(*m*)	**dowry**
dotation(*f*) apports(*m*) en capital assurance(*f*) à capital différé	**Ausstattung**(*f*); Stiftung(*f*) Stiftungskapital Lebensversicherung auf Todes- und Erlebensfall	**endowment** – capital – insurance
douaire(*m*)	**Mitgift**(*f*); lebenslängliches Nießbrauchrecht des verwitweten Ehegatten an 1/3 des Grundbesitzes des verstorbenen (*US*)	**dower**
douanes(*f*) expédition(*f*) en douane déclaration(*f*) en douane droits(*m*) de douane union(*f*) douanière	**Zoll**(*m*); Zollbehörde(*f*) Zollabfertigung; Verzollung Zollerklärung; Zollanmeldung Zollgebühren, –abgaben Zollunion, –verband	**customs** – clearance – declaration – duties – union
double incrimination	**Verbot**(*n*) **der doppelten Strafverfolgung**(*f*) **eines Täters wegen derselben Tat;**	**double jeopardy**
douloureux, pénible	**schädlich;** nachteilig	**hurtful**
doute(*m*) quasi-certitude du jury rendant un verdict de culpabilité, conviction(*f*) dépassant la croyance en un doute raisonnable	**Zweifel**(*m*); Bedenken(*n*) jeder vernünfige Zweifel ausgeschlossen	**doubt** beyond reasonable –
dresser, faire établir, rédiger tirer un cheque dresser une facture	**ausstellen** e-n Scheck – e-e Rechnung –	**make out** – a cheque – an invoice
droit(*m*), intérêt(*m*) acquis	**sicher begründetes Anrecht**(*n*); berechtigte Interesse	**vested interest**
droit(*m*); compétence(*f*) judiciaire	**Gerichtsbarkeit**(*f*); Gerichtshoheit(*f*); Gerichtsstand(*m*); Rechtsprechung(*f*)	**jurisdiction**
toutes matières contentieuses, compétence générale	allgemeine Zuständigkeit	general –
compétence d'exception	besondere Zuständigkeit	special –

FRENCH	GERMAN	ENGLISH
droit(*m*); science(*f*) juridique; législation(*f*), loi(*f*) procédure(*f*)	**Recht**(*n*)	**law**
droit administratif	formelles –, Prozeß–	adjective –
droit aérien	Verwaltungs–	administrative –
droit bancaire	Luft–	air –
droit des faillites	Bank–	banking –
droit des précédents	Konkurs–	bankruptcy –
droit civil	Fall–	case –
droit coutumier, droit commun	Zivil–	civil –
droit communautaire	Gewohnheits–	common –
droit des sociétés	Gemeinschaftsrecht (*EG*)	Community –
droit constitutionnel	Gesellschafts–; Aktien–	company –
droit des obligations	Verfassungs–	constitutional –
droit des sociétés (*US*)	Vertrags–; Schuld–	contract –
droit criminel	Gesellschafts–; Aktien– (*US*)	corporation – (*US*)
droit électoral	Straf–	criminal –
droit communautaire	Wahl–; Wahlgesetz	electoral –
droit du travail	EG-Recht	EEC –
droit de l'environnement	Arbeitsrecht	employment –
droit de la famille	Recht zum Schutz der Umwelt	environmental –
droit fédéral	Familien–	family –
droit financier	Bundes–; Bundesgesetz	federal –
droit fiscal	Finanzgesetz	financial –
droit des assurances	Steuer–	fiscal –
droit international	Versicherungs–	insurance –
droit du travail	internationales –	international –
droit maritime	Arbeits–	labour –
loi martiale, état de siège	See–	maritime –
droit du mariage	Stand–;Kriegs–	martial –
droit commercial	Ehe–	matrimonial –
droit militaire, code de justice militaire	Handels–	mercantile –
droit pénal	Militär(straf)–; Wehr(straf)–	military –
droit positif	Straf–; Strafgesetz	penal –
droit privé	positives Recht	positive –
droit de la procédure	Privat–	private–
droit de la propriété	Verfahrens–	procedural –
droit public	Liegenschafts–; Sachen–	property –
droit romain	öffentliches –	public –
loi fiscale	Römisches –	Roman –
	Steuer–; Steuergesetz	tax –
droit(*m*) **commercial**	**Handelsrecht**(*n*)	**mercantile law**
droit(*m*) **coutumier**	**Gewohnheitsrecht**(*n*)	**customary law**
droit(*m*) **coutumier et jurisprudentiel**	**Gewohnheitsrecht**(*n*); (ungeschriebenes) geme in Recht	**common law**
droit d'accession; avènement(*m*) au trône; assentiment(*m*)	**Zunahme**(*f*); Beitritt(*m*); Neuanschaffung(*f*)	**accession**
acte(*f*) d'entrée en possession	Beitrittsakte (*EG*)	act of –
droit(*m*) **d'auteur,** propriété(*f*) littéraire	**Urheberrecht**(*n*)	**copyright**
droit(*m*) **de la famille**	**Familienrecht**(*n*)	**family law**

FRENCH	GERMAN	ENGLISH
droit(m) de la responsabilité	Recht(n) der unerlaubten Handlungen(f)	law of torts
droit de naissance, droit d'aînesse; patrimoine	Geburtsrecht(n), angestammtes Recht(n)	birthright
droit(m) de préemption	Vorkaufsrecht(n); Bezugsrecht(n)	preemptive right
droit(m) de préférence sur tout ou partie de l'actif présent et à venir d'une société, sous réserve du droit pour la société de modifier cet actif dans le cours normal de ses affaires	schwebendes Sicherungsrecht(n)	floating charge
droit(m) de timbre	Gebührenstempel(m); –marke	stamp duty
droit(m) de visite	Besuchsrecht(n); Verkehrsrecht(n) (zu e-m Kinde)	visiting right
droit(m) de vote	Stimmrecht(n)	voting power
droits de vote (des actionnaires)	Stimmrecht(n) (der Aktieninhaber)(m)	voting rights (of shareholders)
droit(m) du mariage	Eherecht(n)	matrimonial law
droit(m) maritime	See(schiffahrts)recht(n)	maritime law
droit(m) matériel	materielles Recht(n)	substantive law
droits(m) de l'homme	Menschenrecht(n)	human rights
dû(m), droits(m), frais(m), redevance(f)	Gebühren(f), Abgaben(n); Beitrag(m)	dues
dû(m); légitime	geschuldet; zustehend; fällig; gebührend	due
réflexion(f) voulue, mûre réflexion	(nach) reifliche(r) Überlegung	– consideration
échéance(f), (en) temps utile	Fälligkeitsdatum; –termin	– date
procédure judiciaire(f) de sauvegarde de la liberté individuelle	ordnungsgemäßes Verfahren; ordentliches Gerichtsverfahren	– process of law (US)
du ressort de, de la compétence de	erkennbar; gerichtlich verfolgbar; der Gerichtsbarkeit unterworfen	cognisable
ducroire(m)	Delkredere	del credere
dûment, en temps utile	gebührend; ordnungsmäßig; rechtzeitig	duly
duplicité(f), double jeu	(unzulässige) Häufung(f) mehrerer Klagegründe(m) in e-r Klageschrift(f)	duplicity

E

FRENCH	GERMAN	ENGLISH
échantillon(m); sondage(m)	(Stich-)Probe(f); (Waren-)Probe(f), Muster(n)	**sample**
échantillonnage(m)	(Auswahl(f) nach dem) Stichprobenverfahren(m);	**sampling**
échantillonage au hasard	Zufallsstichprobenerhebung	random –
échantillonnage(m) au hasard	Stichprobenerhebung(f)	**random sampling**
échéance(f) date(f) d'échéance	Fälligkeit(f)(stermin)(m) –stag; Verfalltag	**maturity** date of –
échec(m), manquement(m), faillite(f) déni(m) de justice non-comparution(f) non-observation(f) de	Mißerfolg(m); Bankrott(m); Versäumnis(n); Zahlungseinstellung Justizversagen Nichterscheinen (vor Gericht) Nichtbefolgung; –einhaltung; –erfüllung	**failure** – of justice – to appear – to comply with
défaut(m) de paiement	Nichtzahlung; Zahlungsversäumnis	– to pay
échouer, manquer, faire défaut	scheitern; unterliegen; Zahlung(f) einstellen; in Konkurs gehen	**fail (to)**
échu, arriéré, en souffrance	hervorragend; offenstehend, ausstehend	**outstanding**
économies(f) d'échelle	Größenvorteile(m); Rationalisierung(f)	**economies of scale**
écrit(m), écriture(f), souscription(f)	Schreiben; Schriftform(f)	**writing**
ecu	Ecu	**ecu**
effacement, radiation	Löschung(f); Streichung(f)	**deletion**
effacer, radier, supprimer	löschen, streichen	**delete (to)**
effet(m) conséquence(f) légale, effet juridique	Wirkung(f); Folge(f); Kraft(f) Rechtswirkung; –kraft	**effect** legal –
effet(m) payable à vue, traite(f) à vue	Sichtwechsel(m)	**sight bill**
efficace; frappant; solvable date(f) d'entrée en vigueur	effektiv; wirksam Tag des Inkrafttretens	**effective** – date

FRENCH	GERMAN	ENGLISH
efficacité(f), compétence(f)	**Leistungsfähigkeit**(f); Wirksamkeit(f)	**efficiency**
taux(m), courbe(f) d'efficacité de rentabilité	Leistungsverhältnis	– ratio
différence(s) d'efficacité	Leistungsabweichung, Intensitätsabweichung	– variance
effraction(f)	**Einbruch**(m)	**breaking and entering**
égal	**gleich;** gleichberechtigt	**equal**
égalité(f) des droits	Gleichberechtigung; Rechtsgleichheit	– rights
partage(m) des voix	Stimmengleichheit	– votes
égalité(f) **de voix**	**Stimmengleichheit**(f)	**parity of votes**
éjecter, évincer, expulser	**ausweisen;** entfernen; (Amt) entheben	**eject (to)**
éloignement(m)	**Entlegenheit**(f); Ferne(f)	**remoteness**
dommage(m) indirect	Nichtzurechenbarkeit e-s Schadens	– of damage
non-pertinence d'un témoignage	Beweisunerheblichkeit	– of evidence
embarras(m), hypothèque(f)	**Last**(f); (Grundstücks-) Belastung(f); Hypothekenlast(f)	**encumbrance**
émeute	**Aufruhr**(f)	**riot**
émoluments(m), honoraires(m)	**Einkünfte;** Bezüge(m)	**emolument(s)**
empêcher, dissuader	**abschrecken;** verhindern	**deter (to)**
empêcher qqu'un de	jdn abhalten von	– s.o. from
empêcher, exclure	**verbieten,** untersagen; ausschließen	**bar (to)**
retirer une plainte	Rechtsweg ausschließen	– legal proceedings
empêcher, prévenir, exclure	**ausschließen**	**preclude (to)**
empêcher, prévenir	**verhindern;** verhüten	**prevent (to)**
empiéter sur	**übergreifen;** eingreifen	**encroach (to) (upon)**
emploi(m) **rémunéré**	**Erwerbstätigkeit**(f)	**gainful employment**
empoisonner	**vergiften**	**poison (to)**
empreinte(f)	**Abdruck**(m)	**imprint**
empreinte(f) **de la main**	**Handballenabdruck**(m)	**palmprint**
emprisonnement(m)	**Beschränkung**(f); Inhaftierung(f)	**confinement**
emprisonnement cellulaire (au Cecret)	Einzelhaft	solitary –
emprisonnement(m)	**Inhaftierung**(f); Freiheits–, Gefängnisstrafe(f)	**imprisonment**
emprisonner, mettre en prison	**inhaftieren;** ins Gefängnis(n) setzen	**imprison (to)**
emprunteur (n)	**Entleiher**(m); Kredit–, Darlehensnehmer(m)	**borrower**
emprunteur (adj.)	**Leihen,** Borgen; Darlehens–, Kreditaufnahme(f)	**borrowing**

FRENCH	GERMAN	ENGLISH
emprunteur(*m*), débiteur(*m*) sur gages, gageur(*m*)	**Pfandgeber**(*m*); –schuldner(*m*)	**pledgor**
en avant, antérieur; à terme engagement(*m*) d'acheter ou de vendre à un prix fixé, à une date ultérieure	**Termin-**(*m*) –kontrakt	**forward** – contract
transaction(*f*) à terme	–geschäft	– transactions
en cours d'action	**Anhängigkeit**(*f*) **des Verfahrens**	**pendency of action**
en dehors du mariage	**außerehelich**	**extramarital**
en instance, en cours action(*f*) en cours	**anhängig;** schwebend –er Rechtsstreit	**pending** – action
en puissance, incomplet crime(*m*) non parfait droit(*m*) en puissance	**angefangen;** in Entstehung(*f*) begriffen; teilweise begründet unvollkommende Missetat entstehendes od. im Entstehen begriffenes Recht	**inchoate** – crime – right
en tournée, itinérant, ambulant juge(*m*) en tournée	**reisend** Reiserichter	**itinerant** – judge
en trop, en chômage technique, licencié économique	**entlassen;** überflüssig	**redundant**
encaissement(*m*); levée(*f*), perception(*f*); rassemblement(*f*), réunion(*f*); recouvrement(*m*) agence(*f*) de recouvrement ordre(*m*) de recouvrement procédure(*f*) de mise en recouvrement	**Einziehung**(*f*), Inkasso(*n*), Beitreibung(*f*) Inkassostelle Inkassoauftrag Einziehungsverfahren	**collection** – agency – order – procedure
enchère, offre	**Angebot**(*n*)**,** Offerte(*f*); Antrag(*m*), Bewerbung(*f*); Gebot(*n*)	**bid**
enchérisseur(*m*)	**Bietender**(*m*)**,** Steigerer(*m*); Bewerber(*m*)	**bidder**
encourir, subir subir des dégâts subir des pertes	**sich zuziehen;** erleiden; sich (e-r Gefahr) aussetzen Schaden erleiden Verlust erleiden	**incur (to)** – damage – losses
endos, endossement(*m*), approbation(*f*), visa	**Indossament**(*n*)**;** Vermerk(*m*); Bestätigung(*f*)	**endorsement**
endosser, souscrire à	**indossieren;** (auf der Rückseite einer Urkunde) vermerken; zustimmen	**endorse (to)**
endosseur(*m*), concessionnaire(*m*), avaliste(*m*)	**Indossant**(*m*)**;** Girant(*m*); Begeber(*m*)	**endorser**
enfant(*m, f*)	**Kind**(*n*)**,** Nachkomme(*m*)	**child**
enfant(*m, f*) **naturel**	**uneheliches Kind**	**bastard**
enfreindre, mépriser, passer outre à	**nicht beachten;** ignorieren	**disregard (to)**

FRENCH	GERMAN	ENGLISH
enfreindre, violer, empiéter sur	**verletzen (Recht);** verstoßen gegen	**infringe (to)**
enfreindre, violer	**verletzen;** verstoßen; übertreten	**violate (to)**
engagement(m), obligation(f); renvoi(m) à une commission	**Verpflichtung**(f); Übergabe(f); Einlieferung(f)	**commitment**
incarcération(f)	Einlieferung ins Gefängnis/in (Untersuchungs-Haft) nehmen	– to custody, prison
obligation contractuelle	vertragliche Verpflichtung	contractual –
engagement(m)	**Verpflichtung**(f); Abmachung(f); Versprechen(n)	**engagement**
engagement(m) **irrévocable**	**zwingende Verpflichtung**(f)	**binding commitment**
enjoindre, prescrire	**auferlegen;** vorschreiben; (gerichtlich) untersagen	**enjoin (to)**
enlèvement(m)	**Entführung**(f)	**abduction**
enlèvement(m), kidnapping(m), rapt(m) (s'emploie plutôt quand la victime est un enfant)	**Entführung**(f)	**kidnapping**
enquête(f)	**(gerichtliche) Untersuchung**(f); Beweisaufnahme(f)	**inquest**
enquête après mort d'homme menée par un coroner(m)	amtliche Leichenschau	coroner's –
procéder à une enquête	Leichnam gerichtlich untersuchen; obduzieren	to hold an –
enquête(f), investigation(f)	**Untersuchung**(f)	**inquiry**
enquête judiciaire	gerichtliche -	judicial –
enquête officielle	amtliche -	official –
enquête(f), investigation(f)	**Ermittlung**(f); Untersuchung	**investigation**
officier(m) chargé de l'enquête	–sbeamter	– officer
enquête préliminaire	Voruntersuchung	preliminary –
enquêter, faire une enquête	**nachfragen;** sich erkundigen	**inquire (to)**
enregistré, inscrit, immatriculé	**eingetragen**	**registered**
lettre(f) recommandée	eingeschriebener Brief	– letter
courrier(m) recommandé	Einschreiben	– mail
siège(m) social	–er Sitz	– office
enregistrement(m), immatriculation(f), inscription(f)	**Eintragung**(f); Zulassung(f)	**registration**
dépôt(m) d'un brevet	Eintragung in die Patentrolle	patent –
plaque(f) d'immatriculation	Nummernschild; polizeil. Kennzeichen	– plate
dépôt d'une marque de fabrique	Eintragung e-s Warenzeichens	trade mark –
enrichir	**bereichern**	**enrich (to)**
entamer (des poursuites), commencer	**beginnen;** einleiten	**initiate (to)**

FRENCH	GERMAN	ENGLISH
entendre, écouter; instruire	**verhandeln;** hören	**hear (to)**
entrave(f), obstacle(m); cause(f) d'incapacité de contracter	**Behinderung**(f); Hinderungsgrund(f)	**impediment**
entrée(f), article(m); enregistrement(m), déclaration(f)	**Beitritt**(m); Eintrag(m); Buchung(f); Zollanmeldung(f)	**entry**
déclaration en douane de marchandises passibles de droits	Zolldeklaration für zollpflichtige Waren (Zoll)	– for dutiable goods (customs)
immigration(f) clandestine	illegale Einreise	illegal –
passer une écriture (comptabilité)	etw. eintragen, verbuchen (Buchhaltung)	to make an – (bookkeeping)
droit(m) d'entrée, droit de prendre possession	Inbesitznahmerecht; Einreiserecht	right of –
entrepreneur(m)	**Unternehmer**(m)	**entrepreneur**
entreprise(f)	**Unternehmen**(n); Betrieb(m); Geschäft(n)	**enterprise**
entreprise(f), spéculation(f), risque(m)	**Wagnis**(n); Unternehmen(n); Risiko(n)	**venture**
association(f), entreprise en participation	Joint Venture; Gemeinschaftsunternehmen	joint –
entrer, enregistrer	**eintreten;** einbringen, erheben	**enter (to)**
conclure un accord (avec)	e-n Vertrag mit jmd abschließen	– into an agreement (with)
environnement(m) (US)	**Innen-**	**Interior** (US)
ministère(m) de l'environnement (US)	–ministerium(n) (US)	Department of the – (US)
ministre(m) de l'environnement (US)	–minister(m) (US)	Secretary of the – (US)
envisager, confronter	**gegenüberstellen;** konfrontieren	**confront (to)**
confronter les témoins	Zeugen gegenüberstellen	– witnesses
envoi(m) **de fonds,** versement(m), traite(f), chèque(m)	**Überweisung**(f)	**remittance**
épouse(f), femme(f)	**Ehefrau**(f)	**wife**
époux(m) **survivant**	**überlebender Ehegatte**	**surviving spouse**
équilibre(m)	**Gleichgewicht**(n)	**equilibrium**
équité(f), principes(m) de la justice (opp. droit formel)	**Billigkeit**(f); Unparteilichkeit(f)	**equity**
tribunal(m) qui applique les principes de l'équité	Billigkeitsgericht	court of –
capital(m) effectif, fonds(m) propres	Eigenkapital; Beteiligungskapital	– capital
équivalence(f)	**Gleichwertigkeit**(f)	**equivalence**
erreur(f), faux raisonnement	**Trugschluß**(m); Irrtum(m)	**fallacy**
erreur(f), méprise(f)	**Irrtum**(m); Fehler(m)	**mistake**
erreur sur les faits	Tatsachenirrtum	– of fact
faute(f) de droit	Rechtsirrtum	– of law

FRENCH	GERMAN	ENGLISH
erreur(f) erreur judiciaire	**Irrtum**(m)**; Fehler**(m)*; Versehen*(n) Fehlspruch; Rechtsirrtum; Fehler des Gerichts	**error** judicial –
erreur(f) **fondamentale**	**Kardinalfehler**(m)	**cardinal error**
erreur(f) **judiciaire, déni**(m) de justice	**Fehlurteil**(n)**; Justizirrtum(m)	**miscarriage of justice**
erreur(f) **judiciaire**	**fehlerhaftes Gerichtsverfahren**	**mistrial**
erreur(f) **sur le nom d'une partie**	**falsche Benennung**(f)**; Namensirrtum(m)	**misnomer**
erroné	**irrtümlich; unrichtig**	**erroneous**
escroc(m)	**Schwindler**(m)**; Betrüger(m)	**swindler**
escroc(m)**, chevalier**(f) d'industrie	**Schieber**(m)**; korrupter Beamter(m)	**grafter**
escroquerie(f)**, détournement**(m)**, abus**(m) de confiance	**Veruntreuung**(f)**; Unterschlagung(f)	**embezzlement**
escroquerie(f)	**Schwindel**(m)**; Betrug(m)	**swindle**
espèce(f)**, genre**(m)**, nature**(f) (paiement, règlement) en nature	**Art**(f)**; Gattung(f) in natura; – Waren	**kind** in –
espion(m)	**Spion**(m)	**spy**
essai(m) **préliminaire, vérification**(f) **préalable**	**Vortest**(m)	**pretest**
essayer, entreprendre, tâcher de	**versuchen; unternehmen**	**attempt (to)**
'establishment', classes(f) dirigeantes; fondation(f), assiette(f), établissement(m) établissement bancaire maison(f) de commerce siège(m) social	**Gründung**(f)**; Unternehmen(n); Feststellung(f) Bankinstitut Geschäftsbetrieb Ort der Niederlassung	**establishment** banking – business – place of –
établir	**gründen; nachweisen; bestätigen**	**establish (to)**
établir, prouver le bien- fondé	**substantiieren; begründen**	**substantiate (to)**
État(m)**, Commonwealth**	**Gemeinwesen**(n)**; Staat(m), Nation(f)	**commonwealth**
état(m)**, condition**(f); mode(m, f) légal de possession; biens(m) immeubles; patrimoine(m); masse(f) des biens succession(f) partage(m) d'une succession agent(m) immbilier bien(m) mobiliers	**Vermögen**(n)**; Nachlaß(m); Grundeigentum(n); Anwesen(n) Nachlaß Aufteilung des Nachlasses, Erbauseinandersetzung Grundstücksmakler; Immobilienhändler Mobiliarvermögen; beweglicher Nachlaß	**estate** deceased's – distribution of an – – agent personal –

FRENCH	GERMAN	ENGLISH
état(m) de fait	Tatbestand(smerkmale)	operative fact
état(m) matrimonial	Familienstand(m)	marital status
étendre, prolonger, proroger	verlängern	extend (to)
reculer l'échéance d'un paiement	Zahlungsfrist –	– a payment term
étiqueter, munir d'une fiche	Anhängezettel(m), – versehen	tag (to)
étranger, ressortissant étranger	Ausländer(m); Fremder(m)	alien
étrangler	erwürgen; strangulieren	strangle (to)
être déchu de, perdre par confiscation	verwirken; einbüßen	forfeit (to)
être le complice de	Beihilfe(f) leisten, begünstigen	aid and abet
étude(f) d'avocat, d'avoué (US)	Rechtsanwaltsbüro(n) (US)	law office (US)
eurodevise(m), euromonnaie(f)	Eurowährung(f)	Euro-currency
évaluation(f); estimation(f), détermination(f) du montant d'impôt	Bewertung(f); Festsetzung(f); (Schaden-)Feststellung(f); (Steuer-)Veranlagung	assessment
évaluation(f) des préjudices (dégâts)	Festsetzung einer Entschädigungssumme	– of damages
évasion(f), fraude(f)	Ausweichen; Umgehung(f); Vermeidung(f)	evasion
fraude(f) fiscale	Steuerhinterziehung	tax –
éventuel, conditionnel, fortuit	abhängig	contingent
honoraires éventuels engagement(m) éventuel; tierce caution	Erfolgshonorar Eventualverbindlichkeiten	– fee – liabilities
éviction(f), expulsion	Zwangsräumung(f); Heraussetzung(f)	eviction
ordre(m) d'expulsion	Räumungsbefehl, –urteil	– order
examen(m), étude(f), visite(f)	Zeugenvernehmung(f); Verhör(n)	examination
contre-interrogatoire interrogatoire(m)	Kreuzverhör Hauptvernehmung (durch die benennende Partei)	cross–– direct –
audition(f) d'un témoin autopsie(f)	Zeugenvernehmung Leichenschau; Obduktion	– of witness post-mortem –
examen(m) radioscopique	Roentgenuntersuchung(f)	X-ray examination
examiner de très près, enquêter minutieusement	genau prüfen; (Stimmen) nachzählen	scrutinise (to)

FRENCH	GERMAN	ENGLISH
exclusion(*f*), empêchément(*m*)	**Hinderung**(*f*)(**sgrund**)(*m*); rechtshemmender(*m*) Einwand(*m*); Rechtsverwirkung	**estoppel**
écartement(*m*) du bénéfice de certains droits par acte notarié	Verwirkung des Einwands gegen den Inhalt einer gesiegelten Urkunde;	– by deed
déchéance(*f*) de ses droits par jugement	Ausschluß der nochmaligen Prozeßführung über denselben Streitgegenstand	– by judgment
exclusion(*f*), prévention(*f*)	**Ausschluß**(*m*)	**preclusion**
exécuteur(*m*), **exécutrice**(*f*) **(testamentaire)**	**Vollstrecker**(*m*); Erbschaftsverwalter(in)(*m*, *f*), Testamentsvollstrecker(in)	**executor, executrix**
exécution(*f*) exécution d'un testament	**Ausfertigung**(*f*) e-s Testaments	**execution** – of a will
exécution(*f*) **d'un jugement**	**Vollstreckung**(*f*) **e-s Urteils**	**enforcement of a judgment**
exécution(*f*) **d'un contrat ordonnée par le cour**	**vertragserfallung nach gerichtsurteil**	**specific performance**
exempter, exonérer	**befreien**; freistellen; ausnehmen	**exempt (to)**
exonérer, dispenser disculper qqu'un, exonérer qqu'un de ses responsabilités(*f*)	**entlasten**; entbinden jdn von einer Schuld oder Haftung befreien	**exonerate (to)** – s.o. from guilt or liability
expatrier	**ausbürgern**	**expatriate (to)**
expédier	**versenden**, liefern; konsignieren; hinterlegen	**consign (to)**
expédition(*f*) **de marchandises**	**Sendung**(*f*)	**consignment**
expérimental, provisoire	**versuchsweise**	**tentative**
expiration(*f*), cessation(*f*), échéance(*f*) expiration(*f*) d'un contrat	**Ablauf**(*m*); Erlöschen(*n*); Verfall(*m*) Ablauf e-s Vertrags	**expiration, expiry** – of a contract
exploit(*m*), ordonnance(*f*), acte(*m*) judiciaire	**gerichtliche Anweisung**(*f*)/ **Verfügung**(*f*); Klageschrift(*f*); Schriftstück	**writ**
ordonnance de saisie-arrêt	Arrestbefehl; Pfändungs-, Zwangsvallstreckung Vollstreckungsbefehl;	– of attachment
ordonnance d'exécution injonction(*f*) de déférer un accusé devant le tribunal	gerichtliche Anordnung eines Haftprüfungstermins; Vorführungsbefehlim	– of enforcement – of execution
exploit de saisie-exécution séquestre(*m*) judiciaire	Beschlagnahmeverfügung (gerichtliche Einsetzung e-s Zwangsverwalters)	– of habeas corpus– of sequestration
assignation(*f*), citation (à comparaître)	Prozeßladung mit Klageschrift	– of summons
exposé(*m*), dossier(*m*)	**schriftl. Beauftragung**(*f*) **und Information**(*f*) (des Barrister durch den Solicitor) zur Vertretung vor Gericht; Schriftsatz; Auftrag, Mandat	**brief**

FRENCH	GERMAN	ENGLISH
exposé; constitution(*f*) de dossier	**Information**(*f*); Bestellung(*f*) eines vor Gericht(*n*) auftretenden Anwalts; Anweisung, Unterweisung; Einsatzbesprechung	**briefing**
exposé des motifs d'une loi, attendus d'un arrêt; préambule(*m*)	**Präambel**(*f*); Eingangsformel(*f*)	**preamble**
expropriation(*f*)	**Landenteignung**(*f*)	**expropriation of land**
exproprier, déposséder	**enteignen**	**expropriate (to)**
expulser	**ausschließen;** ausweisen	**expel (to)**
expulsion(*f*)	**Vertreibung**(*f*); Ausweisung(*f*); Ausschluß(*m*)	**expulsion**
extinction(*f*) **d'un droit**; confusion(*f*); fusion(*f*), unification(*f*)	**Zusammenschluß**(*m*); Fusion(*f*)	**merger**
clause(*f*) de fusion	Zusammenschlußklausel	– clause
extortion(*f*)	**Erpressung**(*f*)	**extortion**
extrader	**ausliefern**	**extradite (to)**
extradition(*f*)	**Auslieferung**(*f*)	**extradition**
extrajudiciaire	**außergerichtlich**	**extrajudicial**
extraterritoriaux(*f*)	**exterritorial;** außerhalb des Hoheitsgebiets(*n*)	**extraterritorial**

F

FRENCH	GERMAN	ENGLISH
facture(f) **pro forma,** facture pour la forme	**Proformarechnung**(f)	**pro forma invoice**
faculté(f), liberté(f), droit(m) de faire qque chose faculté de droit	**Lehrkörper**(m) juristische Fakultät	**faculty** – of laws
faculté(f), option(f); droit(m) de souscription	**Option**(f)	**option**
failli, banqueroutier	**Konkursschuldner**(m); Zahlungsunfähiger(m); Gemeinschuldner(m)	**bankrupt**
être déclaré en faillite prononcer la faillite de qqu'un se déclarer en faillite faire faillite	bankrott erklärt werden jdn für bankrott erklären Konkurs (Bankrott) anmelden in Konkurs gehen (geraten); bankrott machen	to be declared – to declare s.o. – to declare oneself – to go –
faillite(f)	**Bankrott**(m), Konkurs(m); Zahlungseinstellung(f)	**bankruptcy**
tribunal(m) de faillite procédure(f) de faillite se mettre en faillite, deposer son bilan	Konkursgericht Konkursverfahren e-n Antrag auf Konkurseröffnung stellen Konkurs anmelden	– court proceedings in – to present a – petition
faillite volontaire	freiwilliger Konkurs	voluntary –
faire connaître, publier, rendre public	**veröffentlichen**	**publish (to)**
faire de l'obstruction, entraver entraver l'action de la justice	**behindern;** hemmen Gerichtsverfahren behindern	**obstruct (to)** – legal procedure
faire saisir un article non payé	**wieder in Besitz**(m) **nehmen;** zurücknehmen	**repossess (to)**
faire une enquête, vérifier	**ermitteln;** untersuchen	**investigate (to)**
fait(m), réalité(f) fait brut	**Tatsache**(f); Umstand(m) beweiserhebliche Tatsache; beweisbare Tatsache	**fact** evidentiary –
point(m) de fait	strittige Tatsachen; zu beweisende –	– in issue
fait pertinent, fait essentiel	wesentliche Tatsache	material –

FRENCH	GERMAN	ENGLISH
fait(m) de mourir en laissant un testament	Testierfähigkeit(f)	testacy
fait(m) de mourir intestat, sans testament	Sterben ohne Hinterlassung(f) eines Testaments	intestacy
fait de prétendre faussement que l'on est marié à une certaine personne	Vorspiegelung(f) des Bestehens e-r Ehe(f)	jactitation of marriage
fait(m) réfutatif	entlastende Tatsache(f)	infirmative fact
falsification(f), trucage(m), contrefaçon(f)	Verfälschung(f)	falsification
falsifier, fausser, dénaturer	verfälschen	falsify (to)
familial(m); national(m)	inländisch; innerstaatlich; Familien–	domestic
économie(f) nationale droit(m) interne	Binnenwirtschaft inländisches, innerstaatliches Recht	– economy – law
fatal, mortel accident(m) mortel blessures(f) ayant entraîné la mort	tödlich –er Unfall –e Verletzung	fatal – accident – injury
faussaire(m), contrefacteur(m)	Fälscher(m)	forger
fausse(f) constitution des parties	unzulässige Klageverbindung(f)	misjoinder
faute(f), négligence(f), imperfection(f) responsabilité(f) de la faute	Schuld(f); Verschulden; Fehler(m) vom Verschulden abhängige Haftung; Fehleranfälligkeit (EDV)	fault – liability
faux, contrefaçon(f), falsification(f), supposition(f)	Fälschung(f)	forgery
faux, erroné témoignage(m) faux prétextes(m) fallacieux	falsch; unwahr falsches Zeugnis falsche Darstellung, Behauptung	false – testimony – pretence
fédéral cour(f) fédérale juridiction(f) fédérale	Bundes- –gericht –gerichtsbarkeit, Zuständigkeit der Bundesgerichte	federal – court – jurisdiction
fermer, clore(m) clôture(f) de la procédure	schließen; einstellen; beenden Verfahren einstellen	close (to) – the proceedings
fiançailles(f)	Verlobung(f)	betrothal
fictif, simulé contrat(m) fictif	fiktiv; Schein- Scheinvertrag	fictitious, fictive – contract

213

FRENCH	GERMAN	ENGLISH
fidéicommis(*m*), tutelle(*f*); garde(*m*), dépôt(*m*); 'trust'(*m*), concentration(*f*) verticale d'entreprises; confiance(*f*)	**Treuhandverhältnis**(*n*); – vermögen(*n*)	**trust**
bénéficiaire(*m*) de la tutelle	Treuhandsbegünstigter	– beneficiary
acte(*m*) fiduciaire	Treuhandvertrag;	– deed
biens(*m*) placés sous tutelle	Treuhandvermögen	– property
fiduciaire(*m*) (*n et adj.*), dépositaire(*m, f*)	**Treuhänder**(*m*); Vermögensverwalter(*m*)	**fiduciary**
filiale(*f*)	**Tochtergesellschaft**(*f*)	**subsidiary company**
filière(*f*); vestige(*m*), trace(*f*)	**Spur**(*f*); Anzeichen(*n*)	**trace**
fin(*f*), terme(*m*)	**Ende**(*n*); Ziel(*n*); Absicht(*f*)	**end**
finance(*f*)	**Finanzwesen**(*n*)	**finance**
gestion(*f*) financière	betriebliche Finanzwirtschaft; Unternehmensfinanzierung	business –
société(*f*) de financement	Finanzierungsgesellschaft; Kreditinstitut für Kundenfinanzierung	– company
financier, financiére	**finanziell;** Finanz-	**financial**
audit(*m*) financier	Buchprüfung	– audit
budget(*m*) financier	Finanzplan	– budget
contrats(*m*) à terme	Finanztermingeschäfte	– futures
garantie(s)(*f*) financière(s)	Finanzgarantie	– guarantee
institution(*f*) financière	Kredit-, Finanzinstitut	– institution
marché(*m*) financier	Finanz-, Kreditmarkt	– market
lois(*f*) de finances	Finanzgesetzgebung	– legislation
management(m) financier	Finanzmanagement	– management
bilan(*m*), état(*m*) des finances	Finanzbericht; Handelsbilanz (*US*)	– statement
fisc(*m*)	**Finanzamt**(*n*)	**Inland Revenue**
fisc(*m*), trésor(*m*) (public) ministre(*m*) des finances, 'chancelier(*m*) de l'échiquier' (*UK*)	**Staatskasse**(*f*); Fiskus(*m*) Finanzminister (*UK*)	**exchequer** Chancellor of the Exchequer
fiscal, fiscale fisc(*m*) contrôle(*m*) fiscal	**Finanz-;** Steuer- –behörde(*f*) –kontrolle, –aufsicht	**fiscal** – authority – control
fixer d'avance, prédéterminer	**vorherbestimmen**	**predetermine (to)**
flotter; émettre, lancer	**frei schwanken;** in Umlauf(*m*) bringen	**float (to)**
lancer un emprunt	Anleihe auflegen od. begeben	– a loan
foi(*f*), confiance(*f*) de bonne foi	**Glaube**(*m*) in bösem Glauben, wider Treu und Glauben	**faith** in bad –
de mauvaise foi	in gutem Glauben; nach Treu und Glauben	in good –

FRENCH	GERMAN	ENGLISH
fond(*m*), substance(*f*); mérite(*m*)	**Tatsachen**(*f*) **und Rechtspunkte**(*m*); materielle Umstände(*m*)	**merits**
jugement(*m*) au fond	Entscheidung in der Sache selbst, Entscheidung nach materiellem Recht	decision on the –
rejet(*m*) (d'une plainte) pour manque de fondement	Klageabweisung aufgrund e-r Sachentscheidung	dismissal on the –
fond(*m*) **de tutelle**	**Treuhandfonds**(*m*)	**trust fund**
fondation(*f*), institution(*f*); fondement(*m*)	**Stiftung**(*f*)	**foundation**
fondation charitable	– mit gemeinnützigem Zweck	charitable –
fondé à réclamer des dommages-intérêts	**zum Schadensersatz**(*m*) **berechtigt sein**	**entitled to damages**
fonds(*m*) **consolidés** *(UK)*, rentes(*f*) perpétuelles	**konsolidierte Staatsanleihen**(*f*); Konsols *(UK)*	**consols** *(UK)*
fonds(*m*) **d'apport,** capital(*m*) d'apport	**Anfangs-/Einlagekapital**(*n*); Gründungs–	**initial fund/capital**
fonds(*m*) **dominant**	**herrschendes Grundstück**(*n*) **(bei Grunddienstbarkeit)**	**dominant tenement**
forçat(*m*), déporté(*m, f*), bagnard(*m*); détenu(*m*) d'un pénitencier *(US)*	**Strafgefangener**(*m*); Sträfling(*m*); Verurteilter(*m*)	**convict**
force(*f*), vigueur(*f*), résistance(*f*)	**Kraft**(*f*); Macht(*f*)	**strength**
en vertu de, au regard de	aufgrund von; unter Berufung auf	on the – of
force(*f*) de la loi	Gesetzeskraft	– of law
force(*f*)	**Kraft**(*f*)	**force**
de force, par force	zwangsweise, mit Gewalt	by –
force de la loi	Gesetzes–	– of law
(cas de) force majeure	höhere Gewalt	*force majeure*
forcé	**Zwangs-**	**forced**
emprunt(*m*) forcé	–anleihe(*f*)	– loan
vente(*f*) forcée	–verkauf(*m*)	– sale
forcer, contraindre	**zwingen;** nötigen	**compel (to)**
forcer à faire	**drängen;** zwingen	**impel (to)**
forclore saisir, mettre fin à un prêt	**ausschließen;** verfallen lassen; präkludieren	**foreclose (to)**
formel, régulier, absolu, conventionnel	**formal;** formell	**formal**
vice de forme	Formfehler	– error
fornication(*f*)	**außerehelicher Geschlechtsverkehr**(*m*); Unzucht(*f*)	**fornication**
forum(*m*); tribunal(*m*) compétent (et son siège)	**Forum**(*n*); Gremium(*n*)	**forum**
fournir, prévoir, stipuler	**bestimmen;** beschaffen	**provide (to)**
fournisseur(*m*)	**Lieferant**(*m*)	**supplier**

FRENCH	GERMAN	ENGLISH
fractionnel, divisionnaire (*adj.*)	**Teil-**(*m*)	**fractional**
titre(*m*) fractionnel	–schein	– certificate
action(*f*) fractionnelle	Aktienspitzen	– share
frais(*m*) **de manutention**	**Bearbeitungsgebühren**(*f*); Umschlagspesen(*n*)	**handling charges**
franco avion	**f.o.p.** (Frei an Flugzeug)(*n*)	**FOP** (free on plane)
franco bord	**f.o.b.** (Frei an Bord)	**FOB** (free on board)
franco camion	**Frei Lastwagen**(*m*)	**FOT** (free on truck)
franco quai	**f.a.s.** (Frei Langsseite Seeschiff)	**FAS** (free alongside ship)
franco quai	**f.o.q.** (Frei Kai)(*m*)	**FOQ** (free on quay)
franco wagon	**f.o.r.** (Frei Bannstation(*f*), Eisenbahnwaggon(*m*))	**FOR** (free on rail)
frapper d'incapacité légale, interdire	**unfähig** machen; für unfähig erklären	**incapacitate (to)**
fraude(*f*), tromperie(*f*), abus(*m*) de confiance	**Betrug**(*m*); Veruntreuung(*f*); arglistige Täuschung(*f*)	**fraud**
fret(*m*), cargaison(*f*), transport(*m*) de marchandises; frais(*m*) de transport	**Fracht**(*f*)	**freight**
transport par avion	Luft–	air –
transport maritime	See–	ocean (sea) –
fruits(*m*) **civils,** fruits du travail agricole	**Ernte(ertrag)**(*f*); Früchte auf dem Halm(*m*)	**emblements**
frustration(*f*); anéantissement(*m*); impossibilité(*f*) d'exécuter un contrat	**Vereitelung**(*f*); Verhinderung(*f*)	**frustration**
frustrer, faire échouer, déjouer	**besiegen;** vereiteln; zu Fall(*m*) bringen; aufheben	**defeat (to)**
fugitif recherché par la justice	**flüchtiger Rechtsbrecher**(*m*)	**fugitive from justice**
fuir	**entlaufen;** durchgehen	**elope (to)**

G

FRENCH	GERMAN	ENGLISH
gage(*m*), promesse(*f*), nantissement(*m*), voeu(*m*)	**Pfand**(*n*); Versprechen	**pledge**
gager, mettre en gage	**verpfänden;** geloben	**pledge (to)**
gain(*m*), profit(*m*), bénéfice(*m*)	**Gewinn**(*m*); Verdienst(*m*); Erwerb(*m*)	**gain**
gain(s)(*m*), salaire(*m*), bénéfice(*m*)	**Ertrag**(*m*); Einkommen(*n*)	**earning(s)**
bénéfice, gains bruts (nets)	Brutto– (Netto–)einkommen	gross (net) –
gang(*m*), bande(*f*) de malfaiteurs; convoi(*m*) de prisonniers (*US*)	**(Arbeiter–)Kolonne;** Schicht(*f*)	**gang**
garant(*m*), caution(*f*), répondant(*m*), avaliste	**Bürge**(*m*); Garant(*m*)	**guarantor**
garantie(*f*), caution(*f*); aval(*m*), cautionnement(*m*)	**Bürgschaft(sleistung)**(*f*); Sicherheit(*f*); Garantie(*f*)	**guarantee** (*cf.* surety)
garantie absolue	selbstschuldnerische Bürgschaft	absolute –
garantie collatérale	Nebenbürgschaft	collateral –
garantie conditionnelle	Ausfallbürgschaft	conditional –
garantie(*f*), caution(*f*), garant(*m*); sûreté(*f*), certitude(*f*)	**Bürge**(*m*); Garant(*m*); Sicherheitsleistung(*f*)	**surety**
garde, garde d'un enfant; détention(*f*), état(*m*) d'arrestation	**Haft**(*f*); Obhut(*f*), Sorgerecht(*n*); Verwahrung(*f*)	**custody**
détention préventive	Untersuchungshaft; Sicherungsverwahrung	preventive –
détention à fins de protection	Schutzhaft	protective –
bonne(*f*) garde	sichere Aufbewahrung; Verwahrung	safe –
garde(*m*), tutelle(*f*)	**Vormundschaft**(*f*); Schutz(*m*), Obhut(*f*)	**guardianship**
garde(*f*); syndic(*m*)	**Verwahrer**(*m*); Vormund(*m*) (*US*); Treuhänder(*m*)	**custodian**
gardien(*m*)	**Vorsteher**(*m*); Aufsichtsbeamter(*m*)	**warden**
gardien(*m*) **de la paix**	**Sicherheitsbeamter**(*m*)	**peace officer**

FRENCH	GERMAN	ENGLISH
garnir, orner; saisir	**Drittschuldnerpfändung**(f) **vornehmen;** Drittschuldner(m) ein Zahlungsverbot zustellen	**garnish (to)**
gaspillage(m), déchets(m)	**Verschwendung**(f); Abfall(m); Wertminderung(f)	**waste**
gaspiller	**verschwenden;** vergeuden	**squander (to)**
gendarmerie(f)	**Polizei**(f)	**constabulary**
gêné, embarassé; grevé(f) d'hypothèques	**in Geldverlegenheit**(f); Zahlungsschwierigkeit(f)	**embarrassed**
général(m) homme(m) d'affaires	**General-** –bevollmächtiger(m); allgemeiner Handelsvertreter(m)	**general** – agent
avaries(f) communes entrepreneur(m) général dommages-intérêt(m) qui découlent naturellement de la plainte	Große Havarie –unternehmer Gesamtschaden; allgemeiner Schaden	– average – contractor – damages
privilège(m) général assemblée(f) générale	allgemeines Pfandrecht Mitgliederversammlung; Hauptversammlung	– lien – meeting
associé(m) ordinaire	unbeschränkt (persönlich)haftender Gesellschafter	– partner
société(m) en nom collectif	allgemeine offene Handelsgesellschaft; allgemeine Personengesellschaft	– partnership
génocide(m)	**Genozid**(m); Völkermord(m)	**genocide**
gibet(m), potence(f)	**Gerüst**(n); Schafott(n)	**scaffold**
gouvernement(m) de l'État	**Regierung**(f)	**government**
grâce(f), amnistie(f)	**Begnadigung**(f); Straferlaß(m)	**pardon**
grâce(f), clémence(f), pitié(f) euthanasie(f)	**Gnade**(f) Euthanasie; Tötung auf Verlangen	**mercy** – killing
recours(m) en grâce	–ngesuch	petition for –
grâce(f), pardon(m), amnistie(f) loi(f) d'amnistie	**Gnade**(f) –nfrist, Nachfrist	**grace** – act of
Grand Chancelier d'Angleterre	**Lordkanzler**(m)	**Lord High Chancellor**
greffier(m)	**Urkundsbeamter**(m) der **Geschäftsstelle**(f); Leiter der Gerichtskanzlei	**clerk of court**
grever, gêner	**belasten;** erschweren	**encumber (to)**
grever, gêner	**hypothekarisch belasten**	**incumber (to),** alternative spelling of encumber

FRENCH	GERMAN	ENGLISH
grief(*m*); injustice(*f*)	**Beschwerdegrund**(*m*), Klage–; Mißstand(*m*)	**grievance**
commission(*f*) du contentieux administratif	Arbeiter-Beschwerdeausschuß; Schlichtungsausschuß	– committee
procédure(*f*) de règlement des différends	Beschwerdeverfahren	– procedure
redresser un tort	Übelstand, Mißstand abhelfen	to redress a –
gros(*m*), grossier, trop fort; brut(*m*)	**schwer**	**gross**
négligence(*f*) coupable	grobe Fahrlässigkeit	– negligence
grossiste	**Großhändler**(*m*)	**wholesaler**
groupe(*m*), réunion(*f*) (de spécialistes); panneau(*m*), tableau(*m*)	**Gremium**(*n*); Ausschuß(*m*)	**panel**
jury(*m*)	Geschworene(nliste)	jury –
groupement(*m*) **(de sociétés)**	**Firmengruppe**(*f*), Konzern(*m*)	**group (of companies)**

H

FRENCH	GERMAN	ENGLISH
habeas corpus	**Habeas Corpus;** richterliche Haftprüfung(*f*)	**habeas corpus**
habitat(*m*)	**Heimat**(*f*); Habitat(*n*)	**habitat**
Haye (La) Convention(*f*) de La Haye, Tribunal(*m*) de La Haye	**Haag**(*m*) –er Abkommen –er Schiedshof	**Hague (The)** – Convention – Tribunal
handicap(*m*), inaptitude(*f*)	**Hindernis**(*n*); Benachteiligung(*f*); Behinderung(*f*)	**handicap**
harcèlement(*m*)	**Belästigung**(*f*)	**harassment**
harceler, tourmenter	**belästigen**	**harass (to)**
harmonisation(*f*)	**Angleichung**(*f*) (*EG*)	**harmonisation** (*EEC*)
harmoniser, concilier	**angleichen;** harmonisieren	**harmonise (to)**
hasardeux, risqué, dangereux	**gefährlich;** nicht verkehrssicher	**unsafe**
haschisch(*m*)	**Haschisch**(*n*)	**hashish**
haute trahison	**Hochverrat**(*m*); Landesverrat(*m*)	**high treason**
héréditaire	**erblich**	**hereditary**
héritage(*m*), succession(*f*); procédure(*f*) en matière de succession	**Erbschaft**(*f*); Erbe(*n*)	**inheritance**
droits(*m*) successoraux	Erbschaftssteuer	– tax
hériter (de)	**erben**	**inherit (to)**
héritier(*m*), **héritière**(*f*); héritier ab intestat héritier légal héritier naturel seul héritier, héritier unique héritier désigné par disposition testamentaire légataire(*m, f*) universel	**Erbe**(*m*) Intestats– gesetzlicher – – durch Geburtsrecht Allein– Testaments– Allein–	**heir** intestate – legal – natural – sole – testamentary – universal –
hold-up(*m*), braquage(*m*) (*fam.*), attaque(*f*) à main armée	**Überfall**(*m*); Hindernis(*n*)	**hold-up**
homicide(*m, f*), meurtre(*m*)	**Tötung**(*f*) (s. Mord)	**homicide** (*cf. murder*)

FRENCH	GERMAN	ENGLISH
homicide(*m, f*)	**Totschlag**(*m*)	**manslaughter**
homme(*m*) **de loi,** juriste(*m*); avocat(*m*) (*surtout US*)	**(Rechts-)Anwalt**(*m*)	**lawyer**
homologation(*f*), ratification(*f*), entérinement(*m*)	**Ratifizierung**(*f*); Bestätigung(*f*)	**ratification**
honoraire(s), cachet(*m*), cotisation(*f*); terre(*f*) ou droit réel transmissible	**Gebühr**(*f*); Vergütung(*f*)	**fee**
honoraires d'avocat	Anwaltshonorar	counsel's –
frais(*m*) de justice	Gerichtskosten, –gebühren	court –
propriété inconditionelle	Eigentumsrecht bedingungsloses Eigentum(*m*)	– simple
droits de patente(*f*)	Lizenzgebühr	licence –
honorer, respecter	**honorieren;** einlösen	**honour (to)**
honorer un chèque	e-n Scheck einlösen	– a cheque
hors usine	**ab Fabrik**(*f*)	**ex factory**
huissier	**Gerichtsdiener**(*m*); Justizwachtmeister(*m*)	**usher**
huissier(*m*)	**Hilfsbeamter**(*m*); Gerichtsdiener(*m*); Gerichtsvollzieher(*m*) Gutsverwalter	**bailiff**
hypothécaire	**hypothekarisch;** pfandrechtlich	**hypothecary**
hypothèque(*f*)	**Grundpfandrecht**(*n*); Hypothek(*f*)	**mortgage**
hypothèque sur biens mobiliers	Mobiliarhypothek	chattel –
obligation(*f*) hypothécaire	Hypothekenpfandbrief, –urkunde	– bond
contrat(*m*) d'hypothèque, acte hypothécaire	Hypothekenbrief;	– deed
emprunt(*m*), prêt(*m*) hypothécaire	Hypothekendarlehen; –anleihe	– loan
hypothéquer	**hypothekarisch belasten;** verpfänden	**mortgage (to)**
hypothétique(*f*)	**hypothetisch;** mutmaßlich;	**hypothetical**

I

FRENCH	GERMAN	ENGLISH
idée(*f*) **directrice**	**Leitgedanke**(*m*)	**guiding idea**
identification(*f*) carte(*f*) d'identité acte(*m*) de notoriété signe(*m*) d'identification	**Identifizierung**(*f*) Kennkarte, Personalausweis Kennkarte, Personalausweis Erkennungs–, Kennzeichen	**identification** – card – certificate – mark
identifier	**identifizieren**	**identify (to)**
identité(*f*) fausse(*f*) identité erreur(*f*) sur la personne	**Identität**(*f*) gefälschte – Personenverwechslung	**identity** false – mistaken –
ignorance(*f*)	**Unwissenheit**(*f*); Unkenntnis(*n*)	**ignorance**
ignorant	**unwissend;** unkundig	**ignorant**
illégal, illicite	**illegal;** rechtswidrig	**illegal**
illégal, illicite	**rechtswidrig;** unzulässig	**illicit**
illégalement, à tort	**unangemessen;** übermäßig	**unduly**
illégalité	**Illegalität**(*f*); Rechtswidrigkeit(*f*)	**illegality**
illégitime	**unehelich;** unrechtmäßig	**illegitimate**
illégitime, indu allégation(*f*) sans fondement	**ungebührlich;** ungehörig –e Behauptung	**undue** – allegation
illettré, analphabète	**Analphabet**(*m*)	**illiterate**
imitation(*f*)**,** factice, faux(*f*)	**Nachahmung**(*f*)	**imitation**
immigration(*f*)	**Einwanderung**(*f*)	**immigration**
immobilisation(*f*)**,** fermeture(*f*)	**Betriebseinstellung**(*f*)**;** Stillegung(*f*)	**shut-down**
immobilisé(*f*)**,** fixe immobilisations(*f*) coûts(*m*) fixes prix(*m*) fixe	**fest;** festliegend Anlagevermögen Fixkosten Festpreis; festgesetzter Preis	**fixed** – assets – costs – price
immunité(*f*)**,** exemption(*f*)**,** exonération(*f*) immunité diplomatique immunité juridique	**Immunität**(*f*) diplomatische – gerichtliche –	**immunity** diplomatic – judicial –
impartialité	**Unparteiischkeit**(*f*)**;** Objektivität(*f*)	**impartiality**

FRENCH	GERMAN	ENGLISH
implicite, tacite, absolu consentement(*m*) tacite garantie(*f*) implicite	**stillschweigend;** mit einbegriffen stillschweigende Zustimmung –e Garantie, konkludente Garantie	**implicit, implied** – assent – warranty
importation(*f*) importateur(*m*) licence(*f*) d'importation contingents(*m*) d'importation restrictions(*f*) à l'importation	**Einfuhr**(*f*) –vertreter –lizenz –quote –beschränkungen	**import** – agent – licence – quota – restrictions
imposer, prélever, frapper de, saisir lever un impôt, percevoir une taxe faire une saisie-exécution	**erheben** Steuer – beschlagnahmen; in Besitz nehmen	**levy (to)** – a tax – distress
imposer à, obliger à	**verpflichten;** zwingen	**obligate (to)**
imposition(*f*), charges(*f*) fiscales, fiscalité(*f*) convention(*f*) relative à la double imposition	**Besteuerung**(*f*); Kostenfestsetzung(*f*) Doppelbesteuerungsabkommen	**taxation** double – agreement
impossible à vérifier	**nicht zu ermitteln;** nicht feststellbar	**unascertainable**
impôt(*m*), taxe(*f*), imposition(*f*)	**Auferlegung**(*f*); Verhängung(*f*); Abgabe(*f*)	**imposition**
impôt(*m*), taxe(*f*), contribution(*f*) impôt surles donations impôt sur le revenu impôt indirect impôt sur les successions impôt municipal, impôt local 'poll tax', capitation(*f*) calcul(*m*) d'imposition, assiette(*f*) de l'impôt le fisc fraude(*f*) fiscale fraude fiscale loi(*f*) fiscale déclaration(*f*) d'impôts taxe sur la valeur ajoutée (TVA) impôt retenu à la source	**Steuer**(*m*) Schenkungs– Einkommens– indirekte – Erschafts– Kommunal– Kopf–, Kommunal– –veranlagung –behörde –hinterziehung; –vermeidung –betrug –gesetz; –recht –erklärung Mehrwert– (MwSt) Abzug– Quellen–	**tax** gift – income – indirect – inheritance – municipal – poll – – assessment – authority – evasion – fraud – law – return value added – (VAT) withholding –
impôt(*m*) **sur les bénéfices exceptionnels**	**Sondergewinnsteuer**(*m*); Mehrgewinnsteuer(*m*)	**excess profits tax**
impôt(*m*) **sur les salaires**	**Sozialversicherungsbeitrag**(*m*)	**payroll tax**
impôts(*m*) **locaux** *(UK)*	**Gemeindesteuer**(*m*) *(UK)*	**rates** *(UK)*
impropre, incorrect, irrégulier usage(*m*) abusif	**ungehörig** –e, unsachgemäße Verwendung, Mißbrauch	**improper** – use
impuni	**unbestraft;** ungeahndet	**unpunished**

FRENCH	GERMAN	ENGLISH
imputer, attribuer, accuser	zuschreiben; zur Last legen	impute (to)
inaliénable revendication(f) inaliénable droit(m) inaliénable	unabdingbar –e Forderung –es Recht	inalienable – claim – right
inattaquable	unangreifbar; nicht zu widerlegen	unassailable
incapacité(f) incapacité légale	Unfähigkeit(f) Geschäfts–, Rechts–	incapacity legal –
incapacité(f); infirmité(f), invalidité(f) pension(f) d'invalidité incapacité légale incapacité partielle incapacité permanente	Unfähigkeit(f) Invaliditätsrente; (Kriegs–) Beschädigtenrente Rechts–, Prozeßunfähigkeit teilweise Erwerbs–, Arbeitsunfähigkeit dauerhafte Erwerbs–, Arbeitsunfähigkeit	disability – pension legal – partial – permanent –
incapacité(f), impuissance(f)	Unfähigkeit(f); Unvermögen(n)	inability
incapacité(f) de témoigner; infamie(f)	Ehrlosigkeit(f), Schande(f); Verlust(m) der bürgerlichen Ehrenrechte	infamy
incendiaire	Brandstifter(m); durch Brandstiftung(f) verursacht	incendiary
inceste(m)	Inzest(m)	incest
incidence(f), répercution(f) (de la fiscalité)	Wirkung(f)	impact
incitation(f), provocation(f) (au crime, au délit)	Anstiftung(f); Aufwiegelung(f)	incitement
incitation(f) au crime, au délit	Anstiftung(f), Begünstigung(f); Vorschub(m)	abetment
inciter, pousser, fomenter	anstiften; aufhetzen	instigate (to)
inciter qqu'un (à)	anstiften; aufwiegeln	incite (to) s.o.
incompatible, inconciliable intérêts(m) inconciliables	unvereinbar –e Interessen	incompatible – interests
incompétent, non qualifié (pour) preuve(f) irrecevable incapable, interdit (aliéné, etc.) témoin(m) récusé, non qualifié	unfähig; unzurechnungsfähig (US), geschäftsunfähig unzulässiges Beweismittel Geschäftsunfähiger (US) unzulässiger Zeuge	incompetent – evidence – person – witness
inconditionnel, sans condition	bedingungslos; uneingeschränkt	unconditional
incontesté, sans rival	unbestritten; unangefochten	unchallenged
incontesté; remporté sans opposition (scrutin, élection)	unbestritten; unbestreitbar	uncontested

FRENCH	GERMAN	ENGLISH
incorporation(f), fusion(f), constitution(f); octroi(m) de la personnalité morale	**Gründung**(f) (e-r juristischen **Person**(f), **Kapitalgesellschaft**)(f)	**incorporation**
certificat(m) de constitution	–sbescheinigung;	certificate of –
statut(m) de constitution de société	–urkunde	charter of –
incorporel	**immateriell;** nicht körperlich	**incorporeal**
biens(m) incorporels	–e Gegenstände	– property
droits(m) incorporels	Immaterialgüterrechte	– rights
incorruptible	**unbestechlich**	**incorruptible**
incrimination(f) **de soi-même**	**Selbstbezichtigung**(f)	**self-incrimination**
inculper, accuser, incriminer	**anklagen**	**indict (to)**
poursuivre qqu'un pour un crime	jdn e-s Verbrechens –	– s.o. for a crime
indécent	**ungehörig;** anstößig	**indecent**
indéchiffrable, incompréhensible	**unleserlich;** nicht zu entziffern	**undecipherable**
indemniser, dédommager	**schadlos halten**	**indemnify (to)**
indemnité(f)	**Schadloshaltung**(f); Abfindung(f); Freistellung(f)	**indemnity**
indemnité(f), dommages-intérêts(m)	**Schadensersatz**(m); Entschädigung(-ssumme)(f)	**damages**
dommages-intérêts conditionnels	bedingt zuerkannter Schadensersatzanspruch	contingent –
dommages-intérêts incidents	Schadenersatz für Aufwendungen bei Vertragserfüllung	incidental –
dommages liquidés	im voraus der Höhe nach bestimmter Schadensersatz; Vertragsstrafe	liquidated –
dommages-intérêts symboliques ('un franc symbolique')	nomineller Schadensersatz	nominal –
dommages-intérêts non liquidés	(der Höhe nach noch) unbestimmter Schadensersatz	unliquidated –
indéniable	**unbestreitbar;** unleugbar	**undeniable**
indice(m)	**Anhaltspunkt**(m)	**clue**
indigent, nécessiteux	**Bedürftiger**(m)	**indigent**
indigent(m), économiquement faible	**Bedürftiger**(m); Unterstützungsempfänger(m)	**pauper**
indisponible	**nicht verfügbar**	**unavailable**
individuel, indivis; séparé; plusieurs	**einzeln;** gesondert	**several**
indulgence(f); jour(m) de grâce, délai de paiement	**Stundung**(f); Nachsicht(f), Milde(f)	**indulgence**
inévitable, incontournable	**unvermeidbar**	**unavoidable**

FRENCH	GERMAN	ENGLISH
inexactitude(*f*), imprécision(*f*)	**Ungenauigkeit**(*f*); Unrichtigkeit(*f*)	**inaccuracy**
infliger	**auferlegen;** zufügen	**inflict (to)**
informateur(*m*)	**Anzeigenerstatter**(*m*); Denunziant(*m*); Spitzel(*m*)	**informer**
information(*f*) **confidentielle**	**Verschlußsache**(*f*); unter Geheimschutz gestellte Information(*f*)	**classified information**
information(*f*) **confidentielle**	**vertrauliche Mitteilung**(*f*), – Information(*f*)	**confidential information**
information(s)(*f*); acte(*m*) d'accusation émanant du ministère public; dénonciation(*f*), délation(*f*)	**Nachricht**(*f*); Mitteilung(*f*); Strafanzeige(*f*); Anklage(*f*)	**information**
renseignements(*m*) confidentiels	vertrauliche Mitteilung	confidential –
échange(*m*) de renseignements	Informationsaustausch	exchange of –
infraction(*f*) **imputée**	**zur Last gelegte Tat**(*f*)	**alleged offence**
infraction(*f*), violation(*f*)	**Verletzung**(*f*), Übertretung(*f*), Verstoß(*m*)	**breach**
rupture de contrat manquement(*m*) au devoir (aux obligations), forfaiture(*f*)	Vertragsbruch, –verletzung Pflichtverletzung, –vergehen	– of contract – of duty
violation de la loi infraction aux règles indiscrétion(*f*), violation de la confidentialité	Gesetzesverletzung, Rechtsbruch Ordnungswidrigkeit Verletzung der Geheimhaltungspflicht	– of law – of rules – of secrecy
infraction(*f*), violation(*f*)	**Verletzung**(*f*); Verstoß(*m*); Übertretung(*f*)	**violation**
en contravention de la loi atteinte(*f*) à la vie privée	ein Gesetz übertreten Verletzung der Privatsphäre; – der Intimspäre	in – of the law – of privacy
infraction(*f*), violation(*f*)	**Verletzung**(*f*); Verstoß(*m*)	**infraction**
infraction, violation (d'une loi), contrefaçon	**(Rechts-)Verletzung**(*f*); Verstoß(*m*); Zuwiderhandlung(*f*)	**infringement**
contrefaçon(*f*) en matière de droits d'auteur	Urheberrechtsverletzung	– of copyright
contrefaçon en matière de brevet	Patentverletzung	– of patent
infraction(*f*) **à la législation sur les stupéfiants**	**Drogendelikt**(*n*) (*s. Rauschgift*)(*n*)	**drug offence** (*cf. narcotics*)
infraction(*f*) **à la législation sur les stupéfiants**	**Rauschgiftverbrechen**(*m*)	**narcotics crime**
infraction(*f*) **à la loi,** tort(*m*) fait à qqu'un	**Unrecht**(*n*); Rechtsverletzung(*f*); Delikt(*n*)	**wrong**
injonction(*f*)	**gerichtl. Verfügung**(*f*); Gerichtsbeschluß(*m*)	**court order**

FRENCH	GERMAN	ENGLISH
injuste, déloyal, inéquitable concurrence(*f*) déloyale pratiques(*f*) commerciales déloyales	**unredlich; ungerecht** unlauterer Wettbewerb unlautere Marktmethoden	**unfair** – competition – market practices
injuste enrichissement(*m*) sans cause	**ungerecht; unbillig** ungerechtfertigte Bereicherung	**unjust** – enrichment
injustifié, non motivé	**ungerechtfertigt**	**unjustified**
inapplicable	**nicht (ein-)klagbar;** nicht vollstreckbar	**unenforceable**
innocence(*f*)	**Schuldlosigkeit(*f*);** Unschuld(*f*)	**innocence**
innocent(*m*)	**schuldlos;** unschuldig	**innocent**
innocent(*m*)	**unschuldig**	**not guilty**
insolvabilité(*f*), mise(*f*) en liquidation judiciaire	**Zahlungsunfähigkeit(*f*);** Insolvenz(*f*)	**insolvency**
insolvable	**zahlungsunfähig;** insolvent	**insolvent**
instance(*f*), circonstance(*f*), preuve(*f*) tribunal(*m*) supérieur tribunal inférieur	**Instanz(*f*)** höheres Gericht; höhere – Vorinstanz; untere –	**instance** court of higher – court of lower –
instance(*f*) en cours	**Nebenprozess(*m*);** Zwischenverfahren	**mesne process**
instigateur(*m*), auteur(*m*)	**Anstifter(*m*);** Aufhetzer(*m*)	**instigator**
instituer, fonder, établir engager une action en justice engager des poursuites judiciaires	**einleiten;** erheben eine Klage erheben gerichtliches Verfahren einleiten	**institute (to)** – an action – legal proceedings
insuffisance(*f*)	**Unangemessenheit(*f*);** Unzulänglichkeit(*f*)	**inadequacy**
insulte(*f*), injure(*f*), affront(*m*) injure grave	**Beleidigung(*f*)** gröbliche –	**insult** gross –
intégration horizontale(*f*)	**horizontale Integration(*f*)**	**horizontal integration**
intenter un procès à, poursuivre qqu'un en justice poursuivre qqu'un en dommages-intérêts poursuivre qqu'un en diffamation	**verklagen;** Klage einreichen auf Schadenersatz verklagen wegen übler Nachrede verklagen	**sue (to)** – for damages – for malicious slander
intention(*f*) ou état de fait **présumé;** incidence(*f*), répercussion(*f*) implicitement incidences financières	**Verwicklung(*f*);** innewohnende Bedeutung(*f*); (stillschweigende) Folgerung stillschweigend; durch sinngemäße Auslegung die finanziellen Folgen, Auswirkungen	**implication** by – the financial –(s)
interdiction(*f*), interdit(*m*), défense(*f*)	**Verbot(*n*)**	**interdiction**

FRENCH	GERMAN	ENGLISH
interdire, mettre hors-la-loi, prohiber	**verbieten;** Sperre verhängen über	**ban (to)**
interdit(*m*)**,** prohibé	**verboten**	**prohibited**
intéressement(*m*) **sur les bénéfices**	**Beteiligungen**(*f*) *(pl.)*	**participating interest**
intérêt(*m*) **de report**	**(Börse)**(*f*) **Report**(*m*); Kursaufschlag(*m*)	**contango**
marché(*m*) des reports	Reportgeschäft	– business
taux(*m*) de report	Reportsatz, Prolongationssatz	– rate
intérêt(s)(*m*); titre(*m*), droit(*m*); parti(*m*), groupe(*m*)	**Anrecht**(*n*)**;** Beteiligung(*f*); Zins(*m*)	**interest**
intérêts composés	Zinseszins	compound –
participation(*f*) de contrôle	ausschlaggebender Kapitalanteil	controlling –
intérêts moratoires	Verzugszinsen	– on overdue payment
participation majoritaire	Mehrheitsbeteiligung	majority –
intérêts simples	einfache, gewöhnliche Zinsen	simple –
droit acquis	wohlerworbenes, sicher begründetes Anrecht	vested –
interjeter, confier (des valeurs), placer, remettre	**einreichen;** vorbringen	**lodge (to)**
déposer une réclamation	Anspruch geltend machen	– a claim
interjeter appel	Berufung einlegen	– an appeal
interjeter appel, faire appel d'une décision; former un recours	**anrufen,** sich wenden an	**appeal (to)**
interlocutoire	**einstweilig;** vorläufig	**interlocutory**
jugement(*m*)	Zwischenurteil	– judgment
interlocutoire		
intermédiaire(*m*)**,** personne(*m*) interposée	**Vermittler**(*m*)	**intermediary**
intermédiaire, revendeur(*m*)	**Zwischenhändler**(*m*)**;** Vermittler(*m*)	**middleman**
international	**international;** zwischenstaatlich	**international**
interne, intérieur	**intern;** inländisch, Binnen-	**internal**
interner	**internieren**	**intern (to)**
interprétation(*f*)	**Auslegung**(*f*)**;** Erklärung(*f*)	**interpretation**
interpréter, analyser	**auslegen**	**construe (to)**
interrogatoire(*m*)**,** interrogation(*f*)	**Befragung**(*f*)**;** Verhör(*n*), Vernehmung(*f*)	**interrogation**
interrogatoire(*m*)	**Verhör**(*n*)**;** Befragung(*f*)	**questioning**
interroger, mettre en doute	**verhören;** in Zweifel(*m*) ziehen	**question (to)**
interroger un suspect; filtrer, trier; masquer, protéger	**überprüfen;** untersuchen	**screen (to)**
étudier les risques de sécurité	Sicherheitsrisiken überprüfen	– security risks

FRENCH	GERMAN	ENGLISH
intervenir	eingreifen; Prozeß(*m*) beitreten	intervene
intervenir (dans un procès); accepter (un arbitrage); s'affilier, adhérer à	verbinden	join (to)
unir par les liens du mariage	jdn trauen	– in matrimony
intervention(*f*)	Eingriff(*m*); Prozeßbeitritt(*m*)	intervention
intestat	ohne Testament verstorben	intestate
intimé(*f*)	Beklagter(*m*) (Berufungs–, Beschwerde–, Revision–)	appellee
intitulé(*m*); prémisses(*f*); local(*m*), (les) lieux(*m*), (l')immeuble(*m*)	Geschäftsräume(*m*); Betriebsräume(*m*)	premises
introduction(*f*) d'un texte juridique	einleitende Erklärung(*f*); Präambel(*f*); Darstellung(*f*)	recitals
intrus (dans une propriété privée)	Besitzstörer; Rechtsverletzer	trespasser
inventaire(*m*), stock(*m*); bilan(*m*) de faillite (*US*)	(Lager-)Bestand(*m*); Inventar(*n*); Inventur(*f*)	inventory
investissement(*m*), placement de fonds	Investition(*f*); (Kapital-)Anlage, Beteiligung(*f*)	investment
banque(*f*) d'affaires (*US*)	Investitionsbank; Emissions–Investment–,	– bank (*US*)
société(*m*) de placement (de portefeuill(e)	Kapitalanlagegesellschaft	– company
fonds(*m*) de placement	Investitionsfonds	– fund
société d'investissement	Kapitalanlagegesellschaft	– trust
inviolé	unverletzlich; unversehrt	inviolate
invoquer	sich berufen auf	invoke (to)
invoquer la loi	– eine Rechtsvorschrift, e-n Gesetzeserlaß	– an enactment
irrecevable, illicite, inadmissible	unzulässig	inadmissible
témoignage(*m*) irrecevable	–e Beweismittel; nicht zugelassenes Beweismaterial	– evidence
irréfragable	unwiderlegbar	irrebuttable
présomption(*f*) absolue	–e Rechtsvermutung	– presumption
irréfutable	unwiderlegbar	irrefutable
irréprochable	zuverlässig; nicht widerlegbar	unimpeachable
irresponsable, insolvable	unverantwortlich; nicht haftbar	irresponsible
irrévocable, non recouvrable	unwiderruflich	irrevocable
lettre(*f*) de crédit irrévocable	–es Akkreditiv	– letter of credit
ivresse(*f*); empoisonnement(*m*)	(Be-)Trunkenheit(*f*)	intoxication

J

FRENCH	GERMAN	ENGLISH
jeux(*m*) **de hasard,** jeux d'argent	**Glücksspiel**(*n*)	**gambling**
jouissance(*f*)**,** exercice(*m*) d'un droit	**Genuß**(*n*)**;** Nießbrauch(*m*)	**enjoyment**
possession(*f*)	Eigentumsausübung	– of property
judiciaire, juridique	**gerichtlich;** richterlich	**judicial**
acte(*m*) judiciaire	richterliche Handlung	– act
ressort(*m*) territorial d'un tribunal	Gerichtsbezirk	– district
reconnaissance(*f*) d'un fait par la justice	Kenntnisnahme des Gerichts	– notice
pouvoir judiciaire	richterliche Gewalt; Justizgewalt	– power
procédure(*f*) judiciaire	Gerichtsverhandlung	– proceeding
révision(*f*) judiciaire	gerichtliche Überprüfung	– review
système(*m*) judiciaire	Gerichtswesen	– system
judiciaire (*adj.*)**;** magistrature(*f*) (*n*)	**Gerichtswesen**(*n*)**;** Rechts–; Richterstand(*m*)	**judiciary**
judiciaire, juridique, légal	**juristisch;** Rechts-	**juridical**
juge(*m*)**,** magistrat(*m*)	**Richter**(*m*)	**judge**
juge de cour d'appel	Berufungs–	appellate –
magistrat assesseur	Hilfs–	assistant –
juge du siège	Einzelrichter, im Büroweg entscheidender Richter	– in chambers
président(*m*) du tribunal	Gerichtspräsident; vorsitzender Richter	presiding –
(juge)(*m*) **des référés**	**unter Ausschluß**(*m*) **der Öffentlichkeit**(*f*)	**in chambers**
juge(*m*) **non-professionel**	**Laienrichter**(*m*)	**lay judge**
jugement(*m*)**,** arrêt(*m*)**,** décision(*f*)	**Urteil**(*n*) (Zivilrecht)(*n*)**;** Zuerkennung(*f*)**,** Zusprechung(*f*)	**adjudgment**
jugement(*m*)**,** décision(*f*)**,** prononcé d'un jugement; adjudication(*f*)**,**	**Entscheidung**(*f*)**,** Urteil(*n*)**;** Zuerkennung(*f*)**,** Zuschlag(*m*)	**adjudication**
jugement déclaratif de faillite	Eröffnung eines Konkursverfahrens, Konkurseröffnung	– of bankruptcy

FRENCH	GERMAN	ENGLISH
jugement(*m*), décision(*f*) judiciaire	**Urteil**(*n*)	**judgment**
jugement déclaratoire	Feststellungs–	declaratory –
jugement définitif	End–	definitive –
jugement final	rechtskräftiges –; End–	final –
jugement interlocutoire	Zwischen–	interlocutory –
jugement rendu à l'unanimité	Anerkenntnis–	– by consent
jugement par défaut	Versäumnis–	– by default
créancier dont la dette est ajugée due par le cour	Vollstreckungsgläubiger	– creditor
débiteur(*m*) dont la dette est ajugée due par le cour	Urteilsschuldner	– debtor
jugement sommaire	– im abgekürzten, summarischen Verfahren	summary –
prononcer une sentence	– erlassen, verkünden	to award –
rendre un jugement	– erlassen	to deliver –
jugement(*m*) **définitif, sans appel**	**Endurteil**(*n*); rechtskräftiges Urteil(*n*)	**final judgment/ decree/sentence**
jugement exécutoire	**Vollstreckungsurteil**(*n*)	**executory decree**
jugement(*m*) **ordonnant le cumul des peines**	**zusätzliche Strafzumessung**	**consecutive sentences**
juger, mettre en jugement; essayer	**(gerichtlich) verhandeln,** untersuchen	**try (to)**
juger une affaire (au tribunal)	Prozeß führen; über eine Sache verhandeln	– a case
juger, statuer, rendre un arrêt	**erkennen,** entscheiden, Recht(*n*) sprechen	**adjudicate (to)**
mettre (qqu'un) en faillite	Schuldner für zahlungsunfähig erklären; Konkurs(verfahren) über das Vermögen des Schuldners eröffnen	– s.o. bankrupt
juré, membre(*m*) du jury	**Geschworener**(*m*)	**juror**
juré en désaccord avec le reste du jury	**nicht Zustimmende(r)**(*f*, *m*), **widersprechende(r)**(*f*, *m*) **Geschworene(r)**(*f*, *m*)	**dissenting juror**
juridiction(*f*), lieu(*m*) du jugement	**Gerichtsstand**(*m*); Zuständigkeit(*f*)	**venue**
juridiction(*f*) **du premier degré**	**Vorinstanz**(*f*); unteres Gericht(*n*)	**lower court**
jurisprudence(*f*), droit jurisprudentiel	**Fallrecht**(*n*); Präzedenzrecht(*n*)	**case law**
juriste(*m*), légiste(*m*); homme(*m*) de loi (*US*), avocat	**Jurist**(*m*); Rechtsgelehrter(*m*)	**jurist**
jury(*m*)	**Schwurgericht**(*n*); Geschworene	**jury**
jury de conseil	beratende Jury	advisory –
jury d'accusation (*US*)	Anklagejury (*US*)	grand – (*US*)
jury de jugement (*US*)	Urteilsjury (*US*)	petty – (*US*)
procès(*m*) conduit devant un jury	Schwurgerichtsverfahren	trial by –
jury du procès	Geschworene in e-m Prozeß; Urteilsjury	trial –

FRENCH	GERMAN	ENGLISH
jury(*m*) **d'accusation** *(US)*	**Anklagejury**(*f*) *(US)*	**grand jury** *(US)*
juste, équitable réclamation(*f*) en accord avec les principes de l'équité	**billig;** gerecht Billigkeitsanspruch	**equitable** – claim
juste, impartial libre échange dans des conditions de réciprocité loyale procès(*m*) équitable	**gerecht;** billig; fair Praxis der Nichtdiskriminierung im Außenhandel ordentliches Gerichtsverfahren; unparteiisches Verfahren	**fair** – trade practices – trial
justice(*f*), équité(*f*); administration(*f*) de la justice; titre(*m*) donné aux magistrats	**Gerechtigkeit**(*f*); Rechtspflege(*f*); Richter(*m*) (Titel)	**justice**
justifier, soutenir	**rechtfertigen;** verteidigen; beanspruchen	**vindicate (to)**
juvénile tribunal(*m*) pour enfants crime(*m*) ou délit commis par un mineur délinquance(*f*) juvénile délinquant(*m, f*) juvénile, accusé(*m*) mineur	**Jugend-** –gericht(*n*) –verbrechen –kriminalität(*f*) jugendlicher Straftäter(*m*)	**juvenile** – court – crime – delinquency – delinquent, offender

L

FRENCH	GERMAN	ENGLISH
lancer (un mandat d'arrêt), émettre, publier	**erlassen; ausstellen**	**issue (to)**
rendre un arrêt de justice	e-n Gerichtsbeschluß erlassen	– a court order
délivrer une citation à comparaître	Prozeßladung (mit Klageschrift) ergehen lassen	– a writ of summons
donner des instructions	Vorschriften erlassen	– instructions
émettre des actions	Wertpapiere ausgeben (s. Aktien)	– securities (cf. share)
latent, caché(m)	**verborgen;** heimlich	**latent**
le droit, la justice, le bien; droit(m), titre(m), privilège(m)	**Recht(sanspruch)**(m)	**right**
droits civils	Grundrechte; bürgerliche Ehrenrechte	civil –(s)
droits de l'homme	Menschenrechte	human –(s)
propriété(f) intellectuelle	immaterielle Rechte	intangible –(s)
droit d'appel	Berufungsrecht; Rechtsmittel	– of appeal
droit(m) de recours	Entschädigungsrecht	– of redress
droit de passage	Vorfahrtsrecht; Wegerecht	– of way
droits acquis en vertu de la constitution	wohlerworbene, wohlbegründete Rechte	vested –
légal, licite, légitime	**gesetzlich;** rechtmäßig; rechtsgültig	**lawful**
majorité(f) (légale)	Volljährigkeit	– age
héritier(m) légitime	gesetzlicher, rechtmäßiger Erbe	– heir

FRENCH	GERMAN	ENGLISH
légal, licite, légitime, judiciaire, juridique	**gesetzmäßig;** rechtmäßig; rechtsgültig; juristisch	**legal**
âge(m) de la majorité légale	Volljährig-, Mündigkeit	– age
assistance(f) judiciaire	Armenrecht, Prozeßkostenhilfe (UK); unentgeltliche Beratungshilfe (US)	– aid
capacité(f) judiciaire	Rechts-, Geschäftsfähigkeit	– capacity
compétence judiciaire	Geschäftsfähigkeit	– competence
incapacité(f) légale	Geschäftsunfähigkeit; Prozeßunfähigkeit (US)	– disability
excuse(f) légale	Schuldausschließungsgrund; rechtliche erhebliche Einwendung(f)	– excuse
incapacité légale	Geschäftsunfähigkeit	– incapacity
responsabilité(f) légale	gesetzlicher Haftpflicht; – Haftung	– liability
personne(f) morale	juristische (rechtsfähige) Person	– person
poursuites(f) judiciaires	Gerichtsverfahren; Prozeß	– proceedings
représentant(m, f) légal	Vertreter in Rechtssachen; gesetzlicher Vertreter; Nachlaßverwalter(m)	– representative
statut(m) légal	Rechtsstellung; –position	– status
légaliser, authentifier, certifier	**legalisieren;** beglaubigen	**legalise (to)**
légataire(m, f)	**Testamentserbe**(m); Vermächtnisnehmer(m)	**devisee**
légataire(m, f)	**Vermächtnisnehmer**(m); Erbe(m)	**legatee**
légataire(m) **universel**	**Restnachlaßempfänger**(m)	**residuary legatee**
légiférer	**Gesetze geben**(n), – machen, – erlassen	**legislate (to)**
législatif, législative	**gesetzgebend**	**legislative**
assemblée(f) législative	–e Versammlung	– assembly
pouvoir(m) législatif	–e Gewalt; Legislative	– power
législation(f)	**Gesetzgebung**(f); Gesetze(n)	**legislation**
législation(f) **facultative,** non impérative	**Kannbestimmungen**(f)	**permissive legislation**
légitime, justifié	**legitim;** rechtmäßig, gesetzmäßig; ehelich	**legitimate**
légitime défense(f), autodéfense	**Notwehr**(f); Selbstverteidigung(f)	**self-defence**
légitimer, justifier	**rechtfertigen**	**justify (to)**
legs(m)	**Vermächtnis**(n); Legat(m); Erbteil(n)	**bequest**
legs(m)	**Vermächtnis**(n); Erbe(m)	**legacy**
legs à payer d'une source spécifiée	beschränktes Gattungsvermächtnis	demonstrative –
legs universel	Gattungsvermächtnis; Geldsummenvermächtnis	general –
léguer	**testamentarisch vermachen;** vererben	**bequeath (to)**

FRENCH	GERMAN	ENGLISH
lettre(f) procuration(f) lettre(f) de crédit déclaration(f) d'intention	**Brief**(m); Schreiben (schriftlicher) Vollmacht Akkreditiv Absichtserklärung	**letter** – of attorney – of credit – of intent
libération(f), décharge(f) libération conditionnelle dégrevage libération de prison	**Entlassung**(f); Entlastung(f); Entladung(f), Löschen Strafaussetzung zur Bewährung; bedingte Entlassung Entlastung; Entschuldung Freilassung	**discharge** conditional – – from an encumbrance – from prison
libérer, relaxer, élargir, renoncer, délier, décharger	**freilassen;** entlassen	**release (to)**
liberté(f)	**Freiheit**(f)	**liberty** (cf. freedom)
liberté(f), franchise(f), immunité(f) liberté d'association liberté religieuse, liberté du culte liberté d'expression liberté de la presse liberté du commerce	**Freiheit**(f) Versammlungs– Religions– Rede– Presse– Handels–	**freedom** – of assembly – of religion – of speech – of the press – of trade
liberté(f), privilège(m); droit(m) électoral; minimum de couverture(f) (assurance)	**Konzession**(f)	**franchise**
liberté surveillée; liberté conditionnelle en liberté(f) surveillée contrôleur(m) judiciaire	**Entlassung**(f) **auf Bewährung**(f); bedingter Straferlaß(m) gegen Ehrenwort freigelassen Bewährungsbeamter	**parole** on – – officer
liberté surveillée(f), mise(f) à l'épreuve; essai à l'épreuve, à l'essai contrôleur(m) judiciaire	**Bewährung**(f) auf – –sbeamter	**probation** on – – officer
libre, en franchise, exempt franco quai franco bord franco avion franco quai franco wagon franco camion port(m) libre libre-échange	**frei** Frei Längsseite Seeschiff Frei an Bord Frei an Flugzeug Frei Kai Frei Bahnstation, Eisenbahnwaggon Frei Lastwagen Freihafen Freihandel	**free** – alongside ship (FAS) – on board (FOB) – on plane (FOP) – on quay (FOQ) – on rail (FOR) – on truck (FOT) – port – trade
libre d'hypothèques	**unbelastet;** hypothekenfrei	**unencumbered**
licencié(f) **en droit**	**niedrigster akademischer Grad**(m) **der jurist. Fakultät**(f)	**LLB**
licenciement(m) **économique**	**(betriebsbedingte) Entlassung**(f)	**redundancy**

FRENCH	GERMAN	ENGLISH
lieu(m), endroit(m), place(f) siège(m) d'une société	**Ort**(m) Geschäftssitz; geschäftliche Niederlassung	**place** – of business
lieu de livraison lieu d'accomplissement (d'un contrat) lieu de résidence	Liefer–; Erfüllungs– Wohn-, Aufenthalts–	– of delivery – of performance – of residence
lieu(m) **du crime**	**Tatort**(m)	**scene of crime**
lignée(f), origine(f)	**Abstammung**(f); Herkunft	**parentage**
limitation(f), prescription(f), restriction(f)	**Verjährung**(f)	**limitation**
prescription d'action période(f) de prescription droit(m) de prescription	Klage– –sfrist –sgesetz	– of actions – period statute of –
limite(f), période(f), durée(f), terme(m), fin(f)	**Zeitdauer**(m); Fachausdruck(m)	**term**
durée d'un bail délai(m) de congé durée des fonctions	Miet-, Pachtzeit Kündigungsfrist Amtszeit	– of a lease – of notice – of office
limité, restreint société(f) dans laquelle la responsabilité des associés est limitée (société anonyme, société à responsabilité(f) limitée)	**beschränkt**; begrenzt Kapitalgesellschaft mit (Haftungsbeschränkung)	**limited** – company
responsabilité limitée commanditaire(m) société(f) en commandite simple	beschränkte Haftung beschränkt haftender Gesellschafter; Kommanditist Kommanditgesellschaft	– liability – partner – partnership
limiter la portée d'une déclaration	**Erklärung**(f) **unter Einschränkungen**(f) **abgeben**	**qualify (to) a statement**
liquidateur(m)	**Konkursverwalter**(m); Liquidator(m)	**liquidator**
liquidation(f) entrer en liquidation liquidation volontaire	**Liquidation**(f) in – gehen –aufgrund Gesellschaftsbeschlusses; freiwillige –	**liquidation** to go into – voluntary –
liquidé, certain créance(f) liquide dommages-intérêts(m) par contrat	**beziffert** auf eine bestimmte Summe –e Forderung –er Schadensersatz; vereinbarte Vertragsstrafe	**liquidated** – claim – damages
liquider liquider une société	**abwickeln**; in Liquidation gehen Liquidation e-r Gesellschaft durchführen	**liquidate (to)** – a company
liste(f) **des actionnaires**	**Gesellschaftsverzeichnis**(n); Liste der Aktionäre	**list of shareholders**
litige(m), procès(m)	**Prozeß**(m); Rechtsstreit(m)	**litigation**
litigieux	**strittig**	**litigious**

FRENCH	GERMAN	ENGLISH
livraison(f) **à court terme**	**Minderlieferung**(f); unvollständige Lieferung(f)	**short delivery**
locataire(m, f), tenancier(m), concessionnaire(m, f)	**Mieter**(m); Pächter(m); Leasingnehmer(m)	**lessee**
locataire(m), tenancier(m), usufruitier(m)	**Mieter**(m); Pächter(m)	**tenant**
locataire(m) **à bail,** emphytéote(m)	**Mieter**(m); Pächter(m)	**leaseholder**
location(f), louage(m); embauchage(m); salaire(m) vente(m) à tempérament	**Miete**(f); Einstellung(f); Heuer(m) Teilzahlungs–, Abzahlungskauf (UK)	**hire** – -purchase
location(f), usufruit(m), droits(m) du tenant	**Mietverhältnis**(n); Pacht–(f)	**tenancy**
location-vente(f), crédit-bail(m), leasing(m)	**(ver-)mieten;** (ver-)pachten;	**leasing**
logement(m), résidence(f)	**Aufenthalt**(m); Wohnung(f)	**dwelling**
logistique	**Logistik**(f)	**logistics**
loi, ordonnance(f), décret(m)	**Gesetzeserlaß**(m); Gesetzeskraftverleihung(f)	**enactment**
loi(f) **habilitante**	**Ermächtigungsgesetz**(n)	**enabling Act**
loi(f) **martiale**	**Kriegsrecht**(n); Standrecht(n)	**martial law**
lois(m) **de la chasse**	**Jagdgesetz**(n), (Jagd)	**game law (hunting)**
louer, embaucher donner en location, louer	**mieten** ver–	**hire (to)** – out
louer; adjuger un contrat de travaux publics	**vermieten;** verpachten; zulassen	**let (to)**
loyer(m); prix(m) de location	**Miete**(f); Pacht(f)	**rent**

M

FRENCH	GERMAN	ENGLISH
machinations(f) **et intrigues**(f)	**planen und Ränke schmieden**	**scheming and planning**
macro-économie(f)	**Makroökonomie**(f)	**macroeconomics**
magistrat(m), juge(m)	**Ehrenamtlicherichter**(m)	**magistrate**
magistrature(f); période(f) d'exercice d'un juge	**Gerichtsbarkeit**(f); Rechtsprechung(f)	**judicature**
main(f) **d'oeuvre,** salariés(m); travail(m), labeur(m)	**Arbeit**(f)(skräfte(f), –nehmer)(m)	**Labor** (US), **labour**
Ministère(m) du Travail	–sministerium (US)	Department of –
travaux(m) forcés	Zwangs–	forced –
conflit(m) du travail	–skampf	– conflict, dispute
droit(m) du travail	–srecht	– law
permis(m) de travail	–sgenehmigung	– permit
organisations(f) ouvrières, ouvriers(m) syndiqués	gewerkschaftlich organisierte Arbeitnehmer	organised –
Bureau(m) International du travail (BIT)	Internationales –samt, IAA	International – Organisation
maire(m)	**Bürgermeister**(m)	**mayor**
maison(f) **de correction**	**Straf(vollzugs)anstalt**(f) (US); Gefängnis(n)	**correctional institution**
maitre(m) **en droit**	**höherer akademischer Grad der jurist. Fakultät**(f)	**LLM**
majoration(f) **d'héritage;** accroissement(m) organique	**Zuwachs**(m); Zunahme(m); Anwachsen(n)	**accretion**
majorité(f) (n), majoritaire (adj.)	**Mehrheit**(f)	**majority**
majorité absolue	absolute –	absolute –
vote(m) majoritaire	–sbeschluß; –swahl	– vote
majorité requise	qualifizierte –	qualified –
mal(m), **tort**(m), préjudice(m)	**Schaden**(m)	**harm**
lésion(f) corporelle	körperlicher –; Körperverletzung	bodily –
malfaiteur(m)	**Täter**(m); Verbrecher(m)	**malefactor**
malhonnêteté(f)	**Unredlichkeit**(f); Unehrlichkeit(f)	**dishonesty**

FRENCH	GERMAN	ENGLISH
malpropre, déloyal jeu(m) déloyal, malveillance(f) (par ext., crime, meurtre)	**unredlich** unfaires Spiel; Verbrechen	**foul** – play
mandat(m), décret(m), ordre(m), arrêté(m) injonction(f)	**Befehl**(m); Verfügung(f)	**order**
ordonnance(f) de mise en détention	gerichtliche Verfügung; Gerichtsbeschluß Haftbefehl	court – detention –
ordonnance d'extradition ordonnance interlocutoire	Auslieferungsbefehl; –beschluß Zwischenverfügung; einstweilige Verfügung	extradition – interlocutory –
ordonnance de ne pas faire	richterlicher Verbot; einstweilige Verfügung	restraining –
mandat(m), pouvoir(m), certificat(m), bon(m) de souscription	**Ermächtigung**(f); Bescheinigung(f); Haftbefehl(m)	**warrant**
ordonnance de saisie-exécution	Arrestbefehl; Pfändungsbeschluf	distress –
mandat de perquisition ordre d'arrestation ordonnance de saisie procuration(f), pouvoir	Durchsuchungsbefehl Haftbefehl Beschlagnahmeverfügung Prozeßvollmacht e-s Anwalts (zur Erklärung e-s Anerkenntnisses vor Geicht)	search – – of arrest – of attachment – of attorney
mandat(m), procuration(f)	**Auftrag**(m); Mandat(n)	**mandate**
mandat(m) **d'un magistrat;** feuille(f) de contributions; précepte(m), principe(m)	**(gerichtliche) Anweisung**(f); Regel(f)	**precept**
mandataire(m), représentant dûment désigné	**Anwalt**(m); Rechtsbeistand(m); Bevollmächtigter(m, f)	**attorney**
avocat (US) conseiller et représentant légal du gouvernement	Rechtsanwalt, –anwältin (US) Generalstaatsanwalt; Kronanwalt; Justizminister	--at-law (US) – -general
procuration	Vollmacht(surkunde); Prozeßvollmacht (US)	letter of –
mandat pouvoirs	Vollmacht; Vertretungsbefugnis; Prozeßvollmacht	power of –
mandataire(m), fondé de pouvoir; procuration(f), mandat(m)	**(Stimmrechts-)Vollmacht**(f); (Stimmrechts-)Vertreter(m)	**proxy**
manqué, avorté, inopérant	**erfolglos,** ergebnislos	**abortive**
manquement(f), défaillance(f)	**Nichterfüllung**(f); Unterlassung(f); (Zahlungs-) Verzug(m)	**default**
défaut(m) de comparution	Nichterscheinen (vor Gericht); Versäumnis der Einlassung	– of appearance
jugement(m) par défaut	Versäumnisurteil	judgment by –
marchandise(f), denrées(f)	**(Handels-)Artikel**(m); Ware; Rohstoff(m)	**commodity**

FRENCH	GERMAN	ENGLISH
marché place(f) du marché prix(m) courant du marché part(f) du marché valeur(f) marchande	**Markt**(m) Marktplatz –preis; Kurswert –anteil –wert; Kurswert; Verkehrswert	market – place – price – share – value
marché(m) **des changes**	**Devisenmarkt**(m)	foreign exchange market
marché(m) **monétaire**	**Geldmarkt**(m)	money market
mari(m)	**Ehemann**(m); Gatte(m)	husband
mariage(m)	**Ehe**(f)(stand)(m)	matrimony
mariage(m) contrat(m) de mariage dispense(f) de bans contrat de mariage mariage simulé	**Heirat**(f); Ehe(f) Ehevertrag Heiratserlaubnis Ehevertrag Scheinehe	marriage – articles – licence – settlement sham –
mariage(m) né dans le mariage, filiation(f) légitime né hors du mariage, filiation naturelle	**Ehe(stand)**(m) ehelich geboren nichtehelich geboren	wedlock born in – born out of –
maritime, marin assurance(f) maritime	**See(schiffahrt)**(f) –(transport)versicherung	marine – insurance
marque(f) **(de fabrique et de commerce)** marque déposée	**Warenzeichen**(n); Handelsmarke(f) eingetragenes Warenzeichen	trade mark registered –
matériel(m)**,** réel, essentiel preuve(f) matérielle fait(m) essentiel	**wesentlich** beweiserhebliche Zeugenaussage –e Tatsache	material – evidence – fact
matricide(m, f)	**Muttermord**(m)	matricide
mauvais, faux créance(f) irrécouvrable mauvaise foi	**zweifelhaft; unzureichend** zweifelhafte Außenstände (pl.); uneinbringliche Forderung böser Glaube	bad – debt – faith
mauvais traitement	**Mißhandlung**(f)	maltreatment
médecine(m) **légale**	**Gerichtsmedizin**(f)	forensic medicine
médiateur(m)	**Ombudsmann**(m); Beschwerdekommissar(m)	ombudsman
médical(m) certificat(m) médical expertise(f) médicale	**ärztlich;** medizinisch ärztliches Attest medizinischer Sachverständigenbeweis	medical – certificate – evidence
méfait(m); prévarication(f)	**rechts,** gesetzwidrige Handlung(f), –s Verhalten	malfeasance
mémento(m)**,** rappel(m) pour mémoire	**Mahnung**(f); Beanstandung(f)	reminder
menace(f)	**(Be)Drohung**(f)	menace
menace(f)	**Drohung**(f)	threat

FRENCH	GERMAN	ENGLISH
menacer, proférer des menaces	**drohen**	**threaten (to)**
menées(f) **commerciales,** transactions boursières	**Geschäfte**(n); Transaktionen; Geschäftsverbindungen	**dealings**
menottes(f)	**Handschellen**(f)	**handcuffs**
mental(m) cruauté(f) mentale aberration(f) mentale hôpital(m) psychiatrique incapacité(f) mental soins(m) psychiatriques	**geistig** seelische Grausamkeit Geistesstörung psychiatrisches Krankenhaus; –e Anstalt Geisteskrankheit Pflege der Geisteskranken	**mental** – cruelty – disorder – hospital, home – incapacity – nursing
mépris(m), outrage(m), manque de respect outrage civil outrage à magistrat(s) outrage délictueux	**Mißachtung**(f); Geringschätzung(f) Ungehorsam gegenüber gerichtlichem Gebot Mißachtung des Gerichts strafbare Mißachtung des Gerichts; Ungebühr vor Gericht	**contempt** civil – – of court criminal –
mercantilisme(m)	**Geschäftemacher**(m); Schieber(m)	**profiteering**
mesure(f), démarches mesure coercitive mesure licite mesure de précaution mesures préventives	**Maßnahme**(f) Zwangs– rechtmäßige – Vorsichts– vorbeugende –	**measure** coercive – lawful – precautionary – preventive –
mesures(f) **de contrainte**	**Zwangsmaßnahmen**(f)	**coercive measures**
mettre en accusation, récuser, contester récuser un témoin	**anklagen;** anfechten; in Zweifel ziehen die Glaubwürdigkeit eines Zeugen anzweifeln (US)	**impeach (to)** – a witness
mettre en danger, compromettre	**gefährden**	**jeopardise (to)**
mettre en litige, contester	**prozessieren**	**litigate (to)**
mettre en gage, gager	**verpfänden**	**pawn (to)**
mettre hors-la-loi, proscrire, prohiber	**ächten;** für unrechtmäßig erklären	**outlaw (to)**
meurtre(m), assassinat(m) tentative(f) de meurtre assassinat (US) homicide(m, f) par imprudence, involontaire (US)	**Mord**(m) –versuch schwerer – leichter –	**murder** attempted – first-degree – (US) second-degree – (US)
meurtre(m), tuerie(f) euthanasie(f)	**Tötung**(f) Gnadentod, Euthanasie	**killing** mercy –
micro-économie(f)	**Mikroökonomie**(f)	**microeconomics**
militaire code(m) de justice militaire, droit(m) militaire police(m) militaire tribunal(m) militaire	**Militär-**(n) –(straf)recht(n); Wehr(straf)recht(n); –polizei(f) –gericht(n)	**military** – law – police – tribunal

FRENCH	GERMAN	ENGLISH
mille(m) marin	Seemeile(f)	nautical mile
mineur(m)	Unmündiger(m) (s. Minderjähriger)	infant (cf. minor)
mineur(m)	Minderjähriger(m), (s. Unmündiger)	minor (cf. infant)
mineur(m), peu important vol(m) simple infraction(f) mineure, contravention(f) larcin(m)	geringfügig; unbedeutend Bagatelldiebstahl Übertretung; Bagatelldelikt Bagatelldiebstahl	petty – larceny – offence – theft
ministère(m) de l'intérieur (UK)	Innenministerium(n) (UK)	Home Office (UK)
ministre(m) de l'intérieur (UK)	Innenminister(m) (UK)	Home Secretary (UK)
minorité(f) participation(f) minoritaire participation minoritaire	Minderheit(f) –sbeteiligung; Anteile in Fremdbesitz Fremdanteil	minority – interest – share
mise en accusation	Anklage(verlesung)(f); gerichtliche Belangung	arraignment
mise(f) en cause (US)	Streitverkündung(f) (US)	interpleader (US)
mise(f) en liberté, élargissement; cession(f) de propriété; décharge(f); mise(f) en vente; libération(f)de capitaux relaxe, mise en liberté	Freilassung(f); Erlösung; Entlastung Haftentlassung	release – from custody
mise(f) en oeuvre, application mise en oeuvre d'une politique application(f) d'un règlement	Durchführung(f); Erfüllung(f) (politisches) Programm in die Tat umsetzen Durchführung von Bestimmungen	implementation – of a policy – of regulations
mobile(m), ressort(m), raison(f), motif(m) raison(f), mobile principal(e)	Beweggrund(f); Motiv(n) Haupt–	motive main/principal –
monétaire système(m) monétaire unité(f) monétaire	Währungs- –system(n) –einheit(f)	monetary – system – unit
monogamie	Monogamie(f)	monogamy
monopole(m), droit(m) d'exclusivité	Monopol(n)	monopoly
monopoliser	monopolisieren; für sich allein in Anspruch nehmen	monopolise (to)
monter un coup contre qqu'un (fam.), inventer	jdn lügnerisch bezichtigen	frame (to) s.o.
moratoire(m)	Moratorium(n), Stillhalteabkommen(n)	moratorium
morgue(f), institut(m) médico-légal	Leichenhalle(f)	mortuary

FRENCH	GERMAN	ENGLISH
mort, décès	**Ableben**(n); Tod(m)	**decease**
mort(f) **civile,** perte(f) d'un droit, perte par confiscation	**Verwirkung**(f); Verlust(m); Beschlagnahme(f)	**forfeiture**
expiration(f) d'un brevet	Patentverlust	– of a patent
déchéance(f) d'une police d'assurance	Versicherungsverfall	– of an insurance
perte de biens par confiscation	Eigentumsverlust; Vermögenseinziehung	– of property
mortalité(f)	**Sterblichkeit**(f)	**mortality**
taux(m) de mortalité	–sziffer	– rate
statistiques(m) de mortalité	–sstatistik	– statistics
mortel, léthal	**tödlich**	**lethal**
motion(f), requête(f), demande(f)	**Antrag**(m)	**motion**
demande d'ajournement	Vertagungs–	– for adjournment
demande tendant à juger à nouveau la même affaire	– auf Wiederaufnahme des Verfahrens	– for new trial
moyens(m), **façons**(f); ressources(f) financières	**Mittel**(n)	**means**
moyens de pression	Zwangs–	– of coercion
moyens de preuve	Beweis–	– of evidence
moyen de paiement, méthode de paiement	Zahlungs–	– of payment
multilatéral, plurilatéral	**multilateral**	**multilateral**
municipalité(f); circonscription(f) électorale urbaine	**Stadtbezirk**(m); Gemeinde, Kreis(m)	**borough**
mutinerie(f)	**Meuterei**(f)	**mutiny**
mutuel	**gegenseitig**	**mutual**
assurance(f) mutuelle	Versicherung auf Gegenseitigkeit	– insurance
société(f) d'assurances mutuelles	Versicherungsverein auf Gegenseitigkeit	– insurance company
donation(f) au dernier survivant	–es Testament	– will

N

FRENCH	GERMAN	ENGLISH
national assemblée(f) nationale monnaie(f) nationale dette(f) publique revenu(m) national sécurité(f) sociale droit(m) interne, droit national territoire(m) national	**National-** –versammlung(f) Landeswährung Staatsschuld Volkseinkommen Sozialversicherung (UK) Landesrecht, innerstaatliches –, einzelstaatliches(EG) Recht Staats–, Hoheitsgebiet	**national** – assembly – currency – debt – income – insurance – law – territory
nationalisation(f)	**Verstaatlichung**(f)	**nationalisation**
naturalisation demande(f) de naturalisation décret(m) de naturalisation	**Einbürgerung**(f) –santrag –surkunde	**naturalisation** application for – certificate of –
naturel héritier(m) naturel personne physique, individu(m)	**natürlich-** Erbe durch Geburtsrecht natürliche Person	**natural** – heir – person
né dans (hors) (des liens) du mariage	**(un-)ehelich geboren**	**born in (out of) wedlock**
nécessité(f)	**Notwendigkeit**(f); Bedürfnis(n)	**necessity**
négligence(f) **contributoire**	**Mitverschulden**(n); mitwirkendes Verschulden	**contributory negligence**
négligence(f), délai(m) tardif pour faire valoir un droit	**(schuldhafte) Unterlassung;** Versäumnis(n) (in der Geltendmachung(f) e-s Anspruchs; Verwirkung(f)	**laches**
négligence(f) **professionnelle,** faute(f)	**gesetzeswidrige Handlung**(f); standeswidriges Verhalten	**malpractice**
négligence(f) négligence, faute(f) de nature délictuelle	**Vernachlässigung**(f); Unterlassung(f) grobe Fahrlässigkeit	**neglect** gross –

FRENCH	GERMAN	ENGLISH
négligence(f), incurie(f), imprudence(f)	**Fahrlässigkeit**(f); Verschulden	**negligence**
part(f) de responsabilité de la victime dans un accident	Mitverschulden	contributory –
négligence criminelle	strafbare Fahrlässigkeit	criminal –
négligence, faute(f) de nature délictuelle	grobe Fahrlässigkeit	gross –
négociable	**begebbar;** umlauffähig	**negotiable**
instrument(m) (commercial) négociable	–es Wertpapier	– instrument
titre(m) négociable	–es Wertpapier	– security
négociant, marchand; courtier(m) de change, cambiste(m) (US); 'dealer'(m), trafiquant(m) de stupéfiant	**Händler**(m); Wertpapier–(n)	**dealer**
net	**netto;** rein	**net**
actif(m) net	Reinvermögen	– assets
revenu(m) net	Nettoeinkommen; Reinertrag	– income
résultat(m) net	Endergebnis	– result
valeur(f) nette	Reinvermögen; Eigenkapital	– worth
neutralité(f)	**Neutralität**(f)	**neutrality**
législation(f) de neutralité	–sgesetzgebung	– legislation
politique(f) de neutralité	–spolitik	– policy
nier, contester	**in Abrede**(f) **stellen;** leugnen; verweigern	**deny (to)**
nom(m) **commercial,** raison(f) sociale,enseigne(f)	**Handelsname**(m) **Firmenname**(m);	**trade name**
nommer, désigner	**ernennen;** nominieren	**nominate (to)**
non armé, sans armes	**unbewaffnet**	**unarmed**
non attesté, non certifié	**unbeglaubigt;** unbestätigt	**unattested**
non autorisé, illégal, illicite	**nicht ermächtigt;** unbefugt	**unauthorised**
non confirmé; léonin	**unbestätigt**	**unconfirmed**
non convertible	**unwiderlegbar**	**uncontrovertible**
non échu	**noch nicht fällig**	**unmatured**
non engagé, libre, neutraliste	**nicht gebunden,** blockfrei	**uncommitted**
non exercé	**verborgen;** still	**dormant**
non fondé, sans fondement(m)	**unbegründet;** grundlos	**unfounded**
accusation(f) sans fondement	–e Beschuldigung	– accusation
non intentionnel, involontaire	**unbeabsichtigt;** ungewollt	**unintentional**
non pertinent, inconsistant	**Unerheblichkeit**(f)	**irrelevance**
non pertinent, sans effet	**unerheblich;** nicht zur Sache gehörig	**irrelevant**

FRENCH	GERMAN	ENGLISH
non qualifié; sans réserves(f)	**unzuständig; uneingeschränkt**	**unqualified**
non valable, inopérant	**unwirksam;** wertlos	**nugatory**
non vérifié	**nicht bestätigt**	**unverified**
non-	**Nicht-**	**non-**
-acceptation(f)	–annahme; Annaheverweigerung	-acceptance
-comparution(f)	–erscheinen	-appearance
-conformité(f), insoumission(f), refus(m) de se conformer	–befolgung, –efüllung	-compliance
-litigieux	–streitig; kontradiktorisch	-contentious
inexistant	– vorhanden	-existent
négligence(f) simple	(pflichtwidrige) Unterlassung, Nichterfüllung	-feasance
-observation(f)	–befolgung, –beachtung	-observance
pays(m) non-membre de la CEE	Drittländer(pl.) (EG)	-member country (EEC)
inexécution(f)	–erfüllung, –leistung	-performance
-résident(m)	– ansässig; im Ausland ansässig	-resident
il ne s'en suit pas	irrige Folgerung; unschlüssig	non sequitur
non-dénonciation(f), recel(m); forfaiture(f)	**(pflichtwidrige) Nichtanzeige** e-r strafbaren Handlung(f)	**misprision**
non-respect prémédité d'un contrat	**antizipierter Vertragsbruch(m);** vor Fälligkeit erklärte Erfüllungsverweigerung oder Verhalten, das beabsichtigten Vertragsbruch andeutet	**anticipatory breach**
non-valable, sans effet légal	**(rechts-)ungültig**	**invalid**
notaire(m)	**Notar(m)**	**notary public**
notification(f) d'un acte, d'une mesure	**Handlungsanzeige(f)**	**notification of an act**
nouveau procès(m)	**Wiederaufnahmeverfahren(n);** erneute Verhandlung(f)	**retrial**
nouvelle audition(f)	**erneute Verhandlung(f);** Berufung(f)(sverfahren)(n)	**rehearing**
nu	**bloß,** nackt, dürftig, arm	**bare**
nuire, blesser	**schädigen;** verletzen	**harm (to)**
nul et de nul effet, vide	**nichtig;** unwirksam	**void**
nul et non avenu	(null und) nichtig; ungültig	null and –
nul et non avenu	**(null und) nichtig**	**null and void**
nullité(f)	**Nichtigkeit(f);** Ungültigkeit(f)	**nullity**
action(f) en nullité	Nichtigkeitsklage	– action
nullité de mariage	absolute Nichtigkeit der Ehe	– of marriage

O

FRENCH	GERMAN	ENGLISH
objecter, récuser (un témoin)	**einwenden;** beanstanden	**object (to)**
objectif, sans parti-pris	**unvoreingenommen;** unparteiisch	**unbiased**
objection(f), récusation(f) (d'un témoin)	**Einwand**(m); Beanstandung(f)	**objection**
rejeter une objection	e-n Einspruch zurückweisen	overrule an –
admettre une objection	e-r Einwendung stattgeben	sustain an –
obligation(f), engagement(m)	**Schuldurkunde**(f), –schein(m); Wertpapier(n), Obligation(f), Schuldverschreibung(f); Haftungsversprechen(n), Bürgschaft(f), Garantieerklärung(f); Zollverschluß(m)	**bond**
titre(m) au porteur	Inhaberobligation, –schuldverschreibung	bearer –
obligation d'État, rente d'État	Staatsanleihen, –papiere, –schuldverschreibungen	government –
obligation amortissable	tilgbare Obligation, kündbare Obligation	redeemable –
bon d'épargne	(staatl.) Sparbrief; Sparschuldverschreibung (US)	savings –
obligation(f), reconnaissance(f) de dette	**Verbindlichkeiten** (Sammelbegriff für alle ungesicherten, langfristigen –); Rückzollschein	**debenture**
obligation(f), devoir(m), engagement(m)	**Verpflichtung**(f); Schuldverhältnis(n); Auflage(f)	**obligation**
obligation accessoire	akzessorische Verpflichtung; Nebenpflicht	accessory –
devoir de secret	gemeinsame Verpflichtung; Gesamtverpflichtung	joint –
obligation conjointe	Verpflichtung zur Geheimhaltung	– of secrecy
obligation à titre principal	Hauptpflicht; Hauptverbindlichkeit	principal –
obligation(f) **contractuelle**	**Vertragsbeziehung**(f); Rechtsbeziehung(f) zwischen den unmittelbaren Vertragsparteien	**privity in contract**
obligatoire	**verpflichtend;** obligatorisch	**obligatory**

FRENCH	GERMAN	ENGLISH
obligatoire, forcé(f)	**obligatorisch;** zwangsweise	**compulsory**
administration(f) forcée	Zwangsverwaltung	– administration
engagement(m) obligatoire	Zwangsverpflichtung	– commitment
jonction(f) d'instances	notwendige Streitgenossenschaft	– joinder
obligatoire	(US)	
liquidation(f) judiciaire	Zwangsliquidation	– liquidation
obligatoire, impératif	**obligatorisch;** zwingend	**mandatory**
obliger, engager, lier	**binden;** verpflichten	**bind (to)**
s'engager	sich verpflichten (etwas zu tun)	– oneself
oblitérer, effacer	**(aus)löschen;** unkenntlich machen	**obliterate (to)**
occupant(m), locataire(m, f),	**Besitzer**(m); Inhaber(m);	**occupant**
usufruitier(m, f)	Bewohner(m)	
occupation(f), possession(f)	**Besitz**(m)(**-ergreifung**)(f)	**occupancy**
odieux, abominable	**anstößig;** belästigend	**obnoxious**
officiel (adj.);	**amtlich**	**official**
fonctionnaire(m) (n),		
représentant(m) officiel		
acte(m) officiel	Amtshandlung	– act
administrateur(m) officiel	Konkursverwalter; – bestellter	– administrator
	Nachlaßverwalter	
autorisation(f) officielle	–e Genehmigung	– authorisation
publication(f) officielle	Amtsblatt	– journal
liquidateur(m) judiciaire	Konkursverwalter	– receiver
cachet(m) réglementaire	Amts–, Dienstsiegel	– seal
secret(m) d'État	Amts–, Dienstverschwiegenheit	– secrecy
officier, célébrer	**amtieren**	**officiate (to)**
officier habilité à recevoir	**Urkundsperson**(f); zur	**commissioner for**
les déclarations sous	Abnahme(f) von Eiden berechtigter	**oaths**
serment(m)	Jurist	
offre(f), proposition(f)	**Angebot**(n); Offerte(f)	**offer**
cours(m) d'offre	Angebotspreis; Briefkurs	– price
offre(f), soumission(f)	**(Leistungs-/Zahlungs-/**	**tender**
	Lieferungs-/Submissions-)	
	Angebot(n) Andienung	
offre(f) **de conditions plus**	**Minderangebot**(n); Unter–	**underbid**
avantageuses		
oligopole(m)	**Oligopol**(n)	**oligopoly**
omettre	**auslassen;** unterlassen	**omit (to)**
omission(f), négligence(f)	**Auslassung**(f); Unterlassung(f)	**omission**
omission(f), oubli(m),	**Versehen**	**oversight**
bévue(f)		
opérations(f), livraisons(f) à	**Termingeschäfte**(n); (Termin-)	**futures (forward)**
terme; cotation à terme		
commande(m) à terme,	Terminkontrakt	futures contract
contrat à terme		
instruments(m) financiers	Finanztermingeschäfte	financial future(s)
à terme		
marché(m) des instruments	Termingeschäft	futures business
à terme		
option(f) sur contrat à	Option auf e-n Terminkontrakt	future(s) option
terme		

FRENCH	GERMAN	ENGLISH
opinion(f) avis(m) en accord	**Meinung**(f); Urteilsbegründung(f) zustimmendes Votum mit v.d. Mehrheit abweichender Begründung	**opinion** concurring –
avis de la minorité	mit der Mehrheitsentscheidung nicht übereinstimmende Stellungnahme e-s Richters	dissenting –
opinion publique	öffentliche Meinung	public –
opinion(f) **préconçue**	**Vorurteil**(n); Befangenheit(f), Voreingenommenheit(f)	**bias**
parti pris personnel	persönliches Vorurteil	personal –
opposant	**streitende Partei**(f), anfechtende –	**contestant**
opposant	**(Prozeß-)Gegner**(m)	**opponent**
oppression(f)	**Unterdrückung**(f)	**oppression**
ordinaire assemblée(f) générale ordinaire	**ordentlich** –e Hauptversammlung	**ordinary** – general meeting
ordonnance(f), décret(m), règlement(m)	**Verordnung**(f); Erlaß(m)	**ordinance**
ordonnance(f), décision(f) d'un juge sur un point de droit	**(amtliche oder gerichtliche)** **Enscheidung**(f); Anordnung(f)	**ruling**
ordonnance(f) **de ne pas faire**	**einstweilige Verfügung**(f); richterliches Verbot(n)	**restraining order**
ordonnance(f) **prohibitoire,** ordonnance prononçant une interdiction	**einstweilige Verfügung**(f) **(zur Unterlassung)**(f)	**prohibitory injunction**
ordre(m) **d'arrestation** *(US)*	**Haftbefehl**(m) *(US)*	**capias** *(US)*
original, initial, primitif *(adj.);* original(m, f) (n) prix(m) d'achat d'origine acte(m) primordial juridiction(f) de première instance	**ursprünglich;** Anschaffungskosten Originalurkunde erstinstanzliche Zuständigkeit; Gericht erster Instanz	**original** – acquisition cost – document – jurisdiction
origine(f), provenance(f) certificat(m) d'origine pays(m) d'origine	**Ursprung**(f); Herkunft(f) –szeugnis –sland	**origin** certificate of – country of –
orphelin(m)	**Waise**(f)	**orphan**
otage(m)	**Geisel**(f)	**hostage**
ouï-dire(f)	**Hörensagen**(n)	**hearsay**
outrage(m); atrocité(f)	**Gewalttätigkeit**(f); Ausschreitung(f); grobe Beleidigung(f)	**outrage**
ouvert, public(m), libre, accessible tribunal(m) siégeant en public crédit(m) à capital variable	**öffentlich;** zugänglich für in öffentlicher Verhandlung; revolvierender Kredit	**open** – court – end credit

P

FRENCH	GERMAN	ENGLISH
partie(f), fraction(f)	**Teil**(n); Partei(f)	**part**
passage(m) **au travers**	**Leugnen;** Bestreiten (des klägerischen Vorbringens)	**traverse** (CL)
passage(m) **de frontière**	**Grenzübergang**(m); –übertritt(m)	**border crossing**
passage(m) **obscur dans la rédaction d'un jugement,** incertitude(f)	**Unbestimmtheit**(f); Unsicherheit(f)	**uncertainty**
passer outre, outrepasser	**sich hinwegsetzen über;** außer Kraft(f) setzen	**override (to)**
paiement(m), règlement(m), versement(m); paye(f), rémunération(f)	**Zahlung**(f)	**payment**
paiement d'avance, paiement par anticipation	Voraus–, An–	advance –
paiement différé	aufgeschobene –; Raten–	deferred –
paiement partiel	Teil–, Raten–	part –
paiement intégral	volle (Ein)–	– in full
paiement en nature	Naturalleistung	– in kind
conditions(f) de paiement	–sbedingungen	terms of –
pair(m); pair du royaume (UK)	**Ebenbürtige(r)**(m); Adlige(r)(m)	**peer**
par tête	**pro**(m) **kopf**	**per capita**
parafer, émarger	**abzeichnen,** unterzeichnen; paraphieren	**initial (to)**
paragraphe(m)	**Absatz**(m); Abschnitt(m)	**paragraph**
paragraphe(m), sous-section(f)	**Unterabschnitt**(m)	**subsection**
paraître, apparaître, comparaître	**erscheinen;** auftreten; den Anschein haben	**appear (to)**
ester en justice, comparaître dans un tribunal	vor Gericht erscheinen	– in court
parenté(m) **par alliance**	**Verwandtschaft**(f); Schwägerschaft(f)	**affinity**
parent(m, f), allié(m, f)	**(Bluts-)Verwandtschaft**(m); Angehörige(r)(m)	**kin**
parent le plus proche	der (die) nächste(r) Verwandte(r)	next of –

FRENCH	GERMAN	ENGLISH
parent(m, f) **le plus proche**	**Verwandte**(m, f); nächste Familienangehörige(m, f)	**next of kin**
parjure(m), faux serment(m), faux témoignage(m)	**Meineid**(m)	**perjury**
parlement(m) loi(f)	**Parlament**(n) Gesetz	**Parliament** Act of –
paroisse(f)	**(Kirchen-)Gemeinde**(f)	**parish**
part(m) **d'héritage** réserve(f) légale	**Erbteil**(n) gesetzliche Rücklagen	**portion (of an estate)** reserved by law for an heir
part(f) **de participation**	**prozentualer Anteil**(m)	**percentage share**
partage(m), répartition(f), morcellement(m) répartition d'un héritage	**Teilung**(f) Erb(schafts)–; Erbauseinandersetzung	**partition** – of an estate
participation(f) certificat(m) de participation prêt(m) en participation	**Beteiligung**(f); Teilhabe(f) Anteilschein Konsortialkredit; Gemeinschaftsdarlehen	**participation** – certificate – loan
partie(f); parti(m) (politique) partie opposée, partie adverse partie indispensable partie lésée partie opposée, partie adverse tiers(m), tierce personne	**(Prozeß-)Partei**(f) Gegen-; Prozeßgegner notwendiger Streitgenosse Verletzte(r); Geschädigte(r) Gegen– Dritte(r); Nebenintervenient	**party** adverse – indispensable – injured – opposite – third –
partie(f) **chagrinée**, partie(f) perdante (dans une décision judiciaire)	**beschwerte Partei**	**aggrieved party**
partie(f) **indispensable**	**notwendige Streitpartei**(f)	**indispensable party**
partie(f) **opposée**, partie adverse	**Gegenpartei**(f)	**opposing (opposite) party**
paternité(f) reconnaissance(f) de paternité	**Vaterschaft**(f) –sanerkenntnis	**paternity** acknowledgement of –
payable, exigible dettes(f) passives	**zahlbar**; fällig Verbindlichkeiten; Passiva	**payable** accounts –
payé, acquitté, versé, rémunéré capital(m) versé actions(f) libérées police(f) d'assurances libérée	**bezahlt** eingezahltes Kapital (v.d. Aktionären) voll eingezahltes Kapital prämien-, beitragsfreie Police	**paid** --in capital --up shares/stock --up policy
payer, acquitter, régler; rétribuer, rémunérer	**(be-)zahlen**	**pay (to)**
payeur(m), tiré (d'un effet)	**Zahler**(m)	**payer**

FRENCH	GERMAN	ENGLISH
pays(m) **hôte,** pays d'accueil	**Gastland**(n); Aufnahmestaat(m)	**host country**
pays(m) **membre**	**Mitgliedsstaat**(m)	**member State**
pays membre invité (CEE)	**Gaststaat**(m) (EG)	**host member State** (EEC)
peine(f), amende(f), forfait(m) d'indemenité	**Strafe**(f)	**penalty**
peine capitale, peine de mort	Todes–	death –
dédit(m), clause(f) pénale	Vertragsstrafeklausel	– clause
sous peine de	bei e-r Strafe von	under – of
peine capitale, peine de mort	**Todesstrafe**(f)	**death penalty**
pénal	**straf-(rechtlich)**	**penal**
action(f) pénale	–klage	– action
droit(m) pénal	–recht	– law
travaux(m) forcés	Zuchthaus(strafe); Zwangsarbeit	– servitude
pénitencier(m)	**Strafgefängnis**(n)	**penitentiary**
pension(f) **alimentaire**	**Unterhalt(sbetrag)**(m)	**alimony**
pension(f) **alimentaire;** défense(f) de ses droits; maintien(m), conservation(f)	**Unterhalt**	**maintenance**
contribution(f) à l'entretien	–sbeitrag(m)	– contribution
responsabilité(f) en matière d'aliments	–sverpflichtung(f)	– liability
pension(f) **alimentaire**	**Unterstützung**(f); (s. Unterhalt)	**support** (cf. alimony)
péril(m), danger(m)	**Gefahr**(f); Risiko(n)	**peril**
fortune(f) de mer	Seerisiken, Gefahren auf See (pl.)	– of the sea
danger(m) encouru pendant le transport	Transportgefahr	– of transportation
périmer, se périmer, tomber en désuétude; devenir disponible	**erlöschen;** außer Kraft treten	**lapse (to)**
période(f) **de jouissance,** période d'occupation d'un emploi	**(Land)Besitzrecht**(n); Amtsinnehabung(f)	**tenure**
permis(m), autorisation(f), concession(f), brevet(m)	**Genehmigung**(f); Konzession(f); Lizenz(f)	**licence, license** (US)
permis de conduire	Führerschein	driving –
plaque(f) d'immatriculation	Nummernschild; Kraftfahrzeug-Zulassungsnummer	– plate
certificat(m) de extrait (d'acte) de mariage	Heiratserlaubnis, –genehmigung	marriage –
permis(m), licence(f), autorisation(f)	**Genehmigung**(f)	**permit**
permis de construire	Bau–	building –
autorisation d'exporter (d'importer)	Export– (Import–)	export (import) –
permis de travail	Arbeits–	labour –
permis(m) **de conduire**	**Führerschein**(m)	**driving licence**

FRENCH	GERMAN	ENGLISH
permis(m) de travail	Arbeitsgenehmigung(f); -erlaubnis(n)	work permit
permissible, tolérable	zulässig; erlaubt	permissible
perpétuité(f)	unbegrenzte Dauer(f)	perpetuity
perquisition(f), fouille, recherche(f)	Suche(f); Fahndung(f)	search
mandat(m) de perquisition	Durchsuchungsbefehl	– warrant
perquisition(f) droit(m) d'effectuer une perquisition	Durchsuchung(f) Durchsuchungsrecht	visit and search – right
persécuter, harceler	verfolgen; belästigen	persecute (to)
persécution(f), harcèlement(m)	Verfolgung(f); Belästigung(f)	persecution
personne(f), individu(m) personne morale personne morale personne physique	Person(f) juristische – juristische – natürliche –	person artificial – legal – natural –
personne(f) décédée, le défunt	Verstorbener(m); Erblasser(m)	deceased, decedent
personnel présence(f) en personne signalement(m) biens(m) personnels, biens propres caution(f) personnelle	persönlich –e Anwesenheit –e Beschreibung bewegliches Vermögen –e Bürgschaft	personal – attendance – description – property, personalty – surety
personnes(f) à charge	(Familien-)Angehörige(f); Unterhaltsberechtigte; Hinterbliebene	dependants
persuader, convaincre	überzeugen; überreden	persuade (to)
persuasion(f); conviction(f); confession(f) religieuse	Überzeugung(f); Überredung(f)	persuasion
perte(f), déficit(m), déperdition(f)	Verlust(m); Schaden(m)	loss
pertes reportées sur les années futures	Verlustvortrag	– carried (brought) forward
déficit annuel, pertes annuelles	Verlust für das betreffende Jahr	– for the year
perte, déperdition du capital	Kapitalverlust	– of capital
perte d'intérêt(s)	Zinsverlust	– of interest
perte totale	Totalschaden; Totalverlust	total –
pertinence(f)	Relevanz(f); Wichtigkeit(f)	relevancy
pertinent, applicable, approprié, utile	relevant; erheblich	relevant
philosophie(f) du droit droit(m) comparé médecine(f) légale	Rechtswissenschaft(f) vergleichende – Gerichtsmedizin	jurisprudence comparative – medical –

FRENCH	GERMAN	ENGLISH
physique	**physisch;** körperlich	**physical**
handicap(*m*) physique, invalidité(*f*)	Körperbehinderung	– disability
constrainte(*f*) physique	physicher Zwang	– duress
lésion(*f*) corporelle	Körperverletzung	– harm
invalidité	unheilbare Impotenz	– incapacity
blessures(*f*) corporelles	Körperverletzung	– injury
inventaire(*m*) détaillé	körperliche Bestandsaufnahme; Inventur	– inventory
pickpocket(*m*)	**Taschendieb**(*m*)	**pickpocket**
pièce(*f*) à conviction	**Beweisstück**(*n*)	**exhibit**
piller, saccager	**plündern**	**pillage (to)**
placement(*m*) de valeurs	**Plazierung**(*f*) **von Wertpapieren;** Unterbringung –(*f*)	**placement of securities** (*US*), **placing of securities** (*UK*)
plaider, soumettre	**vorlegen;** beantragen	**submit (to)**
soumettre une demande d'agrément	Genehmigungsantrag einreichen	– an application for approval
demander à la cour de dire que	dem Gericht zur Entscheidung stellen	– that the court declare
plaider	**plädieren;** vor Gericht vorbringen	**plead (to)**
plaider coupable (non coupable)	sich schuldig (nicht schuldig) bekennen	– guilty (not guilty)
plaider la cause de qqu'un	**e-n Rechtsstreit für jdn führen**	**conduct (to) somebody's cause**
plaideur(*m*)	**Prozeßpartei**(*f*)**;** prozeßführende Partei(*f*)	**litigant**
plaignant	**Beschwerdeführer**(*m*)**;** Erstatter(*m*) e-r Strafanzeige(*f*); Kläger(*m*)	**complainant**
plaignant(*m*), requérant(*m*), demandeur(*m*)	**Kläger**(*m*)	**plaintiff**
plainte(*f*)	**Klage**(*f*)**;** Klageschrift(*f*); Beschwerde(*f*)	**complaint**
plainte(*f*)	**Klage**(*f*)**;** Beschwerde(*f*)	**plaint**
poinçon(*m*), cachet	**Feingehaltsstempel**(*m*)**;** Kennzeichen	**hallmark**
poison(*m*)	**Gift**	**poison**
police(*f*)	**Polizei**(*f*)	**police**
la police	–behörde	– authority
officier(*m*) de police	Polizist	– constable
tribunal(*m*) de police	–gericht	– court
forces(*f*) de police, corps(*m*) de police	–(truppe)	– force
inspecteur(*m*) de police	–kommissar	– inspector
policier	–beamter	– officer
poste(*f*) de police	–revier; –wache	– station

FRENCH	GERMAN	ENGLISH
police(f) **(d'assurance)**; politique, ligne(f) de conduite	**(Versicherungs-)Police**(f)	**policy**
assuré, détenteur(m) d'une police d'assurance	Versicherungsnehmer	– holder
prendre, contracter une police d'assurance	e-e Versicherung abschließen	to take out a –
police(m) **montée**, police à cheval	**berittene Polizei**(f)	**mounted police**
pollution(f) **des eaux**	**Wasserverunreinigung**(f); Gewässerverschmutzung(f)	**water pollution**
population(f)	**Bevölkerung**(f); Einwohner(zahl)(m)	**population**
portée(f), champ(m) d'action, compétence(f)	**Bereich**(m); Rahmen(m)	**scope**
qui sont du ressort de, qui relève de	im Rahmen von	within the – of
portefeuille(m) **(d'actions, de valeurs)**	**Portefeuille**(n)	**portfolio**
porter; adopter	**unterstützen**, durchbringen, einbringen	**carry (to)**
faire passer une proposition	e-n Antrag annehmen	– a motion
adopter une résolution	e-n Beschluß durchbringen	– a resolution
porter atteinte ou préjudice, compromettre, affaiblir	**beeinträchtigen**; verschlechtern	**impair (to)**
porteur(m) **de titres,** actionnaire(m)	**Aktieninhaber**(m); Anteilseigner(m)	**stockholder**
porteur	**Träger**(m), Überbringer(m) (s. Inhaber, Besitzer)	**bearer** (cf. holder)
titre(m) au porteur	Inhaberobligation, Inhaberschuldverschreibung	– bond
attestation au porteur	Inhaberzertifikat	– certificate
titres, valeurs au porteur	Inhaberpapiere	– securities
port(m)	**Hafen**(m)	**port**
(les) autorités(f) portuaires	–behörde	– authority
droits(m) portuaires	–gebühren	– charges
posséder	**besitzen**; zugeben	**own (to)**
possesseur(m), détenteur(m)	**Besitzer**(m); Inhaber(m)	**possessor**
possession(f)	**Besitz**(m)	**possession**
possession effective	tatsächlicher, unmittelbarer –	actual –
possession de fait	unberechtigter –; Ersitzung	adverse –
date(f) d'entrée en possession	Datum der Inbesitznahme, der –ergreifung	date of taking –
post-nuptial(f)	**nachehelich**	**post-nuptial**
pot-de-vin(m)	**Bestechung**(f)	**bribe**
potence(f), gibet(m)	**Galgen**(m)	**gallows**

FRENCH	GERMAN	ENGLISH
poursuite(*f*)**,** accusation(*f*), action(*f*) publique; ministère(*m*) public; plaignant(*m*)	**Strafverfolgung**(*f*)**;** Anklageerhebung(*f*)	**prosecution**
poursuivre (traduire) en justice, mettre en accusation	**vor Gericht**(*n*) **stellen;** anklagen; zur Anklage(*f*) vernehmen	**arraign**
poursuivre en justice intenter une action	**anklagen;** strafrechtlich verfolgen Prozeß betreiben, – führen	**prosecute (to)** an action
poursuivre (une enquête), suivre, continuer	**verfolgen;** betreiben	**pursue (to)**
pouvoir; énergie(*f*), puissance(*f*) pouvoir de désignation procuration(*f*) (écrite), mandat(*m*) (de faire) agir investi de pouvoirs spéciaux	**Vollmacht**(*f*)**;** Befugnis(*n*) Ernennungsrecht Vollmacht mit Spezialvollmacht handeln; mit besonderer Befugnis handeln	**power** – of appointment – of attorney to act with special –(s)
pratiquer la discrimination	**diskriminieren;** unterscheiden	**discriminate (to)**
pratiques(*f*) **commerciales restrictives**	**Wettbewerbsbeschränkungen**(*f*)**;** Kartelle(*n*)	**restrictive trade practices**
précaire possession(*f*) précaire droit(*m*) accordé à titre précaire	**widerruflich;** kündbar jederzeit entziehbarer Besitz widerruflich gewährtes Recht	**precarious** – posession – right
précéder	**vorhergehen**	**forego (to)**
prédécesseur(*m*)	**Vorgänger**(*m*)	**predecessor**
prédécès(*m*)	**vorher erfolgter Tod**(*m*)**;** vorzeitiger erfolgter Tod(*m*)	**predecease**
préjudice(*m*)**,** lésion(*f*) (d'un droit), tort(*m*), dommage(*m*) blessure(*f*) accidentelle lésion(*f*) corporelle accident(*m*) du travail incapacité(*f*) permanente blessure	**Verletzung**(*f*)**;** Schaden(*m*) Unfallverletzung Körperverletzung Betriebs-, Arbeitsunfall Dauerschaden; lebenslängliche Körperbeschädigung Personenschaden; Körperverletzung	**injury** accidental – bodily – occupational – permanent – personal –
préjudice(*m*)**,** tort(*m*); préjugé(*m*) sans préjudice de	**Vorurteil**(*n*)**;** Beeinträchtigung(*f*); Schaden unbeschadet; unter Vorbehalt; ohne Verbindlichkeit	**prejudice** without – to
préliminaire, préalable(*m*) témoignage(*m*) préliminaire audience(*f*) préliminaire instruction(*f*) (d'une affaire), enquête(*f*) préliminaire	**vorläufig** vorläufige Beweisaufnahme gerichtl.Voruntersuchung Voruntersuchung	**preliminary** – evidence – hearing – investigation
préméditation(*f*)**,** malveillance(*f*)	**böse Absicht**(*f*)	**malice**
préméditation(*f*)	**Vorbedacht**(*m*)	**premeditation**

FRENCH	GERMAN	ENGLISH
prémédité	vorsätzlich	premeditated
prémédité	Vorbedacht(m) in böswilliger Absicht	prepense
prémédité, délibéré	berechnet, er-; kalkuliert	calculated
prémédité, intentionnel	vorsätzlich; absichtlich	intentional
prémédité, volontaire assassinat(m), homicide(m, f) volontaire	vorsätzlich; absichtlich Mord; Totschlag	wilful – murder
abus(m) de jouissance, dégâts commis intentionnellement	vorsätzliche Substanzschädigung; – Wertminderung	– waste
premier, d'origine	erste, erster, erstes, an erster Stelle	first
assassinat(m)	schwerer Mord	-degree (murder) (US)
privilèges(m) privilégiées délinquant(m) primaire	erstrangiges Pfandrecht Ersttäter; Nichtvorbestrafter	– lien – offender
premier président(f) d'une cour	Oberrichter(m); Vorsitzender(m, f) e-s hohen Gerichts, Präsident des Obersten Bundesgerichtshofs	chief justice
prendre recueillir des témoignages	nehmen Beweis aufnehmen, erheben; Zeugenaussage hören	take (to) – evidence
prendre en charge, reprendre	übernehmen	– over
recueillir le serment de qqu'un	jdn vereidigen	– the oath of s.o.
prénom(m)	Vorname(m); Tauf-	given name
prénuptial contrat(m) de mariage	vorehelich –er güterrechtlicher Vertrag; Ehevertrag	antenuptial – settlement
prérogative(f), privilège(m)	Vorrecht(n); Prärogativ(n)	prerogative
prescription(f)	Verjährung(f); Vorschrift(f)	prescription
prescrire, ordonner	verjähren; vorschreiben	prescribe (to)
présenter porter témoignage	einreichen; vorbringen Beweismittel beibringen	present (to) – evidence
préserver les preuves	Beweissicherung(f)	perpetuate (to) evidence
président(m)	Vorsitzender(m), Präsident(m); Obmann(m)	chairman
président(m) du tribunal	Vorsitzender(m); Vorsitz(m) führender Richter(m)	presiding judge
présomptif preuve(f) par déduction, par présomption	mutmaßlich Wahrscheinlichkeits–, Indizienbeweis	presumptive – evidence
présomption(f), preuve(f) indirecte	Indizienbeweis(m)	circumstantial evidence

FRENCH	GERMAN	ENGLISH
présomption(f)	**Vermutung**(f)	**presumption**
décès(m) présumé	Todes–	– of death
présomption de fait	Tatsachen–	– of fact
présomption d'innocence	Unschulds–	– of innocence
intention(f) présumée	Folgerung daß Vorsatz vorlag	– of intent
présomption de titre	Eigentums–	– of title
présumer	**vermuten**; annehmen	**presume (to)**
prétendant(m)	**Heuchler**(m); Prätendent(m)	**pretender**
prétendre, faire semblant de	**vorspiegeln**; vortäuschen	**pretend (to)**
prêt(m), emprunt(m)	**Darlehen**(n)	**loan**
prêt sur garantie	besichertes –; Bürgschaftskredit	– against a guarantee
accord(m) de prêt, d'emprunt	–svertrag; Kreditvertrag	– agreement
prêt remboursable sur demande, argent à vue	kurzfristiges –	– at call
prêt à intérêt(s)	verzinsliches –	– at interest
capital(m) d'emprunt	–skapital; Anleihekapital	– capital
intérêt(m) sur emprunt	–szinsen; Anleihezinsen	– interest
prêt hypothécaire	Hypotheken–	mortage –
emprunt garanti	gesichertes –	secured –
prêter	**(ver-, aus-)leihen**; leisten	**lend (to)**
prêteur(m)	**Darlehensgeber**(m); Kredit–; Verleiher(m)	**lender**
prêteur(m) **sur gages**	**Pfandgläubiger**(m)	**pawnee**
preuve(f); épreuve(f)	**Nachweis**(m), Beleg(m); Beweis(m)	**proof**
charge(f) de la preuve	Beweislast	burden of –
preuve manifeste	eindeutiger Beweis	positive –
preuve de créance	Forderungsnachweis	– of claim
preuve de culpabilité	Schuldbeweis	– of guilt
justification(f) d'identité	Identitätsnachweis	– of identity
preuve littérale	schriftlicher Beweis	written –
preuve(f) **concluante,** pertinente	**schlüssiger (zwingender) Beweis**	**conclusive evidence**
preuve(f) **corroborante**	**bestätigende Zeugenaussage**(f)	**corroborating evidence**
preuve(f); homologation(f) (d'un testament); vérification(f)	**Testamentsbestätigung**(f)	**probate**
preuve(f) **suffisante**	**hinreichender Beweis**(m); Glaubhaftmachung(f)	**substantial evidence**

FRENCH	GERMAN	ENGLISH
preuve(f) **testimoniale,** témoignages(m)	**Beweis**(m)**(material)**(n); Nachweis(m); Zeugenaussage(f)	**evidence**
preuve recevable	zulässiger Beweis	admissible –
charge(f) de la preuve	Beweislast, –pflicht	burden of –
présomptions(f), preuve indirecte	Indizienbeweis	circumstantial –
preuve concluante, pertinente	schlüssiger (zwingender) Beweis	conclusive –
preuve directe	unmittelbarer Beweis	direct –
preuve authentique, notoriété(f) de droit	Urkundenbeweis	documentary –
faux(f)témoignage	falsche Zeugenaussage	false –
preuve indirecte	mittelbarer Beweis	indirect –
témoignage, déposition(f) orale	mündlicher Beweis; Beweis durch Zeugenaussagen	oral –
preuve par déduction, par présomption	Wahrscheinlichkeits–, Indizienbeweis	presumptive –
meilleure preuve	primäres Beweismittel; Beweismittel erster Ordnung	primary –
preuve par vue di lieux	Augenscheinsbeweis; Beweis durch Augenscheinnahme	real –
prévenir, éviter	**ablenken; abwenden; verhüten**	**avert (to)**
prévenir des dégâts	Schaden abwenden	– damage
prévenir la violence	Gewalt abwenden	– violence
prévenir; informer qqu'un de ses droits (police)	**(ver-)warnen**	**caution (to)**
préventif, préventive; de précaution	**Vorsichts-;** vorbeugend	**precautionary**
mesures(f) de précaution, mesures préventives	–maßregeln treffen	– measures
préventif	**vorbeugend;** verhütend	**preventive**
détention(f) préventive	Sicherungsverwahrung	– detention
prévu(f) **par la loi,** légal, statutaire, réglementaire	**gesetzlich**	**statutory**
prime(f) **à la hausse;** option(f) d'achat	**Kaufoption**(f); Vorprämie(f)	**call option**
prime(f), agio(m); récompense(f); prix convenu(m); profit net(m); reprise(f) (en cas de location)	**Prämie**(f)	**premium**
prime d'assurance	Versicherungs–	insurance –
obligations(f) à primes	Sparprämienanleihen	– bonds
salaire(m) supplémentaire (exceptionnel)	–nlohn	– wage
prime(f) **de sauvetage,** indemnité de remorquage; sauvetage(m), renflouement(m); récupération de matériels et marchandises après sauvetage(m)	**Bergung**(f); Altmaterialverwertung(f)	**salvage**
société(f) de sauvetage	Bergungsgesellschaft	– company
contrat(m) de sauvetage	Bergungsvertrag	– contract
frais(m) de sauvetage	Bergungskosten	– costs

FRENCH	GERMAN	ENGLISH
principe(*m*) conducteur	Grundprinzipien(*n*)	guiding principles
principe(*m*) auquel on ne peut déroger	maßgebliches Prinzip(*n*)	overriding principle
priorité(*f*), privilège(*m*); hypothèque(*f*) clause(*f*) de priorité ordonnance(*f*) de priorité	Vorrang(*m*); Priorität(*f*) Rangfolge, Reihenfolge Prioritätsklausel	priority order of – – clause
prisée(*f*) et estimation, expertise(*f*), évaluation, inventaire(*m*)	Bewertung(*f*); Schätzwert(*m*)	valuation
prison(*f*)	Gefängnis(*n*)	prison
prison(*f*), maison(*f*) d'arrêt	Gefängnis(*n*)	gaol, also spelled jail
prison(*f*) pour jeunes détenus (*US*), maison de correction(*f*)	Jugendhaftanstalt(*f*) (*US*)	reformatory (*US*)
prisonnier(*m*), prisonnière(*m*)	Gefangener(*m*); Häftling	prisoner
privation(*f*), destitution(*f*) privation de liberté	Beraubung(*f*); Entziehung(*f*); Verlust(*m*) Freiheitsberaubung; –entziehung	deprivation – of liberty
privé, particulier(*m*) société(*f*) à responsabilité limitée (SARL), société privée entreprise(*f*) privée droit(*m*) privé droit privé international action(*f*) en justice privée vente(*f*) de gré à gré secteur(*m*) privé	privat; nicht öffentlich personenbezogene Kapitalgesellschaft; (*etwa:* Gesellschaft mit beschränkter Haftung) Privatunternehmen; freie Marktwirtschaft Privat-, Zivilrecht internationales Privatrecht Privatklage Privatverkauf; freihändiger Verkauf Privatsektor; Privatwirtschaft	private – company – enterprise – law – international law – prosecution – sale – sector
privilège(*m*); incident(*m*); qui appartient	Vorfall(*m*); Ereignis(*n*)	incident
privilège(*m*), droit(*m*) de rétention, nantissement privilège général privilège sur les biens privilège particulier droit de rétention	Pfandrecht(*n*); Zurückbehaltungsrecht(*n*) allgemeines Pfandrecht Zurückbehaltungsrecht an Vermögen(swerten) Pfandrecht an e-r bestimmten Sache Zurückbehaltungsrecht (das Besitz der Sache voraussetzt)	lien general – – on assets particular – possessory –
privilège(*m*), droit(*m*) préférentiel	Vorzugsrecht(*n*)	preferential right
privilège(*m*) spécial	Pfandrecht(*n*) an e-r bestimmten Sache(*f*)	particular lien

FRENCH	GERMAN	ENGLISH
prix, attribution(f); jugement(m) sentence(f) arbitrale	**Belohnung**(f); Zuerkennung(f); Schiedsurteil(n); Rechtsspruch	**award**
prononcement d'une sentence (d'un jugement)	Urteil sprechen, (durch Urteil) zuerkennen	– of a judgment
prix(m), cours(f), cote(f) cartel(m) des prix contrôle(m) des prix discrimination(f) des prix indice(m) des prix limite(f) de prix	**Preis**(m) –kartell –kontrolle –diskriminierung –index –grenze	**price** – cartel – control – discrimination – index – limit
prix(m) **de rachat**	**Vorprämienkurs**(m)	**call price**
prix(m) **de revient,** prix de fabrication	**Gestehungskosten;** Einzelkosten	**prime cost**
prix(m) **du catalogue**	**Listenpreis**(m); Katalogpreis(m)	**list price**
probabilité(f)	**Wahrscheinlichkeit**(f)	**probability**
probant fait(m) probant force(f) probante	**beweisrechtlich** beweiserhebliche Tatsache Beweiswert; Beweiskraft	**probative** – fact – value
procéder à un nouvel interrogatoire, réexaminer	**nochmals vernehmen;** erneut überprüfen	**re-examine (to)**
procédure(f); cabinet(m), clientèle(f); pratique(f), méthode(f)	**Praxis**(f); Verfahren	**practice**
manoeuvre(f), procédure(f) légale procédure civile usages(m) commerciaux	Anwaltspraxis Zivilverfahren Handelspraktikten	legal – civil – trade –(s)
procédure(f) **connexe**	**Verfahren außerhalb der Streitverhandlung**(f); Nebenverfahren	**collateral proceeding(s)**
procédures(f) **d'avant-procès,** procédure gracieuse	**Vorverfahren**(n)	**pre-trial procedure**
procès(m)	**(Zivil-)Prozeß**(m); Rechtsstreit(m); Klage(f)	**lawsuit**
procès(m); essai(m)	**Gerichtsverhandlung**(f); Verfahren(n)	**trial**
action(f) civile jugement(m) sommaire	Zivilverfahren Hauptverhandlung ohne Geschworene	civil – summary –
procés conduit devant un jury première instance cour(f) jugeant en juge(m) du fond	Schwurgerichtsverfahren Prozeßgericht; Instanz Tatrichter; Richter der ersten Instanz	– by jury – court – judge
procès-verbal(m), compte-rendu(m)	**Protokoll**(n); Niederschrift(f)	**minutes**
processus(m), procédé(m), méthode(f) action(f) en justice, procès huissier	**gerichtliche Verfügung**(f); Verfahren(n) gerichtliches Verfahren Zusteller (e-r gerichtlichen Verfügung)	**process** juridical – – server

FRENCH	GERMAN	ENGLISH
procurateur(*m*); fondé(*m*) de pouvoir; agent(*m*) d'affaires	**Bevollmächtigter**(*m*); Anwalt(*m*)	**procurator**
procuration,(*f*) mandat(*m*)	**Vollmacht**(*f*); Besorgung(*n*)	**procuration**
production(*f*), fabrication(*f*), présentation(*f*)	**Produktion**(*f*); Herstellung(*f*)	**production**
droits(*m*) de licence	Herstellungslizenz	– licence
droits de fabrication	Herstellungsrecht	– rights
produit(*m*) **fini**, résultat(*m*)	**Endprodukt**(*n*)	**end-product**
produits(*m*) **semi-finis**	**Halbfabrikate**(*n*)	**semifinished goods**
professionnel (*adj.*)	**beruflich**	**occupational**
accident(*m*) du travail	Betriebs–, Berufsunfall	– accident
maladie(*f*) professionnelle	Berufskrankheit	– disease
profit(*m*), bénéfice(*m*), boni(*m*), gain(*m*), prime(*f*)	**Gewinn**(*m*); Ertrag(*m*); Nutzen(*m*)	**profit**
profitable, avantageux	**nutznießend**; nutzbringend, vorteilhaft	**beneficial**
titre de droit en équité	Nutzungsrecht, Nießbrauchrecht; materieller Eigentumsanspruch	– interest
prohiber, interdire	**verbieten**	**prohibit (to)**
prohibition(*f*), défense(*f*), interdiction(*f*)	**Verbot**(*n*); Prohibition(*f*)	**prohibition**
projet(*m*) **d'acte**	**Entwurf**(*m*); Konzept(*n*)	**draft**
avant-projet de loi	Gesetzesentwurf, –vorlage	– Bill
projet de contrat	Vertragsentwurf	– contract
projet(*m*) **de loi**	**Schriftstück**(*n*), Urkunde(*f*); Rechnung(*f*); Gesetzentwurf(*m*), –vorlage; Wechsel, Tratte; Geldschein (*US*), Banknote(*f*)	**bill**
projet de loi gouvernemental	Regierungsvorlage	government –
lettre(*f*) de change	(gezogener) Wechsel, Tratte	– of exchange
résumé(*m*) des chefs d'accusation	Anklageschrift	– of indictment
connaissement(*m*)	Konnossement, Seefrachtbrief; (Binnenschiffahrt) Ladeschein	– of lading
promesse(*f*)	**Versprechen**(*n*); Zusage(*f*)	**promise**
promettre	**versprechen**	**promise (to)**
promulgation(*f*), proclamation(*f*)	**Bekanntmachung**(*f*); Veröffentlichung(*f*)	**promulgation**
propriétaire(*m, f*), possesseur(*m*)	**Eigentümer**(*m*); Eigner(*m*)	**owner**
propriétaire(*m, f*)	**Eigentümer**(*m*)	**proprietor**
propriétaire(*m*) **foncier**	**Grundeigentümer**(*m*)	**freeholder**
propriété(*f*), possession(*f*)	**Eigentum(srecht)**(*n*); Besitz(*m*)	**ownership**
nue-propriété(*f*)	bloßes Eigentumsrecht (ohne Nutzungen)	bare –
propriété(*f*) dans l'indivision	Miteigentum; gemeinsames Eigentum	joint –

FRENCH	GERMAN	ENGLISH
propriété(*f*) **indivise,** bien(*m*) indivis	**ungeteiltes Vermögen**(*n*)	**undivided property**
propriété(*f*) **intellectuelle**	**geistiges Eigentum**(*n*)	**intellectual property**
propriété(*f*) **foncière,** biens(*m*) immobiliers	**Grundvermögen**(*n*); Liegenschaften(*n*)	**landed property**
prospectus(*m*), appel(*m*) à souscription publique	**Prospekt**(*m*); Einführungs–(*m*); Werbeschrift(*f*)	**prospectus**
protecteur(*m*)	**schützend**	**protective**
protéger, sauvegarder	**schützen**	**protect (to)**
prouvé, qui a fait ses preuves, attesté	**erwiesen**	**proved, proven**
prouver, établir, justifier, attester	**beweisen;** belegen	**prove (to)**
provision(*f*) **sur honoraires d'avocat**; arrhes(*f*); cachet(*m*)	**Anwaltsbestellung**(*f*); Gebührenvorschuß(*m*)	**retainer**
provisoire, transitoire, intérimaire; intérim(*m*)	**Zwischen-**	**interim**
décret(*m*) intérimaire	–urteil(*n*)	– decree
rapport(*m*) provisoire	–bericht(*m*)	– report
provisoire, temporaire, conservatoire	**vorläufig**	**provisional**
ordonnance(*f*) de référé mesure(*f*) provisoire, recours(*m*) dans le cadre d'un jugement(*m*) avant dire droit	einstweilige Verfügung –er Rechtsbehelf; einstweilige Anordnung	– injunction – remedy
provocation(*f*)	**Herausforderung**(*f*)	**provocation**
provoquer, inciter	**herausfordern**	**provoke (to)**
proxénétisme(*m*) **commettre**	**Kuppelei betreiben;** Vorschub(*m*) leisten	**pander (to)**
psychopathe(*m, f*)	**Psychopath**(*m*)	**psychopath**
public (*adj.*); public(*m*) (*n*)	**öffentlich**	**public**
vente(*f*) aux enchères publiques	–e Versteigerung; Zwangsversteigerung	– auction
pouvoirs(*m*) publics	–e Behörde	– authority
société(*f*) anonyme	Kapitalgesellschaft	– company
dépenses(*f*) publiques	–e Ausgaben; Ausgaben der –en Hand	– expenditure
fonds(*m*) publics	–e Mittel	– funds
système(*m*) de santé publique	staatlicher Gesundheitsdienst	– health system
audience(*f*) publique	–e Verhandlung	– hearing
jour(*m*) férié, fête légale	gesetzlicher Feiertag	– holiday
avis(*m*) au public	–e Bekanntmachung	– notice
propriété(*f*) publique	Staatseigentum; Eigentum der – en Hand	– property
ministère(*f*) public	Staatsanwalt	– prosecutor
secteur(*m*) public	–er Sektor; –e Hand	– sector
services(*m*) publics	Versorgungsunternehmen (Elektrizität, Gas, Wasser)	– utilities

FRENCH	GERMAN	ENGLISH
publication(f), avis(m) public	**Veröffentlichung**(f)	**publication**
punitif, vindicatif	**nachtragend;** strafend	**vindictive**
pur, non édulcoré	**unverfälscht;** echt	**unadulterated**
putatif	**vermeintlich;** mutmaßlich	**putative**

Q

FRENCH	GERMAN	ENGLISH
qualité(*f*), vertu en vertu de	**Tugend**(*f*); Wert(*m*) kraft; aufgrund von	**virtue** by – of
qualité(*f*); statut(*m*), condition(*f*) contrôle(*m*), agrément(*m*) de la qualité plainte portant sur la qualité	**Qualität**(*f*) –sabnahme(prüfung) –sbeanstandung	**quality** – approval – complaint
quarantaine(*f*)	**Quarantäne**(*f*)	**quarantine**
quasi-certitude du jury, conviction(*f*) dépassant la croyance en un doute raisonnable	**jeder Zweifel ausgeschlossen;** (Beweisergebnis, das jeden vernünftigen Zweifel ausschließt)	**beyond reasonable doubt**
quatre sociétés du barreau (les)	**(Gebäude**(*n*) **der vier alten) Innungen**(*f*) **der Barrister**(*m*) **in London;** Berufsorganisation(*f*) der Barrister(*m*)	**Inns of Court** *(UK)*
question(*f*), point(*m*) litigieux, objet(*m*) du litige; émission(*f*); conséquence(*f*) question de fait question de droit question finale	**Streitfrage**(*f*) strittige Tatfrage; Tatbestand strittige Rechtsfrage entscheidungs–, rechtserhebliche Streitfrage	**issue** – of fact – of law ultimate –
question(*f*), interrogation(*f*)	**Frage**(*f*); Beanstandung(*f*)	**query**
questionnaire(*m*)	**Fragebogen**(*m*)	**questionnaire**
qui a un quorum	**beschlußfähig**	**quorum (to be a)**
quittance(*f*), quitus(*m*), acquit(*m*)	**Abfindung**(*f*); Entlastung(*f*); Quittung(*f*)	**quittance**
quorum(*m*), quantum(*m*)	**Quorum**(*n*); Beschlußfähigkeit(*f*)	**quorum**
quota(*f*), contingent; quote- part(*f*); cotisation(*f*)	**Quote**(*f*); Kontingent(*n*)	**quota**

R

FRENCH	GERMAN	ENGLISH
rabais(*m*), remise(*f*), réduction(*f*)	**Nachlaß**(*m*); Rabatt(*m*)	**rebate**
radiation(*f*) **d'un avocat du barreau**	**Ausschluß**(*m*) **aus der Anwaltschaft**	**disbarment**
raison(*f*), cause(*f*) motif(*m*) d'appel	**Grund**(*m*) Rechtsmittelbegründung; Berufungsbegründung	**ground** – for appeal
considérants	Urteilsbegründung	grounds for judgment
raison(*f*) **sociale**, nom(*m*) commercial, enseigne(*f*)	**Firmenname**(*m*); Handelsname(*m*)	**trade name**
raison(*f*) **sociale**	**Firmenname**(*m*); Bezeichnung(*f*) (der Firma)	**firm name**
raisonnable	**vernünftig**; angemessen; zumutbar; gerechtfertigt	**reasonable**
quasi-certitude du jury rendant un verdict, conviction(*f*) dépassant la croyance en un doute raisonnable	jeder vernünftige Zweifel ausgeschlossen	beyond – doubt
rançon(*f*) exiger une rançon de qqu'un	**Lösegeld**(*n*) – von jdm fordern	**ransom** demand (to) a – from s.o.
rapport(*m*), proportion(*f*), raison(*f*), quotient(*m*), coefficient(*m*)	**Verhältnis**(*n*); Koeffizient(*m*)	**ratio**
ratio(*f*) d'autonomie financière	Verschuldungsgrad; –koeffizient	debt-equity –
coefficient de trésorerie	Liquiditätsquote; Deckungsgrad	liquidity –
rapport(*m*), rendement(*m*), production(*f*)	**Ertrag**(*m*); Rendite(*f*); Effektivverzinsung(*f*)	**yield**
rassembler, réunir, citer	**einberufen**; laden; sich versammeln	**convene (to)**
tenir une réunion des actionnaires	e-e Hauptversammlung, Gesellschafter einberufen	– a shareholders' meeting
rationaliser	**rationalisieren**	**rationalise (to)**
rationalisation(*f*)	**Rationalisierung**(*f*)	**rationalisation**

FRENCH	GERMAN	ENGLISH
rationnement(m)	Rationierung(f); Bewirtschaftung(f)	rationing
ravages(m), dégâts(m) causer des ravages	Verwüstung(f); Unheil(n) – anrichten	havoc to wreak –
réaction(f), réponse(f)	(Klage)Beantwortung(f); Erwiderung(f)	response
réaffecter; opérer une nouvelle cession	rückübertragen; –abtreten	reassign (to)
réalisable, résoluble, résiliable	kündbar; befristet	terminable
réaliser; convertir en espèces; se rendre compte de qque chose vendre des biens	realisieren; veräußern Eigentum veräußern	realise (to) – property
réassurance(f), contre-assurance(f)	Rückversicherung(f)	reinsurance
recel(m) de marchandises volées	Hehlerei(f)	receiving of stolen goods
receleur(m); destinataire(m), réceptionnaire(m); liquidateur(m) administrateur(m) judiciaire (pour faillite)	Konkursverwalter(m) (vorläufiger) –; Zwangsverwalter	receiver official –
recette(m) marginale	Grenzeinnahmen	marginal revenue
recettes(f), rendement(m); retour(m) des invendus; statistiques(m), résultats	(Kapital)ertrag(m); Gewinn(m); Rendite(f)	returns
recevable, acceptable	zulässig, erlaubt; zulassungsberechtigt	admissible
recevable, plausible sommes à encaisser, dettes actives	ausstehend Außenstände	receivable accounts –
recevoir, admettre	(Geschäftsbeziehungen) unterhalten; in Erwägung(f) ziehen	entertain (to)
recherche(f) et développement (R & D)	Forschung(f) und Entwicklung(f) (F & E)	research and development (R & D)
réciprocité(f)	Gegenseitigkeit(f)	reciprocity
réciproque, bilatéral	gegenseitig	reciprocal
recommandations(f) du juge aux jurés (US)	Rechtsbelehrung(f) der Geschworenen (US)	instructions to jury (US)
récompense(f), dédommagement(m)	Belohnung(f); Entschädigung(f)	recompense
récompense(f)	Belohnung(f); Vergütung(f)	reward
reconstitution(f), reconstruction(f)	Wiederaufbau(m); Reorganisation(f)	reconstruction

FRENCH	GERMAN	ENGLISH
recours(*m*) recours contre un tiers	**Regreß**(*m*); Rückgriff(*m*) gegen Dritte Regreß nehmen	**recourse** – against a third party
recrutement(*m*) **par un** **'chasseur de têtes'**; braconnage(*m*)	**Wildern**	**poaching**
rectification(*f*), redressement(*m*)	**Richtigstellung**(*f*); Berichtigung(*f*)	**rectification**
reçu(*m*), récépissé(*m*)	**Quittung**(*f*); Empfangsschein	**receipt**
récupérer	**wiedererlangen; –gutmachen**	**retrieve (to)**
récupérer; mettre en valeur	**zurückfordern;** urbar machen	**reclaim (to)**
reddition(*f*); abandon(*m*), abdication(*f*)	**Abtretung**(*f*); Aufgabe(*f*)	**surrender**
rédiger, mettre à jour; fausser un bilan, gonfler les comptes	**auf den neuesten Stand**(*m*) **bringen;** höher bewerten; zuschreiben	**write (to) up**
redouter, craindre; appréhender, arrêter	**festnehmen,** verhaften; ergreifen, fassen; befürchten	**apprehend (to)**
redresser, rétablir, réparer un tort	**Abhilfe**(*f*) **schaffen;** wiedergutmachen	**redress (to)**
réel, tangible actif corporel, biens tangibles	**materiell;** erheblich materielle Vermögenswerte; Sachvermögen	**tangible** – assets
réel, véritable, effectif, concret perte réelle possession effective prix(*m*) réel; prix d'achat profit(*m*) réel valeur(*f*) marchande	**wirklich,** tatsächlich, effektiv; gegenwärtig tatsächlicher Verlust unmittelbarer Besitz Tagespreis, Marktpreis; Anschaffungskosten echter Gewinn, tatsächlich erzielter Gewinn tatsächlicher od. wirklicherWert; Effektivwert Tageswert	**actual** – loss – possession – price – profit – value
réel, vrai biens(*m*) immobiliers preuve(*f*) par vue de lieux revenu(*m*) réel biens immobiliers	**dinglich;** unbeweglich; effektiv Grundeigentum; unbewegliches Vermögen Augenscheinsbeweis; Beweis durch Augenscheinnahme immobiliarvermögen Realeinkommen	**real** – estate – evidence – income – property
réévaluation(*f*), réimposition(*f*)	**Neuveranlagung**(*f*); Neufestsetzung(*f*)	**reassessment**
réévaluation(*f*)	**Aufwertung**(*f*); Neubewertung(*f*)	**revaluation**
réévaluer, réviser la cote de, réimposer	**neu veranlagen; –** festsetzen	**reassess (to)**
réexaminer, reconsidérer	**neu erwägen;** nachprüfen	**reconsider (to)**
ré-exportation(*f*)	**Wiederausfuhr**(*f*)	**re-exportation**

FRENCH	GERMAN	ENGLISH
référence(f), renvoi(m), mention	**Bezugnahme**(f); Betreff(m)	**reference**
en fonction (de)	unter Bezugnahme	by –
refinancement(m)	**Refinanzierung**(f)	**refinancing**
réformer, révoquer, casser casser, révoquer un jugement, une sentence	**aufheben;** stornieren; rückbuchen Urteil aufheben	**reverse (to)** – a judgment
refuge(m)	**Zufluchtsort**(m); Hafen(m)	**haven**
refuge(m), asile(m)	**Zuflucht**(f)	**refuge**
réfugié(m)	**Flüchtling;** Heimatvertriebener(m)	**refugee**
refus(m), déni(m)	**Weigerung**(f); Absage(f)	**refusal**
refuser	**verweigern;** absagen	**refuse (to)**
réfutable	**widerlegbar**	**refutable**
réfuter une preuve, une présomption	**widerlegen;** entkräften	**rebut (to)**
régime(m) **cellulaire,** isolement carcéral	**Einzelhaft**(f)	**solitary confinement**
registre(m), livre(m); teneur(f) de registre (US), greffier(m), archiviste(m)	**Register**(n); Verzeichnis(n); Registerführer(m) (US); Gerichts –, Standesbeamter(M)	**register**
registre(m) **de la Lloyd**	**Lloyd's Register**(m)	**Lloyd's Register**
règle(f) **de procédure,** règle de droit immuable; disposition(f)	**Regel**(f); Bestimmung(f); Verordnung(f)	**rule**
règlement(m) **à l'amiable**	**außergerichtliche od. gütliche Einigung**(f)	**out-of-court settlement**
réglements(m) (CEE)	**Verordnungen**(f) (EG)	**regulations** (EEC)
Règles Fédérales de Procédure Civile (US)	**Bundeszivilprozeßordnung**(f) (US)	**Federal Rules of Civil Procedure** (US)
réhabilitation(f), redressement(m), rétablissement(m)	**Rehabilitierung**(f)	**rehabilitation**
réinscrire une affaire au rôle	**wiedereinsetzen in den vorigen Stand**(m); klageabweisendes Urteil aufheben	**reinstate (to) a court matter**
réintégrande(f); montant(m) alloué par jugement; recouvrement(m), récupération; reprise(f) redressement(m)	**(Wieder)Erlangung**(f); Beitreibung(f)	**recovery**
reprise(f) de dommages-intérêts	Erlangung von Schadensersatz	– of damages
rejet(m), réfaction(f)	**Nichtanerkennung**(f); Zurückweisung(f)	**disallowance**
rejeter, renoncer à	**verzichten auf;** nicht anerkennen; dementieren	**disclaim (to)**
rejeter, refuser	**ablehnen;** zurückweisen	**reject (to)**

FRENCH	GERMAN	ENGLISH
relais(m) **de mer**	**aus dem Meer**(n) **gewonnenes Land**(n); Marschen(f)	**innings (lands reclaimed from the sea)**
relatif à une personne morale ou sociale actif(m) social corps(m) constitué, personne morale actions(f) d'une société	**körperschaftlich;** korporativ Gesellschaftsvermögen Körperschaft, juristische Person Aktien	**corporate** – assets – body – stock
rembourser, restituer, ristourner	**rückvergüten**	**refund (to)**
remmettre (qqu'un entre les mains de la justice)	**übergeben,** aushändigen; (s. abtreten)	**hand (to) over** (cf. surrender)
remplir, exécuter, suppléer à pourvoir à une vacance remplir un formulaire	**füllen;** bekleiden; besetzen eine freie Stelle besetzen ein Formular ausfüllen	**fill (to)** – a vacancy – in a form
rémunérateur, payant; paiement(m) agent(m) payant banquier(m) payant	**zahlend** Zahlstelle zweitbeauftragte Bank	**paying** – agent – banker
rémunération(f), allocation(f), indemnité(f)	**Vergütung**(f); Honorar(n)	**remuneration**
rencontre, réunion(f), assemblée(f), meeting(m) assemblée générale assemblée générale des créanciers	**Versammlung**(f); Besprechung(f) Jahreshauptversammlung Gläubigerversammlung	**meeting** general – – of creditors
rendre, déclarer rendre un arrêt prononcer un jugement	**verkünden** ein (Scheidungs-) Urteil –, erlassen ein Urteil –	**pronounce (to)** – a decree – a judgment
renforcer, épauler; endosser; financer	**unterstützen;** begünstigen; gegenzeichnen	**back (to)**
renoncer à, abandonner un droit; se déroger	**aufgeben;** Verzicht(m) leisten	**waive (to)**
renonciation(f), désistement(m), abandon(m) renonciation tacite désistement de revendication, d'instance, d'action renonciation à un (des) droit (s) abandon d'un droit de propriété	**Aufgabe**(f); (Verzicht-)Leistung(f) ausdrücklicher (od. stillschweigender) Verzicht(m) Anspruchsaufgabe Rechtsverzicht Rechtsverzicht	**waiver** express (or implied) – – of claim – of rights – of title
renonciation(f) **explicite à un droit**; refus(m) d'une charge	**Verzichtleistung**(f), –serklärung; Widerruf(m)	**disclaimer**
renseignements(m) **privilégiés**	**durch Aussageverweigerungsrecht**(n) geschützte Mitteilung(f)	**privileged information**

270

FRENCH	GERMAN	ENGLISH
rentabilité*(f)*	Rentabilität*(f)*; Wirtschaftlichkeit*(f)*	**profitability**
rentrée*(f)*, rentrée en possession d'un bien-fonds *(US)*	Wiederinbesitznahme*(f)*; Rückgriff*(m)*	**regress**
renvoi*(m)*, congédiement*(m)*, rejet*(m)*, licenciement*(m)*	Entlassung*(f)*; Zurückweisung*(f)*; Einstellung*(f)*	**dismissal**
classement d'une affaire	Klageabweisung	– of an action
renvoyer, congédier, destituer, licencier	entlassen; abweisen, zurückweisen	**dismiss (to)**
rejeter un appel, débouter d'un appel	Berufung verwerfen, zurückweisen	– an appeal
réparation*(f)*, redressement*(m)*; secours*(m)*, aide*(f)*	Rechtshilfe*(f)*	**relief**
conclusions*(f)* acceptées	beantragte –; Gegenstand der Leistungsklage	affirmative –
demande*(m)* d'assistance	Klageantrag; Sachantrag	claim for –
jugement*(m)* déclaratif	deklaratorischer Rechtsschutz	declaratory –
répartie*(f)*	Erwiderung*(f)*; Duplik*(f)*	**rejoinder**
répartir, attribuer, ventiler, lotir	zuteilen, zumessen; anteilmäßig verteilen	**apportion (to)**
répondre; réagir, être l'intimé	erwidern; Klageerwiderung*(f)* einreichen	**respond (to)**
répondre de, garantir	einstehen für; sich verbürgen für	**vouch (to) for**
réponse*(f)*, réplique*(f)*	antworten, entsprechen; Folge leisten; sich richten nach	**answer**
réfutation*(f)* d'une accusation, réplique du défendeur*(m)*	sich wegen einer Anklage oder Beschuldigung verantworten	– to a charge
répréhensible	zu beanstanden; unzulässig	**objectionable**
représaille(s)*(f)*, mesure*(f)* de rétorsion; remboursement*(m)*	Vergeltung*(f)*(smaßnahmen)	**retaliation**
répressif	Straf-*(f)*	**punitive**
justice*(f)* répressive, justice pénale	–justiz	– justice
réprimande*(f)*, critique*(f)*	Kritik*(f)*, Tadel*(m)*, Rüge*(f)*	**censure**
motion*(f)* de censure	Mißtrauensantrag	motion of –
répudiation*(f)*, abandon*(m)*	Aufgabe*(f)*; Verzicht	**relinquishment**
répudiation*(f)* (d'une succession), renoncement*(m)*, abandon*(m)*	Verzicht*(m)*(leistung)*(f)*; Aufgabe*(f)*	**renunciation**
requérant*(m)*	Antragsteller*(m)*; Kläger*(m)*	**petitioner**
requête*(f)*, appel*(m)*, pétition*(f)*	Antrag*(m)*	**petition**
recours en droit	Berufungs–	appeal –
recours*(m)* en grâce	Gnadengesuch	– for pardon or commutation of penalty

FRENCH	GERMAN	ENGLISH
requète de révision pénale	**Aktenanforderung**(*f*); Revisionsantrag(*f*)	**certiorari**
réserve(*f*), provision(*f*), couverture(*f*)	**Rücklage**(*f*); Reserve(*f*)	**reserve**
fonds(*m*) de réserve	Rückstellung für Eventualverbindlichkeiten	contingency –
réserve légale	gesetzliche Mindestreserven; – Rücklagen;	legal –
réserve de réévaluation	Neubewertungsrücklage	revaluation –
réserve(*f*) **technique**	**versicherungstechnische Rücklagen**(*f*)	**technical reserve**
résidence(*f*), domicile(*m*)	**Wohnsitz**(*m*); Domizil(*n*)	**residence**
résidence officielle	Amtssitz	official –
domicile habituel	ständiger Wohnsitz	permanent –
résidence(*f*) **habituelle**	**ständiger Aufenthaltsort**(*m*); - Wohnsitz(*m*)	**permanent residence**
résiliation(*f*), extinction(*f*), cessation(*f*), expiration(*f*)	**Beendigung**(*f*)	**termination**
congé(*m*)	– des Arbeitsverhältnisses durch Kündigung	notice of –
résiliation, expiration d'un contrat	Vertrags–	– of a contract
résister lors de son arrestation	**sich der Verhaftung**(*f*) **widersetzen**	**resist (to) arrest**
résolution(*f*), délibération(*f*), ordre(*m*) du jour	**Beschluß**; Resolution(*f*)	**resolution**
respect(*m*)	**Einhaltung**(*f*)	**observance**
respect de la loi	– der Gesetze	– of the law
respect(*m*) **de la loi**	**Gesetzestreue**(*f*)	**obedience to the law**
respectueux des lois	**gesetzestreu**	**law-abiding**
responsabilité(*f*)	**Verantwortlichkeit**(*f*); Rechenschaftspflicht(*m*), Rechnungslegungspflicht; Strafmündigkeit	**accountability**
responsabilité(*f*), obligation(*f*), passif	**Haftung**(*f*); Verbindlichkeit(*f*)	**liability**
obligation future; dépenses(*f*) imprévues	Eventual-	contingent –
passif exigible à court terme	kurzfristige Verbindlichkeiten (*pl.*)	current –
responsabilité conjointe	gemeinsame Haftung; Gesamthaftung	joint –
responsabilité limitée	beschränkte Haftung	limited –
responsabilité personnelle	persönliche Haftung	personal –
responsabilité inconditionnelle	Gefährdungshaftung; verschuldensunabhängige Haftung	strict –
responsabilité(*f*) **stricte**	**strenge (verschuldensunabhängige) Haftung**(*f*) Gefährdungshaftung	**strict liability**

FRENCH	GERMAN	ENGLISH
responsable	**verantwortlich,** unterworfen; abhängig; zugänglich für	**amenable**
passible d'amende(s)	e-r Geldstrafe unterliegend	– to fines
responsable (de); assujetti à, tenu de; passible de, sujet à	**haftbar;** verantwortlich	**liable**
responsable; compétent	**haftbar;** haftpflichtig	**responsible**
restitution(f), réparation(f), dommages-intérêt(s)(m)	**Rückerstattung**(f); Wiederherstellung(f) des früheren Rechtszustands	**restitution**
restitution	**Rückgabe**(f); Wiederherstellung(f)	**restoration**
restreindre, limiter, réduire	**beschränken;** ein–	**restrict (to)**
résumé(m), abrégé(m), sommaire(m); extrait(m); analyse(f)	**Auszug**(m), Abriß(m); Zusammenfassung(f)	**abstract**
extrait du répertoire des mutations de propriété	Eigentumsnachweis	– of title
résumé(m) **du juge à l'intention des jurés**	**Schlußplädoyer**(m); Rechtsbelehrung(f) d. Geschworenen Zusammenfassung	**summing-up**
résumé(m) ou extrait du jugement; bordereau(m) d'un dossier de procédure; registre(m) des jugements rendus; récépissé(m) de douane	**Urteilsregister**(n), –liste; Etikett(n); Inhaltsverzeichnis(n); Lieferschein; Zollquittung	**docket**
retenir, détenir, garder	**in Haft nehmen;** zurück–, einbehalten	**detain (to)**
retirer, ôter	**e-r Pfründe berauben;** Einkommen entziehen	**disendow (to)**
retirer, se retirer	**zurückziehen;** widerrufen; zurücktreten	**withdraw (to)**
rétractation(f)	**Widerruf**(m)	**retraction**
retrait(m)	**Rücknahme**(f); Abhebung(f); Rücktritt(m)	**withdrawal**
retrait d'argent	Geldabhebung	– of money
retraite(f)	**Ruhestand**(m); Rücktritt(m)	**retirement**
retraite(f), pension(f) pension d'invalidité pension de vieillesse, retraite vieillesse allocation(f) de retraite caisse(f) de retraite assurance(f) retraite	**Pension**(f); Rente(f) Invalidenrente Altersrente Pensionsleistungen Pensionsfonds Rentenversicherung; Pensionsversicherung	**pension** disability – old age – – benefits – fund – insurance
rétrocession(f)	**Wiederabtretung**(f); Retrozession(f)	**retrocession**

FRENCH	GERMAN	ENGLISH
réunion(*f*), union(*f*) jonction(*f*) d'instances	**Beitritt**(*m*); Verbindung(*f*) Klagehäufung; Anspruchshäufung	**joinder** – of actions/claims
jonction d'instance des défendeur	Mitverklagen (weiterer Parteien)	– of defendants
acceptation(*f*) d'un arbitrage	Festlegung der zu entscheidenden streitigen Fragen	– of issue
jonction d'instances	Bildung e-r Streitgenossenschaft;	– of parties
jonction des appels	Nebenintervention Rechtsmittelverbindung	– of remedies
réussir à avoir, obtenir, se procurer; garantir	**sichern**; sicherstellen	**secure (to)**
garantir un prêt (une créance)	Sicherheit für ein Darlehen leisten	– a loan (debt)
obtenir un témoignage	Beweise sicherstellen	– evidence
révéler	**enthüllen**; offenbaren	**reveal (to)**
revenu(*m*), rapport(*m*), rentes(*f*)	**(Staats)Einkommen**(*n*); Steuereinnahmen(*m*)	**revenue**
revenu(*m*), rendement(*m*); remboursement(*m*), ristourne; renvoi(*m*), réexpédition(*f*)	**Rückerstattung**(*f*); Steuererklärung(*f*); Ertrag(*m*) Vermögensangabe	**return**
rendement(*m*) d'un actif	Gesamtkapitalrentabilität	– on assets
rentabilité(*f*) du capital (investi)	Kapitalertrag	– on capital
rendement sur investissement (RSI)	Ertrag aus Kapitalanlage; Kapitalrendite	– on investment (ROI)
revenu(*m*) **locatif**	**Mieteinnahmen**(*f*); Pacht–(*f*)	**rental income**
révision(*f*) **en appel**	**Überprüfung**(*f*) **e-s Urteils (durch Rechtsmittelgericht)**	**review on appeal**
révocation(*f*), abrogation(*f*), annulation(*f*)	**Widerruf**(*m*)	**revocation**
annulation d'un appel d'offres	Zurücknahme e-s Angebots	– of a tender
annulation d'un testament	– des Testaments	– of a will
révoquer, abroger, revenir sur une promesse	**widerrufen**; aufheben	**revoke (to)**
risque(*m*), aléa(*m*), péril(*m*) contrôle(*m*) des pertes marge(*f*) de risque	**Risiko**(*n*) –management –spanne	**risk** – management – margin
rixe(*f*), bagarre(*f*), échaufourrée(*f*)	**Handgemenge**(*n*); Prügelei(*f*)	**scuffle**
royauté(*f*), princes(*m*) du sang	**Königtum**(*n*); Lizenzgebühr(*f*)	**royalty**
rupture(*f*) **(de contrat)**, séparation(*f*)	**Trennung**(*f*)	**severance**
cessation(*f*) d'actions en justice	Klagen–	– of legal actions
indemnité(*f*) de licenciement, de rupture de contrat	Entlassungsabfindung; Härteausgleich	– pay

S

FRENCH	GERMAN	ENGLISH
sabotage(m)	Sabotage(f)	sabotage
s'abstenir de	verzichten auf	forgo (to)
saccager, piller	durchwühlen; plündern	ransack (to)
sacrilège(m)	Sakrileg(n); Kirchenschändung(f)	sacrilege
sain, sûr dépôt(m) en garde dépôt en coffre-fort	sicher -e Verwahrung; Depot Tresor; Aufbewahrung (im Tresor)	safe – custody – deposit
sain et sauf, indemne	unversehrt; unbeschädigt	unharmed
saisie(f), confiscation(f) saisie des biens et effets saisie immobilière	Beschlagnahme(m) – bewegliches Vermögens – unbewegliches Vermögens; – von Grundbesitz	seizure – of chattels – of real estate
saisie-arrêt(f), opposition(f)	Forderungspfändung(f); Verbot(n) (dem Drittschuldner)(m) Zahlung(f) zu leisten	garnishment
saisie-exécution(f); l'objet saisi	Inbesitznahme(f); Beschlagnahme(f)	distraint
saisir, confisquer	ergreifen; beschlagnahmen	seize (to)
saisir, opérer une saisie	in Besitz(m) nehmen; mit Beschlag(m) (Arrest)(m) belegen	distrain (to)
sanction(f), ratification(f), approbation(f) sanction pénale	Sanktion(f); Bestätigung(f) Strafmaßnahmen	sanction punitive –
sanctionner, ratifier	(offiziell) genehmigen; sanktionieren	sanction (to)
sanitaire	sanitär; hygienisch	sanitary
sans importance, non pertinent témoignage(m) non pertinent	unerheblich –er Beweis	immaterial – evidence
sans précédent	ohne Präzedenzfall(m); beispiellos	unprecedented
sans protection(f), sans emballage(m)	ungeschützt; ungedeckt	unprotected
sans scrupules(m)	skrupellos	unscrupulous

FRENCH	GERMAN	ENGLISH
santé(*f*) dispensaire(*m*), centre(*m*) de soins certificat(*m*) médical risque(*m*) pour la santé assurance(*f*) maladie santé(*f*) publique	**Gesundheit**(*f*) medizinisches Versorgungszentrum –szeugnis, –sattest –srisiko Krankenversicherung (öffentliches) –swesen;	**health** – centre – certificate – hazard – insurance public –
satisfaction(*f*), réparation(*f*), purge(*f*)	**Befriedigung**(*f*); Bezahlung(*f*); Erfüllung(*f*)	**satisfaction**
sauvegarder, prendre des mesures de protection protéger les intérêts de qqu'un	**sichern;** wahrnehmen jds Interessen wahren	**safeguard (to)** – a person's interests
sauver; économiser, épargner sauver la vie de qqu'un	**retten** jdm das Leben retten	**save (to)** – a person's life
scandaliser, indigner	**Anstoß**(*m*) **erregen;** empören	**scandalise (to)**
sciemment	**wissentlich**	**knowingly**
science(*f*)	**(Natur)wissenschaft**(*f*)	**science**
scrutin(*m*)**,** tour(*m*) de scrutin scrutin secret	**Wahl**(*f*)**,** Abstimmung(*f*); Stimmzettel(*m*); Wahlgang(*m*) geheime Wahl, – Abstimmung	**ballot** secret –
(se) cacher se soustraire à l'action de la justice	**sich verstecken** sich der Strafverfolgung entziehen	**hide (to)** – from justice
se confesser, avouer	**gestehen;** bekennen	**confess (to)**
se parjurer, faire un faux serment, un faux témoignage	**Meineid**(*m*) **leisten**	**perjure (to)**
se porter garant de qqu'un, pour qqu'un	**Kaution**(*f*) **stellen,** für jdn Sicherheit(*f*) leisten	**go (to) bail for s.o.**
se rendre; renoncer à renoncer à une succession	**ausliefern;** übergeben Besitzrecht am Nachlaß e-s Verstorbenen aufgeben	**surrender (to)** – a deceased's estate
se retenir, s'abstenir	**Abstand**(*m*) **nehmen von**	**refrain (to)**
se soustraire à la justice, fuir	**flüchtig werden;** (sich dem Gericht) entziehen	**abscond (to)**
secret(*m*) clause(*f*) de secret	**Geheimhaltung**(*f*)**;** Verschwiegenheit(*f*) Geheimhaltungsklausel	**secrecy** – clause
secret Loi(*f*) relative aux secrets d'État	**Geheimnis**(*n*) Gesetz zum Schutz von Staatsgeheimnissen	**secret** Official Secrets Act
section(*f*), article(*m*) (d'une loi)	**Paragraph**(*m*)**;** Abschnitt(*m*)	**section**
sécurité(*f*), sûreté(*f*)	**Sicherheit**(*f*)	**safety**

FRENCH	GERMAN	ENGLISH
sécurité(f), sûreté(f) nantissement(m)	**Bürgschaft**(f); Sicherheit(f) Nebensicherheit; Deckung durch Hinterlegung von Effekten	**security** collateral –
garantie(f) hypothécaire intérêt(s)(m) garanti(s)	hypothekarische Sicherheit Sicherungsrecht an beweglichen oder unbeweglichen Sachen	– by mortgage – interest
forces(f) de sécurité risque(m) sécuritaire	Sicherheitspolizei Sicherheitsrisiko	– police – risk
sécurité(f) **d'emplois**	**Arbeitsplatzsicherheit**(f)	**employment security**
séduction(f)	**Anlockung**(f); Verführung(f), Anwerbung(f)	**enticement**
sentence(f), condamnation(f), jugement(m)	**(Straf)Urteil**(n); Strafe(f)	**sentence**
arrêt(m) de mort, condamnation à mort, peine(f) de mort	Todesurteil	death –
condamnation à perpétuité condamnation à une peine de prison	lebenslängliche Freiheitsstrafe Gefängnisstrafe	life – prison –
condamnation avec sursis	Strafaussetzung (zur Bewährung)	suspended –
prononcer une condamnation à l'encontre de qqu'un	Strafurteil fällen, verkünden	to pass – on s.o.
séparation(f) **(des époux)** séparation(f) juciciaire (des époux)	**Gerichtliche Trennung**(f) Ehetrennung; Aufhebung der ehelichen Gemeinschaft	**separation** judicial –
séquestration(f), mise(f) sous séquestre	**Zwangsverwaltung**(f); Sequestration(f)	**sequestration**
serment(m) déférer le serment à qqu'un sous serment	**Eid**(m) jdn e-n Eid abnehmen; vereidigen unter –	**oath** administer the – to s.o. under –
service(m) **d'affacturage**; achat(m) ferme de créances	**Factoring**(n) **(Forderungsankauf)**(m)	**factoring**
services(m) **publics**; commodités(f)	**Versorgungsunternehmen**(n); –werte(m)	**utilities**
servitude(f), droit(m) d'usage	**Grunddienstbarkeit**(f)	**easement**
servitude(f) travaux forcés	**Dienstbarkeit**(f) Zuchthaus (strafe); Zwangsarbeit	**servitude** penal –
session(f) **plénière**	**Plenarsitzung**(f)	**plenary session**
seul, unique seul bénéficiaire	**allein**; einzig Alleinbegünstigter	**sole** – beneficiary
sévérité(f), rigueur(f); violence(f)	**Härte**(f); Strenge(f)	**severity**
gravité(f) d'un crime, d'un délit	Schwere e-r Straftat, e-s Delikts	– of an offence

FRENCH	GERMAN	ENGLISH
shérif(*m*)	**(oberster)**(*m*) **Verwaltungsbeamter**	**sheriff**
préfet(*m*) (*Angleterre*) capitaine(*m*) de gendarmerie (*US*)	Vollstreckungsbeamter (*England*) Vollstreckungsbeamter; Polizeichef (*US*)	– (*England*) – (*US*)
shérif(*m*) (*US*)	**Polizeihauptmann**(*m*) (*US*); Vollstreckungsbeamter(*m*)	**marshal** (*US*)
SICAV	**offener Investmentfonds**	**unit trust**
siège(*m*), charge(*f*), office(*m*) siège du gouvernement le siège social de la société	**Sitz**(*m*) Regierungssitz; Firmen–	**seat** – of government the company's –
signataire(*m*) **d'un affidavit,** d'une attestation; témoin(*m*) déposant	**vereidigter Zeuge**(*m*); Aussteller(*m*) (e-s Affidavit)	**deponent**
signataire(*m*), souscripteur(*m*)	**Unterzeichner**(*m*)	**signatory**
signature(*m*), visa(*m*) signature personnelle devant témoin	**Unterschrift**(*f*) eigenhändige – bestätigt	**signature** personal – witnessed
simulacre(*m*); mannequin(*m*); homme(*m*) de paille; factice (*adj.*)	**Strohmann**(*m*); Schein–	**dummy**
simulacre(*m*) **de procès**	**Scheinprozeß**(*m*)	**mock trial**
simulateur(*m*)	**Simulant**(*f*)	**malingerer**
simulation(*f*), absentéisme(*m*)	**simulieren**	**malingering**
simulation(*f*), faux(*f*) semblant fausses allégations, moyens(*m*) frauduleux	**Vorwand**(*m*) Vorspiegelung falscher Tatsachen	**pretence** false –
site(*m*), terrain(*m*) (à bâtir), *par ext.* chantier	**Lage**(*f*); Standort(*m*); Bauplatz(*m*)	**site**
social les services sociaux assurance(*f*) sociale système(*m*) de sécurité sociale bien-être(*m*) social assistant(e)(*m, f*) social(e)	**sozial** –verwaltung –versicherung –versicherungssystem –fürsorge; Wohlfahrt –fürsorger; Wohlfahrtsbeamter	**social** – administration – insurance – security system – welfare – worker
société(*f*), association(*f*) établissement(*m*) de crédit foncier coopérative(*f*) société constituée	**Gesellschaft**(*f*) Bausparkasse Genossenschaft; Konsumverein rechtsfähige Gesellschaft; eingetragene –	**society** building – cooperative – incorporated –
société(*f*) **à responsabilité non limitée**	**(Kapital-)Gesellschaft**(*f*) **mit unbeschränkter Haftung**(*f*)	**unlimited company**
société(*f*) **commerciale**	**Handelsgesellschaft**(*f*)	**trading** company

FRENCH	GERMAN	ENGLISH
société(f) mère	Dachgesellschaft(f); Muttergesellschaft(f)	parent company
société(f) par actions anonyme	Kapitalgesellschaft(f)	joint-stock company
société(f) prête-nom	Scheingesellschaft(f); vorgeschobene Gesellschaft(f)	dummy company
solidaire, collectif, conjoint	gemeinsam	joint
action(f) collective	−es Vorgehen	− action
garde(m, f) conjointe d'un enfant	−es Sorgerecht	− custody
codéfendeur(m)	Mitbeklagter	− defendant
intérêt(m) commun	−es Interesse	− interest
responsabilité(f) conjointe	−e Haftung; Gesamthaftung	− liability
copropriété(f)	−es Eigentum; Miteigentum	− ownership
codemandeur(m)	Mit−, Nebenkläger	− plaintiff
responsabilité solidaire	−e Verantwortung; Solidarhaftung	− responsibility
coentreprise(f), opération(f) conjointe, association(f) en participation	Joint Venture; Gemeinschaftsuntenehmen	− venture
sollicitation(f)	Bitte(f), Ersuchen	solicitation
solvabilité(f)	Zahlungsfähigkeit(f); Solvenz(f)	solvency
marge(f) de solvabilité	Liquiditätsmarge	− margin
taux(m) de solvabilité	Solvenzkennzahl	− ratio
sommaire	summarisch; kurz	summary
jugement(m) sommaire	Urteil im abgekürzten (beschleunigten) Verfahren	− judgment
procédure(f) sommaire	summarisches (abgekürztes) Verfahren	− proceedings
somme(f) globale, somme forfaitaire	Pauschalbetrag(m); Abfindungsbetrag(m)	lump sum
souches(f), familles(f), lignées(f)	Stämmen; (Parentelen)	stirpes
par souches	(Erbfolge) nach Stämmen	per −
soumettre, asujettir	unterwerfen; aussetzen	subject (to)
faire subir de mauvais traitements à qqu'un	Mißhandlung aussetzen	− s.o. to maltreatment
soumission(f); engagement(m), promesse(f); entreprise(f) commerciale	Verpflichtung(serklärung)(f); Unternehmen(n)	undertaking
sous pair	unter pari; unter dem Nennwert	under par
souscrire	unterzeichnen; − schreiben	subscribe (to)
sous-entrepreneur(m), sous-traitant	Subunternehmer(m); Nach−; Unterlieferant(m)	subcontractor
sous-estimer	unterbewerten; underschätzen	underrate (to)
sous-jacent, fondamental	zugrundeliegend	underlying
raisons(f) cachées	−e Ursachen, −e Beweggründe	− motives
sous-location(f)	Untervermietung(f); −pacht(f)	sublease
soussigné (le)	Unterzeichnete(r)(m)	undersigned (the)

FRENCH	GERMAN	ENGLISH
soutenir	aufrecht erhalten; bestätigen	uphold (to)
soutenir, être complice, aider	anstiften, begünstigen; Vorschub(m) leisten	abet (to)
soutenir, supporter accepter un pourvoi accorder une objection	stattgeben; aufrechterhalten e-m Berufungsantrag stattgeben e-r Einwendung stattgeben	sustain (to) – an appeal – an objection
spéculation(f)	Spekulation(f); Vermutung(f)	speculation
stagiaire(m)	auf – Freigelassener(m); auf Probe(f) Eingestellter(m)	probationer
statistiques(m) démographiques	Personenstandsstatistik(f); Bevölkerungsstatistik	vital statistics
statut(m), capacité(f) juridique état(m) statut légal, union(f) état(m) matrimonial, état de mariage	Status(m) Personenstand; Rechtsposition(f) Familienstand	status legal – marital –
strangulation(f)	Erwürgung(f)	strangulation
subjectif	subjektiv; unsachlich	subjective
subornation(f) (de témoins), intimidation(f), menaces(f)	Einschüchterung(f)	intimidation
subrogation(f)	Subrogation(f); Rechtsübergang(m)	subrogation
substitut(m)	Stellvertreter(m), stellvertretendes Mitglied	alternate
subversif	subversiv; staatsgefährdend	subversive
succession(f)	Nachlaß(m); Erbschaft(f)	deceased's estate
succession(f), descendance(f), héritiers(m) succession ab intestat droits(m) de succession, droits successifs	Erbfolge(f) Intestat–; gesetzliche – –recht; Erbberechtigung	succession intestate – right of –
suicide(m)	Suizid(m); Selbstmord(m)	suicide
sujet(m) (à), soumis (à), sous réserve (de), redevable (de) soumis au droit coutumier asujetti aux stipulations	abhängig von; vorbehaltlich nach derzeit gültigem Recht vorbehaltlich der Bestimmungen von	subject – to current law – to the provisions of
superflu, au chômage, licencié économique	entlassen; überflüssig	redundant
supériorité(f), prépondérance(f), supériorité(f) numérique supériorité des preuves du demandeur	Übergewicht(n); Überwiegen überzeugender Beweis	preponderance – of evidence
supposition(f), déduction(f), inférence(f)	Folgerung(f); Rückschluß(m)	inference

FRENCH	GERMAN	ENGLISH
suppression(f)	**Unterdrückung**(f); Verheimlichung(f)	**suppression**
dissimulation(f), destruction(f) de preuves	Unterdrückung von Beweismaterial	– of evidence
sur place, 'loco'	**Loco-Konto**(n)	**loco**
surestaries(f), droits(m) de surestarie; magasinage, droits(m) de magasinage	**Überliegezeit**(f); Überliegegeld	**demurrage**
surseoir, suspendre surseoir à l'exécution	**aufhalten;** einstellen; aussetzen (Zwangs)Vollstreckung einstellen, aufschieben	**stay (to)** – execution
suspendre l'audience	Verfahren aussetzen	– proceedings
sursis(m), commutation(f) de peine de mort	**Strafvollstreckungsaufschub**(m)	**reprieve**
sursis(m), délai(m), répit(m)	**Fristverlängerung**(f); Vollstreckungsaufschub(m)	**respite**
surveillance(f)	**Überwachung**(f); Kontrolle(f)	**surveillance**
surveiller, vérifier, contrôler	**überwachen;** kontrollieren	**monitor (to)**
survivant	**Überlebende(r)**(m); Hinterbliebene(r)(m)	**survivor**
suspension(f); vacation(f), suspension(f), interruption(f)	**Schwebezustand**(m); Unentschiedenheit(f)	**abeyance**
suspension(f), surséance(f) arrêt(m) de paiement surséance de jugement	**Einstellung**(f); Aufhebung(f) Zahlungseinstellung Aussetzen der Strafe zur Bewährung	**suspension** – of payments – of sentence
suspicion, soupçon(m)	**Verdacht**(m); Argwohn(m)	**suspicion**
syndic(m) **de faillite**	**Konkursverwalter**(m)	**trustee in bankruptcy**
syndicat(m)	**Gewerkschaft**(f)	**trade union**
syndicat(m) **de garantie,** groupe(m) de souscription	**Versicherungskonsortium**(f); Emissions–(f)	**underwriting syndicate**
Système(m) **Monétaire Européen** (SME)	**Europäisches Währungssystem** (EWS)	**European Monetary System (EMS)**

T

FRENCH	GERMAN	ENGLISH
tableau(*m*) **de financement**	**Kapitalflußrechnung**(*f*)	**funds statement**
tacite consentement(*m*) tacite	**stillschweigend** –e Zustimmung	**tacit** – consent
tarif(*m*), barème(*m*) tarif protecteur législation(*f*) douanière	**(Zoll**(*m*)**)Tarif**(*m*)**;** Satz(*m*) Schutzzoll Zollgesetzgebung	**tariff** protective – – legislation
taux(*m*), cours(*m*), tarif(*m*) taux de conversion taux d'escompte taux de change taux d'intérêt taux de rendement	**Satz**(*m*)**;** Kurs(*m*) Umrechnungskurs Diskontsatz Wechselkurs Zinssatz Ertragsrate; Rentabilität	**rate** conversion – discount – exchange – – of interest – of return
taux(*m*) **uniforme**	**Pauschalsatz**(*m*)**;** Pauschalgebühr(*f*)	**flat rate**
témoignages(*m*) **contradictoires**	**sich widersprechende** **Beweise**(*m*), sich widersprechende Zeugenaussage(*f*)	**conflicting evidence**
témoignages(*m*) **concordants**	**verstärkender Beweis**(*m*)**;** erdrückendes Beweismaterial(*n*)	**cumulative evidence**
témoignage(*m*) **oral**	**mündliche Zeugenaussage**(*f*)	**oral testimony**
témoin(*m*) témoin à décharge témoin à charge témoin instrumentaire du testament	**Zeuge**(*m*) Entlastungs–; vom Beklagten/ Angeklagten benannter – Belastungs–; – der Anklage Testaments–	**witness** – for the defence – for the prosecution – to a will
témoin(*m*) **oculaire**	**Augenzeuge**(*m*)	**eyewitness**
tendancieux, non impartial, partial	**voreingenommen**, befangen, parteiisch	**biased**
teneur(*m*) **de registre,** greffier(*m*), archiviste(*m*) directeur(*m*) de l'enregistrement de sociétés	**Registerführer**(*m*)**;** Gerichts–(*m*), Standesbeamter(*m*) Führer des Gesellschaftsregisters	**registrar** the – of companies

FRENCH	GERMAN	ENGLISH
tenir, détenir; être investi; conclure, juger; obliger	**besitzen;** für Recht(n) erkennen	**hold (to)**
avoir confiance (en)	als Treuhänder verwalten	– in trust
détenir des actions	Aktien besitzen	– shares
tentative(f) **de perpétration d'un crime**	**versuchtes Verbrechen**(n); versuchte Straftat	**attempted crime**
tenue(f) **(d'une réunion);** portefeuille(m), disponibilités; ferme(f), tenure(f); holding(m)	**Beteiligung**(f)	**holding**
participation(f) majoritaire	Mehrheits–	majority –
tenure(f) **à bail,** propriété(f) louée à bail	**Mietbesitz**(m); Pachtbesitz(m); Mietgrundstück(n); Pachtland(n)	**leasehold**
tenure(f) **en propriété perpétuelle et libre**	**Grundeigentum**(n); (zeitl. unbeschränktes) Eigentumsrecht(n) (an Grundbesitz)	**freehold**
terrain(m) **communal, banal**	**Gemeindeland**(n); Allmende	**common land**
territoire(m)	**(Staats-, Hoheits-)Gebiet**(n); Territorium(f)	**territory**
territoire d'un état membre (de la CEE)	Mietgliedsstaat-Gebiet *(EG)*	member State – *(EEC)*
testament(m) dernières volontés et testament	**Testament**(n) –; letztwillige Verfügung	**testament** last will and –
testament(m)	**letztwillige Verfügung; s.** Testament(n)	**will** *(cf. testament)*
donation(f) au dernier survivant, testament mutuel	gemeinschaftliche(s) (wechselbezügliche(s)) –	joint (mutual) –
acte de dernières volontés homologation(f) d'un testament	Testament Testamentsbestätigung	last – and testament probate of –
établir un testament	Testament als gültig bestätigen	to prove a –
testateur(m)	**Erblasser**(m); Vermächtnisgeber(m)	**devisor**
testateur(m)	**Vermächtnisgeber**(m); Erblasser(m)	**legator**
testateur(m), **testatrice**(f)	**Erblasser(in)**(m, f); Testator(m)	**testator, testatrix**
texte(m), loi(f) inopérant(e)	**unwirksame, ungültige Rechtsvorschrift**(f), Verordnung(f)	**inoperative enactment**
tiers(m), tierce personne(m) mise(f) en cause assurance(f) de responsabilité civile responsabilité(f) civile	**Dritte(r)**(m, f) Streitverkündung Haftpflichtversicherung; Fremdversicherung Haftpflicht	**third party** third-party action third-party insurance third-party liability
tirage(m), tiré à part	**(Sonder-)Abdruck**(m)	**offprint**
tiré(m), accepteur(m); intervenant(f), donneur d'aval	**Annehmer**(m); Akzeptant(m) (e-s Wechsels)	**acceptor**

FRENCH	GERMAN	ENGLISH
tiré(*m*) **(d'un effet),** payeur(*m*) (d'une lettre de change)	**Bezogener**(*m*); Trassat(*m*)	**drawee**
tireur(*m*), souscripteur(*m*)	**Aussteller**(*m*); Trassant(*m*)	**drawer**
titre(*m*) **de propriété**; titre nobiliaire; intitulé(*m*) (d'une action)	**Eigentum(srecht)**(*n*); Titel(*m*)	**title**
transfert de droit	Rechtsübertragung; Forderungsabtretung	assignment of –
de propriété exclusive détenteur(*m*) d'un titre (de propriété)	ausschließliches Besitzrecht Titelinhaber	exclusive – --holder
titre(*m*) **privilégié** (*US*)	**Vorzugsaktie**(*f*) (*US*)	**preferred stock** (*US*)
titres(*m*), fonds(*m*), valeurs(*f*) boursières	**Wertpapiere**(*n*); Effekten	**securities**
valeurs cotées titres remboursables valeurs mobilières librement cessibles	börsenfähige – einlösbare Wertpapiere übertragbare –	listed – redeemable – transferrable –
titulaire(*m*) **d'un poste**	**Amtsinhaber**(*m*)	**incumbent**
tontine(*f*)	**Tontine**(*f*); lotterieähnliche Rentenversicherung(*f*) auf den Erlebensfall	**tontine**
tort(*m*)	**unerlaubte** Handlung(*f*); zivilrechtliches Delikt(*n*)	**tort**
droit(*m*) de la responsabilité	Recht der unerlaubten Handlungen; Deliktsrecht	– law of torts
torture(*f*)	**Folterung**(*f*)	**torture**
tournée(*f*), ronde(*m*) (de police)	**(Polizei-)Runde**(*f*), Rundgang(*m*)	**beat (police)**
(toutes les) installations (d'une maison)	**Einrichtungsgegenstände**(*m*)	**fixtures and fittings**
trafic(*m*), circulation(*f*), transport(*m*)	**Verkehr**(*m*)	**traffic**
accident(*m*) de la circulation	–sunfall	– accident
infraction(*f*) au code de la route	–sdelikt	– offence
contrevenant(*m*) au code de la route	–ssünder	– offender
infraction au code de la route	Verletzung der –svorschriften	– violation
trahison(*f*)	**Verrat**(*m*); Treubruch(*m*)	**betrayal**
trahison(*f*)	**Landesverrat**(*m*); Hochverrat(*m*)	**treason**
traité(*m*), pacte(*m*), convention(*f*)	**(Staats)Vertrag**(*m*)	**treaty**
traite(*f*) **à vue**	**Sichtwechsel**(*m*)	**demand bill**
Traité(*m*) **de Rome** (*CEE*)	**(Die Römischen) Verträge** (*EG*)	**Treaty of Rome** (*EEC*)
traitement(*m*), appointement(*m*), salaire(*m*)	**Gehalt**(*m*); Besoldung(*f*)	**salary**

FRENCH	GERMAN	ENGLISH
tranche(*f*)	Tranche(*f*)	tranche
transaction(*f*), compromis(*m*), arrangement(*m*); gestion(*f*), conduite d'une affaire	Geschäft(svorgang)(*n*); Durchführung(*f*)	transaction
transfert(*m*), mutation(*f*), transmission(*f*), virement(*m*) transmission de propriété cession(*f*) d'actions transmission de titre constitutif propriété	Übertragung(*f*) Vermögens–; Eigentums– Aktien– Forderungs–; Eigentums–	transfer – of property – of shares – of title
transgresseur(*m*) de la loi	Rechtsbrecher(*m*); Gesetzesübertreter(*m*)	law-breaker
transgresseur(*m*)	Übertreter(*m*); Missetäter(*m*)	transgressor
transgression(*f*), infraction(*f*), violation(*f*) violation d'une loi	Übertretung(*f*); Verletzung(*f*) Gesetzesübertretung	transgression – of a law
transit(*m*), passage(*m*), trajet(*m*), route(*f*) dommages(*m*) causés au cours du transport marchandises(*f*) en transit port(*m*) de transit	Transit(*m*); Transport(*m*) Schaden auf dem Transport Transitgüter, –waren Transithafen	transit damage in – – goods – port
transitaire(*m*), expéditionnaire(*m*)	Beförderung(*f*); Versand(*m*); Spedition(*f*)	forwarding
transitoire, passager	vorübergehend	transitory
transport(*m*), transmission(*f*) tout mode de transmission de propriété transport d'immeubles acte(*m*) de cession	Übertragung(*f*); Beförderung(*f*) Vermögens–, Eigentumsübertragung Grundstücksauflassung; Übertragungs–, Auflassungsurkunde	conveyance – of property – of real estate deed of –
transport(*m*), charroi(*m*)	Beförderung(*f*); Transport(kosten)(*m*)	haulage
transporteur(*m*)	Beförderer(*m*); Spediteur(*m*); Frachtführer(*m*)	carrier
traître	Verräter(*m*)	traitor
travail(*m*) à la pièce, travail à la tâche	Akkordarbeit(*f*)	piecework
travail(*m*) (travaux) en cours	unfertige Erzeugnisse(*n*); in Gang befindliche Arbeit(*f*)	work in progress
travailleur(*m*) indépendant	Selbständiger(*m*)	self-employed person
tribunal(*m*), cour(*f*) de justice tribunal traitant les affaires financières (Allemagne)	Gericht(shof)(*m*); Tribunal(*n*) Finanzgericht	tribunal – for tax and other financial matters (Germany)
tribunal(*m*) de police	Amtsgericht(*n*); erstinstanzliches Gericht(*n*)	magistrates' court

FRENCH	GERMAN	ENGLISH
tribunal(*m*) **des successions et des tutelles**	**Nachlaßgericht**(*n*)	**probate court**
tribunal(*m*) **inférieur,** tribunal de première instance	**unteres Gericht**(*n*)**;** Instanzgericht(*n*)	**inferior court**
tribunal(*m*) **maritime**	**See(schiffahrt)gericht, –amt**	**Admiralty court**
tribunal(*m*) **supérieure**	**höhere Instanz**(*f*)**;** übergeordnetes Gericht	**superior court**
troc(*m*) échange	**Tausch**(*m*) Tauschgeschäft; Barter–, Kompensations–	**barter** – transaction
tromper, duper	**hintergehen,** betrügen; verleiten	**beguile (to)**
tromper, tricher, escroquer	**betrügen,** beschwindeln; übervorteilen	**cheat (to)**
tromperie(*f*)**,** fraude(*f*)	**Täuschung**(*f*)**;** Betrug(*m*)	**deceit**
trompeur(*m*)**,** mensonger, déloyal	**täuschend;** irreführend; trügerisch	**deceptive**
truquer, maquiller, contrefaire	**fälschen;** nachmachen	**fake (to)**
tutelle(*f*)**;** pupille(*m, f*)**;** service(*m*), salle(*f*) d'hôpital; surveillance(*f*)	**Mündel**(*n*)**;** Stadtbezirk(*m*)	**ward**
tuteur(*m, f*)**,** conseil(*m*) judiciaire, curateur(*m*)	**Vormund**(*m*)**;** Hüter(*m*)	**guardian**
TVA (taxe sur la valeur ajoutée)	**MwSt** (Mehrwertsteuer)(*m*)	**VAT** (value added tax)

U

FRENCH	GERMAN	ENGLISH
'understatement', litote(f)	Untertreibung(f); Unterbewertung(f)	understatement
unilatéral	einseitig; voreingenommen	one-sided
urbain	städtisch	urban
urgence, situation(f) critique loi(f) d'exception vente(f) forcée	Not(zu)stand(m); Notfall(m) Notstandsverordnung, –gesetz Notverkauf	emergency – law – sale
urgent	dringend; eilig	urgent
usage(m) de moyens dilatoires	mutwilliges (dilatorisches) Parteivorbringen	sham pleading
usufruit(m)	Nutzungsrecht(n); Nießbrauch(m)	usufruct
usure(f)	Wucher(zinsen)(m)	usury
usurier	Wucherer(m)	usurer
usurpation(f), intrusion(f), empiètement(m)	Eindringen; Besitzstörung(f)	intrusion
usurpation(f) de droits, empiètement(f) sur la propriété d'autrui	Übergriff(m), Eingriff(m) in jds Rechte(f)	encroachment (upon s.o.'s rights)
utile, actif, productif, instrumental	behilflich; mitwirkend	instrumental
contribuer à	beitragen zu, mitwirken bei	to be – in
utilisateur(m) final	Endabnehmer(m); Endanwender(m)	end-user

V

FRENCH	GERMAN	ENGLISH
vacance(f), emploi(m) vacant, poste(f) à pourvoir	**freie, unbesetzte Stelle**	**vacancy**
vacances(f) **judiciaires,** suspension(f) d'audience; intersession(f) parlementaire	**(Sitzungs)**(f)**Unterbrechung**(f); Pause(f)	**recess**
vacant, libre	**frei, unbesetzt**	**vacant**
vagabond(m)**,** clochard(m)	**Landstreicher**	**vagrant**
vagabondage(m)	**Landstreicherei**	**vagrancy**
valeur(f)	**Wert**(m)	**worth**
valeur(f) valeur comptable valeur marchande valeur de rachat	**Wert**(m)**;** Valuta(f) Buchwert; buchmäßiger Wert Marktwert Rückkaufswert	**value** book – market – surrender –
valeur(f) **au pair**	**Nennwert**(m)**;** Nominalwert(m)	**par value**
valeur comptable, prix(m) d'inventaire	**Buchwert**(m)**;** buchmäßiger Wert(m)	**book value**
valeur(f) **nominale**	**Nennwert**(m)	**nominal value**
valeurs(f) **mobilières librement cessibles**	**übertragbare Wertpapiere**(f)	**transferable securities**
valeurs(f) **non cotées**	**nicht notierte Wertpapiere**(f)	**unlisted securities**
valide, régulier, valable, recevable	**(rechts)gültig;** in Kraft(f); stichhaltig	**valid**
valider	**für (rechts)gültig erklären;** bestätigen	**validate (to)**
validité(f)	**(Rechts)Gültigkeit**(f)**;** Laufzeit(f)	**validity**
vandaliser	**böswillig zerstören**	**vandalise**
vandalisme(m)	**Vandalismus**(m)**;** böswillige Sachbeschädigung(f)	**vandalism**
vendeur(m)	**Verkäufer**(m)	**seller**
vendeur(m) **de biens immobiliers,** vendeur, apporteur	**Verkäufer**(m)	**vendor**
vengeance(f)	**Rache**(f)	**revenge**
vengeance(f)	**Rache**(f)	**vengeance**

FRENCH	GERMAN	ENGLISH
vente(*f*), distribution, cession	**Verfügung**(*f*); Erledigung(*f*); Veräußerung(*f*)	**disposal**
droit(*m*) de libre disposition	Verfügungsrecht	right of –
verdict(*m*)	**(Urteils-)Spruch**(*m*); Entscheidung(*f*)	**verdict**
verdict pour démandeur ou défendeur (*procédure civile*); verdict de culpabilité ou d'acquittement (*procédure criminelle*)	Entscheidung (für Kläger od. Beklagten) (Zivilprozeß); Schuld– od. Freispruch (Strafprozeß)	general –
détermination(*f*) des faits de procédure	Feststellung des Tatbestandes	special –
verdict de culpabilité	Schuldspruch; Erkennen auf 'schuldig'	– of guilty
verdict d'acquittement	Freispruch; Erkennen auf 'nicht schuldig'	– of not guilty
vérifiable, contrôlable	**verifizierbar**; nachprüfbar	**verifiable**
vérifier, apurer, faire un audit	**(Bücher**(*m*), **Rechnungen**(*f*)) **prüfen**; Revision(*f*) durchführen	**audit (to)**
vérifier, contrôler	**verifizieren**; beglaubigen, nachprüfen	**verify (to)**
verser au dossier, classer, archiver	**einreichen**; zu den Akten nehmen	**file (to)**
se pourvoir en appel	ein Rechtsmittel (Berufung, usw.) einlegen	– an appeal
déposer une requête	ein Gesuch (Antrag) einreichen	– a petition
vice-, -adjoint; député(*m*); substitut(*m*) (d'un juge)	**Abgeordneter**(*m*); Stellvertreter(*m*)	**deputy**
victime(*f*)	**Opfer**(*m*); Geschädigter(*m*); Verletzter(*m*)	**victim**
vie(*f*)	**Leben**(*n*)	**life**
prison(*f*) à perpétuité, emprisonnement(*m*) à vie	–slängliche Freiheitsstrafe	imprisonment for –
assurance(*f*) vie, assurance sur la vie	–sversicherung	– assurance/insurance
violation(*f*) **de domicile**, effraction(*f*)	**Einbruchdiebstahl**(*m*)	**housebreaking**
violation(*f*) **de propriété**	**widerrechtliches Betreten**	**trespassing**
violence(*f*), contrainte(*f*)	**Zwang**(*m*); Nötigung(*f*)	**duress**
agir à son corps défendant sous la contrainte	unter Zwang handeln	to act under –
violence(*f*), voies(*f*) de fait	**Gewalt**(*m*)(-tätigkeit)(*f*)	**violence**
violeur(*m*)	**Vergewaltiger**(*m*)	**rapist**
voie(*f*) **de recours**, moyen(*m*) de droit, dédommagement(*m*)	**Rechtsbehelf**(*m*)	**remedy**
ordonnance(*f*) de référé, mesure(*f*) provisoire	vorläufiger –	provisional –

FRENCH	GERMAN	ENGLISH
voies(f) **de fait**	**Gewaltanwendung**(f); Körperverletzung(f), Mißhandlung(f), tätlicher Angriff	**battery**
coups(m) et blessures	schwere tätliche Beleidigung (Mißhandlung); Körperverletzung	assault and –
voix(f) **prépondérante**	**ausschlaggebende Stimme**(f)	**casting vote**
vol(m)	**Diebstahl**(m)	**theft**
vol(m) vol important larcin(m)	**Diebstahl**(m) schwerer – leichter –	**larceny** grand – petty –
vol(m) **à l'étalage**	**Ladendiebstahl**(m)	**shoplifting**
vol(m) **qualifié** vol à main armée vol qualifié avec violences	**Raub**(m); Beraubung(f) bewaffneter Raubüberfall gewalttätige(r) –	**robbery** armed – – with violence
voler, dérober	**stehlen**	**steal (to)**
volontaire concordat préventif de la faillite aveu(m) spontané	**freiwillig;** unentgeltlich freiwilliger Vergleich freiwilliges Geständnis	**voluntary** – composition – confession
volonté (délibérée)	**Wille**(m)**;** -nsäußerung(f)	**volition**
voyou(m), vandale(m, f), hooligan(m)	**Rowdy**(m)	**hooligan**

FRENCH	GERMAN	ENGLISH
zéro(*m*)	**null**	**zero**
'zero-base budgeting' (ZBB)	Budgetierung auf –basis	--base budgeting (ZBB)
coupon(*m*) zéro (sans intérêt)	–kupon	– coupon
valeur(*m*) nulle	–wert	– value
zone(*m*), district(*m*), quartier(*m*)	**Zone**(*f*); Gebiet(*n*)	**zone**
zone frontière	Grenzgebiet	border –
zone dangereuse	Gefahrenzone	danger –
zone franche, zone libre	Frei(hafen)zone	free –
zone militaire	Militärgebiet	military –
tarif(*m*) de zone	Zonentarif	– tariff

German/English/French

A

GERMAN	ENGLISH	FRENCH
(ab-, ver-)leugnen; nichts zu tun haben mit; verstoßen	**disown (to)**	**désavouer,** renier
ab Fabrik(f)	**ex factory**	**hors usine**
ab Kai(m)	**ex quay**	**à quai,** dédouané
ab Lager(n)	**ex store**	**disponible**
ab Schiff(n)	**ex ship**	**au débarquement,** à bord
Abänderungsklausel(f)	**derogative clause**	**clause**(f) **dérogatoire**
Abandon(m); Aufgabe(f); Verzicht(leistung)(f); Verlassen(n); Aussetzung(f)	**abandonment**	**abandon**(m)
abandonnieren; zurückziehen; zurücknehmen; fallenlassen	**abandon (to)**	**abandonner,** renoncer
Abdruck(m)	**imprint**	**empreinte**(f)
Abfindung(f); Entlastung(f); Quittung(f)	**quittance**	**quittance**(f), quitus(m), acquit(m)
Abgeordneter(m); Stellvertreter(m)	**deputy**	**vice-,** -adjoint; député(m); substitut(m) (d'un juge)
abhängig	**contingent**	**éventuel,** conditionnel, fortuit
Erfolgshonorar Eventualverbindlichkeiten	– fee – liabilities	honoraires éventuels engagement(m) éventuel; tierce caution
abhängig von; vorbehaltlich	**subject**	**sujet**(m) **(à),** soumis (à), sous réserve (de), redevable (de)
nach derzeit gültigem Recht vorbehaltlich der Bestimmungen von	– to current law – to the provisions of	soumis au droit coutumier asujetti aux stipulations
Abhilfe(f) **schaffen;** wiedergutmachen	**redress (to)**	**redresser,** rétablir, réparer un tort
Abkürzung(f), Auszug(m), Zusammenfassung(f); Einschränkung(f), Beeinträchtigung(f)	**abridgement**	**diminution**(f), restriction(f)
Ablauf(m); Erlöschen(n); Verfall(m) Ablauf e-s Vertrags	**expiration, expiry** – of a contract	**expiration**(f), cessation(f), échéance(f) expiration(f) d'un contrat

GERMAN	ENGLISH	FRENCH
Ableben(*n*); Tod(*m*)	**decease**	**mort**, décès
ablehnen; bestreiten; beanstanden; einen Anspruch in Abrede stellen ein Recht bestreiten, in Frage stellen	**challenge (to)** – a claim – a right	**contester**, défier, interpeller contester une réclamation, une demande contester un droit; attaquer une décision
ablehnen; zurückweisen	**reject (to)**	**rejeter**, refuser
ablenken; abwenden; verhüten Schaden abwenden Gewalt abwenden	**avert (to)** – damage – violence	**prévenir**, éviter prévenir des dégâts prévenir la violence
Ableugnung(*f*), Ver–; s. Verzicht(*m*)	**abnegation** (*cf. waiver*)	**désaveu**(*m*); renonciation(*f*)
Absatz(*m*); Abschnitt(*m*)	**paragraph**	**paragraphe**(*m*)
abschaffen, beseitigen; außer Kraft(*f*) setzen	**abolish (to)**	**abolir**, supprimer
Abschaffung(*f*); Aufhebung(*f*), Außerkraftsetzung(*f*)	**abrogation**	**abrogation**(*f*)
abschrecken; verhindern jdn abhalten von	**deter (to)** – s.o. from	**empêcher**, dissuader empêcher qqu'un de
abschreiben; abbuchen	**write (to) off**	**amortir**, défalquer, annuler
Abschrift(*f*); Ausfertigung(*f*) des Gerichtsprotokolls	**transcript**	**copie**(*f*) **conforme d'un acte judiciaire,** transcription(*f*)
absichtlich, vorsätzlich; (wohl-) überlegt	**deliberate**	**délibéré**(*m*), prémédité, voulu
Abstammung(*f*); Herkunft	**parentage**	**lignée**(*f*), origine(*f*)
Abstand(*m*) **nehmen von**	**refrain (to)**	**se retenir,** s'abstenir
Abteilung(*f*) **des High Court** (*UK*); Gerichtshof erster Instanz	**Queen's Bench Division** (*UK*)	**Cour**(*f*) **du Banc de la Reine** (*UK*)
Abteilung(*f*) **des High Court** (*UK*); Gerichtshof(*m*) erster Instanz(*f*)	**King's Bench** (*UK*)	**Cour**(*f*) **du Banc du Roi** (*UK*)
Abtreibung(*f*)	**abortion**	**avortement**(*m*)
abtreten, übereignen; bestimmen, ernennen Vermögen übertragen	**assign (to)** – property	**donner en partage,** assigner, imposer, déléguer, céder attribuer des biens
abtreten, zedieren; überlassen	**cede (to)**	**céder**
Abtretung(*f*), Übereignung(*f*), Übertragung(*f*) Forderungs–, Anspruchsabtretung Aktienübertragung	**assignment** – of claim – of shares	**assignation**(*f*), affectation(*f*), cession(*f*), transfert(*m*) transfert d'une créance transmission d'actions
Abtretung(*f*); Aufgabe(*f*)	**surrender**	**reddition**(*f*); abandon(*m*), abdication(*f*)

GERMAN	ENGLISH	FRENCH
Abtretung(f); Zession(f); Überlassung(f)	**cession**	**cession**(f)
Abtretungsurkunde	deed of –	acte(m) de cession
Abweichen; Klageänderung(f)	**departure**	**départ**(m); écart(m)
Abweichen von den gesetzlichen Vorschriften	– from statutory regulations	dérogation(f) aux dispositions légales
abweichend; andersdenkend	**dissentient**	**dissident,** opposant
Abweichung(f)	**divergence**	**divergence**(f)
Meinungsverschiedenheit	– of opinion	divergence d'opinions
Abweichung(f); Deviation(f)	**deviation**	**déviation**(f), écart(m); dérogation(f)
abwickeln; in Liquidation gehen	**liquidate (to)**	**liquider**
Liquidation e-r Gesellschaft durchführen	– a company	liquider une société
Abwicklung(f)	**winding up**	**dissolution**(f), liquidation(f)
– e-r Gesellschaft	– of a company	liquidation d'une société
abzeichnen, unterzeichnen; paraphieren	**initial (to)**	**parafer,** émarger
ächten; für unrechtmäßig erklären	**outlaw (to)**	**mettre hors-la-loi,** proscrire, prohiber
Adoption(f), Annahme(f)	**adoption**	**adoption**(f)
Adoptiv-	**adoptive**	**adoptif**
Adresse(f), Anschrift(f); Anrede(f), Ansprache(f)	**address**	**adresse**(f), allocution(f),
Zustellungsadresse	– for service	domicile(m) élu
Anrede des Gerichts	– to the court	plaidoirie(f)
Akkordarbeit(f)	**piecework**	**travail**(m) **à la pièce,** travail à la tâche
Aktenanforderung(f); Revisionsantrag(f)	**certiorari**	**requète de rèvision pénale**
Aktie(f); Gesellschaftsanteil(m)	**share**	**action**(f), valeur(f), part(f)
Gratisaktie	bonus –	action gratuite
Stammaktie	common – (US)	action(f) ordinaire (US)
börsennotierte Aktie	listed –	action cotée (officiellement)
Stammaktie	ordinary –	action ordinaire
Vorzugsaktie	preference –	action privilégiée, de priorité
Namensaktie	registered –	action nominative
Stammaktie mit bedingter (keine Bedingung unterliegemer)	restricted (non-restricted) –	valeur sujette (non sujette) à restriction
Dividendenzahlung (Dividendein Form von)	– dividend	dividende2(m) de l'action
Gratisaktien		
Aktienausgabe; Emission	– issue	émission(f) d'actions
nicht notierte Aktie	unlisted –	action non cotée
Aktienbesitz(m); Anteils–(m)	**shareholding**	**actionnariat**(m)
Aktieninhaber(m); Anteilseigner(m)	**stockholder**	**porteur**(m) **de titres,** actionnaire(m)
Aktionär(f); Antelseigner(m)	**shareholder**	**actionnaire**(m), détenteur(m) d'actions

297

GERMAN	ENGLISH	FRENCH
Aktiva; Vermögen(n)	**asset(s)**	**actif**(m), avoir(m), biens(m), fonds(m), capital(m), masse(f) active
Aktiva und Passiva	– and liabilities	actif et (ensemble de) dettes
Anlagevermögen; Vermögenswerte	capital –	actif immobilisé
Umlaufvermögen; sofort realisierbare Aktiven	current –	actif réalisable, disponible, à court terme
feste Anlagen; Sachanlagen; Anlagevermögen	fixed –	immobilisations(f)
flüssiges Vermögen, flüssige Mittel	liquid –	disponibilités(f)
Alibi(n)	**alibi**	**alibi**(m)
allein; einzig	**sole**	**seul,** unique
Alleinbegünstigter	– beneficiary	seul bénéficiaire
amtieren	**officiate (to)**	**officier,** célébrer
amtlich	**official**	**officiel** (adj.); fonctionnaire(m) (n), représentant(m) officiel
Amtshandlung	– act	acte(m) officiel
Konkursverwalter; – bestellter Nachlaßverwalter	– administrator	administrateur(m) officiel
–e Genehmigung	– authorisation	autorisation(f) officielle
Amtsblatt	– journal	publication(f) officielle
Konkursverwalter	– receiver	liquidateur(m) judiciaire
Amts-, Dienstsiegel	– seal	cachet(m) réglementaire
Amts-, Dienstverschwiegenheit	– secrecy	secret(m) d'État
(amtliche oder gerichtliche) Enscheidung(f); Anordnung(f)	**ruling**	**ordonnance**(f), décision(f) d'un juge sur un point de droit
Amtsgericht(n); erstinstanzliches Gericht(n)	**magistrates' court**	**tribunal**(m) **de police**
Amtsinhaber(m)	**incumbent**	**titulaire**(m) **d'un poste**
(Amts)Siegel(n); Plombe(f), Verschluß(m)	**seal**	**cachet**(m), sceau(m)
seinen Siegel anbringen, beidrücken	to affix one's –	apposer son cachet
unter dem Siegel von; gesiegelt	under the – of	sous le sceau de
an der Börse(m) **notieren;** listenmäßig erfassen	**list (to)**	**coter en Bourse,** cataloguer, enregistrer
Analphabet(m)	**illiterate**	**illettré,** analphabète
Aneignung(f); Bewilligung(f), Bereitstellung(f), Bestimmung(f); Verwendung(f)	**appropriation**	**appropriation**(f), attribution(f), dotation(f), prélèvement(m)
Bereitstellung von Mitteln für bestimmten Zweck	– of funds	détournement(m) de fonds
Vermögensverteilung, Besitzverwendung	– of property	appropriation(f) d'un bien
anerkennen, befolgen	**abide by (to)**	**demeurer;** se conformer, se soumettre

GERMAN	ENGLISH	FRENCH
Anerkennung(f), Genehmigung; ausgesetzte Summe; Beihilfe(f); Vergütung(f); Preisnachlaß(m); (Steuer-Freibetrag)	allowance	**allocation**(f), gratification(f); rabais(m), ristourne(f); pension(f), rente(f), indemnité(f); déduction(f), abattement(m)
jährlicher Abschreibungsbetrag	annual –	amortissement(m) linéaire
Tagegeld(er); Diäten	daily –	indemnités journalières
Aufwandsentschädigung	expense –	indemnités pour frais
Alterszulage	superannuation –	pension de retraite
Anerkennung(f); Anerkenntnis(f); (Empfangs-)Bestätigung(f); Zugeständnis; (notarielle) Beglaubigung	acknowledgement	**constatation**(f), reconnaissance(f)
urkundliche Beglaubigung	– by record	aveu judiciaire
Anerkenntnis der Beanstandung, Beschwerde	– of complaint	récépissé d'une réclamation, d'une plainte
Schuldanerkenntnis	– of debt	reconnaissance de dette
Anfall(m); Auflauf(m) (Zinsen); Entstehung(f) (Anspruch, Recht)	accrual	**date**(f) de survenance; date(f) de naissance (d'un droit); échéance(f)
Anfangs-/Einlagekapital(n); Gründungs–	initial fund/capital	**fonds**(m) d'apport, capital(m) d'apport
anfechten	impugn (to)	**attaquer**, mettre en doute, discuter
Beweismaterial –	– evidence	récuser un témoignage
anfügen; beimessen; verhaften; pfänden	attach (to)	**attacher**, impliquer, imputer; saisir, contraindre par corps
beschlagnahmen und verkaufen	– and sell	saisir et vendre
Anfügung(f); Zuteilung(f); Verhaftung(f); Beschlagnahme(f), Pfändung(f)	attachment	**attachement**(m), fixation(f); saisie(f); opposition(f); mandat(m) d'amener; prise(f) de corps
Vermögensbeschlagnahme	– of property	saisie immobilière
Arrestbefehl; Pfändungsbefehl; Beschlagnahmeverfügung	– order	ordonnance(f) de saisie
anführen, angeben; (Unerwiesenes) behaupten; (bei Gericht) vorbringen, geltend machen	allege (to)	**alléguer**, prétendre, exciper de
Anführung(f), Angabe(f); (unerwiesene) Behauptung(f) Parteivorbringen	allegation	**allégation**(f); chef(m) d'accusation; moyen(m) de défense
Angebot(n), Offerte(f); Antrag(m), Bewerbung(f); Gebot(n)	bid	**enchère**, offre
Angebot(n); Offerte(f)	offer	**offre**(f), proposition(f)
Angebotspreis; Briefkurs	– price	cours(m) d'offre
angefangen; in Entstehung(f) begriffen; teilweise begründet	inchoate	**en puissance**, incomplet
unvollkommene Missetat	– crime	crime(m) non parfait
entstehendes od. im Entstehen begriffenes Recht	– right	droit(m) en puissance

GERMAN	ENGLISH	FRENCH
angegliedert, angeschlossen	**affiliated**	**affilié**(*m*)
Angeklagter(*m*); Beschuldigter(*m*); Täter(*m*)	**culprit**	**coupable;** accusé(*m*), prévenu
angleichen; harmonisieren	**harmonise (to)**	**harmoniser,** concilier
Angleichung(*f*)**;** Annäherung(*f*) Rechtsangleichung, Angleichung von Rechtsvorschriften und Verordnungen (*EG*)	**approximation** – of laws and regulations (*EEC*)	**approximation**(*f*) rapprochement(*m*) des législations et des règlementations(*f*) (*CEE*)
Angleichung(*f*) (*EG*)	**harmonisation** (*EEC*)	**harmonisation**(*f*)
angreifen; tätlich bedrohen od. beleidigen	**assault (to)**	**agresser,** se livrer à des voies de fait sur
angrenzen	**abut (to)**	**confiner**
angrenzend; benachbart	**contiguous**	**contigu, contiguë**
Anhaltspunkt(*m*)	**clue**	**indice**(*m*)
Anhängezettel(*m*), – versehen	**tag (to)**	**étiqueter,** munir d'une fiche
anhängig; schwebend –er Rechtsstreit	**pending** – action	**en instance,** en cours action(*f*) en cours
Anhängigkeit(*f*) **des Verfahrens**	**pendency of action**	**en cours d'action**
anheften, aufkleben; aufdrücken mit e-m Siegel versehen, siegeln	**affix (to)** – a seal	**attacher,** apposer, ajouter sceller (un document), apposer des scellés
ankämpfen gegen; sich jdn zum Gegener(*m*) machen	**antagonise**	**contrarier**
Anklage(*f*), Beschuldigung(*f*); Belastung(*f*), Hypothek(*f*); Obhut(*f*), Sorge(*f*); Gebühr(*f*), Unkosten angeklagt wegen Mordes angeklagt wegen Diebstahls angeklagt wegen Landesverrats, Hochverrats	**charge** – of murder – of theft – of treason	**acte**(*m*) **d'accusation,** inculpation; chef(*m*) d'accusation; réquisitoire(*m*) inculpation(*f*) de meurtre inculpation de vol inculpation de trahison
Anklagejury(*f*) (*US*)	**grand jury** (*US*)	**jury**(*m*) **d'accusation** (*US*)
anklagen, anschuldigen, beschuldigen	**accuse (to)**	**accuser,** incriminer
anklagen, unter Anklage stellen	**charge (to)**	**accuser,** inculper
anklagen jdn e-s Verbrechens –	**indict (to)** – s.o. for a crime	**inculper,** accuser, incriminer poursuivre qqu'un pour un crime
anklagen; anfechten; in Zweifel ziehen die Glaubwürdigkeit eines Zeugen anzweifeln (*US*)	**impeach (to)** – a witness	**mettre en accusation,** récuser, contester récuser un témoin
anklagen; strafrechtlich verfolgen Prozeß betreiben, – führen	**prosecute (to)** an action	**poursuivre en justice** intenter une action
Ankläger(*m*)**;** Vertreter(*m*) der Anklage(*f*) Staatsanwalt	**prosecutor** public –	**accusateur**(*m*)**,** plaignant ministère(*m*) public

GERMAN	ENGLISH	FRENCH
Anklage(verlesung)(f); gerichtliche Belangung	**arraignment**	**mise en accusation**
Anlockung(f); Verführung(f), Anwerbung(f)	**enticement**	**séduction**(f)
Annahme(f); Anerkennung(f); Akzept(n); Zusage(f)	**acceptance**	**acceptation**(f), consentement(m), agrément(m)
Annahme e-s Urteils	– of a judgment	acquiescement à un jugement
annehmen; anerkennen; akzeptieren; antreten (Amt)	**accept (to)**	**accepter,** approuver, agréer
annehmen; verabschieden ein Gesetz verabschieden e-n Beschluß fassen	**pass (to)** – a Bill – a resolution	**adopter,** passer adopter un projet de loi prendre, adopter une résolution
(Straf)Urteil fällen, verkünden	– sentence	prononcer une condamnation
Annehmer(m); Akzeptant(m) (e-s Wechsels)	**acceptor**	**tiré**(m), accepteur(m); intervenant(f), donneur d'aval
annullieren; kündigen, aufheben; für ungültig erklären	**annul**	**annuler,** abroger
Annullierung(f); Aufhebung(f); Ungültigkeitserklärung(f); Rückgängigmachung	**annulment**	**annulation**(f), abrogation(f), résiliation(f), cassation(f)
anordnen, bestimmen; bestellen, ernennen zu e-n Vormund bestellen e-n Treuhänder bestellen	**appoint (to)** – a guardian – a trustee	**désigner,** nommer, établir, choisir désigner un tuteur désigner un trustee
Anordnung(f); Leitung(f); Rechtsbelehrung(f)	**direction**	**direction**(f); **ordre**(m), prescription(f)
Anrecht(n); Beteiligung(f); Zins(m)	**interest**	**intérêt(s)**(m); titre(m), droit(m); parti(m), groupe(m)
Zinseszins ausschlaggebender Kapitalanteil	compound – controlling –	intérêts composés participation(f) de contrôle
Verzugszinsen	– on overdue payment	intérêts moratoires
Mehrheitsbeteiligung einfache, gewöhnliche Zinsen wohlerworbenes, sicher begründetes Anrecht	majority – simple – vested –	participation majoritaire intérêts simples droit acquis
anrufen, sich wenden an	**appeal (to)**	**interjeter appel,** faire appel d'une décision; former un recours
(an-)rufen; vorsprechen; einberufen; einfordern, auffordern (gerichtlich) aufrufen, e-e Sache – jdn auffordern über etwas auszusagen zur Ordnung rufen	**call (to)** – a case – a person to give evidence – to order	**appeler,** citer à comparaître appeler une cause, une affaire appeler un témoin à faire sa déposition ouvrir (une séance)

GERMAN	ENGLISH	FRENCH
ansammeln; horten	**hoard (to)**	**accumuler,** thésauriser
Anscheinsbeweis(m); Glaubhaftmachung(f)	**prima facie evidence**	**commencement**(m) **de preuve**
Anschlag(m); Verschwörung(f)	**plot**	**complot**(m), intrigue(f), conspiration(f); parcelle(f) de terrain
Anschuldigung(f), Beschuldigung(f)	**accusation**	**accusation**(f), incrimination(f)
Anspruch(m); Forderung(f); Behauptung(f); Klagebegehren	**claim**	**créance**(f); revendication(f), requête(f); droit(m) qu'on entend faire valoir en justice
Schadensersatzanspruch, – forderung	– for damages	action(f) en dommages-intérêts
Rechtsmittelanspruch	– for relief	demande(f) de déduction
Gegenanspruch; Widerklage	counter––	demande reconventionnelle
deklaratorischer Anspruch, Feststellungs–	declaratory –	demande déclaratoire
Anspruchsteller(m); Antragsteller(m); Kläger(m)	**claimant**	**demandeur**(m), partie(f) requérante
anstiften, begünstigen; Vorschub(m) leisten	**abet (to)**	**soutenir,** être complice, aider
anstiften; aufhetzen	**instigate (to)**	**inciter,** pousser, fomenter
anstiften; aufwiegeln	**incite (to)** s.o.	**inciter** qqu'un (à)
Anstifter(m); Aufhetzer(m)	**instigator**	**instigateur**(m), auteur(m)
Anstiftung(f), Begünstigung(f); Vorschub(m)	**abetment**	**incitation**(f) **au crime, au délit**
Anstiftung(f); Aufwiegelung(f)	**incitement**	**incitation**(f), provocation(f) (au crime, au délit)
Anstoß(m) **erregen;** empören	**scandalise (to)**	**scandaliser,** indigner
anstößig; belästigend	**obnoxious**	**odieux,** abominable
antizipierter Vertragsbruch(m); vor Fälligkeit erklärte Erfüllungsverweigerung oder Verhalten, das beabsichtigten Vertragsbruch andeutet	**anticipatory breach**	**non-respect prémédité d'un contrat**
Antrag(m)	**petition**	**requête**(f), appel(m), pétition(f)
Berufungs–	appeal –	recours en droit
Gnadengesuch	– for pardon or commutation of penalty	recours(m) en grâce
Antrag(m)	**motion**	**motion**(f), requête(f), demande(f)
Vertagungs–	– for adjournment	demande d'ajournement
– auf Wiederaufnahme des Verfahrens	– for new trial	demande tendant à juger à nouveau la même affaire

GERMAN	ENGLISH	FRENCH
Antragsteller(*m*); Bewerber(*m*); Anmelder(*m*)	**applicant**	**demandeur**(*m*), requérant(*m*), pétitionnaire(*f, m*), ayant(*m*) droit
Antragsteller(*m*); Kläger(*m*)	**petitioner**	**requérant**(*m*)
antworten, entsprechen; Folge leisten; sich richten nach	**answer**	**réponse**(*f*), réplique(*f*)
sich wegen einer Anklage oder Beschuldigung verantworten	– to a charge	réfutation(*f*) d'une accusation, réplique du défendeur(*m*)
Anwalt(*m*), Rechtsbeistand(*m*); Sprecher(*m*), Fürsprecher(*m*)	**advocate**	**avocat**(*m*)
Generalanwalt *(am Gerichtshof der EG)*	– general	avocat général
Kronanwalt *(Schottland)*	Lord Advocate	conseiller et représentant du gouvernment en Écosse
Anwalt(*m*); Rechtsbeistand(*m*)	**solicitor**	**conseiller juridique,** avocat(*m*) non plaidant, avoué
Anwalt(*m*); Rechtsbeistand(*m*); Bevollmächtigter(*m, f*)	**attorney**	**mandataire**(*m*), représentant dûment désigné
Rechtsanwalt, –anwältin *(US)*	--at-law *(US)*	avocat *(US)*
Generalstaatsanwalt; Kronanwalt; Justizminister	– -general	conseiller et représentant légal du gouvernement
Vollmacht(surkunde); Prozeßvollmacht *(US)*	letter of –	procuration
Vollmacht; Vertretungsbefugnis; Prozeßvollmacht	power of –	mandat pouvoirs
Anwalt(*m*); Rechtsbeistand(*m*)	**counsel**	**avocat**(*m*), conseil(*m*); avis(*m*)
Prozeßbevollmächtigter des Klägers	– for the plaintiff	avocat du plaignant
Anklagevertreter	– for the prosecution	représentant(*m*) du ministère public
Anwaltsbestellung(*f*); Gebührenvorschuß(*m*)	**retainer**	**provision**(*f*) **sur honoraires d'avocat;** arrhes(*f*); cachet(*m*)
Anwaltsbüro(*n*), Kanzlei(*f*)	**chambers**	**cabinet**(*m*) **de juge,** d'avocat, étude(*f*) d'avoué
unter Ausschluß der Öffentlichkeit verhandeln	hear in –	juger en chambre du conseil
unter Ausschluß der Öffentlichkeit	in –	en référé
Anwendungsbereich(*m*)	**range of application**	**champ**(*m*) **d'application**
Anzahlung(*f*)	**down-payment**	**accompte (hypothèque, vente à crédit)**
Anzahlung(*f*); Einlage(*f*); Hinterlegung(*f*); Sicherheitsleistung(*f*); Verwahrung(*f*)	**deposit**	**dépôt**(*m*)
Einlagegarantie	– guarantee	dépôt de garantie
anzeigen; denunzieren; (Vertrag)(*m*) kündigen	**denounce (to)**	**dénoncer**

GERMAN	ENGLISH	FRENCH
Anzeigenerstatter(m); Denunziant(m); Spitzel(m)	**informer**	**informateur**(m)
Arbeitsgenehmigung(f); – erlaubnis(n)	**work permit**	**permis**(m) **de travail**
Arbeit(f)(skräfte(f), –nehmer)(m)	**Labor** (US), **labour**	**main**(f) **d'oeuvre,** salariés(m); travail(m), labeur(m)
–sministerium (US)	Department of –	Ministère(m) du Travail
Zwangs–	forced –	travaux(m) forcés
–skampf	– conflict, dispute	conflit(m) du travail
–srecht	– law	droit(m) du travail
–sgenehmigung	– permit	permis(m) de travail
gewerkschaftlich organisierte Arbeitnehmer	organised –	organisations(f) ouvrières, ouvriers(m) syndiqués
Internationales –samt, IAA	International – Organisation	Bureau(m) International du travail (BIT)
Arbeitslosigkeit(f)	**unemployment**	**chômage**(m)
Arbeitsplatzsicherheit(f)	**employment security**	**sécurité**(f) **d'emplois**
Art(f); Gattung(f)	**kind**	**espèce**(f), genre(m), nature(f)
in natura; – Waren	in –	(paiement, règlement) en nature
Artikel(m); Warenposten(n); Abschnitt(m), Paragraph(m); Vertragsbestimmungen (pl.)	**article(s)**	**article**(m), clause(f), stipulation(f), élément(m), dispositions(f)
Gesellschaftsvertrag; Satzung	– of association (UK)	statuts(m) d'une SARL
Gründungsurkunde; Satzung	– of incorporation (US)	statuts d'une société commerciale
Heiratsvertrag	– of marriage	contrat(m) de mariage
ärztlich; medizinisch	**medical**	**médical**(m)
ärztliches Attest	– certificate	certificat(m) médical
medizinischer Sachverständigenbeweis	– evidence	expertise(f) médicale
Assisengericht(n); Geschworenengericht(n), Schwurgericht(n)	**assize court**	**cour**(f) **d'assises**
Asyl(n); Freistatt(f)	**sanctuary**	**asile**(m), refuge(m), sanctuaire(m)
auf – Freigelassener(m); auf Probe(f) Eingestellter(m)	**probationer**	**stagiaire**(m)
auf den neuesten Stand(m) **bringen**; höher bewerten; zuschreiben	**write (to) up**	**rédiger**, mettre à jour; fausser un bilan, gonfler les comptes
Aufbewahrungsort(f); Versteck(n), geheimes Lager(n)	**cache**	**cachette**(f)
aufdecken; enthüllen	**uncover (to)**	**découvrir**
Aufenthalt(m); Wohnung(f)	**dwelling**	**logement**(m), résidence(f)
Aufenthaltsort(m), Wohnsitz(m)	**abode**	**demeure**, résidence
auferlegen; vorschreiben; (gerichtlich) untersagen	**enjoin (to)**	**enjoindre**, prescrire

GERMAN	ENGLISH	FRENCH
auferlegen; zufügen	inflict (to)	infliger
Auferlegung(f); Verhängung(f); Abgabe(f)	imposition	impôt(m), taxe(f), imposition(f)
Aufgabe(f); Verzicht	relinquishment	répudiation(f), abandon(m)
Aufgabe(f); (Verzicht-)Leistung(f)	waiver	renonciation(f), désistement(m), abandon(m)
ausdrücklicher (od. stillschweigender) Verzicht(m)	express (or implied) –	renonciation tacite
Anspruchsaufgabe	– of claim	désistement de revendication, d'instance, d'action
Rechtsverzicht	– of rights	renonciation à un (des) droit (s)
Rechtsverzicht	– of title	abandon d'un droit de propriété
aufgeben; Verzicht(m) leisten	waive (to)	renoncer à, abandonner un droit; se déroger
aufgeschoben; gestundet; zurückgestellt	deferred	différé, ajourné
hinausgeschobene Zahlung; Ratenzahlung (US)	– payment	paiement différé
aufhalten; einstellen; aussetzen (Zwangs)Vollstreckung einstellen, aufschieben	stay (to) – execution	surseoir, suspendre surseoir à l'exécution
Verfahren aussetzen	– proceedings	suspendre l'audience
aufheben, verwerfen	overrule (to)	annuler, passer outre, décider contre
aufheben; für ungültig erklären	quash	casser, infirmer, annuler
aufheben; herabsetzen; aussetzen, einstellen	abate (to)	abolir, annuler
aufheben; rückgängig machen	rescind (to)	casser, annuler, rescinder
aufheben; stornieren; rückbuchen	reverse (to)	réformer, révoquer, casser
Urteil aufheben	– a judgment	casser, révoquer un jugement, une sentence
aufheben; widerrufen; abbestellen	countermand (to)	annuler, rappeler, révoquer
Aufhebung(f); Außerkraftsetzung(f)	repeal	abrogation(f), révocation(f)
Aufhebung(f); Nachlaß(m), Ermäßigung(f); Aussetzung(f), Einstellung(f)	abatement	diminution(f), réduction(f)
Minderungsklage	– of action	action en réduction
Aufhebung(f); Stornierung(f); Rückbuchung(f)	reversal	arrêt(m) d'annulation, réforme(f) d'un jugement en appel
Auflösung(f); Aufhebung(f)	dissolution	dissolution(f)
Auflösung der Ehe	– of marriage	dissolution du mariage
aufnehmen; aufbringen	raise (to)	augmenter; se procurer, réunir
Geldmittel –	– funds	se procurer des fonds, réunir des fonds

GERMAN	ENGLISH	FRENCH
aufrecht erhalten; bestätigen	**uphold (to)**	soutenir
Aufruhr(*f*)	**riot**	émeute
aufschieben	**postpone (to)**	**ajourner,** repousser, différer
aufschieben; (zeitlich od. örtlich) verlegen; vertagen	**adjourn (to)**	**ajourner,** différer, suspendre, remettre, renvoyer
aufschieben; zurückstellen	**defer (to)**	**différer,** ajourner
Aufschub(*m*)	**postponement**	**ajournement**(*m*), report(*m*), renvoi(*m*)
Aufschub(*m*); Zurückstellung(*f*)	**deferment**	**ajournement**(*m*), remise(*f*)
Aufsichtsbehörde(*f*)	**supervisory authority**	**autorités**(*f*) **de contrôle, de surveillance**
Aufstellung(*f*) **der Geschworenenliste**	**impanelling,** alternative spelling of empanelling	**désignation**(*f*) **des membres du jury**
Auftrag(*m*); Mandat(*n*)	**mandate**	**mandat**(*m*), procuration(*f*)
Auftraggeber(*m*); Vorgesetzter(*m*); Hauptschuldner(*m*); Kapital(*n*) Kapital und Zinsen Haupttäter	**principal** – and interest – in the first degree	**auteur**(*m*) **d'un crime ou délit;** débiteur(*m*) principal capital(*m*) et intérêt(s) auteur(*m*) principal d'un crime
Mittäter; Tatgehilfe	– in the second degree	complice
Aufwertung(*f*); Neubewertung(*f*)	**revaluation**	**réévaluation**(*f*)
Augenzeuge(*m*)	**eyewitness**	**témoin**(*m*) **oculaire**
aus dem Meer(*n*) **gewonnenes Land**(*n*); Marschen(*f*)	**innings (lands reclaimed from the sea)**	**relais**(*m*) **de mer**
ausbürgern	**expatriate (to)**	**expatrier**
Ausfertigung(*f*) e-s Testaments	**execution** – of a will	**exécution**(*f*) exécution d'un testament
Ausländer(*m*); Fremder(*m*)	**alien**	**étranger,** ressortissant étranger
auslassen; unterlassen	**omit (to)**	**omettre**
Auslassung(*f*); Unterlassung(*f*)	**omission**	**omission**(*f*), négligence(*f*)
auslegen	**construe (to)**	**interpréter,** analyser
Auslegung(*f*); Erklärung(*f*)	**interpretation**	**interprétation**(*f*)
ausliefern	**extradite (to)**	**extrader**
ausliefern; übergeben Besitzrecht am Nachlaß e-s Verstorbenen aufgeben	**surrender (to)** – a deceased's estate	**se rendre;** renoncer à renoncer à une succession
Auslieferung(*f*)	**extradition**	**extradition**(*f*)
(aus)löschen; unkenntlich machen	**obliterate (to)**	**oblitérer,** effacer
ausschlaggebende Stimme(*f*)	**casting vote**	**voix**(*f*) **prépondérante**
ausschließen	**preclude (to)**	**empêcher,** prévenir, exclure

GERMAN	ENGLISH	FRENCH
ausschließen; ausweisen	expel (to)	expulser
ausschließen; verfallen lassen; präkludieren	foreclose (to)	forclore saisir, mettre fin à un prêt
Ausschluß(m)	preclusion	exclusion(f), prévention(f)
Ausschluß(m) aus der Anwaltschaft	disbarment	radiation(f) d'un avocat du barreau
außer Kraft(f) setzen; ersetzen	supersede (to)	annuler, remplacer, supplanter
außerehelich	extramarital	en dehors du mariage
außerehelicher Geschlechtsverkehr(m); Unzucht(f)	fornication	fornication(f)
außergerichtlich	extrajudicial	extrajudiciaire
außergerichtliche od. gütliche Einigung(f)	out-of-court settlement	règlement(m) à l'amiable
Ausstattung(f); Stiftung(f) Stiftungskapital Lebensversicherung auf Todes- und Erlebensfall	endowment – capital – insurance	dotation(f) apports(m) en capital assurance(f) à capital différé
ausstehend Außenstände	receivable accounts –	recevable, plausible sommes à encaisser, dettes actives
ausstellen	make out	dresser, faire établir, rédiger
e-n Scheck – e-e Rechnung –	– a cheque – an invoice	tirer un cheque dresser une facture
Aussteller(m), Abgeber(m) e-s Affidavit (eidesstattliche Erklärung) (US)	affiant (US)	auteur(m) d'un affidavit (d'un attestation) (US)
Aussteller(m); Trassant(m)	drawer	tireur(m), souscripteur(m)
Austausch(m); Umwandlung(f) Strafumwandlung	commutation – of penalty	commutation(f) commutation de peine
(Auswahl(f) nach dem) Stichprobenverfahren(m); Zufallsstichprobenerhebung	sampling random –	échantillonnage(m) échantillonage au hasard
Ausweichen; Umgehung(f); Vermeidung(f) Steuerhinterziehung	evasion tax –	évasion(f), fraude(f) fraude(f) fiscale
ausweisen; entfernen; (Amt) entheben	eject (to)	éjecter, évincer, expulser
Auszug(m), Abriß(m); Zusammenfassung(f) Eigentumsnachweis	abstract – of title	résumé(m), abrégé(m), sommaire(m); extrait(m); analyse(f) extrait du répertoire des mutations de propriété
Autopsie(f), Obduktion(f)	autopsy	autopsie(f)

B

GERMAN	ENGLISH	FRENCH
Bank(*f*)	**bank**	**banque**(*f*)
Zentral–, Noten–	central –	banque centrale
Clearing–, Giro–	clearing –	banque de virement
Geschäfts–; Handels–	commercial –	banque commerciale
Kredit–	credit –	banque de crédit
Depositen–	deposit –	banque de dépôt
Industrie–	industrial –	banque industrielle
Investitions– *(US)*	investment – *(US)*	banque d'affaires *(US)*
Merchant–	merchant –	banque d'affaires *(UK)*
Banknote(*f*); Papiergeld(*m*)	**banknote**	**billet**(*m*) **de banque**
Bankrott(*m*), Konkurs(*m*);	**bankruptcy**	**faillite**(*f*)
Zahlungseinstellung(*f*)		
Konkursgericht	– court	tribunal(*m*) de faillite
Konkursverfahren	proceedings in –	procédure(*f*) de faillite
e-n Antrag auf	to present a –	se mettre en faillite,
Konkurseröffnung stellen	petition	deposer son bilan
Konkurs anmelden		
freiwilliger Konkurs	voluntary –	faillite volontaire
be—, vereidigt	**sworn**	**assermenté**
eidliche Erklärung	statement	déposition(*f*) sous serment
vereidigter Zeuge	witness	témoin(*m*) sous serment
Bearbeitungsgebühren(*f*);	**handling charges**	**frais**(*m*) **de manutention**
Umschlagspesen(*n*)		
bedingt (durch); abhängig(von)	**conditional**	**conditionnel**
Strafaussetzung zur Bewährung;	– discharge	libération(*f*) conditionnelle
bedingte Entlassung		
auflösende Bedingung (bei	– limitation	héritage(*m*) dévolu sous
Einräumung e-s zeitlich		condition résolutoire
begrenzten Nutzungsrechts)		
bedingt Entlassener	**parolee**	**délinquant**(*m*) **en liberté surveillée**
Bedingungen	**terms**	**clauses**(*f*)**, conditions**(*f*); prix(*m*)
Zahlungs–	– of payment	conditions de paiement
Verkaufs–	– of sale	conditions de vente
Ausschreibungs–, Submissions–	– of tender	conditions(*f*) d'offre
bedingungslos; uneingeschränkt	**unconditional**	**inconditionnel,** sans condition
(Be)Drohung(*f*)	**menace**	**menace**(*f*)

GERMAN	ENGLISH	FRENCH
Bedürftiger(m)	**indigent**	**indigent**, nécessiteux
Bedürftiger(m); Unterstützungsempfänger(m)	**pauper**	**indigent**(m), économiquement faible
beeidigt eidliche Erklärung vereidigter Zeuge	**sworn** statement witness	**assermenté** déposition(f) sous serment témoin(m) sous serment
beeinträchtigen; Abbruch(m) tun; (teilweise) aufheben	**derogate (to)**	**déroger**, porter atteinte à
beeinträchtigen; verschlechtern	**impair (to)**	**porter atteinte ou préjudice,** compromettre, affaiblir
Beeinträchtigung(f); Minderung(f); teilweise Außerkraftsetzung	**derogation**	**dérogation**(f), diminution(f)
Beeinträchtigung(f); Verschlechterung(f) körperliche Behinderung	**impairment** physical –	**affaiblissement**(m), altération(f), diminution(f) infirmité(f)
Beendigung(f)	**termination**	**résiliation**(f), extinction(f), cessation(f), expiration(f)
– des Arbeitsverhältnisses durch Kündigung Vertrags–	notice of – – of a contract	congé(m) résiliation, expiration d'un contrat
Befehl(m); Verfügung(f)	**order**	**mandat**(m), décret(m), ordre(m), arrêté(m)
gerichtliche Verfügung; Gerichtsbeschluß Haftbefehl	court – detention –	injonction(f) ordonnance(f) de mise en détention
Auslieferungsbefehl; –beschluß Zwischenverfügung; einstweilige Verfügung richterlicher Verbot; einstweilige Verfügung	extradition – interlocutory – restraining –	ordonnance d'extradition ordonnance interlocutoire ordonnance de ne pas faire
Beförderer(m); Spediteur(m); Frachtführer(m)	**carrier**	**transporteur**(m)
Beförderung(f); Transport(kosten)(m)	**haulage**	**transport**(m), charroi(m)
Beförderung(f); Versand(m); Spedition(f)	**forwarding**	**transitaire**(m), expéditionnaire(m)
Befragung(f); Verhör(n), Vernehmung(f)	**interrogation**	**interrogatoire**(m), interrogation(f)
befreien; freistellen; ausnehmen	**exempt (to)**	**exempter**, exonérer
Befreiung(f); Verteilung(f); Erlassung(f) Rechtsanwendung; Rechtsprechung	**dispensation** – of justice	**dispense**(f) exercice(m), pratique de la justice
Befriedigung(f); Bezahlung(f); Erfüllung(f)	**satisfaction**	**satisfaction**(f), réparation(f), purge(f)

GERMAN	ENGLISH	FRENCH
begebbar; umlauffähig	**negotiable**	**négociable**
–es Wertpapier	– instrument	instrument(*m*)
		(commercial) négociable
–es Wertpapier	– security	titre(*m*) négociable
beginnen; einleiten	**initiate (to)**	**entamer (des poursuites),**
		commencer
beglaubigte Abschrift	**authenticated copy**	**ampliation**(*f*)
Begnadigung(*f*); Straferlaß(*m*)	**pardon**	**grâce**(*f*), amnistie(*f*)
Begnadigung(*f*); Straferlaß(*m*)	**pardoning**	**action**(*f*) **de gracier,**
		d'amnistier
begrenzen; inhaftieren	**confine (to)**	**détenir**
in Gefängnishaft nehmen	– to prison	envoyer en prison
Begünstigter(*m*) (dem etwas	**grantee**	**concessionnaire**(*m*)
bewilligt, übertragen, verliehen		
wurde)		
behaupten, erklären; vorbringen;	**assert (to)**	**affirmer,** revendiquer,
geltend machen		alléguer
seine Rechte geltend machen;	– one's rights	revendiquer ses droits
auf seine Rechten bestehen		
behaupten; geltend machen	**contend (to)**	**affirmer,** prétendre
Behauptung(*f*); Streit(*m*);	**contention**	**contestation**(*f*), dispute(*f*)
Vorbringen		
behilflich; mitwirkend	**instrumental**	**utile,** actif, productif,
		instrumental
beitragen zu, mitwirken bei	to be – in	contribuer à
behindern; hemmen	**obstruct (to)**	**faire de l'obstruction,**
		entraver
Gerichtsverfahren behindern	– legal procedure	entraver l'action de la
		justice
Behinderung(*f*);	**impediment**	**entrave**(*f*), obstacle(*m*);
Hinderungsgrund(*f*)		cause(*f*) d'incapacité de
		contracter
Behinderung(*f*); Störung(*f*)	**disturbance**	**dérangement,**
		perturbation(*f*), trouble
Störung der öffentlichen	– of public order	atteinte(*f*) à l'ordre public
Ordnung (Ruhe)		
Behörde(*f*); Befugnis(*n*);	**authority**	**autorité**(*f*), mandat(*m*),
Genehmigung(*f*); Vollmacht(*f*)		pouvoir(*m*), compétence(*f*)
Polizeibehörde	police –	la police; autorité
		policière
Verwaltungs–, Staatsbehörde;	public –	pouvoirs publics
öffentliche Gewalt, Staatsgewalt		
beibehalten; beauftragen	**retain (to)**	**choisir,** retenir, conserver
Beihilfe(*f*) **leisten,** begünstigen	**aid and abet**	**être le complice de**
Beilegung(*f*), Vergleich;	**composition**	**arrangement**(*m*)
Zusammensetzung		**transactionnel,**
		concordat(*m*)
beistimmen; beitreten; antreten	**accede (to)**	**accéder à,** entrer en
		possession

GERMAN	ENGLISH	FRENCH
Beitritt(m); Eintrag(m); Buchung(f); Zollanmeldung(f)	**entry**	**entrée**(f), article(m); enregistrement(m), déclaration(f)
Zolldeklaration für zollpflichtige Waren (Zoll)	– for dutiable goods (customs)	déclaration en douane de marchandises passibles de droits
illegale Einreise	illegal –	immigration(f) clandestine
etw. eintragen, verbuchen (Buchhaltung)	to make an – (bookkeeping)	passer une écriture (comptabilité)
Inbesitznahmerecht; Einreiserecht	right of –	droit(m) d'entrée, droit de prendre possession
Beitritt(m); Verbindung(f)	**joinder**	**réunion**(f), union(f)
Klagehäufung; Anspruchshäufung	– of actions/claims	jonction(f) d'instances
Mitverklagen (weiterer Parteien)	– of defendants	jonction d'instance des défendeur
Festlegung der zu entscheidenden streitigen Fragen	– of issue	acceptation(f) d'un arbitrage
Bildung e-r Streitgenossenschaft; Nebenintervention	– of parties – of remedies	jonction d'instances jonction des appels
Rechtsmittelverbindung		
bejahend, Bejahung(f)	**affirmative**	**affirmatif**
Rechtfeststellungsklage (Wiedergutmachung) der Folgen vergangener Diskriminierung (US)	– action (US)	action en constatation un droit mesures(f) pour favoriser les discriminés (US)
Einrede des Beklagten (US) (Zivilprozeß) Behauptung(en) die der Angeklagte glaubhaft zu machen hat (Strafprozeß)	– defence	moyen de défense nouveau détruisant la thèse du demandeur, même si elle était justifiée au moment où la plainte avait été déposée
bekannt	**known**	**connu**, constaté, avéré
bekanntmachen; zur Kenntnis bringen	make –	faire savoir
Bekanntmachung(f); Veröffentlichung(f)	**promulgation**	**promulgation**(f), proclamation(f)
Beklagter(m); Angeklagter(m)	**defendant**	**défenseur**(m), défenderesse(f), accusé,-e
Beklagter(m); Antragsgegner(m); (siehe(m) Berufungsbeklagter)	**respondent**	**défendeur**(m); **intimé**
Beklagter(m) (Berufungs-, Beschwerde-, Revision-)	**appellee**	**intimé**(f)
belasten; erschweren	**encumber (to)**	**grever**, gêner
belastend	**incriminating**	**compromettant**
Belastungsmaterial	– evidence	pièce(f) à conviction
belästigen	**harass (to)**	**harceler**, tourmenter
Belästigung(f)	**harassment**	**harcèlement**(m)
beleidigend; diffamierend; verleumderisch	**defamatory**	**diffamatoire**
beleidigend; verleumderisch	**libellous**	**diffamatoire**

GERMAN	ENGLISH	FRENCH
Beleidigung(f)	**insult**	**insulte**(f), injure(f), affront(m)
gröbliche –	gross –	injure grave
Beleidigung(f); Verleumdung(f); Klage(f)	**libel**	**diffamation**(f), libelle(m), écrit diffamatoire
beliebig; Ermessens-	**discretionary**	**discrétionnaire**
Belohnung(f); Entschädigung(f)	**recompense**	**récompense**(f), dédommagement(m)
Belohnung(f); Vergütung(f)	**reward**	**récompense**(f)
Belohnung(f); Zuerkennung(f); Schiedsurteil(n); Rechtsspruch	**award**	**prix,** attribution(f); jugement(m) sentence(f) arbitrale;
Urteil sprechen, (durch Urteil) zuerkennen	– of a judgment	prononcement d'une sentence (d'un jugement)
Benachrichtigung(f); Anzeige(f)	**notice**	**avis**(m), préavis(m), notification(f), convocation(f)
öffentliche Bekanntmachung	– by publication	notification par voie de presse
Berufungsschrift	– of appeal	déclaration(f) d'appel
Steuerbescheid	– of assessment (tax)	avis d'imposition, avertissement(m) du fisc
Andienung;	– of delivery	accusé de réception
Empfangsbestätigung		
Kündigungsschreiben	– of termination	congé(m)
kündigen	to give –	donner un préavis; signifier son congé (à qqu'un); donner sa démission
(be-)raten; benachrichtigen, verständigen, mitteilen avisieren	**advise (to)**	**conseiller,** recommander, avertir, instruire, aviser de
beratend; konsultativ	**consultative**	**consultatif**
Berater(m)	**consultant**	**consultant**(m), conseil(m), expert(m)
Beratung(f); Konsultation(f)	**consultation**	**consultation**(f), délibération
Beraubung(f); Entziehung(f); Verlust(m)	**deprivation**	**privation**(f), destitution(f)
Freiheitsberaubung; –entziehung	– of liberty	privation de liberté
berechnet, er–; kalkuliert	**calculated**	**prémédité,** délibéré
Bereich(m); Rahmen(m)	**scope**	**portée**(f), champ(m) d'action, compétence(f)
im Rahmen von	within the – of	qui sont du ressort de, qui relève de
bereichern	**enrich (to)**	**enrichir**

GERMAN	ENGLISH	FRENCH
Bergung(f); Altmaterialverwertung(f)	salvage	**prime**(f) **de sauvetage,** indemnité de remorquage; sauvetage(m), renflouement(m); récupération de matériels et marchandises après sauvetage(m)
Bergungsgesellschaft	– company	société(f) de sauvetage
Bergungsvertrag	– contract	contrat(m) de sauvetage
Bergungskosten	– costs	frais(m) de sauvetage
Bericht(m); Aufstellung(f); Auszug(f)	statement	**déclaration**(f), exposé(m), rapport(m), relevé(m)
Schlußbericht; –plädoyer	closing –	plaidoirie(f) finale
Finanzbericht; Rechnungsabschluß	financial –	compte(m) de recettes
Erfolgsrechnung; Ertragsbilanz	income –	déclaration de revenus
Eröffnungsplädoyer	opening –	plaidoirie inaugurale
Kontoauszug; Abrechnung	– of account	relevé de compte
Klagebegründung	– of claim	demande(m) introductive d'instance, conclusion(f) en matière de dommages-intérêts
Klagebeantwortung	– of defence	conclusions de la défense
eidliche (Zeugen)Erklärung	sworn –	déposition(f) sous serment
Berichtigung(f), Bereinigung(f); Angleichung(f); Schlichtung(f), Beilegung (Streit)	adjustment	**ajustement**(m), arrangement(m), régularisation(f), redressement(m), remaniement(m), règlement des créances
Schadensberechnung; Anspruchsregulierung	– of claims	règlement des indemnités
Schadensregulierung, Schadensfeststellung	– of damages	règlement des dommages-intérêts
berittene Polizei(f)	mounted police	**police**(m) **montée,** police à cheval
beruflich	occupational	**professionnel** (adj.)
Betriebs–, Berufsunfall	– accident	accident(m) du travail
Berufskrankheit	– disease	maladie(f) professionnelle
Berufung(f), Revision(f), Beschwerde(f), Einspruch(m)	appeal	**appel**(m), pourvoi(m) en cassation
Rechtsmittelgericht; Berufungsgericht(n)	Court of –	cour(f) d'appel
Berufungsantrag; Berufungsschrift(f); Beschwerdeschrift(f)	appeal (notice of)	**déclaration**(f) **(avis) d'appel**
Berufungsgericht(n); Gericht zweiter Instanz	appellate court	**cour**(f) **d'appel**
Beschlagnahme(m)	seizure	**saisie**(f), confiscation(f)
– bewegliches Vermögens	– of chattels	saisie des biens et effets
– unbewegliches Vermögens; – von Grundbesitz	– of real estate	saisie immobilière

GERMAN	ENGLISH	FRENCH
Beschleunigung(f); vorzeitige Fälligstellung(f) (Wechsel)	**acceleration**	**accélération**(f), réduction(f) (d'un délai), avancement(m) (d'une échéance); prise de possession anticipée
Beschluß(m); Entscheidung(f); Urteil(n) (Zivilprozeß)(m) gerichtliche Entscheidung, Urteil (s. Zivil– od. Strafurteil; Urteilsspruch)	**decision** court – (cf. judgment)	**décision**(f), résolution(f) décision de justice, verdict(m)
Beschluß; Resolution(f)	**resolution**	**résolution**(f), délibération(f), ordre(m) du jour
beschlußfähig	**quorum (to be a)**	**qui a un quorum**
beschränken; ein–	**restrict (to)**	**restreindre**, limiter, réduire
beschränkt; begrenzt Kapitalgesellschaft mit (Haftungsbeschränkung)	**limited** – company	**limité**, restreint société(f) dans laquelle la responsabilité des associés est limitée (société anonyme, société à responsabilité(f) limitée)
beschränkte Haftung beschränkt haftender Gesellschafter; Kommanditist Kommanditgesellschaft	– liability – partner – partnership	responsabilité limitée commanditaire(m) société(f) en commandite simple
Beschränkung(f); Inhaftierung(f) Einzelhaft	**confinement** solitary –	**emprisonnement**(m) emprisonnement cellulaire (au Cecret)
Beschränkung(f); Verhinderung(f); Zurückbehaltung(f)	**restraint**	**contrainte**(f) par corps, emprisonnement(m), séquestration(f)
Beschwerdeführer(m); Erstatter(m) e–r Strafanzeige(f); Kläger(m)	**complainant**	**plaignant**
Beschwerdegrund(m), Klage–; Mißstand(m) Arbeiter-Beschwerdeausschuß; Schlichtungsausschuß Beschwerdeverfahren	**grievance** – committee – procedure	**grief**(m); injustice(f) commission(f) du contentieux administratif procédure(f) de règlement des différends
Übelstand, Mißstand abhelfen	to redress a –	redresser un tort
beschwerte Partei	**aggrieved party**	**partie**(f) **chagrinée,** partie(f) perdante (dans une décision judiciaire)
besiegen; vereiteln; zu Fall(m) bringen; aufheben	**defeat (to)**	**frustrer**, faire échouer, déjouer
Besitz(m) tatsächlicher, unmittelbarer - unberechtigter –; Ersitzung Datum der Inbesitznahme, der – ergreifung	**possession** actual – adverse – date of taking –	**possession**(f) possession effective possession de fait date(f) d'entrée en possession

GERMAN	ENGLISH	FRENCH
besitzen; für Recht(n) erkennen	**hold (to)**	**tenir,** détenir; être investi; conclure, juger; obliger
als Treuhänder verwalten	– in trust	avoir confiance (en)
Aktien besitzen	– shares	détenir des actions
besitzen; zugeben	**own (to)**	**posséder**
Besitzer(m); Inhaber(m)	**possessor**	**possesseur**(m), détenteur(m)
Besitzer(m); Inhaber(m); Bewohner(m)	**occupant**	**occupant**(m), locataire(m, f), usufruitier(m, f)
Besitz(m)(-ergreifung)(f)	**occupancy**	**occupation**(f), possession(f)
Besitz(schuld)klage(f)	**possessory action**	**action**(f) **possessoire**
Besitzstörer; Rechtsverletzer	**trespasser**	**intrus (dans une propriété privée)**
Besitzübertragung(f) **auf Zeit;** Verwahrung(f); Verpfändung(f); anvertrautes Gut, hinterlegte Sache	**bailment**	**contrat**(m) **de dépôt**
Besonderheit(f); Spezialität(f)	**specialty**	**contrat**(m) **formel**
bestätigen, versichern; behaupten; an Eides Statt versichern	**affirm (to)**	**affirmer**
bestätigende Zeugenaussage(f)	**corroborating evidence**	**preuve**(f) **corroborante**
Bestätigung(f), Versicherung(f); Behauptung(f); eidliche Erklärung(f), eidesstattliche Versicherung(f)	**affirmation**	**affirmation**(f) **solennelle;** confirmation(f); ratification(f)
bestechen	**bribe (to)**	**corrompre,** acheter (qqu'un)
Bestechung(f)	**bribe**	**pot-de-vin**(m)
Besteuerung(f); Kostenfestsetzung(f)	**taxation**	**imposition**(f), charges(f) fiscales, fiscalité(f)
Doppelbesteuerungsabkommen	double – agreement	convention(f) relative à la double imposition
bestimmen; beschaffen	**provide (to)**	**fournir,** prévoir, stipuler
Bestimmung(en)(f); Vorschrift(en)(f)	**provision(s)**	**disposition(s)**(f), clause(s)(f), stipulation(s)(f)
einschränkende –	restrictive –	clause(s) restrictive(s)
gesetzliche –	statutory –	disposition(s) statutaire(s)
bestreiten; anfechten	**contest (to)**	**contester,** disputer, attaquer
Bestreitung(f); Ableugnung(f); abschlägiger Bescheid(m)	**denial**	**dénégation**(f), déni(m), démenti(m)
Besuchsrecht(n); Verkehrsrecht(n) (zu e-m Kinde)	**visiting right**	**droit**(m) **de visite**
Beteiligung(f)	**holding**	**tenue**(f) **(d'une réunion);** portefeuille(m), disponibilités; ferme(f), tenure(f); holding(m)
Mehrheits–	majority –	participation(f) majoritaire

GERMAN	ENGLISH	FRENCH
Beteiligung(f); Teilhabe(f) Anteilschein	**participation** – certificate	**participation**(f) certificat(m) de participation
Konsortialkredit; Gemeinschaftsdarlehen	– loan	prêt(m) en participation
Beteiligungen(f) (pl.)	**participating interest**	**intéressement**(m) **sur les bénéfices**
Betriebs- -kapital(n) -aufwendungen(f)	**operating** – capital – expenses	**d'exploitation** capital(m) d'exploitation frais(m) d'exploitation, dépenses(f) de fonctionnement
-ergebnis(n)	– result	résultat(m) d'exploitation
(betriebsbedingte) Entlassung(f)	**redundancy**	**licenciement**(m) **économique**
Betriebseinstellung(f); Stillegung(f)	**shut-down**	**immobilisation**(f), fermeture(f)
Betriebskapital(n); Nettoumlaufvermögen(n)	**working capital**	**capital**(m) **de roulement**
Betrug(m); Veruntreuung(f); arglistige Täuschung(f)	**fraud**	**fraude**(f), tromperie(f), abus(m) de confiance
betrügen, beschwindeln; übervorteilen	**cheat (to)**	**tromper,** tricher, escroquer
(betrügerisch) Veränderungen(f) **vornehmen an etw.;** beeinflussen Beweis fälschen	**tamper (to)** – with evidence	**altérer,** falsifier falsifier une preuve
(Be-)Trunkenheit(f)	**intoxication**	**ivresse**(f); empoisonnement(m)
Bevölkerung(f); Einwohner(zahl)(m)	**population**	**population**(f)
Bevollmächtigter(m); Anwalt(m)	**procurator**	**procurateur**(m); fondé(m) de pouvoir; agent(m) d'affaires
Bewährung(f)	**probation**	**liberté surveillée**(f), mise(f) à l'épreuve; essai
auf – -sbeamter	on – – officer	à l'épreuve, à l'essai contrôleur(m) judiciaire
Beweggrund(f); Motiv(n)	**motive**	**mobile**(m), ressort(m), raison(f), motif(m)
Haupt–	main/principal –	raison(f), mobile principal(e)
bewegliche Sachen(f); Hab und Gut	**goods and chattels**	**biens**(m) **mobiliers**
bewegliches Vermögen(n)	**movables**	**biens**(m) **mobiliers**
beweisen; belegen	**prove (to)**	**prouver,** établir, justifier, attester
Beweislast	**onus of proof**	**charge**(f) **de la preuve**

GERMAN	ENGLISH	FRENCH
Beweis(*m*)**(material)**(*n*); Nachweis(*m*); Zeugenaussage(*f*)	**evidence**	**preuve**(*f*) **testimoniale,** témoignages(*m*)
zulässiger Beweis	admissible –	preuve recevable
Beweislast, –pflicht	burden of –	charge(*f*) de la preuve
Indizienbeweis	circumstantial –	présomptions(*f*), preuve indirecte
schlüssiger (zwingender) Beweis	conclusive –	preuve concluante, pertinente
unmittelbarer Beweis	direct –	preuve directe
Urkundenbeweis	documentary –	preuve authentique, notoriété(*f*) de droit
falsche Zeugenaussage	false –	faux(*f*)témoignage
mittelbarer Beweis	indirect –	preuve indirecte
mündlicher Beweis; Beweis durch Zeugenaussagen	oral –	témoignage, déposition(*f*) orale
Wahrscheinlichkeits–, Indizienbeweis	presumptive –	preuve par déduction, par présomption
primäres Beweismittel; Beweismittel erster Ordnung	primary –	meilleure preuve
Augenscheinsbeweis; Beweis durch Augenscheinnahme	real –	preuve par vue di lieux
Beweispflicht(*f*)**, – last**	**burden of proof**	**charge de la preuve**
beweisrechtlich	**probative**	**probant**
beweiserhebliche Tatsache	– fact	fait(*m*) probant
Beweiswert; Beweiskraft	– value	force(*f*) probante
Beweissicherung(*f*)	**perpetuate (to)** **evidence**	**préserver les preuves**
Beweissicherung(*f*) *(US)*	**perpetuating** **testimony** *(US)*	**la conservation des** **preuves** *(US)*
Beweisstück(*n*)	**exhibit**	**pièce**(*f*) **à conviction**
Bewertung(*f*)**; Festsetzung**(*f*); (Schaden–)Feststellung(*f*); (Steuer–)Veranlagung	**assessment**	**évaluation**(*f*); estimation(*f*), détermination(*f*) du montant d'impôt
Festsetzung einer Entschädigungssumme	– of damages	évaluation(*f*) des préjudices (dégâts)
Bewertung(*f*)**; Schätzwert**(*m*)	**valuation**	**prisée**(*f*) **et estimation,** expertise(*f*), évaluation, inventaire(*m*)
bewilligen; übertragen; zugestehen	**grant** (to)	**accorder, octroyer,** consentir
Bewilligender(*m*); Übertragender(*m*)	**grantor**	**concédant**(*m*), donateur(*m*)
Bewilligung(*f*)**; Übertragung**(*f*); Schenkung(*f*); Beihilfe(*f*); Stipendium	**grant**	**concession**(*f*), octroi; **subvention**(*f*)
(be–)zahlen	**pay (to)**	**payer, acquitter, régler;** rétribuer, rémunérer

GERMAN	ENGLISH	FRENCH
bezahlt	**paid**	**payé,** acquitté, versé, rémunéré
eingezahltes Kapital (v.d. Aktionären) voll	--in capital --up shares/stock	capital(m) versé actions(f) libérées
eingezahltes Kapital prämien-, beitragsfreie Police	--up policy	police(f) d'assurances libérée
beziffert auf eine bestimmte Summe –e Forderung	**liquidated** – claim	**liquidé,** certain créance(f) liquide
–er Schadensersatz; vereinbarte Vertragsstrafe	– damages	dommages-intérêts(m) par contrat
Bezirk(m), Kreis(m) (Bezirks-)Staatsanwalt (US)	**district** – attorney (US)	**district**(m), quartier(m) procureur(m) de la République (US)
(Bundes-)Bezirksgericht (US)	– court (US)	tribunal(m) fédéral de première instance (US)
Gerichtsbezirk	judicial –	ressort(m) territorial d'un tribunal
Bezirk(m) (US)	**precinct** (US)	**circonscription**(f) **électorale** (US)
Bezogener(m); Trassat(m)	**drawee**	**tiré**(m) **(d'un effet),** payeur(m) (d'une lettre de change)
Bezugnahme(f); Betreff(m)	**reference**	**référence**(f), renvoi(m), mention
unter Bezugnahme	by –	en fonction (de)
Bietender(m), Steigerer(m); Bewerber(m)	**bidder**	**enchérisseur**(m)
Bilanz(f), Rechnungsabschluß(m)	**balance sheet**	**bilan**(m) **d'inventaire**
bilateral; gegenseitig	**bilateral**	**bilatéral,** synallagmatique
billig; gerecht Billigkeitsanspruch	**equitable** – claim	**juste,** équitable réclamation(f) en accord avec les principes de l'équité
Billigkeit(f); Unparteilichkeit(f)	**equity**	**équité**(f), principes(m) de la justice (opp. droit formel)
Billigkeitsgericht	court of –	tribunal(m) qui applique les principes de l'équité
Eigenkapital; Beteiligungskapital	– capital	capital(m) efêtif, fonds(m) propres
binden; verpflichten sich verpflichten (etwas zu tun)	**bind (to)** – oneself	**obliger,** engager, lier s'engager
Binnen-; inländisch Heimat, Heimatland	**home** – country	**domicile**(m), foyer(m) pays (terre) natale; pays d'origine
EG-Heimatstaat	– member State (EEC)	pays(m) membre permanent (CEE)
Bitte(f), Ersuchen	**solicitation**	**sollicitation**(f)
Blasphemie(f), Gotteslästerung(f)	**blasphemy**	**blasphème**(m)
bloß, nackt, dürftig, arm	**bare**	**nu**

GERMAN	ENGLISH	FRENCH
(Bluts-)Verwandtschaft(m); Angehörige(r)(m) der (die) nächste(r) Verwandte(r)	kin next of –	parent(m, f), allié(m, f) parent le plus proche
Börse	stock exchange	Bourse(f)
(Börse)(f) Report(m); Kursaufschlag(m) Reportgeschäft Reportsatz, Prolongationssatz	contango – business – rate	intérêt(m) de report marché(m) des reports taux(m) de report
Börsenmakler(m)	stockbroker	agent(m) de change, courtier(m) en valeurs mobilières
börsennotiert –es Unternehmen –e Wertpapiere	listed – company – securities	coté, énuméré société(f) bourse cotée valeurs(f) cotées
Börsennotierung(f); Zulassung(f) Zulassungseinzelheiten (s. Prospekt)	listing – particulars (cf. prospectus)	cotation(f) prospectus(m) d'émission d'action, appel(m) à la souscription
böse Absicht(f)	malice	préméditation(f), malveillance(f)
böswillig –e Handlung; vorsätzlich rechtswidrige Handlung –e Absicht	malicious – act – intent	criminel, fait avec intention de nuire, malveillant acte(m) criminel but(m) délictueux
böswillig zerstören	vandalise	vandaliser
Boykott(m), Sperre(f)	boycott	boycottage(m)
Brandstifter(m); durch Brandstiftung(f) verursacht	incendiary	incendiaire
Brandstiftung(f)	arson	crime(m) d'incendie volontaire
Brief(m); Schreiben (schriftlicher) Vollmacht Akkreditiv Absichtserklärung	letter – of attorney – of credit – of intent	lettre(f) procuration(f) lettre(f) de crédit déclaration(f) d'intention
bringen, tragen, erheben Klage erheben; Prozeß anhängig machen; verklagen	bring (to) – an action	apporter, amener intenter une action en justice
(Bücher(m), Rechnungen(f)) prüfen; Revision(f) durchführen	audit (to)	vérifier, apurer, faire un audit
Buchführung(f); Rechnungslegung(f); Abrechnung(f); Rechnungswesen Buchungsunterlagen, Buchungsbelege Kassenbuchhaltung Kostenrechnung; Betriebskalkulation	accounting – records cash – cost –	comptabilité(f) pièces(f) comptables comptabilité de caisse comptabilité de prix de revient

GERMAN	ENGLISH	FRENCH
Buchhalter(*m*); Buchhaltungsfachmann(*m*); Buchprüfer(*m*) (öffentlich zugelassener) Wirtschaftsprüfer (*US*) (öffentlich zugelassener) Wirtschaftsprüfer (*UK*)	accountant certified public – (*US*) chartered – (*UK*)	**comptable**(*m*) expert(*m*) comptable (*US*) expert comptable (*UK*)
Buchwert(*m*); buchmäßiger Wert(*m*)	**book value**	**valeur comptable,** prix(*m*) d'inventaire
Bundes- -gericht -gerichtsbarkeit, Zuständigkeit der Bundesgerichte	**federal** – court – jurisdiction	**fédéral** cour(*f*) fédérale juridiction(*f*) fédérale
Bundeszentralbank(*f*) (*US*)	**Federal Reserve Bank** (*US*)	**Banque**(*f*) **Fédérale de Réserve** (*US*)
Bundeszivilprozeßordnung(*f*) (*US*)	**Federal Rules of Civil Procedure** (*US*)	**Règles Fédérales de Procédure Civile** (*US*)
Bürge(*m*); Garant(*m*)	**guarantor**	**garant**(*m*), caution(*f*), répondant(*m*), avaliste
Bürge(*m*); Garant(*m*); Sicherheitsleistung(*f*)	**surety**	**garantie**(*f*), caution(*f*), garant(*m*); sûreté(*f*), certitude(*f*)
Bürger(*m*); Staatsbürger(*m*)	**citizen**	**citoyen**(*m*), ressortissant
bürgerlich, staatsbürgerlich; städtisch	**civic**	**civique,** municipal
bürgerlich, zivilrechtlich Zivilprozeß, bürgerlicher Rechtsstreit Zivilgericht Zivilrecht; bürgerliches Recht, Privatrecht zivilrechtliche Haftung Ziviltrauung, standesamtliche Trauung (Staats-)Bürgerrechte (Staats-)Beamter; öffentlicher Bediensteter	**civil** – action – court – law – liability – marriage – rights – servant	**civil,** –e action(*f*) civile tribunal(*m*) civil 'jus civile', droit(*m*) romain; droit civil responsabilité(*f*) civile mariage(*m*) civil droits(*m*) civils; droits civiques fonctionnaire(*m*)
Bürgermeister(*m*)	**mayor**	**maire**(*m*)
Bürgschaft(*f*); Kaution(*f*), Sicherheitsleistung(*f*) Bürgschaftsschein Sicherheitsleistung (Kaution) zulassen Sicherheit anbieten gegen Bürgschaft (Sicherheitsleistung) entlassen, freilassen	**bail** – bond to grant – to offer – to release on –	**caution**(*f*) bon de caution admettre une caution proposer une caution mise en liberté sous caution

GERMAN	ENGLISH	FRENCH
Bürgschaft(f); Sicherheit(f) Nebensicherheit; Deckung durch Hinterlegung von Effekten hypothekarische Sicherheit Sicherungsrecht an beweglichen oder unbeweglichen Sachen Sicherheitspolizei Sicherheitsrisiko	**security** collateral – – by mortgage – interest – police – risk	**sécurité**(f), sûreté(f) nantissement(m) garantie(f) hypothécaire intérêt(s)(m) garanti(s) forces(f) de sécurité risque(m) sécuritaire
Bürgschaft(sleistung)(f); Sicherheit(f); Garantie(f) selbstschuldnerische Bürgschaft Nebenbürgschaft Ausfallbürgschaft	**guarantee** (cf. surety) absolute – collateral – conditional –	**garantie**(f), caution(f); aval(m), cautionnement(m) garantie absolue garantie collatérale garantie conditionnelle

C

GERMAN	ENGLISH	FRENCH
c.i.f. *(s. Fracht)*	CIF	CAF (coût, assurance maritime, fret)*(m)*
Clearingbank*(f)*, Giro-Code*(m)*	clearing bank code	banque*(f)* de virement code*(m)*

D

GERMAN	ENGLISH	FRENCH
Dachgesellschaft(*f*); Muttergesellschaft(*f*)	**parent company**	**société**(*f*) **mère**
Darlehen(*n*) besichertes –; Bürgschaftskredit	**loan** – against a guarantee	**prêt**(*m*), emprunt(*m*) prêt sur garantie
–svertrag; Kreditvertrag	– agreement	accord(*m*) de prêt, d'emprunt
kurzfristiges –	– at call	prêt remboursable sur demande, argent à vue
verzinsliches –	– at interest	prêt à intérêt(s)
–skapital; Anleihekapital	– capital	capital(*m*) d'emprunt
–szinsen; Anleihezinsen	– interest	intérêt(*m*) sur emprunt
Hypotheken-	mortage –	prêt hypothécaire
gesichertes –	secured –	emprunt garanti
Darlehensgeber(*m*); Kredit–; Verleiher(*m*)	**lender**	**prêteur**(*m*)
Datum(*n*); Zeitpunkt(*m*); Termin	**date**	**date**(*f*)
Abschlußtermin; Anmeldeschluß; Abschlußstichtag	closing –	date limite
Verfallstag; Ablauftermin	expiry –	date d'expiration
Tilgungstermin; Einlösungstermin	redemption –	date de remboursement, date d'amortissement
Ablauf–, Enddatum; Tag des Außerkrafttretens	termination –	date de cessation, date de résiliation
Defizit(*n*); Minder–, Fehlbetrag(*m*); Passivsaldo(*m*)	**deficit**	**déficit**(*m*)
delegieren; weiterübertragen Verantwortung übertragen	**delegate (to)** – responsibility	**déléguer** déléguer une responsabilité
Delikt(*n*); unerlaubte Ausführung(*f*) e–r an sich rechtmäßigen Handlung	**misfeasance**	**accomplissement**(*m*) **incorrect d'un acte licite**
Delkredere	**del credere**	**ducroire**(*m*)
Devisen; Umtausch(*m*)	**exchange**	**change**(*m*); transmission(*f*); Bourse(*f*)
Devisenkontrolle	– control	contrôle(*m*) des changes
(Wechsel-)Kursverlust	– loss	perte(*f*) de change
Wechsel–, Devisen–, Umrechnungskurs	– rate	taux(*m*) de change, cours du change

GERMAN	ENGLISH	FRENCH
Devisenmarkt(*m*)	**foreign exchange market**	**marché**(*m*) **des changes**
(Die Römischen) Verträge (*EG*)	**Treaty of Rome** (*EEC*)	**Traité**(*m*) **de Rome** (*CEE*)
Diebstahl(*m*)	**theft**	**vol**(*m*)
Diebstahl(*m*) schwerer – leichter –	**larceny** grand – petty –	**vol**(*m*) vol important larcin(*m*)
Dienstbarkeit(*f*) Zuchthaus (strafe); Zwangsarbeit	**servitude** penal –	**servitude**(*f*) travaux forcés
dilatorisch; aufschiebend dilatorische (od. prozeßhindernde) Einrede	**dilatory** – plea	**dilatoire** exception(*f*) dilatoire
dinglich; unbeweglich; effektiv Grundeigentum; unbewegliches Vermögen Augenscheinsbeweis; Beweis durch Augenscheinnahme immobiliarvermögen Realeinkommen	**real** – estate – evidence – income – property	**réel,** vrai biens(*m*) immobiliers preuve(*f*) par vue de lieux revenu(*m*) réel biens immobiliers
direkt; unmittelbar direkte Kosten, Einzelkosten; leistungsabhängige Kosten unmittelbarer Schaden direkter Nachkomme unmittelbarer Beweis erste Befragung des Zeugen durch die den Zeugen stellende Partei	**direct** – cost – damage – descendant – evidence – examination	**direct** frais(*m*) spéciaux dommages(*m*) directs descendant(*m*) direct preuve(*f*) directe interrogatoire(*m*) direct
Direktion(*f*); Verwaltungsstelle(*f*); Behörde(*f*); Ausschuß(*m*), Gremium(*n*); Verpflegung(*f*) Verwaltungsrat; –ausschuß Beratungsausschuß, –stelle (Gremium der) Direktoren; Vorstand	**board** administrative – advisory – – of directors	**commission**(*f*), conseil(*m*), administration(*f*) comité(*m*) administratif comité consultatif conseil d'administration
diskriminieren; unterscheiden	**discriminate (to)**	**pratiquer la discrimination**
diskriminierend; unterscheidend Ausnahmegesetzgebung diskriminierende Maßnahme diskriminierende Politik diskriminierendes Verfahren unterschiedliche Behandlung	**discriminatory** – legislation – measure – policy – procedure – treatment	**discriminatoire** législation(*f*) d'exception mesure(*f*) discriminatoire politique(*f*) de discrimination, de favoritisme procédure(*f*) d'exception traitement(*m*) discriminatoire
Diskriminierung(*f*); Benachteiligung(*f*)	**discrimination**	**discrimination**(*f*)
Dissens(*m*), Meinungsverschiedenheit(*f*)	**dissent**	**dissentiment**(*m*), différence(*f*) d'opinion
Dividende(*f*)	**dividend**	**dividende**(*m*)

GERMAN	ENGLISH	FRENCH
Dock(n), Kai(m); Anklagebank(f)	**dock**	**banc**(m) **des accusés**
Doktortitel(m) **der juristischen Fakultät**(f)	**LLD**	**docteur**(m) **endroit**
Dokumentenakkreditiv(n)	**documentary credit**	**crédit**(m) **documentaire**
Domizil(n); Wohnsitz(m); Firmensitz(m)	**domicile**	**domicile**(m)
drängen; zwingen	**impel (to)**	**forcer à faire**
dringend; eilig	**urgent**	**urgent**
Dritte(r)(m, f) Streitverkündung Haftpflichtversicherung; Fremdversicherung Haftpflicht	**third party** third-party action third-party insurance third-party liability	**tiers**(m), tierce personne(m) mise(f) en cause assurance(f) de responsabilité civile responsabilité(f) civile
Drittschuldnerpfändung(f) **vornehmen;** Drittschuldner(m) ein Zahlungsverbot zustellen	**garnish (to)**	**garnir,** orner; saisir
Drogendelikt(n) (s. Rauschgift)(n)	**drug offence** (cf. narcotics)	**infraction**(f) **à la législation sur les stupéfiants**
drohen	**threaten (to)**	**menacer,** proférer des menaces
Drohung(f)	**threat**	**menace**(f)
durch Aussageverweigerungsrecht(n) geschützte Mitteilung(f)	**privileged information**	**renseignements**(m) **privilégiés**
Durchführung(f); Erfüllung(f)	**implementation**	**mise**(f) **en oeuvre,** application
(politisches) Programm in die Tat umsetzen Durchführung von Bestimmungen	– of a policy – of regulations	mise en oeuvre d'une politique application(f) d'un règlement
Durchsuchung(f) Durchsuchungsrecht	**visit and search** – right	**perquisition**(f) droit(m) d'effectuer une perquisition
durchwühlen; plündern	**ransack (to)**	**saccager,** piller

E

GERMAN	ENGLISH	FRENCH
Ebenbürtige(r)(*m*); Adlige(r)(*m*)	**peer**	**pair**(*m*); pair du royaume (*UK*)
Ecu	**ecu**	**ecu**
effektiv; wirksam Tag des Inkrafttretens	**effective** – date	**efficace;** frappant; solvable date(*f*) d'entrée en vigueur
Ehebruch(*m*)	**adultery**	**adultère**(*m*)
Ehefrau(*f*)	**wife**	**épouse**(*f*), femme(*f*)
Ehemann(*m*); Gatte(*m*)	**husband**	**mari**(*m*)
Eherecht(*n*)	**matrimonial law**	**droit**(*m*) **du mariage**
Ehe(*f*)**(stand)**(*m*)	**matrimony**	**mariage**(*m*)
Ehe(stand)(*m*) ehelich geboren nichtehelich geboren	**wedlock** born in – born out of –	**mariage**(*m*) né dans le mariage, filiation(*f*) légitime né hors du mariage, filiation naturelle
Ehrenamtlicherichter(*m*)	**magistrate**	**magistrat**(*m*), juge(*m*)
Ehrlosigkeit(*f*), Schande(*f*); Verlust(*m*) der bürgerlichen Ehrenrechte	**infamy**	**incapacité**(*f*) **de témoigner;** infamie(*f*)
Ehrverletzung(*f*); Beleidigung(*f*); Verleumdung(*f*)	**defamation**	**diffamation**(*f*)
Eid(*m*) jdn e-n Eid abnehmen; vereidigen unter –	**oath** administer the – to s.o. under –	**serment**(*m*) déférer le serment à qqu'un sous serment
Eidesstattliche Erklärung(*f*) **od. Versicherung**(*f*), (schriftlich) eidliche Erklärung eidesstattliche, schriftliche Zeugenaussage entgegennehmen eidesstattlich erklären, eidliche schriftliche Erklärung abgeben	**affidavit** evidence taken on – to make an –	**attestation**(*f*), témoignage(*m*) écrit; déposition(*f*) de témoin sous serment déposition de témoin recueillie sous serment faire une déclaration sous serment
eidlich bezeugen; vor Gericht(*n*) aussagen; absetzen	**depose (to)**	**déposer**

GERMAN	ENGLISH	FRENCH
Eigentum(*f*); Vermögen(*n*)	**property**	**biens**(*m*), propriété(*f*), avoirs(*m*), possessions(*f*)
Grundstücke und Gebäude	fixed –	biens immobiliers, immeubles
immaterielle Vermögenswerte	intangible –	biens incorporels
Grundvermögen; Liegenschaften	landed –	biens-fonds, propriété foncière
Sachenrecht	law of –	droit(*m*) de la propriété
Pachtgrundstücke	leasehold –	propriété affermée, louée à bail
bewegliches Vermögen	movable –	biens mobiliers
persönliches Eigentum; bewegliches Vermögen	personal –	biens mobiliers
Staatseigentum; Eigentum der öffentlichen Hand	public –	propriété publique
Eigentümer(*m*)	**proprietor**	**propriétaire**(*m, f*)
Eigentümer(*m*); Eigner(*m*)	**owner**	**propriétaire**(*m, f*), possesseur(*m*)
Eigentums-	**proprietary**	**de propriété**, de propriétaire
–rechte(*n*)	– rights	droits(*m*) de propriété
Eigentum(srecht)(*n*); Besitz(*m*)	**ownership**	**propriété**(*f*), possession(*f*)
bloßes Eigentumsrecht (ohne Nutzungen)	bare –	nue-propriété(*f*)
Miteigentum; gemeinsames Eigentum	joint –	propriété(*f*) dans l'indivision
Eigentum(srecht)(*n*); Titel(*m*)	**title**	**titre**(*m*) **de propriété**; titre nobiliaire; intitulé(*m*) (d'une action)
Rechtsübertragung; Forderungsabtretung	assignment of –	transfert de droit
ausschließliches Besitzrecht	exclusive –	de propriété exclusive
Titelinhaber	– -holder	détenteur(*m*) d'un titre (de propriété)
Eigentumsvorbehalt(*m*)	**reservation of title**	**clause**(*f*) **de restriction d'un titre**
einberufen; laden; sich versammeln	**convene (to)**	**rassembler,** réunir, citer
e-e Hauptversammlung, Gesellschafter einberufen	– a shareholders' meeting	tenir une réunion des actionnaires
Einbrecher(*m*)	**burglar**	**cambrioleur**(*m*)
Einbruch(*m*)	**breaking and entering**	**effraction**(*f*)
Einbruchdiebstahl(*m*)	**housebreaking**	**violation**(*f*) **de domicile**, effraction(*f*)
Einbruch(sdiebstahl)(*m*)	**burglary**	**cambriolage**(*m*)
Einbürgerung(*f*)	**naturalisation**	**naturalisation**
–santrag	application for –	demande(*f*) de naturalisation
–surkunde	certificate of –	décret(*m*) de naturalisation
Eindringen; Besitzstörung(*f*)	**intrusion**	**usurpation**(*f*), intrusion(*f*), empiètement(*m*)

GERMAN	ENGLISH	FRENCH
Einfuhr(*f*) –vertreter –lizenz –quote –beschränkungen	**import** – agent – licence – quota – restrictions	**importation**(*f*) importateur(*m*) licence(*f*) d'importation contingents(*m*) d'importation restrictions(*f*) à l'importation
eingetragen eingeschriebener Brief Einschreiben –er Sitz	**registered** – letter – mail – office	**enregistré**, inscrit, immatriculé lettre(*f*) recommandée courrier(*m*) recommandé siège(*m*) social
eingetragen (als Kapitalgesellschaft)(*f*) Körperschaft rechtsfähige (Handels-) Gesellschaft	**incorporate(d)** – body – company	**constitué**, autorisé, enregistré doté de la personnalité civile, personne(*f*) morale société(*f*) constituée, société enregistrée
eingreifen; Prozeß(*m*) beitreten	**intervene**	**intervenir**
Eingriff(*m*)**;** Prozeßbeitritt(*m*)	**intervention**	**intervention**(*f*)
Einhaltung(*f*) – der Gesetze	**observance** – of the law	**respect**(*m*) respect de la loi
Einheitliche Europäische Akte **(EG)**	**Single European Act** **(EC)**	**Acte**(*m*) **Unique Européen** **(CE)**
Einkünfte; Bezüge(*m*)	**emolument(s)**	**émoluments**(*m*), honoraires(*m*)
einleiten; erheben eine Klage erheben gerichtliches Verfahren einleiten	**institute (to)** – an action – legal proceedings	**instituer,** fonder, établir engager une action en justice engager des poursuites judiciaires
einleitende Erklärung(*f*)**;** Präambel(*f*); Darstellung(*f*)	**recitals**	**introduction**(*f*) **d'un texte** **juridique**
einräumen; zugestehen; gewähren	**concede (to)**	**concéder**
Einrede(*f*)**;** Einlassung(*f*); Klagebeantwortung(*f*) Verteidiger; Anwalt des Beklagten Klagebeantwortung; Verteidigungsvorbringen Entlastungszeuge; von der Verteidigung benannter Zeuge	**defence** – counsel statement of – witness for the –	**défense**(*f*)**;** la défense avocat(*m*) de la défense, défenseur conclusions(*f*) de la défense témoin(*m*) de la défense

GERMAN	ENGLISH	FRENCH
Einrede; Vorbringen	**plea**	**défense**(f), moyens(m) de défense; cause(f) (US), procès(m)
Klageerwiderung	defendant's –	– conclusion(f) de le défense
dilatorische, aufschiebende Einrede	dilatory –	exception(f) dilatoir
Schuldbekenntnis; Schuldigerklärung	– of guilty	aveu(m) de culpabilité fait à l'audience
Nichtigkeitsbeschwerde; – der Rechtsunwirksamkeit	– of nullity	exception de nullité
Gnadengesuch	– for mercy	appel(m) à la clémence, recours(m) en grâce
einreichen; vorbringen	**lodge (to)**	**interjeter,** confier (des valeurs), placer, remettre
Anspruch geltend machen	– a claim	déposer une réclamation
Berufung einlegen	– an appeal	interjeter appel
einreichen; vorbringen	**present (to)**	**présenter**
Beweismittel beibringen	– evidence	porter témoignage
einreichen; zu den Akten nehmen	**file (to)**	**verser au dossier,** classer, archiver
ein Rechtsmittel (Berufung, ua.) einlegen	– an appeal	se pourvoir en appel
ein Gesuch (Antrag) einreichen	– a petition	déposer une requête
Einrichtungsgegenstände(m)	**fixtures and fittings**	**(toutes les) installations (d'une maison)**
Einschüchterung(f)	**intimidation**	**subornation**(f) **(de témoins),** intimidation(f), menaces(f)
einseitig; voreingenommen	**one-sided**	**unilatéral**
Einsichtnahme(f)	**inspection**	**contrôle**(m), inspection(f), vérification(f)
– in Urkunden, Akten	– of documents (US)	remise(f) de documents à la partie adverse
einstehen für; sich verbürgen für	**vouch (to) for**	**répondre de,** garantir
einstellen; fallen lassen	**drop (to)**	**baisser,** diminuer; renoncer à, retirer
Klage fallenlassen, zurücknehmen	– a case	abandonner des poursuites
Einstellung(f); **Aufhebung**(f)	**suspension**	**suspension**(f), surséance(f)
Zahlungseinstellung	– of payments	arrêt(m) de paiement
Aussetzen der Strafe zur Bewährung	– of sentence	surséance de jugement
einstweilig; vorläufig	**interlocutory**	**interlocutoire**
Zwischenurteil	– judgment	jugement(m) interlocutoire
einstweilige Verfügung(f); richterliches Verbot(n)	**restraining order**	**ordonnance**(f) **de ne pas faire**
einstweilige Verfügung(f) **(zur Unterlassung)**(f)	**prohibitory injunction**	**ordonnance**(f) **prohibitoire,** ordonnance prononçant une interdiction

GERMAN	ENGLISH	FRENCH
Eintragung(f); Zulassung(f)	**registration**	**enregistrement**(m), immatriculation(f), inscription(f)
Eintragung in die Patentrolle	patent –	dépôt(m) d'un brevet
Nummernschild; polizeil. Kennzeichen	– plate	plaque(f) d'immatriculation
Eintragung e-s Warenzeichens	trade mark –	dépôt d'une marque de fabrique
eintreten; einbringen, erheben	**enter (to)**	**entrer,** enregistrer
e-n Vertrag mit jmd abschließen	– into an agreement (with)	conclure un accord (avec)
Einwand(m); Beanstandung(f)	**objection**	**objection**(f), récusation(f) (d'un témoin)
e-n Einspruch zurückweisen	overrule an –	rejeter une objection
e-r Einwendung stattgeben	sustain an –	admettre une objection
Einwanderung(f)	**immigration**	**immigration**(f)
einwandfrei	**unobjectionable**	**acceptable,** à qui on ne peut rien reprocher
einwenden; beanstanden	**object (to)**	**objecter,** récuser (un témoin)
Einwilligung(f); Zustimmung(f)	**consent**	**consentement**(m)
in gegenseitigem Einvernehmen; einverständlich	by mutual –	d'un commun accord
Einzelhaft(f)	**solitary confinement**	**régime**(m) **cellulaire,** isolement carcéral
einzeln; gesondert	**several**	**individuel,** indivis; séparé; plusieurs
Einziehung(f), Inkasso(n), Beitreibung(f)	**collection**	**encaissement**(m); levée(f), perception(f); rassemblement(f), réunion(f); recouvrement(m)
Inkassostelle	– agency	agence(f) de recouvrement
Inkassoauftrag	– order	ordre(m) de recouvrement
Einziehungsverfahren	– procedure	procédure(f) de mise en recouvrement
Empfänger(m)	**recipient**	**bénéficiaire**(m), destinataire(m), allocataire(m)
e-n Rechtsstreit für jdn führen	**conduct (to) somebody's cause**	**plaider la cause de qqu'un**
Endabnehmer(m); Endanwender(m)	**end-user**	**utilisateur**(m) **final**
Ende(n); Ziel(n); Absicht(f)	**end**	**fin**(f), terme(m)
Endprodukt(n)	**end-product**	**produit**(m) **fini,** résultat(m)
Endurteil(n); rechtskräftiges Urteil(n)	**final judgment/ decree/sentence**	**jugement**(m) **définitif, sans appel**
Entdeckung(f), Enthüllung(f); Ermittlung(f); Offenlegung(f)	**discovery**	**découverte**(f), divulgation(f)
Entdeckungsverfahren	– proceedings	procédure(f) en vue d'identifier les actifs d'une succession

GERMAN	ENGLISH	FRENCH
enteignen	**expropriate (to)**	**exproprier**, déposséder
enterben	**disinherit (to)**	**déshériter**
Entführung(*f*)	**abduction**	**enlèvement**(*m*)
Entführung(*f*)	**kidnapping**	**enlèvement**(*m*), kidnapping(*m*), rapt(*m*) (s'emploie plutôt quand la victime est un enfant)
entgegengesetzt; sich widersprechend	**contradictory**	**contradictoire**
entgegengesetzt; wechselseitig Wider-, Gegenklage	**cross** --action	**contre-**, anti- action(*f*) reconventionnelle, opposition(*f*)
Anschlußberufung Gegenanspruch	--appeal --claim	appel(*m*) incident revendication(*f*) dans une action reconventionnelle
Kreuzverhör beiderseitig Garantie beiderseitige Haftung	--examination --guarantee --liability	contre-interrogatoire(*m*) contre-garantie(*f*) contre-responsabilité(*f*)
enthüllen; offenbaren	**reveal (to)**	**révéler**
entlassen; abweisen, zurückweisen	**dismiss (to)**	**renvoyer**, congédier, destituer, licencier
Berufung verwerfen, zurückweisen	– an appeal	rejeter un appel, débouter d'un appel
entlassen; überflüssig	**redundant**	**superflu**, au chômage, licencié économique
Entlassung(*f*); Entlastung(*f*); Entladung(*f*), Löschen	**discharge**	**libération**(*f*), décharge(*f*)
Strafaussetzung zur Bewährung; bedingte Entlassung	conditional –	libération conditionnelle
Entlastung; Entschuldigung	– from an encumbrance	dégrevage
Freilassung	– from prison	libération de prison
Entlassung(*f*); Zurückweisung(*f*); Einstellung(*f*)	**dismissal**	**renvoi**(*m*), congédiement(*m*), rejet(*m*), licenciement(*m*)
Klageabweisung	– of an action	classement d'une affaire
Entlassung(*f*) **auf Bewährung**(*f*); bedingter Straferlaß(*m*)	**parole**	**liberté surveillée;** liberté conditionnelle
gegen Ehrenwort freigelassen Bewährungsbeamter	on – – officer	en liberté(*f*) surveillée contrôleur(*m*) judiciaire
entlasten; entbinden jdn von einer Schuld oder Haftung befreien	**exonerate (to)** – s.o. from guilt or liability	**exonérer**, dispenser disculper qqu'un, exonérer qqu'un de ses responsabilités(*f*)
entlastende Tatsache(*f*)	**infirmative fact**	**fait**(*m*) **réfutatif**
entlaufen; durchgehen	**elope (to)**	**fuir**
Entlegenheit(*f*); **Ferne**(*f*) Nichtzurechenbarkeit e-s Schadens	**remoteness** – of damage	**éloignement**(*m*) dommage(*m*) indirect
Beweisunerheblichkeit	– of evidence	non-pertinence d'un témoignage

GERMAN	ENGLISH	FRENCH
Entleiher(*m*); Kredit–, Darlehensnehmer(*m*)	**borrower**	**emprunteur** (*n.*)
entscheiden, erkennen; zuerkennen, zusprechen Schadensersatz zuerkennen, zusprechen	**adjudge** – damages	**adjuger,** déclarer, prononcer sur accorder (allouer) des dommages-intérêts
entscheiden; beschließen 'das Gericht verfügt, daß'	**rule (to)** 'the court rules that'	**décider,** régir, gouverner 'le tribunal a décidé que'
Entscheidung(*f*), Urteil(*n*); Zuerkennung(*f*), Zuschlag(*m*) Eröffnung eines Konkursverfahrens, Konkurseröffnung	**adjudication** – of bankruptcy	**jugement**(*m*), décision(*f*), prononcé d'un jugement; adjudication(*f*), jugement déclaratif de faillite
Entschuldigung(*f*); Rechtfertigung(*f*)	**exculpation**	**disculpation**(*f*)
entwenden; stehlen	**pilfer (to)**	**chaparder,** commettre de menus larcins
Entwendung(*f*); geringfügiger Diebstahl(*m*)	**pilfering, pilferage**	**chapardage**(*m*), larcins(*m*)
Entwurf(*m*); Konzept(*n*) Gesetzesentwurf, –vorlage Vertragsentwurf	**draft** – Bill – contract	**projet**(*m*) **d'acte** avant-projet de loi projet de contrat
e-r Pfründe berauben; Einkommen entziehen	**disendow (to)**	**retirer,** ôter
Erbe(*m*) Intestats- gesetzlicher – – durch Geburtsrecht Allein– Testaments– Allein–	**heir** intestate – legal – natural – sole – testamentary – universal –	**héritier**(*m*), héritière(*f*) héritier ab intestat héritier légal héritier naturel seul héritier, héritier unique héritier désigné par disposition testamentaire légataire(*m*, *f*) universel
erben	**inherit (to)**	**hériter (de)**
Erbfolge(*f*) Intestat–; gesetzliche – –recht; Erbberechtigung	**succession** intestate – right of –	**succession**(*f*), descendance(*f*), héritiers(*m*) succession ab intestat droits(*m*) de succession, droits successifs
Erblasser(*m*); Vermächtnisgeber(*m*)	**devisor**	**testateur**(*m*)
Erblasser(in)(*m*, *f*); Testator(*m*)	**testator, testatrix**	**testateur**(*m*), **testatrice**(*f*)
erblich	**hereditary**	**héréditaire**
erbringen, anführen, beibringen Gründe anführen e-n Beweis erbringen	**adduce (to)** – an argument – evidence	**apporter,** offrir; alléguer invoquer une raison fournir une preuve

GERMAN	ENGLISH	FRENCH
Erbschaft(*f*)**;** Erbe(*n*)	**inheritance**	**héritage**(*m*)**,** succession(*f*)*;* procédure(*f*) en matière de succession
Erbschaftssteuer	– tax	droits(*m*) successoraux
Erbteil(*n*) gesetzliche Rücklagen	**portion (of an estate)** reserved by law for an heir	**part**(*m*) **d'héritage** réserve(*f*) légale
erfolglos, ergebnislos	**abortive**	**manqué,** avorté, inopérant
ergänzen, abändern e-n Gesetzesentwurf, Gesetz abändern	**amend (to)** – a statute	**amender,** modifier, rectifier amender une loi, modifier un règlement
ergänzend; untergeordnet, Hilfs–, Neben–	**ancillary**	**auxiliaire**(*m*)**,** subordonné(*f*), annexe(*f*) à
Ergänzung(*f*)**,** Abänderung(*f*)*;* Zusatz(*m*), Nachtrag(*m*)	**amendment**	**amendement**(*m*)**,** modification(*f*), correction(*f*), rectification(*f*)
ergreifen; beschlagnahmen	**seize (to)**	**saisir,** confisquer
ergreifen; einholen; erreichen; ertappen	**catch (to)**	**attraper**
erheben	**levy (to)**	**imposer,** prélever, frapper de, saisir
Steuer –	– a tax	lever un impôt, percevoir une taxe
beschlagnahmen; in Besitz nehmen	– distress	faire une saisie-exécution
erkennbar; gerichtlich verfolgbar; der Gerichtsbarkeit unterworfen	**cognisable**	**du ressort de,** de la compétence de
erkennen, entscheiden, Recht(*n*) sprechen Schuldner für zahlungsunfähig erklären; Konkurs(verfahren) über das Vermögen des Schuldners eröffnen	**adjudicate (to)** – s.o. bankrupt	**juger,** statuer, rendre un arrêt mettre (qqu'un) en faillite
Erkenntnis(*n*)**;** (gerichtliche) Kenntnisnahme; (richterliche) Zuständigkeit(*f*); Anerkenntnis(*n*)	**cognisance**	**connaissance**(*f*)
erklären; aussagen	**state (to)**	**déclarer,** énoncer, fixer
Erklärung(*f*)**;** Klageschrift(*f*)*;* (Wert-)Angabe(*f*)*;* Zolldeklaration(*f*) Konkurserklärung, -eröffnung Einverständnis–, Zustimmungserklärung Beschwerde Willens–, Absichtserklärung	**declaration** – of bankruptcy – of consent – of dissent – of intention	**déclaration**(*f*)**;** décision(*f*) judiciaire; dispositif(*m*) de jugement déclaration de faillite déclaration de consentement déclaration de désaccord déclaration d'intention; demande(*f*) de naturalisation (*US*)
Erklärung(*f*) **unter Einschränkungen**(*f*) **abgeben**	**qualify (to) a statement**	**limiter la portée d'une déclaration**

GERMAN	ENGLISH	FRENCH
erlassen; ausstellen	**issue (to)**	**lancer (un mandat d'arrêt),** émettre, publier
e-n Gerichtsbeschluß erlassen	– a court order	rendre un arrêt de justice
Prozeßladung (mit Klageschrift) ergehen lassen	– a writ of summons	délivrer une citation à comparaître
Vorschriften erlassen	– instructions	donner des instructions
Wertpapiere ausgeben (s. *Aktien*)	– securities (*cf. share*)	émettre des actions
Erlöschen	**lapse**	**défaillance**(*f*), erreur(*f*); caducité(*f*), extinction; laps(*m*) (de temps)
– e-s Patents	– of patent	déchéance(*f*) d'un brevet
– e-s Rechts	– of rights	déchéance de droits
Fristablauf; Verjährung	– of time	laps de temps
erloschen; außer Kraft treten	**lapse (to)**	**périmer,** se périmer, tomber en désuétude; devenir disponible
erlöschen; verfallen; hinfällig geworden	**lapsed**	**déchu,** périmé, caduc
erloschenes Urheberrecht	– copyright	droit(*m*) d'auteur périmé
verfallene Versicherung	– insurance	assurance(*f*) périmée
Ermächtigung(*f*); Bescheinigung(*f*); Haftbefehl(*m*)	**warrant**	**mandat**(*m*), pouvoir(*m*), certificat(*m*), bon(*m*) de souscription
Arrestbefehl; Pfändungsbeschluf	distress –	ordonnance de saisie-exécution
Durchsuchungsbefehl	search –	mandat de perquisition
Haftbefehl	– of arrest	ordre d'arrestation
Beschlagnahmeverfügung	– of attachment	ordonnance de saisie
Prozeßvollmacht e-s Anwalts (zur Erklärung e-s Anerkenntnisses vor Geicht)	– of attorney	procuration(*f*), pouvoir
Ermächtigungsgesetz(*n*)	**enabling Act**	**loi**(*f*) **habilitante**
Ermessen(*n*); Diskretion(*f*); Klugheit(*f*)	**discretion**	**discrétion**(*f*), pouvoir discrétionnaire
ermitteln, feststellen; sich vergewissern	**ascertain (to)**	**constater,** vérifier, déterminer
Schaden feststellen	– damages	constater les dégâts, déterminer les préjudices
ermitteln; untersuchen	**investigate (to)**	**faire une enquête,** vérifier
Ermittlung(*f*); Untersuchung –sbeamter	**investigation** – officer	**enquête**(*f*), investigation(*f*) officier(*m*) chargé de l'enquête
Voruntersuchung	preliminary –	enquête préliminaire
ernennen; nominieren	**nominate (to)**	**nommer,** désigner
erneute Verhandlung(*f*); Berufung(*f*)(sverfahren)(*n*)	**rehearing**	**nouvelle audition**(*f*)
Ernte(ertrag)(*f*); Früchte auf dem Halm(*m*)	**emblements**	**fruits**(*m*) **civils,** fruits du travail agricole
Erpressung(*f*)	**extortion**	**extortion**(*f*)
Erpressung(*f*); Nötigung	**blackmail**	**chantage**(*m*)

GERMAN	ENGLISH	FRENCH
erscheinen; auftreten; den Anschein haben vor Gericht erscheinen	**appear (to)** – in court	**paraître,** apparaître, comparaître ester en justice, comparaître dans un tribunal
erste, erster, erstes, an erster Stelle schwerer Mord erstrangiges Pfandrecht Ersttäter; Nichtvorbestrafter	**first** -degree (murder) (US) – lien – offender	**premier,** d'origine assassinat(m) privilèges(m) privilégiées délinquant(m) primaire
Ertrag(m); Einkommen(n) Brutto– (Netto-)einkommen	**earning(s)** gross (net) –	**gain(s)**(m), salaire(m), bénéfice(m) bénéfice, gains bruts (nets)
Ertrag(m); Rendite(f); Effektivverzinsung(f)	**yield**	**rapport**(m), rendement(m), production(f)
Erwerbstätigkeit(f)	**gainful employment**	**emploi**(m) **rémunéré**
erwidern; Klageerwiderung(f) einreichen	**respond (to)**	**répondre;** réagir; être l'intimé
Erwiderung(f); Duplik(f)	**rejoinder**	**répartie**(f)
erwiesen	**proved, proven**	**prouvé,** qui a fait ses preuves, attesté
erwürgen; strangulieren	**strangle (to)**	**étrangler**
Erwürgung(f)	**strangulation**	**strangulation**(f)
Europäische Wirtschafts- gemeinschaft (EWG)	**European Economic Community (EEC)**	**Communauté**(f) **économique européenne** (CEE)
Europäisches Währungssystem (EWS)	**European Monetary System (EMS)**	**Système**(m) **Monétaire Européen** (SME)
Eurowährung(f)	**Euro-currency**	**eurodevise**(m), euromonnaie(f)
EWG (Europäische Wirtschaftsgemeinschaft) EG-Recht(n) EG – Gesetzgebung(f)	**EEC (European Economic Community)** – law – legislation	**CEE (Communauté économique européenne)** droit(m) communautaire directives(f) européennes
exterritorial; außerhalb des Hoheitsgebiets(n)	**extraterritorial**	**extraterritoriaux**(f)

F

GERMAN	ENGLISH	FRENCH
Factoring(n) **(Forderungsankauf)**(m)	**factoring**	**service**(m) **d'affacturage;** achat(m) ferme de créances
Fähigkeit(f); Kapazität(f); Inhalt(m)	**capacity**	**capacité**(f); **qualité**(f)
Rechtsfähigkeit; Geschäftsfähigkeit	legal –	capacité légale
dienstliche, amtliche Eigenschaft	official –	exercice des fonctions
Testierfähigkeit	testamentary –	capacité de tester
Fahrerflucht(f)	**hit-and-run driving**	**délit de fuite**
Fahrlässigkeit(f); Verschulden	**negligence**	**négligence**(f), incurie(f), imprudence(f)
Mitverschulden	contributory –	part(f) de responsabilité de la victime dans un accident
strafbare Fahrlässigkeit	criminal –	négligence criminelle
grobe Fahrlässigkeit	gross –	négligence, faute(f) de nature délictuelle
Fahrnis(n), bewegliches Vermögen(n)	**chattels**	**biens** (m) **meubles**
Fall(m); Rechts–, Streitsache(f); Prozeß(m)	**case**	**cas**(m), affaire(f)
der zur Entscheidung stehende Fall; der vorliegende Fall	– at issue	espèce
Berufungssache	– on appeal	affaire dont la Cour d'Appel est saisie
Strafsache; Strafprozeß	criminal –	affaire criminelle
Jugendsache	juvenile –	affaire concernant un mineur
schwebende, anhängige Streitsache	pending –	affaire en cours d'instance, affaire pendante devant
Fälligkeit(f)**(stermin)**(m) –stag; Verfalltag	**maturity** date of –	**échéance**(f) date(f) d'échéance
Fallrecht(n); Präzedenzrecht(n)	**case law**	**jurisprudence**(f), droit jurisprudentiel
falsch; unwahr	**false**	**faux,** erroné
falsches Zeugnis	– testimony	témoignage(m) faux(f)
falsche Darstellung, Behauptung	– pretence	prétextes(m) fallacieux
falsche Benennung(f); Namensirrtum(m)	**misnomer**	**erreur**(f) **sur le nom d'une partie**

GERMAN	ENGLISH	FRENCH
falsche Darstellung(f)	misrepresentation	conduite(f) visant à induire en erreur
arglistige Täuschung; wissentlich falsche Angaben	fraudulent –	fraude(f) pénale
Irreführung durch Vorspiegelung falscher Tatsachen	– of facts	déformation(f) des faits
fälschen; nachmachen	fake (to)	truquer, maquiller, contrefaire
Fälscher(m)	forger	faussaire(m), contrefacteur(m)
Fälschung(f)	forgery	faux, contrefaçon(f), falsification(f), supposition(f)
(Familien-)Angehörige(f); Unterhaltsberechtigte; Hinterbliebene	dependants	personnes(f) à charge
Familienbeihilfe(f); Familienzulage(f)	family allowance	allocation(s)(f) familiale(s)
Familienrecht(n)	family law	droit(m) de la famille
Familienstand(m)	marital status	état(m) matrimonial
f.a.s. (Frei Langsseite Seeschiff)	FAS (free alongside ship)	franco quai
fehlerhaftes Gerichtsverfahren	mistrial	erreur(f) judiciaire
Fehlurteil(n); Justizirrtum(m)	miscarriage of justice	erreur(f) judiciaire, déni(m) de justice
feindlich, gegnerisch; nachteilig; entgegenstehend	adverse	adverse, opposé
Unterbilanz; passive Bilanz	– balance	balance(f) (commerciale) déficitaire
Zeuge der Gegenseite; feindlicher Zeuge	– witness	témoin(m) de la partie adverse
Feingehaltsstempel(m); Kennzeichen	hallmark	poinçon(m), cachet
fest; festliegend	fixed	immobilisé(f), fixe
Anlagevermögen	– assets	immobilisations(f)
Fixkosten	– costs	coûts(m) fixes
Festpreis; festgesetzter Preis	– price	prix(m) fixe
Festnahme(f), Verhaftung(f); Begriff(m), Vorstellung(f); Befürchtung(f)	apprehension	appréhension(f), arrestation(f), prise de corps; crainte(f)
festnehmen, verhaften; ergreifen, fassen; befürchten	apprehend (to)	redouter, craindre; appréhender, arrêter
festnehmen, verhaften; (Verfahren)(n) aussetzen; anhalten	arrest	arrestation(f), prise(f) de corps, placement(m) en détention; saisie(f) (de biens); contrainte(f) par corps
Haftbefehl; Beschlagnahmeverfügung	warrant of –	mandat d'arrêt
feststellend; (rechts-)erklärend; deklaratorisch	declaratory	déclaratoire
Feststellungsurteil	– judgment	jugement(m) déclaratoire

GERMAN	ENGLISH	FRENCH
Feuerversicherung(f)	**fire insurance**	**assurance**(f) **incendie**
fiktiv; Schein- Scheinvertrag	**fictitious, fictive** – contract	**fictif,** simulé contrat(m) fictif
Finanz-; Steuer- –behörde(f) –kontrolle, –aufsicht	**fiscal** – authority – control	**fiscal, fiscale** fisc(m) contrôle(m) fiscal
Finanzamt(n)	**Inland Revenue**	**fisc**(m)
finanziell; Finanz- Buchprüfung Finanzplan Finanztermingeschäfte Finanzgarantie Kredit-, Finanzinstitut Finanz-, Kreditmarkt Finanzgesetzgebung Finanzmanagement Finanzbericht; Handelsbilanz (US)	**financial** – audit – budget – futures – guarantee – institution – market – legislation – management – statement	**financier, financiére** audit(m) financier budget(m) financier contrats(m) à terme garantie(s)(f) financière(s) institution(f) financière marché(m) financier lois(f) de finances management(m) financier bilan(m), état(m) des finances
finanziell unabhängig; nicht auf fremde Hilfe angewiesen	**self-supporting**	**autosuffisant**
Finanzwesen(n) betriebliche Finanzwirtschaft; Unternehmensfinanzierung Finanzierungsgesellschaft; Kreditinstitut für Kundenfinanzierung	**finance** business – – company	**finance**(f) gestion(f) financière société(f) de financement
Firmengruppe(f)**,** Konzern(m)	**group (of companies)**	**groupement**(m) **(de sociétés)**
Firmenname(m)**;** Bezeichnung(f) (der Firma)	**firm name**	**raison**(f) **sociale**
flüchtig werden; (sich dem Gericht) entziehen	**abscond (to)**	**se soustraire à la justice,** fuir
flüchtiger Rechtsbrecher(m)	**fugitive from justice**	**fugitif recherché par la justice**
Flüchtling; Heimatvertriebener(m)	**refugee**	**réfugié**(m)
(Flugzeug-)(n)**Entführung**(f)	**hijacking**	**détournement**(m) **(d'avion)**
flüssig; liquid(e) Umlaufkapital flüssige Mittel; Bargeld	**liquid** – assets – funds	**disponible,** liquide liquidités(f) disponibilités(f)
f.o.b. (Frei an Bord)	**FOB** (free on board)	**franco bord**
folgern, schließen	**infer (to)**	**conclure**
Folgerung(f)**;** Rückschluß(m)	**inference**	**supposition**(f)**,** déduction(f), inférence(f)
Folterung(f)	**torture**	**torture**(f)
f.o.p. (Frei an Flugzeug)(n)	**FOP** (free on plane)	**franco avion**
f.o.q. (Frei Kai)(m)	**FOQ** (free on quay)	**franco quai**
f.o.r. (Frei Bannstation(f), Eisenbahnwaggon(m))	**FOR** (free on rail)	**franco wagon**

GERMAN	ENGLISH	FRENCH
Forderungspfändung(*f*); Verbot(*n*) (dem Drittschuldner)(*m*) Zahlung(*f*) zu leisten	**garnishment**	**saisie-arrêt**(*f*), opposition(*f*)
Forderungsrecht(*n*); obligatorischer Anspruch(*m*)	**chose in action**	**créance**(*f*), titre de créance; droit(*m*) incorporel permettant une action en justice
formal; formell	**formal**	**formel,** régulier, absolu, conventionnel
Formfehler	– error	vice de forme
formelle Anklageschrift(*f*)	**indictment**	**acte**(*m*) **d'accusation,** inculpation(*f*)
formloser Vertrag(*m*)	**simple contract**	**convention**(*f*) **verbale,** contrat(*m*) tacite, contrat sous seing privé
Forschung(*f*) **und Entwicklung**(*f*) (F & E)	**research and development (R & D)**	**recherche**(*f*) **et développement** (R & D)
Forum(*n*); Gremium(*n*)	**forum**	**forum**(*m*); tribunal(*m*) compétent (et son siège)
Fracht(*f*)	**freight**	**fret**(*m*), cargaison(*f*), transport(*m*) de marchandises; frais(*m*) de transport
Luft–	air –	transport par avion
See–	ocean (sea) –	transport maritime
Frachter(*m*); Verlader(*m*), Verfrachter(*m*)	**freighter**	**affréteur**(*m*); navire(*m*) marchand; wagon(*m*) de marchandises
Frage(*f*); Beanstandung(*f*)	**query**	**question**(*f*), interrogation(*f*)
Fragebogen(*m*)	**questionnaire**	**questionnaire**(*m*)
frei, unbesetzt	**vacant**	**vacant,** libre
frei	**free**	**libre,** en franchise, exempt
Frei Längsseite Seeschiff	– alongside ship (FAS)	franco quai
Frei an Bord	– on board (FOB)	franco bord
Frei an Flugzeug	– on plane (FOP)	franco avion
Frei Kai	– on quay (FOQ)	franco quai
Frei Bahnstation, Eisenbahnwaggon	– on rail (FOR)	franco wagon
Frei Lastwagen	– on truck (FOT)	franco camion
Freihafen	– port	port(*m*) libre
Freihandel	– trade	libre-échange
Frei Lastwagen(*m*)	**FOT** (free on truck)	**franco camion**
frei schwanken; in Umlauf(*m*) bringen	**float (to)**	**flotter;** émettre, lancer
Anleihe auflegen od. begeben	– a loan	lancer un emprunt
freie, unbesetzte Stelle	**vacancy**	**vacance**(*f*), emploi(*m*) vacant, poste(*f*) à pourvoir
Freiheit(*f*)	**liberty** (*cf. freedom*)	**liberté**(*f*)

GERMAN	ENGLISH	FRENCH
Freiheit(f)	**freedom**	**liberté**(f), franchise(f), immunité(f)
Versammlungs–	– of assembly	liberté d'association
Religions–	– of religion	liberté religieuse, liberté du culte
Rede–	– of speech	liberté d'expression
Presse–	– of the press	liberté de la presse
Handels–	– of trade	liberté du commerce
freilassen; entlassen	**release (to)**	**libérer**, relaxer, élargir, renoncer, délier, décharger
Freilassung(f); Erlösung; Entlastung	**release**	**mise**(f) **en liberté**, élargissement; cession(f) de propriété; décharge(f) mise(f) en vente; libération(f) de capitaux
Haftentlassung	– from custody	relaxe, mise en liberté
freisprechen, lossprechen, entbinden	**absolve (to)**	**acquitter**, absoudre
freisprechen (von e-r Anklage); abtragen (Schuld); entbinden von (Pflicht)	**acquit (to)**	**acquitter**, décharger
Freispruch(m)	**acquittal**	**acquittement**(m), décharge(f), quitus(m)
Freistellungsklausel(f); Haftungsausschluß–(f)	**exemption clause**	**clause**(m) **d'exonération**, clause d'exemption
freiwillig; unentgeltlich	**voluntary**	**volontaire**
freiwilliger Vergleich	– composition	concordat préventif de la faillite
freiwilliges Geständnis	– confession	aveu(m) spontané
Freizeichnungsklausel(f)	**exclusion clause**	**clause**(m) **d'exclusion**, refus(m) d'admission
Frist(f); Zeitbeschränkung(f)	**time-limit**	**délai**(m), limite(f) de temps
Fristverlängerung(f); Vollstreckungsaufschub(m)	**respite**	**sursis**(m), délai(m), répit(m)
Führerschein(m)	**driving licence**	**permis**(m) **de conduire**
füllen; bekleiden; besetzen	**fill (to)**	**remplir**, exécuter, suppléer à
eine freie Stelle besetzen	– a vacancy	pourvoir à une vacance
ein Formular ausfüllen	– in a form	remplir un formulaire
für (rechts)gültig erklären; bestätigen	**validate (to)**	**valider**
Fürsorge(f) **(soziale)**	**welfare (social)**	**bien-être social**, prévoyance(f) sociale, service(m) social
Wohlfahrtsausschuß	– committee	comité(m) de bienfaisance
Sozialarbeiter(in)	– officer	assistant(e)(m) social(e)

340

G

GERMAN	ENGLISH	FRENCH
Galgen(m)	**gallows**	**potence**(f), gibet(m)
Garantie(f); Gewährleistung(f)	**warranty**	**clause**(f) **pénale du contrat,** garantie(f); autorisation(f), justification(f)
Gastland(n); Aufnahmestaat(m)	**host country**	**pays**(m) **hôte,** pays d'accueil
Gaststaat(m) (EG)	**host member State** (EEC)	**pays membre invité** (CEE)
GATT (Allgemeines Zoll- und Handelsabkommen)	**GATT** (General Agreement on Tariffs and Trade)	**Accord**(m)**Général sur les Tarifs Douaniers et le Commerce**
(Gebäude(n) **der vier alten) Innungen**(f) **der Barrister**(m) **in London;** Berufsorganisation(f) der Barrister(m)	**Inns of Court** (UK)	**les quatre sociétés du barreau**
Gebühr(f); Vergütung(f)	**fee**	**honoraire(s),** cachet(m), cotisation(f); terre(f) ou droit réel transmissible
Anwaltshonorar	counsel's –	honoraires d'avocat
Gerichtskosten, –gebühren	court –	frais(m) de justice
Eigentumsrecht; bedingungsloses Eigentum(m)	– simple	propriété incondifionelle
Lizenzgebühr	licence –	droits de patente(f)
Gebühren(f), Abgaben(n); Beitrag(m)	**dues**	**dû**(m), droits(m), frais(m), redevance(f)
gebührend; ordnungsmäßig; rechtzeitig	**duly**	**dûment,** en temps utile
Gebührenerlaß(m)	**remission of charges**	**détaxe**(f)
Gebührenstempel(m); –marke	**stamp duty**	**droit**(m) **de timbre**
Geburtsrecht(n), angestammtes Recht(n)	**birthright**	**droit de naissance,** droit d'aînesse; patrimoine
Gefahr(f); Risiko(n)	**hazard**	**danger**(m), risque(m); jeu(m) de hasard
Gefahr(f); Risiko(n)	**peril**	**péril**(m), danger(m)
Seerisiken, Gefahren auf See (pl.)	– of the sea	fortune(f) de mer
Transportgefahr	– of transportation	danger(m) encouru pendant le transport

GERMAN	ENGLISH	FRENCH
gefährden	**jeopardise (to)**	**mettre en danger,** compromettre
Gefährdung(*f*) Verbot der doppelten Strafverfolgung eines Täters wegen derselben Tat	**jeopardy** double –	**danger**(*m*), risque(*m*) être traduit en justice pour un crime ou un délit dont on a déjà eu à répondre
gefährlich; nicht verkehrssicher	**unsafe**	**hasardeux,** risqué, dangereux
Gefangener(*m*); gefangen; für den Eigenbedarf(*m*)	**captive**	**captif, captive**(*m, f*)
Gefangener(*m*); Häftling	**prisoner**	**prisonnier**(*m*), **prisonnière**(*m*)
Gefängnis(*n*)	**gaol,** also spelled jail	**prison**(*f*), maison(*f*) d'arrêt
Gefängnis(*n*)	**jail**	**prison**(*f*), maison(*f*) d'arrêt
Gefängnis(*n*)	**prison**	**prison**(*f*)
Gegenforderung(*f*), –anspruch(*m*)	**counterclaim**	**demande**(*f*) **reconventionnelle**
Gegenklage(*f*), –beschuldigung(*f*)	**countercharge**	**contre-accusation**(*f*)
Gegenpartei(*f*)	**opposing (opposite) party**	**partie**(*f*) **opposée,** partie adverse
gegenseitig	**reciprocal**	**réciproque,** bilatéral
gegenseitig Versicherung auf Gegenseitigkeit Versicherungsverein auf Gegenseitigkeit –es Testament	**mutual** – insurance – insurance company – will	**mutuel** assurance(*f*) mutuelle société(*f*) d'assurances mutuelles donation(*f*) au dernier survivant
Gegenseitigkeit(*f*)	**reciprocity**	**réciprocité**(*f*)
gegenüberstellen; konfrontieren Zeugen gegenüberstellen	**confront (to)** – witnesses	**envisager,** confronter confronter les témoins
Gegner(*m*), gegnerische Partei(*f*), Prozeßgegner(*m*)	**adversary**	**adversaire**(*m*), partie(*f*) adverse, contradicteur(*m*)
Gehalt(*m*); Besoldung(*f*)	**salary**	**traitement**(*m*), appointement(*m*), salaire(*m*)
geheimes Einverständnis(*n*); stillschweigende Einwilligung(*f*)	**connivance**	**collusion**(*f*), complicité(*f*)
Geheimhaltung(*f*); Verschwiegenheit(*f*) Geheimhaltungsklausel	**secrecy** – clause	**secret**(*m*) clause(*f*) de secret
Geheimnis(*n*) Gesetz zum Schutz von Staatsgeheimnissen	**secret** Official Secrets Act	**secret** Loi(*f*) relative aux secrets d'État
Geisel(*f*)	**hostage**	**otage**(*m*)

GERMAN	ENGLISH	FRENCH
geistig	**mental**	**mental**(m)
seelische Grausamkeit	– cruelty	cruauté(f) mentale
Geistesstörung	– disorder	aberration(f) mentale
psychiatrisches Krankenhaus;	– hospital, home	hôpital(m) psychiatrique
–e Anstalt		
Geisteskrankheit	– incapacity	incapacité(f) mental
Pflege der Geisteskranken	– nursing	soins(m) psychiatriques
geistiges Eigentum(n)	**intellectual property**	**propriété**(f) **intellectuelle**
Geldmarkt(m)	**money market**	**marché**(m) **monétaire**
Geldstrafe(f)	**fine**	**amende**(f)
unter Androhung e-r Geldstrafe	under penalty of (a)	sous peine d'amende
	–	
Gemeindeland(n); Allmende	**common land**	**terrain**(m) **communal,** banal
Gemeindesteuer(m) (UK)	**rates** (UK)	**impôts**(m) **locaux** (UK)
gemeinsam	**joint**	**solidaire,** collectif, conjoint
–es Vorgehen	– action	action(f) collective
–es Sorgerecht	– custody	garde(m, f) conjointe d'un enfant
Mitbeklagter	– defendant	codéfendeur(m)
–es Interesse	– interest	intérêt(m) commun
–e Haftung; Gesamthaftung	– liability	responsabilité(f) conjointe
–es Eigentum; Miteigentum	– ownership	copropriété(f)
Mit-, Nebenkläger	– plaintiff	codemandeur(m)
–e Verantwortung; Solidarhaftung	– responsibility	responsabilité solidaire
Joint Venture; Gemeinschaftsuntenehmen	– venture	coentreprise(f), opération(f) conjointe, association(f) en participation
Gemeinschaft(f) (EG); Gemeinde(f)	**community**	**collectivité**(f)
gemeinschaftliche Rechtsvorschriften (EG)	Community legislation (EC)	législation(f) communautaire (CE)
Gemeinwesen(n); Staat(m), Nation(f)	**commonwealth**	**État**(m), Commonwealth
genau prüfen; (Stimmen) nachzählen	**scrutinise (to)**	**examiner de très près,** enquêter minutieusement
Genehmigung(f)	**permit**	**permis**(m), licence(f), autorisation(f)
Bau–	building –	permis de construire
Export– (Import–)	export (import) –	autorisation d'exporter (d'importer)
Arbeits–	labour –	permis de travail
Genehmigung(f); Konzession(f); Lizenz(f)	**licence, license** (US)	**permis**(m), autorisation(f), concession(f), brevet(m)
Führerschein	driving –	permis de conduire
Nummernschild; Kraftfahrzeug-Zulassungsnummer	– plate	plaque(f) d'immatriculation
Heiratserlaubnis, –genehmigung	marriage –	certificat(m) de extrait (d'acte) de mariage

343

GERMAN	ENGLISH	FRENCH
General- –bevollmächtiger(m); allgemeiner Handelsvertreter(m) Große Havarie –unternehmer Gesamtschaden; allgemeiner Schaden	**general** – agent – average – contractor – damages	**général**(m) homme(m) d'affaires avaries(f) communes entrepreneur(m) général dommages-intérêt(m) qui découlent naturellement de la plainte
allgemeines Pfandrecht Mitgliederversammlung; Hauptversammlung unbeschränkt (persönlich)haftender Gesellschafter allgemeine offene Handelsgesellschaft; allgemeine Personengesellschaft	– lien – meeting – partner – partnership	privilège(m) général assemblée(f) générale associé(m) ordinaire société(m) en nom collectif
generell, alles umfassend; Gesamt– Blankovollmacht	**blanket** – authority	**d'application**(f) **générale** carte blanche
Genossenschaft(f); Konsumverein(m)	**cooperative society**	**coopérative,** société(f) coopérative
Genozid(m); Völkermord(m)	**genocide**	**génocide**(m)
Genuß(n); Nießbrauch(m)	**enjoyment**	**jouissance**(f), exercice(m) d'un droit
Eigentumsausübung	– of property	possession(f)
gerecht; billig; fair Praxis der Nichtdiskriminierung im Außenhandel	**fair** – trade practices	**juste,** impartial libre échange dans des conditions de réciprocité loyale
ordentliches Gerichtsverfahren; unparteiisches Verfahren	– trial	procès(m) équitable
gerecht; rechtmäßig	**just**	**conforme à la loi,** juste, équitable
Gerechtigkeit(f); Rechtspflege(f); Richter(m) (Titel)	**justice**	**justice**(f), équité(f); administration(f) de la justice; titre(m) donné aux magistrats

GERMAN	ENGLISH	FRENCH
Gericht(*n*)	**court**	**cour**(*f*) **de justice,** tribunal
Verwaltungs–	administrative –	tribunal administratif
Schieds–	arbitration –	tribunal d'arbitrage
erstinstanzliches – für mehrere Bezirke (*US*)	circuit –	tribunal de première instance (*US*)
– für Zivilsachen	civil –	tribunal civil
Grafschafts–; Kreis– (*US*); Amts–	county –	tribunal de première instance
Berufungs–	– of appeal	cour d'appel
– für Strafsachen, Strafkammer	criminal –	cour(*f*) de juridiction criminelle
(Bundes-)Bezirksgericht (*US*)	district – (*US*)	tribunal(*m*) fédéral de première instance (*US*)
Bundes–	federal –	cour fédérale
unteres –; Instanzgericht	inferior –	tribunal inférieure
erstinstanzliches Gericht (ohne Geschworene); Amts–	magistrates' –	tribunal de première instance
Polizei–	police –	tribunal de police
Nachlaß–	probate – (*US*)	tribunal des successions et des tutelles (*US*)
einzelstaatliches – (*US*)	state –	tribunal d'État
höhere Instanz; übergeordnetes –	superior –	tribunal supérieure
Oberster Gerichtshof; Oberstes Bundes– (*US*) höheres Berufungs–	supreme –	cour suprême
erkennendes –; – erster Instanz	trial –	tribunal de première instance
gerichtlich; richterlich	**judicial**	**judiciaire,** juridique
richterliche Handlung	– act	acte(*m*) judiciaire
Gerichtsbezirk	– district	ressort(*m*) territorial d'un tribunal
Kenntnisnahme des Gerichts	– notice	reconnaissance(*f*) d'un fait par la justice
richterliche Gewalt; Justizgewalt	– power	pouvoir judiciaire
Gerichtsverhandlung	– proceeding	procédure(*f*) judiciaire
gerichtliche Überprüfung	– review	révision(*f*) judiciaire
Gerichtswesen	– system	système(*m*) judiciaire
gerichtlich verhandeln, untersuchen	**try (to)**	**juger,** mettre en jugement; **essayer**
Prozeß führen; über eine Sache verhandeln	– a case	juger une affaire (au tribunal)
gerichtliche Anweisung(*f*); Regel(*f*)	**precept**	**mandat**(*m*) **d'un magistrat;** feuille(*f*) de contributions; précepte(*m*), principe(*m*)
Gerichtliche Trennung(*f*)	**separation**	**séparation**(*f*) **(des époux)**
Ehetrennung; Aufhebung der ehelichen Gemeinschaft	judicial –	séparation(*f*) juciciaire (des époux)
(gerichtliche) Untersuchung(*f*); Beweisaufnahme(*f*)	**inquest**	**enquête**(*f*)
amtliche Leichenschau	coroner's –	enquête après mort d'homme menée par un coroner(*m*)
Leichnam gerichtlich untersuchen; obduzieren	to hold an –	procéder à une enquête

GERMAN	ENGLISH	FRENCH
gerichtliche Verfügung(f), Anordnung(f)	**injunction**	**arrêt**(m) **de suspension,** de sursis; jugement(m) avant faire droit; injonction(f), ordre
einstweilige Verfügung (auf Unterlassung)	interim –	ordonnance(f) de référé
einstweilige Verfügung (zur Vornahme einer Handlung)	mandatory –	commandement(m) du tribunal
endgültige gerichtliche Verfügung (zur Unterlassung)	perpetual –	ordonnance définitive
einstweilige Verfügung (zur Unterlassung); gerichtliches Verbot	preventive –	ordonnance de ne pas faire
einstweilige Verfügung (zur Unterlassung);	prohibitive –	ordonnance de ne pas faire
einstweilige Verfügung	temporary –	ordonnance temporaire
gerichtliche Verfügung(f); Gerichtsbeschluß(m)	**court order**	**injonction**(f)
gerichtliche Verfügung(f)/ **Anweisung**(f); Klageschrift(f); Schriftstück	**writ**	**exploit**(m), ordonnance(f), acte(m) judiciaire
Arrestbefehl; Pfändungs-, Zwangsvallstreckung	– of attachment	ordonnance de saisie-arrêt
Vollstreckungsbefehl;	– of enforcement	ordonnance d'exécution
gerichtliche Anordnung eines Haftprüfungstermins; Vorführungsbefehlim	– of execution	injonction(f) de déférer un accusé devant le tribunal
Beschlagnahmeverfügung (gerichtliche Einsetzung e-s Zwangsverwalters)	– of habeas corpus– of sequestration	exploit de saisie-exécution séquestre(m) judiciaire
Prozeßladung mit Klageschrift	– of summons	assignation(f), citation (à comparaître)
gerichtliche Verfügung(f); Verfahren(n)	**process**	**processus**(m), procédé(m), méthode(f)
gerichtliches Verfahren	juridical –	action(f) en justice, procès
Zusteller (e-r gerichtlichen Verfügung)	– server	huissier
gerichtliche Vorladung(f)	**summons**	**citation**(f) **à comparaître,** assignation(f)
jdn eine Ladung zustellen	to serve a – on s.o.	assigner qqu'un (à comparaître)
Gerichtsakte(f); Prozeßakte(f)	**court record**	**procès-verbal**(m)
Gerichtsbarkeit(f); Gerichtshoheit(f); Gerichtsstand(m); Rechtsprechung(f)	**jurisdiction**	**juridiction**(f); compétence(f) judiciaire
allgemeine Zuständigkeit	general –	toutes matières contentieuses, compétence générale
besondere Zuständigkeit	special –	compétence d'exception
Gerichtsbarkeit(f); Rechtsprechung(f)	**judicature**	**magistrature**(f); période(f) d'exercice d'un juge
Gerichtsdiener(m); Justizwachtmeister(m)	**usher**	**huissier**

GERMAN	ENGLISH	FRENCH
Gericht(shof)(*m*); Tribunal(*n*)	**tribunal**	**tribunal**(*m*), cour(*f*) de justice
Finanzgericht	– for tax and other financial matters (Germany)	tribunal traitant les affaires financiéres (Allemagne)
Gerichtsmedizin(*f*)	**forensic medicine**	**médecine**(*m*) **légale**
Gerichtsstand(*m*); Zuständigkeit(*f*)	**venue**	**juridiction**(*f*), lieu(*m*) du jugement
Gerichtsverhandlung(*f*); Verfahren(*n*)	**trial**	**procès**(*m*); essai(*m*)
Zivilverfahren	civil –	action(*f*) civile
Hauptverhandlung ohne Geschworene	summary –	jugement(*m*) sommaire
Schwurgerichtsverfahren	– by jury	procés conduit devant un jury première instance
Prozeßgericht; Instanz	– court	cour(*f*) jugeant en
Tatrichter; Richter der ersten Instanz	– judge	juge(*m*) du fond
Gerichtswesen(*n*); Rechts–; Richterstand(*m*)	**judiciary**	**judiciaire** (*adj.*); magistrature(*f*) (*n*)
geringfügig; unbedeutend	**petty**	**mineur**(*m*), peu important
Bagatelldiebstahl	– larceny	vol(*m*) simple
Übertretung; Bagatelldelikt	– offence	infraction(*f*) mineure, contravention(*f*)
Bagatelldiebstahl	– theft	larcin(*m*)
Gerüst(*n*); Schafott(*n*)	**scaffold**	**gibet**(*m*), potence(*f*)
gesamtschuldnerisch; solidarisch	**jointly and severally**	**conjointement et solidairement**
gesamtschuldnerisch haftbar	– liable	solidairement et conjointement responsable
Geschäftemacher(*m*); Schieber(*m*)	**profiteering**	**mercantilisme**(*m*)
Geschäfte(*n*); Transaktionen; Geschäftsverbindungen	**dealings**	**menées**(*f*) **commerciales**, transactions boursières
(Geschäftsbeziehungen) unterhalten; in Erwägung(*f*) ziehen	**entertain (to)**	**recevoir**, admettre
geschäftsführender Direktor(*m*); Generaldirektor(*m*)	**managing director**	**administrateur**(*m*) **délégué**(*m*), administrateur(*m*) gérant
Geschäftsräume(*m*); Betriebsräume(*m*)	**premises**	**intitulé**(*m*); prémisses(*f*); local(*m*), (les) lieux(*m*), (l')immeuble(*m*)
Geschäft(svorgang)(*n*); Durchführung(*f*)	**transaction**	**transaction**(*f*), compromis(*m*), arrangement(*m*); gestion(*f*), conduite d'une affaire
geschlossen	**closed-end**	**à capital limité**, fixe
–e (Investment-)gesellschaft	– (investment) company	société à capital fixe

GERMAN	ENGLISH	FRENCH
geschuldet; zustehend; fällig; gebührend	**due**	**dû**(*m*)**;** légitime
(nach) reifliche(r) Überlegung	– consideration	réflexion(*f*) voulue, mûre réflexion
Fälligkeitsdatum; –termin	– date	échéance(*f*), (en) temps utile
ordnungsgemäßes Verfahren; ordentliches Gerichtsverfahren	– process of law (*US*)	procédure judiciaire(*f*) de sauvegarde de la liberté individuelle
geschützt; gedeckt; heimlich	**covert**	**couvert**
Geschworener(*m*)	**juror**	**juré,** membre(*m*) du jury
Gesellschaft(*f*)	**society**	**société**(*f*)**,** association(*f*)
Bausparkasse	building –	établissement(*m*) de crédit foncier
Genossenschaft; Konsumverein rechtsfähige Gesellschaft; eingetragene –	cooperative – incorporated –	coopérative(*f*) société constituée
Gesellschafter(*m*)	**partner**	**associé**(*m*)
persönlich (unbeschränkt) haftender –	general –	commandité(*m*)
Kommanditist; beschränkt haftender –	limited –	commanditaire(*m*)
Gesellschaftsverzeichnis(*n*)**;** Liste der Aktionäre	**list of shareholders**	**liste**(*f*) **des actionnaires**
Gesetze geben(*n*)**,** – machen, – erlassen	**legislate (to)**	**légiférer**
Gesetzeserlaß(*m*)**;** Gesetzeskraftverleihung(*f*)	**enactment**	**loi,** ordonnance(*f*), décret(*m*)
gesetzestreu	**law-abiding**	**respectueux des lois**
Gesetzestreue(*f*)	**obedience to the law**	**respect**(*m*) **de la loi**
Gesetzesvollzug(*m*)	**law enforcement**	**application**(*f*) **de la loi**
gesetzeswidrige Handlung(*f*)**;** standeswidriges Verhalten	**malpractice**	**négligence**(*f*) **professionnelle,** faute(*f*)
gesetzgebend	**legislative**	**législatif,** législative
–e Versammlung	– assembly	assemblée(*f*) législative
–e Gewalt; Legislative	– power	pouvoir(*m*) législatif
Gesetzgebung(*f*)**;** Gesetze(*n*)	**legislation**	**législation**(*f*)
gesetzlich	**statutory**	**prévu**(*f*) **par la loi,** légal, statutaire, réglementaire
gesetzlich; rechtmäßig; rechtsgültig	**lawful**	**légal,** licite, légitime
Volljährigkeit	– age	majorité(*f*) (légale)
gesetzlicher, rechtmäßiger Erbe	– heir	héritier(*m*) légitime

GERMAN	ENGLISH	FRENCH
gesetzmäßig; rechtmäßig; rechtsgültig; juristisch	**legal**	**légal,** licite, légitime, judiciaire, juridique
Volljährig-, Mündigkeit	– age	âge(m) de la majorité légale
Armenrecht, Prozeßkostenhilfe (UK); unentgeltliche Beratungshilfe (US)	– aid	assistance(f) judiciaire
Rechts-, Geschäftsfähigkeit	– capacity	capacité(f) judiciaire
Geschäftsfähigkeit	– competence	compétence judiciaire
Geschäftsunfähigkeit; Prozeßunfähigkeit (US)	– disability	incapacité(f) légale
Schuldausschließungsgrund; rechtliche erhebliche Einwendung(f)	– excuse	excuse(f) légale
Geschäftsunfähigkeit	– incapacity	incapacité légale
gesetzlicher Haftpflicht; – Haftung	– liability	responsabilité(f) légale
juristische (rechtsfähige) Person	– person	personne(f) morale
Gerichtsverfahren; Prozeß	– proceedings	poursuites(f) judiciares
Vertreter in Rechtssachen; gesetzlicher Vertreter; Nachlaßverwalter(m)	– representative	représentant(m, f) légal
Rechtsstellung; –position	– status	statut(m) légal
Gesetz(n); Statut(en)(n); Satzung(f)	**statute**	**acte(m) législatif,** loi(f) écrite (opp. 'common law')
Geständnis(n); Bekenntnis(n)	**confession**	**confession(f),** aveu(m)
gestehen; bekennen	**confess (to)**	**se confesser,** avouer
Gestehungskosten; Einzelkosten	**prime cost**	**prix(m) de revient,** prix de fabrication
Gesundheit(f)	**health**	**santé(f)**
medizinisches Versorgungszentrum	– centre	dispensaire(m), centre(m) de soins
–szeugnis, –sattest	– certificate	certificat(m) médical
–srisiko	– hazard	risque(m) pour la santé
Krankenversicherung	– insurance	assurance(f) maladie
(öffentliches) –swesen;	public –	santé(f) publique
Gewalt(f) anwenden	**resort (to) to violence**	**avoir recours à la violence**
Gewaltanwendung(f); Körperverletzung(f), Mißhandlung(f), tätlicher Angriff	**battery**	**voies(f) de fait**
schwere tätliche Beleidigung (Mißhandlung); Körperverletzung	assault and –	coups(m) et blessures
Gewalt(m)(-tätigkeit)(f)	**violence**	**violence(f),** voies(f) de fait
Gewalttätigkeit(f); Ausschreitung(f); grobe Beleidigung(f)	**outrage**	**outrage(m);** atrocité(f)
Gewerkschaft(f)	**trade union**	**syndicat(m)**
Gewinn(m); Ertrag(m); Nutzen(m)	**profit**	**profit(m),** bénéfice(m), boni(m), gain(m), prime(f)

349

GERMAN	ENGLISH	FRENCH
Gewinn(m); Verdienst(m); Erwerb(m)	**gain**	**gain**(m), profit(m), bénéfice(m)
Gewißheit(f), Sicherheit(f); Rechtssicherheit(f)	**certainty**	**certitude**(f), conviction(f)
Sicherheits-, Gewißheitsgrad	degree of –	degré(m) de certitude
Gewohnheitsrecht(n)	**customary law**	**droit**(m) **coutumier**
Gewohnheitsrecht(n); (ungeschriebenes) geme in Recht	**common law**	**droit**(m) **coutumier et jurisprudentiel**
gewöhnlicher Aufenthaltsort(m)	**habitual residence**	**domicile**(m) **habituel**
Gift	**poison**	**poison**(m)
Girokonto(n) (UK); Postgirokonto(n)	**giro account**	**CCP** (compte courant postal)
Glaube(m)	**faith**	**foi**(f), confiance(f)
in bösem Glauben, wider Treu und Glauben	in bad –	de bonne foi
in gutem Glauben; nach Treu und Glauben	in good –	de mauvaise foi
Gläubiger(m); Kreditgeber(m)	**creditor**	**créditeur**(m), créancier(m)
Glaubwürdigkeit(f)	**credibility**	**crédibilité**(f)
gleich; gleichberechtigt	**equal**	**égal**
Gleichberechtigung; Rechtsgleichheit	– rights	égalité(f) des droits
Stimmengleichheit	– votes	partage(m) des voix
Gleichgewicht(n)	**equilibrium**	**équilibre**(m)
Gleichwertigkeit(f)	**equivalence**	**équivalence**(f)
Glücksspiel(n)	**gambling**	**jeux**(m) **de hasard,** jeux d'argent
Gnade(f)	**mercy**	**grâce**(f), clémence(f), pitié(f)
Euthanasie; Tötung auf Verlangen	– killing	euthanasie(f)
–ngesuch	petition for –	recours(m) en grâce
Gnade(f)	**grace**	**grâce**(f), pardon(m), amnistie(f)
–nfrist, Nachfrist	– act of	loi(f) d'amnistie
Grad(m); Rang(m); (s. Mord)	**degree** (cf. murder)	**degré**(m)
Grafschaft(f); Verwaltungsbezirk(m)	**county**	**comté**(m)
Grafschaftsrat; Bezirksausschuß	– council	conseil(m) général
Grafschaftsgericht; Kreisgericht (US); Amtsgericht	– court	tribunal(m) de première instance
Grausamkeit(f)	**cruelty**	**cruauté**(f), mauvais traitements(m)
seelische Grausamkeit	mental –	cruauté mentale, excès(m) et injures(f) graves
Gremium(n); Ausschuß(m)	**panel**	**groupe**(m), réunion(f) (de spécialistes); panneau(m), tableau(m)
Geschworene(nliste)	jury –	jury(m)
Grenzeinnahmen	**marginal revenue**	**recette**(m) **marginale**

GERMAN	ENGLISH	FRENCH
Grenzkosten	marginal cost	coût(m) marginal
Grenzübergang(m); –übertritt(m)	border crossing	passage(m) de frontière
Größenvorteile(m); Rationalisierung(f)	economies of scale	économies(f) d'échelle
Großhändler(m)	wholesaler	grossiste
Grund(m) Rechtsmittelbegründung; Berufungsbegründung	ground – for appeal	raison(f), cause(f) motif(m) d'appel
Urteilsbegründung	grounds for judgment	considérants
Grundbuch(n); Kataster(m)	land register	cadastre(m), registre(m) du cadastre
Grunddienstbarkeit(f)	easement	servitude(f), droit(m) d'usage
Grundeigentümer(m)	freeholder	propriétaire(m) foncier
Grundeigentum(n); (zeitl. unbeschränktes) Eigentumsrecht(n) (an Grundbesitz)	freehold	tenure(f) en propriété perpétuelle et libre
gründen; nachweisen; bestätigen	establish (to)	établir
Grundpfandrecht(n); Hypothek(f) Mobiliarhypothek	mortgage chattel –	hypothèque(f) hypothèque sur biens mobiliers
Hypothekenpfandbrief, –urkunde Hypothekenbrief	– bond – deed	obligation(f) hypothécaire contrat(m) d'hypothèque, acte hypothécaire
Hypothekendarlehen; –anleihe	– loan	emprunt(m), prêt(m) hypothécaire
Grundprinzipien(n)	guiding principles	principe(m) conducteur
Grundstücke(n); Immobilien	realty	biens(m) immobiliers
Grundstücksauflassungsurkunde(f); Verzichtsurkunde(f)	quitclaim deed	acte(m) de transfert d'un droit ou d'un titre par voie de reconciliation(f), mais sans garantie de validité
Grundstücksmakler(m) (US); Immobilien–	realtor (US)	agent(m) immobilier (US)
Gründung(f); Unternehmen(n); Feststellung(f)	establishment	'establishment', classes(f) dirigeantes; fondation(f), assiette(f), établissement(m)
Bankinstitut Geschäftsbetrieb Ort der Niederlassung	banking – business – place of –	établissement bancaire maison(f) de commerce siège(m) social
Gründung(f) (e-r juristischen Person(f), Kapitalgesellschaft)(f)	incorporation	incorporation(f), fusion(f), constitution(f); octroi(m) de la personnalité morale
–sbescheinigung;	certificate of –	certificat(m) de constitution
–urkunde	charter of –	statut(m) de constitution de société
Grundvermögen(n); Liegenschaften(n)	landed property	propriété(f) foncière, biens(m) immobiliers

GERMAN	ENGLISH	FRENCH
Gruppenklage(*f*); von einer Interessengruppe angestrengte Klage(*f*)	**class action** *(US)*	**action**(*f*) **de groupe** *(US)*
Gruppenversicherung(*f*)	**group insurance**	**assurance**(*f*) **collective**
gültig; zahlungsfähig sichere Forderung in gutem Glauben, nach Treu und Glauben	**good** – debts – faith	**bon**(*m*) créance(*f*) recouvrable bonne foi(*f*)
Gutachter(*m*); Sachverständiger(*m*); Havariekommissar(*m*)	**surveyor**	**contrôleur**(*m*), inspecteur(*m*), expert(*m*)
gütlich; freundschaftlich gütliche Einigung, Regelung; Vergleich	**amicable** – settlement	**amiable** arrangement(*m*) à l'amiable

H

GERMAN	ENGLISH	FRENCH
Haag(*m*) –er Abkommen –er Schiedshof	**Hague (The)** – Convention – Tribunal	**La Haye** Convention(*f*) de La Haye tribunal(*m*) de La Haye
Habeas Corpus; richterliche Haftprüfung(*f*)	**habeas corpus**	**habeas corpus**
Hafen(*m*) –behörde –gebühren	**port** – authority – charges	**port**(*m*) (les) autorités(*f*) portuaires droits(*m*) portuaires
Haft(*f*); Obhut(*f*), Sorgerecht(*n*); Verwahrung(*f*)	**custody**	**garde,** garde d'un enfant; détention(*f*), état(*m*) d'arrestation
Untersuchungshaft; Sicherungsverwahrung	preventive –	détention préventive
Schutzhaft	protective –	détention à fins de protection
sichere Aufbewahrung; Verwahrung	safe –	bonne(*f*) garde
haftbar; haftpflichtig	**responsible**	**responsable; compétent**
haftbar; verantwortlich	**liable**	**responsable (de)**; assujetti à, tenu de; passible de, sujet à
Haftbefehl(*m*) (*US*)	**capias** (*US*)	**ordre**(*m*) **d'arrestation** (*US*)
Haftung(*f*); Verbindlichkeit(*f*)	**liability**	**responsabilité**(*f*), obligation(*f*), passif
Eventual-	contingent –	obligation future; dépenses(*f*) imprévues
kurzfristige Verbindlichkeiten (*pl.*)	current –	passif exigible à court terme
gemeinsame Haftung; Gesamthaftung	joint –	responsabilité conjointe
beschränkte Haftung	limited –	responsabilité limitée
persönliche Haftung	personal –	responsabilité personnelle
Gefährdungshaftung; verschuldensunabhängige Haftung	strict –	responsabilité inconditionnelle
Hagelversicherung(*f*)	**hail insurance**	**assurance**(*f*) **contre la grêle**
Halbfabrikate(*n*)	**semifinished goods**	**produits**(*m*) **semi-finis**
Handballenabdruck(*m*)	**palmprint**	**empreinte**(*f*) **de la main**
(Handels-)Artikel(*m*); Ware; Rohstoff(*m*)	**commodity**	**marchandise**(*f*), denrées(*f*)

GERMAN	ENGLISH	FRENCH
Handelsgesellschaft(f)	**trading** company	**société**(f) **commerciale**
Handelsname(m); Firmenname(m);	**trade name**	**nom**(m) **commercial** **raison**(f) **sociale**,enseigne(f)
Handelsrecht(n)	**mercantile law**	**droit**(m) **commercial**
Handgemenge(n); Prügelei(f)	**scuffle**	**rixe**(f), bagarre(f), échauffourrée(f)
Händler(m); Wertpapier–(n)	**dealer**	**négociant,** marchand; courtier(m) de change, cambiste(m) (US); 'dealer'(m), trafiquant(m) de stupéfiant
Handlungsanzeige(f)	**notification of an act**	**notification**(f) **d'un acte,** d'une mesure
Handschellen(f)	**handcuffs**	**menottes**(f)
Härte(f); Strenge(f)	**severity**	**sévérité**(f), rigueur(f); violence(f)
Schwere e-r Straftat, e-s Delikts	– of an offence	gravité(f) d'un crime, d'un délit
Haschisch(n)	**hashish**	**haschisch**(m)
Haushalt(ung)svorstand(m)	**householder**	**chef**(m) **de famille;** locataire(m, f), propriétaire(m, f)
Hausieren	**peddling**	**colportage**(m)
Hehlerei(f)	**receiving of stolen** **goods**	**recel**(m) **de marchandises** **volées**
Heimat(f); Habitat(n)	**habitat**	**habitat**(m)
Heimfall(m) **herrenlosen** **Vermögens an den Staat**(m); Staatserbrecht	**escheat**	**déshérence**(f), bien(m) tombé en déshérence
Heirat(f); Ehe(f) Ehevertrag Heiratserlaubnis Ehevertrag Scheinehe	**marriage** – articles – licence – settlement sham –	**mariage**(m) contrat(m) de mariage dispense(f) de bans contrat de mariage mariage simulé
Helfershelfer(m), Gehilfe(m)	**aider and abettor**	**complice**(m)
herausfordern	**provoke (to)**	**provoquer,** inciter
Herausforderung(f)	**provocation**	**provocation**(f)
herrschendes Grundstück(n) **(bei** **Grunddienstbarkeit)**	**dominant tenement**	**fonds**(m) **dominant**
hervorragend; offenstehend, ausstehend	**outstanding**	**échu,** arriéré, en souffrance
Heuchler(m); Prätendent(m)	**pretender**	**prétendant**(m)
Hilfe(leistung)(f), Beistand(m); Förderung(f), Beihilfe(f); Rechtsbeistand	**aid**	**aide**(f), assistance(f), secours(m)
Hilfsbeamter(m); Gerichtsdiener(m); Gerichtsvollzieher(m) Gutsverwalter	**bailiff**	**huissier**(m)

GERMAN	ENGLISH	FRENCH
Hindernis(n)**;** Benachteiligung(f); Behinderung(f)	**handicap**	**handicap**(m)**,** inaptitude(f)
Hinderung(f)**(sgrund)**(m)**;** rechtshemmender(m) Einwand(m); Rechtsverwirkung	**estoppel**	**exclusion**(f)**,** empêchément(m)
Verwirkung des Einwands gegen den Inhalt einer gesiegelten Urkunde;	– by deed	écartement(m) du bénéfice de certains droits par acte notarié
Ausschluß der nochmaligen Prozeßführung über denselben Streitgegenstand	– by judgment	déchéance(f) de ses droits par jugement
hineinziehen; verwickeln	**implicate (to)**	**compromettre,** impliquer
hinreichender Beweis(m)**;** Glaubhaftmachung(f)	**substantial evidence**	**preuve**(f) **suffisante**
hintergehen, betrügen; verleiten	**beguile (to)**	**tromper,** duper
Hinterleger(m)**;** Einzahler(m)	**depositor**	**déposant**(m)
hinzuwählen; kooptieren	**coopt (to)**	**coopter**
Hochverrat(m)**;** Landesverrat(m)	**high treason**	**haute trahison**
höhere Instanz(f)**;** übergeordnetes Gericht	**superior court**	**tribunal**(m) **supérieure**
höherer akademischer Grad der jurist. Fakultät(f)	**LLM**	**maître**(m) **en droit**
honorieren; einlösen e-n Scheck einlösen	**honour (to)** – a cheque	**honorer,** respecter honorer un chèque
Hörensagen(n)	**hearsay**	**ouï-dire**(f)
horizontale Integration(f)	**horizontal integration**	**intégration horizontale**(f)
hypothekarisch; pfandrechtlich	**hypothecary**	**hypothécaire**
hypothekarisch belasten	**incumber (to),** alternative spelling of encumber	**grever,** gêner
hypothekarisch belasten; verpfänden	**mortgage (to)**	**hypothéquer**
Hypothekengläubiger(m)**;** Pfandgläubiger(m)	**mortgagee**	**créancier hypothécaire**
Hypothekenschuldner(m)**;** Verpfänder(m)	**mortgagor**	**débiteur**(m) **hypothécaire**
hypothetisch; mutmaßlich;	**hypothetical**	**hypothétique**(f)

I

GERMAN	ENGLISH	FRENCH
(ideeller) Firmenwert(*m*)	**goodwill**	**achalandage**(*m*), fonds(*m*) de commerce; profit(*m*) net
identifizieren	**identify (to)**	**identifier**
Identifizierung(*f*)	**identification**	**identification**(*f*)
Kennkarte, Personalausweis	– card	carte(*f*) d'identité
Kennkarte, Personalausweis	– certificate	acte(*m*) de notoriété
Erkennungs–, Kennzeichen	– mark	signe(*m*) d'identification
Identität(*f*)	**identity**	**identité**(*f*)
gefälschte –	false –	fausse(*f*) identité
Personenverwechslung	mistaken –	erreur(*f*) sur la personne
illegal; rechtswidrig	**illegal**	**illégal,** illicite
Illegalität(*f*); Rechtswidrigkeit(*f*)	**illegality**	**illégalité**
immateriell; nicht körperlich	**incorporeal**	**incorporel**
–e Gegenstände	– property	biens(*m*) incorporels
Immaterialgüterrechte	– rights	droits(*m*) incorporels
immaterielle Vermögenswerte(*m*)	**intangible assets**	**actif incorporel**
Immobilien; Liegenschaften	**immovables**	**biens**(*m*) **immobiliers**
Immunität(*f*)	**immunity**	**immunité**(*f*), exemption(*f*), exonération(*f*)
diplomatische –	diplomatic –	immunité diplomatique
gerichtliche –	judicial –	immunité juridique
in Abrede(*f*) **stellen;** leugnen; verweigern	**deny (to)**	**nier,** contester
in Besitz(*m*) **nehmen;** mit Beschlag(*m*) (Arrest)(*m*) belegen	**distrain (to)**	**saisir,** opérer une saisie
in doppelter Ausfertigung(*f*) **(Urkunden)**(*f*); zweiteilig	**bipartite**	**biparti,** bilatéral
in Geldverlegenheit(*f*); Zahlungsschwierigkeit(*f*)	**embarrassed**	**gêné,** embarassé; grevé(*f*) d'hypothèques
in gutem Glauben; gutgläubig, redlich	**bona fide**	**bonne foi**(*f*)
gutgläubiger Inhaber (Eigentümer)	– holder	détenteur(*m*) de bonne foi
solides Angebot	– offer	offre(*f*) ferme(*f*)
in Haft nehmen; zurück–, einbehalten	**detain (to)**	**retenir,** détenir, garder

GERMAN	ENGLISH	FRENCH
in Verwahrung(f) **nehmen** (gerichtlich od. behördlich)	**impound (to)**	**déposer (des documents au greffe)**; saisir, confisquer
Inbesitznahme(f); Beschlagnahme(f)	**distraint**	**saisie-exécution**(f); l'objet saisi
Inbesitznahme(f); Beschlagnahme(f); Not(lage)(f)	**distress**	**détresse**(f), désespoir(m); saisie(f) en cas de non-paiement du loyer
indirekte Steuer(m); Verbrauchssteuer(m); Gewerbesteuer(m)	**excise tax**	**contributions**(f) **indirectes**, impôt(m) indirect
Indizienbeweis(m)	**circumstantial evidence**	**présomptions**(f), preuve(f) indirecte
Indossament(n); Vermerk(m); Bestätigung(f)	**endorsement**	**endos**, endossement(m), approbation(f), visa
Indossament(n); Vermerk(m), Bestätigung(f)	**indorsement,** alternative spelling of endorsement	**approbation**(f) **(d'un appel)**; visa(m); appui(m), soutien(m)
Indossant(m); Girant(m); Begeber(m)	**endorser**	**endosseur**(m), concessionnaire(m), avaliste(m)
indossieren; (auf der Rückseite einer Urkunde) vermerken; zustimmen	**endorse (to)**	**endosser,** souscrire à
Informant(m); Gewährsmann(m)	**informant**	**dénonciateur**(m), délateur(m)
Information(f); Bestellung(f) eines vor Gericht(n) auftretenden Anwalts; Anweisung, Unterweisung; Einsatzbesprechung	**briefing**	**exposé**; constitution(f) de dossier
Inhaber(m); Besitzer(m) Treuhänder Aktien–	**holder** – in trust – of shares, shareholder	**détenteur**(m), porteur(m) détenteur(m) de bonne foi actionnaire(m)
inhaftieren; ins Gefängnis(n) setzen	**imprison (to)**	**emprisonner,** mettre en prison
Inhaftierung(f); Freiheits–, Gefängnisstrafe(f)	**imprisonment**	**emprisonnement**(m)
inländisch; innerstaatlich; Familien– Binnenwirtschaft inländisches, innerstaatliches Recht	**domestic** – economy – law	**familial**(m); national(m) économie(f) nationale droit(m) interne
Innen– –ministerium(n) (US)	**Interior** (US) Department of the – (US)	**environnement**(m) (US) ministère(m) de l'environnement (US)
–minister(m) (US)	Secretary of the – (US)	ministre(m) de l'environnement (US)
Innenminister(m) (UK)	**Home Secretary** (UK)	**ministre**(m) **de l'intérieur** (UK)
Innenministerium(n) (UK)	**Home Office** (UK)	**ministère**(m) **de l'intérieur** (UK)

GERMAN	ENGLISH	FRENCH
Insasse(*m*)	**inmate**	**détenu**(*m*), interné(*m, f*)
Instanz(*f*)	**instance**	**instance**(*f*), circonstance(*f*), preuve(*f*)
höheres Gericht; höhere – Vorinstanz; untere –	court of higher – court of lower –	tribunal(*m*) supérieur tribunal inférieur
intern; inländisch, Binnen-	**internal**	**interne**, intérieur
international; zwischenstaatlich	**international**	**international**
internieren	**intern (to)**	**interner**
Investition(*f*); (Kapital-)Anlage, Beteiligung(*f*) Investitionsbank; Emissions– Investment–, Kapitalanlagegesellschaft Investitionsfonds Kapitalanlagegesellschaft	**investment** – bank *(US)* – company – fund – trust	**investissement**(*m*), placement de fonds banque(*f*) d'affaires *(US)* société(*m*) de placement (de portefeuill(e) fonds(*m*) de placement société d'investissement
Inzest(*m*)	**incest**	**inceste**(*m*)
Irrtum(*m*); Fehler(*m*) Tatsachenirrtum Rechtsirrtum	**mistake** – of fact – of law	**erreur**(*f*), méprise(*f*) erreur sur les faits faute(*f*) de droit
Irrtum(*m*); Fehler(*m*); Versehen(*n*) Fehlspruch; Rechtsirrtum; Fehler des Gerichts	**error** judicial –	**erreur**(*f*) erreur judiciaire
irrtümlich; unrichtig	**erroneous**	**erroné**

J

GERMAN	ENGLISH	FRENCH
Jagdgesetz(n), (Jagd)	**game law (hunting)**	**lois**(m) **de la chasse**
Jahreseinkommen(n); (jährliche) Rente(f), Annuität(f)	**annuity**	**annuité**(f); rente viagière(f)
Jahr(n)	**year**	**année**(f), exercice(m)
Kalender–	calendar –	année civile
Geschäfts–; Rechnungs–	financial –	année budgétaire, exercice financier
Steuer– (UK); Haushalts–, Rechnungs–	fiscal –	année fiscale
Geburts–	– of birth	année de naissance
jd belasten; beschuldigen	**incriminate (to) s.o.**	**accuser qqu'un**
jdn lügnerisch bezichtigen	**frame (to) s.o.**	**monter un coup contre qqu'un** (fam.), inventer
jeder Zweifel ausgeschlossen; (Beweisergebnis, das jeden vernünftigen Zweifel ausschließt)	**beyond reasonable doubt**	**quasi-certitude du jury,** conviction(f) dépassant la croyance en un doute raisonnable
jn zu einer Geldstrafe(f) **verurteilen;** mit einer Geldstrafe belegen	**fine (to) s.o.**	**condamner qqu'un à une amende**
Jugend–	**juvenile**	**juvénile**
–gericht(n)	– court	tribunal(m) pour enfants
–verbrechen	– crime	crime(m) ou délit commis par un mineur
–kriminalität(f)	– delinquency	délinquance(f) juvénile
jugendlicher Straftäter(m)	– delinquent, offender	délinquant(m, f) juvénile, accusé(m) mineur
Jugendhaftanstalt(f) (US)	**reformatory** (US)	**prison**(f) **pour jeunes détenus** (US), maison de correction(f)
Jurist(m); Rechtsgelehrter(m)	**jurist**	**juriste**(m), légiste(m); homme(m) de loi (US), avocat
juristisch; Rechts–	**juridical**	**judiciaire,** juridique, légal

K

GERMAN	ENGLISH	FRENCH
Kabinett(*n*); Ministerium(*n*)	**cabinet**	**cabinet**(*m*), conseil(*m*) des ministres
Kabinetts-, Regierungsausschuß	– committee	commission(*f*) du conseil des ministres
Kabinettssitzung	– meeting	réunion(*f*) du cabinet, du conseil des ministres
Kannbestimmungen(*f*)	**permissive legislation**	**législation**(*f*) **facultative,** non impérative
Kanzler(*m*); Richter(*m*) od. Vorsitzender(*m*) (des Court of Chancery)	**chancellor**	**chancelier**(*m*)
Schatzkanzler; Finanzminister	Chancellor of the Exchequer	chancelier de l'Échiquier, ministre(*m*) des finances
Lordkanzler	Lord Chancellor	le Grand Chancelier d'Angleterre
Kapital-(*n*) –verbrechen	**capital** (*criminal law*) – crime	**capital**(*m*) crime(*m*) punissable de la peine capitale
Todesstrafe	– punishment	peine(*f*) capitale, peine de mort
Kapital(*n*); Vermögen(*n*) Eigenmittelrelation	**capital** – adequacy ratio	**capital**(*m*) rapport(*m*) d'adéquation du capital
Kapitalvorschuß	– advance	prêt(*m*) pour constitution de capital
(Kapital-)Veräußerungsgewinn; realisierter Kursgewinn	– gain	plus(*f*)-value
Kapitalanteil	– holding	possession(*f*) de capital
Kapitalbeteiligung	– interest	intérêt(*m*) du capital
Kapitalmarkt	– market	marché(*m*) des capitaux
Kapitalverzinsung	– return	rendement(*m*), rentabilité du capital
Aktienkapital; Stammkapital	– stock	capital social
voll eingezahltes Kapital	paid-up –	capital versé
Aktien-, Stamm-; Betriebskapital	share –	capital actions
Kapital einfordern(*n*); Einzahlung(*f*) verlangen	**call-up of capital**	**appel**(*m*) **de fonds**
(Kapital)ertrag(*m*); Gewinn(*m*); Rendite(*f*)	**returns**	**recettes**(*f*), rendement(*m*); retour(*m*) des invendus; statistiques(*m*), résultats

GERMAN	ENGLISH	FRENCH
Kapitalflußrechnung(f)	funds statement	tableau(m) de financement
Kapitalgesellschaft(f)	joint-stock company	société(f) par actions
(Kapital-)Gesellschaft(f); Firma(f)	company	compagnie(f), société(f), entreprise(f)
angeschlossenes Unternehmen; Konzern-	affiliated –	filiale(m)
Schwestergesellschaft angegliederte Gesellschaft; Beteiligungs-	associated	associée(f)
Dachgesellschaft	– controlling	société mère
Holding-, Dachgesellschaft	– holding –	holding, société de participations financières
eingetragene (rechtsfähige) Gesellschaft	incorporated –	société constituée
Kapitalgesellschaft	joint-stock –	société de capitaux, par actions
Gesellschaft mit beschränkter Haftung	private –	société à responsabilité limitée (SARL)
Aktiengesellschaft	public –	société anonyme
Handelsgesellschaft	trading –	société commerciale
(Kapital-)Gesellschaft(f) mit unbeschränkter Haftung(f)	unlimited company	société(f) à responsabilité non limitée
Kardinalfehler(m)	cardinal error	erreur(f) fondamentale
Kaskoversicherung(f) (Schiffs-, Flugzeug-)	hull insurance	assurance(f) d'un navire hors cargaison
Kauf(m); Erwerb(m)	purchase	achat(m)
Kaufoption(f); Vorprämie(f)	call option	prime(f) à la hausse; option(f) d'achat
Kaufvertrag(m)	sales contract	contrat(m) de vente
kausal bedingt mittelbarer Schaden, Folgeschaden	consequential – damage	conséquent, consécutif dommage(m) indirect
Kausalzusammenhang(m)	causal connection	connection causal, relation(f) de causalité
Kaution(f) stellen, für jdn Sicherheit(f) leisten	go (to) bail for s.o.	se porter garant de qqu'un, pour qqu'un
Kinderbeihilfe(f), Kindergeld(n)	children's allowance	allocation familiale
Kind(n), Nachkomme(m)	child	enfant(m, f)
(Kirchen-)Gemeinde(f)	parish	paroisse(f)
Klage(f), Verfahren(n), Rechtsstreit(m); Handlung(f), Vorgehen	action	action(f)
Schadensersatzklage, Klage auf Entschädigung	– for damages	demande(m) de dommages-intérêts
Feststellungsklage	– for declaration	demande de décision judiciaire
Unterlassungsklage	– for injunction	demande d'injonction
Klage erheben, anstrengen; jdn verklagen, gegen jdn Klage erheben	to bring an – against s.o.	intenter un procès à, contre, qqu'un
Klage abweisen	to dismiss an –	rejeter une action (en justice)

GERMAN	ENGLISH	FRENCH
Klage(*f*); Beschwerde(*f*)	**plaint**	**plainte**(*f*)
Klage(*f*); Klageschrift(*f*); Beschwerde(*f*)	**complaint**	**plainte**(*f*)
(Klage)Beantwortung(*f*); Erwiderung(*f*)	**response**	**réaction**(*f*), réponse(*f*)
klagen auf Testamentsanerkennung(*f*)	**propound (to) a will**	**demander l'homologation d'un testament**
Klagepunkt(*m*)	**count**	**compte**(*m*), calcul(*m*); chef(*m*) d'accusation
erster Klagepunkt	of the first –	au premier chef
zweiter Klagepunkt	of the second –	au second chef
Kläger(*m*)	**plaintiff**	**plaignant**(*m*), requérant(*m*), demandeur(*m*)
Kläger(*m*) (Berufungs–, Revisions–, Rechtsmittel–); Beschwerdeführer(*m*)	**appellant**	**appellant**(*m*)
Klausel(*f*); Absatz(*m*); Vereinbarung(*f*)	**clause**	**clause**(*f*)
Freizeichnungsklausel; Befreiungsklausel	exemption –	clause d'exonération
Strafklausel, Strafbestimmung	penalty –	clause pénale, dédit
Kodizil(*n*); Testamentsnachtrag(*m*); Zusatz(*m*)	**codicil**	**codicille**(*m*), avenant(*m*)
kollektiv(*n*), gesamt(*f*)	**collective**	**collectif, collective**
Tarifvertrag; Kollektivvertrag	– agreement, bargain	convention(*f*) collective
Tarifverhandlungen	– bargaining	négociation(*f*) pour convention collective
Kollektivschuld	– guilt	culpabilité(*f*) collective
gemeinsame Kapitalanlagegesellschaft, Investmentgesellschaft	– investment company	société(*f*) de placement
Gesamtverpflichtung, –schuld; Kollektivhaftung	– liability	responsabilité(*f*) collective
Kollusion(*f*); geheimes (unerlaubtes) Einverständnis(*n*)	**collusion**	**collusion**(*f*), connivence(*f*)
Komitee(*n*), Ausschuß(*m*)	**committee**	**comité**(*m*), conseil(*m*)
Gläubigerausschuß	creditors', liquidation –	délégation(*f*) des créanciers
Parlaments–; Sonder–; Untersuchungsausschuß	select –	commission(*f*) d'enquête parlementaire
Ständiger Ausschuß	standing –	comité de direction; réunion des présidents
Komplize(*m*); Mittäter(*m*), Mitschuldiger(*m*, *f*); Helfershelfer(*m*)	**accomplice**	**complice**(*m*)
Kondominium; Eigentumswohnung(*f*) (US)	**condominium**	**condominium**(*m*), copropriété(*f*) immobilière
Konfiszierung(*f*); Beschlagnahme(*f*)	**confiscation**	**confiscation**(*f*)
Königtum(*n*); Lizenzgebühr(*f*)	**royalty**	**royauté**(*f*), princes(*m*) du sang

GERMAN	ENGLISH	FRENCH
Konkurrenz(f); Wettbewerb Wettbewerbsklausel unlauterer Wettbewerb	**competition** – clause unfair –	**concurrence**(f) clause(f) de concurrence concurrence déloyale

Konkursschuldner(m);
Zahlungsunfähiger(m);
Gemeinschuldner(m)
  bankrott erklärt werden
  jdn für bankrott erklären
	bankrupt
	
	to be declared –
	to declare s.o. –
		failli, banqueroutier
		
		être déclaré en faillite
		prononcer la faillite de
		  qqu'un

Konkurs (Bankrott) anmelden in Konkurs gehen (geraten); bankrott machen	to declare oneself – to go –	se déclarer en faillite faire faillite
Konkursverwalter(m)	**trustee in bankruptcy**	**syndic**(m) **de faillite**
Konkursverwalter(m); Liquidator(m)	**liquidator**	**liquidateur**(m)
Konkursverwalter(m)	**receiver**	**receleur**(m); destinataire(m), réceptionnaire(m); liquidateur(m)
(vorläufiger) –; Zwangsverwalter	official –	administrateur(m) judiciaire (pour faillite)
Konsens(m); Übereinstimmung(f)	**consensus**	**consensus**
Konsignatar; Empfänger	**consignee**	**destinataire**
Konsignation(f); Hinterlegung(f) (Schottland)	**consignation**	**consignation**(f)
konsolidieren; zusammenlegen	**consolidate (to)**	**consolider,** codifier
konsolidiert	**consolidated**	**consolidé**(m), unifié, capitalisé
konsolidierte Staatsanleihen(f); Konsols (UK)	**consols** (UK)	**fonds**(m) **consolidés** (UK), rentes(f) perpétuelles
Konsolidierung(f); Vereinigung(f) Prozeß–, Klagenverbindung Zusammenlegung (od. Fusion) von Gesellschaften	**consolidation** – of actions – of companies	**consolidation**(f), fusion(f) jonction(f) d'instances fusion de sociétés
Konsortium(n); (Recht der) eheliche(n) Lebensgemeinschaft(f)	**consortium**	**consortium**(m); mariage(m) légitime
Konzession(f)	**franchise**	**liberté**(f), privilège(m); droit(m) électoral; minimum de couverture(f) (assurance)
Konzession(f); Zugeständnis(n); Zulassung(f)	**concession**	**concession**(f); dégrèvement(m)
körperliche Züchtigung(f); Prügelstrafe(f)	**corporal punishment**	**châtiment**(m) **corporel**
Körperschaft(f); juristische Person(f)	**corporation**	**corporation**(f), guilde(f), corps(m) constitué, corps(m) de métier

GERMAN	ENGLISH	FRENCH
Körperschaft(f)**; Vereinigung(f);** Gremium(n), Organ(n) Verwaltungsgremium, -behörde, -stelle juristische Person; Körperschaft	**body** administrative – – corporate	**corps**(m) instance(f) administrative personne morale, corps constitué
körperschaftlich; korporativ Gesellschaftsvermögen Körperschaft, juristische Person Aktien	**corporate** – assets – body – stock	**relatif à une personne morale ou sociale** actif(m) social corps(m) constitué, personne morale actions(f) d'une société
Korpus delicti; Tatbestand (eines Verbrechens)	**corpus delicti**	**corps**(m) **du délit**
(Kosten) bestreiten; aufkommen für	**defray (to)**	**défrayer**
Kraft(f) zwangsweise, mit Gewalt Gesetzes– höhere Gewalt	**force** by – – of law *force majeure*	**force**(f) de force, par force force de la loi (cas de) force majeure
Kraft(f)**; Macht**(f) aufgrund von; unter Berufung auf Gesetzeskraft	**strength** on the – of – of law	**force**(f)**,** vigueur(f), résistance(f) en vertu de, au regard de force(f) de la loi
kränken, jdn in seinem Recht verletzen	**aggrieve (to)**	**chagriner,** blesser, causer de la peine
Kredit(m)**; Darlehen(n);** Guthaben(n)	**credit**	**crédit**(m)
Kreis(m)**, Bezirk(m)** erstinstanzliches Gericht für mehrere Bezirke *(US)* Strafrichter; Richter	**circuit** – court *(US)* – judge	**circuit**(m) tribunal(m) de première instance *(US)* juge(m) de la Crown Court et de la county court (Angleterre)
Kriegsrecht(n)**; Standrecht(n)**	**martial law**	**loi**(f) **martiale**
Kriegsrisikoversicherung(f)	**war risk insurance**	**assurance**(f) **sur les risques de guerre**
kriminell; strafbar; strafrechtlich Strafverfahren; strafrechtliche Verfolgung; Anklage wegen e-s Verbrechens Gericht für Strafsachen; Strafkammer Strafrecht Strafregister; Vorstrafe(nverzeichnis)	**criminal** – action – charge – court – law – record	**criminel**(m) *(n. et adj.)* action(f) au criminel inculpation(f) de crime cour(f) de juridiction criminelle droit(m) pénal, droit criminel casier(m) judiciaire
Kritik(f)**,** Tadel(m), Rüge(f) Mißtrauensantrag	**censure** motion of –	**réprimande**(f)**,** critique(f) motion(f) de censure

GERMAN	ENGLISH	FRENCH
Krone(f) Gericht für Strafsachen und einige Zivilsachen *(England und Wales)*	**Crown** – Court	**Couronne**(f) **(l'État)** cour d'assises
kündbar; befristet	**terminable**	**réalisable,** résoluble, résiliable
Kuppelei betreiben; Vorschub(m) leisten	**pander (to)**	**proxénetisme**(m) **commettre**

L

GERMAN	ENGLISH	FRENCH
laden; auffordern, zu erscheinen jdn vor Gericht laden	**summon (to)** – s.o. before the court	**convoquer,** mander, citer citer qqu'un à comparaître devant le tribunal
Ladendiebstahl(*m*)	**shoplifting**	**vol**(*m*) **à l'étalage**
Lage(*f*)**;** Standort(*m*); Bauplatz(*m*)	**site**	**site**(*m*)**,** terrain(*m*) (à bâtir), *par ext.* chantier
(Lager-)Bestand(*m*)**;** Inventar(*n*); Inventur(*f*)	**inventory**	**inventaire**(*m*)**,** stock(*m*); bilan(*m*) de faillite (*US*)
Laienrichter(*m*)	**lay judge**	**juge**(*m*) **non-professionel**
(Land)Besitzrecht(*n*)**;** Amtsinnehabung(*f*)	**tenure**	**période**(*f*) **de jouissance,** période d'occupation d'un emploi
Landenteignung(*f*)	**expropriation of land**	**expropriation**(*f*)
Landesverrat(*m*)**;** Hochverrat(*m*)	**treason**	**trahison**(*f*)
Landstreicher	**vagrant**	**vagabond**(*m*)**,** clochard(*m*)
Landstreicherei	**vagrancy**	**vagabondage**(*m*)
langfristig –er Kredit –e Verbindlichkeit	**long-term** – credit – debt	**à long terme** crédit(*m*) à long terme créance(*f*) à long terme
Last(*f*)**;** (Grundstücks-) Belastung(*f*); Hypothekenlast(*f*)	**encumbrance**	**embarras**(*m*)**,** hypothèque(*f*)
Leben(*n*) –slängliche Freiheitsstrafe –sversicherung	**life** imprisonment for – – assurance/ insurance	**vie**(*f*) prison(*f*) à perpétuité, emprisonnement(*m*) à vie assurance(*f*) vie, assurance sur la vie
ledig (Familienstand)(*m*)	**single (marital status)**	**célibataire**(*m, f*)
legalisieren; beglaubigen	**legalise (to)**	**légaliser,** authentifier, certifier
Legislative(*f*)**;** gesetzgebende Körperschaft(*f*)	**legislature**	**corps**(*m*) **législatif,** législature(*f*)
legitim; rechtmäßig, gesetzmäßig; ehelich	**legitimate**	**légitime,** justifié

GERMAN	ENGLISH	FRENCH
Lehre(*f*), Doktrin(*f*)	**doctrine**	**doctrine**(*f*)
Lehrkörper(*m*)	**faculty**	**faculté**(*f*), liberté(*f*), droit(*m*) de faire qque chose
juristische Fakultät	– of laws	faculté de droit
Leichenhalle(*f*)	**mortuary**	**morgue**(*f*), institut(*m*) médico-légal
Leihen, Borgen; Darlehens–, Kreditaufnahme(*f*)	**borrowing**	**emprunteur** (*adj.*)
Leistung(*f*); Erfüllung(*f*)	**performance**	**accomplissement**(*m*), résultats(*m*); prestation(*f*)
Teilerfüllung eines Abkommens	part – of an agreement	éxécution(*f*) partielle d'une convention
Leistungsfähigkeit(*f*); Wirksamkeit(*f*)	**efficiency**	**efficacité**(*f*), compétence(*f*)
Leistungsverhältnis	– ratio	taux(*m*), courbe(*f*) d'efficacité de rentabilité
Leistungsabweichung, Intensitätsabweichung	– variance	différence(s) d'efficacité
(Leistungs-/Zahlungs-/ Lieferungs-/Submissions-) Angebot(*n*) Andienung	**tender**	**offre**(*f*), soumission(*f*)
Leitgedanke(*m*)	**guiding idea**	**idée**(*f*) **directrice**
letztwillige Verfügung; s. Testament(*n*)	**will** (*cf. testament*)	**testament**(*m*)
gemeinschaftliche(s) (wechselbezügliche(s)) –	joint (mutual) –	donation(*f*) au dernier survivant, testament mutuel
Testament Testamentsbestätigung	last – and testament probate of –	acte de dernières volontés homologation(*f*) d'un testament
Testament als gültig bestätigen	to prove a –	établir un testament
letztwillige Verfügung(*f*) **(Vermächtnis**(*n*) **über Grundbesitz)**(*m*)	**devise**	**disposition**(*f*) **testamentaire de biens immobiliers**
Leugnen; Bestreiten (des klägerischen Vorbringens)	**traverse** *(CL)*	**passage**(*m*) **au travers**
Lieferant(*m*)	**supplier**	**fournisseur**(*m*)
Liquidation(*f*) in – gehen –aufgrund Gesellschaftsbeschlusses; freiwillige –	**liquidation** to go into – voluntary –	**liquidation**(*f*) entrer en liquidation liquidation volontaire
Liquidität(*f*) –sgrad	**liquidity** – ratio	**disponibilité**(*f*), liquidité(*f*) taux(*m*) de liquidité
Liste(*f*); Aufstellung(*f*); Anhang(*m*); Zeitplan(*m*)	**schedule**	**annexe**(*f*), avenant(*m*); cédule(*f*); programme(*m*), horaire(*m*)
Listenpreis(*m*); Katalogpreis(*m*)	**list price**	**prix**(*m*) **du catalogue**
Lizenzgeber(*m*); Konzessionserteiler(*m*)	**licensor**	**concédant**

GERMAN	ENGLISH	FRENCH
Lizenznehmer(*m*); Konzessionsinhaber(*m*)	**licensee**	**concessionnaire**(*m, f*)
Lloyd's Register(*m*)	**Lloyd's Register**	**registre**(*m*) **de la Lloyd**
Loco-Konto(*n*)	**loco**	**sur place, 'loco'**
Logistik(*f*)	**logistics**	**logistique**
Lordkanzler(*m*)	**Lord High Chancellor**	**Grand Chancelier d'Angleterre**
löschen, streichen	**delete (to)**	**effacer,** radier, supprimer
Löschung(*f*); Streichung(*f*)	**deletion**	**effacement,** radiation

Lösegeld(*n*)
   – von jdm fordern
	ransom
	   demand (to) a –
	   from s.o.
		rançon(*f*)
		   exiger une rançon de
		   qqu'un

M

GERMAN	ENGLISH	FRENCH
Mahnung(*f*); Beanstandung(*f*)	**reminder**	**mémento**(*m*), rappel(*m*) pour mémoire
Makler(*m*), Vermittler(*m*)	**broker**	**courtier**(*m*), agent(*m*) de change
Makroökonomie(*f*)	**macroeconomics**	**macro-économie**(*f*)
Management(*n*)	**management**	**direction**(*f*), administration(*f*), gestion(*f*), gérance(*f*), exploitation(*f*); management(*m*), technique de gestion
Unternehmensführung; Geschäftsleitung	company –	gestion de société
Abrechnungsausschuß	– committee	comité(*m*) chargé des comptes de gestion
Verwaltungsgesellschaft	– company	société(*f*) de gérance
Manager(*m*); Geschäftsführer(*m*)	**manager**	**directeur**(*m*), gérant(*m*), gestionnaire(*m*)
Mangel(*m*); Fehlbetrag(*m*), Minderbetrag(*m*)	**deficiency**	**découvert**(*m*)
Markt(*m*)	**market**	**marché**
Marktplatz	– place	place(*f*) du marché
–preis; Kurswert	– price	prix(*m*) courant du marché
–anteil	– share	part(*f*) du marché
–wert; Kurswert; Verkehrswert	– value	valeur(*f*) marchande
Massenverhaftung(*f*)	**mass arrest**	**arrestation**(*f*) **massive**
maßgebliche Klausel(*f*)	**overriding clause**	**clause**(*f*) **dérogatoire**
maßgebliches Prinzip(*n*)	**overriding principle**	**principe**(*m*) **auquel on ne peut déroger**
Maßnahme(*f*)	**measure**	**mesure**(*f*), démarches
Zwangs–	coercive –	mesure coercitive
rechtmäßige –	lawful –	mesure licite
Vorsichts–	precautionary –	mesure de précaution
vorbeugende –	preventive –	mesures préventives
materiell; erheblich	**tangible**	**réel,** tangible
materielle Vermögenswerte; Sachvermögen	– assets	actif corporel, biens tangibles
materielles Recht(*n*)	**substantive law**	**droit**(*m*) **matériel**

GERMAN	ENGLISH	FRENCH
Mehrgewinn(*m*); Übergewinn(*m*)	**excess profits**	**bénéfice**(*m*) **actualisé net**
Mehrheit(*f*)	**majority**	**majorité**(*f*) (*n*), **majoritaire** (*adj.*)
absolute –	absolute –	majorité absolue
–sbeschluß; –swahl	– vote	vote(*m*) majoritaire
qualifizierte –	qualified –	majorité requise
Meineid(*m*)	**perjury**	**parjure**(*m*), faux serment(*m*), faux témoignage(*m*)
Meineid(*m*) **leisten**	**perjure (to)**	**se parjurer,** faire un faux serment, un faux témoignage
Meinung(*f*); Urteilsbegründung(*f*) zustimmendes Votum mit v.d. Mehrheit abweichender Begründung	**opinion** concurring –	**opinion**(*f*) avis(*m*) en accord
mit der Mehrheitsentscheidung nicht übereinstimmende Stellungnahme e-s Richters	dissenting –	avis de la minorité
öffentliche Meinung	public –	opinion publique
Meinungsverschiedenheit(*f*); Widerspruch(*m*)	**disagreement**	**désaccord**(*m*)
melden; mitteilen	**notify (to)**	**aviser,** signifier, avertir
Menschenrecht(*n*)	**human rights**	**droits**(*m*) **de l'homme**
Meuterei(*f*)	**mutiny**	**mutinerie**(*f*)
Mietbesitz(*m*); Pachtbesitz(*m*); Mietgrundstück(*n*); Pachtland(*n*)	**leasehold**	**tenure**(*f*) **à bail,** propriété(*f*) louée à bail
Miete(*f*); Einstellung(*f*); Heuer(*m*)	**hire**	**location**(*f*), louage(*m*); embauchage(*m*); salaire(*m*) vente(*m*) à tempérament
Teilzahlungs–, Abzahlungskauf (*UK*)	-purchase	
Miete(*f*); Pacht(*f*)	**rent**	**loyer**(*m*); prix(*m*) de location
Miet(e)(*f*); Pacht(*f*) Pachtvertrag (landwirtschaftliche Grundstücke, Betrieb)	**lease** agricultural (farm) –	**bail**(*m*), concession(*f*) bail à ferme
Pachtvertrag (Pachtland) Mietvertrag	land – – agreement	bail à ferme contrat(*m*) de bail
Mieteinnahmen(*f*); Pacht–(*f*)	**rental income**	**revenu**(*m*) **locatif**
mieten ver–	**hire (to)** – out	**louer,** embaucher donner en location, louer
Mieter(*m*); Pächter(*m*)	**leaseholder**	**locataire**(*m*) **à bail,** emphytéote(*m*)
Mieter(*m*); Pächter(*m*)	**tenant**	**locataire**(*m*), tenancier(*m*), usufruitier(*m*)
Mieter(*m*); Pächter(*m*); Leasingnehmer(*m*)	**lessee**	**locataire**(*m, f*), tenancier(*m*), concessionnaire(*m, f*)

GERMAN	ENGLISH	FRENCH
Mietverhältnis(n); Pacht-(f)	**tenancy**	**location**(f), usufruit(m), droits(m) du tenant
Mikroökonomie(f)	**microeconomics**	**micro-économie**(f)
mildern; herabsetzen	**mitigate (to)**	**atténuer**
mildernde Umstände	**extenuating circumstances**	**circonstances**(f) **atténuantes**
mildernde Umstände(m)	**mitigating circumstances**	**circonstances**(f) **atténuantes**
Milderung(f)	**mitigation**	**adoucissement**(m)
Herabsetzung des Schadensersatzes	– of damages	réduction(f) de dommages-intérêts
Strafmilderung	– of penalty	réduction de peine
Militär-(n)	**military**	**militaire**
–(straf)recht(n); Wehr(straf)recht(n);	– law	code(m) de justice militaire, droit(m) militaire
–polizei(f)	– police	police(m) militaire
–gericht(n)	– tribunal	tribunal(m) militaire
Minderangebot(n); Unter-	**underbid**	**offre**(f) **de conditions plus avantageuses**
Minderheit(f)	**minority**	**minorité**(f)
–sbeteiligung; Anteile in Fremdbesitz	– interest	participation(f) minoritaire
Fremdanteil	– share	participation minoritaire
Minderjähriger(m), (s. Unmündiger)	**minor** (cf. infant)	**mineur**(m)
Minderlieferung(f); unvollständige Lieferung(f)	**short delivery**	**livraison**(f) **à court terme**
Mißachtung(f); Geringschätzung(f)	**contempt**	**mépris**(m), outrage(m), manque de respect
Ungehorsam gegenüber gerichtlichem Gebot	civil –	outrage civil
Mißachtung des Gerichts	– of court	outrage à magistrat(s)
strafbare Mißachtung des Gerichts; Ungebühr vor Gericht	criminal –	outrage délictueux
Mißbrauch(m)	**misuse**	**abus**(m), mauvais usage(m)
Mißbrauch(m); Beschimpfung(f); Mißhandlung(f)	**abuse**	**abus**(m), excès(m); viol(m)
Mißerfolg(m); Bankrott(m); Versäumnis(n); Zahlungseinstellung	**failure**	**échec**(m), manquement(m), faillite(f)
Justizversagen	– of justice	déni(m) de justice
Nichterscheinen (vor Gericht)	– to appear	non-comparution(f)
Nichtbefolgung; –einhaltung; –erfüllung	– to comply with	non-observation(f) de
Nichtzahlung; Zahlungsversäumnis	– to pay	défaut(m) de paiement
Mißhandlung(f)	**maltreatment**	**mauvais traitement**
Mißkredit(m); schlechter Ruf(m); Unglaubwürdigkeit(f)	**discredit**	**discrédit**(m), déconsidération(f)
Mißstand(m); Schaden(m); Unheil(n)	**mischief**	**dégâts**(m), dommages(m), méfait(m)

GERMAN	ENGLISH	FRENCH
Mitbeklagter(*m*, *f*), Neben–; Mitangeklagter(*m*, *f*)	**co-accused, co-defendant**	**co-défendeur**(*m*), co-accusé(*m*)
Miterbe(*m*), Neben–	**coheir**	**cohéritier**(*m*)
Mitgift(*f*); Aussteuer(*m*)	**dowry**	**dot**(*f*)
Mitgift(*f*); lebenslängliches Nießbrauchrecht des verwitweten Ehegatten an 1/3 des Grundbesitzes des verstorbenen (*US*)	**dower**	**douaire**(*m*)
Mitgliedsstaat(*m*)	**member State**	**pays**(*m*) **membre**
Mittäter(*m*); Komplize(*m*), Mitschuldiger(*m*, *f*)	**accessory**	**complice**(*m*); **accessoire**(*m*)
Mittäterschaft(*m*) (*StrafR*); Mitschuld(*f*); Tatbeteiligung(*f*)	**complicity**	**complicité**(*f*)
Mittel(*n*)

   Zwangs–
   Beweis–
   Zahlungs– | **means**

  – of coercion
  – of evidence
  – of payment | **moyens**(*m*), façons(*f*); ressources(*f*) financières
  moyens de pression
  moyens de preuve
  moyen de paiement, méthode de paiement |
Mittel(*n*); Urkunde(*f*)	**instrument**	**acte**(*m*) **juridique**, document(*m*) officiel, élément(*m*) de preuve écrite
Mitverschulden(*n*); mitwirkendes Verschulden	**contributory negligence**	**négligence**(*f*) **contributoire**
Mitversicherung(*f*)	**co-insurance**	**coassurance**(*f*)
Monogamie(*f*)	**monogamy**	**monogamie**
monopolisieren; für sich allein in Anspruch nehmen	**monopolise (to)**	**monopoliser**
Monopol(*n*)	**monopoly**	**monopole**(*m*), droit(*m*) d'exclusivité
Moratorium(*n*), Stillhalteabkommen(*n*)	**moratorium**	**moratoire**(*m*)
Mord(*m*)
–versuch
schwerer –
leichter –	**murder**
attempted –
first-degree – (*US*)
second-degree – (*US*)	**meurtre**(*m*), assassinat(*m*) tentative(*f*) de meurtre assassinat (*US*) homicide(*m*, *f*) par imprudence, involontaire (*US*)
multilateral	**multilateral**	**multilatéral, plurilatéral**
Mündel(*n*); Stadtbezirk(*m*)	**ward**	**tutelle**(*f*); pupille(*m*, *f*); service(*m*), salle(*f*) d'hôpital; surveillance(*f*)
mündliche Zeugenaussage(*f*)	**oral testimony**	**témoignage**(*m*) **oral**
mutmaßlich
Wahrscheinlichkeits–, Indizienbeweis	**presumptive**
– evidence	**présomptif**
preuve(*f*) par déduction, par présomption
Muttermord(*m*)	**matricide**	**matricide**(*m*, *f*)

GERMAN	ENGLISH	FRENCH
Mutterschaftsgeld(*n*); – leistungen(*f*)	**maternity benefit**	**allocation**(*f*) **de maternité**
mutwilliges (dilatorisches) Parteivorbringen	**sham pleading**	**usage**(*m*) **de moyens dilatoires**
MwSt (Mehrwertsteuer)(*m*)	**VAT** (value added tax)	**TVA** (taxe sur la valeur ajoutée)

N

GERMAN	ENGLISH	FRENCH
Nachahmung(*f*)	**imitation**	**imitation**(*f*), factice, faux(*f*)
Nachahmung(*f*); Fälschung(*f*)	**counterfeit**	**contrefaçon**, faux
Nachahmung(*f*); Fälschung(*f*)	**counterfeiting**	**contrefaçon**
nachehelich	**post-nuptial**	**post-nuptial**(*f*)
nachfragen; sich erkundigen	**inquire (to)**	**enquêter**, faire une enquête
Nachkommenschaft(*f*); Abkomme(*m*)	**offspring**	**descendance**(*f*)
Nachlaß(*m*); Erbschaft(*f*)	**deceased's estate**	**succession**(*f*)
Nachlaß(*m*); Rabatt(*m*)	**rebate**	**rabais**(*m*), remise(*f*), réduction(*f*)
Nachlaßgericht(*n*)	**probate court**	**tribunal**(*m*) **des successions et des tutelles**
Nachricht(*f*); Mitteilung(*f*); Strafanzeige(*f*); Anklage(*f*)	**information**	**information(s)**(*f*); acte(*m*) d'accusation émanant du ministère public; dénonciation(*f*), délation(*f*)
vertrauliche Mitteilung	confidential –	renseignements(*m*) confidentiels
Informationsaustausch	exchange of –	échange(*m*) de renseignements
Nachteil(*m*); Schaden(*m*); Beeinträchtigung(*f*)	**detriment**	**détriment**(*m*), préjudice(*m*), perte(*f*)
nachtragend; strafend	**vindictive**	**punitif,** vindicatif
Nachweis(*m*), Beleg(*m*); Beweis(*m*)	**proof**	**preuve**(*f*); épreuve(*f*)
Beweislast	burden of –	charge(*f*) de la preuve
eindeutiger Beweis	positive –	preuve manifeste
Forderungsnachweis	– of claim	preuve de créance
Schuldbeweis	– of guilt	preuve de culpabilité
Identitätsnachweis	– of identity	justification(*f*) d'identité
schriftlicher Beweis	written –	preuve littérale
Narbe(*f*)	**scar**	**cicatrice**(*f*)
-n und blaue Flecken	scars and bruises	cicatrices et contusions

GERMAN	ENGLISH	FRENCH
National-	**national**	**national**
–versammlung(f)	– assembly	assemblée(f) nationale
Landeswährung	– currency	monnaie(f) nationale
Staatsschuld	– debt	dette(f) publique
Volkseinkommen	– income	revenu(m) national
Sozialversicherung (UK)	– insurance	sécurité(f) sociale
Landesrecht, innerstaatliches –, einzelstaatliches(EG) Recht	– law	droit(m) interne, droit national
Staats–, Hoheitsgebiet	– territory	territoire(m) national
natürlich-	**natural**	**naturel**
Erbe durch Geburtsrecht	– heir	héritier(m) naturel
natürliche Person	– person	personne physique, individu(m)
(Natur)wissenschaft(f)	**science**	**science(f)**
Neben-	**incidental**	**accidentel,** éventuel, accessoire
–klage(f)	– action	poursuites sur incident
–ausgaben; –kosten	– expenses, incidentals	faux frais
Nebeneinkünfte	**perquisites**	**avantages(m) accessoires,** gratifications(f)
Nebenprozess(m); Zwischenverfahren	**mesne process**	**instance(f) en cours**
nehmen	**take (to)**	**prendre**
Beweis aufnehmen, erheben; Zeugenaussage hören	– evidence	recueillir des témoignages
übernehmen	– over	prendre en charge, reprendre
jdn vereidigen	– the oath of s.o.	recueillir le serment de qqu'un
nennen, betiteln; berechtigen	**entitle (to)**	**donner le droit de**
Nennwert(m)	**nominal value**	**valeur(f) nominale**
Nennwert(m); Nominalwert(m)	**par value**	**valeur(f) au pair**
netto; rein	**net**	**net**
Reinvermögen	– assets	actif(m) net
Nettoeinkommen; Reinertrag	– income	revenu(m) net
Endergebnis	– result	résultat(m) net
Reinvermögen; Eigenkapital	– worth	valeur(f) nette
neu erwägen; nachprüfen	**reconsider (to)**	**réexaminer,** reconsidérer
neu veranlagen; – festsetzen	**reassess (to)**	**réévaluer,** réviser la cote de, réimposer
Neutralität(f)	**neutrality**	**neutralité(f)**
–sgesetzgebung	– legislation	législation(f) de neutralité
–spolitik	– policy	politique(f) de neutralité
Neuveranlagung(f); Neufestsetzung(f)	**reassessment**	**réévaluation(f),** réimposition(f)

GERMAN	ENGLISH	FRENCH
Nicht-	**non**	**non-**
–annahme; Annaheverweigerung	–acceptance	–acceptation(*f*)
–erscheinen	–appearance	–comparution(*f*)
–befolgung, –efüllung	–compliance	–conformité(*f*), insoumission(*f*), refus(*m*) de se conformer
–streitig; kontradiktorisch	–contentious	litigieux
– vorhanden	–existent	inexistant
(pflichtwidrige) Unterlassung, Nichterfüllung	–feasance	négligence(*m*) simple
–befolgung, –beachtung	–observance	–observation(*f*)
Drittländer(*pl.*) *(EG)*	–member country *(EEC)*	pays(*m*) non-membre de la CEE
–erfüllung, –leistung	–performance	inexécution(*f*)
– ansässig; im Ausland ansässig	–resident	–résident(*m*)
irrige Folgerung; unschlüssig	*non sequitur*	il ne s'en suit pas
nicht beachten; ignorieren	**disregard (to)**	**enfreindre,** mépriser, passer outre à
nicht befolgen; mißachten	**disobey (to)**	**désobéir**
nicht bestätigt	**unverified**	**non vérifié**
nicht (ein-)klagbar; nicht vollstreckbar	**unenforceable**	**inapplicable**
nicht erfüllen; zurückweisen	**dishonour (to)**	**déshonorer**
e-n Wechsel nicht bezahlen, –einlösen	– a bill	refuser le paiement d'une traite, ne pas honorer une traite
nicht ermächtigt; unbefugt	**unauthorised**	**non autorisé,** illégal, illicite
nicht gebunden, blockfrei	**uncommitted**	**non engagé,** libre, neutraliste
nicht notierte Wertpapiere(*f*)	**unlisted securities**	**valeurs**(*f*) **non cotées**
nicht verfügbar	**unavailable**	**indisponible**
nicht zu ermitteln; nicht feststellbar	**unascertainable**	**impossible à vérifier**
nicht Zustimmende(r)(*f, m*), widersprechende(r)(*f, m*) Geschworene(r)(*f, m*)	**dissenting juror**	**juré en désaccord avec le reste du jury**
Nichtanerkennung(*f*); Zurückweisung(*f*)	**disallowance**	**rejet**(*m*), réfaction(*f*)
Nichterfüllung(*f*); Unterlassung(*f*); (Zahlungs-) Verzug(*m*)	**default**	**manquement**(*f*), défaillance(*f*)
Nichterscheinen (vor Gericht); Versäumnis der Einlassung	– of appearance	défaut(*m*) de comparution
Versäumnisurteil	judgment by –	jugement(*m*) par défaut
nichtig; unwirksam	**void**	**nul et de nul effet,** vide
(null und) nichtig; ungültig	null and –	nul et non avenu
Nichtigkeit(*f*); Ungültigkeit(*f*)	**nullity**	**nullité**(*f*)
Nichtigkeitsklage	– action	action(*f*) en nullité
absolute Nichtigkeit der Ehe	– of marriage	nullité de mariage

GERMAN	ENGLISH	FRENCH
Niederschrift(*f*); Urkunde(*f*); Protokoll	**record**	**document**(*m*), dossier(*m*)
Gerichtsakte	court –	dossier du tribunal
Vorstrafenregister	criminal –	casier(*m*) judiciaire
Beweisaufnahme	– of evidence	procès-verbal(*m*) de témoignage
niedrigster akademicher Grad(*m*) **der jurist. Fakultät**(*f*)	**LLB**	**licencié**(*f*) **en droit**
noch nicht fällig	**unmatured**	**non échu**
nochmals vernehmen; erneut überprüfen	**re-examine (to)**	**procéder à un nouvel interrogatoire,** réexaminer
Notar(*m*)	**notary public**	**notaire**(*m*)
Note(*f*); Schein(*m*)	**note**	**billet**(*m*), bordereau(*m*), facture(*f*), bulletin(*m*)
(Luft-)Frachtbrief	consignment –	lettre(*f*) de voiture
Gutschriftanzeige	credit –	facture d'avoir, bordereau de crédit
Diskontabrechnung	discount –	bordereau d'escompte
Eigenwechsel; Schuldschein	promissory –	billet à ordre
Versandanzeige; Schiffszettel	shipping –	permis(*m*) d'embarquement
Notwehr(*f*); Selbstverteidigung(*f*)	**self-defence**	**légitime défense**(*f*), autodéfense
notwendige Streitpartei(*f*)	**indispensable party**	**partie**(*f*) **indispensable**
Notwendigkeit(*f*); Bedürfnis(*n*)	**necessity**	**nécessité**(*f*)
Not(zu)stand(*m*); Notfall(*m*)	**emergency**	**urgence,** situation(*f*) critique
Notstandsverordnung, –gesetz	– law	loi(*f*) d'exception
Notverkauf	– sale	vente(*f*) forcée
null	**zero**	**zéro**(*m*)
Budgetierung auf –basis	– -base budgeting (ZBB)	'zero-base budgeting' (ZBB)
–kupon	– coupon	coupon(*m*) zéro (sans intérêt)
–wert	– value	valeur(*m*) nulle
(null und) nichtig	**null and void**	**nul et non avenu**
Nutzen(*m*), Vorteil(*m*); Hilfe(*f*), Begünstigung(*f*); Versicherungsleistung	**benefit**	**avantage**(*m*)
Sachleistungen	benefits in kind	avantages en nature
Krankengeld, –unterstützung	sickness –	prestation(*f*) maladie
Arbeitslosenunterstützung	unemployment –	indemnité(*f*) de chômage
nutznießend; nutzbringend, vorteilhaft	**beneficial**	**profitable,** avantageux
Nutzungsrecht, Nießbrauchrecht; materieller Eigentumsanspruch	– interest	titre de droit en équité
Nutzungsberechtigter(*m*), Begünstigter(*m*); Empfangsberechtigter Leistungsempfänger; Anspruchsberechtigter	**beneficiary**	**bénéficiaire**(*m, f*), ayant(*m*) droit
Nutzungsrecht(*n*); Nießbrauch(*m*)	**usufruct**	**usufruit**(*m*)

O

GERMAN	ENGLISH	FRENCH
Obduktion(f)	**post-mortem**	**autopsie**(f)
Oberhaus(n) (UK)	**House of Lords** (UK)	**Chambre**(f) **des Lords** (UK)
Oberrichter(m); Vorsitzender(m, f) e-s hohen Gerichts, Präsident des Obersten Bundesgerichtshofs	**chief justice**	**premier président**(f) **d'une cour**
Oberster(m) **Gerichtshof**(m); Oberstes Bundesgericht (US); höheres Berufungsgericht	**supreme court**	**cour**(f) **suprême**
(oberster)(m) **Verwaltungsbeamter** Vollstreckungsbeamter (England) Vollstreckungsbeamter; Polizeichef (US)	**sheriff** – (England) – (US)	**shérif**(m) préfet(m) (Angleterre) capitaine(m) de gendarmerie (US)
obligatorisch; zwangsweise Zwangsverwaltung Zwangsverpflichtung notwendige Streitgenossenschaft (US) Zwangsliquidation	**compulsory** – administration – commitment – joinder – liquidation	**obligatoire,** forcé(f) administration(f) forcée engagement(m) obligatoire jonction(f) d'instances obligatoire liquidation(f) judiciaire
obligatorisch; zwingend	**mandatory**	**obligatoire,** impératif
offener Investmentfonds	**unit trust**	**SICAV**
offenkundige Handlung(f)	**overt act**	**acte**(m) **manifeste**
Offenlegung(f); Bekanntgabe(f)	**disclosure (of)**	**communication**(f) **de pièces**

GERMAN	ENGLISH	FRENCH
öffentlich	**public**	**public** *(adj.)*; public*(m)* *(n)*
–e Versteigerung; Zwangsversteigerung	– auction	vente*(f)* aux enchères publiques
–e Behörde	– authority	pouvoirs*(m)* publics
Kapitalgesellschaft	– company	société*(f)* anonyme
–e Ausgaben; Ausgaben der –en Hand	– expenditure	dépenses*(f)* publiques
–e Mittel	– funds	fonds*(m)* publics
staatlicher Gesundheitsdienst	– health system	système*(m)* de santé publique
–e Verhandlung	– hearing	audience*(f)* publique
gesetzlicher Feiertag	– holiday	jour*(m)* férié, fête légale
–e Bekanntmachung	– notice	avis*(m)* au public
Staatseigentum; Eigentum der –en Hand	– property	propriété*(f)* publique
Staatsanwalt	– prosecutor	ministère*(f)* public
–er Sektor; –e Hand	– sector	secteur*(m)* public
Versorgungsunternehmen (Elektrizität, Gas, Wasser)	– utilities	services*(m)* publics
öffentlich; zugänglich für	**open**	**ouvert**, public*(m)*, libre, accessible
in öffentlicher Verhandlung;	– court	tribunal*(m)* siégeant en public
revolvierender Kredit	– end credit	crédit*(m)* à capital variable
(offiziell) genehmigen; sanktionieren	**sanction (to)**	**sanctionner,** ratifier
ohne Möglichkeit*(f)* **der Verbindung***(f)* **mit der Außenwelt**	**incommunicado**	**au secret**
ohne Präzedenzfall*(m)***;** beispiellos	**unprecedented**	**sans précédent**
ohne Testament verstorben	**intestate**	**intestat**
Oligopol*(n)*	**oligopoly**	**oligopole***(m)*
Ombudsmann*(m)***;** Beschwerdekommissar*(m)*	**ombudsman**	**médiateur***(m)*
Opfer*(m)***;** Geschädigter*(m)*; Verletzter*(m)*	**victim**	**victime***(f)*
Option*(f)*	**option**	**faculté***(f)***,** option*(f)*; droit*(m)* de souscription
ordentlich	**ordinary**	**ordinaire**
–e Hauptversammlung	– general meeting	assemblée*(f)* générale ordinaire
ordnungswidriges Verhalten*(n)***;** ärgernis*(n)* erregendes Benehmen	**disorderly conduct**	**conduite***(f)* **contraire aux bonnes moeurs**
Ort*(m)*	**place**	**lieu***(m)***,** endroit*(m)*, place*(f)*
Geschäftssitz; geschäftliche Niederlassung	– of business	siège*(m)* d'une société
Liefer–	– of delivery	lieu de livraison
Erfüllungs–	– of performance	lieu d'accomplissement (d'un contrat)
Wohn–, Aufenthalts–	– of residence	lieu de résidence
Ortsstatuten*(n)***;** Gemeindeverordnung*(f)*; Satzung*(f)*; Geschäftsordnung	**by-laws**	**arrêté municipal ou communal;** statuts*(m)* d'une société

P

GERMAN	ENGLISH	FRENCH
Paragraph(*m*); Abschnitt(*m*)	**section**	**section**(*f*), article(*m*) (d'une loi)
Parlament(*n*) Gesetz	**Parliament** Act of –	**parlement**(*m*) loi(*f*)
Patentinhaber(*m*)	**patentee**	**Breveté**(*m*), titulaire(*m*) d'un brevet d'invention

Patent(*n*)
 	
–verletzung
–recht; –gesetz
–rechte
	patent
	
	– infringement
	– law
	– rights
		brevet d'invention (*n*);
		breveté (*adj.*), patenté (*adj.*)
		  contrefaçon(*f*)
		  droit(*m*) des brevets
		  propriété(*f*) industrielle

Pauschalbetrag(*m*); Abfindungsbetrag(*m*)	**lump sum**	**somme**(*f*) **globale**, somme forfaitaire
Pauschalsatz(*m*); Pauschalgebühr(*f*)	**flat rate**	**taux**(*m*) **uniforme**
Pension(*f*); Rente(*f*) Invalidenrente Altersrente Pensionsleistungen Pensionsfonds Rentenversicherung; Pensionsversicherung	**pension** disability – old age – – benefits – fund – insurance	**retraite**(*f*), pension(*f*) pension d'invalidité pension de vieillesse, retraite vieillesse allocation(*f*) de retraite caisse(*f*) de retraite assurance(*f*) retraite
peremptorisch; zwingend zwingendes Argument Ablehnung der Geschworenen ohne Angabe von Gründen peremptorischer Einwand	**peremptory** – argument – challenge – defence	**décisif**, absolu, péremptoire argument(*m*) décisif exception(*f*) péremptoire, récusation(*f*) de jurés défense(*f*) au fond
Person(*f*) juristische – juristische – natürliche –	**person** artificial – legal – natural –	**personne**(*f*), individu(*m*) personne morale personne morale personne physique
Personengesellschaft(*f*) Kommanditgesellschaft	**partnership** limited –	**association**(*f*), société(*f*), participation(*f*) société en commandite simple
Personenstandsstatistik(*f*); Bevölkerungsstatistik	**vital statistics**	**statistiques**(*m*) **démographiques**

GERMAN	ENGLISH	FRENCH
persönlich	**personal**	**personnel**
–e Anwesenheit	– attendance	présence(f) en personne
–e Beschreibung	– description	signalement(m)
bewegliches Vermögen	– property, personalty	biens(m) personnels, biens propres
–e Bürgschaft	– surety	caution(f) personnelle
Pfandgeber(m); –schuldner(m)	**pledgor**	**emprunteur**(m), débiteur(m) sur gages, gageur(m)
Pfandgläubiger(m)	**pawnee**	**prêteur**(m) **sur gages**
Pfand(n); Versprechen	**pledge**	**gage**(m), promesse(f), nantissement(m), voeu(m)
Pfandnehmer(m); –gläubiger(m)	**pledgee**	**créancier**(m) **gagiste**(m), prêteur(m) sur gages
Pfandrecht(n); Zurückbehaltungsrecht(n)	**lien**	**privilège**(m), droit(m) de rétention, nantissement
allgemeines Pfandrecht	general –	privilège général
Zurückbehaltungsrecht an Vermögen(swerten)	– on assets	privilège sur les biens
Pfandrecht an e-r bestimmten Sache	particular –	privilège particulier
Zurückbehaltungsrecht (das Besitz der Sache voraussetzt)	possessory –	droit de rétention
Pfandrecht(n) **an e-r bestimmten Sache**(f)	**particular lien**	**privilège**(m) **spécial**
Pflicht(f); Aufgabe(f); Abgabe(f)	**duty**	**devoir**(m), obligation(f); fonction(f), responsabilité(f); service(m) commandé; droit(m), impôt(m), taxe(f)
Zollgebühr	customs –	droits de douane
Pflichtverletzung(f), Vergehen(n); Kriminalität(f)	**delinquency**	**délinquence**(f)
Jugendkriminalität	juvenile –	délinquence juvénile
(pflichtwidrige) Nichtanzeige e-r strafbaren Handlung(f)	**misprision**	**non-dénonciation**(f), recel(m); forfaiture(f)
physisch; körperlich	**physical**	**physique**
Körperbehinderung	– disability	handicap(m) physique, invalidité(f)
physischer Zwang	– duress	constrainte(f) physique
Körperverletzung	– harm	lésion(f) corporelle
unheilbare Impotenz	– incapacity	invalidité
Körperverletzung	– injury	blessures(f) corporelles
körperliche Bestandsaufnahme; Inventur	– inventory	inventaire(m) détaillé
plädieren; vor Gericht vorbringen	**plead (to)**	**plaider**
sich schuldig (nicht schuldig) bekennen	– guilty (not guilty)	plaider coupable (non coupable)
(plädierender)(m) **Anwalt**(m); Barrister(m)	**barrister**	**avocat**(m), avocate à la Cour
planen und Ränke schmieden	**planning and scheming**	**machinations**(f) **et intrigues**(f)

GERMAN	ENGLISH	FRENCH
Plazierung(f) **von Wertpapieren;** Unterbringung –(f)	**placement of securities** (US), **placing of securities** (UK)	**placement**(m) **de valeurs**
Plenarsitzung(f)	**plenary session**	**session**(f) **plénière**
plündern	**pillage (to)**	**piller,** saccager
Polizei(f)	**constabulary**	**gendarmerie**(f)
Polizei(f) –behörde Polizist –gericht –(truppe) –kommissar –beamter –revier; –wache	**police** – authority – constable – court – force – inspector – officer – station	**police**(f) la police officier(m) de police tribunal(m) de police forces(f) de police, corps(m) de police inspecteur(m) de police policier poste(f) de police
Polizeihauptmann(m) (US); Vollstreckungsbeamter(m)	**marshal** (US)	**shérif**(m) (US)
(Polizei-)Runde(f), Rundgang(m)	**beat (police)**	**tournée**(f), ronde(m) (de police)
Portefeuille(n)	**portfolio**	**portefeuille**(m) **(d'actions, de valeurs)**
Postleitzahl(f) (US)	**zipcode** (US)	**code**(m) **postal** (US)
Präambel(f); Eingangsformel(f)	**preamble**	**exposé des motifs d'une loi,** attendus d'un arrêt; préambule(m)
Prämie(f) Versicherungs– Sparprämienanleihen –nlohn	**premium** insurance – – bonds – wage	**prime**(f), agio(m); récompense(f); prix convenu(m); profit net(m); reprise(f) (en cas de location) prime d'assurance obligations(f) à primes salaire(m) supplémentaire (exceptionnel)
Praxis(f); Verfahren Anwaltspraxis Zivilverfahren Handelspraktikten	**practice** legal – civil – trade –(s)	**procédure**(f); cabinet(m), clientèle(f); pratique(f), méthode(f) manoeuvre(f), procédure(f) légale procédure civile usages(m) commerciaux
Präzedenzfall(m)	**precedent**	**décision**(f) **judiciaire faisant jurisprudence;** précédent(m)
Preis(m) –kartell –kontrolle –diskriminierung –index –grenze	**price** – cartel – control – discrimination – index – limit	**prix**(m), cours(f), cote(f) cartel(m) des prix contrôle(m) des prix discrimination(f) des prix indice(m) des prix limite(f) de prix

GERMAN	ENGLISH	FRENCH
(Preis) angaben(f); notieren	**quote (to)**	**coter (une valeur);** faire un devis; se référer à, rappeler
Preisangabe(f); –angebot(n); Notierung(f)	**quotation**	**cotation**(f), cours(m); référence(f)
privat; nicht öffentlich personenbezogene Kapitalgesellschaft; (etwa: Gesellschaft mit beschränkter Haftung)	**private** – company	**privé,** particulier(m) société(f) à responsabilité limitée (SARL), société privée
Privatunternehmen; freie Marktwirtschaft	– enterprise	entreprise(f) privée
internationales Privatrecht	– international law	droit privé international
Privat–, Zivilrecht	– law	droit(m) privé
Privatklage	– prosecution	action(f) en justice privée
Privatverkauf; freihändiger Verkauf	– sale	vente(f) de gré à gré
Privatsektor; Privatwirtschaft	– sector	secteur(m) privé
pro(m) **kopf**	**per capita**	**par tête**
Produkthaftpflichtversicherung(f)	**product liability insurance**	**assurance**(f) **contre les défauts de fabrication**
Produktion(f); Herstellung(f)	**production**	**production**(f), fabrication(f), présentation(f)
Herstellungslizenz	– licence	droits(m) de licence
Herstellungsrecht	– rights	droits de fabrication
Proformarechnung(f)	**pro forma invoice**	**facture**(f) **pro forma,** facture pour la forme
Prospekt(m); Einführungs–(m); Werbeschrift(f)	**prospectus**	**prospectus**(m), appel(m) à souscription publique
Protokoll(n); Niederschrift(f)	**minutes**	**procès-verbal**(m), compte-rendu(m)
prozentualer Anteil(m)	**percentage share**	**part**(f) **de participation**
Prozeß(m); Klage(f)	**suit**	**action**(f) **civile,** poursuite(f), procès(m)
Prozeß(m); Rechtsstreit(m)	**litigation**	**litige**(m), procès(m)
(Prozeß–)Gegner(m)	**opponent**	**opposant**
prozessieren	**litigate (to)**	**mettre en litige,** contester
(Prozeß–)Partei(f) Gegen–; Prozeßgegner	**party** adverse –	**partie**(f); parti(m) (politique) partie opposée, partie adverse
notwendiger Streitgenosse	indispensable –	partie indispensable
Verletzte(r); Geschädigte(r)	injured –	partie lésée
Gegen–	opposite –	partie opposée, partie adverse
Dritte(r); Nebenintervenient	third –	tiers(m), tierce personne

GERMAN	ENGLISH	FRENCH
Prozeßpartei(*f*); prozeßführende Partei(*f*)	**litigant**	**plaideur**(*m*)
Prozeßrecht(*n*); Verfahrens–(*n*)	**procedural law**	**code**(*m*) **de procédure**
psychische Leiden(*n*)	**pain and suffering**	**blessures**(*f*) **et souffrances**(*f*)
Psychopath(*m*)	**psychopath**	**psychopathe**(*m, f*)

Q

GERMAN	ENGLISH	FRENCH
Qualität(f)	**quality**	**qualité**(f); statut(m), condition(f)
–sabnahme(prüfung)	– approval	contrôle(m), agrément(m) de la qualité
–sbeanstandung	– complaint	plainte portant sur la qualité
Quarantäne(f)	**quarantine**	**quarantaine**(f)
quittieren; Empfang(m) bescheinigen	**receipt (to)**	**acquitter**
Quittung(f); Empfangsschein	**receipt**	**reçu**(m), récépissé(m)
Quorum(n); Beschlußfähigkeit(f)	**quorum**	**quorum**(m), quantum(m)
Quote(f); Kontingent(n)	**quota**	**quota**(f), contingent; quote-part(f); cotisation(f)

R

GERMAN	ENGLISH	FRENCH
Rache(f)	**revenge**	**vengeance**(f)
Rache(f)	**vengeance**	**vengeance**(f)

Rat(m); Benachrichtigung(f), Mitteilung(f); Avis
  juristische Beratung, Rechtsbeistand
	advice
	  legal –
		avis(m), conseil(m)
		  avis(m) d'un homme de loi

Rat(m); Versammlung(f); Ortsbehörde(n)
  Weisung, Verfügung, Richtlinie(des Rats)
  Ratsbeschluß
  Rat der Europäischen Gemeinschaft
  Sicherheitsrat der Vereinten Nationen
	council
	  Council directive
	
	  Council decision
	  Council of the EEC
	
	  UN Security Council
		conseil(m), assemblée(f)
		  directive(f) du conseil
		
		  décision(f) du conseil
		  le Conseil de la CE
		
		  le Conseil de sécurité des Nations Unies

Ratenkauf(m)	**instalment purchase**	**achat**(m) à tempérament
Ratifizierung(f); Bestätigung(f)	**ratification**	**homologation**(f), ratification(f), entérinement(m)
rationalisieren	**rationalise (to)**	**rationaliser**
Rationalisierung(f)	**rationalisation**	**rationalisation**(f)
Rationierung(f); Bewirtschaftung(f)	**rationing**	**rationnement**(m)

Raub(m); Beraubung(f)
  bewaffneter Raubüberfall
  gewalttätige(r) –
	robbery
	  armed –
	  – with violence
		vol(m) **qualifié**
		  vol à main armée
		  vol qualifié avec violences

räumen; ausziehen; aufgeben	**vacate (to)**	**annuler,** résilier, évacuer, démissionner
Rauschgiftverbrechen(m)	**narcotics crime**	**infraction**(f) **à la législation sur les stupéfiants**

realisieren; veräußern
 	
  Eigentum veräußern
	realise (to)
	
	  – property
		réaliser; convertir en espèces; se rendre compte de qque chose
		  vendre des biens

GERMAN	ENGLISH	FRENCH
Rechnungsprüfung(*f*); Revision(*f*)	**audit, auditing**	**audit**(*f*), vérification(*f*), apurement(*m*)
Steuerprüfung	tax –	vérification de comptabilité par le fisc
rechtfertigen	**justify (to)**	**légitimer,** justifier
rechtfertigen; verteidigen; beanspruchen	**vindicate (to)**	**justifier,** soutenir
Recht(*n*)	**law**	**droit**(*m*); science(*f*) juridique; législation(*f*), loi(*f*)
formelles –, Prozeß–	adjective –	procédure(*f*)
Verwaltungs–	administrative –	droit administratif
Luft–	air –	droit aérien
Bank–	banking –	droit bancaire
Konkurs–	bankruptcy –	droit des faillites
Fall–	case –	droit des précédents
Zivil–	civil –	droit civil
Gewohnheits–	common –	droit coutumier, droit commun
Gemeinschaftsrecht *(EG)*	Community –	droit communautaire
Gesellschafts–; Aktien–	company –	droit des sociétés
Verfassungs–	constitutional –	droit constitutionnel
Vertrags–; Schuld–	contract –	droit des obligations
Gesellschafts–; Aktien– *(US)*	corporation – *(US)*	droit des sociétés *(US)*
Straf–	criminal –	droit criminel
Wahl–; Wahlgesetz	electoral –	droit électoral
EG-Recht	EEC –	droit communautaire
Arbeitsrecht	employment –	droit du travail
Recht zum Schutz der Umwelt	environmental –	droit de l'environnement
Familien–	family –	droit de la famille
Bundes–; Bundesgesetz	federal –	droit fédéral
Finanzgesetz	financial –	droit financier
Steuer–	fiscal –	droit fiscal
Versicherungs–	insurance –	droit des assurances
internationales –	international –	droit international
Arbeits–	labour –	droit du travail
See–	maritime –	droit maritime
Stand–;Kriegs–	martial –	loi martiale, état de siège
Ehe–	matrimonial –	droit du mariage
Handels–	mercantile –	droit commercial
Militär(straf)–; Wehr(straf)–	military –	droit militaire, code de justice militaire
Straf–; Strafgesetz	penal –	droit pénal
positives Recht	positive –	droit positif
Privat–	private–	droit privé
Verfahrens–	procedural –	droit de la procédure
Liegenschafts–; Sachen–	property –	droit de la propriété
öffentliches –	public –	droit public
Römisches –	Roman –	droit romain
Steuer–; Steuergesetz	tax –	loi fiscale
Recht(*n*) **der unerlaubten Handlungen**(*f*)	**law of torts**	**droit**(*m*) **de la responsabilité**
rechts, gesetzwidrige Handlung(*f*), –s Verhalten	**malfeasance**	**méfait**(*m*); prévarication(*f*)

GERMAN	ENGLISH	FRENCH
Recht(sanspruch)(*m*)	**right**	**le droit,** la justice, le bien; droit(*m*), titre(*m*), privilège(*m*)
Grundrechte; bürgerliche Ehrenrechte	civil –(s)	droits civils
Menschenrechte	human –(s)	droits de l'homme
immaterielle Rechte	intangible –(s)	propriété(*f*) intellectuelle
Berufungsrecht; Rechtsmittel	– of appeal	droit d'appel
Entschädigungsrecht	– of redress	droit(*m*) de recours
Vorfahrtsrecht; Wegerecht	– of way	droit de passage
wohlerworbene, wohlbegründete Rechte	vested –	droits acquis en vertu de la constitution
(Rechts-)Anwalt(*m*)	**lawyer**	**homme**(*m*) **de loi,** juriste(*m*); avocat(*m*) (*surtout US*)
Rechtsanwaltsbüro(*n*) (*US*)	**law office** (*US*)	**étude**(*f*) **d'avocat,** d'avoué (*US*)
Rechtsbehelf(*m*)	**remedy**	**voie**(*f*) **de recours,** moyen(*m*) de droit, dédommagement(*m*)
vorläufiger -	provisional –	ordonnance(*f*) de référé, mesure(*f*) provisoire
Rechtsbelehrung(*f*) **der Geschworenen** (*US*)	**instructions to jury** (*US*)	**recommandations**(*f*) **du juge aux jurés** (*US*)
Rechtsbrecher(*m*); Gesetzesübertreter(*m*)	**law-breaker**	**transgresseur**(*m*) **de la loi**
(rechts)gültig; in Kraft(*f*); stichhaltig	**valid**	**valide,** régulier, valable, recevable
(Rechts)Gültigkeit(*f*); Laufzeit(*f*)	**validity**	**validité**(*f*)
Rechtshilfe(*f*)	**relief**	**réparation**(*f*), redressement(*m*); **secours**(*m*), aide(*f*)
beantragte –; Gegenstand der Leistungsklage	affirmative –	conclusions(*f*) acceptées
Klageantrag; Sachantrag	claim for –	demande(*m*) d'assistance
deklaratorischer Rechtsschutz	declaratory –	jugement(*m*) déclaratif
Rechtshilfeersuchen	**letters rogatory**	**commission**(*f*) **rogatoire**
Rechtsnachfolger(*m*); Zessionar(*m*); Erwerber(*m*)	**assignee**	**cessionnaire**(*m*); syndic(*m*), administrateur-séquestre(*m*)
Rechtsprechung(*f*) **nach equity-Recht**(*n*)**;** Kanzleigericht	**chancery**	**chancellerie**(*f*)
Gericht(*n*), das nach den Grundsätzen des equity urteilt	court of –	tribunal(*m*) jugeant en 'equity'
(rechts-)ungültig	**invalid**	**non-valable,** sans effet légal
(Rechts-)Verletzung(*f*)**;** Verstoß(*m*); Zuwiderhandlung(*f*)	**infringement**	**infraction,** violation (d'une loi), contrefaçon
Urheberrechtsverletzung	– of copyright	contrefaçon(*f*) en matière de droits d'auteur
Patentverletzung	– of patent	contrefaçon en matière de brevet
Rechtsvorgänger(*m*); Zedent(*m*); Übertragender(*m*); Abtreter(*m*)	**assignor**	**cédant**(*m*)

GERMAN	ENGLISH	FRENCH
rechtswidrig; unzulässig	**illicit**	**illégal**, illicite
Rechtswissenschaft(f)	**jurisprudence**	**philosophie**(f) **du droit**
vergleichende –	comparative –	droit(m) comparé
Gerichtsmedizin	medical –	médecine(f) légale
Refinanzierung(f)	**refinancing**	**refinancement**(m)
Regel(f); Bestimmung(f);	**rule**	**règle**(f) **de procédure**, règle
Verordnung(f)		de droit immuable;
		disposition(f)
Regelung(f); Beilegung(f);	**settlement**	**arrangement**(m),
Abfindung(f)		règlement(m), transaction(f);
		disposition(f) de biens,
		liquidation(f)
außergerichtliche Regelung	out-of-court –	arrangement à l'amiable
Regelung auf	– by arbitration	règlement arbitral
schiedsgerichtlichem Weg		
Regierung(f)	**government**	**gouvernement**(m) **de l'État**
Registerführer(m); Gerichts–(m),	**registrar**	**teneur**(m) **de registre,**
Standesbeamter(m)		greffier(m), archiviste(m)
Führer des Gesellschaftsregisters	the – of companies	directeur(m) de
		l'enregistrement de
		sociétés
Register(n); Verzeichnis(n);	**register**	**registre**(m), livre(m);
Registerführer(m) (US);		teneur(f) de registre (US),
Gerichts –, Standesbeamter(M)		greffier(m), archiviste(m)
Regreß(m); Rückgriff(m)	**recourse**	**recours**(m)
gegen Dritte Regreß nehmen	– against a third party	recours contre un tiers
Rehabilitierung(f)	**rehabilitation**	**réhabilitation**(f),
		redressement(m),
		rétablissement(m)
reisend	**itinerant**	**en tournée**, itinérant,
		ambulant
Reiserichter	– judge	juge(m) en tournée
Reiseversicherung(f)	**travel insurance**	**assurance**(f) **voyage**
relevant; erheblich	**relevant**	**pertinent**, applicable,
		approprié, utile
Relevanz(f); Wichtigkeit(f)	**relevancy**	**pertinence**(f)
Rentabilität(f);	**profitability**	**rentabilité**(f)
Wirtschaftlichkeit(f)		
Restnachlaßempfänger(m)	**residuary legatee**	**légataire**(m) **universel**
retten	**save (to)**	**sauver**; économiser,
		épargner
jdm das Leben retten	– a person's life	sauver la vie de qqu'un
Richter(m)	**judge**	**juge**(m), magistrat(m)
Berufungs–	appellate –	juge de cour d'appel
Hilfs–	assistant –	magistrat assesseur
Einzelrichter, im Büroweg	– in chambers	juge du siège
entscheidender Richter		
Gerichtspräsident; vorsitzender	presiding –	président(m) du tribunal
Richter		

GERMAN	ENGLISH	FRENCH
Richterbank(*f*); Gericht(*n*); Richterschaft(*m*)	**bench**	**banc**(*m*)
(richterlicher) Haftbefehl	– warrant	mandat(*m*) d'arrêt décerné sur le siège
richterlicher Beamter(*m*) **zur Untersuchung**(*f*) **der Todesursache**(*f*)	**coroner**	**'coroner'**(*m*)
Richtigstellung(*f*); Berichtigung(*f*)	**rectification**	**rectification**(*f*), redressement(*m*)
Richtlinie(*f*); Anordnung(*f*) (*EG*) EG-Rat Richtlinie	**directive** (*EC law*) Council –	**directive**(*f*) directive du Conseil
Richtlinien(*f*)	**guidelines**	**directives**(*f*)
Risiko(*n*) –management –spanne	**risk** – management – margin	**risque**(*m*), aléa(*m*), péril(*m*) contrôle(*m*) des pertes marge(*f*) de risque
Roentgenuntersuchung(*f*)	**X-ray examination**	**examen**(*m*) **radioscopique**
Rowdy(*m*)	**hooligan**	**voyou**(*m*), vandale(*m, f*), hooligan(*m*)
Rückerstattung(*f*); Steuererklärung(*f*); Ertrag(*m*) Vermögensangabe	**return**	**revenu**(*m*), rendement(*m*); remboursement(*m*), ristourne; renvoi(*m*), réexpédition(*f*)
Gesamtkapitalrentabilität Kapitalertrag	– on assets – on capital	rendement(*m*) d'un actif rentabilité(*f*) du capital (investi)
Ertrag aus Kapitalanlage; Kapitalrendite	– on investment (ROI)	rendement sur investissement (RSI)
Rückerstattung(*f*); Wiederherstellung(*f*) des früheren Rechtszustands	**restitution**	**restitution**(*f*), réparation(*f*), dommages-intérêt(s)(*m*)
Rückgabe(*f*); Wiederherstellung(*f*)	**restoration**	**restitution**
Rückgängigmachung(*f*), Ungültig–; Aufhebung(*f*), Widerruf(*m*); Kündigung(*f*)	**cancellation**	**annulation**(*f*)
Aufhebungs–, Kündigungs–, Rücktrittsklausel	– clause	clause(*f*) de résiliation, clause résolutoire
Rückkauf(*m*); Einlösung(*f*); Tilgung(*f*)	**redemption**	**amortissement**(*m*), rachat(*m*), remboursement(*m*), faculté(*f*) de réméré
Tilgung e-r Hypothek Rückkauf von Wertpapieren Tilgungskurs	– of a mortgage – of securities – rate	purge(*f*) d'hypothèque amortissement de titres taux(*m*) de remboursement, d'amortissement
gesetzliches Rückkaufsrecht	– right	droit(*m*) de rachat
Rücklage(*f*); Reserve(*f*)	**reserve**	**réserve**(*f*), provision(*f*), couverture(*f*)
Rückstellung für Eventualverbindlichkeiten	contingency –	fonds(*m*) de réserve
gesetzliche Mindestreserven; – Rücklagen;	legal –	réserve légale
Neubewertungsrücklage	revaluation –	réserve de réévaluation

GERMAN	ENGLISH	FRENCH
Rücknahme(f); Abhebung(f); Rücktritt(m)	**withdrawal**	**retrait**(m)
Geldabhebung	– of money	retrait d'argent
rücksichtslos; böswillig	**wanton**	**capricieux,** absurde, dévergondé
mutwillige Verletzung	– injury	blessure(f) accidentelle
rückübertragen; –abtreten	**reassign (to)**	**réaffecter**; opérer une nouvelle cession
rückvergüten	**refund (to)**	**rembourser,** restituer, ristourner
Rückversicherung(f)	**reinsurance**	**réassurance**(f)**,** contre-assurance(f)
Ruhestand(m); Rücktritt(m)	**retirement**	**retraite**(f)

S

GERMAN	ENGLISH	FRENCH
s. verschwören; sich heimlich verabreden	**conspire (to)**	**conspirer,** comploter
Sabotage(*f*)	**sabotage**	**sabotage**(*m*)
Sachen; körperliche Gegenstände	**corporeal property**	**biens corporels**
Sakrileg(*n*)**;** Kirchenschändung(*f*)	**sacrilege**	**sacrilège**(*m*)
sanitär; hygienisch	**sanitary**	**sanitaire**
Sanktion(*f*)**;** Bestätigung(*f*)	**sanction**	**sanction**(*f*), ratification(*f*), approbation(*f*)
Strafmaßnahmen	punitive –	sanction pénale
Satz(*m*)**;** Kurs(*m*)	**rate**	**taux**(*m*), cours(*m*), tarif(*m*)
Umrechnungskurs	conversion –	taux de conversion
Diskontsatz	discount –	taux d'escompte
Wechselkurs	exchange –	taux de change
Zinssatz	– of interest	taux d'intérêt
Ertragsrate; Rentabilität	– of return	taux de rendement
Satzung(*f*) (*UK*); Statut(*n*) (e-r Kapitalgesellschaft)(*f*), Gründungsvertrag(*m*)	**memorandum of association** (*UK*)	**acte**(*m*) **constitutif d'une société** (*UK*)
Schaden(*m*)	**harm**	**mal**(*m*), tort(*m*), préjudice(*m*)
körperlicher –; Körperverletzung	bodily –	lésion(*f*) corporelle
Schaden(*m*)**;** Beschädigung(*f*); Verlust(*m*)	**damage**	**dommage**(*m*), dégât(*m*)
tatsächlicher Schaden	actual –	dommage réel
mittelbarer Schaden; Folgeschaden	consequential –	dommage indirect
strafbare Sachbeschädigung	criminal –	dégâts criminels
unmittelbarer Schaden	direct –	dommage direct
Gesamtschaden; allgemeiner Schaden	general –	dommage général
Teilschaden	partial –	dommage partiel

GERMAN	ENGLISH	FRENCH
Schadensersatz(*m*);	**damages**	**indemnité**(*f*), dommages-intérêts(*m*)
Entschädigung(-ssumme)(*f*)		
bedingt zuerkannter Schadensersatzanspruch	contingent –	dommages-intérêts conditionnels
Schadenersatz für Aufwendungen bei Vertragserfüllung	incidental –	dommages-intérêts incidents
im voraus der Höhe nach bestimmter Schadensersatz; Vertragsstrafe	liquidated –	dommages liquidés
nomineller Schadensersatz	nominal –	dommages-intérêts symboliques ('un franc symbolique')
(der Höhe nach noch) unbestimmter Schadensersatz	unliquidated –	dommages-intérêts non liquidés
Schadensersatzklage(*f*)	**remedial action**	**action**(*f*) **en recours**
Schadenversicherung(*f*); Unfall-Haftpflichtversicherung(*f*) *(US)*	**casualty insurance**	**assurance**(*f*) **contre les accidents**
schädigen; verletzen	**harm (to)**	**nuire** blesser
schädlich; nachteilig	**hurtful**	**douloureux,** pénible
schadlos halten	**indemnify (to)**	**indemniser,** dédommager
Schadloshaltung(*f*); Abfindung(*f*); Freistellung(*f*)	**indemnity**	**indemnité**(*f*)
Scheidung(*f*)	**divorce**	**divorce**(*m*)
Ehescheidungsverfahren	– proceedings	action(*f*) en divorce
Scheingesellschaft(*f*); vorgeschobene Gesellschaft(*f*)	**dummy company**	**société**(*f*) **prête-nom**
Scheinprozeß(*m*)	**mock trial**	**simulacre**(*m*) **de procès**
scheitern; unterliegen; Zahlung(*f*) einstellen; in Konkurs gehen	**fail (to)**	**échouer,** manquer, faire défaut
Schenkung(*f*); Zuwendung	**gift**	**don**(*m*)
beschränkte (aus bestimmten Mitteln erfüllte) Schenkung	demonstrative –	legs(*m*) à payer d'une source spécifiée
Schenkung zu treuen Händen	– in trust	don placé sous tutelle
Schenkungssteuer	– tax	impôt(*m*) sur les donations
Schenkungsempfänger(*m*); Begünstigter(*m*)	**donee**	**donataire**(*m*), bénéficiaire(*m*)
Schenkungsgeber(*m*); Stifter(*m*)	**donor**	**donneur**(*m*), donateur(*m*)
Schieber(*m*); korrupter Beamter(*m*)	**grafter**	**escroc**(*m*), chevalier(*f*) d'industrie
Schiebung(*f*), Korruption(*f*); Bestechungsgeld(*n*)	**graft**	**concussion**(*f*), corruption(*f*) de fonctionnaires
Schieds(gerichts)verfahren(*n*); Schiedsgerichtsbarkeit(*f*); Arbitrage(geschäft)	**arbitration**	**arbitrage**(*m*)
Schiedsspruch	– award	sentence(*f*) arbitrale
Schiedsstelle, Schlichtungsstelle	– board	commission(*f*) arbitrale
Schiedsklausel	– clause	clause(*f*) compromissoire
Schiedsgericht(shof)	– tribunal	tribunal(*m*) arbitral
Schiedsrichter(*m*)	**arbitrator**	**arbitre**(*m*), amiable compositeur

GERMAN	ENGLISH	FRENCH
Schiedsrichter(m); Sachverständiger(m)	**referee**	**arbitre**(m), amiable compositeur
Schiffsagentur(f)	**shipping agency**	**agence**(f) **maritime,** agence(f) d'affrètement
Schiffseigner(m); Reeder(m)	**shipowner**	**armateur**(m)
Schiffsmakler(m)	**shipbroker**	**courtier**(m) **maritime**
Schiffsmakler(m); Seehafenspediteur(m)	**shipping agent**	**agent maritime,** commissionnaire(m) chargeur
schlechtes (ordnungswidriges) Verhalten; Verletzung(f) der Amtspflich	**misconduct**	**adultère**(m); mauvaise gestion, inconduite(f)
Schlichter(m); Vermittler(m)	**mediator**	**conciliateur**(m), médiateur(m)
Schlichtung(f); Vermittlung(f)	**mediation**	**conciliation**(f), médiation(f), intervention(f) amicale
schließen; einstellen; beenden Verfahren einstellen	**close (to)** – the proceedings	**fermer,** clore(m) clôture(f) de la procédure
Schließung(f); Schluß(m); Abschluß(m) Schluß der Debatte	**closure** – of debate	**clôture**(f) clôture des débats
schlüssiger (zwingender) Beweis	**conclusive evidence**	**preuve**(f) **concluante,** pertinente
Schlußplädoyer(m)	**closing address**	**allocution**(f), plaidoirie(f) finale
Schlußplädoyer(m); Rechtsbelehrung(f) d. Geschworenen Zusammenfassung	**summing-up**	**résumé**(m) **du juge à l'intention des jurés**
Schmuggel(m)	**smuggling**	**contrebande**(f)
Schreiben; Schriftform(f)	**writing**	**écrit**(m), écriture(f), souscription(f)
schriftl. Beauftragung(f) **und Information**(f) (des Barrister durch den Solicitor) zur Vertretung vor Gericht; Schriftsatz; Auftrag, Mandat	**brief**	**exposé**(m), dossier(m)
Schriftsätze(m)	**pleadings**	**(les) débats**(m)
Schriftstück(n), Urkunde(f); Rechnung(f); Gesetzentwurf(m), –vorlage; Wechsel, Tratte; Geldschein (US), Banknote(f) Regierungsvorlage	**bill** government –	**projet**(m) **de loi** projet de loi gouvernemental
(gezogener) Wechsel, Tratte Anklageschrift	– of exchange – of indictment	lettre(f) de change résumé(m) des chefs d'accusation
Konnossement, Seefrachtbrief; (Binnenschiffahrt) Ladeschein	– of lading	connaissement(m)
Schuld(f)	**guilt**	**culpabilité**(f)

GERMAN	ENGLISH	FRENCH
Schuld(f); Forderung(f) zweifelhafte Forderung Schuldurkunde (pl.) Außenstände bevorrechtigte Schuld, Forderung	**debt** doubtful – instrument of – outstanding – preferential –	**dette**(f), créance(f) créance douteuse titre(m) de créance dette à recouvrer créance préférentielle
Schuld(f); Verschulden; Fehler(m) vom Verschulden abhängige Haftung; Fehleranfälligkeit (EDV)	**fault** – liability	**faute**(f), négligence(f), imperfection(f) responsabilité(f) de la faute
Schuldanerkenntnis(n); Eigenwechsel(m)	**promissory note**	**billet**(m) **à ordre,** promesse écrite de payer sa dette
schuldhaft; strafbar	**culpable**	**coupable;** volontaire
(schuldhafte) Unterlassung; Versäumnis(n) (in der Geltendmachung(f) e-s Anspruchs); Verwirkung(f)	**laches**	**négligence**(f), délai(m) tardif pour faire valoir un droit
schuldig nicht – s. – bekennen Urteil auf-	**guilty** not – to plead – verdict of –	**coupable**(m, f) innocent, non coupable plaider coupable verdict(m) de culpabilité
schuldlos; unschuldig	**innocent**	**innocent**(m)
Schuldlosigkeit(f); Unschuld(f)	**innocence**	**innocence**(f)
Schuldner(m); Darlehens–, Kreditnehmer(m)	**debtor**	**débiteur**(m)
Schuldurkunde(f), –schein(m); Wertpapier(n), Obligation(f), Schuldverschreibung(f); Haftungsversprechen(n), Bürgschaft(f), Garantieerklärung(f); Zollverschluß(m) Inhaberobligation, – schuldverschreibung Staatsanleihen, – papiere, –schuldverschreibungen tilgbare Obligation, kündbare Obligation (staatl.) Sparbrief; Sparschuldverschreibung (US)	**bond** bearer – government – redeemable – savings –	**obligation**(f), engagement(m) titre(m) au porteur obligation d'État, rente d'État obligation amortissable bon d'épargne
schützen	**protect (to)**	**protéger,** sauvegarder
schützend	**protective**	**protecteur**(m)
schwebendes Sicherungsrecht(n)	**floating charge**	**droit**(m) **de préférence sur tout ou partie de l'actif présent et à venir d'une société, sous réserve du droit pour la société de modifier cet actif dans le cours normal de ses affaires**
Schwebezustand(m); Unentschiedenheit(f)	**abeyance**	**suspension**(f); vacation(f), suspension(f), interruption(f)

GERMAN	ENGLISH	FRENCH
Schweigegeld(n)	**hush money**	**argent**(m) **donné à qqu'un pour prix de son silence**
schwer	**gross**	**gros**(m), grossier, trop fort; brut(m)
grobe Fahrlässigkeit	– negligence	négligence(f) coupable
Schwindel(m); Betrug(m)	**swindle**	**escroquerie**(f)
Schwindler(m); Betrüger(m)	**swindler**	**escroc**(m)
Schwurgericht(n); Geschworene	**jury**	**jury**(m)
beratende Jury	advisory –	jury de conseil
Anklagejury (US)	grand – (US)	jury d'accusation (US)
Urteilsjury (US)	petty – (US)	jury de jugement (US)
Schwurgerichtsverfahren	trial by –	procès(m) conduit devant un jury
Geschworene in e-m Prozeß; Urteilsjury	trial –	jury du procès
Scrip(m); Zwischenschein(m)	**scrip**	**bon**(m), document(m), titre(m), certificat(m)
–inhaber	--holder	porteur(m) de titre, détenteur(m) de documents
Seehandel(m)	**seaborne trade**	**commerce**(m) **maritime**
Seemeile(f)	**nautical mile**	**mille**(m) **marin**
See(schiffahrt)(f)	**marine**	**maritime,** marin
–(transport)versicherung	– insurance	assurance(f) maritime
See(schiffahrt)gericht, –amt	**Admiralty court**	**tribunal**(m) **maritime**
See(schiffahrts)recht(n)	**maritime law**	**droit**(m) **maritime**
Segment(n); Sparte(f)	**segment**	**branche**(f), segment(m)
Marktsegment	market –	secteur(m) du marché
Selbständiger(m)	**self-employed person**	**travailleur**(m) **indépendant**
Selbstbezichtigung(f)	**self-incrimination**	**incrimination**(f) **de soi-même**
Selbstfinanzierung(f)	**self-financing**	**autofinancement**(m)
Sendung(f)	**consignment**	**expédition**(f) **de marchandises**
Sexualverbrechen	**sex crime**	**crime**(m) **d'ordre sexuel**
sich aneignen; bewilligen, bereitstellen; bestimmen, verwenden	**appropriate (to)**	**approprier,** allouer, répartir, doter, prélever
sich berufen auf	**invoke (to)**	**invoquer**
– eine Rechtsvorschrift, e-n Gesetzeserlaß	– an enactment	invoquer la loi
sich der Verhaftung(f) **widersetzen**	**resist (to) arrest**	**résister lors de son arrestation**
sich hinwegsetzen über; außer Kraft(f) setzen	**override (to)**	**passer outre,** outrepasser

GERMAN	ENGLISH	FRENCH
sich vergleichen, einigen mit s-n Gläubigern einen Vergleich schließen	**compound (to)** – with one's creditors	**composer,** transiger s'arranger avec ses créanciers
sich verstecken sich der Strafverfolgung entziehen	**hide (to)** – from justice	**(se) cacher** se soustraire à l'action de la justice
sich widersprechende Beweise(*m*)**,** sich widersprechende Zeugenaussage(*f*)	**conflicting evidence**	**témoignages**(*m*) **contradictoires**
sich zuziehen; erleiden; sich (e-r Gefahr) aussetzen Schaden erleiden Verlust erleiden	**incur (to)** – damage – losses	**encourir,** subir subir des dégâts subir des pertes
sicher –e Verwahrung; Depot Tresor; Aufbewahrung (im Tresor)	**safe** – custody – deposit	**sain,** sûr dépôt(*m*) en garde dépôt en coffre-fort
sicher begründetes Anrecht(*n*)**;** berechtigte Interesse	**vested interest**	**droit**(*m*), intérêt(*m*) acquis
Sicherheit(*f*)	**safety**	**sécurité**(*f*), sûreté(*f*)
Sicherheit geleistet(*f*)**;** Kaution gestellt	**bailed**	**admis**(*m, f*) **à caution**
Sicherheitsbeamter(*m*)	**peace officer**	**gardien**(*m*) **de la paix**
Sicherheitsversprechen(*n*)**;** Kautions–	**recognisance**	**caution**(*f*) **juridique**
sichern; sicherstellen Sicherheit für ein Darlehen leisten Beweise sicherstellen	**secure (to)** – a loan (debt) – evidence	**réussir à avoir,** obtenir, se procurer; garantir garantir un prêt (une créance) obtenir un témoignage
sichern; wahrnehmen jds Interessen wahren	**safeguard (to)** – a person's interests	**sauvegarder,** prendre des mesures de protection protéger les intérêts de qqu'un
Sicherungsgegenstand(*m*)**;** Nebensicherheit(*f*); Verwandte(r) in der Seitenlinie	**collateral**	**additionnel,** indirect; nantissement(*m*); parent(*m*) en ligne colatérale
Sicherungsgeschäft(*n*)**;** Deckungsgeschäft(*n*)	**hedge**	**couverture**(*f*), arbitrage(*m*), contrepartie(*f*)
Sichtwechsel(*m*)	**demand bill**	**traite**(*f*) **à vue**
Sichtwechsel(*m*)	**sight bill**	**effet**(*m*) **payable à vue,** traite(*f*) à vue
Simulant(*f*)	**malingerer**	**simulateur**(*m*)
simulieren	**malingering**	**simulation**(*f*), absentéisme(*m*)
Sittenpolizei(*f*)	**vice squad**	**brigade**(*f*) **mondaine,** brigade des moeurs
sittenwidrig; gegen Treu und Glauben verstoßend	**unconscionability**	**absence de scrupules**

GERMAN	ENGLISH	FRENCH
Sittlichkeitsvergehen	**sexual offence**	**délit**(m) **d'ordre sexuel**
Sitz(m)	**seat**	**siège**(m), charge(f), office(m)
Regierungssitz;	– of government	siège du gouvernement
Firmen–	the company's –	le siège social de la société
Sitzung(f)	**session**	**audience**(f), session(f), séance(f)
Gericht tagt	court in –	tribunal(m) en session, en séance
öffentliche –	open –	audience publique
(Sitzungs)(f)**Unterbrechung**(f); Pause(f)	**recess**	**vacances**(f) **judiciaires,** suspension(f) d'audience; intersession(f) parlementaire
skrupellos	**unscrupulous**	**sans scrupules**(m)
(Sonder-)Abdruck(m)	**offprint**	**tirage**(m)**,** tiré à part
Sondergewinnsteuer(m); Mehrgewinnsteuer(m)	**excess profits tax**	**impôt**(m) **sur les bénéfices exceptionnels**
sozial	**social**	**social**
–verwaltung	– administration	les services sociaux
–versicherung	– insurance	assurance(f) sociale
–versicherungssystem	– security system	système(m) de sécurité sociale
–fürsorge; Wohlfahrt	– welfare	bien-être(m) social
–fürsorger; Wohlfahrtsbeamter	– worker	assistant(e)(m, f) social(e)
Sozialversicherungsbeitrag(m)	**payroll tax**	**impôt**(m) **sur les salaires**
Sparkasse(f)	**savings bank**	**caisse**(f) **d'épargne**
Spekulation(f)**;** Vermutung(f)	**speculation**	**spéculation**(f)
Spion(m)	**spy**	**espion**(m)
Sponsor(m)**;** Geldgeber(m)	**sponsor**	**caution**(f)**,** garant(m); caution personnelle d'un immigrant (US); parrain(m), commanditaire(m), 'sponsor'
Spot(m)	**spot**	**disponible**; lieu(m) précis, point; message(m) publicitaire
–markt	– market	march(m)é au comptant
–kurs; Kassakurs	– rate	cours(f) du disponible
–geschäft; Kassageschäft	– transaction	opération(f) au comptant
Spur(f)**;** Anzeichen(n)	**trace**	**filière**(f)**;** vestige(m), trace(f)
(Staats-, Hoheits-)Gebiet(n)**;** Territorium(f)	**territory**	**territoire**(m)
Mietgliedsstaat-Gebiet (EG)	member State – (EEC)	territoire d'un état membre (de la CEE)
Staatsbürgerschaft(m)**,** Staatsangehörigkeit(f)	**citizenship**	**citoyenneté**(f)**,** nationalité(f)
(Staats)Einkommen(n)**;** Steuereinnahmen(m)	**revenue**	**revenu**(m)**,** rapport(m), rentes(f)

GERMAN	ENGLISH	FRENCH
Staatskasse(*f*)**;** Fiskus(*m*) Finanzminister *(UK)*	**exchequer** Chancellor of the Exchequer	**fisc**(*m*)**,** trésor(*m*) (public) ministre(*m*) des finances, 'chancelier(*m*) de l'échiquier' *(UK)*
Staatsschuldverschreibung *(US),* firmeneigene –; Schatzanweisung *(UK)*	**treasury bond**	**bon du trésor (à long terme)**
(Staats)Vertrag(*m*)	**treaty**	**traité**(*m*)**,** pacte(*m*), convention(*f*)
Stadtbezirk(*m*)**;** Gemeinde, Kreis(*m*)	**borough**	**municipalité**(*f*)**;** circonscription(*f*) électorale urbaine
städtisch	**urban**	**urbain**
Stämmen; (Parentelen)	**stirpes**	**souches**(*f*)**,** familles(*f*), lignées(*f*)
(Erbfolge) nach Stämmen	*per –*	par souches
ständiger Aufenthaltsort(*m*)**;** - Wohnsitz(*m*)	**permanent residence**	**résidence**(*f*) **habituelle**
stattgeben; aufrechterhalten e-m Berufungsantrag stattgeben e-r Einwendung stattgeben	**sustain (to)** – an appeal – an objection	**soutenir,** supporter accepter un pourvoi accorder une objection
Status(*m*)	**status**	**statut**(*m*)**,** capacité(*f*) juridique
Personenstand; Rechtsposition(*f*)	legal –	état(*m*) statut légal, union(*f*)
Familienstand	marital –	état(*m*) matrimonial, état de mariage
stehlen	**steal (to)**	**voler,** dérober
Stellvertreter(*m*)**,** stellvertretendes Mitglied	**alternate**	**substitut**(*m*)
Sterben ohne Hinterlassung(*f*) **eines Testaments**	**intestacy**	**fait**(*m*) **de mourir intestat,** sans testament
Sterblichkeit(*f*) –sziffer –sstatistik	**mortality** – rate – statistics	**mortalité**(*f*) taux(*m*) de mortalité statistiques(*m*) de mortalité

GERMAN	ENGLISH	FRENCH
Steuer(m)	**tax**	**impôt**(m), taxe(f), contribution(f)
Schenkungs–	gift –	impôt surles donations
Einkommens–	income –	impôt sur le revenu
indirekte –	indirect –	impôt indirect
Erschafts–	inheritance –	impôt sur les successions
Kommunal–	municipal –	impôt municipal, impôt local
Kopf–, Kommunal–	poll –	'poll tax', capitation(f)
–veranlagung	– assessment	calcul(m) d'imposition, assiette(f) de l'impôt
–behörde	– authority	le fisc
–hinterziehung; –vermeidung	– evasion	fraude(f) fiscale
–betrug	– fraud	fraude fiscale
–gesetz; –recht	– law	loi(f) fiscale
–erklärung	– return	déclaration(f) d'impôts
Mehrwert– (MwSt)	value added – (VAT)	taxe sur la valeur ajoutée (TVA)
Abzug– Quellen–	withholding –	impôt retenu à la source
(Stich-)Probe(f); (Waren-) Probe(f), Muster(n)	**sample**	**échantillon**(m); **sondage**(m)
Stichprobenerhebung(f)	**random sampling**	**échantillonnage**(m) **au hasard**
Stichtag(m); (letzter) Termin(m); Anmeldeschluss(n)	**deadline**	**date limite,** date de clôture
Stiftung(f)	**foundation**	**fondation**(f), institution(f); fondement(m)
– mit gemeinnützigem Zweck	charitable –	fondation charitable
(stillschweigend) einwilligen; sich fügen in; dulden	**acquiesce (to)**	**acquiescer,** consentir
stillschweigend; mit einbegriffen stillschweigende Zustimmung –e Garantie, konkludente Garantie	**implicit, implied** – assent – warranty	**implicite,** tacite, absolu consentement(m) tacite garantie(f) implicite
(stillschweigende) Einwilligung(f); **Sichfügen**(n); Duldung(f)	**acquiescence**	**acquiescement**(m), assentiment(m), consentement(m)
stillschweigend –e Zustimmung	**tacit** – consent	**tacite** consentement(m) tacite
Stimmengleichheit(f)	**parity of votes**	**égalité**(f) **de voix**
Stimmrecht(n)	**voting power**	**droit**(m) **de vote**
Stimmrecht(n) **(der Aktieninhaber)**(m)	**voting rights (of shareholders)**	**droits de vote (des actionnaires)**
(Stimmrechts-)Vollmacht(f); (Stimmrechts-)Vertreter(m)	**proxy**	**mandataire**(m), fondé de pouvoir; procuration(f), mandat(m)
Störung(f)	**nuisance**	**acte**(m) **dommageable,** désagrément
Besitz– od. Eigentums– (der Einzelnen)	private –	atteinte(f) aux droits privés, trouble(m) de jouissance
– der Allgemeinheit; öffentliches ärgernis	public –	atteinte aux droits du public

GERMAN	ENGLISH	FRENCH
Straf-(f) –justiz	**punitive** – justice	**répressif** justice(f) répressive, justice pénale
Strafaussetzung(f) **zur Bewährung**(f)	**suspended sentence**	**condamnation**(f) **avec sursis**
Strafe(f) Kollektiv–	**punishment** collective –	**châtiment**(m), peine(f), sanction(f), punition(f) peine collective
Strafe(f) Todes– Vertragsstrafeklausel bei e-r Strafe von	**penalty** death – – clause under – of	**peine**(f), amende(f), forfait(m) d'indemenité peine capitale, peine de mort dédit(m), clause(f) pénale sous peine de
Strafe(f) **umwandeln**	**commute (to) a penalty**	**commuer une peine**
(straf-)erschwerende, strafverschärfende Umstände	**aggravating circumstances**	**circonstances**(f) **aggravantes**
Strafgefangener(m); Sträfling(m); Verurteilter(m)	**convict**	**forçat**(m), déporté(m, f), bagnard(m); détenu(m) d'un pénitencier (US)
Strafgefängnis(n)	**penitentiary**	**pénitencier**(m)
straf-(rechtlich) –klage –recht Zuchthaus(strafe); Zwangsarbeit	**penal** – action – law – servitude	**pénal** action(f) pénale droit(m) pénal travaux(m) forcés
Straftat(f); Delikt(n) strafbare Handlung Verbrechen, schweres Vergehen Jugendstraftat	**offence** criminal – indictable – juvenile –	**crime**(m), délit(m), acte(m) délictueux, toute violation(f) de la loi crime, infraction(f) pénale acte délictueux, crime, délit délit commis par un mineur
(Straf)Urteil(n); Strafe(f) Todesurteil lebenslängliche Freiheitsstrafe Gefängnisstrafe Strafaussetzung (zur Bewährung) Strafurteil fällen, verkünden	**sentence** death – life – prison – suspended – to pass – on s.o.	**sentence**(f), condamnation(f), jugement(m) arrêt(m) de mort, condamnation à mort, peine(f) de mort condamnation à perpétuité condamnation à une peine de prison condamnation avec sursis prononcer une condamnation à l'encontre de qqu'un
Strafverfolgung(f); Anklageerhebung(f)	**prosecution**	**poursuite**(f), accusation(f), action(f) publique; ministère(m) public; plaignant(m)

GERMAN	ENGLISH	FRENCH
Strafvollstreckungsaufschub(*m*)	**reprieve**	**sursis**(*m*), commutation(*f*) de peine de mort
Straf(vollzugs)anstalt(*f*) *(US)*; *Gefängnis*(*n*)	**correctional institution**	**maison**(*f*) **de correction**
streitende Partei(*f*), anfechtende–	**contestant**	**opposant**
Streitfrage(*f*)	**issue**	**question**(*f*), point(*m*) litigieux, objet(*m*) du litige; émission(*f*); conséquence(*f*)
strittige Tatfrage; Tatbestand	– of fact	question de fait
strittige Rechtsfrage	– of law	question de droit
entscheidungs–, rechtserhebliche Streitfrage	ultimate –	question finale
Streitverkündung(*f*) *(US)*	**interpleader** *(US)*	**mise**(*f*) **en cause** *(US)*
strenge (verschuldensunabhängige) Haftung(*f*) Gefährdungshaftung	**strict liability**	**responsabilité**(*f*) **stricte**
strittig	**litigious**	**litigieux**
Strohmann(*m*); Schein–	**dummy**	**simulacre**(*m*); mannequin(*m*); homme(*m*) de paille; factice *(adj.)*
Stundung(*f*); Nachsicht(*f*), Milde(*f*)	**indulgence**	**indulgence**(*f*); jour(*m*) de grâce, délai de paiement
subjektiv; unsachlich	**subjective**	**subjectif**
Subrogation(*f*); Rechtsübergang(*m*)	**subrogation**	**subrogation**(*f*)
substantiieren; begründen	**substantiate (to)**	**établir,** prouver le bien-fondé
Subunternehmer(*m*); Nach–; Unterlieferant(*m*)	**subcontractor**	**sous-entrepreneur**(*m*), sous-traitant
subversiv; staatsgefährdend	**subversive**	**subversif**
Suche(*f*); Fahndung(*f*)	**search**	**perquisition**(*f*), fouille, recherche(*f*)
Durchsuchungsbefehl	– warrant	mandat(*m*) de perquisition
Suizid(*m*); Selbstmord(*m*)	**suicide**	**suicide**(*m*)
summarisch; kurz	**summary**	**sommaire**
Urteil im abgekürzten (beschleunigten) Verfahren	– judgment	jugement(*m*) sommaire
summarisches (abgekürztes) Verfahren	– proceedings	procédure(*f*) sommaire
Sündenbock(*m*)	**scapegoat**	**bouc**(*m*) **émissaire**

T

GERMAN	ENGLISH	FRENCH
Taschendieb(*m*)	**pickpocket**	**pickpocket**(*m*)
Tat(*m*), Handlung(*f*), Akt(*m*); Urkunde(*f*); Gesetz(*n*)	**act**	**acte**(*m*), action(*f*), mesure(*f*), loi(*m*)
höhere Gewalt, Naturereignis	– of God	cas(*m*) de force majeure
Deliktshandlung, strafbare Handlung, Straftat	criminal –	acte relevant du droit pénal, fait pénalement punissable
Tatbestand(smerkmale)	**operative fact**	**état**(*m*) **de fait**
Täter(*m*)	**offender**	**criminel,** délinquant(*m*), contrevenant
Erst–, Nichtvorbestrafter	first –	délinquant primaire
Gewohnheits–	habitual –	récidiviste(*m*)
jugendlicher –	juvenile –	délinquant juvénile
Täter(*m*); Verbrecher(*m*)	**malefactor**	**malfaiteur**(*m*)
tätl. Angriff(*m*); Bedrohung(*f*); Gewaltanwendung(*f*)	**assault**	**agression**(*f*), attaque(*f*), voies de fait
schwere tätliche Beleidigung (Mißhandlung); Körperverletzung	– and battery	coups(*m*) et blessures
Tatort(*m*)	**scene of crime**	**lieu**(*m*) **du crime**
Tatsache(*f*); Umstand(*m*)	**fact**	**fait**(*m*), réalité(*f*)
beweiserhebliche Tatsache; beweisbare Tatsache	evidentiary –	fait brut
strittige Tatsachen; zu beweisende –	– in issue	point(*m*) de fait
wesentliche Tatsache	material –	fait pertinent, fait essentiel
Tatsachen(*f*) **und Rechtspunkte**(*m*); materielle Umstände(*m*)	**merits**	**fond**(*m*), substance(*f*); mérite(*m*)
Entscheidung in der Sache selbst, Entscheidung nach materiellem Recht	decision on the –	jugement(*m*) au fond
Klageabweisung aufgrund e-r Sachentscheidung	dismissal on the –	rejet(*m*) (d'une plainte) pour manque de fondement
Tausch(*m*)	**barter**	**troc**(*m*)
Tauschgeschäft; Barter–, Kompensations–	– transaction	échange

GERMAN	ENGLISH	FRENCH
täuschend; irreführend; trügerisch	**deceptive**	**trompeur**(*m*), mensonger, déloyal
Täuschung(*f*); Betrug(*m*)	**deceit**	**tromperie**(*f*), fraude(*f*)
Teil-(*m*)	**fractional**	**fractionnel,** divisionnaire (*adj.*)
–schein	– certificate	titre(*m*) fractionnel
Aktienspitzen	– share	action(*f*) fractionnelle
Teil(*n*); Partei(*f*)	**part**	**partie**(*f*), fraction(*f*)
Teilung(*f*)	**partition**	**partage**(*m*), répartition(*f*), morcellement(*m*)
Erb(schafts)–; Erbauseinandersetzung	– of an estate	répartition d'un héritage
Termin-(*m*)	**forward**	**en avant,** antérieur; à terme
–kontrakt	– contract	engagement(*m*) d'acheter ou de vendre à un prix fixé, à une date ultérieure
–geschäft	– transactions	transaction(*f*) à terme
Termingeschäfte(*n*); (Termin-)	**futures (forward)**	**opérations**(*f*), livraisons(*f*) à terme; cotation à terme
Terminkontrakt	futures contract	commande(*m*) à terme, contrat à terme
Finanztermingeschäfte	financial future(s)	instruments(*m*) financiers à terme
Termingeschäft	futures business	marché(*m*) des instruments à terme
Option auf e-n Terminkontrakt	future(s) option	option(*f*) sur contrat à terme
testamentarisch vermachen; vererben	**bequeath (to)**	**léguer**
Testament(*n*) –; letzwillige Verfügung	**testament** last will and –	**testament**(*m*) dernières volontés et testament
Testamentsbestätigung(*f*)	**probate**	**preuve**(*f*); homologation(*f*) (d'un testament); vérification(*f*)
Testamentserbe(*m*); Vermächtnisnehmer(*m*)	**devisee**	**légataire**(*m, f*)
testierfähig; verfügungs– testierfähig sein	**disposing** of – mind	**disposition**(*f*) de bonne disposition
Testierfähigkeit(*f*)	**testacy**	**le fait de mourir en laissant un testament**
Tochtergesellschaft(*f*)	**subsidiary company**	**filiale**(*f*)
Todesstrafe(*f*)	**death penalty**	**peine capitale,** peine de mort
tödlich	**lethal**	**mortel,** léthal
tödlich	**fatal**	**fatal,** mortel
–er Unfall	– accident	accident(*m*) mortel
–e Verletzung	– injury	blessures(*f*) ayant entraîné la mort

GERMAN	ENGLISH	FRENCH
Tontine(*f*); lotterieähnliche Rentenversicherung(*f*) auf den Erlebensfall	**tontine**	**tontine**(*f*)
Totenschein(*m*); Sterbeurkunde(*f*)	**death certificate**	**acte**(*m*) **de décès**, extrait(*m*) mortuaire
Totschlag(*m*)	**manslaughter**	**homicide**(*m, f*)
Tötung(*f*) Gnadentod, Euthanasie	**killing** mercy –	**meurtre**(*m*), tuerie(*f*) euthanasie(*f*)
Tötung(*f*) (s. Mord)	**homicide** (*cf. murder*)	**homicide**(*m, f*), meurtre(*m*)
Träger(*m*), Überbringer(*m*) (s. Inhaber, Besitzer)	**bearer** (*cf. holder*)	**porteur**
Inhaberobligation, Inhaberschuldverschreibung	– bond	titre(*m*) au porteur
Inhaberzertifikat	– certificate	attestation au porteur
Inhaberpapiere	– securities	titres, valeurs au porteur
Tranche(*f*)	**tranche**	**tranche**(*f*)
Transit(*m*); Transport(*m*)	**transit**	**transit**(*m*), passage(*m*), trajet(*m*), route(*f*)
Schaden auf dem Transport	damage in –	dommages(*m*) causés au cours du transport
Transitgüter, –waren	– goods	marchandises(*f*) en transit
Transithafen	– port	port(*m*) de transit
Trennung(*f*)	**severance**	**rupture**(*f*) **(de contrat),** séparation(*f*)
Klagen–	– of legal actions	cessation(*f*) d'actions en justice
Entlassungsabfindung; Härteausgleich	– pay	indemnité(*f*) de licenciement, de rupture de contrat
Treuhänder(*m*); Vermögensverwalter(*m*)	**fiduciary**	**fiduciaire**(*m*) (*n et adj.*), dépositaire(*m, f*)
Treuhandfonds(*m*)	**trust fund**	**fond**(*m*) **de tutelle**
Treuhandverhältnis(*n*); –vermögen(*n*)	**trust**	**fidéicommis**(*m*), tutelle(*f*); garde(*m*), dépôt(*m*); 'trust'(*m*), concentration(*f*) verticale d'entreprises; **confiance**(*f*)
Treuhandsbegünstigter	– beneficiary	bénéficiaire(*m*) de la tutelle
Treuhandvertrag;	– deed	acte(*m*) fiduciaire
Treuhandvermögen	– property	biens(*m*) placés sous tutelle
Trugschluß(*m*); Irrtum(*m*)	**fallacy**	**erreur**(*f*), faux raisonnement
Trunkenheit(*f*) **am Steuer**(*m*)	**drunken driving**	**conduite**(*f*) **en état d'ivresse**
Tugend(*f*); Wert(*m*) kraft; aufgrund von	**virtue** by – of	**qualité**(*f*), vertu en vertu de

U

GERMAN	ENGLISH	FRENCH
Übeltäter(m)**;** Rechtsverletzer(m)	**wrongdoer**	**auteur**(m) **d'un méfait,** délinquant(m)
Überalterung(f) (technisch oder wirtschaftlich); Wertminderung(f) wegen –	**obsolescence**	**désuétude**(f), obsolescence(f), caducité(m); **amortissement**(m) **industriel**
Übereinkommen, Einverständnis(n); Vergleich(m); Abmachung(f)	**accord**	**accord**(m), consentement(m)
vergleichsweise Erfüllung; außergerichtlicher Vergleich	– and satisfaction	novation(f) éxécutée
übereinstimmen; zusammentreffen	**concur (to)**	**approuver,** accéder à
Übereinstimmung, Einvernehmen(n); Einverständnis(n); Abmachung(f); Abkommen, Vertrag(m); Tarifvertrag(m)	**agreement**	**accord**(m), convention(f), contrat(m), traité(m), acte(m), règlement(m), acte(m)
vorehelicher Vertrag verbindliches Abkommen	antenuptial – binding –	contrat de mariage convention(f) liant les parties
gegenseitige Vereinbarung; gegenseitiges Einvernehmen Lohnabkommen; Lohnvereinbarung	mutual – wage –	accord de gré à gré accord sur les salaires, convention salariale
Übereinstimmung(f)	**concordance**	**concordance**(f)
Übereinstimmung(f)**;** Zusammentreffen Kompetenzkonflikt; konkurrierende Zuständigkeit	**concurrence** – of jurisdiction	**approbation**(f), accord(m); conflit(m), concurrence(f) compétence(f) simultanée de plusieurs tribunaux
Überfall(m)**;** Hindernis(n)	**hold-up**	**hold-up**(m), braquage(m) (fam.), attaque(f) à main armée
Überfall(m)**;** Razzia(f)	**raid**	**descente**(f)**,** rafle(f) de police, raid
überfällig; rückständig	**overdue**	**arriéré,** impayé, en souffrance
Überführung(f)**;** Schuldspruch(m), Verurteilung(f)	**conviction**	**condamnation**(f)

GERMAN	ENGLISH	FRENCH
übergeben, aushändigen; (s. abtreten)	**hand (to) over** *(cf. surrender)*	**remmettre** (qqu'un entre les mains de la justice)
übergeben; begehen; verüben strafbare Handlung, Verbrechen begehen	**commit (to)** – a crime	**commettre,** perpétrer commettre, perpétrer un crime
Übergeber(*m*)**;** Hinterleger(*m*), Verpfänder(*m*)	**bailor**	**déposant**(*m*)
Übergewicht(*n*)**;** Überwiegen	**preponderance**	**supériorité**(*f*)**,** prépondérance(*f*), supériorité(*f*) numérique supériorité des preuves du demandeur
überzeugender Beweis	– of evidence	
übergreifen; eingreifen	**encroach (to) (upon)**	**empiéter sur**
Übergriff(*m*)**,** Eingriff(*m*) in jds Rechte(*f*)	**encroachment (upon s.o.'s rights)**	**usurpation**(*f*) **de droits,** empiètement(*f*) sur la propriété d'autrui
Überlebende(r)(*m*)**;** Hinterbliebene(r)(*m*)	**survivor**	**survivant**
überlebender Ehegatte	**surviving spouse**	**époux**(*m*) **survivant**
Überlegenheit(*f*)**,** bestimmender Einfluß(*m*)	**ascendancy**	**ascendance**(*f*)
Überliegezeit(*f*)**;** Überliegegeld	**demurrage**	**surestaries**(*f*)**,** droits(*m*) de surestarie; magasinage, droits(*m*) de magasinage
Übernehmer(*m*)**;** Depositar(*m*), Verwahrer(*m*)	**bailee**	**dépositaire**(*m*)
überprüfen; untersuchen	**screen (to)**	**interroger un suspect;** filtrer, trier; masquer, protéger
Sicherheitsrisiken überprüfen	– security risks	étudier les risques de sécurité
Überprüfung(*f*) **e-s Urteils (durch Rechtsmittelgericht)**	**review on appeal**	**révision**(*f*) **en appel**
übertragbare Wertpapiere(*f*)	**transferable securities**	**valeurs**(*f*) **mobilières librement cessibles**
Übertragender(*m*)**;** Zedent(*m*)	**transferor**	**cédant**(*m*)**,** endosseur(*m*)
Übertragung(*f*)**,** Verpachtung(*f*); Ableben(*n*), Tod(*m*)	**demise**	**cession**(*f*) **à bail;** décès(*m*)
Übertragung(*f*)	**transfer**	**transfert**(*m*)**,** mutation(*f*), transmission(*f*), virement(*m*)
Vermögens–; Eigentums– Aktien– Forderungs–; Eigentums-	– of property – of shares – of title	transmission de propriété cession(*f*) d'actions transmission de titre constitutif propriété
Übertragung(*f*)**;** Beförderung(*f*) Vermögens–, Eigentumsübertragung Grundstücksauflassung; Übertragungs–, Auflassungsurkunde	**conveyance** – of property – of real estate deed of –	**transport**(*m*)**,** transmission(*f*) tout mode de transmission de propriété transport d'immeubles acte(*m*) de cession

GERMAN	ENGLISH	FRENCH
(Übertragungs-)(f)Empfänger(m); Zessionar(m)	transferee	cessionnaire(m)
Übertreter(m); Missetäter(m)	transgressor	transgresseur(m)
Übertretung(f); Verletzung(f)	transgression	transgression(f), infraction(f), violation(f)
Gesetzesübertretung	– of a law	violation d'une loi
überwachen; kontrollieren	monitor (to)	surveiller, vérifier, contrôler
Überwachung(f); Kontrolle(f)	surveillance	surveillance(f)
Überweisung(f)	remittance	envoi(m) de fonds, versement(m), traite(f), chèque(m)
Überweisung(f), Einlieferung(f); Verhaftung(f)	committal	délégation(f); renvoi(m); incarcération
Anordnung der Hauptverhandlung (Strafprozeß)	– for trial	renvoi devant la cour d'assises; mise(f) en accusation
überzeugen; überreden	persuade (to)	persuader, convaincre
Überzeugung(f); Überredung(f)	persuasion	persuasion(f); conviction(f); confession(f) religieuse
üble Nachrede(f); (mündliche Beleidigung)(f)	slander	diffamation(f) verbale
umwandelbar; konvertierbar konvertierbare Papiere	convertible – securities	convertible titres(m) convertibles
umwandeln; –wechseln, –tauschen	convert (to)	convertir, transformer, changer
unabdingbar	inalienable	inaliénable
–e Forderung	– claim	revendication(f) inaliénable
–es Recht	– right	droit(m) inaliénable
unangemessen; übermäßig	unduly	illégalement, à tort
Unangemessenheit(f); Unzulänglichkeit(f)	inadequacy	insuffisance(f)
unangreifbar; nicht zu widerlegen	unassailable	inattaquable
unbeabsichtigt; ungewollt	unintentional	non intentionnel, involontaire
unbeglaubigt; unbestätigt	unattested	non attesté, non certifié
unbegrenzte Dauer(f)	perpetuity	perpétuité(f)
unbegründet; grundlos	unfounded	non fondé, sans fondement(m)
–e Beschuldigung	– accusation	accusation(f) sans fondement
unbelastet; hypothekenfrei	unencumbered	libre d'hypothèques
unbeschränkt; endgültig; rechtskräftig	absolute	absolu, irrévocable
unbeschränkte Macht, – Gewalt einwandfreier Beweis	– power – proof	pouvoir absolu preuve(f) irréfutable
unbestätigt	unconfirmed	non confirmé; léonin

GERMAN	ENGLISH	FRENCH
unbestechlich	**incorruptible**	**incorruptible**
unbestimmter Schadensersatz(*m*); unbezifferte Schadensforderung	**unliquidated damages**	**dommages-intérêts**(*m*) **non liquidés**
Unbestimmtheit(*f*); Unsicherheit(*f*)	**uncertainty**	**passage**(*m*) **obscur dans la rédaction d'un jugement,** incertitude(*f*)
unbestraft; ungeahndet	**unpunished**	**impuni**
unbestreitbar; unleugbar	**undeniable**	**indéniable**
unbestritten; unangefochten	**unchallenged**	**incontesté,** sans rival
unbestritten; unbestreitbar	**uncontested**	**incontesté;** remporté sans opposition (scrutin, élection)
unbewaffnet	**unarmed**	**non armé,** sans armes
unehelich; unrechtmäßig	**illegitimate**	**illégitime**
(un-)ehelich geboren	**born in (out of) wedlock**	**né dans (hors) (des liens) du mariage**
uneheliches Kind	**bastard**	**enfant**(*m, f*) **naturel**
unerheblich	**immaterial**	**sans importance,** non pertinent
–er Beweis	– evidence	témoignage(*m*) non pertinent
unerheblich; nicht zur Sache gehörig	**irrelevant**	**non pertinent,** sans effet
Unerheblichkeit(*f*)	**irrelevance**	**non pertinent,** inconsistant
unerlaubte Handlung(*f*); zivilrechtliches Delikt(*n*)	**tort**	**tort**(*m*)
Recht der unerlaubten Handlungen; Deliktsrecht	– law of torts	droit(*m*) de la responsabilité
unfähig; unzurechnungsfähig (*US*), geschäftsunfähig	**incompetent**	**incompétent,** non qualifié (pour)
unzulässiges Beweismittel	– evidence	preuve(*f*) irrecevable
Geschäftsunfähiger (*US*)	– person	incapable, interdit (aliéné, etc.)
unzulässiger Zeuge	– witness	témoin(*m*) récusé, non qualifié
unfähig machen; für unfähig erklären	**incapacitate (to)**	**frapper d'incapacité légale,** interdire
Unfähigkeit(*f*)	**incapacity**	**incapacité**(*f*)
Geschäfts-, Rechts–	legal –	incapacité légale
Unfähigkeit(*f*)	**disability**	**incapacité**(*f*); infirmité(*f*), invalidité(*f*)
Invaliditätsrente; (Kriegs-) Beschädigtenrente	– pension	pension(*f*) d'invalidité
Rechts-, Prozeßunfähigkeit	legal –	incapacité légale
teilweise Erwerbs-, Arbeitsunfähigkeit	partial –	incapacité partielle
dauerhafte Erwerbs-, Arbeitsunfähigkeit	permanent –	incapacité permanente
Unfähigkeit(*f*); Unvermögen(*n*)	**inability**	**incapacité**(*f*)**,** impuissance(*f*)

GERMAN	ENGLISH	FRENCH
Unfallversicherung(*f*)	**accident insurance**	**assurance**(*f*) **contre les accidents**
unfertige Erzeugnisse(*n*); in Gang befindliche Arbeit(*f*)	**work in progress**	**travail**(*m*) **(travaux) en cours**
ungebührlich; ungehörig –e Behauptung	**undue** – allegation	**illégitime,** indu allégation(*f*) sans fondement
ungehörig –e, unsachgemäße Verwendung, Mißbrauch	**improper** – use	**impropre,** incorrect, irrégulier usage(*m*) abusif
ungehörig; anstößig	**indecent**	**indécent**
Ungehorsam; Gehorsamsverweigerung	**disobedience**	**désobéissance**(*f*)
Ungenauigkeit(*f*); Unrichtigkeit(*f*)	**inaccuracy**	**inexactitude**(*f*), imprécision(*f*)
ungerecht; unbillig ungerechtfertigte Bereicherung	**unjust** – enrichment	**injuste** enrichissement(*m*) sans cause
ungerechtfertigt	**unjustified**	**injustifié,** non motivé
ungeschützt; ungedeckt	**unprotected**	**sans protection**(*f*), sans emballage(*m*)
ungesetzlich; rechtswidrig	**unlawful**	**contraire à la loi,** séditieux, illégal, illicite
ungesichert; ungedeckt	**unsecured**	**à découvert**(*m*), sans garantie, sur notoriété(*f*)
ungeteiltes Vermögen(*n*)	**undivided property**	**propriété**(*f*) **indivise,** bien(*m*) indivis
ungültig machen; annullieren	**nullify (to)**	**annuler**
ungültig machen; für ungültig erklären	**invalidate (to)**	**casser,** abroger, invalider, annuler
unleserlich; nicht zu entziffern	**undecipherable**	**indéchiffrable,** incompréhensible
unmittelbare Ursache(*f*)	**proximate cause**	**cause**(*f*) **immédiate**
Unmündiger(*m*) (*s. Minderjähriger*)	**infant** (*cf. minor*)	**mineur**(*m*)
Unparteiischkeit(*f*); Objektivität(*f*)	**impartiality**	**impartialité**
unrechtmäßige Handlung(*f*)	**wrongful act**	**acte**(*m*) **illégal**
Unrecht(*n*); Rechtsverletzung(*f*); Delikt(*n*)	**wrong**	**infraction**(*f*) **à la loi,** tort(*m*) fait à qqu'un
unredlich unfaires Spiel; Verbrechen	**foul** – play	**malpropre,** déloyal jeu(*m*) déloyal, malveillance(*f*) (par ext., crime, meurtre)
unredlich; ungerecht unlauterer Wettbewerb unlautere Marktmethoden	**unfair** – competition – market practices	**injuste,** déloyal, inéquitable concurrence(*f*) déloyale pratiques(*f*) commerciales déloyales

GERMAN	ENGLISH	FRENCH
Unredlichkeit(f); Unehrlichkeit(f)	**dishonesty**	**malhonnêteté**(f)
Unruhe(f); Störung(f)	**disorder**	**désordre**(m)
unschuldig	**not guilty**	**innocent**(m)
unter Ausschluß(m) **der Öffentlichkeit**(f)	**in camera**	**à huis clos**
unter Ausschluß(m) **der Öffentlichkeit**(f)	**in chambers**	**(juge)**(m) **des référés**
unter pari; unter dem Nennwert	**under par**	**sous pair**
unter Strafandrohung(f) **laden** einen Zeugen -	**subpoena (to)** – a witness	**assigner à comparaître** assigner un témoin à comparaître
Unterabschnitt(m)	**subsection**	**paragraphe**(m), **sous-**section(f)
unterbewerten; underschätzen	**underrate (to)**	**sous-estimer**
Unterbrechung(f); Einstellung(f) Aussetzung e-s Verfahrens; Klagerücknahme	**discontinuance** – of an action	**cessation**(f), abandon(m) désistement(m) d'action
Unterdrückung(f)	**oppression**	**oppression**(f)
Unterdrückung(f); Verheimlichung(f) Unterdrückung von Beweismaterial	**suppression** – of evidence	**suppression**(f) dissimulation(f), destruction(f) de preuves
unteres Gericht(n); Instanzgericht(n)	**inferior court**	**tribunal**(m) **inférieur,** tribunal de première instance
Unterhalt	**maintenance**	**pension**(f) **alimentaire;** défense(f) de ses droits; maintien(m), conservation(f)
–sbeitrag(m)	– contribution	contribution(f) à l'entretien
–sverpflichtung(f)	– liability	responsabilité(f) en matière d'aliments
Unterhalt(sbetrag)(m)	**alimony**	**pension**(f) **alimentaire**
Unternehmen(n); Betrieb(m); Geschäft(n)	**enterprise**	**entreprise**(f)
Unternehmer(m)	**entrepreneur**	**entrepreneur**(m)
Unternehmerhaftpflichtversich-erung(f), Arbeitgeberversicherung	**employer's liability insurance**	**l'assurance responsabilité**(f) **des patrons**
Unterschrift(f) eigenhändige – bestätigt	**signature** personal – witnessed	**signature**(m), visa(m) signature personnelle devant témoin
unterstützen, durchbringen, einbringen e-n Antrag annehmen	**carry (to)** – a motion	**porter;** adopter faire passer une proposition
e-n Beschluß durchbringen	– a resolution	adopter une résolution
unterstützen; begünstigen; gegenzeichnen	**back (to)**	**renforcer,** épauler; endosser; financer

411

GERMAN	ENGLISH	FRENCH
Unterstützung(f); Deckung(f); Indossierung(f) finanzielle Unterstützung	**backing** financial –	**appui**(m), couverture(f); remboursement(m) soutien financier
Unterstützung(f); (s. Unterhalt)	**support** (cf. alimony)	**pension**(f) **alimentaire**
Unterstützungsverein(m); Versicherungsverein(m) auf Gegenseitigkeit(f)	**friendly society**	**amicale**(f), société(f) de recours mutuel
Untersuchung(f) gerichtliche - amtliche -	**inquiry** judicial – official –	**enquête**(f), investigation(f) enquête judiciaire enquête officielle
Untersuchungsergebnis(n); Befund(m) (tatsächliche) Feststellungen des Gerichts Zwischenentscheidung Richterspruch; Gerichtsurteil; richterliche Feststellungen	**findings** court's – interlocutory – judicial –	**données**(f), constatations(f) conclusions(f) du tribunal, verdict conclusions interlocutoires conclusions d'un tribunal
Untersuchungshaft(f); Anordnung der Haftfortdauer	**remand**	**ajournement**(m), renvoi(m)
(Untersuchungs-)Haft(f); Festnahme(f); Zurückhaltung(f), Beschlagnahme	**detention**	**détention**
Untertreibung(f); Unterbewertung(f)	**understatement**	'**understatement**', litote(f)
Untervermietung(f); –pacht(f)	**sublease**	**sous-location**(f)
unterwerfen; aussetzen Mißhandlung aussetzen	**subject (to)** – s.o. to maltreatment	**soumettre**, asujettir faire subir de mauvais traitements à qqu'un
unterzeichnen; – schreiben	**subscribe (to)**	**souscrire**
Unterzeichner(m)	**signatory**	**signataire**(m), souscripteur(m)
Unterzeichnete(r)(m)	**undersigned (the)**	**le soussigné**
unverantwortlich; nicht haftbar	**irresponsible**	**irresponsable**, insolvable
unvereinbar –e Interessen	**incompatible** – interests	**incompatible**, inconciliable intérêts(m) inconciliables
unverfälscht; echt	**unadulterated**	**pur**, non édulcoré
unverletzlich; unversehrt	**inviolate**	**inviolé**
unvermeidbar	**unavoidable**	**inévitable**, incontournable
unvermindert	**unabated**	**d'égale intensité**
unversehrt; unbeschädigt	**unharmed**	**sain et sauf**, indemne
unverteilter Gewinn(m); nicht ausgeschütteter –; s. unverteilter Reingewinn	**undistributed profits** (cf. unappropriated)	**bénéfices**(m) **non distribués**
unverteilter Reingewinn(m); Bilanzgewinn(m)	**unappropriated profits**	**bénéfices**(m) **non distribués**
unverzinsliche Schuld(f); nicht-zinstragende Forderung(f)	**passive debt**	**dette**(f) **passive**

GERMAN	ENGLISH	FRENCH
unvoreingenommen; unparteiisch	**unbiased**	**objectif,** sans parti-pris
unvorhergesehenes Ereignis(*n*); Eventualfall(*m*)	**contingency**	**contingence**(*f*), cas(*m*) imprévu
Reserve für unvorhergesehen Ausgaben; Rückstellung für Eventualverbindlichkeiten; Sicherheitsrücklage	– reserve	fonds(*m*) de réserve
unwiderlegbar	**irrefutable**	**irréfutable**
unwiderlegbar	**uncontrovertible**	**non convertible**
unwiderlegbar	**irrebuttable**	**irréfragable**
–e Rechtsvermutung	– presumption	présomption(*f*) absolue
unwiderruflich	**irrevocable**	**irrévocable,** non recouvrable
–es Akkreditiv	– letter of credit	lettre(*f*) de crédit irrévocable
unwirksam; wertlos	**nugatory**	**non valable,** inopérant
unwirksame, ungültige Rechtsvorschrift(*f*), Verordnung(*f*)	**inoperative enactment**	**texte**(*m*), loi(*f*) inopérant(e)
unwissend; unkundig	**ignorant**	**ignorant**
Unwissenheit(*f*); Unkenntnis(*n*)	**ignorance**	**ignorance**(*f*)
unzulässig	**inadmissible**	**irrecevable,** illicite, inadmissible
–e Beweismittel; nicht zugelassenes Beweismaterial	– evidence	témoignage(*m*) irrecevable
(unzulässige) Häufung(*f*) **mehrerer Klagegründe**(*m*) **in e-r Klageschrift**(*f*)	**duplicity**	**duplicité**(*f*), double jeu
unzulässige Klageverbindung(*f*)	**misjoinder**	**fausse**(*f*) **constitution des parties**
unzuständig; uneingeschränkt	**unqualified**	**non qualifié;** sans réserves(*f*)
Urheber(*m*); Begründer(*m*)	**originator**	**créateur**(*m*), promoteur(*m*)
Urheberrecht(*n*)	**copyright**	**droit**(*m*) **d'auteur,** propriété(*f*) littéraire
Urkunde(*f*), Vertrag(*m*); Tat(*f*), Handlung(*f*)	**deed**	**action**(*f*), acte(*m*); acte notarié
Abtretungsurkunde	– of assignment	acte attributif de biens
Beitrittsurkunde; Einwilligungserklärung	– of consent	déclaration(*f*) de consentement
Übertragungs-, Auflassungsurkunde (bei Grundeigentum)	– of conveyance	acte de cession
Treuhandvertrag; Sicherungsübereignung	– of trust	acte fiduciaire
Urkunde(*f*); Verfassungs-, Verleihungs-, Gründungsurkunde(*f*)	**charter**	**charte**(*f*), statuts(*m*), privilège(*m*)
Gründungsurkunde einer Gesellschaft	– of a company	acte(*m*), statuts d'association d'une compagnie, d'une société

GERMAN	ENGLISH	FRENCH
Urkundsbeamter(*m*) **der Geschäftsstelle**(*f*)**;** Leiter der Gerichtskanzlei	**clerk of court**	**greffier**(*m*)
Urkundsperson(*f*)**;** zur Abnahme(*f*) von Eiden berechtigter Jurist	**commissioner for oaths**	**officier habilité à recevoir les déclarations sous serment**(*m*)
Ursache(*f*)**,** Grund(*m*); Rechtsfall(*m*), –streit, –sache	**cause**	**cause**(*f*)**,** raison(*f*)
Anfechtungsgrund	– of appeal	motif(*m*) de l'appel
Klage–, Beschwerdegrund	– of complaint	motif de la plainte
Verdachtsgrund	– of suspicion	raison de soupçonner
Ursprung(*f*)**;** Herkunft(*f*)	**origin**	**origine**(*f*)**,** provenance(*f*)
–szeugnis	certificate of –	certificat(*m*) d'origine
–sland	country of –	pays(*m*) d'origine
ursprünglich;	**original**	**original, initial, primitif (adj.);** original(*m, f*) (*n.*)
Anschaffungskosten	– acquisition cost	prix(*m*) d'achat d'origine
Originalurkunde	– document	acte(*m*) primordial
erstinstanzliche Zuständigkeit; Gericht erster Instanz	– jurisdiction	juridiction(*f*) de première instance
Urteil(*n*)	**judgment**	**jugement**(*m*)**,** décision(*f*) judiciaire
Feststellungs–	declaratory –	jugement déclaratoire
End–	definitive –	jugement définitif
rechtskräftiges –; End–	final –	jugement final
Zwischen–	interlocutory –	jugement interlocutoire
Anerkenntnis–	– by consent	jugement rendu à l'unanimité
Versäumnis–	– by default	jugement par défaut
Vollstreckungsgläubiger	– creditor	créancier dont la dette est ajugée due par le cour
Urteilsschuldner	– debtor	débiteur(*m*) dont la dette est ajugée due par le cour
– im abgekürzten, summarischen Verfahren	summary –	jugement sommaire
– erlassen, verkünden	to award –	prononcer une sentence
– erlassen	to deliver –	rendre un jugement
Urteil(*n*)**;** Verfügung(*f*); Verordnung(*f*) (*s. Urteilsspruch*)	**decree** (*cf. judgment*)	**décret**(*m*)**,** décision(*f*) d'ordre judiciaire ou administratif
rechtskräftiges Scheidungsurteil	– absolute	jugement définitif
vorläufiges Scheidungsurteil	– nisi	jugement provisoire; jugement interlocutoire
Scheidungsurteil	divorce –	jugement de divorce
Endurteil, rechtskräftiges Urteil	final –	jugement final
Urteil(*n*) (Zivilrecht)(*n*); Zuerkennung(*f*), Zusprechung(*f*)	**adjudgment**	**jugement**(*m*)**,** arrêt(*m*), décision(*f*)
Urteilsregister(*n*)**,** –liste; Etikett(*n*); Inhaltsverzeichnis(*n*); Lieferschein; Zollquittung	**docket**	**résumé**(*m*) **ou extrait du jugement;** bordereau(*m*) d'un dossier de procédure; registre(*m*) des jugements rendus; récépissé(*m*) de douane

GERMAN	ENGLISH	FRENCH
(Urteils-)Spruch(*m*); Entscheidung(*f*)	**verdict**	**verdict**(*m*)
Entscheidung (für Kläger od. Beklagten) (Zivilprozeß); Schuld– od. Freispruch (Strafprozeß)	general –	verdict pour démandeur ou défendeur (*procédure civile*); verdict de culpabilité ou d'acquittement (*procédure criminelle*)
Feststellung des Tatbestandes	special –	détermination(*f*) des faits de procédure
Schuldspruch; Erkennen auf 'schuldig'	– of guilty	verdict de culpabilité
Freispruch; Erkennen auf 'nicht schuldig'	– of not guilty	verdict d'acquittement

V

GERMAN	ENGLISH	FRENCH
Vandalismus(*m*); böswillige Sachbeschädigung(*f*)	**vandalism**	**vandalisme**(*m*)
Vaterschaft(*f*) –sanerkenntnis	**paternity** acknowledgement of –	**paternité**(*f*) reconnaissance(*f*) de paternité
(ver-, aus-)leihen; leisten	**lend (to)**	**prêter**
verantwortlich, unterworfen; abhängig; zugänglich für e-r Geldstrafe unterliegend	**amenable** – to fines	**responsable** passible d'amende(s)
Verantwortlichkeit(*f*); Rechenschaftspflicht(*m*), Rechnungslegungspflicht; Strafmündigkeit	**accountability**	**responsabilité**(*f*)
veräußern, übertragen (Rechte)	**alienate (to) (rights)**	**aliéner,** transférer, détourner, céder
verbergen; verheimlichen; verschleiern; verschweigen	**conceal (to)**	**dissimuler,** cacher
Verbergen(*n*)**;** Verheimlichung(*f*); Verschleierung(*f*); Verschweigen Unterdrücken von Beweismaterial	**concealment** – of evidence	**dissimulation**(*f*); recel(*m*) dissimulation de preuves
verbieten	**prohibit (to)**	**prohiber,** interdire
verbieten, untersagen; ausschließen Rechtsweg ausschließen	**bar (to)** – legal proceedings	**empêcher,** exclure retirer une plainte
verbieten; Sperre verhängen über	**ban (to)**	**interdire,** mettre hors-la-loi, prohiber
verbinden jdn trauen	**join (to)** – in matrimony	**intervenir (dans un procès);** accepter (un arbitrage); s'affilier, adhérer à unir par les liens du mariage
Verbindlichkeiten (Sammelbegriff für alle ungesicherten, langfristigen –); Rückzollschein	**debenture**	**obligation**(*f*), reconnaissance(*f*) de dette
verborgen; heimlich	**latent**	**latent,** caché(*m*)

GERMAN	ENGLISH	FRENCH
verborgen; still	**dormant**	**non exercé**
verboten	**prohibited**	**interdit**(*m*), prohibé
Verbot(*n*)	**interdiction**	**interdiction**(*f*), interdit(*m*), défense(*f*)
Verbot(*n*); Prohibition(*f*)	**prohibition**	**prohibition**(*f*), défense(*f*), interdiction(*f*)
Verbot(*n*); Untersagung(*f*)	**inhibition**	**défense**(*f*) **expresse,** interdiction(*f*), prohibition
Verbot(*n*) **der doppelten Strafverfolgung**(*f*) **eines Täters wegen derselben Tat**	**double jeopardy**	**double incrimination**
Verbraucher(*m*)	**consumer**	**consommateur**(*m*), usager(*m*)
Konsumkredit; Konsumenten–	– credit	crédit(*m*) à la consommation
Konsumgüter; Verbrauchs–	– goods	biens de consommation
Index der Verbraucherpreise	– price index	indice(*m*) des prix à la consommation
Verbraucherschutz	– protection	protection(*f*) des consommateurs
Verbrechen; strafbare Handlung(*f*), Straftat(*f*)	**crime**	**crime**(*m*)
Verdacht(*m*); Argwohn(*m*)	**suspicion**	**suspicion,** soupçon(*m*)
vereidigter Zeuge(*m*); Aussteller(*m*) (e-s Affidavit)	**deponent**	**signataire**(*m*) **d'un affidavit,** d'une attestation; témoin(*m*) déposant
Vereitelung(*f*); Verhinderung(*f*)	**frustration**	**frustration**(*f*); anéantissement(*m*); impossibilité(*f*) d'exécuter un contrat
Verfahren außerhalb der Streitverhandlung(*f*); Nebenverfahren	**collateral proceeding(s)**	**procédure**(*f*) **connexe**
Verfahren(*n*); Prozeß(*m*)	**proceedings**	**acte**(*m*) **de procédure,** procès(*m*); délibérations(*f*); marche(*f*) à suivre
Schieds(gerichts)verfahren	arbitration –	procédure(*f*) d'arbitrage
Gerichtsverfahren	court –	procès(*m*)
Ehescheidungsverfahren	divorce –	instance(*f*) en divorce
Konkursverfahren	– in bankruptcy	procédure en faillite
Schnellverfahren; summarisches Verfahren	summary –	procédure sommaire
verfälschen	**falsify (to)**	**falsifier,** fausser, dénaturer
Verfälschung(*f*)	**falsification**	**falsification**(*f*), trucage(*m*), contrefaçon(*f*)
(Ver-)Fälschung(*f*)	**adulteration**	**altération**(*f*)
Münzverfälschung	– of coinage	falsification(*f*) de monnaie
Verfälschung von Nahrungsmitteln, Lebensmittelfälschung	– of food	fraude(*f*) alimentaire

GERMAN	ENGLISH	FRENCH
Verfassung(f); Gründung(f); Beschaffenheit(f)	**constitution**	**constitution**(f)
verfassungsmäßig, –rechtlich	**constitutional**	**constitutionnel**(m), **constitutionelle**(f)
Verfassungsgericht; ordentliches Bundesgericht	– court	tribunal(m) constitutionnel
Verfassungsrecht	– law	droit(m) constitutionnel
verfassungswidrig	**unconstitutional**	**anticonstitutionnel**
verfolgen; belästigen	**persecute (to)**	**persécuter,** harceler
verfolgen; betreiben	**pursue (to)**	**poursuivre (une enquête),** suivre, continuer
Verfolgung(f); Belästigung(f)	**persecution**	**persécution**(f), harcèlement(m)
Verfügung(f); Erledigung(f); Veräußerung(f)	**disposal**	**vente**(f), distribution, cession
Verfügungsrecht	right of –	droit(m) de libre disposition
Verfügungsgewalt(f); Anordnung(f); Bestimmung(f)	**disposition**	**disposition testamentaire,** cession(f) (de biens)
Verführung(f)	**seduction**	**corruption**(f), séduction(f)
Vergeltung(f)(smaßnahmen)	**retaliation**	**représaille(s)**(f), mesure(f) de rétorsion; remboursement(m)
Vergewaltiger(m)	**rapist**	**violeur**(m)
vergiften	**poison (to)**	**empoisonner**
Vergütung(f); Honorar(n)	**remuneration**	**rémunération**(f), allocation(f), indemnité(f)
Verhältnis(n); Koeffizient(m)	**ratio**	**rapport**(m), proportion(f), raison(f), quotient(m), coefficient(m)
Verschuldungsgrad; –koeffizient	debt-equity –	ratio(f) d'autonomie financière
Liquiditätsquote; Deckungsgrad	liquidity –	coefficient de trésorerie
verhandeln; hören	**hear (to)**	**entendre,** écouter; instruire
Verhandlung(f)	**hearing**	**audience**(f), débats(m) (d'un procès); interrogatoire(m) d'un accusé
Haftverhandlung	detention –	audience concernant la détention
Schlußverhandlung, Schlußtermin;	final –	audience de jugement
– e-s Falls	– of a case	instruction(f) d'une affaire
Zeugenvernehmung	– of witnesses	audition des témoins
Voruntersuchung	preliminary –	audience préliminaire
öffentliche Verhandlung	public –	audience publique
verhindern; verhüten	**prevent (to)**	**empêcher,** prévenir
verhören; in Zweifel(m) **ziehen**	**question (to)**	**interroger,** mettre en doute
Verhör(n)**; Befragung**(f)	**questioning**	**interrogatoire**(m)
verifizierbar; nachprüfbar	**verifiable**	**vérifiable,** contrôlable

GERMAN	ENGLISH	FRENCH
verifizieren; beglaubigen, nachprüfen	**verify (to)**	**vérifier,** contrôler
verjähren; vorschreiben	**prescribe (to)**	**prescrire,** ordonner
Verjährung(*f*)	**limitation**	**limitation**(*f*), prescription(*f*), restriction(*f*)
Klage–	– of actions	prescription d'action
–sfrist	– period	période(*f*) de prescription
–sgesetz	statute of –	droit(*m*) de prescription
Verjährung(*f*); Vorschrift(*f*)	**prescription**	**prescription**(*f*)
Verkäufer(*m*)	**seller**	**vendeur**(*m*)
Verkäufer(*m*)	**vendor**	**vendeur**(*m*) **de biens immobiliers,** vendeur, apporteur
Verkehr(*m*)	**traffic**	**trafic**(*m*), circulation(*f*), transport(*m*)
–sunfall	– accident	accident(*m*) de la circulation
–sdelikt	– offence	infraction(*f*) au code de la route
–ssünder	– offender	contrevenant(*m*) au code de la route
Verletzung der –svorschriften	– violation	infraction au code de la route
verklagen; Klage einreichen	**sue (to)**	**intenter un procès à,** poursuivre qqu'un en justice
auf Schadenersatz verklagen	– for damages	poursuivre qqu'un en dommages-intérêts
wegen übler Nachrede verklagen	– for malicious slander	poursuivre qqu'un en diffamation
verkünden ein (Scheidungs-) Urteil –, erlassen	**pronounce (to)** – a decree	**rendre,** déclarer rendre un arrêt
ein Urteil –	– a judgment	prononcer un jugement
verlängern	**extend (to)**	**étendre,** prolonger, proroger
Zahlungsfrist –	– a payment term	reculer l'échéance d'un paiement
Verlängerungsklausel(*f*); Report–(*m*)	**continuation clause**	**clause**(*f*) **de report**
Verlassen; Fahnenflucht	**desertion**	**désertion**(*f*)
verletzen; Schaden zufügen	**hurt (to)**	**blesser**
verletzen; verstoßen; übertreten	**violate (to)**	**enfreindre,** violer
verletzen (Recht); verstoßen gegen	**infringe (to)**	**enfreindre,** violer, empiéter sur

GERMAN	ENGLISH	FRENCH
Verletzung(f), Übertretung(f), Verstoß(m)	**breach**	**infraction**(f), violation(f)
Vertragsbruch, –verletzung	– of contract	rupture de contrat
Pflichtverletzung, -vergehen	– of duty	manquement(m) au devoir (aux obligations), forfaiture(f)
Gesetzesverletzung, Rechtsbruch	– of law	violation de la loi
Ordnungswidrigkeit	– of rules	infraction aux règles
Verletzung der Geheimhaltungspflicht	– of secrecy	indiscrétion(f), violation de la confidentialité
Verletzung(f); Schaden(m)	**injury**	**préjudice**(m), lésion(f) (d'un droit), tort(m), dommage(m)
Unfallverletzung	accidental –	blessure(f) accidentelle
Körperverletzung	bodily –	lésion(f) corporelle
Betriebs-, Arbeitsunfall	occupational –	accident(m) du travail
Dauerschaden; lebenslängliche Körperbeschädigung	permanent –	incapacité(f) permanente
Personenschaden; Körperverletzung	personal –	blessure
Verletzung(f); Verstoß(m)	**infraction**	**infraction**(f), violation(f)
Verletzung(f); Verstoß(m); Übertretung(f)	**violation**	**infraction**(f), violation(f)
ein Gesetz übertreten	in – of the law	en contravention de la loi
Verletzung der Privatsphäre; – der Intimspäre	– of privacy	atteinte(f) à la vie privée
Verleumdung(f) **durch die Presse**	**press libel**	**diffamation**(m) **publiée dans un journal**
Verlobung(f)	**betrothal**	**fiançailles**(f)
Verlust(m); Schaden(m)	**loss**	**perte**(f), déficit(m), déperdition(f)
Verlustvortrag	– carried (brought) forward	pertes reportées sur les années futures
Verlust für das betreffende Jahr	– for the year	déficit annuel, pertes annuelles
Kapitalverlust	– of capital	perte, déperdition du capital
Zinsverlust	– of interest	perte d'intérêt(s)
Totalschaden; Totalverlust	total –	perte totale
Vermächtnisgeber(m); Erblasser(m)	**legator**	**testateur**(m)
Vermächtnis(n); Erbe(m)	**legacy**	**legs**(m)
beschränktes Gattungsvermächtnis	demonstrative –	legs à payer d'une source spécifiée
Gattungsvermächtnis; Geldsummenvermächtnis	general –	legs universel
Vermächtnis(n); Legat(m); Erbteil(n)	**bequest**	**legs**(m)
Vermächtnisnehmer(m); Erbe(m)	**legatee**	**légataire**(m, f)
vermeintlich; mutmaßlich	**putative**	**putatif**
(ver-)mieten; (ver-)pachten;	**leasing**	**location-vente**(f), crédit-bail(m), leasing(m)
vermieten; verpachten; zulassen	**let (to)**	**louer;** adjuger un contrat de travaux publics

GERMAN	ENGLISH	FRENCH
Vermieter(*m*); Verpächter(*m*); Leasinggeber(*m*)	**lessor**	**bailleur**(*m*), loueur(*m*) à bail
Vermittler(*m*)	**intermediary**	**intermédiaire**(*m*), personne(*m*) interposée
Vermittler(*m*); Schlichter(*m*)	**conciliator**	**conciliateur**(*m*), arbitre(*m*)
Vermögen(*n*); Nachlaß(*m*); Grundeigentum(*n*); Anwesen(*n*)	**estate**	**état**(*m*), condition(*f*); mode(*m, f*) légal de possession; biens(*m*) immeubles; patrimoine(*m*); masse(*f*) des biens
Nachlaß	deceased's –	succession(*f*)
Aufteilung des Nachlasses, Erbauseinandersetzung	distribution of an –	partage(*m*) d'une succession
Grundstücksmakler; Immobilienhändler	– agent	agent(*m*) immbilier
Mobiliarvermögen; beweglicher Nachlaß	personal –	bien(*m*) mobiliers
Vermögen(*n*) **mit Belastungen**(*f*) **od. Auflagen**	**onerous property**	**biens**(*m*) **onéreux**
vermuten; annehmen	**presume (to)**	**présumer**
Vermutung(*f*)	**presumption**	**présomption**(*f*)
Todes–	– of death	décès(*m*) présumé
Tatsachen–	– of fact	présomption de fait
Unschulds–	– of innocence	présomption d'innocence
Folgerung daß Vorsatz vorlag	– of intent	intention(*f*) présumée
Eigentums–	– of title	présomption de titre
Vernachlässigung(*f*); Unterlassung(*f*)	**neglect**	**négligence**(*f*)
grobe Fahrlässigkeit	gross –	négligence, faute(*f*) de nature délictuelle
vernünftig; angemessen; zumutbar; gerechtfertigt	**reasonable**	**raisonnable**
jeder vernünftige Zweifel ausgeschlossen	beyond – doubt	quasi-certitude du jury rendant un verdict, conviction(*f*) dépassant la croyance en un doute raisonnable
veröffentlichen	**publish (to)**	**faire connaître**, publier, rendre public
Veröffentlichung(*f*)	**publication**	**publication**(*f*), avis(*m*) public
Verordnung(*f*); Erlaß(*m*)	**ordinance**	**ordonnance**(*f*), décret(*m*), règlement(*m*)
Verordnungen(*f*) *(EG)*	**regulations** *(EEC)*	**règlements**(*m*) *(CEE)*
verpfänden	**pawn (to)**	**mettre en gage**, gager
verpfänden; geloben	**pledge (to)**	**gager**, mettre en gage
verpflichten; zwingen	**obligate (to)**	**imposer à**, obliger à
verpflichtend; obligatorisch	**obligatory**	**obligatoire**

GERMAN	ENGLISH	FRENCH
Verpflichtung(f); Abmachung(f); Versprechen(n)	**engagement**	**engagement**(m)
Verpflichtung(f); Schuldverhältnis(n); Auflage(f)	**obligation**	**obligation**(f), devoir(m), engagement(m)
akzessorische Verpflichtung; Nebenpflicht	accessory –	obligation accessoire
gemeinsame Verpflichtung; Gesamtverpflichtung	joint –	devoir de secret
Verpflichtung zur Geheimhaltung	– of secrecy	obligation conjointe
Hauptpflicht; Hauptverbindlichkeit	principal –	obligation à titre principal
Verpflichtung(f); Übergabe(f); Einlieferung(f)	**commitment**	**engagement**(m), obligation(f); renvoi(m) à une commission
Einlieferung ins Gefängnis/in (Untersuchungs-Haft) nehmen	– to custody, prison	incarcération(f)
vertragliche Verpflichtung	contractual –	obligation contractuelle
Verpflichtung(serklärung)(f); Unternehmen(n)	**undertaking**	**soumission**(f); engagement(m), promesse(f); entreprise(f) commerciale
Verrat(m); Treubruch(m)	**betrayal**	**trahison**(f)
Verräter(m)	**traitor**	**traître**
Versammlung(f); Besprechung(f)	**meeting**	**rencontre**, réunion(f), assemblée(f), meeting(m)
Jahreshauptversammlung	general –	assemblée générale
Gläubigerversammlung	– of creditors	assemblée générale des créanciers
verschärfter Schadensersatz(m)	**exemplary damages**	**dommages-intérêts**(m) **pour préjudice moral**
verschlimmern; erschweren, verschärfen	**aggravate (to)**	**aggraver**; accroître
Verschlimmerung(f); Erschwerung(f), Verschärfung(f)	**aggravation**	**aggravation**(f)
Verschlußsache(f); unter Geheimschutz gestellte Information(f)	**classified information**	**information**(f) **confidentielle**
verschwenden; vergeuden	**squander (to)**	**gaspiller**
Verschwendung(f); Abfall(m); Wertminderung(f)	**waste**	**gaspillage**(m), déchets(m)
Verschwörung(f); geheime Absprache(f)	**conspiracy**	**conspiration**(f), complot(m)
Versehen	**oversight**	**omission**(f), oubli(m), bévue(f)
versenden, liefern; konsignieren; hinterlegen	**consign (to)**	**expédier**
Versicherer(m); Garant(m)	**underwriter**	**assureur**(m), souscripteur(m)
Versicherer(m); Versicherungsträger(m)	**insurer**	**assureur**

GERMAN	ENGLISH	FRENCH
Versicherter(m) (s. Versicherungsnehmer)(m)	**insured person** (cf. policyholder)	**assuré** (–e)
Versicherung(f)	**insurance**	**assurance**(f)
Unfall–, Schadens–	accident, casualty –	assurance contre les accident
Fluggast–	air passenger –	assurance sur voyage aérien
– gegen alle Verfahren und Risiken	all-risk –	assurance tous risques
Renten–	annuity –	assurance viagère
Kraftfahrzeug–	automobile –	assurance automobile
Einbruchdiebstahl–	burglary –	assurance contre le cambriolage
Fracht–; Güter–	cargo –	assurance sur faculté (de marchandises)
Mit–	co--	coassurance
Kollektiv–; Gruppen–	collective –	assurance de groupe
Kredit–	credit –	assurance contre les risques de crédit
Invaliditäts–	disablement –	assurance invalidité
Betriebshaftpflicht–; Arbeitgeberhaftpflicht–	employers' liability –	assurance contre les accidents du travail
Ausfuhrkredit–;	export credit –	assurance contre les risques de crédit à l'exportation
Feuer–	fire –	assurance incendie
Fracht–	freight –	assurance du fret
Gesamtwert–	full value –	assurance pourla totalité de la valeur déclarée
Waren–	goods –	assurance marchandises
Hagel–	hail –	assurance contre la grêle
Kranken–	health –	assurance maladie
Rechtsschutz–	legal expenses –	assurance sur les frais de justice
Haftpflicht–	liability –	assurance responsabilité civile
Lebens–	life –	assurance sur la vie
Leibrenten–	life annuity –	assurance de rente viagère
Betriebsunterbrechungs–	loss of profit –	assurance sur le manque à gagner
(Reise-)Gepäck–	luggage –	assurance sur les bagages
See(transport)–	marine –	assurance maritime
– auf Gegenseitigkeit	mutual –	assurance mutuelle
Alters–	old age pension –	assurance de rente vieillesse
Regen–	pluvious –	assurance contre les dégâts causés par la pluie
Sach–; Vermögens–	property –	assurance immobilière
Sozial–	social –	assurance(s) sociale(s)
Transport–	transport –	assurance transports
Reise–	travel –	assurance voyages
Arbeitslosen–	unemployment –	assurance chômage
Wasserschaden–	water-damage –	assurance contre les dégâts d'eau
Versicherungskonsortium(f); Emissions–(f)	**underwriting syndicate**	**syndicat**(m) **de garantie**, groupe(m) de souscription

GERMAN	ENGLISH	FRENCH
(Versicherungs-)Police(f)	**policy**	**police**(f) **(d'assurance)**; politique, ligne(f) de conduite
Versicherungsnehmer	– holder	assuré, détenteur(m) d'une police d'assurance
e-e Versicherung abschließen	to take out a –	prendre, contracter une police d'assurance
versicherungstechnische Rücklagen(f)	**technical reserve**	**réserve**(f) **technique**
versöhnen; in Einklang bringen	**reconcile (to)**	**ajuster,** apurer; concilier, réconcilier
Versöhnung(f), Schlichtung(f)	**conciliation**	**conciliation**(f), arbitrage(m)
Versöhnung(f); (Konten)Abstimmung(f)	**reconciliation**	**accord**(m), réconciliation(f)
Versorgungsunternehmen(n); –werte(m)	**utilities**	**services**(m) **publics**; commodités(f)
versprechen	**promise (to)**	**promettre**
Versprechen(n); Zusage(f)	**promise**	**promesse**(f)
Verstaatlichung(f)	**nationalisation**	**nationalisation**(f)
verstärkender Beweis(m); erdrückendes Beweismaterial(n)	**cumulative evidence**	**témoignages**(m) **concordants**
Verstorbener(m); Erblasser(m)	**deceased, decedent**	**personne**(f) **décédée,** le défunt
versuchen; unternehmen	**attempt (to)**	**essayer,** entreprendre, tâcher de
versuchsweise	**tentative**	**expérimental,** provisoire
versuchtes Verbrechen(n); versuchte Straftat	**attempted crime**	**tentative**(f) **de perpétration d'un crime**
Verteilung(f); Distribution(f)	**distribution**	**distribution**(f), répartition(f), partage(m)
Ausschüttung der Dividende	– of dividends	paiement(m) des dividendes
Vermögensverteilung	– of property	partage des biens
Vertrag(m); Abkommen(n)	**contract**	**contrat**(m), convention(f), pacte(m)
zweiseitiger Vertrag	bilateral –	contrat bilatéral
Vertragsrecht	– law	droit(m) des obligations
einseitig verpflichtender Vertrag	unilateral –	contrat unilatéral
Vertragsabrede(f); Verpflichtung(f); Zusicherung(f)	**covenant**	**contrat**(m), convention(f), pacte(m)
Vertragsbeziehung(f); Rechtsbeziehung(f) zwischen den unmittelbaren Vertragsparteien	**privity in contract**	**obligation**(f) **contractuelle**
vertragserfallung nach gerichtsurteil	**specific performance**	**exécution**(f) **d'un contrat ordonnée par le cour**
Vertragspartei(f); Lieferant(m); Unternehmer(m)	**contractor**	**contractant**(m), adjudicataire(m), entrepreneur(m)
Vertrauen; Verlaß(m)	**reliance**	**confiance**(f)

GERMAN	ENGLISH	FRENCH
vertrauliche Mitteilung(f), – Information(f)	**confidential information**	**information**(f) **confidentielle**
Vertreibung(f); Ausweisung(f); Ausschluß(m)	**expulsion**	**expulsion**(f)
Vertreter(m), Makler(m); Bevollmächtigter(m), Handlungsbeauftragter(m)	**agent**	**agent**(m), représentant(m), préposé(m); mandataire(m), fondé de pouvoirs
Bankagent; Vertreter e-r Bank	bank –	agent(m) bancaire
Kommissionsvertreter, Kommissionär	commission –	commissionnaire(m) en marchandises
Exportagent	export –	commissionnaire exportateur
Alleinvertreter	sole –	agent exclusif, dépositaire exclusif
veruntreuen; unterschlagen	**embezzle (to)**	**détourner**, escroquer (des fonds)
Veruntreuung(f); Unterschlagung(f)	**embezzlement**	**escroquerie**(f), détournement(m), abus(m) de confiance
verurteilen; für unbrauchbar erklären	**condemn (to)**	**condamner**
Verurteilung(f); Unbrauchbarerklärung(f)	**condemnation**	**condamnation**(f)
Verwahrer(m); Depositar(m); Hinterlegungsstelle	**depositary**	**dépositaire**(m); consignation(f)
Verwahrer(m); Vormund(m) (US); Treuhänder(m)	**custodian**	**garde**(f); syndic(m)
verwalten; handhaben, vollstrecken; als Nachlaßverwalter(m) tätig sein	**administer (to)**	**administrer**, gérer, appliquer
Eid abnehmen; jdn vereidigen	– an oath	déférer le serment
Recht sprechen, Recht anwenden; Gerechtigkeit walten lassen	– justice	rendre la justice
Verwaltung(f); Führung(f), Leitung(f); Amtsperiode(f)	**administration**	**administration**(f), gestion(f), régie(f)
Regierung (US)	– (US)	le gouvernement (fédéral) (US)
verwaltungs(technisch)	**administrative**	**administratif**
Verwaltungsrecht	– law	droit(m) administratif
Verwandte(m, f); nächste Familienangehörige(m, f)	**next of kin**	**parent**(m, f) **le plus proche**
Verwandtschaft(f); Schwägerschaft(f)	**affinity**	**parenté**(m) **par alliance**
(ver-)warnen	**caution (to)**	**prévenir**; informer qqu'un de ses droits (police)
verweigern; absagen	**refuse (to)**	**refuser**

GERMAN	ENGLISH	FRENCH
Verwicklung(f); innewohnende Bedeutung(f); (stillschweigende) Folgerung	**implication**	**intention**(f) **ou état de fait présumé**; incidence(f), répercussion(f)
stillschweigend; durch sinngemäße Auslegung	by –	implicitement
die finanziellen Folgen, Auswirkungen	the financial –(s)	incidences financières
verwirken; einbüßen	**forfeit (to)**	**être déchu de,** perdre par confiscation
Verwirkung(f); Verlust(m); Beschlagnahme(f)	**forfeiture**	**mort**(f) **civile,** perte(f) d'un droit, perte par confiscation
Patentverlust	– of a patent	expiration(f) d'un brevet
Versicherungsverfall	– of an insurance	déchéance(f) d'une police d'assurance
Eigentumsverlust; Vermögenseinziehung	– of property	perte de biens par confiscation
Verwüstung(f); Unheil(n)	**havoc**	**ravages**(m), dégâts(m)
– anrichten	to wreak –	causer des ravages
verzichten; aufgeben	**renounce (to)**	**abandonner,** renoncer à, se démettre de, répudier
verzichten auf	**forgo (to)**	**s'abstenir de**
verzichten auf; nicht anerkennen; dementieren	**disclaim (to)**	**rejeter,** renoncer à
Verzicht(m)**(leistung)**(f); Aufgabe(f)	**renunciation**	**répudiation**(f) **(d'une succession),** renoncement(m), abandon(m)
Verzichtleistung(f), –serklärung; Widerruf(m)	**disclaimer**	**renonciation**(f) **explicite à un droit**; refus(m) d'une charge
Vollmacht(f); Befugnis(n)	**power**	**pouvoir**; énergie(f), puissance(f)
Ernennungsrecht	– of appointment	pouvoir de désignation
Vollmacht	– of attorney	procuration(f) (écrite), mandat(m) (de faire)
mit Spezialvollmacht handeln; mit besonderer Befugnis handeln	to act with special –(s)	agir investi de pouvoirs spéciaux
Vollmacht(f); Besorgung(n)	**procuration**	**procuration,**(f) mandat(m)
Vollstrecker(m); Erbschaftsverwalter(in)(m, f), Testamentsvollstrecker(in)	**executor, executrix**	**exécuteur**(m), **exécutrice**(f) **(testamentaire)**
Vollstreckung(f) e-s Urteils	**enforcement of a judgment**	**exécution**(f) **d'un jugement**
Vollstreckungsgläubiger(m); (Pfändungs-)Pfandgläubiger(m) (US); Partei die Forderungspfändung(f) bewirkt hat	**garnisher**	**créancier saisissant**
Vollstreckungsurteil(n)	**executory decree**	**jugement exécutoire**
Vollziehung(f) **des Eheaktes**	**consummation of marriage**	**consommation**(f) **du mariage**

GERMAN	ENGLISH	FRENCH
vor Gericht(*n*) **stellen; anklagen;** zur Anklage(*f*) vernehmen	**arraign**	**poursuivre (traduire) en justice,** mettre en accusation
Vorausnahme(*f*); Vorauszahlung(*f*); Vorgriff(*m*)	**anticipation**	**anticipation**(*f*); exercice(*m*) anticipé d'un droit
Vorbedacht(*m*)	**premeditation**	**préméditation**(*f*)
Vorbedacht(*m*) **in böswilliger Absicht**	**prepense**	**prémédité**
Vorbedingung(*f*)	**prerequisite (condition)**	**condition**(*f*) **préalable**(*m*), prérequis
Vorbehaltsklausel(*f*); Rücktritts-, Schutz-;	**escape clause**	**clause**(*f*) **de sauvegarde**
vorbeugend; verhütend Sicherungsverwahrung	**preventive** – detention	**préventif** détention(*f*) préventive
vorehelich –er güterrechtlicher Vertrag; Ehevertrag	**antenuptial** – settlement	**prénuptial** contrat(*m*) de mariage
voreingenommen, befangen, parteiisch	**biased**	**tendancieux,** non impartial, partial
Vorfall(*m*); Ereignis(*n*)	**incident**	**privilège**(*m*); incident(*m*); qui appartient
Vorgänger(*m*)	**predecessor**	**prédécesseur**(*m*)
vorgefaßte Schlußfolgerung(*f*)	**preconceived conclusion**	**conclusions**(*f*) **préconçues**
vorher erfolgter Tod(*m*); vorzeitiger erfolgter Tod(*m*)	**predecease**	**prédécès**(*m*)
vorherbestimmen	**predetermine (to)**	**fixer d'avance,** prédéterminer
vorhergehen	**forego (to)**	**précéder**
Vorinstanz(*f*); unteres Gericht(*n*)	**lower court**	**juridiction**(*f*) **du premier degré**
Vorkaufsrecht(*n*); Bezugsrecht(*n*)	**preemptive right**	**droit**(*m*) **de préemption**
vorläufig	**provisional**	**provisoire,** temporaire, conservatoire
einstweilige Verfügung –er Rechtsbehelf; einstweilige Anordnung	– injunction – remedy	ordonnance(*f*) de référé mesure(*f*) provisoire, recours(*m*) dans le cadre d'un jugement(*m*) avant dire droit
vorläufig vorläufige Beweisaufnahme	**preliminary** – evidence	**préliminaire,** préalable(*m*) témoignage(*m*) préliminaire
gerichtl.Voruntersuchung Voruntersuchung	– hearing – investigation	audience(*f*) préliminaire instruction(*f*) (d'une affaire), enquête(*f*) préliminaire

GERMAN	ENGLISH	FRENCH
vorläufige Hinterlegung(*f*) **e-r Urkunde**(*f*); bei e-m Treuhänder(*m*) hinterlegte Urkunde(*f*)	**escrow**	**dépôt**(*m*) **fiduciaire**, dépôt conditionnel
vorlegen; beantragen Genehmigungsantrag einreichen	**submit (to)** – an application for approval	**plaider**, soumettre soumettre une demande d'agrément
dem Gericht zur Entscheidung stellen	– that the court declare	demander à la cour de dire que
Vormund(*m*); **Hüter**(*m*)	**guardian**	**tuteur**(*m, f*), **conseil**(*m*) judiciaire, curateur(*m*)
Vormundschaft(*f*); **Schutz**(*m*), Obhut(*f*)	**guardianship**	**garde**(*m*), tutelle(*f*)
Vorname(*m*); **Tauf-**	**given name**	**prénom**(*m*)
Vorprämienkurs(*m*)	**call price**	**prix**(*m*) **de rachat**
Vorrang(*m*); **Priorität**(*f*)	**priority**	**priorité**(*f*), **privilège**(*m*); hypothèque(*f*)
Rangfolge, Reihenfolge Prioritätsklausel	order of – – clause	clause(*f*) de priorité ordonnance(*f*) de priorité
Vorrecht(*n*); **Prärogativ**(*n*)	**prerogative**	**prérogative**(*f*), **privilège**(*m*)
Vorsatz(*m*)	**intent**	**dessein**(*m*), **motif**(*m*), **but**(*m*), **intention**(*f*)
strafrechtlicher – böswillige Absicht betrügerische Absicht	criminal – evil – fraudulent –	but délictueux intention criminelle intention frauduleuse
vorsätzlich	**premeditated**	**prémédité**
vorsätzlich; absichtlich	**intentional**	**prémédité**, intentionnel
vorsätzlich; absichtlich Mord; Totschlag	**wilful** – murder	**prémédité**, volontaire assassinat(*m*), homicide(*m, f*) volontaire
vorsätzliche Substanzschädigung; – Wertminderung	– waste	abus(*m*) de jouissance, dégâts commis intentionnellement
Vorsichts-; vorbeugend	**precautionary**	**préventif, préventive;** de précaution
–maßregeln treffen	– measures	mesures(*f*) de précaution, mesures préventives
Vorsitzender(*m*), **Präsident**(*m*); Obmann(*m*)	**chairman**	**président**(*m*)
Vorsitzender(*m*); **Vorsitz**(*m*) führender Richter(*m*)	**presiding judge**	**président**(*m*) **du tribunal**
vorspiegeln; vortäuschen	**pretend (to)**	**prétendre**, faire semblant de
Vorspiegelung(*f*) **des Bestehens e-r Ehe**(*f*)	**jactitation of marriage**	**fait de prétendre faussement que l'on est marié à une certaine personne**
Vorsteher(*m*); Aufsichtsbeamter(*m*)	**warden**	**gardien**(*m*)
Vortest(*m*)	**pretest**	**essai**(*m*) **préliminaire**, vérification(*f*) préalable

GERMAN	ENGLISH	FRENCH
vorübergehend	**transitory**	**transitoire**, passager
Vorurteil(*n*); Beeinträchtigung(*f*); Schaden	**prejudice**	**préjudice**(*m*), tort(*m*); préjugé(*m*)
unbeschadet; unter Vorbehalt; ohne Verbindlichkeit	without – to	sans préjudice de
Vorurteil(*n*); Befangenheit(*f*), Voreingenommenheit(*f*)	**bias**	**opinion**(*f*) **préconçue**
persönliches Vorurteil	personal –	parti pris personnel
Vorverfahren(*n*)	**pre-trial procedure**	**procédures**(*f*) **d'avant-procès**, procédure gracieuse
Vorwand(*m*)	**pretence**	**simulation**(*f*), faux(*f*) semblant
Vorspiegelung falscher Tatsachen	false –	fausses allégations, moyens(*m*) frauduleux
Vorzugsaktie(*f*) (*UK*)	**preference share** (*UK*)	**action**(*f*) **privilégiée** (*UK*), action de priorité
Vorzugsaktie(*f*) (*US*)	**preferred stock** (*US*)	**titre**(*m*) **privilégié** (*US*)
Vorzugsrecht(*n*)	**preferential right**	**privilège**(*m*), droit(*m*) préférentiel

GERMAN	ENGLISH	FRENCH
Wagnis(*n*); Unternehmen(*n*); Risiko(*n*)	**venture**	**entreprise**(*f*), spéculation(*f*), risque(*m*)
Joint Venture; Gemeinschaftsunternehmen	joint –	association(*f*), entreprise en participation
Wahl(*f*), Abstimmung(*f*); Stimmzettel(*m*); Wahlgang(*m*)	**ballot**	**scrutin**(*m*), tour(*m*) de scrutin
geheime Wahl, – Abstimmung	secret –	scrutin secret
Wahrscheinlichkeit(*f*)	**probability**	**probabilité**(*f*)
Währung(*f*); Umlauf(*m*), Laufzeit(*f*)	**currency**	**circulation**(*f*), cours(*f*) de l'argent; devise(*m*), monnaie
Laufzeit e-s Vertrags	– of a contract	devise d'un contrat
Devisenvergehen	– offence	infraction(*f*) à la réglementation des changes
Währungsbeschränkungen	– restrictions	réglementation(*f*) des changes
Währungs-	**monetary**	**monétaire**
–system(*n*)	– system	système(*m*) monétaire
–einheit(*f*)	– unit	unité(*f*) monétaire
Waise(*f*)	**orphan**	**orphelin**(*m*)
Warenzeichen(*n*); Handelsmarke(*f*)	**trade mark**	**marque**(*f*) **(de fabrique et de commerce)**
eingetragenes Warenzeichen	registered –	marque déposée
Wasserschadenversicherung(*f*)	**water damage insurance**	**assurance**(*f*) **sur les dégâts des eaux**
Wasserverunreinigung(*f*); Gewässerverschmutzung(*f*)	**water pollution**	**pollution**(*f*) **des eaux**
Weigerung(*f*); Absage(*f*)	**refusal**	**refus**(*m*), déni(*m*)
Wert(*m*)	**worth**	**valeur**(*f*)
Wert(*m*); Valuta(*f*)	**value**	**valeur**(*f*)
Buchwert; buchmäßiger Wert	book –	valeur comptable
Marktwert	market –	valeur marchande
Rückkaufswert	surrender –	valeur de rachat

GERMAN	ENGLISH	FRENCH
Wertpapiere(n); Effekten	**securities**	**titres**(m), **fonds**(m), **valeurs**(f) **boursières**
börsenfähige –	listed –	valeurs cotées
einlösbare Wertpapiere	redeemable –	titres remboursables
übertragbare –	transferrable –	valeurs mobilières librement cessibles
wesentlich	**material**	**matériel**(m), réel, essentiel
beweiserhebliche Zeugenaussage	– evidence	preuve(f) matérielle
–e Tatsache	– fact	fait(m) essentiel
Wettbewerbsbeschränkungen(f); Kartelle(n)	**restrictive trade practices**	**pratiques**(f) **commerciales restrictives**
Wideraufbau(m); Reorganisation(f)	**reconstruction**	**reconstitution**(f), reconstruction(f)
widerlegbar	**refutable**	**réfutable**
widerlegen; entkräften	**rebut (to)**	**réfuter une preuve**, une présomption
(widerrechtlich) Besitz(m) **entziehen**; zur Räumung(f) zwingen	**dispossess (to)**	**déposséder**, dessaisir, exproprier
widerrechtliche Aneignung(f)/ **Verwendung**(f); Veruntreuung(f)	**misappropriation**	**abus**(m) **de confiance**
(widerrechtliche) Vorenthaltung(f) **(Grundbesitz)**; Haftbefehl	**detainer**	**détention**(f), prise de possession
widerrechtliches Betreten	**trespassing**	**violation**(f) **de propriété**
Widerruf(m)	**retraction**	**rétractation**(f)
Widerruf(m)	**revocation**	**révocation**(f), abrogation(f), annulation(f)
Zurücknahme e-s Angebots	– of a tender	annulation d'un appel d'offres
– des Testaments	– of a will	annulation d'un testament
widerrufen; aufheben	**revoke (to)**	**révoquer**, abroger, revenir sur une promesse
widerruflich; kündbar	**precarious**	**précaire**
jederzeit entziehbarer Besitz	– posession	possession(f) précaire
widerruflich gewährtes Recht	– right	droit(m) accordé à titre précaire
widersprechen; in Abrede stellen	**contradict (to)**	**contredire**
Widerspruch(m); Unstimmigkeit(f); Abweichung(f)	**discrepancy**	**désaccord**(m), contradiction(f)
Widerspruch(m); Widerrede(f)	**contradiction**	**contradiction**(f), contredit(m)
wieder in Besitz(m) **nehmen**; zurücknehmen	**repossess (to)**	**faire saisir un article non payé**
Wiederabtretung(f); Retrozession(f)	**retrocession**	**rétrocession**(f)
Wiederaufnahmeverfahren(n); erneute Verhandlung(f)	**retrial**	**nouveau procès**(m)
Wiederausfuhr(f)	**re-exportation**	**ré-exportation**(f)

GERMAN	ENGLISH	FRENCH
wiedereinsetzen in den vorigen Stand(*m*); klageabweisendes Urteil aufheben	reinstate (to) a court matter	réinscrire une affaire au rôle
wiedererlangen; -gutmachen	retrieve (to)	récupérer
(Wieder)Erlangung(*f*); Beitreibung(*f*)	recovery	réintégrande(*f*); montant(*m*) alloué par jugement; recouvrement(*m*), récupération; reprise(*f*) redressement(*m*)
Erlangung von Schadensersatz	– of damages	reprise(*f*) de dommages-intérêts
Wiederinbesitznahme(*f*); Rückgriff(*m*)	regress	rentrée(*f*), rentrée en possession d'un bien-fonds (*US*)
wild; unzivilisiert	savage	brutal(*m*), féroce
Wilddieb(*m*)	poacher	chasseur(*m*) de têtes (*fam.*); braconnier(*m*)
Wildern	poaching	recrutement(*m*) par un 'chasseur de têtes'; braconnage(*m*)
Wille(*m*); -nsäußerung(*f*)	volition	volonté (délibérée)
wirklich, tatsächlich, effektiv; gegenwärtig	actual	réel, véritable, effectif, concret
tatsächlicher Verlust	– loss	perte réelle
unmittelbarer Besitz	– possession	possession effective
Tagespreis, Marktpreis; Anschaffungskosten	– price	prix(*m*) réel; prix d'achat
echter Gewinn, tatsächlich erzielter Gewinn	– profit	profit(*m*) réel
tatsächlicher od. wirklicherWert; Effektivwert Tageswert	– value	valeur(*f*) marchande
Wirkung(*f*)	impact	incidence(*f*), répercution(*f*) (de la fiscalité)
Wirkung(*f*); Folge(*f*); Kraft(*f*) Rechtswirkung; -kraft	effect legal –	effet(*m*) conséquence(*f*) légale, effet juridique
wirtschaftlich; gewerblich; geschäftlich; handelsüblich	commercial	commercial
Handelsvertretung	– agency	agence(*f*) de renseignements commerciaux
Geschäftsbank; Handels–	– bank	banque(*f*) commerciale
Handelsgericht	– court	tribunal(*m*) commercial
Handelsrecht; –gesetz	– law	droit(*m*) commercial
Handelsregister	– register	registre(*m*) de commerce
Wirtschaftsbeauftragter(*m*)	economic agent	agent(*m*) économique
wissentlich	knowingly	sciemment
Wohnort(*m*) betreffend; Heimats–	domiciliary	domiciliaire

GERMAN	ENGLISH	FRENCH
Wohnsitz(*m*); Domizil(*n*)	**residence**	**résidence**(*f*)**,** domicile(*m*)
Amtssitz	official –	résidence officielle
ständiger Wohnsitz	permanent –	domicile habituel
Wucherer(*m*)	**usurer**	**usurier**
Wucher(zinsen)(*m*)	**usury**	**usure**(*f*)

Y

GERMAN	ENGLISH	FRENCH
Yard(*n*), Elle(*f*); Hof(*m*); Scotland Yard (Langenmaß = 91,44 cm)	**yard**	**chantier**(*m*); **cour**(*f*); unité de mesure: 1 yard = 3 pieds = 91,44 cm

Z

GERMAN	ENGLISH	FRENCH
zahlbar; fällig Verbindlichkeiten; Passiva	**payable** accounts –	**payable,** exigible dettes(f) passives
zahlend	**paying**	**rémunérateur,** payant; paiement(m)
Zahlstelle zweitbeauftragte Bank	– agent – banker	agent(m) payant banquier(m) payant
Zahler(m)	**payer**	**payeur**(m), tiré (d'un effet)
Zahlung(f)	**payment**	**paiement**(m), règlement(m), versement(m); paye(f), rémunération(f)
Voraus-, An-	advance –	paiement d'avance, paiement par anticipation
aufgeschobene –; Raten- Teil-, Raten- volle (Ein)- Naturalleistung –sbedingungen	deferred – part – – in full – in kind terms of –	paiement différé paiement partiel paiement intégral paiement en nature conditions(f) de paiement
Zahlungsempfänger(m)	**payee**	**bénéficiaire**(m), porteur(m) d'un effet
Zahlungsfähigkeit(f); Solvenz(f) Liquiditätsmarge Solvenzkennzahl	**solvency** – margin – ratio	**solvabilité**(f) marge(f) de solvabilité taux(m) de solvabilité
zahlungsunfähig; insolvent	**insolvent**	**insolvable**
Zahlungsunfähigkeit(f); Insolvenz(f)	**insolvency**	**insolvabilité**(f), mise(f) en liquidation judiciaire
Zeitdauer(m); Fachausdruck(m)	**term**	**limite**(f), période(f), durée(f), terme(m), fin(f)
Miet-, Pachtzeit Kündigungsfrist Amtszeit	– of a lease – of notice – of office	durée d'un bail délai(m) de congé durée des fonctions
Zeuge(m) Entlastungs-; vom Beklagten/ Angeklagten benannter – Belastungs-; – der Anklage	**witness** – for the defence – for the prosecution	**témoin**(m) témoin à décharge témoin à charge
Testaments-	– to a will	témoin instrumentaire du testament
Zeugenaussage(f)	**testimony**	**déposition**(f) **d'un témoin,** attestation(f), témoignage(m)

GERMAN	ENGLISH	FRENCH
Zeugenaussage(f); Beweisaufnahmeprotokoll(n); Hinterlegung(f); Absetzung(f)	**deposition**	**déposition**(f)
eidliche Zeugenaussage	– of evidence	témoignage(m)
Zeugenaussage	– of witness	déposition d'un témoin
Zeugenvernehmung(f); Verhör(n)	**examination**	**examen**(m), étude(f), visite(f)
Kreuzverhör	cross--	contre-interrogatoire
Hauptvernehmung (durch die benennende Partei)	direct –	interrogatoire(m)
Zeugenvernehmung	– of witness	audition(f) d'un témoin
Leichenschau; Obduktion	post-mortem –	autopsie(f)
Zeugnis(n), Bescheinigung(f); Urkunde(f); Anteilschein(m)	**certificate**	**certificat**(m), attestation
Geburtsurkunde	birth –	acte(m) de naissance
Einlagezertifikat; Depot–, Hinterlegungsschein	– of deposit	certificat de dépôt
Ursprungszeugnis; Herkunftsbescheinigung	– of origin	certificat d'origine
Sterbeurkunde; Totenschein	death –	acte de décès
Gesundheitsattest; –zeugnis	health –	billet(m) de santé
Heiratsurkunde	marriage –	acte de mariage
(Zivil-)Prozeß(m); Rechtsstreit(m); Klage(f)	**lawsuit**	**procès**(m)
Zoll(m); Zollbehörde(f)	**customs**	**douanes**(f)
Zollabfertigung; Verzollung	– clearance	expédition(f) en douane
Zollerklärung; Zollanmeldung	– declaration	déclaration(f) en douane
Zollgebühren, –abgaben	– duties	droits(m) de douane
Zollunion, –verband	– union	union(f) douanière
(Zoll(m))**Tarif**(m); Satz(m)	**tariff**	**tarif**(m), barème(m)
Schutzzoll	protective –	tarif protecteur
Zollgesetzgebung	– legislation	législation(f) douanière
Zone(f); Gebiet(n)	**zone**	**zone**(m), district(m), quartier(m)
Grenzgebiet	border –	zone frontière
Gefahrenzone	danger –	zone dangereuse
Frei(hafen)zone	free –	zone franche, zone libre
Militärgebiet	military –	zone militaire
Zonentarif	– tariff	tarif(m) de zone
zu beanstanden; unzulässig	**objectionable**	**répréhensible**
Zufall(m), zufälliges Ereignis(n)	**fortuitous event**	**cas**(m) **fortuit**
Zuflucht(f)	**refuge**	**refuge**(m), asile(m)
Zufluchtsort(m); Hafen(m)	**haven**	**refuge**(m)
Zugang(m); Zutritt(m); Zugriff (EDV)(m)	**access**	**accès**, abord
zugrundeliegend	**underlying**	**sous-jacent**, fondamental
–e Ursachen, –e Beweggründe	– motives	raisons(f) cachées
zulassen, aufnehmen; zugeben, zugestehen; anerkennen	**admit (to)**	**admettre**, concéder, avouer, laisser passer, accepter
e-n Anspruch anerkennen	– a claim	reconnaître une prétention, admettre un recours

GERMAN	ENGLISH	FRENCH
zulässig, erlaubt; zulassungsberechtigt	**admissible**	**recevable**, acceptable
zulässig; erlaubt	**permissible**	**permissible**, tolérable
Zulassung(f), Aufnahme(f), Eintritt(m); Eingeständnis(n); Anerkenntnis(n); Geständnis(n)	**admission**	**admission**(f), accès(m), acceptation(f), aveu(m)
Anerkenntnis der Einrede	– of plea	aveu(m) judiciaire
Zulassungsbedingungen	– requirements	conditions(f) d'admission
zum Schadensersatz(m) **berechtigt sein**	**entitled to damages**	**fondé à réclamer des dommages-intérêts**
zumessen	**mete (to) out**	**assigner**, décerner
Zunahme(f); Beitritt(m); Neuanschaffung(f)	**accession**	**droit d'accession**; avènement(m) au trône; assentiment(m)
Beitrittsakte *(EG)*	act of –	acte(f) d'entrée en possession
Zunahme(f); (Wert-)Zuwachs(m)	**increment**	**d'accroissement**
zur Last gelegte Tat(f)	**alleged offence**	**infraction**(f) imputée
Zurückbehaltung(f); Ein–	**withholding**	**détention**(f), dissimulation(f), refus(m)
Verschweigen von Beweisen	– of evidence	dissimulation de preuve
Abzugssteuer; Quellensteuer	– tax	impôt(m) retenu à la source
zurückfordern; urbar machen	**reclaim (to)**	**récupérer**; mettre en valeur
zurückkaufen; einlösen; tilgen	**redeem (to)**	**amortir**, racheter, rembourser
zurückziehen; widerrufen; zurücktreten	**withdraw (to)**	**retirer**, se retirer
Zusammenleben; Lebensgemeinschaft	**cohabitation**	**cohabitation**(f), concubinage(m), union(f) libre
Zusammenschluß(m); Fusion(f)	**merger**	**extinction**(f) **d'un droit**; confusion(f); fusion(f), unification(f)
Zusammenschlußklausel	– clause	clause(f) de fusion
zusätzliche Strafzumessung	**consecutive sentences**	**jugement**(m) **ordonnant le cumul des peines**
zuschreiben; zur Last legen	**impute (to)**	**imputer**, attribuer, accuser
zuständig; befugt; maßgeblich; sachverständig geschäftsfähig	**competent**	**compétent**
sachverständiger Rat	– advice	avis(m) qualifié
zuständige Behörde	– authority	autorité(f) compétente
zulässiges (und schlüssiges) Beweismaterial	– evidence	preuve(f) recevable
zuständiges Gericht	court of – jurisdiction	tribunal(m) compétent
Zuständigkeit(f); Befugnis(n); Geschäftsfähigkeit(f)	**competence, competency**	**compétence**(f), capacité(f)

GERMAN	ENGLISH	FRENCH
Zustellung(f)	**service**	**assignation**(f), signification(f); service(m)
– durch Hilfsbeamten – e-r Vorladung	– by bailiff – of summons	signification par huissier signification de convocation
Zustimmung(f), **Genehmigung**(f)	**assent**	**assentiment**(m), agrément(m), approbation(f)
zuteilen, zumessen; anteilmäßig verteilen	**apportion (to)**	**répartir**, attribuer, ventiler, lotir
zuteilen; vergeben; aufteilen; bestimmen für	**allocate**	**allouer**, affecter, attribuer
Zuteilung(f); Zuweisung(f); Aufteilung(f)	**allocation**	**allocation**(f), assignation(f), ventilation(f), répartition(f)
Mittelvergabe, Mittelzuweisung; Kapitalbewilligung, Kapitalverwendung Gewinnzurechnung Aktienzuteilung	– of funds – of profits – of shares	affectation(f) de fonds répartition(f) des bénéfices attribution(f) d'actions
Zuteilung(f); Zuweisung(f); Zuerkennung(f); Verteilung(f)	**allotment**	**attribution**(f), affectation(f), répartition(f); part(f), portion(f)
Vermögenszuteilung; Besitzverteilung	– of property	lotissement(m)
zuverlässig; nicht widerlegbar	**unimpeachable**	**irréprochable**
Zuwachs(m); Zunahme(m); Anwachsen(n)	**accretion**	**majoration**(f) **d'héritage**; accroissement(m) organique
Zuwiderhandlung(f); Übertretung(f); Verstoß(m) Zuwiderhandlung in Verletzung von	**contravention** in – of	**contravention**(f), infraction(f) en violation de
Zwang(m), Nötigung(f); Beschränkung(f)	**constraint**	**contrainte**, obligation; privation(f) de liberté, internement(m)
unter Zwang handeln	to act under –	agir sous la contrainte
Zwang(m); Nötigung(f)	**coercion**	**coercition**(f), contrainte(f)
Zwang(m); Nötigung(f)	**compulsion**	**contrainte**(f), violence(f)
Zwang(m); Nötigung(f) unter Zwang handeln	**duress** to act under –	**violence**(f), contrainte(f) agir à son corps défendant sous la contrainte
Zwangs- –anleihe(f) –verkauf(m)	**forced** – loan – sale	**forcé** emprunt(m) forcé vente(f) forcée
Zwangsmaßnahmen(f)	**coercive measures**	**mesures**(f) **de contrainte**
Zwangsräumung(f); Heraussetzung(f) Räumungsbefehl, –urteil	**eviction** – order	**éviction**(f), expulsion ordre(m) d'expulsion
Zwangsverwaltung(f); Sequestration(f)	**sequestration**	**séquestration**(f), mise(f) sous séquestre

GERMAN	ENGLISH	FRENCH
(zwangsweise) durchführen; gerichtlich geltend machen; vollstrecken	**enforce (to)**	**appliquer,** faire exécuter
Zweck(*m*); Absicht(*f*)	**purpose**	**but**(*m*), objet(*m*), dessein(*m*), affectation(*f*)
Zweideutigkeit(*f*); Ungewißheit(*f*), Unklarheit(*f*) versteckter Dissens	**ambiguity** latent –	**ambiguïté**(*f*) imprécision d'un texte légal
Zweifel(*m*); Bedenken(*n*) jeder vernünfige Zweifel ausgeschlossen	**doubt** beyond reasonable –	**doute**(*m*) quasi-certitude du jury rendant un verdict de culpabilité, conviction(*f*) dépassant la croyance en un doute raisonnable
zweifelhaft; unzureichend zweifelhafte Außenstände *(pl.);* uneinbringliche Forderung böser Glaube	**bad** – debt – faith	**mauvais,** faux créance(*f*) irrécouvrable mauvaise foi
Zweigstelle(*f*), –niederlassung(*f*), Filiale(*f*), Nebenstelle(*f*); Branche, Sparte	**branch**	**branche**(*f*), succursale(*f*), agence(*f*)
Zweitausfertigung(*f*); Gegenstück(*n*)	**counterpart**	**contrepartie**(*f*); duplicata(*m*)
zwingen; nötigen	**compel (to)**	**forcer,** contraindre
zwingende Verpflichtung(*f*)	**binding commitment**	**engagement**(*m*) **irrévocable**
Zwischen- –urteil(*n*) –bericht(*m*)	**interim** – decree – report	**provisoire,** transitoire, intérimaire; intérim(*m*) décret(*m*) intérimaire rapport(*m*) provisoire
Zwischenhändler(*m*); Vermittler(*m*)	**middleman**	**intermédiaire,** revendeur(*m*)